S0-BYT-855

JOB

VOLUME 15

THE ANCHOR YALE BIBLE is a fresh approach to the world's greatest classic. Its object is to make the Bible accessible to the modern reader; its method is to arrive at the meaning of biblical literature through exact translation and extended exposition, and to reconstruct the ancient setting of the biblical story, as well as the circumstances of its transcription and the characteristics of its transcribers.

THE ANCHOR YALE BIBLE is a project of international and interfaith scope: Protestant, Catholic, and Jewish scholars from many countries contribute individual volumes. The project is not sponsored by any ecclesiastical organization and is not intended to reflect any particular theological doctrine. Prepared under our joint supervision, THE ANCHOR YALE BIBLE is an effort to make available all the significant historical and linguistic knowledge which bears on the interpretation of the biblical record.

THE ANCHOR YALE BIBLE is aimed at the general reader with no special formal training in biblical studies; yet it is written with the most exacting standards of scholarship, reflecting the highest technical accomplishment.

This project marks the beginning of a new era of cooperation among scholars in biblical research, thus forming a common body of knowledge to be shared by all.

William Foxwell Albright
David Noel Freedman
GENERAL EDITORS

THE ANCHOR YALE BIBLE

JOB

◆

Introduction, Translation,
and Notes

by

MARVIN H. POPE

THE ANCHOR YALE BIBLE

Yale University Press · New Haven and London

NEW HANOVER COUNTY
PUBLIC LIBRARY
201 CHESTNUT STREET
WILMINGTON, NC 28401

First published in 1965 by Doubleday, a division of Random House, Inc. First Yale University Press impression 2008.

Copyright © 1965, 1973 by Yale University as assignee from Doubleday, a division of Random House, Inc.

All rights reserved.

This book may not be reproduced, in whole or in part, including illustrations, in any form (beyond that copying permitted by Sections 107 and 108 of the U.S. Copyright Law and except by reviewers for the public press), without written permission from the publishers.

Printed in the United States of America.

ISBN 978-0-300-14075-0

Library of Congress Catalog Card Number 65-12361

A catalogue record for this book is available from the British Library.

This paper meets the requirements of ANSI/NISO Z39.48-1992 (Permanence of Paper).

PREFACE

The Book of Job, like other great classics of world literature, can never be translated or interpreted definitively. Many of the shortcomings of the present effort are known to the author and more will doubtless be noted by critical readers. It is hoped only that in minor details this effort may afford some slight advances. What is relatively new herein derives mostly from the Ugaritic texts, documents which have already shed so much light on the Old Testament that they must be considered one of the most significant archaeological discoveries of our time and which, even after more than a quarter century of study, have not been fully exploited.

The scope of the introductory materials was difficult to decide, since readers will vary widely in their acquaintance with the Bible in general and the Book of Job in particular. The order, too, was something of a problem, but the reader may solve this for himself by perusing the various parts of the Introduction in any order or measure, as the need is felt for orientation or background.

The NOTES to the translation follow the text. Emendations are discussed in the NOTES and are not placed in a separate critical apparatus which would be meaningful only to those who have some knowledge of Semitic philology and textual criticism and thus would not need such an instrument to discover how the translation deviates from the received text. The attempted explanations of textual and exegetical difficulties and the remedies proposed are often complex and involved, but this, in the nature of the case, could scarcely be avoided. Especially where new suggestions are offered, it seemed appropriate to present the argument in some detail. Liberties taken with the text may strike some readers as extreme, while a few may incline to still more radical measures.

The debt to others is too great to be reckoned or acknowledged. Those familiar with the literature of biblical criticism will be able to trace lines of dependence even when no documentation is given.

Of modern commentaries, Dhorme's was most useful. The frequent notice of Tur-Sinai's views is an index to their provocative originality, and even though the present writer was often unable to agree, they still served to force a radical reconsideration of some of the time-honored means of glossing over difficulties.

Dr. David Noel Freedman is due a special note of thanks for his thorough critical editing of the manuscript. So many of his suggestions have been adopted, or more often adapted, that it would be difficult to acknowledge every item and insight which in some measure might be credited to him.

Dr. William F. Albright also read the manuscript and gave of his time to discuss some of the many problems. With all modern students of the Bible and the ancient Near East, the writer stands greatly and gratefully in the debt of this master scholar.

Dean John Perry Miller of the Graduate School of Yale University kindly provided a subvention for stenographic assistance from the John Morris Whiton Fund and for this the writer is most grateful.

The writer is indebted to Mrs. Marca Anderson for her skill and patience in typing the manuscript and to Messrs. Robert Neff and Gene Tucker for assistance in proofreading. Professor John Marks of Princeton University perused the Introduction and caught a number of errors and incongruities that had escaped previous readers. The galley proofs were read by Mr. David Robertson; by virtue of his acumen and knowledge, he called to my attention many discrepancies and omissions. The author's helpmeet suffered vicariously with him the torments of the task and resisted the urge to counsel him to curse Job and die; she was patient to the end which she was glad to expedite by typing and inserting addenda and corrigenda. The flaws that remain are solely the fault of the writer.

In this third edition several new interpretations have been adopted and adapted from the many striking suggestions offered by M. Dahood in his first volume on the Psalms, *Psalms I, 1–50* (THE ANCHOR BIBLE, vol. 16) and some corrections and minor revisions made.

Many of the corrections in the second and third editions came from alert and critical readers, and particularly from my students in a recent seminar on Job: Messrs. Curtiss Hoffman, William

Horwitz, and Stephen Kaufman. I am especially grateful to Professor Francis I. Andersen of the Church Divinity School of the Pacific who called my attention to numerous errors. The indexes were prepared with the help of Mrs. Ellen Geller and Mrs. Faith Richardson to whom I am beholden.

Some explanations and apologies are in order for the changes, additions and deletions of this edition. Materials for a third edition of this work were submitted in the spring of 1967, but for various reasons there was delay in the resetting of the galley and page proofs. Meanwhile new and important studies appeared which had to be taken into account, most notably the monograph by A. C. M. Blommerde, the second and third volumes of M. Dahood's *Psalms* which contain numerous references to Job, and lastly the Targum from Cave XI of Qumran. The efforts to update this third edition have been hampered by inexorable pressures of time and the distractions of sundry other chores, so that the results are not entirely satisfactory but must serve until there is opportunity for more extensive and drastic revision. Many of the changes in the final stages of this revision have again been provoked and influenced by the give and take of seminar discussions, in particular with Messrs. Bernard Paetzold, Bruce Zuckerman, and Dr. Walter L. Michel. Dr. Michel's unpublished dissertation, "The Ugaritic Texts and the Mythological Expressions in the Book of Job (including a new translation of and philological notes on the Book of Job)" (University of Wisconsin, 1970), was most useful, particularly for the thorough survey of recent literature. Discussions with Dr. Michel on Ugaritic and possible mythological allusions in Job were very helpful, even though agreement was not always reached. Special thanks are due Mr. Bruce Zuckerman for assistance in all phases of this revision and in particular for his attention to passages of special interest or difficulty in the Qumran Targum and for many acute observations and creative suggestions. Credit is acknowledged in connection with some specific items, but instances in which expressions of appreciation might be offered are too numerous, hence this general note of thanks to Mr. Zuckerman. Thanks are also due to Professor Stephen A. Kaufman of the University of Chicago who kindly supplied data to be included in his review article on "The Job Targum from Qumran" to be published in JAOS. Finally, I am grateful to Dr. Michel for providing indexes of the new material in this edition.

Marvin H. Pope

CONTENTS

Preface v

Principal Abbreviations XI

Introduction XV

Summary of the Content of the Book of Job XV
The Problem of Literary Integrity XXIII
The Literary Form of the Book XXX
The Date of the Book XXXII
The Authorship of the Book XL
The Place of the Book in the Canon XLII
Textual Problems XLIII
The Language of the Book XLVII
Problems of Prosody L
Parallel Literature LVI
Old Testament Affinities LXXI
The Purpose and Teaching of the Book LXXIII

Selected Bibliography LXXXV

Translation and Notes

1. The Testing of Job (i 1–22) 1
2. More Drastic Measures (ii 1–13) 18
3. Job's Protest (iii 1–11; 16; 12–15; 17–26) 26
4. Eliphaz Remonstrates (iv 1–21) 34
5. Eliphaz's Discourse (*continued*) (v 1–27) 40
6. Job's Reply to Eliphaz (vi 1–30) 48
7. Job's Reply (*continued*) (vii 1–21) 57
8. Bildad's First Discourse (viii 1–22) 64
9. Job's Reply to Bildad (ix 1–35) 68
10. Job's Reply (*continued*) (x 1–22) 78
11. Zophar's First Discourse (xi 1–20) 83
12. Job's Reply to Zophar (xii 1–25) 88
13. Job's Reply (*continued*) (xiii 1–27) 96
14. Job's Reply (*concluded*) (xiv 1–2; xiii 28; xiv 3–22) 104
15. Eliphaz's Second Discourse (xv 1–35) 112
16. Job's Reply to Eliphaz (xvi 1–22) 121

17. Job's Reply (*continued*) (xvii 1–16) 127
18. Bildad's Second Discourse (xviii 1–21) 132
19. Job's Reply to Bildad (xix 1–29) 138
20. Zophar's Second Discourse (xx 1–29) 149
21. Job's Reply to Zophar (xxi 1–34) 155
22. Eliphaz's Third Discourse (xxii 1–30) 163
23. Job's Reply to Eliphaz (xxiii 1–17) 170
24. Job's Reply (*continued*) (xxiv 1–3; 9; 21; 4–8; 10–14b; 15; 14c; 16–17) 174
25. Bildad's Third Discourse (xxv 1–6; xxvi 5–14) 180
26. Job's Reply to Bildad; Zophar's Third Discourse (xxvii 1; xxvi 1–4; xxvii 2–23; xxiv 18–20; 22–25) 187
27. Poem on the Inaccessibility of Wisdom (xxviii 1–28) 197
28. Job's Peroration (xxix 1–10; 21–25; 11–20) 207
29. Job's Peroration (*continued*) (xxx 1–31) 217
30. Job's Final Oath (xxxi 1–8; 38–40b; 9–14; 23; 15–22; 24–37; 40c) 225
31. Elihu Intervenes (xxxii 1–22) 240
32. Elihu Attempts to Refute Job (xxxiii 1–33) 245
33. Elihu's Second Speech (xxxiv 1–37) 254
34. Elihu's Third Speech (xxxv 1–16) 262
35. Elihu's Fourth and Final Speech (xxxvi 1–28; 31; 29–30; 32–33) 266
36. Elihu's Final Speech (*continued*) (xxxvii 1–18; 21; 19–20; 22–24) 278
37. The Theophany: Yahweh's First Discourse (xxxviii 1–41) 288
38. Yahweh's First Discourse (*continued*) (xxxix 1–30) 304
39. Job Challenged; Yahweh's Second Discourse (xl 1–24; xli 1–8) 316
40. Yahweh's Second Discourse (*continued*) (xli 9–34) 335
41. Job Recants; Epilogue (xlii 1–17) 347

Indexes 355
Authors 357
Subjects 362
Words 369
Biblical References 376
Koranic References 406
Rabbinic References 407
Ugaritic References 408

Key to the Text 409

PRINCIPAL ABBREVIATIONS

1. Publications

AfO	Archiv für Orientforschung
AJSL	American Journal of Semitic Languages and Literatures
ANEP	*The Ancient Near East in Pictures,* ed. J. B. Pritchard, 1954
ANET	*Ancient Near Eastern Texts Relating to the Old Testament,* ed. J. B. Pritchard, 2d ed., 1955
ARW	Archiv für Religionswissenschaft
ATR	Anglican Theological Review
BA	The Biblical Archaeologist
BANE	*The Bible and the Ancient Near East,* ed. G. E. Wright, 1961
BASOR	Bulletin of the American Schools of Oriental Research
BDB	F. Brown, S. R. Driver, and C. A. Briggs, eds., of Wilhelm Gesenius' *Hebrew and English Lexicon of the Old Testament,* 2d ed., Oxford, 1952
BH	*Biblia Hebraica,* ed. Kittel-Kahle
BIES	Bulletin of the Israel Exploration Society
BJPES	Bulletin of the Jewish Palestine Exploration Society
BJRL	Bulletin of the John Rylands Library
BO	Bibliotheca Orientalis
BWANT	Beiträge zur Wissenschaft vom Alten und Neuen Testaments
BWL	*Babylonian Wisdom Literature,* by W. G. Lambert, 1960
BZAW	Beihefte zur Zeitschrift für die alttestamentliche Wissenschaft
CAD	*The Assyrian Dictionary,* Oriental Institute of the University of Chicago, 1956–
CBQ	Catholic Biblical Quarterly
CIS	*Corpus Inscriptionum Semiticarum*
ET	Expository Times
EUP	*El im ugaritischen Pantheon,* by O. Eissfeldt, 1951
EUT	*El in the Ugaritic Texts,* by M. Pope, VTS, II, 1955
FuF	Forschungen und Fortschritte

GKC	*Gesenius' Hebrew Grammar,* ed. E. Kautzsch, revised by A. E. Cowley, 2d Eng. ed., 1910
HTR	Harvard Theological Review
HUCA	Hebrew Union College Annual
ICC	International Critical Commentary
IDB	The Interpreter's Dictionary of the Bible, 1962
IEJ	Israel Exploration Journal
JAOS	Journal of the American Oriental Society
Jastrow	Marcus Jastrow, comp. *A Dictionary of the Tarqumim, The Talmud Babli and Yerushalmi, and the Midrashic Literature,* 1950
JBL	Journal of Biblical Literature and Exegesis
JBR	Journal of Bible and Religion
JCS	Journal of Cuneiform Studies
JJS	Journal of Jewish Studies
JNES	Journal of Near Eastern Studies
JPOS	Journal of the Palestine Oriental Society
JQR	Jewish Quarterly Review
JR	Journal of Religion
JRAS	Journal of the Royal Asiatic Society
JSS	Journal of Semitic Studies
JTS	Journal of Theological Studies
KAI	*Kanaanäische und aramäische Inschriften,* by H. Donner and W. Röllig, 3 vols., 1960–64.
KB	L. Koehler and W. Baumgartner, *Lexicon in Veteris Testamenti Libros,* 1953
MGWJ	Monatsschrift für Geschichte und Wissenschaft des Judentums
MVAG	Mitteilungen der vorderasiatisch-aegyptischen Gesellschaft
NWSPJ	"Northwest Semitic Philology and Job," by M. Dahood, in *The Bible in Current Catholic Thought,* ed. John L. McKenzie, 1962
OLZ	Orientalistische Literaturzeitung
PEQ	Palestine Exploration Quarterly
PNWSP	*Proverbs and Northwest Semitic Philology,* by M. Dahood, Rome, 1963
PSALMS I, II, III	*PSALMS I, 1–50; PSALMS II, 51–100; PSALMS III, 101–150,* by M. Dahood (AB vols. 16, 17, 17A), 1965, 1968, 1970
1QH	Qumran Hymns of Thanksgiving
1QS	Qumran Manual of Discipline
RB	Revue biblique
REJ	Revue des études juives

RES	Revue des études semitiques
RHPR	Revue d'histoire et de philosophie religieuses
RHR	Revue de l'histoire des religions
TB	Talmud Babli
ThR	Theologische Rundschau
TLZ	Theologische Literaturzeitung
TS	Theological Studies
TZ	Theologische Zeitschrift, Basel
UH	*Ugaritic Handbook* (Analecta Orientalia 25), by C. H. Gordon, Rome, 1947
UHP	*Ugaritic-Hebrew Philology,* by M. Dahood, Rome, 1965
UT	*Ugaritic Textbook,* 4th ed. (Rome, 1965) of C. H. Gordon's *Ugaritic Grammar.* Unless otherwise specified, parenthetic references to Ugaritic texts are to this volume.
VT	Vetus Testamentum
VTS	Vetus Testamentum Supplements
WIANE	*Wisdom in Israel and in the Ancient Near East,* eds. M. Noth and D. W. Thomas, VTS, III, 1955
WO	Die Welt des Orients
WZKM	Wiener Zeitschrift für die Kunde des Morgenlandes
ZA	Zeitschrift für Assyriologie und verwandte Gebiete
ZAW	Zeitschrift für die alttestamentliche Wissenschaft
ZDMG	Zeitschrift der deutschen morgenländischen Gesellschaft
ZNW	Zeitschrift für die neutestamentliche Wissenschaft und die Kunde der älteren Kirche

2. Versions

AB	The Anchor Bible, 1964–
AT	The Bible: An American Translation: The Old Testament, eds. J. M. P. Smith et al., The New Testament, ed. E. J. Goodspeed, 1931
BJ	La Bible de Jérusalem, 1956
CCD	Confraternity of Christian Doctrine, 1944–69
IB	The Interpreter's Bible, 1952–57
JPS	Jewish Publication Society of America: The Holy Scriptures, 1917
KJ	The King James, or Authorized Version of 1611
LXX	The Septuagint
NAB	New American Bible, 1970
NEB	The New English Bible, 1970
MT	Masoretic Text

Qumran Targum (11Q tg Job) *Le Targum de Job de la Grotte XI de Qumran,* édité et traduit par J. P. M. van der Ploeg et A. S. van der Woude, avec collaboration de B. Jongeling, Koninklijke nederlandse Akademie van Wetenschappen. Leiden: Brill, 1972

RSV	The Revised Standard Version, 1946, 1952
RV	The Revised Version, 1885
Targ.	Targum, Aramaic translations or paraphrases
TEV	Today's English Version. Job for Modern Man, 1971
Syr.	Syriac version, the Peshitta
Vulg.	The Vulgate

3. Other Abbreviations

Akk.	Akkadian
Ar.	Arabic
Aram.	Aramaic
Eg.	Egyptian
Gr.	Greek
Heb.	Hebrew
Lat.	Latin
NT	New Testament
OT	Old Testament
Sem.	Semitic
Sum.	Sumerian
TB	Talmud Babli
Ugar.	Ugaritic

INTRODUCTION

"You have heard of the patience of Job, and you have seen the purpose of the Lord, how the Lord is merciful and compassionate." This traditional view of the patient Job, as it is stated in the New Testament Epistle of James (v 11), is familiar to nearly everyone. It is, however, scarcely a balanced view, since it ignores the thrust of more than nine tenths of the book and appears to take account only of the beginning and end of the story. The vehement protests of the supposedly patient Job will surprise and even shock any who expect to find the traditional patient and pious sufferer throughout. In spite of sporadic attempts of ancient scribes and translators to soften the impact of some of the near blasphemous tirades, the fact cannot be mistaken that Job bluntly calls into question divine justice and providence. The extreme case of Job's unmerited woes, as with any and every instance of seemingly senseless suffering, raises the ultimate questions of divine justice (theodicy) and the meaning and purpose of life. To such disturbing questions there is probably no better introduction than the Book of Job. For the understanding and appreciation of such an ancient literary work, a considerable fund of information is necessary. The introductory material that follows is intended to supply some of the essential background and to point up the major problems without exhausting the subject or, hopefully, the reader.

Perhaps the best way to begin the process of introduction to the Book of Job is with a brief summary of its content.

Summary of the Content of the Book of Job

The Book of Job falls into five unequal parts:

I. Prologue (chs. i–ii)
II. Dialogue or Symposium (iii–xxxi)

III. The Elihu Speeches (xxxii–xxxvii)
IV. Theophany (xxxviii–xlii 6)
V. Epilogue (xlii 7–17)

I. THE PROLOGUE introduces the hero as a man of exemplary rectitude and piety, blessed with wealth and a happy family for whom he is particularly solicitous (i 1–5). At a session of the divine assembly, Yahweh[1] calls the Satan's attention to Job's unexampled probity and piety and the Satan questions the disinterested character of this piety and suggests that Job bereft of his material blessings would curse Yahweh to his face. The implied wager is accepted by Yahweh who grants the Satan permission to test Job by any means short of an assault on his person (i 6–12). The Satan strips Job of all his possessions, even his children, but Job accepts the calamity with resignation and instead of cursing Yahweh, as the Satan had predicted, he utters a blessing (i 13–22). Yahweh taunts the Satan who replies to the effect that Job has not been really tested since he himself remained unharmed. This time the Satan is given leave to do anything except take Job's life (ii 1–6). The Satan proceeds to afflict Job with a terrible disease. Job sits among the ashes and scrapes himself with a potsherd. His wife urges him to curse God and die, but he upbraids her for her folly and reaffirms his resignation to God whom he refuses to accuse (ii 7–10). Three friends—Eliphaz, Bildad, and Zophar—hear of his calamity and

[1] A very brief explanation of the word "Yahweh" may be in order. The name of the God of Israel was regarded, in post-exilic times, as too holy to be uttered and the word *'ăḏônay*, "my Lord[s]," was pronounced in its stead. When the vowel signs were added to the consonants of the sacred text, the vowels of the word *'ăḏônay* were put with the consonants of the ineffable name (YHWH), but every Jew knew that the consonants of the holy name were not to be sounded, but rather the consonants of the surrogate 'DNY. Christian ignorance of this taboo resulted in the blending of the vowels of the surrogate with the consonants of the name to produce the form JEHOVAH which, despite its sonorous quality, is a morphological monstrosity with no claim to legitimacy except the several centuries of misguided usage. Already in the sixteenth century (A.D.), Mercerus suggested that the original pronunciation of the name was Yahwe. Clement of Alexandria transliterated the name in Greek as *Iaoué* and Theodoret of Cyrrhus reported that the Samaritans pronounced it as *Iabé*. Whether this form—Yahwe—is older or younger than the shorter forms *yāh, yāhû, yĕhô>yô*, (as it occurs in Israelite personal names such as *yĕhô/yô-nāṯān*, Jonathan ["Y has given"], *yirmĕyāh/yāhû*, Jeremiah ["Y is exalted (?)"], and the cry *hallĕlû-yāh*, ["praise ye Yah"]) is uncertain. As to the origin and meaning of the name, there are a number of different theories and a considerable literature which cannot be discussed here. Cf. B. W. Anderson, "God, names of," IDB, II, pp. 407–17.

come to condole him. So appalled are they at his misery that they sit seven days in silence (ii 11–13).

II. The Dialogue. Job breaks the silence with a bitter complaint, cursing his birth, longing for release through death, questioning the reason for existence in the face of such misery (iii). Eliphaz ventures to reply, beginning gingerly, but soon warms up to chide Job for failure to bear up under adversity (iv 1–6). He affirms the doctrine of individual retribution (iv 7–11) and recounts a terrifying apparition of a spirit who asks how mortal man can be just or pure to God who does not so regard even his angels (iv 12–21). There is thus no prospect of help from any of the (lesser) gods (holy ones) (v 1). The fool is suddenly visited with disaster (v 2–5). Man is born for trouble (v 6–7). Job has no recourse but to God, whose providence destroys the wicked but chastens and saves the righteous. Job can still be restored to prosperity and security (v 8–27). Job replies to Eliphaz that the extremity of his anguish justifies the bitterness of his complaint (vi 1–5), that Eliphaz's arguments are insipid, even putrid (vi 6–7). Again he pleads for death as an escape from his suffering (vi 8–13). His friends he charges with disloyalty and betrayal (vi 14–23). He challenges the friends to prove the guilt which they assume is his (vi 24–30). Man's life is painful and short (vii 1–10), so why does not God leave him alone?

Bildad answers, characterizing Job's speech as a big wind (viii 1–2). How can he charge God with injustice (viii 3)? His children must have sinned and got only what they deserved (viii 4). If only Job would appeal to God, he might be restored (viii 5–7). Bildad appeals to the lessons of experience and history which, he alleges, prove that the wicked always meet with disaster, but the righteous are saved, and so may Job also be saved (viii 8–22). Job admits that man cannot be justified before God (ix 1–4), who makes the issue a question of power so that man cannot contend with him (ix 5–21). God makes no distinction between the innocent and the guilty, but destroys both alike. Earth is controlled by the wicked. Justice is blind. If God is not responsible for all this, then who is (ix 22–24)? Life is fleeting, but what use the struggle when there is no hope? Even though he were clean, God would souse him in muck (ix 25–31). Job appeals for an arbiter to ensure fair play. He asks God to put aside his club and allow him to speak freely, but God will not do this (ix 32–35). Sick of life, Job resolves to speak out and question God (x 1–3). Can God see through human eyes? Does God share man's limitations? Why, then does he persecute man (x 4–7)? Man is but clay, flesh, and bone (x 8–11). Life, love, and providential care God once granted Job, but all the while he was plotting to undo him (x 12–13). God is constantly alert for opportunity to harm Job (x 14–17). Why did he allow him to be born? Why not let him alone for a little while before he goes down to the land of darkness (x 18–22)?

Zophar charges Job with brazenly pleading innocence in order to silence men, but were God to speak Job's guilt would be made clear (xi 1–5). God's greatness is beyond man's comprehension (xi 6–12). Job, therefore, ought to appeal to God for mercy and forgiveness and be restored to favor (xi 13–19). The wicked have no refuge or hope (xi 20).

Job replies with sarcastic praise of the wisdom of his friends (xii 1–2). But he is not inferior to them (xii 3). He contrasts his misery with the prosperity of the wicked (xii 4–6). Beasts, birds, and fishes all know that God has the power and exercises such control as there is in the world (xii 7–25). This Job also knows as well as the friends (xiii 1–2). They lie in order to defend God and their arguments are worthless (xiii 3–12). Job ventures to stake his life on a direct challenge and appeal to God. All he asks is that God give him a fair hearing, dispensing with terror and intimidation, and that specific indictment be made (xiii 13–23). But God instead continues to harass him (xiii 24–28). Life is brief and full of trouble, so why does God not give man some respite (xiv 1–6)? There is no hope in the hereafter (xiv 7–12). If only there were such a hope, he would wait his turn (xiv 13–15). But the only prospect is extinction (xiv 18–22).

Eliphaz begins the second round by dubbing Job's speech hot air and gross impiety (xv 1–4). Job is insincere and his own mouth convicts him (xv 4–6). Was he the first man ever born? Is he privy to the divine secrets? Is wisdom his personal monopoly? Does he know something his friends do not know, men older than Job's father (xv 7–10)? Job is mad to berate God (xv 11–13). Even the angels are not pure before God, so how could sinful man be clean (xv 14–16)? The wisdom of the ages is that the wicked always suffer (xv 17–35).

Job replies that he has heard enough of such flatulent nonsense (xvi 1–3). Were the tables turned, he could offer them such verbiage (xvi 4–5). He charges God with vicious and unprovoked assaults (xvi 6–17). He cries out for vindication, appealing for the help of a witness in heaven, an arbiter to intercede for him with God, as a man would do for his friend (xvi 18–22). Life is ebbing. Mockery is all he gets from his friends (xvii 1–5) and from God (xvii 6). His hope is the grave and maggots (xvii 13–16).

Bildad accuses Job of setting word snares. He resents being regarded as stupid by one who is raving mad (xviii 1–4a). Does Job expect the world to be changed for his sake (xviii 4b, c)? The woes of the wicked are elaborated (xviii 5–21).

Job charges the friends with tormenting and taunting him (xix 1–5). God has afflicted him unjustly (xix 6–12). Family, friends, servants, and wife are alienated from him. His friends persecute him as does God (xix 13–22). Job makes his appeal to the future and asserts his faith in ultimate vindication in spite of death (xix 23–27). (The last two verses of this chapter are jumbled and probably misplaced.)

Zophar is profoundly disturbed (xx 1–3). The apparent triumph of the wicked can be only momentary. No matter how prosperous or powerful the wicked may become, they will perish like dung, fly like a dream, be swept away by disaster (xx 4–29).

Job urges close attention to his words. He feels justified in his complaint against God (xxi 1–6). He gives the lie to the assertion of the friends, pointing to the undisturbed prosperity of the wicked (xxi 7–18). The argument that God punishes the children of the wicked is no answer to the difficulty (xxi 19–21). Death comes alike to all, without regard to one's merits. The wicked escape disaster and go in peace to their death (xxi 22–23). The "comfort" and "answers" of the friends are false (xxi 34).

Eliphaz opens his third speech with the point that God derives no benefit from man's rectitude or piety (xxii 1–3). Certainly it is not for piety that Job is being punished (xxii 4). Actually it must be that Job is very wicked. He has oppressed the poor, the widow, the orphan (xxii 5–9). This must be the reason disaster has befallen him (xxii 10–11). God sees and punishes evil (xxii 12–20). Job, therefore, is again advised to yield, submit, repent, return to God, and be restored to prosperity, even to the position of interceding for others with God (xxii 21–30).

Job wishes to find God and to come into legal contest with him (xxiii 1–7). But God eludes him (xxiii 8–9). Even though God must know that Job is innocent (xxiii 10–12), he continues to terrorize him (xxiii 13–17). Violence and oppression are rampant in the world (xxiv 1–17).

(xxiv 18–20, 22–25 belong in the mouth of one of the friends rather than in Job's. The displacement may have been made deliberately in order to confuse the issue and nullify Job's argument.)

Chapters xxiv–xxvii are thoroughly scrambled. The third speech of Bildad (xxv) is quite brief and not very similar to his preceding discourses. A considerable part of Job's reply (xxvii 8–23) presents the viewpoint of the friends which Job all the while has denied and refuted. The third speech of Zophar is missing entirely. Some rearrangement is obviously necessary and it is possible to apportion the material in several ways to make reasonably consistent the continuation of the argument. Various rearrangements have been proposed. We submit that the simplest and most satisfactory expedient is to augment Bildad's abbreviated discourse of xxv with the beautiful paean to God's power in xxvi 5–14 and to supply the missing speech of Zophar from the incongruous parts of Job's speech, xxvii 8–23, to which may be added appropriately xxiv 18–20, 22–25.

Virtually all critics are agreed that the poem on wisdom, xxviii, is extraneous. It is put into the mouth of Job with no effort being made to correlate or integrate it with the rest of Job's discourse. The burden of its message is that wisdom far exceeds in value any precious material on or in the earth, and is completely inaccessible to man except through piety.

Job's final speech in the Dialogue is introduced by xxvi 2–4 and xxvii 2–6 and then continued by xxix–xxxi. Job reaffirms his innocence and integrity (xxvii 2–6). He recalls with longing his former blessed estate when he was prosperous and happy in the favor of God, respected by all as a benefactor of the poor and champion of the oppressed (xxix). And now he is derided and insulted by young upstarts and the very dregs of society, racked by loathsome and painful disease, assailed by God, ready for death and the infernal world (xxx). Job now resorts to a series of denials, or negative confessions. He declares that he has imposed an interdict on his eyes to never so much as look upon folly (emending the word "virgin"). He swears, with terrible self-imprecations, that he never committed a long catalogue of sins; never acquired wealth by means of injustice; never abused his land or tenants (transposing xxxi 38–40 after xxxi 8); never committed adultery, maltreated slaves, the poor, widows; never put his confidence in riches; never worshiped the sun and moon; never rejoiced at his foe's misfortune; never permitted the men of his household even to contemplate indulging in the sport of homosexual abuse of strangers, or turned a guest over to the mob. Here Job rests his case, affixes his signature, challenges God to answer him and write an indictment (xxxi).

III. THE ELIHU SPEECHES. The three friends cease to answer Job because he maintains his righteousness. But a young man named Elihu, who had listened to the Dialogue and was angered by Job's self-righteousness and the failure of the friends to confute him, injects himself belatedly into the argument (xxxii 1–5).

Elihu apologizes profusely for his brashness in presuming to lecture his elders. He reminds them, however, that wisdom does not necessarily come with old age, rather it is a gift of God. Since his elders have failed to confute Job, he will make the effort. He is bloated with words and must give them vent. He will speak impartially and without flattery (xxxii 6–22). He now turns his attention to Job. He assures Job that they can debate on equal terms, since he (Elihu) is only a man and not God (xxxiii 1–7). Elihu proceeds to summarize Job's argument: that God persecutes him although he is innocent and ignores his protest and appeal (xxxiii 8–13). But God does answer man in various ways, especially by means of dreams. God may afflict a man with illness in order to chasten or warn him (xxxiii 14–22). An angel may intervene on behalf of the afflicted man and plead his cause and win his restoration to health and redemption from death, when and if the afflicted man admits and repents his guilt. Thus God time and again redeems men such as Job (xxxiii 23–30). If Job has no reply to these assertions, he should keep quiet and listen to more instruction from Elihu (xxxiii 31–33).

Elihu proceeds in his second discourse to charge Job with blasphemy in his denial of divine justice. God, Elihu insists, is just and he does reward and punish. Job's challenge of this fundamental doctrine adds rebellion to his sin (xxxiv).

Elihu in his third uninterrupted speech addresses himself to Job's assertion that neither sin nor piety appear to make a difference to God. Elihu's answer is that God is too exalted to be benefited or harmed by what man does, but God, nevertheless, does reward and punish. If God ignores a man's appeal, it is only because he knows that it is deceitful and insincere. In charging God with ignoring transgression, Job speaks falsely and out of ignorance (xxxv).

In his fourth and final speech, Elihu continues to defend God's justice. Not even kings are exempt from divine supervision. If a sinner repents, he is restored to prosperity; if not, he dies. Affliction may thus be the means by which a man finds deliverance. This could be the case with Job. God is exalted and his power and providence are beyond man's understanding. God makes the rain, the storms, thunder, lightning, and snow. Can Job even comprehend, much less do such things? The violent thunderstorm reveals God's power, yet he is just and never oppresses. Men, therefore, should fear him (xxxvi–xxxvii).

IV. THE THEOPHANY. Yahweh now answers Job from out of a storm. Who is Job to speak out of ignorance? What does he know of the founding of the earth, the subjugation of the violent sea, the dawn of day, the depths of the infernal regions, the expanse of the earth, the abodes of light and darkness, the treasure houses of the snow and ice, the ordering of the constellations and the rains (xxxviii 1–38)? Can Job provide food for the lion and the raven? Does he know the birth season of the wild goats, the habits of the wild ass? Could he domesticate the wild bull (xxxviii 39–xxxix 12)? The ostrich is described in some detail (xxxix 13–18). Does Job give the war horse his power and courage? (xxxix 19–25.) Is it by Job's wisdom that the hawk and eagle soar and find prey (xxxix 26–30)? Yahweh challenges Job to answer, but Job admits his smallness and promises to say no more (xl 1–5).

Again Yahweh speaks to Job out of the storm and challenges him to show that he has divine powers. If Job can do such things as thunder and humble the proud and the wicked, then Yahweh will admit that Job can save himself (xl 7–14). Next Job is invited to consider Behemoth (not the hippopotamus, but a mythical bovine [?] monster) whose power is described (xl 15–23). He is challenged to grapple Leviathan (not the crocodile, but a mythical marine monster) whose fearsome might is detailed at considerable length (xl 24–xli 26).

Job answers with humble acknowledgment of God's omnipotence and his own ignorance. Heretofore he had only hearsay knowledge. Now that he has seen God for himself, he recants and repents in dust and ashes (xlii 1–6, but omitting vss. 3a, 4 as mistakenly repeated from xxxviii 2, 3b and xl 7b).

V. THE EPILOGUE. Yahweh rebukes Eliphaz and the other two friends for not having spoken the truth about him, as had Job. He commands them to offer sacrifice and have Job pray for them so that they may escape divine reprisal. Yahweh then restores Job's fortunes and doubles the property he had lost. Job's relatives come to visit him and eat with him and offer condolences and gifts. A new family is provided, seven (fourteen?) sons and three very beautiful daughters. Job lives one hundred and forty years (longer?) and sees his progeny to the fourth generation, and dies in contented old age (xlii 7–17).

THE PROBLEM OF LITERARY INTEGRITY

To summarize the contents of the Book of Job raises the question of its literary unity and integrity. The same issue is raised by the problem of classifying the work in its literary form because the whole suggests a sort of piecemeal composition.

The problem of literary integrity is most immediately evident in the incongruities and inconsistencies between the Prologue-Epilogue and the Dialogue. The Prologue presents to us the traditional pious and patient saint who retained his composure and maintained his integrity through all the woes inflicted on him and refused to make any accusation of injustice against Yahweh, but rather continued to bless the god who had afflicted him. In the Dialogue we meet quite a different Job whose bitter complaints and charges of injustice against God shock his pious friends who doggedly defend divine justice and persistently reaffirm the doctrine of exact individual retribution.[1a] In view of these attitudes, the Epilogue, in which the friends, not Job, are rebuked for not having spoken the truth about Yahweh comes as something of a shock. In the Dialogue Job effectively demolishes the friends' doctrine that wickedness is always punished and virtue always rewarded. But in the final settlement in the Epilogue this dogma is sustained by the highly artificial manner in which Job is both compensated for his pains and restored to health and prosperity. There are other minor incongruities, for example, in the Prologue-Epilogue Job is scrupulous in his observance of the sacrificial cultus, but the Dialogue betrays not the slightest

[1a] Cf. H. L. Ginsberg, "Job the Patient and Job the Impatient," *Conservative Judaism* 21/3 (1967), 12–28.

interest in this particular concern and in his final apology for his life Job makes no claim on this account. The names used for God are different in the Prologue-Epilogue and the Dialogue; the former uses Yahweh and Elohim while the latter employs variously the terms El, Eloah, Elohim, and Shaddai. The temper and mood of the Prologue-Epilogue and of the Dialogue are quite distinct: the Prologue reflects a rather detached and impersonal attitude toward the cruel experiment to test the basis of Job's piety; by contrast the Dialogue is highly charged with emotion and the anguish of a tortured soul. The literary forms are also different: the Prologue-Epilogue is in prose, though in its epic style a number of lines have such poetic quality that we have ventured to arrange portions of the Prologue as poetry; the Dialogue is in poetry throughout. In view of these incongruities, critics have generally regarded the Prologue-Epilogue and the Dialogue as having diverse authorship and origin, although some have thought the author of the Dialogue composed the Prologue-Epilogue as the setting for his work. Most critics, however, regard the Prologue-Epilogue as part of an ancient folk tale which the author of the Dialogue used as the framework and point of departure for his poetic treatment of the problem of suffering. Whether this ancient folk tale was in written form or transmitted orally, it had probably attained a relatively fixed form and content which the author of the Dialogue could not modify in any radical fashion. It has epic style and the charm and flavor of an oft told tale. Ezek xiv 14, 20 indicates that there was a legendary figure named Job, of great antiquity—like Noah and Danel[2] (the ancient prototype of the biblical Daniel now known to us from the Ugaritic epic).[3] The great antiquity of the literary motif of the righteous suf-

[2] See S. Spiegel, "Noah, Danel, and Job," *Louis Ginzberg Jubilee Volume*, 1945, pp. 305–55; M. Noth, "Noah, Daniel and Hiob in Ezekiel XIV," VT 1 (1951), 251–60.

[3] Since the Ugaritic texts are mentioned so often in this study, and because they have not received as much publicity as the Dead Sea scrolls, it may be well to give a brief explanation of their nature and their importance for Semitic and biblical studies.

In 1928 a peasant plowing his field at Minet el Beida (White Harbor) on the coast of North Syria near Latakia made the initial discovery which led to the excavation of the nearby mound of Ras Shamra. Since 1929 (interrupted only by World War II) the distinguished French archaeologist C. F. A. Schaeffer has excavated at Ras Shamra, finding with each campaign important new materials. The first campaign in 1929 unearthed a batch of clay tablets inscribed in a hitherto unknown cuneiform (wedge-shaped) script. The script was deciphered with amazing speed by two European Semitists, the French scholar É. Dhorme and the German H. Bauer, each working independently. The methodology they used is reminiscent of that used in Edgar Allan Poe's story "The Gold Bug." Since the script had only thirty symbols, it was assumed to be alphabetic. The locale suggested that the language was most likely Semitic. Both guesses proved correct as the two scholars found combinations of symbols that made sense. Happily in some of the texts there were little wedges separating words. Now, in all the Semitic languages the word for "three" (e.g., Akk. *šalāš*, Heb. *šālôš*, Ar. *ṯalāṯ*, Aram. *tĕlāt*) begins and ends with the same letter—an occurrence which is relatively rare. Thus when a combination of three symbols appeared with the first and third identical, it was surmised that this was the word for "three." With two letters tentatively identified, other likely combinations were sought, as for example, the word for "king," *mlk*, (the script is purely consonantal, except for the representation of the vowels with the glottal stop) has the same letter in the middle as does the word for "three." Thus these two words give the symbols for *m, l, k,* and *ṯ* and open up more possibilities for testing these values in other groups of symbols. Following this method, the two scholars were able in less than a year to match most of the symbols with the linear alphabet; the remaining gaps were quickly filled by W. F. Albright and others.

The ancient name of the city turned out to be "Ugarit," a name long known from Akkadian documents as an important Syrian city in the second millennium B.C. and now brought to light and made part of history. One of the first tablets discovered was a liturgy or incantation to protect Ugarit from harm by foreign enemies. At the end of one of the mythological texts there was mention of Niqmad, king of Ugarit (*nqmd mlk ugrt*). With the excavation of the Royal Palace and the recovery of its archives, the political history of the city during two centuries (ca. 1390–1190 B.C.) is now known in some detail (cf. M. Liverani, *Storia di Ugarit*, Studi Semitici, VI, Rome, 1962).

The initial decipherment of the script on the basis of a few short texts, mostly lists of gods and offerings, was thoroughly tested and proved on the longer texts exhumed in succeeding years. Most important for our present interests are the mythological poems which tell us of the liaisons, intrigues, and conflicts of the gods: of El, the (sometime) head of the pantheon, father of gods; of Baal-Hadad the weather-god whose rains fertilize the earth and whose death and resurrection mean the departure and return of fertility; of Baal's "sister" and consort, the violent virgin 'Anat; of Baal's enemies Mot (Death) and Yamm (Sea); of the master artisan Koshar; and a plethora of lesser gods. Besides the mythological texts, there are two long poems dealing with a King Keret whose experiences resemble those of Job in some respects and a certain Dan(i)el whose son Aqhat paid with his life for refusing to relinquish his bow to the goddess 'Anat. There are a number of smaller mythological texts and fragments, some letters, and even a few texts dealing with the treatment of sick horses.

These documents were copied in the fourteenth century B.C., but some of the myths were probably composed several centuries earlier. In any case, these texts are the second oldest body of Semitic literature at our disposal, since only Akkadian documents furnish older material in a Semitic language. There is no warrant here for entering into a discussion of the still moot issue of the linguistic affinities of the dialect of Ugarit, W. F. Albright's designation as "North Canaanite" has been widely used, but A. Goetze (*Language* 17 [1941], 127–38) has shown that in several important features Ugaritic differs from "Canaanite" and he suggested that it may be more closely referer has been established by S. N. Kramer's recovery of a Sumerian poetic essay dating from ca. 2000 B.C. dealing with the same problem as the Book of Job and giving an answer very much like that offered in the Epilogue.[4] How much of the ancient folk tale is preserved by the Prologue-Epilogue and what modifications the author of the poetic Dialogue had to make in the old story is impossible, at this time, to determine. Probably very little of the old tale has been lost because the Prologue and Epilogue together present a fairly complete story. It may be that the older prose tale included an episode in which the friends counseled Job (as his wife had done) to curse God and die. This would explain God's censure of the friends and praise of Job in the Epilogue. It is not likely that the rebuke to the friends was added to reconcile the Prologue-Epilogue with the Dialogue, for, although it is clear that Job had the better of the argument, the Epilogue betrays no awareness that the doctrine of retribution had been refuted or even questioned.

The essential unity of the Dialogue (iii–xxxi) has not been seriously questioned. Though textual and exegetical difficulties abound in this section, a marked unity in style and consistency in the opposing viewpoints suggest a single author. It is clear that the author's sympathy is with Job, but he attempts to be fair to the friends' viewpoint, sparing no effort to present their arguments fully. Some of the difficulties in the Dialogue, particularly in Job's speeches, appear to have been produced by pious tampering with the text by well-meaning meddlers who felt compelled to mitigate Job's shocking charges against God. Considerable effort and ingenuity appears to have been expended in this effort and sometimes a very clever twist is given to the sense, but generally the attempt is unsuccessful and betrayed by the context. In some cases it would appear that

---

lated to "Amorite" (known from the great number of West Semitic personal names in Akkadian documents). In any case, Ugaritic is related to Canaanite, just how closely remains to be shown. More important for our present interest is the light which these texts shed on the Old Testament. Many references to the Ugaritic texts will be found in the NOTES on the translation. These will serve to demonstrate something of the value of these texts in the study of the Old Testament.

For further information, the reader may refer to the article "Ugarit" by A. Kapelrud in IDB, IV, pp. 724–32, and the short bibliography there given. The best translation of the texts is that of H. L. Ginsberg in ANET, pp. 129–55.

[4] S. N. Kramer, "Man and his God: A Sumerian Variation on the 'Job' Motif," in WIANE, pp. 170–82.

failing to alter the sense, effort has been made to obscure it. The Masoretes on occasion indulge in this activity by imposing a tendentious vocalization on the consonantal text. The most extensive meddling with the text has occurred in chapters xxiv–xxvii where Bildad's third speech is vestigial and Zophar's is missing altogether. Here, Job suddenly expounds the friends' viewpoint which he had all along denied. Some critics have considered this dislocation accidental, but it was more likely a deliberate attempt to refute Job's argument by confusing the issue. The commentaries suggest various rearrangements of chapters xxiv–xxvii, but the order we have adopted appears the simplest and most satisfactory.[5]

The poem on Wisdom (xxviii)[6] is almost universally recognized as extraneous. Its style and language, however, show similarities to those of the rest of the Dialogue and some scholars have regarded it as an independent composition by the same author, though not an integral part of the Book of Job. It is hardly appropriate in Job's mouth since the burden of its message—that wisdom, the secrets of the universe and of divine providence are inaccessible to man—does not comport with Job's desire to bring God into court, as it were, and question him. The poem has some affinities with the Theophany and might have been better interpolated there. Despite its extraneous character, we may be grateful that the poem has been preserved, for it is one of the finest in the Old Testament.

The Elihu speeches (xxxii–xxxvii)[7] are rejected as interpolations by many critics who regard them as having scant value either as literature or as a solution to the problem of evil. Their style is diffuse and pretentious, a large part of the content of the four discourses being devoted to prolix and pompous prolegomena. For the most part Elihu's arguments merely echo what the friends have already said repeatedly, yet he has the effrontery to offer them as if they were novel and decisive. If Elihu has anything distinctive to contribute, it is the elaboration of the idea that suffering may be disciplinary (xxxiii 14–33), already suggested by Eliphaz in his first speech (v 17). In spite of these considerations, a few critics regard Elihu's diatribes as the climax of the work and the author's best

[5] G. A. Barton, "The Composition of Job 24–30," JBL 30 (1911), 66–77; R. H. Pfeiffer, *Introduction to the Old Testament*, 1941, p. 671.

[6] Cf. H. H. Rowley, "The Book of Job and Its Meaning," BJRL 41 (1958), 191, n. 2.

[7] Cf. W. A. Irwin, "The Elihu Speeches in the Criticism of the Book of Job," JR 17 (1937), 37–47.

word on the problem of evil.[8] There are, of course, many phraseological parallels between the Dialogue and the Elihu speeches, but these are easily explicable as imitation by the author of the Elihu speeches. It is difficult to believe that the author of the Dialogue would repeat the argument of the friends through the mouth of Elihu and represent it as something new. It seems more likely that the author of the Elihu speeches, shocked at Job's blasphemous accusations against God, and disappointed at the failure of the friends to silence him, and perhaps equally dissatisfied with the content of the divine speeches, felt impelled to attempt some vindication of divine justice. The author could not, of course, make the attempt after Yahweh had spoken and had humbled Job, but he had to get into the argument before the Theophany. His lavish apologies for presuming to speak at all, and his reassurances to Job that he is after all only a man and not God, may reflect more his own misgivings about intervening ahead of the deity than concern for deference to his elders. Elihu sets the stage for the divine discourses by anticipating and bolstering the weak points in their argument. This could be regarded as the foresight of a single author or the hindsight of an interpolator. The strongest evidence that the Elihu speeches are interpolated is the fact that Elihu is completely ignored in the Epilogue. It is true that the Satan is also passed over in the Epilogue, but he had already completed his role in the Prologue and had no part in the Dialogue. If the Elihu speeches were an integral part of the Dialogue, and if a single author valued them as highly as Elihu did, one would expect some recognition of this in the attribution of praise and blame in the Epilogue.

Yahweh's speeches from the storm[9] have been regarded as secondary by some critics who reason that the author of the Elihu speeches could not have known them, else he would not have dared intrude. We have already noted, however, that Elihu could scarcely be permitted to speak after the divine discourses. Moreover, Job's challenge, "Here is my signature, / Let Shaddai answer me," demands a divine response and not repetition of a discredited dogma by a young upstart. Yahweh's first speech has been praised as a work of genius unequaled in world literature, surpassing all other attempts to describe the greatness of God and the marvels of his creation.

[8] Cf. O. Eissfeldt, *Einleitung in das Alte Testament,* 2d ed., 1956, pp. 561 f.
[9] Eissfeldt, *Einleitung . . . ,* pp. 563 ff.

Critics who do not regard it as an original part of the work give a much less enthusiastic appraisal of the poem's literary and theological value. Some see in it only brutal irony and utter lack of concern for man's predicament.

The authenticity of Yahweh's second speech is less widely accepted than that of the first. The poems on the mythological monsters Behemoth and Leviathan (generally misunderstood as the hippopotamus and the crocodile) which make up almost the entire second speech are commonly considered spurious and inferior. Nevertheless, the second speech also has its champions, and some critics regard it as the climax of the book and a more original form of the divine reply than the first speech. A second speech by Yahweh after Job had been humbled and silenced seems like nagging, but it could be regarded as driving the lesson home. Job is only silenced at the end of the first speech (xl 3–5); after the second speech he is not only subdued but repentant (xlii 6).[10]

The discrepancies between the Epilogue and other parts of the book have already been noted. Most striking is the fact that in the Epilogue the friends are rebuked, not Job, as is the case in the divine speeches. Kaufmann[11] explains the inconsistency by suggesting that the friends were reprimanded because they had taken the easy way of contending with conventional clichés and empty phrases, while Job had challenged God out of a moral duty to speak the truth before him. Job had indeed already charged the friends with asserting a lie in order to curry favor with God, and had warned them that God would rebuke such hypocritical sycophancy. Job's rehabilitation, in which he receives a bonus for his pains, appears to confirm the very doctrine of retribution which Job had so effectively refuted in the Dialogue. This incongruity, however, was unavoidable. In the old folk tale on which the Book of Job was based, as in its Mesopotamian prototypes, the hero must certainly have been restored and rewarded in the end. The author was naturally limited by the prefabricated materials with which he had to work and could not have taken a great deal of liberty with a familiar story. How else could the book have been brought to a conclusion? It would certainly not do to leave Job in his misery after God had

[10] See M. Burrows, "The Voice from the Whirlwind," JBL 47 (1928), 117–32.

[11] Y. Kaufmann, *The Religion of Israel,* tr. and abr. from the Hebrew by M. Greenberg, 1960, p. 335.

vindicated him, although the doubling of his material possessions is a highly artificial device and incompatible with Job's realistic observations in the Dialogue.

The Book of Job in its present form can hardly be regarded as a consistent and unified composition by a single author. Nevertheless, there is a considerable degree of organic unity despite the incongruities. Even the Elihu speeches, though probably interpolated,[12] are blended into the whole with such skill that some scholars have seen Elihu as a reflex of the author of the Dialogue.

The Literary Form of the Book

A good deal of the considerable discussion[13] of the literary form of the Book of Job has been unprofitable. The naïve view that it represents sober history need not be taken seriously,[14] but it may very well be that there was a historical personage behind the story. Rabbi Simeon-ben-Laqish opined that Job never existed and that the story is simply a poetic comparison or parable (*māšāl*) (cf. Midrash Rabba Gen lxvii; TB, Baba Bathra 15a). The term is very fitting since Job is in a sense the type of any and every man who experiences the mystery of seemingly senseless and undeserved suffering. The notion that Job, like the Suffering Servant of Yahweh in Isa lii 13–liii 12, represents the nation Israel in a sort of historical allegory is intriguing. Certainly, if the work was composed in the exilic or early post-exilic period, as many critics believe, it would be difficult if not impossible for the author to ignore the parallel between the sufferings of the individual and the nation.[15] There is, however, not the slightest suggestion of interest in the fate of the nation Israel betrayed anywhere in the book. The choice of a descendant of Esau as the representative righteous sufferer would rule out any likelihood that the narrator had in mind the nation Israel or Judah.

Theodore of Mopsuestia in the fourth century regarded the Book

[12] Cf. Rowley, BJRL 41 (1958), 189, n. 1.

[13] For bibliography and summary, cf. K. Kuhl, "Neuere Literaturkritik des Buches Hiob," ThR 21 (1953), 163–205, 257–317; "Vom Hiobbuche und seinen Problemen," ThR 22 (1954), 261–316; Eissfeldt, *Einleitung* . . . , pp. 558–78.

[14] Cf. Rowley, BJRL 41 (1958), 172, n. 3.

[15] Rowley, BJRL 41 (1958), 200, n. 1.

of Job as being modeled on the Greek dramas.[16] Theodore Beza[17] considered the book as a tragedy and Milton regarded it as an epic. The Homeric epics have been compared, but actually have little in common, with Job.[18] More appropriate is the comparison with the tragic dramas of Aeschylus, Sophocles, and Euripides, but even here the similarity is less in form than in an occasional ideological parallel. H. M. Kallen has argued that the Book of Job actually has the form of a Greek tragedy,[19] including the chorus and the denouement by means of the *deus ex machina* (Yahweh from the storm). The dialogues of Plato have been mentioned for comparison, but there is scant similarity between the long poetic monologues of the so-called Dialogue of the Book of Job and the brief, precise, and analytical conversations of Plato's Dialogues.

In point of fact, there is no single classification appropriate to the literary form of the Book of Job. It shares something of the characteristics of all the literary forms that have been ascribed to it, but it is impossible to classify it exclusively as didactic, dramatic, epic, or anything else. The book viewed as a unit is *sui generis* and no single term or combination of terms is adequate to describe it.[20] Definition of literary form generally presumes literary unity and this point is still disputed with regard to the Book of Job.

[16] J. P. Migne, *Patrologia,* LXVI (1864), 697 f.

[17] *Job Expounded* (1589?), Preface, pp. 3 ff.

[18] Cf. Rowley, BJRL 41 (1958), 168, n. 3.

[19] H. M. Kallen, *The Book of Job as a Greek Tragedy Restored,* 1918.

[20] Cf. Pfeiffer, *Introduction . . . ,* p. 684. Ginsberg, *Conservative Judaism* 21/3 (1967), 12–28, sees the formation of the book as follows: (A) The book of the Patient Job, i 1–ii 8, wherein Job's piety is put to the test and proved genuine and disinterested; (B) ii 9–10, Job's wife fails to appreciate his point of view and is rebuked; (C) ii 11–13, Job's friends arrive; (D) a section, now missing, in which Job's friends urge him, as his wife has done, to repudiate the God who had treated him so cruelly; (E) chapters xxvii and xxviii, Job's indignant rejoinder to the blasphemous suggestion of the friends; (F) perhaps a second lost passage containing a divine address to Job similar to Gen xxii 13, 16–18, in which Job is told that he has passed the test and will be rewarded; (G) xlii 7–17, the friends are rebuked and Job rewarded. Thus the Patient Job is a sort of super-Abraham. Job the Impatient is presented in chapters iii–xlii (minus xxvii and xxviii) wherein "A great genius has taken advantage of a chink in the armor of the orthodox doctrine of retribution, in order to drive a wedge into it." The poet switched the roles traditionally assigned to Job and his friends, and Job became the protestant and the friends the champions of orthodoxy.

The Date of the Book

Rabbinic opinions as to the date of the Book of Job range from the era of the patriarchs (ca. 2100–1550 B.C.) down to the Persian period. Bar Qappara supposed that Job lived in the time of Abraham, and Abba ben Kahana, that he was a contemporary of Jacob whose daughter he married (TB, Baba Bathra 15b). The oldest rabbinic opinion (TB, Baba Bathra 14b) ascribes authorship of the book to Moses. Other traditions connect Job with Jethro and Balaam who were consulted by Pharaoh on the question of the Israelites' genocide, Job's woes being regarded as punishment for his failure to protest this crime (TB, Sanhedrin 106a, Soṭah 11a). The Book of Yashar (a folkloristic retelling of the biblical narrative from Adam to Joshua, probably composed in Italy in the twelfth century) relates a variant of this tradition. In the apocryphal appendix to the LXX, Job is identified with Jobab the king of Edom, grandson of Esau (Gen xxxvi 33) and great-great-grandson of Abraham.

While ordinarily little store may be set by such uncritical traditional opinions, they are not to be brushed aside without due consideration. These early datings were doubtless suggested by the patriarchal background reflected in the folk tale, the Prologue-Epilogue. The patriarchal setting of the Prologue-Epilogue appears as authentic in detail and coloring as that of the patriarchal narratives in Genesis. Job's wealth, like Abraham's, consists of cattle and slaves (Job i 3, xlii 12; Gen xii 16, xxxii 5). As in the Balaam story (Num xxiii 1, 14, 29), religious belief and practice are simple. There is no priesthood or central shrine and the patriarch himself offers sacrifice (Job i 5, xlii 8). The Sabeans and Chaldeans are represented as nomadic raiders with no hint of their later political and economic importance (Job i 15, 17). The unit of money mentioned in Job xlii 11 is met elsewhere only in Gen xxxiii 19 and Josh xxiv 32. Job's longevity is surpassed only by the antediluvians (Gen v) and approximated by Abraham's (Gen xxv 7). The Prologue-Epilogue also presents a number of literary features and motifs which are characteristic of Semitic epic, as known from Akkadian literature and more recently from the Ugaritic texts. These epic literary features appear as a sort of substratum which may well derive from a very ancient Job epic.[21] That there was an ancient Job legend, and perhaps a Job epic, which served as the basis of the biblical narrative, is suggested by the allusion to Job in Ezek xiv 14, 20 where he is associated with the ancient worthies Noah and Danel. It had long been appreciated that the Danel mentioned in connection with Noah and Job implied a Dan(i)el legend older than that of the biblical Book of Daniel whose historical setting is given as the Neo-Babylonian and early Persian periods.[22] This more ancient Danel we now know in a long epic poem from Ugarit dating about a millennium earlier than the Babylonian Exile. From Ugarit also we have another long epic poem which has certain affinities with the story of Job. The Keret epic[23] tells of a king whose entire family was wiped out in a series of catastrophes. He fell victim to disease and was confronted with the prospect of death, but restored to health and resumed his rule. And with the aid and favor of the god El, Keret acquired a new wife and begot a second series of children. The poem is incomplete and we do not know exactly what was its central concern, but the motifs of loss and restoration of family and health are similar to central motifs of the Job story.

Mesopotamian parallels to Job have continued to increase since the early days of the recovery and interpretation of cuneiform documents. The first composition to be recognized as a parallel to the Book of Job was the text entitled "I Will Praise the Lord of Wisdom" (*ludlul bēl nēmeqi*) which became widely known as the "Babylonian Job."[24] Though the earliest extant copies of this text come from the library of Ashurbanipal (669–633 B.C.), the date of composition, in the opinion of experts, goes back to Cassite times (ca. 1600–1150 B.C.).[25] That there were still older Akkadian compositions on the subject of seemingly innocent suffering is indicated by J. Nougayrol's discovery in the Louvre of a fragment of such

21 N. M. Sarna, "Epic Substratum in the Prose of Job," JBL 76 (1957), 13–25.

22 Spiegel, *Louis Ginzberg Jubilee Volume*, pp. 305–55; Noth, VT 1 (1951), 251–60.

23 H. L. Ginsberg, "The Legend of King Keret, a Canaanite Epic of the Bronze Age," BASOR, Suppl. Studies 2–3, 1946; ANET, pp. 142–49; J. Gray, *The Krt Text in the Literature of Ras Shamra, a Social Myth of Ancient Canaan*, Documenta et Monumenta Orientis Antiqui, V, 1955.

24 Full citation of the literature is given by W. G. Lambert in BWL, pp. 27 f.

25 Cf. Lambert, BWL, p. 26.

a poem which dates from the end of the First Dynasty of Babylon.[26] Behind these Akkadian compositions dealing with the problem of suffering lay still older Sumerian prototypes which are now just beginning to be recovered. A Sumerian text dealing with the same problem as the biblical Book of Job has been pieced together by S. N. Kramer[27] from fragments that had long lain unrecognized in museums thousands of miles apart. This Sumerian version of the Job motif is not very similar to the so-called "Babylonian Job," but is as close as the latter to the biblical Job. The Sumerian text dates from about the same time as the Akkadian text, that is, ca. 1700 B.C., but it is likely that it derives from a composition as early as the Third Dynasty of Ur, ca. 2000 B.C., if not earlier. Thus the literary parallels to Job go back to the second millennium B.C. and enhance the probability that an ancient legend or epic lies behind the biblical story and even that the Dialogue may be much older than commonly supposed.

Among early Christian savants, Eusebius suggested a pre-Mosaic date and Gregory of Nazianzus assigned the book to the time of Solomon. Few modern scholars have concurred with such early dates. In the last century, a number of critics, mostly German, have inclined to the seventh century. In more recent decades a date between the sixth and the fourth centuries has been favored.[28] The observation of W. F. Albright represents the general informed opinion: "In any case, it remains exceedingly probable that the author of Job lived in the cosmopolitan atmosphere of the sixth or fifth century B.C., and he was certainly conversant with a wide range of lost pagan Northwest-Semitic literature, though Hebrew was still his literary (probably no longer his spoken) language."[29] An early postexilic date was suggested already by the tannaite rabbis Johanan and Eleazar who supposed that Job was one of those who returned from the Babylonian captivity (cf. TB, Baba Bathra 15a; Talmud Yerushalmi, Soṭah 8; Midrash Rabba Gen lvii). The dating of Job in the sixth or fifth century B.C. inevitably raises the question of the

[26] J. Nougayrol, "Une version ancienne du 'Juste souffrant,'" RB 59 (1952), 239–50. Lambert, however, declares (BWL, p. 11, n. ii) that there is no evidence that this text deals with a righteous sufferer.

[27] Kramer, in WIANE, pp. 170–82.

[28] For a survey of opinions on the date of Job, cf. Pfeiffer, *Introduction . . .*, pp. 675–78.

[29] W. F. Albright, "Some Canaanite-Phoenician Sources of Hebrew Wisdom," in WIANE, p. 14.

relation to the Second Isaiah, and especially to the Servant Poems and the Suffering Servant passage of Isa lii 13–liii 12.[30] There is no need here to enter into a discussion of the complexities connected with the interpretation of the Servant Poems and the question whether the Servant represents an individual, or the nation, or both (through the fluidity of the concept of corporate personality). It is sufficient to stress here that Job is clearly concerned with the problem of individual suffering and that poetic compositions of this nature go back at least to the early part of the second millennium B.C. As for the literary relationship between Job and the Second Isaiah, R. H. Pfeiffer has argued convincingly that Job has priority.[31] An early post-exilic date seems doubtful in view of the following considerations. If the author were a Judean or a Jew who had experienced either the shock of national disaster or the joy of restoration, it would seem inevitable that to him the story of Job would be a parable of his nation's fate and destiny. If this were the case, it is most remarkable that the author nowhere gives any hint of this purpose. If the author of Job were a non-Israelite writing in the sixth or fifth century B.C., the lack of concern for the fate of Israel would be natural enough. However, if he were an Israelite, his concealment of any national concern would be remarkable. The reference to the humiliation of dignitaries and potentates and the destruction of nations in xii 17–25 has been taken as an allusion to the Babylonian Exile of Judah, but the terms are in no way specific. If the author of Job had experienced the national tragedy, his reaction is strange for he betrays no nationalist concerns.[32,32a]

30 Cf. Pfeiffer, *Introduction . . .*, p. 476.

31 R. H. Pfeiffer, "The Priority of Job over Is. 40–55," JBL 46 (1927), 202–6.

32 There are, nonetheless, those who divine Israelite nationalist concerns in the book. Cf. C. L. Feinberg, "Job and the Nation Israel," *Bibliotheca Sacra* 96 (1939), 405–11; 97 (1940), 27–33, 211–16; M. Susman, *Das Buch Hiob und das Schicksal des jüdischen Volkes,* 1948; D. Gonzalo Maeso, "Sentido nacional en el libro de Job," *Estudios Biblicos* 9 (1950), 67–81. B. D. Napier, *Song of the Vineyard,* 1962, pp. 339–43, pursues the analogy of Job/Israel in a very striking way through the parts of the Book of Job.

32a The late A. Guillaume, in his *Studies in the Book of Job,* 1968, offers a novel theory of the date and authorship of Job. The book, he maintains, was written in the second half of the sixth century by a Jew in Arabia. Basing his speculations on the Nabonidus-Cyrus Chronicle, the verse account of Nabonidus' exploits, and the Harran Inscriptions of Nabonidus, Guillaume places the composition of the book between 552 and 542 B.C., during Nabonidus' sojourn in Tema. Nabonidus came with military forces, occupied Tema, slew the king, plundered the land and persecuted the populace. Job himself, according to

Moreover, the choice of an Edomite as the hero of the story would have been an affront to nationalist sentiments for it was the Edomites in particular who rejoiced in the humiliation of Judah and took full advantage of their brothers' misfortune, thus intensifying the enmity and hatred that had long existed between the two related peoples.[33]

Lacking positive evidence of early post-exilic background, some critics have felt constrained to bring the date of the Book of Job down to the fifth or even the fourth century. The presence of the Satan in the Prologue may be evidence of Persian influence. This

---

Guillaume, fell victim to these depredations, as described in i 17; the Chaldeans formed themselves into three bands and made a raid on Job's camels, killing the attendants. Even though there was a considerable Jewish community in the Hijaz and a significant part of Nabonidus' army was presumably Jews, Job's property was plundered by the invaders and he himself escaped slavery and possible death by paying a ransom (vi 22). Thus was set the stage for Job's arguments with his friends and his God. The sufferings of Job and of the homeless poor forced to flee to barren lands and subsist on roots and herbs (xxx 3 ff.) were caused by Nabonidus and his troops as alluded to in xii 6. Nabonidus brought with him his patron deity, the moon-god Sin, and this, Guillaume suggests, is mentioned in xii 6c, "the one who brings a god in his hand." Ordinarily the introduction of another god into the well-stocked Arabian pantheon would have caused no stir, but to the Jewish community of Tema, suffering discrimination because of their monotheistic faith, it would be cause for criticism of God's tolerance. The author of the Book of Job protested that he had never been tempted to idolatry (xxxi 26–28) and therefore had expected to live a long and prosperous life (xxix 18), but instead had become a homeless outcast, forced to consort with the rabble whom he previously deemed unfit to associate with his dogs (xxx 1). The Babylonian occupation of Job's homeland came to an end after ten years and the Lord restored Job's prosperity (xlii 10 ff.). The turn for the better came soon after 542 B.C. which would be the approximate date of the composition of the book. The Jewish community in the Hijaz was comparatively wealthy at that time because they were able to give Job money and gold jewelry (xlii 11). His relatives and friends, as soon as it was safe, provided him with the capital to restore his ravaged estate. The Book of Job thus begins with the suffering occasioned by armed invasion and ends with the departure of the enemy. The Epilogue is not just "a happy ending," but a historical record of what actually happened to the righteous sufferer. Guillaume finds throughout the book allusions to the contemporary historical events and local conditions which he assumes.

Just when and how the Jewish community came to the Hijaz, and in particular the family of the author of the Book of Job, is a matter for speculation. They may have come during the conquests of Nebuchadnezzar in 597 and 586, which would allow time for a second and third generation to master the Arabic language. Since Job's wealth and social position seem to imply a long and honorable past in his adopted land, his forebears may have come as refugees as early as the Assyrian conquest of 722 B.C.

On Guillaume's view of the language of the Book of Job, see below.

33 Cf. M. Haller, "Edom in Urteil der Propheten," BZAW 41 (1925), 109–17.

particular designation of one of the members of the heavenly court may very well have been grafted onto the original tale.[34] The Satan does not figure in the Epilogue, which lays the responsibility for Job's misfortunes entirely on Yahweh (xlii 11). Comparison of II Sam xxiv 1 and I Chron xxi 1 suggests that the Satan may be a parvenu in the Prologue. But, leaving aside the question of the origin of the Satan,[35] the motif of the divine assembly (in which the Satan is only a member) is a feature of early Near Eastern theology encountered in Mesopotamian literature and in the Ugaritic mythological texts.[36] It is also echoed in some of the Psalms and in Second Isaiah[37] as a poetic archaism long after the concept had ceased to have real force. The celestial court scene in the Prologue of the Book of Job bears more resemblance to the vision of Micaiah ben Imlah (I Kings xxii 9–23), which reflects ideas of the ninth century B.C., than to the vision of the high priest's trial in the heavenly court in Zechariah iii, in spite of the parallel use of the definite article before the word. Apart from the reference to the Satan, there is scant ground for dating the Prologue-Epilogue in the post-exilic period. In view of the Mesopotamian and Syrian parallels dating from the second millennium B.C., it would not be unreasonable to suppose that there was an ancient Job legend and epic circulating in Palestine-Syria in pre-exilic times. The author of the Dialogue, as well as the later editors and redactors, may have made considerable changes in the ancient folk tale of Job, but must have retained the chief features of a story already well known. The Dialogue itself is difficult to date. The ideas championed by Job's friends were normative in Mesopotamian theology from the early second millennium B.C.[38] A dialogue between a sufferer and a comforter, or rather heckler, is represented by the Babylonian Theodicy composed between the fourteenth and the eighth centuries B.C., probably ca. 1000 B.C.[39] The fact that the Dialogue of the Book of Job presents three "comforters" rather than one is in itself no strong reason for assuming the influence of Greek philosophical

[34] Cf. Rowley, BJRL 41 (1958), 186, n. 5.

[35] Cf. R. Schärf, *Die Gestalt des Satans im Alten Testament,* 1948, Bibliography, pp. 177–83.

[36] Cf. EUT, pp. 48 f.

[37] Cf. F. M. Cross, Jr., "The Council of Yahweh in Second Isaiah," JNES 12 (1953), 274–77.

[38] Cf. Lambert, BWL, pp. 10 f., 14–20.

[39] Lambert, BWL, p. 67.

dialogues. The sufferer in the Babylonian Theodicy questions divine justice in much the same spirit as Job. The effort to date the Dialogue on the basis of theology is also precarious. The theology of the ancient Near East was remarkably homogeneous over a long period of time.[40] A practical monotheism seems implicit throughout the Book of Job, but there is no unanimity among scholars as to when the doctrine of monotheism arose. The use of the divine name Shaddai harks back to the patriarchal era, whether as a genuine token or as a studied archaism.

The Israeli scholar Y. Kaufmann[41] contends for a pre-exilic date for Job, although not all of his arguments are cogent. According to Kaufmann, the legend of Job's trials at the instance of Satan belong, with the stories of the Flood, Sodom and Gomorrah, and Jonah, to the ancient moralistic literature of Israel. The antiquity of the prose framework, Kaufmann feels, is vouched for by its highly naïve images of God. A theophany in the full light of day such as we have in Job is last mentioned in the Elijah story, I Kings xix. What we can still comprehend of the poetry of Job is, according to Kaufmann, classical Hebrew at its best, but he goes on to observe that the "contacts with Ugaritic, Aramaic, and Arabic are most naturally understood as arising out of the antique literary dialect that the author employed; it is this that makes the reading of the book so difficult."[42] Kaufmann admits that the author may have known and have been influenced by the wisdom of the "Easterners," but he insists on the "Israelite" character of the work. Kaufmann draws an analogy with the story of Jonah the non-Israelite background of which he[43] explains by the fact that it deals with a general, universal moral problem. It should be noted, however, that Jonah is depicted as a "Hebrew," which is not the case with Job. One is inclined to share Kaufmann's view that the book "was composed in the golden age of Israel's creativity, the age before the Exile," but the original "Israelite" character of the work and the specific dates for the various parts of the book remain in doubt.

R. Gordis,[43a] in support of his view that the Book of Job was composed in the period of the Second Temple, in "the heyday of Wisdom

[40] Cf. Morton Smith, "The Common Theology of the Ancient Near East," JBL 71 (1952), 135–47.

[41] *The Religion of Israel,* pp. 334–38.

[42] *The Religion of Israel,* p. 338.

[43] *The Religion of Israel,* p. 283.

[43a] *The Book of God and Man: A Study of Job,* 1965, pp. 216 ff.

literature, when concern with the individual became paramount in religious thought," appeals to presumed dependence on Deutero-Isaiah. "The prophet of the Exile developed the insight that suffering was not necessarily the consequence and proof of sin and applied it to the destiny of the nation. The poet, who knew the writings of Deutero-Isaiah, transferred this idea to the lot of the individual. Moreover, while Deutero-Isaiah must still debate faith in one God against the polytheism rampant in Babylonia, Job takes monotheism for granted." Both these points are moot. The notion that concern for the fate of the individual developed later than concern for the nation needs reconsideration in view of the fact that Mesopotamians were writing about the problem of individual suffering more than a millennium before the Exile and the Second Temple. The alleged monotheism of Job is not explicit, as it is in Deutero-Isaiah. Moreover, there are scholars who would place the development of monotheism much earlier than Deutero-Isaiah.

Gordis argues that the phraseological parallel between Isa xli 20 and Job xii 9 indicates dependency on the part of the latter. But since this is the only place in the Dialogue of Job where the Tetragrammaton YHWH is used, and since some manuscripts read here *'ĕlôah,* it appears more likely that the original reading was *'ĕlôah* and that the reading in Job xii 9 was secondarily conformed to the parallel in Isa xli 20.

Another argument adduced by Gordis for a date in the early second Commonwealth is that Job is familiar with the idea of an afterlife, but like Qoheleth and other Wisdom writers finds himself unable to accept it. "That he was able to dismiss it with no argument suggests the earlier period of the Second Temple, when the idea was beginning to make headway but had not yet won general acceptance." This argument is nullified simply by noting that a similar situation obtains in the Ugaritic epic of Aqhat (2 Aqht vi 33–38) when the young hero is offered immortality (*bl mt,* "no death") by the goddess 'Anat, but rejects the idea as impossible.

> Then answered hero Aqhat:
> "Lie not to me, O Virgin,
> For to a hero thy lies are loathsome.
> Mortal, what fate gets he?
> What gets a mortal as destiny?
> Glaze they will pour on my head,

Lye on the top of my pate.
The common death I will die,
I indeed will die."

One could as well argue that Job should be dated in the middle of the second millennium B.C., on the basis of its parallel attitude toward afterlife with the Aqhat epic, as in the middle of the first millennium on the basis of the parallel with Qoheleth.

H. L. Ginsberg[43b] inclines to the view that the book was produced in the late Persian Period, but does not insist on this.

The fact that the dates proposed by authorities, ancient and modern, span more than a millennium is eloquent testimony that the evidence is equivocal and inconclusive. Even the mention of Job by Jesus Ben Sira (Ecclesiasticus xlix 9) in the second century B.C. does not prove that the present Book of Job was known to Ben Sira, for the allusion is to Ezekiel's mention of the tradition of a righteous Job. The recovery of portions of a Targum of Job from the Qumran Caves indicate that the book must have been in circulation for some time before the first century B.C. While the completed book may be as late as the third century B.C., it may also be several centuries earlier. Parts of the book may have very early antecedents. We have noted the probability of the existence of an ancient Job legend among the western Semites. The treatment of the problem of theodicy and innocent suffering in poetic discourse and dialogue by the eastern Semites, and by the Sumerians, as early as the second millennium B.C. gives reason to suppose that the western Semites could have produced similar works at about the same time. The date of the Book of Job, then, is still an open question and will remain so until more convincing arguments can be given for assigning it to any given century. The seventh century B.C. seems the best guess for the date of the Dialogue. We may hope that discoveries and researches in the not too distant future will make possible more confident and precise estimates.

The Authorship of the Book

It is scarcely possible to speak of the author of any biblical book in the modern sense of the word, for virtually all biblical books are

[43b] *Conservative Judaism* 21/3 (1967), 24.

composite in some degree, as were most literary productions in the ancient Near East. Many different hands and minds must have contributed to the formation of the Gilgamesh Epic, before it reached its more or less standard or canonical form. The Book of Job, in the opinion of most biblical scholars, bears evidences of such compositeness. Yet, in the heart of the book, in the Dialogue (chs. iii–xxxi), there is a characteristic literary excellence which suggests the influence of a single personality. This person we can know only through his work, and it is altogether likely that he will remain forever anonymous, like the author of the great poems of the latter half of the Book of Isaiah. There can be no question that we are confronted with a poet of genius, for his work has been acclaimed as one of the great masterpieces of world literature. He must have been a profoundly religious person, sensitive to the tragic predicament of humanity, especially to individual suffering. The poet had himself probably experienced physical and mental agony, since it is hard to understand how one could have written thus without personal knowledge of suffering. The sincerity and depth of the poet's thought and feeling, his keen insight into human nature, the vivid beauty and the raw realism of his metaphors and similes give his work the power to move men's minds and hearts in every time and place.

There is no certainty that the author was an Israelite. Some parts of the book may suggest familiarity with the prophetic, and didactic writings of the Old Testament, but there is nothing very specific or definite. Job's bitter outcry recalls some of the biblical psalms of lamentation (Pss xxxviii, lxxxviii, cii). Lamentation, however, was a common literary genre in the ancient Near East. There are figures of speech in the Book of Job that comport with a Palestinian background, but again there is nothing that could not be taken as reflecting some other part of the ancient Semitic world as well. The author appears to be acquainted with Egypt and perhaps had traveled widely. In any event, his familiarity with world literature is evidenced by numerous allusions to mythological motifs now known from ancient literature of Mesopotamia and Syria. We may be sure that the author belonged to the intellectual elite of his day. Recent studies of ancient Near Eastern Wisdom Literature indicate that "wisdom" had a strongly international and cosmopolitan flavor.[44] The seeker of wisdom in the ancient world, even as today, tended to

[44] Cf. WIANE, *passim*.

ignore geographical boundaries and political barriers. The author of the Book of Job cannot be precisely placed temporally or geographically, but this is of no great consequence for he speaks to and for all humanity about a problem that has perplexed thinking and feeling men in all times and places. Ginsberg[44a] has affirmed "that the author was a Jew, 100 per cent." (It is not clear whether the percentage applies to Ginsberg's certainty or to the author's Jewishness, or to both.) One good reason why the author can be only a Jew, according to Ginsberg, is his horror at the injustice in the world, as expressed, for example, in xxi 6. "Now this reaction is possible only in Israel," Ginsberg asserts. Without wishing to detract from ancient Israel's merited praise for concern about social justice and sensitivity to injustice, at least on the part of some gifted spokesmen, it does not seem reasonable to deny the possibility of this basically human reaction to non-Israelites. The section on Parallel Literature below, condensed as it is, may serve to mitigate the assurance of Ginsberg's assertion. Ginsberg, of course, is thoroughly familiar with the Parallel Literature and mentions it in connection with the assertion cited, but finds the horrified reaction to injustice exclusively Israelite.

The Place of the Book in the Canon

The Book of Job finds its place in the last of the three divisions of the Hebrew scriptures, the Sacred Writings, or Hagiographa.[45] Despite the unsettling character of the book, its right to be included in the Canon was never challenged, except by Theodore of Mopsuestia. Among the Writings its position has varied somewhat. The Talmud gives the order of the Writings as Ruth, Psalms, Job, Proverbs, Ecclesiastes, Song of Songs, Lamentations, Daniel, Esther, Ezra, Chronicles. In Codex Alexandrinus the order is Psalms, Job, Proverbs, but Cyril of Jerusalem, Epiphanius, Jerome, Rufinus, and the Apostolic Canons attest to the order Job, Psalms, Proverbs. In Jewish usage the poetic trilogy is designated by two sets of initials corresponding to the two orders, Job, Proverbs, Psalms (*'mt*), and Psalms, Job, Proverbs (*t'm*). The Latin Church Fathers men-

[44a] *Conservative Judaism* 21/3 (1967), 28.

[45] Cf. P. Katz, "The Old Testament Canon in Palestine and Alexandria," ZNW 47 (1956), 191–217; p. 208 on Job.

tion other orders, but the order favored by St. Jerome, with Job in the initial position, was fixed by the Council of Trent and this official order of the Vulgate has been generally followed in modern western versions of the Scriptures.

Textual Problems

In fairness to the reader, it should be explained that the translation offered in this volume—as with every attempt to translate an ancient text—glosses over a multitude of difficulties and uncertainties. The Book of Job is textually the most vexed in the Old Testament,[46] rivaled only by Hosea which has the advantage of being much shorter. The expedient of omitting the more difficult passages has been considered, but rejected because it is hard to decide how to grade degrees of difficulty and uncertainty and to know when to despair. The size of the Book of Job would be greatly reduced if all the difficult passages were omitted. In any case, the reasons for omissions would have to be explained in detail. Accordingly, it seemed wise to attempt to explain the nature and crux of the difficulties and to choose what appear to be the best solutions or expedients, thus keeping omissions to a minimum.

It is possible in some cases to "improve" the Hebrew text by comparison with the Greek,[47] but more often recourse to the Greek complicates rather than clarifies a problem. The oldest form of the Greek text was considerably shorter than the Hebrew. In Origen's time the current Greek version had some four hundred lines fewer than the Hebrew. Origen supplied the missing lines from Theodotion's translation of the Hebrew and marked these added lines with an asterisk. A Coptic version of Job, published in 1899, agrees in the main with the pre-Origen text, generally omit-

[46] G. Beer, *Der Text des Buches Hiob*, 1897; G. R. Driver, "Problems in Job," AJSL 52 (1935–36), 160–70; "Problems in the Hebrew Text of Job," in WIANE, pp. 72–93; H. Orlinsky, "The Textual Criticism of the Old Testament," BANE, 1961, pp. 113–32.

[47] J. Ziegler, "Der textkritische Wert der Septuaginta des Buches Job," *Miscellanea Biblica* 2 (1934), 277–96; H. Orlinsky, "Some Corruptions in the Greek Text of Job," JQR 26 (1935–36), 133–45; "The Septuagint—Its Use in Textual Criticism," BA 9 (1946), 23–34; "Studies in the Septuagint of the Book of Job," HUCA 28 (1957), 53–74; 29 (1958), 229–71; 30 (1959), 153–67; J. W. Wevers, "Septuaginta-Forschungen," ThR 22 (1954), 85–138, 171–90 (Hiob, pp. 187–90).

ting the passages which Origen marked with asterisks. The relation of the Hebrew and Greek texts of Job is thus similar to that of the Book of Jeremiah where the Greek is also a good deal shorter than the Hebrew. While a few scholars have supposed that the shorter Greek version represents the earlier form of the text, the weight of the evidence is against them. The gaps in the old Greek text do not relieve but rather increase the difficulties by removing the context of the remaining passages. The translator of the pre-Origen Greek version, apparently unable to understand or translate some of the lines, simply omitted them, just as a modern translator may be tempted to do. This simple expedient of passing over difficulties would certainly spare the translator and interpreter much pain, but would leave the reader dissatisfied and curious to know what was omitted and why. The Greek version of Job in many passages may be regarded as more of a paraphrase than a translation, although the line between translation and paraphrase is difficult to draw. Some students of the Greek text have seen theological bias on the part of the Greek translator which led him to obscure or radically alter the sense of the Hebrew.[48] An eminent specialist in the Greek text, however, has effectively defended the translator of Job against the charges of theological bias in a number of instances.[49] The factor of theological concern or bias cannot, of course, be completely eliminated by any translator or interpreter, ancient or modern. The famous passage Job xiii 15 illustrates the influence of theological interests on the part of both the Jewish scribes and the Greek translator. Contrast of KJ and RSV renderings of this passage will serve to point up a certain theological bias on the part of the Masoretes, the scholars who fixed the standard vocalization of the Hebrew text. The difference between "Though he slay me, yet will I trust in him" and "Behold, he will slay me; I have no hope" is explained by a very minor matter of orthography. The consonantal text has the negative particle *l'* before the last verb which would thus mean "I do not hope/fear" (the verb apparently means to tremble with expectancy, either in hope or fear). The Masoretes were able to twist the sense of the passage radically, and contrary

[48] H. S. Gehman, "The Theological Approach of the Greek Translator of Job 1–15," JBL 68 (1949), 231–40; D. H. Gard, *The Exegetical Method of the Greek Translator of the Book of Job,* JBL Monograph Series, VIII, 1952.

[49] Orlinsky, HUCA 28 (1957), 53–74; 29 (1958), 229–71; 30 (1959), 153–67; 32 (1961), 239–68.

to the context, by proposing a slight change in the spelling of the negative particle *lô(')* in order to interpret it as the preposition with the object suffix, "to/for/in him?," properly spelled *lô(w)*. (This difference in spelling of the homophones for "not" and "to him" is the basis for the difference in Ps c 3, "It is he that made us, and we are his / And not we ourselves.") The elimination of the negative particle enabled the Masoretes to turn Job's defiant and bitter protest against divine injustice into an affirmation of complete trust and submission. The Greek translator did not think of this clever and simple twist, for had he known it he would almost certainly have adopted it here. The Greek translator could do little more to mitigate Job's blasphemy than to muddle the sense a bit: "Though the Mighty One lay hand on me, since he has already begun, I will speak and plead before him."

The other ancient versions are scarcely more helpful than the Greek in the task of reconstituting and interpreting the Hebrew. The Syriac Peshitta, like the Greek, was made directly from the Hebrew, and is often useful in the clarification of obscure Hebrew words. The Targum (Aramaic paraphrase) offers many curious interpretations, but makes little contribution to the solution of textual difficulties. Two portions of a Targum of Job have been found at Qumran, a very small fragment from Cave IV and a more sizable piece from Cave XI. These fragments have yet to be published and their textual value assessed, but they should prove very interesting. It has been suggested that this Targum may be the one condemned by the Apostle Paul's teacher, Rabbi Gamaliel I, and thus one of the earliest Targums committed to writing.[50]

[Since the writing of the preceding paragraph, the Job Targum from Cave XI of Qumran has been published; see the Preface and Principal Abbreviations. The document is officially designated 11 Q tg Job, but in this work is simply referred to as "the Qumran Targum." Nothing is preserved before the middle of chapter xvii of the MT and up to chapter xxxii the text is very fragmentary, but thereafter the remains become progressively more extensive, with some fairly substantial passages between xxxvii 10 and xlii 11 where the document ends. The editors, Professors J. van der Ploeg and A. S. van der

[50] F. M. Cross, Jr., *The Ancient Library of Qumran*, 1958, p. 26. For a preliminary report, cf. J. van der Ploeg, "Le Targum de Job de la grotte 11 de Qumran," *Mededelingen der Koninklijke Akademie van Wetenschappen*, Deel 25, No. 9 (Amsterdam, 1962), 545–57.

Woude, conclude on the basis of palaeography that the manuscript belongs to the first century of the present era. The language of the document, however, suggests that the origins of the text go back as far as the first part of the second century B.C. Accordingly, the Job Targum from Qumran is the oldest Targum so far known. The long-disputed question whether written Targums existed in Jesus' day is now settled and we have a fair sample of just such a document. The language of the Qumran Targum of Job and of the Genesis Apocryphon, we may safely assume, must be very similar to the Aramaic spoken by Jesus and his followers, and by the Palestinian peasantry. Whether the text of the Qumran Targum of Job is the same as that which Rabbi Gamaliel suppressed cannot be determined, but the possibility is now very real and provocative of serious speculation. The translation is on the whole remarkably similar to the MT, but there are numerous differences. In many instances the translation tends to agree more with the LXX than with the MT, but there are also peculiar differences from both. The Qumran Targum thus complicates the already complex problems of the textual history of the Book of Job and much study will be required to clarify details and appraise their significance. The integrity of the MT receives strong support from the Qumran Targum, but there are also many instances where the two cannot be reconciled. A notable contribution of the Qumran Targum is the confirmation of the order, or disorder, presented by MT chapters xxiv–xxvii. Enough is preserved of these chapters to show that the sequence corresponds to that of MT and thus the incompletion or disruption of the third cycle of speeches is attested in the earliest witness to the text. (The antiquity of this condition, however, does not remove the difficulty or obviate the necessity of sorting out the confused strains of the argument presented by those chapters.) One of the most striking differences between the MT, LXX, and the Qumran Targum is the conclusion of the latter at xlii 11.

The publication of the Job Targum came only a short time before the deadline for submission of final revisions for this third edition, and there was no time for a thorough study. Nevertheless, it seemed imperative to take account of this exciting new material, without going too deeply into the difficulties and problems, and to provide for those who might be interested, some indication of the nature, scope, and significance of this new data. If some readers feel that either too little or too much attention is given to the Qumran Targum, they may be appeased, or further vexed, by the apology that several lengthy notes were omitted because the problems were confounded rather than alleviated by the discussion. A number of detailed investigations will have to be devoted to the Qumran Targum before we can know what to make of the textual tangles. M.H.P.]

The Latin version, or Vulgate, was translated directly from the Hebrew text current in St. Jerome's day, at the end of the fourth century. Jerome, however, sometimes translated literally and sometimes rather freely. He had as a tutor a rabbi of Lydda who inevitably influenced his pupil along lines of traditional Jewish exegesis. Jerome was also influenced by Origen's Hexapla (an arrangement of the Hebrew text and a transliteration of the Hebrew in Greek letters alongside the versions of Aquila, Symmachus, Theodotion, and the Alexandrian version, as revised by Origen, in six parallel columns) which he had studied and translated into Latin. It is thus necessary to use considerable discretion in correcting the Hebrew text on the basis of Jerome's Latin.

The Masoretic Hebrew remains our primary source for the Book of Job, even though in many places the text is corrupt or obscure and has to be emended in order to yield any acceptable sense. Modern researches and discoveries have helped to clarify many difficulties both in the text and the interpretation of Job. The mythological texts from the ancient city of Ugarit have been especially valuable for the light thrown on biblical poetry in general and on the Book of Job in particular. In the NOTES will be found reference to some of the contributions made by the Ugaritic texts in respect to specific passages. In spite of recent progress in biblical studies, many textual and exegetical difficulties remain and the Book of Job has more than its share of these. Biblical scholars are aware of these difficulties, but it is only fair to let the interested reader know when there is uncertainty and disagreement about the meaning of a given passage.

THE LANGUAGE OF THE BOOK

In addition to the textual difficulties already mentioned, the Book of Job also presents formidable linguistic and philological problems. Sometimes it is hard to say whether the difficulty of a given passage is more a philological than a textual problem. There are more *hapax legomena* (words which occur only once) and rare words in Job than in any other biblical book. Many of these unique words, as well as the large number of rare words, may be explained from cognates[51] in one or another of the other Semitic languages. (The term "Semitic" is properly a purely linguistic term, coined in 1781 by A. L. Schloezer to designate the family of closely related languages which include Babylonian-Assyrian, Canaanite, Aramaic, Arabic, and Ethiopic. Canaanite includes Hebrew, Phoenician, Moabite, Edomite, and possibly also Ugaritic.[52] People whose mother tongue is one of these Semitic languages are correctly called Semites, but the word ought not to be used as an ethnic term since the peoples who spoke and still speak these languages are of diverse genetic make-up and admixtures.) The problems of Job, however, are not simply lexical, but also morphological and syntactic. The language is ostensibly Hebrew, but with so many peculiarities that some scholars have wondered whether it might not be influenced by some other Semitic dialect. The Edomite connections of the story, its setting and the provenience of the characters, led critics such as Voltaire, Herder, and Renan to suggest that the poem echoes the famed wisdom of Edom (I Kings iv 30). It has been supposed that the author was an Edomite rather than a Jew.[53] The Edomites were recognized as very close relatives of the Israelites, so close that biblical tradition represents the eponymous ancestors of the two peoples as twin brothers (Gen xxv 23 ff.). The language of the Edomites was also very close to that of the Israelites, which came to be termed "Hebrew," but in the Old Testament the language of the Israelites is referred to only as "Canaanite" (Isa xix 18, literally "the lip of Canaan") and "Jewish" (II Kings xviii 26, 28= Isa xxxvi 11, 13=II Chron xxxii 18; Neh xiii 24). The neighboring Canaanite dialects of the Israelites, Ammonites, Moabites, and Edomites were certainly very much alike, to judge from the famous Moabite Stone or Mesha Stela. Unfortunately, we have virtually

[51] Saadia already in the tenth century explained ninety (not seventy) unique and rare words of the OT on the basis of cognates.

[52] For a discussion of recent developments in this area, cf. W. J. Moran, "The Hebrew Language in Its Northwest Semitic Background," BANE, pp. 54–72.

[53] Cf. R. H. Pfeiffer, "Edomitic Wisdom," ZAW 44 (1926), 13–25; Pfeiffer, *Introduction* . . . , p. 680.

no linguistic materials that can be classed as Edomite, except for a few proper names.[54]

It was first suggested by Ibn Ezra that the Book of Job was translated from another language—an idea held by a few modern scholars. Some have thought that the original language was Arabic.[55] It is true that there are a number of words in Job not attested elsewhere in the Old Testament and for which the clue to the meaning is found in Arabic. The explanation is quite obvious—Arabic has by far the richest vocabulary and literature of all the Semitic languages and is the best known. The suggestion that the Book of Job was translated from Arabic may be dismissed as highly improbable.[55a]

It is generally conceded that the language of the Book of Job has a strong Aramaic tinge. There are many features of phonology and morphology that are characteristically Aramaic. Hebrew and Aramaic words are often juxtaposed as synonyms in the poetic parallelism. A certain amount of this sort of mixture is normal for biblical and post-biblical Hebrew. The language of Job, however, contains far more than the normal admixture of Aramaic, more than any other book of the Old Testament. The Israeli scholar Tur-Sinai[56]

[54] Eliezer ben Yehudah, "The Edomitic Language," JPOS 1 (1921), 113–15.

[55] Cf. F. H. Foster, "Is the Book of Job a Translation from an Arabic Original?", AJSL 49 (1932–33), 21–45.

[55a] The theory of the Arabic origin of the Book of Job was advocated by A. Guillaume, "The Arabic Background of the Book of Job," in *Promise and Fulfilment: Essays Presented to S. H. Hooke,* 1963, pp. 106–27, and *Studies in the Book of Job,* 1968. The linguistic difficulties of the book, according to Guillaume, are the result of a centuries-long failure to perceive that it was written by a poet whose language was impregnated through and through with Arabic, that the book was written in Arabia, and furthermore that the very first chapter tells us where (Tema) and almost exactly when (i.e., between 552 and 542 B.C., during or immediately following Nabonidus' sojourn in Tema). The most concise statement of Guillaume's view is confused. In commenting on xv 22 (*Studies . . . ,* p. 95), he says: "I have endeavoured to prove that the Book of Job was written in and probably for Arabic speaking Hebrew readers and consequently one must take into account the possibility that an Arabic word or a Hebrew word used in an Arabic sense lies before us." Presumably the intent was to convey that the language is Hebrew strongly influenced by Arabic, especially in the meanings of certain words. Some of Guillaume's appeals to Arabic are striking, but few are wholly convincing. Resort to Arabic would have justification apart from Guillaume's theory since Arabic is our richest resource of lexical data and must be considered in almost all Semitic studies, but with caution. Guillaume posits some rather dubious phonological relations and ignores relevant Ugaritic data.

[56] N. H. Tur-Sinai (H. Torczyner), *The Book of Job: A New Commentary,* 1957, pp. xxx–xl.

has offered a characteristically bold explanation. It is, he maintains, not a matter of hybrid language, but of partial translation from an Aramaic original. Since Hebrew and Aramaic are closely related, much of the supposed Aramaic original would be readily intelligible to readers of Hebrew. To make the Aramaic poetry accessible to the Hebrew reader, it was necessary only to turn the more difficult and obscure words and phrases into Hebrew. The halfway translator would seem to have been somewhat half-witted, for it is alleged that in many cases he mistook the sense of the original Aramaic and mistranslated. This hodgepodge of Aramaic and Hebrew naturally gave the Masoretes trouble and led them to erroneous vocalizations of the consonantal text. The original language of Job, according to Tur-Sinai, is Babylonian Aramaic of the sixth century B.C. and the incomplete translation into Hebrew was made in Palestine some generations later. Tur-Sinai offers many ingenious suggestions in applying his translation theory to the interpretation of the text of Job, but very little that carries conviction. No satisfactory explanation has yet been given for the strong Aramaic coloring of the language of Job. Some of the apparent linguistic difficulties may be occasioned by our lack of knowledge. The recovery of the mythological texts of ancient Ugarit has added considerably to our knowledge of early Northwest Semitic poetry and it is to be hoped that further discoveries will contribute more information. In the meantime, we have to do the best we can with the text as we now have it. It is often impossible to make sense of a passage without in some way emending or tampering with the text. The text has certainly been tampered with before and has suffered greatly in transmission. It would, however, be extremely naïve for anyone to place too much confidence in any of the ingenious and learned textual restorations and emendations contained in the commentaries and the extensive periodical literature on Job. This *caveat* applies fully both to what is old and what is new in the NOTES of the present work.

PROBLEMS OF PROSODY

There is no warrant for attempting here a detailed discussion of the poetics of the Book of Job since this would necessarily involve discussion of definitions of poetry and a consideration of the ancient poetry of the Egyptians, Sumerians, Akkadians, and western Semites as background for biblical poetry.[57] A few words of explanation, however, may be helpful to any who are unfamiliar with the nature and forms of Old Testament poetry. The fact that some of the Old Testament is poetry was recognized already by the Masoretes who devised a special system of accents for Psalms, Proverbs, and Job. Ibn Ezra and other Jewish commentators had some inkling of the importance of the principle of poetic parallelism for the interpretation of certain biblical passages, but it was the English savant Bishop Robert Lowth who first fully appreciated and described the essential nature of Hebrew poetry in his epoch-making study *De sacra poesi Hebraeorum* in 1753. The basic principle of Hebrew poetry, as Lowth discovered, is *parallelismus membrorum,* that is the repetition, elaboration, or variation of the sense of a line. Lowth identified three types of parallelism; synonymous, antithetic, and synthetic.

In synonymous parallelism the same thought is repeated exactly in synonymous terms, as in Deut xxxii 1–2:

Hear, O heavens, what I speak;
Let the earth hear the words of my mouth.

Let my message drop as the rain,
Let my speech distil as the dew,

Like mist upon the verdure,
Like showers upon the grass.

The term antithetic parallelism may be confusing but a few examples will serve to clarify the matter. The antithesis is not in terms of contradiction, thesis and antithesis, but in opposite aspects of the same idea. Proverbs x–xvi is composed largely of couplets in antithetic parallelism which contrasts the good and the evil aspects of various attitudes and conduct, for example, Prov x 1 ff.:

A wise son delights a father;
But a foolish son is a mother's grief.

[57] W. S. Golénischeff, "Parallélisme symmétrique en ancien égyptien," in *Studies Presented to F. L. Griffith,* 1932, pp. 86–96; W. F. Albright, "The Old Testament and Canaanite Language and Literature," CBQ 7 (1945), 1–31; C. L. Feinberg, "The Poetic Structure of the Book of Job and the Ugaritic Literature," *Bibliotheca Sacra* 103 (1946), 283–92; G. D. Young, "Ugaritic Prosody," JNES 9 (1950), 124–33.

Ill-gotten treasures will not avail;
But virtue saves from death.

Yahweh lets no just appetite hunger;
But the craving of the wicked he thwarts.

A slack hand makes a poor man;
But a busy hand makes rich.

It is difficult to find a clear case of antithetic parallelism in the Book of Job. Certainly iii 3 is not to be classed as such (so Terrien, IB, III, p. 894a), since no contrast is intended between the day of birth and the night of conception—both alike are damned.

The term "synthetic parallelism" is a rather infelicitous catch-all for a great variety of artful elaborations and departures from synonymy. Since Lowth's day many new terms have been introduced in attempts to describe the multiplicity of variations in poetic parallelism: emblematic, climactic, introverted, complete, incomplete, external, internal, among others. The proliferation of terms by modern critics in an attempt to describe the variant types of poetic parallelism testifies to the imagination, freedom, and skill of the poets who were able to employ this device without falling into monotony.[58] The Ugaritic mythological poems, dating from the middle of the second millennium B.C., exhibit virtually all the patterns and variations of parallelism found in the Old Testament.

The problem of Hebrew metrics[59] and the relative length of poetic lines remains unsolved. In poetry there are three mechanisms for achieving rhythm: symmetry in the number of syllables, the alternation of short and long syllables, the alternation of stressed and unstressed syllables. The counting of syllables or the alternation of short and long syllables in Hebrew poetry has yielded no patterns. Following the studies of Sievers,[60] the common view is that Hebrew

[58] G. B. Gray, *The Forms of Hebrew Poetry,* 1915; T. H. Robinson, "Basic Principles of Hebrew Poetic Form," in *Festschrift für Alfred Bertholet,* 1950, pp. 438–50; "Hebrew Poetic Form: The English Tradition," in VTS, I, 1953, pp. 128–49; J. Muilenburg, "A Study in Hebrew Rhetoric: Repetition and Style," in VTS, I, 1953, pp. 97–111; F. Horst, "Die Kennzeichen der hebräischen Poesie," ThR 21 (1953), 97–121.

[59] W. R. Arnold, "The Rhythms of the Ancient Hebrews," in *Old Testament and Semitic Studies in Memory of W. R. Harper,* I, 1908, pp. 165–204; A. Maecklenburg, "Einführung in die Probleme der hebräischen Metrik," WZKM 46 (1939), 1–46; S. Mowinckel, "Zum Problem der hebräischen Metrik," in *Festschrift für Alfred Bertholet,* pp. 379–94.

[60] E. Sievers, *Metrische Studien,* I, 1901; II, 1904–5; III, 1907.

prosody derives its rhythm from alternations in stress. The difficulty is that we know very little about the stress patterns of ancient Hebrew speech. It is certain that the word stress changed through the centuries, so that it is hard to say what the stress system was at the time of composition of a given passage of poetry. As yet no unanimity of view has been achieved as to the scansion of Hebrew poetic lines, or the number and distribution of stressed syllables in a line, or the maximum number of unstressed syllables a line can carry. The basic unit appears to be the couplet or bicolon, but there are also tricola and quatrains. The number of stressed syllables in the line is assumed to determine the meter. Thus in Deut xxxii 2a

ya'ărōp̄ kammāṭār liqḥî	Let my message drop as the rain,
tizzal kaṭṭal 'imrāṯî	Let my speech distil as the dew.

we have a bicolon or distich with three stresses in each colon so that the meter is called 3+3. Other metrical combinations are 2+2, 4+4, 4+2, 4+3, and 3+2. The 3+2 is often called Qinah Rhythm because it is characteristic of the funeral dirge (*qînāh*),[61] but it is not uncommon in other types of poetry. There are occasionally asymmetrical couplets which have the shorter line first. Attempts to find regular combinations of lines have not been eminently successful.[62] To achieve rigidly regular patterns of meter and of strophes in any of the longer poems of the Old Testament almost invariably requires too much cutting and patching to be convincing. The counting of syllables, unstressed and stressed, in lines where the text is above suspicion shows such irregularity as to cast doubt on emendations made purely on the grounds of metric theory. Transliteration of the opening lines of Job's lament, iii 3–10, will serve as a sample to illustrate the character of the poetry of Job and lack of rigid metrical pattern:

[61] H. Jahnow, *Das hebräische Leichenlied*, BZAW 36 (1923).

[62] S. Terrien (IB, III, pp. 894 ff.) presents the first speech of Eliphaz as a model of strophic composition, but it is difficult to find regularity of patterns throughout the poems. Cf. M. Löhr, "Beobachtungen zur Strophik im Buche Hiob," BZAW 33 (1918), 303–21; W. A. Irwin, "Poetic Structure in the Dialogue of Job," JNES 5 (1946), 26–39; P. W. Skehan, "Strophic Patterns in the Book of Job," CBQ 23 (1961), 129–43.

	Syllables	*Stresses*
yô'ḇáḏ yốm 'iwwā́leḏ bố	7	4
wĕhalláylāh 'āmár hōrā́h ḡā́ḇer	10	4
hayyốm hahû́' yĕhî́ ḥṓšeḵ	8	4
'al-yiḏrĕšḗhû 'ĕlốah mimmá'al	10	3
wĕ'al-tôp̄á' 'ālā́yw nĕhārā́h	9	3
yīḡ'ā́lûhû ḥṓšeḵ wĕṣalmā́weṯ	9	3
tiškán 'ālā́yw 'ănānā́h	7	3
yĕḇa'ăṯû́hû kimrîrế yốm	9	3?
halláylāh hahû́' yiqqāḥḗhû 'ṓp̄el	11	4
'al-yiḥáḏ bîmế šānā́h	7	3?
bĕmispár yĕrāḥî́m 'al-yāḇố'	9	3
hinnḗh halláylah hahû́' yĕhî́ ḡalmû́ḏ	11	5?
'al-tāḇố' rĕnānā́h ḇố	7	3?
yiqqĕḇû́hû 'ōrĕrế yốm	8	3?
hā'ăṯiḏî́m 'ôrḗr liwyāṯā́n	9	3
yeḥšĕḵû́ kôḵĕḇế nišpố	8	3?
yĕqáw lĕ'ốr wā'ā́yin	7	3
wĕ'al-yir'éh bĕ'ap̄'appế šáḥar	10	3?
kî́ lố' sāḡár dalṯế biṭnî́	8	3/4/5?
wayyastḗr 'āmā́l mē'ênā́y	8	3

In counting the syllables of the preceding lines we have included those with reduced vowels as they once represented full short vowels in open unaccented syllables. If one were to add the inflexional endings which the words once had, several syllables would be added to each line. Whether this latter consideration will help reduce the discrepancies in the number of syllables in parallel lines is a question that calls for further investigation.[63] The wavering in the estimation of the number of stresses in the lines stems from the uncertainty as to whether we should count the "construct" relation of nouns, as "in the days of the year" (*bîmê šānāh*), as having a single stress. In order to balance the stresses in parallel lines it is often necessary to be inconsistent in this regard, and to count the construct sometimes as a single stress, sometimes as a double. Further, in order to achieve balance or regularity in the number of stresses in parallel lines, it is often necessary to count or discount supposed secondary stresses or accents. There are other problems, too, but the foregoing comments may suffice to indicate something of the nature of the difficulties and the uncertainties.

It may be advisable to say a word about the present attempt to translate the poetry of Job. From the brief sample given in transliteration, it is apparent that the original is characterized by brevity and terseness rarely reflected in translation. The first two lines of Job's lament, for example, contain seven and ten syllables, whereas the traditional English rendering takes ten and fourteen syllables, respectively. The first line of the Twenty-third Psalm, *YHWH rô'î lô' 'eḥsar,* will serve as a fairly typical example of the brevity of the Hebrew, four short words in contrast to the nine words of the traditional English rendering. In the present translation, an effort has been made to achieve brevity and terseness commensurate with the original, although it is too difficult to try to match word for word or syllable for syllable. Sometimes it is impossible to render a line in intelligible English without using many more words or syllables than in the original. In general, the translation is rather literal and often follows even the word order of the original where this makes reasonably acceptable English, although there is no rigorous effort to be consistent on this score.

The line between poetry and prose is sometimes rather difficult to draw and it will be noted that some parts of the Prologue have been arranged as poetry although the characteristic parallelism is

[63] D. N. Freedman, "Archaic Forms in Early Hebrew Poetry," ZAW 72 (1960), 101–7.

absent. The same might have been done in the Epilogue because there too one feels an almost poetic rhythm in the flow of the words, but this is perhaps more marked in the translation than in the original.

Parallel Literature

The Bible cannot be properly studied or understood apart from its background and environment which comprises the whole ancient Near East. Since the middle of the last century, a great deal of new light has been shed on the Bible, especially on the Old Testament, by the recovery of considerable portions of the ancient literatures of Egypt, Mesopotamia, Syria, and Anatolia. The most important and interesting of these ancient documents, especially those that bear on the Old Testament, have been made easily accessible in translation.[64]

The problem with which the Book of Job is concerned also exercised the sages of ancient Egypt and Mesopotamia. An Egyptian text[65] dating from the end of the third millennium B.C. presents the debate of a man with his soul as to the expediency of suicide when life has become intolerable. The man's soul attempts to dissuade him from seeking death. The man proposes to seek death by fire, but his soul refuses to condone this form of escape. Somewhat like Job, the man longs for an advocate among the gods and thinks of himself as pleading his case before the divine tribunal. "Pleasant would be the defense of a god for the secrets of my body." The man's soul opposes the various arguments in favor of self-destruction, but is finally won over by the contention that life is not worth living since there is no justice or love in the world:

> (One's) fellows are evil;
> The friends of today do not love.
>
> . . . . . .

[64] The best by far is ANET. W. G. Lambert's BWL presents the Akkadian texts in translation, transliteration, and autograph, with introductions, bibliography, and notes.

[65] Cf. John A. Wilson, "Egyptian Didactic Tales. A Dispute over Suicide," ANET, pp. 405 ff.

Hearts are rapacious:
Every man seizes his fellow's goods.

. . . .

The gentle man has perished,
(But) the violent man has access to everybody.

. . . .

Goodness is rejected everywhere.

. . . .

. . . .

There are no righteous;
The land is left to those who do wrong.

. . . .

To whom can I speak today?
I am laden with wretchedness
For lack of an intimate (friend).
To whom can I speak today?
The sin which treads the earth,
It has no end.

The weary sufferer looks on death as release from the miseries of life, as recovery from an illness, as escape from bondage. The prospect of death is altogether pleasant:

Death is in my sight today
Like the odor of myrrh
Like sitting under an awning on a breezy day.[66]

Death is further compared to the change from foul weather to fair, to return home from a long journey or from captivity. The man's soul agrees to go along with him and to share the fate of the beyond. The final argument which wins the debate—that life in the beyond will be transformed and the dead will become living gods and share in the divine prerogatives—was not one which was available or acceptable to the author of the Dialogue of the Book of Job. It is interesting to note that in literary form the Egyptian Dispute over Suicide bears some similarity to Job in that it begins and ends with prose sections, the middle section being a poetic soliloquy by the wretched man.

[66] The passages quoted are the translation of Wilson, ANET, pp. 405 ff.

The Egyptian "Tale of the Eloquent Peasant,"[67] dating from the early second millennium B.C., has certain affinities with the Book of Job. The text is introduced by a prose prologue and epilogue and the central portion of the text is composed of nine semi-poetic appeals for justice on the part of the eloquent peasant. The peasant, having been maltreated and robbed by a vassal of the Chief Steward, has his complaint brushed aside as a matter of no consequence. The persistent peasant, however, refuses to be squelched. He argues his case before the Chief Steward himself and even charges the high official with lack of concern for justice. Justice, he argues, should be done for the gods' sake. "Do justice for the sake of the Lord of Justice." Justice is immortal. "Now justice lasts unto eternity; it goes down into the necropolis with him who does it. When he is buried and interred, his name is not wiped out on earth, (but) is remembered for goodness. That is a principle of the word of god." Though the peasant fears that he may be put to death for his bold insistence, he nevertheless persists in his demand for justice and welcomes death as a thirsty man goes for water or a suckling child for milk. Justice at last triumphs and the wronged peasant is rewarded with the property of the villain who had despoiled him. Although the issue of this Egyptian story is social justice and no complaint is made against the gods, still the attitude of the peasant is similar to that of Job. He prefers death rather than submission to injustice.

The problem of suffering receives a good deal of attention in Mesopotamian literature. From fragments of Sumerian texts excavated at Nippur, S. N. Kramer[68] has recovered portions of a literary composition having greater affinities with Job than any other Mesopotamian document previously known. The poem deals with a man who, like Job, had been prosperous and healthy but is afflicted with disease and pain. His lament is strikingly reminiscent of Job[69]:

[67] Cf. John A. Wilson, "The Protests of the Eloquent Peasant," ANET, pp. 407–10. Again the quotations are from Wilson's translation.

[68] Cf. *Biblical Parallels from Sumerian Literature.* Handbook on the Special Exhibit in Honor of the American-Jewish Tercentenary, 1654–1954. Text by S. N. Kramer, with the collaboration of E. I. Gordon. Philadelphia: the University Museum, University of Pennsylvania, 1954, pp. 22 f.; Kramer, in WIANE, pp. 170–82.

[69] The quotations are from S. N. Kramer, *History Begins at Sumer,* ch. 15, "Suffering and Submission: The First 'Job,'" Anchor Books ed., 1959, pp. 114–18.

You have doled out to me suffering ever anew,
I entered the house, heavy is the spirit,
I, the man, went out to the street, oppressed is the heart,
With me, the valiant, my righteous shepherd has become angry, has looked upon me inimically.
My herdsman has sought out evil forces against me who am not his enemy,
My companion says not a true word to me,
My friend gives the lie to my righteous word,
The man of deceit has conspired (?) against me,
And you, my god, do not thwart him . . .
I, the wise, why am I bound to the ignorant youths?
Food is all about, yet my food is hunger,
On the day shares were allotted to all my allotted share was suffering.

Instead of berating his god, the sufferer pleads for mercy:

My god, the day shines bright over the land, for me the day is black.
The bright day, the good day has . . . like the . . .
Tears, lament, anguish and depression are lodged within me,
Suffering overwhelms me like one chosen for nothing but tears,
Evil fate holds me in its hand, carries off my breath of life,
Malignant sickness bathes my body . . .
My god, you who are my father who begot me, lift up my face.
Like an innocent cow, in pity . . . the groan,
How long will you neglect me, leave me unprotected?
Like an ox . . . . ,
How long will you leave me unguided?

The sufferer then admits his guilt in affirming the dictum of the ancients that all men are sinners:

They say—valiant sages—a word righteous and straightforward:
"Never has a sinless child been born to its mother,
. . . . a sinless youth has not existed from of old."

Restoration follows the supplication and confession:

The man's bitter tears which he had wept his god heard,
When the lamentation and wailing which filled him had soothed for the man the heart of his god,

The righteous words, the artless words, uttered by him, his god accepted,
His words which the man prayerfully confessed,
Pleased the . . . . . flesh (?) of his god, and his god withdrew his hand from the evil word.

. . . .

The encompassing sickness-demon, which had spread wide its wings, he swept away (?),
The . . . . , which had smitten him like a . . . . , he dissipated,
The demon of fate, who had been placed there in accordance (?) with his verdict (?), he turned aside (?),
He turned the man's suffering into joy.

The Sumerian poem and the Book of Job have marked similarities as well as differences. It is important to note that both end on the same note of humble acquiescence before the inscrutable divine will. The Sumerian composition is the earliest treatment of the problem of suffering in Mesopotamia, the forerunner of similar compositions considered below.

The Mesopotamian view that evil is an integral part of the cosmic order is well illustrated by the poem quoted above. Basic to Sumerian theology[70] was the notion that man's misfortunes result from sin which taints all. The problem of justice is not so acute in such a view, since any human suffering could be regarded as merited. When evil befalls a man, there is no recourse but to admit one's guilt and praise one's god and plead for mercy. The god to whom the man addresses himself is his personal god who acts as advocate on behalf of his human client in the assembly of the great gods where fates are decided.[71] This Mesopotamian notion appears to be very much like that implicit in Job's appeal for an umpire (ix 33), a heavenly witness (xvi 19, 21), or a vindicator (xix 25–27). The attitude of Job's comforters in the Dialogue is essentially the same as that presupposed in the Sumerian composition: that the victim must have sinned and has no hope but to confess and plead for forgiveness and restoration.

[70] Cf. S. N. Kramer, "Sumerian Theology and Ethics," HTR 49 (1956), 45–62.
[71] Cf. Kramer, *History Begins at Sumer*, p. 107.

Let a human being utter constantly the exaltedness of his god,
Let a man praise artlessly the words of his god,

. . . . . .

Let his lament soothe the heart of his god,
For a human being without a god would not obtain food.[72]

The best-known parallel to Job is a text with the Akkadian title *ludlul bēl nēmeqi,* "I Will Praise the Lord of Wisdom."[73] This text is sometimes referred to as "The Poem of the Righteous Sufferer," or "The Babylonian Job." It has lately been suggested that perhaps a better title would be "The Babylonian Pilgrim's Progress."[74] The date of composition is set by W. G. Lambert[75] in the Cassite period (ca. 1600–1150 B.C.). The title reveals the poem's purpose: it is a thanksgiving hymn for deliverance from distress. The hero of the poem is smitten by disease. His god and goddess, his benevolent angel, his protecting spirit have forsaken him. His strength is gone, his appearance is dismal, his dignity flown. Resort to liver omens and dreams fails to explain his condition. He is terrified by nightmares. The king is incensed against him. Courtiers and underlings plot against him and slander him. His once eloquent voice is silenced, his once proud head lowered, his robust heart enfeebled with fear, his once mighty arms paralyzed. He who once strode as a noble is now ignored like a slave. His friends and even his family are alienated and hostile. Daily there is sighing, nightly lamentation, monthly wailing, yearly gloom. Like a dove he mourns all his days, for a song he utters groans. With weeping his eyes are inflamed, with tears his eyelids swollen. He survived a year, but things got worse. He prayed to his god and goddess, but got no response. Again omens and dreams gave no help and the incantation priest could not appease the divine wrath. What strange conditions, the sufferer observed. He was being treated like one who had not made libations to his god, or at meal time invoked his goddess, like one who had not prayed, who had done nothing on sacred days, had despised sabbaths, and neglected divine rites, had sworn a solemn oath frivolously. On the contrary, he had been most observant and punctilious in prayer and supplication and had taught those

72 Kramer, *Biblical Parallels . . . ,* p. 22.
73 Cf. R. H. Pfeiffer, ANET, pp. 434–37.
74 Lambert, BWL, p. 27.
75 BWL, p. 26.

under him to reverence the gods and the king. He is puzzled and dismayed at the fickleness of the gods and mankind's consequent insecurity[76]:

Would that I knew that these things are pleasing to a god!
What seems good to one, to a god may be evil.
What in one's mind is bad, to his god may seem proper.
Who then can know the will of the gods in heaven?
The counsel of the infernal gods, who can understand?
Where have mankind learned the way of a god?
He who was yesterday alive, is dead today,
One moment dejected, suddenly exuberant.
One minute he sings a happy song,
The next instant, he moans like a mourner.
Like opening and shutting, their condition changes.
When hungry they are like corpses,
Sated they emulate their gods.
In prosperity they think to scale heaven,
In adversity complain of going to hell.
At these things I am appa[lled]; their significance I do not understand.

The sufferer gives a detailed and gruesome description of his symptoms which by contrast make Job's physical woes seem rather mild: headache, cough, cramp, pain in the neck, throbbing in the chest, burning sensation in the bowels, diarrhea, fever, chills, emaciation, fainting spells, unconscious stupor, paralysis, locomotor ataxia, choking, inability to eat or drink. He goes on to describe his distress:

Extremely protracted is the malady.
From fasting my face is changed.
My flesh is flabby, my blood ebbs.

. . . . . .

I am taken to a bed of bondage; to leave is pain.
My house has turned to my prison.

. . . . . .

[76] The passages cited from the "Babylonian Job," the "Theodicy," and the "Dialogue of Pessimism," unless otherwise indicated, are renderings of the present writer who makes thereby no claim of proficiency as an Assyriologist. The renderings are based in the main on the excellent study of W. G. Lambert. The interpretations of other leading specialists have also been compared and checked against the texts as autographed, transcribed, and translated by Lambert.

With writhing my muscles are riven,
My limbs splayed and knocked askew.
In my dung I spend the night like an ox,
I am soiled like a sheep with my excrement.

. . . .

No god came to my rescue or grasped my hand,
My goddess showed no pity, nor came to my side.
Open was the grave, ready my shroud,
While I was not yet dead, the weeping was finished.

In spite of the dismal prospect, the sufferer appears to express a firm faith in his ultimate recovery and vindication, which is reminiscent of Job xix 25. There are, however, textual difficulties at this point, both in Job and in the Akkadian text, as W. G. Lambert[77] observes. R. H. Pfeiffer[78] rendered the lines in question:

> But I know the day on which my tears will cease,
> On which in the midst of the protecting deities their divinity will show mercy.

Lambert[79] translates:

> But I know the day for my whole family,
> When among my friends, their Sun-god will have mercy.

The third tablet of the text begins with a phrase which, according to Lambert, is of great importance for the understanding of the whole poem. The phrase, "His hand was heavy upon me," recalls Job xxiii 2b. Lambert[80] suggests that the writer avoids using the god's name and gives only dark hints that the almighty Marduk is the ultimate cause of the trouble. Job was not so reticent, but laid the blame directly and explicitly on God. In three dreams there appear to the sufferer (whose name, we now learn, is *Šubši-mešrê-Šakkan*) two men and a woman who perform rites of lustration and exorcism and announce that Marduk has sent healing and prosperity. The heart of merciful Marduk was appeased. He received the prayers of the sufferer, caused the wind to bear away his offenses, and dismissed all his woes, sending the (personified)

77 BWL, p. 23.
78 ANET, p. 436a.
79 BWL, p. 46, lines 119 f.
80 BWL, p. 23.

Headache, Cough, and Cramp back to their infernal abodes and removing all the other assorted miseries. The poem, in keeping with its title, ends with a long hymn in praise of Marduk. The greater part of the text is devoted to praise of Marduk for the restoration of his ruined servant. Very little effort is made to probe the problem of theodicy. As Lambert observes, the author appears to shy away from this question because of its blasphemous implications, but under the surface he is "perplexed by the same problem as Job." Marduk rules the world, but allows even his most devoted servant to suffer. As with Job, no adequate answer is offered beyond the assurance that Marduk who smote will also heal. The moral is explicitly drawn in lines quoted in the commentary[81]:

> He who has sinned in regard to Esagil [Marduk's temple], from my case [literally "hand"] let him see.
> On the mouth of the lion who was eating me,
> Marduk put a muzzle.

Even from the brief sketch above, it is obvious that the Akkadian poem also has striking similarities and dissimilarities with the Book of Job. In both a prominent personage, distinguished for piety and rectitude, is suddenly laid low by disease. Both victims, in varying degrees, question divine justice. Both give long and gruesome descriptions of their ailments. Both are finally restored to health. There are, however, marked differences, especially in literary form. The Akkadian poem, as far as it is preserved, is entirely in poetic monologue. The attitudes of the sufferers differ markedly. The Mesopotamian stresses his ritual piety, Job his ethical probity. The Mesopotamian is reluctant to charge the great god with injustice in direct and straightforward language, as Job does. It is not unlikely that the author of Job was familiar with the Akkadian poem, although there is probably no direct literary dependence.

Another Akkadian text generally known as the Babylonian Theodicy[82] also has marked affinities with Job. It has been called the Babylonian Ecclesiastes, but it has perhaps less in common with that book than with Job. The composition (according to Lambert)[83] dates from ca. 1000 B.C. It is a dialogue about human suffering

[81] Lambert, p. 56.

[82] Cf. R. H. Pfeiffer, "A Dialogue about Human Misery," ANET, pp. 438–40; Lambert, BWL, pp. 63–91.

[83] BWL, p. 67.

and divine justice between a sufferer and a friend. The poem consisted originally of twenty-seven stanzas of eleven lines each. The lines of each stanza begin with the same syllable and the acrostic of the twenty-seven syllables spell *a-na-ku sa-ag-gi-il ki-[i-na-am u]b-bi-ib ma-aš-ma-šu ka-ri-bu ša i-li u šar-ri,* "I, Saggil-kinam-ubbib, incantation priest, worship god and king." The plaintiff's name, which means "O Saggil (i.e., Marduk's temple) declare the righteous one pure," expresses the hope of vindication and his piety and loyalty are affirmed by the rest of the acrostic.

The sufferer opens the dialogue with an appeal to his erudite friend to hear his tale of anguish. He was a youngest child, orphaned and left without a guardian. The friend answers with polite sympathy, but suggests that the sufferer's attitude is imbecilic. He asserts that whoever reveres the gods has protection and prosperity. The sufferer replies with a description of his condition that belies the doctrine asserted by the friend. He is a physical wreck, emaciated and enfeebled. Grief has blackened his features. The wine of life has failed. The friend again suggests that the sufferer is mentally deranged. He recommends prayer and pursuit of justice, which will bring mercy and pardon. The sufferer appeals to the world of nature. The wild ass, did it ever attend to divine oracles? The fierce lion who devours the choicest flesh, did it make offerings to appease the goddess' anger? What of the *nouveau riche,* did he weigh out precious metal to the goddess Mami? The sufferer, by contrast, has not stinted with offerings, prayers, blessings, and regular sacrifices to his god and goddess. The friend replies that the god's counsel is remote. The wild ass and the predatory lion get the arrow and the pit. The wealthy upstart the king burns at the stake before his appointed time. Does the sufferer wish to go the same way? If not, he should seek the gracious favor of the god. The sufferer protests that those who neglect the god prosper, while those who pray are impoverished. From his youth the sufferer has sought the will of his god, but he bore a useless yoke for his god decreed destitution instead of wealth. The rascal prospers, while he (the righteous one) is abased. So back and forth goes the argument. The friend continues to insist that the godless and dishonest are properly punished, but who bears the yoke of his god never lacks food (though it may be sparse). The sufferer maintains that the evidence is quite the contrary. The god does nothing to impede evil. Social and economic conditions are the inverse of justice. What good has it done him, that he bowed to his god? He is treated with contempt by the dregs of humanity, as well as by the rich. The friend declares such charges blasphemous. The divine mind is remote, like the center of the heavens, and men cannot understand it. A cow's first calf may be puny, but her next one twice as big. A first child may be a weakling, but the second a mighty hero. In any case, man cannot understand the divine counsel. The sufferer points out how men praise a tyrant trained in murder and abase a humble man who has done no harm, justify a criminal and banish a righteous, god-fearing man, rob the poor to fill the [coffers] of the spoilers with gold, aid the powerful and ruin the weak. Even him, helpless as he is, an upstart persecutes. The friend is forced to admit that mankind is perverse. The gods made them that way:

Primeval king Narru, creator of mankind,
Glorious Zulummar who nipped the clay,
Queen who fashioned them, lady Mami,
Bestowed on mankind perverse speech,
With lies, not truth, endowed them ever.
Ardently they speak the rich man's favor,
"A King!" they say, "Wealth walks at his side!"
Like a thief, they maltreat the poor man,
Heap slander on him, plot his murder,
Criminally, every evil they inflict on him, because he has no help;
Horribly, they destroy him, extinguish him like a flame.

The sufferer makes a final appeal for sympathy from his friend and help from the gods:

Be kind, my friend, hear my woe
Help me! Look on my misery. Would that you could understand.
Humble, receptive, suppliant am I.
A moment's help I have not seen.
The city streets I meekly walked,
My voice unraised, my speech kept low,
My head I lifted not, at the ground I looked.
Like a slave I did not——in the company of my peers,
Help may he give, the god who rejected me,
Mercy may she show, the goddess who [abandoned me].
The shepherd Shamash the people god-like . . .

The ending of the Babylonian Theodicy is very strange. We are not told what finally happens to the plaintiff. Whether he was relieved and restored because he called on the mercy of the god, or was left in his misery, we can only surmise. In any case, no real effort is made to solve the problem. The final admission of the friend that men are sinful because the gods made them so is a part of the actual problem and contributes nothing to the solution. The composition is remarkable in that the negative and pessimistic conclusion is allowed to stand.

There are many striking parallels between this document and the biblical books of Job and Ecclesiastes. There are also striking differences. It is quite possible that the author of Job had some acquaintance, most likely indirect, with this composition.

The Akkadian poem called "A Pessimistic Dialogue between Master and Servant,"[84] or "The Dialogue of Pessimism,"[85] like the Egyptian "Dispute over Suicide," has some affinities with Job. The master calls his obsequious[86] slave and proposes to follow various activities. To each proposal the slave responds with enthusiastic approval and praises the proposed pursuit. The master immediately changes his mind and the nimble-witted slave changes his tune and points out the danger and futility of the said endeavor:

"Slave, attend me." "Here, my lord, here."
"I will love a woman." "Love, my lord, love.
The man who loves a woman, pain and trouble forgets."
"No, slave, I will not love a woman."
"Love not, my lord, love not.
Woman is a pit, a hole, a ditch
Woman is an iron dagger, a sharp one that cuts his throat."

"Slave, attend me." "Here, my lord, here."
"Quick, fetch me water for my hands and give it to me.
Sacrifice to my god I would make." "Do, my lord, do.
The man who makes sacrifice to his god, his heart is happy.
Loan on loan he makes."
"No, slave, sacrifice to my god I'll not make."

[84] R. H. Pfeiffer, ANET, pp. 437–38.

[85] Lambert, BWL, pp. 139–49.

[86] E. A. Speiser, "The Case of the Obliging Servant," JCS 8 (1954), 98–105, has interpreted the composition as social satire rather than "ponderous philosophizing." Lambert (BWL, p. 139, n. 1) has no objection to adding the word "humorous" to the title.

"Make not, my lord, make not.
You will teach the god to trot after you like a dog."

. . . .

"Slave, attend me." "Here, my lord, here."
"Good for my country I would do." "So do, my lord, do.
The man who does good for his country
His deed is put in Marduk's bowl(?)"
"No, slave, I will not do good for my country."
"Do not, my lord, do not.
Mount the mounds of ancient ruins and walk about.
See the skulls of late or early.
Which was the villain, which the benefactor?"

Every human pursuit, pleasure, power, wealth, love, worship, charity, patriotism, is vanity. The master then asks, "So then, what is good?" The slave answers:

To break my neck and your neck
And be thrown in the river. That is good.
Who is tall (enough) to ascend to heaven?
Broad (enough) to compass the netherworld?

The master replies:

No, slave, I will kill you and send you ahead of me.

The slave has the last word:

And, my lord, could you live even three days longer?

Whether the slave means that the master could not look after himself for even three days, or whether he would not wish to continue a life void of meaning, the cynicism and pessimism of effete Mesopotamian society is eloquently attested. Unlike the eloquent Egyptian peasant, the muddle-headed Mesopotamian magnate suffers from ennui rather than physical pain or social injustice. The date of this composition is uncertain, but Lambert[87] points out that the mention of the iron dagger is a clue, as well as the fact that the variations in the manuscripts indicate the copying tradition had not yet become fixed. The document has, perhaps, more in common with Ecclesiastes than with Job, but all three share a common spirit of protest against the seeming futility of human existence.

[87] BWL, p. 141.

According to E. A. Speiser[87a] the major Mesopotamian treatments of the problem of theodicy share the common conclusion that "although the blameless may be exposed to suffering, deliverance is sure to come to him in the end. The ways of the gods are indeed inscrutable, but the truly meritorious need never despair of ultimate salvation. The emphasis, in short, is not so much on the trials of the sufferer as on the miracle of final deliverance. Our three versions of the Mesopotamian counterpart of Job, spread though they are over a total span of more than a millennium, are in full agreement on this significant affirmation."

In Indian literature there is a story, first told in the Markandeya Purana,[88] which is similar in theme to that of Job. Among the gods at an assembly of the god Indra a discussion arose as to whether there was on earth a man perfectly righteous. Most of the gods doubted that such a one existed, but the goddess Vasishta nominated a certain king Hariscandra for this distinction. The god Shiva doubted that Vasishta's candidate could qualify and tested him with a series of calamities like Job's. Hariscandra was bereft of his wealth, his kingdom, his wife and only son, but he preserved his rectitude and was at last restored and rewarded. Despite the similarities, direct interdependence between the stories of Hariscandra and Job is unlikely.

The mystery of suffering is a major theme of Greek literature. The fatalism which characterizes the ancient Greek attitude toward life was probably inherited from their warring ancestors. A fatalistic view of life is natural and inevitable among peoples inured to the ups and downs of constant warfare. Like a good soldier, man must take life as it comes, sharing the hardships and meager rations along with the spoils. To demand or take more than one's proper share in life is *hubris,* insubordination, arrogance, presumption. The gods set the proper limits for man and it is for man to know his place and stay within the bounds set for him. Any overweening transgression of the limits is certain to incite the jealousy of the gods and bring down on the culprit the divine wrath, or *nemesis.* The prudent man is ever mindful of the insurmountable barrier and the inviolable line between himself and his superiors, the gods. The dictum of the

87a Cf. *The Idea of History in the Ancient Near East,* ed. R. C. Dentan, 1958, p. 69; *Oriental and Biblical Studies: Collected Writings of E. A. Speiser,* eds. J. J. Finkelstein and M. Greenberg, 1967, pp. 307 f.

88 Cf. E. Pargiter, *The Markandeya Purana,* translated with notes (*Bibliotheca Indica,* vol. 125, 1904), pp. 32–61.

Delphic Apollo, "Know thyself" is a warning to puny man not to forget his limitations and proper place in the scheme of things. Similarly, the maxim, "Nothing in excess" is not simply an exhortation to moderation in all things but an admonition against *hubris.* The safe way for man is to stay in his place and never to incite the ire of the gods. The common theme of Greek tragedy is the fate of those who dare risk the vengeance of the jealous gods. The divine will always prevails and man's misguided heroism is suicidal. The tragedy laments the sad spectacle of puny man's ridiculous defiance of the inexorable will of the gods.[89] While the tragedies of Sophocles and Euripides have much in common with Job's mood in the Dialogue, it is commonly conceded that Aeschylus' *Prometheus Bound*[90] has greater affinities with Job than has any other of the classical tragedies. Prometheus chained to a rock by order of Zeus as punishment for having brought mankind the gift of fire defiantly protests the injustice of his fate. Prometheus, however, is no mere man but an immortal Titan, a god wronged by the hated Zeus in retaliation for an unauthorized boon bestowed on mankind. Bound to the bare cliff, exposed to sun and storm, he wishes Zeus had rather hurled him into the unfathomed gloom of the netherworld where at least he would be hidden and exempt from heaven's and earth's contempt. His sympathizers, the nymphs and Ocean, urge him to beg pardon and mercy. But he refuses to placate the perpetrator of such monstrous injustice. It is Zeus himself who must relent and loose his bonds and recompense him for the pain and dishonor. Hermes vainly tries to persuade Prometheus to forsake his rebellious hate and propitiate Zeus in humility, lest still worse tortures be visited on him in Hades. As earth and sea convulse to engulf him in more infernal tortures, Prometheus goes down with the defiant cry, "O Earth, behold my wrong."

The similarities between Job and Prometheus are notable, but so too the differences. There is no mystery in Prometheus' pains. He knows the reason for his unjust torture. He knows and hates Zeus' character, and expects from him no mercy, although at times he

[89] Cf. M. P. Nilsson, "Religion as Man's Protest against the Meaninglessness of Events," *Bulletin de la société royale des lettres de Lund,* 1953–54, II, pp. 25–92.

[90] Cf. C. J. Lindblom, "Job and Prometheus, a Comparative Study," *Dragma Martino P. Nilsson,* 1939, pp. 280–87; W. A. Irwin, "Prometheus and Job," JR 30 (1950), 90–108; H. G. May, "Prometheus and Job: The Problem of the God of Power and the Man of Wrath," ATR 34 (1954), 240–46.

expresses a wistful longing for justice very much like Job's. The Promethean spirit of defiance and refusal to bow to wrong, in spite of every terror, is also Job's. If the Book of Job ended with the Dialogue and Job's defiant challenge to God, the parallel would be very striking. We have, however, no ground for supposing that at any stage of the composition[91] Job had an ending like that of Aeschylus' *Prometheus Bound.* The conclusion of the Job story was already set by an ancient tradition going back to the beginning of the second pre-Christian millennium. In spite of the parallels between Job and Prometheus and other Greek tragedies, there is no compelling evidence of direct interdependence.

Old Testament Affinities

Though there is nothing quite like the Book of Job either in the Old Testament or in any other literature, there are, nonetheless, materials and literary forms in the Old Testament with overtones of Job. The author(s) of Job could have been influenced by some of the biblical materials, or, what is more likely, a common fund of ancient literary traditions was drawn upon. The various literary genres represented in Job—narrative, dialogue, hymn, lament, proverb, oracle—are common constituents of Old Testament literature. The narrative portions of Job, in spite of the patriarchal setting, are not very similar to the patriarchal sagas of Genesis. The folk tale of Job is perhaps closer to the story of Ruth than to any other biblical narrative. A large part of Job's discourses are to be classified as lament (iii 3–26, vi 2–vii 21, ix 25–x 22, xiii 23–xiv 22, xvi 6–xvii 9, xix 7–20, xxiii, xxix 1–xxxi 37). The lament was a common genre of Mesopotamian literature in which the sick and the persecuted poured out their complaints in order to obtain divine mercy and forgiveness. The lament of the sick is thus a sort of liturgy for healing. Some of the Psalms, or parts of Psalms, fall in the category of lament, for example, xxii 2–19, xxxviii, lxxxviii. Parts of Job's speeches, for example, v 9–16, ix 4–12,

[91] Cf. K. Fullerton, "The Original Conclusion to the Book of Job," ZAW 42 (1924), 116–35; A. Alt, "Zur Vorgeschichte des Buches Hiob," ZAW 55 (1937), 265–68; C. J. Lindblom, "La composition du livre de Job," *Bulletin de la société royale des lettres de Lund,* 1944–45, III, pp. 111–205; G. Fohrer, "Zur Vorgeschichte and Komposition des Buches Hiob," VT 6 (1956), 249–67.

xii 13–25, xxvi 5–14, xxxiv 18–20, and to a lesser extent parts of the discourses of the friends, for example, xi 7–11, xxv 2–6, are hymns. Of the hymns of the Hebrew Psalter, Ps civ in particular has many contacts with Job (cf. Ps civ 6–9 with Job xxxviii 8–11; Ps civ 21, 27 with Job xxxviii 39–41; Ps civ 30 with Job xii 10; Ps civ 32 with Job ix 5, xxvi 11). Ps civ appears to have been influenced by the beautiful hymn of Akhenaton to the sun-disk Aton.

The Old Testament has little to offer by way of poetic dialogue, and almost nothing that may be compared to the Dialogue of the Book of Job. Abraham engages in dialogue with Yahweh in interceding for Sodom and Gomorrah, Gen xviii 22–32, and Amos intercedes for Israel, Amos vii 1–9, viii 1–3. Abraham's bargaining with Ephron the Hittite, Gen xxiii 3–16, is interesting though prosaic dialogue. The calls of Moses—Exod iii 2–iv 17—Isaiah—Isa vi—Jeremiah—Jer i 1–10—consist of brief dialogues between the caller and the one called.

Mere mention of these brief dialogues makes it clear that we have to look outside the Old Testament for prototypes of the extended poetic Dialogue of the Book of Job. The closest parallel to the Dialogue of the Book of Job, both in form and subject matter, is found in the Babylonian Theodicy. The dialogue was a feature of still older Sumero-Akkadian Fables or Contest Literature in which usually there are two disputants, such as The Eagle and the Snake, The Tamarisk and the Palm, The Ox and the Horse. In The Fable of the Fox, however, there are three other participants in the dispute, the Wolf, the Dog, and the Lion. The Fable of the Fox was probably composed either in the Old Babylonian period, or in the Cassite period, and had Sumerian antecedents.[92] There is thus no need to look to later Greek philosophical dialogue to find several participants in a debate.

The speeches of Job and his "comforters" are spiced with bits and pieces of proverbial wisdom, for example, iv 8–11, v 1–7, viii 11–19, xii 11–12, xiv 1–2. The latter half of Eliphaz's second speech, xv 17–35, is an extended proverbial discourse. Proverbs are often obscure and there are many puzzling passages in Job which appear to be proverbial sayings whose import eludes the mod-

[92] Cf. Lambert, BWL, pp. 150–212, and E. I. Gordon, "A New Look at the Wisdom of Sumer and Akkad," BO 17 (1960), 122–52, especially 144–47.

ern interpreter, as it may also have eluded ancient copyists and translators. The Book of Job, of course, falls in the category of Wisdom Literature. The speeches of the friends are orthodox or conservative wisdom, while Job's discourses may be termed "anti-wisdom wisdom."

The Purpose and Teaching of the Book

It has been generally assumed that the purpose of the book is to give an answer to the issue with which it deals, the problem of divine justice or theodicy.[93] This question is raised inevitably by any and every instance of seemingly unmerited or purposeless suffering, and especially the suffering of a righteous man. Job's case, whether real or imaginary, poses the problem in the most striking possible way. A man of exemplary rectitude and piety is suddenly overwhelmed with disasters and loathsome disease. How can such a situation be reconciled with divine justice and benevolent providence? It must be admitted first and last that the Book of Job fails to give a clear and definitive answer to this question. This, however, does not mean that the book is to be discounted as a magnificent misadventure or a conspicuous failure. The problem of theodicy continues to thwart all attempts at rational solution. Virtually every basic argument that has been adduced in connection with the problem is touched on in the Book of Job. Of the various attitudes suggested in the different parts of the book, it is difficult to say which, if any, was intended as decisive.

The Prologue presents Job's woes as imposed by the Satan with the permission and approval of Yahweh in order to determine whether Job's piety was completely unselfish. Some interpreters find the question of theodicy resolved here in advance. The reader is given a glimpse behind the scenes and made privy to the plot within the celestial council. The action is prompted by Yahweh himself

[93] J. J. Stamm, *Das Leiden des Unschuldigen in Babylon und Israel*, 1946; I. J. Gerber, *The Psychology of the Suffering Mind*, 1951; H. H. Rowley, *Submission in Suffering and Other Essays*, 1951; A. R. King, *The Problem of Evil: Christian Concepts and the Book of Job*, 1952; E. F. Sutcliffe, *Providence and Suffering in the Old and New Testaments*, 1955; J. Scharbert, *Der Schmerz im Alten Testament*, 1955; R. J. Williams, "Theodicy in the Ancient Near East," *Canadian Journal of Theology* 2 (1956), 14–26.

when he calls the Satan's attention to Job as a paragon of virtue and provokes him into questioning the basis and the genuineness of Job's piety. Yahweh himself sets the limits of the testing and Job endures all with magnificent calm and without protest or complaint. Thus is proved to gods and men that disinterested virtue and piety are possible. The victory is seen in Job's confession of unshakable trust:

> Yahweh gave, Yahweh took away.
> Blessed be Yahweh's name.

and

> Shall we accept good from God,
> And not accept evil?

Some interpreters have regarded this as approaching the profoundest insight of both the Old Testament and the New, the doctrine of vicarious atonement by an innocent victim, as the Suffering Servant of the Lord (Isa lii 13–liii 12), or the Cross of Christian faith. Helpful as this insight may be, it derives from the hindsight of Christian faith and experience rather than from any hint in the biblical story. It is one thing for a rational person to choose to suffer or risk suffering for a cause, but it is quite another to become the victim of suffering which appears to have no meaning. We are informed in the Prologue that Job was innocent. The question naturally rises, why the devilish sadistic experiment to see if he had a breaking point? (This is reminiscent of a pessimistic Mesopotamian myth which represents the production of human deformities as a drunken diversion of the gods at the end of a spree celebrating the creation of mankind as slaves for the gods.)[94] H. H. Rowley[95] has given an interesting and useful answer to this difficulty. In assuring us that Job's sufferings were innocent, the author makes an important contribution to the problem. Job, of course, was not aware that God reckoned him as righteous. If he had known he was merely being tried, it would have been no real test and there could be no meaning in this for the man who has to suffer without knowing why. The issue at stake in the testing of Job was not simply the winning of a wager, idle or diabolical, but the vindication of mutual

[94] Cf. S. N. Kramer, *Sumerian Mythology*, 1961, pp. 68–75; H. and H. A. Frankfort, J. A. Wilson, T. Jacobsen, *Before Philosophy: The Intellectual Adventure of Ancient Man*, 1949, pp. 175–79.

[95] BJRL 41 (1958), 167–207.

faith of God in man and man in God. The Job of the Prologue thus agrees with the distorted sense of xiii 15,

Though he slay me, yet will I trust in him.

He would have been willing to be damned for the glory of God. One may admire such faith without raising the question how this sort of damnation may reflect on the character of God or redound to his glory.

In the Dialogue the question is treated in a radically different fashion. The friends argue that Job must have sinned and earned his woes because God is just and rewards and punishes. Any apparent exception to this rule is unreal, or only temporary. But Job vehemently denies that he has sinned, at least not seriously enough to merit such misery as has been inflicted on him. Justice, he argues, often appears abortive in the world and for this God must be held responsible. Hence Job infers that God has no concern for justice or for human feelings. The Dialogue thus makes little contribution to the solution of the problem. Actually it is scarcely appropriate to call this section of the book a dialogue. There is not here the give-and-take of philosophical disputation aimed at the advancement of understanding and truth. Rather each side has a partisan point of view which is reiterated *ad nauseam* in long speeches. There is no real movement in the argument. Attempts to find progression in the debate and subtle differences in the character and personality of the three friends are labored and unconvincing.[96] It is true that the friends grow progressively vehement in their indictment of Job. Their exasperation appears to mount round by round as Job steadfastly refuses to accept their argument—that God is always just and therefore he must be guilty—or their advice—that he admit his guilt and plead for mercy. As the exchange continues, Job grows more serene in his despair, as he gropes and grasps for an answer. He wishes to argue his case with God, but he cannot find God nor force him to grant a fair hearing. Job asks for an umpire to ensure fair treatment. It has been suggested that in Job's appeal to a mediator, an umpire or witness, we have a sort of prophetic testimony to the necessity for a Christ, a being both human and divine who could effect a reconciliation between God and

[96] W. A. Irwin, "An Examination of the Progress of Thought in the Dialogue of Job," JR 13 (1933), 150–64; Terrien, IB, III, p. 901b, n. 125.

Job.[97] This theory appears to have some merit and validity, but it is doubtful whether this person should be described as messianic. It appears likely that behind Job's appeal to a mediator, an umpire or witness (ix 33) lies the ancient Mesopotamian idea of a personal god whose function and duty it was to look after his client's interest and plead his cause before the great gods in the divine assembly.[98] This conception appears to be related more closely to the belief in guardian angels than to messianism, although the figure of the Messiah as Paraclete seems to derive from this sphere of ideas rather than from royal ideology. Job reverts to his appeal to an umpire or friendly witness in xvi 19, 21 (the verb in the latter passage being cognate with the term rendered "umpire" in ix 33). Job uses what seems to be legal jargon, and his tribulations take on the aspect of a legal process. All that he demands is a fair trial, the right of friendly witness, and of defense counsel.

Beginning with a plea to be allowed to escape his misery through death, Job in chapter xiv considers the possibility of an afterlife. This thought is entertained only momentarily, however, as he dismisses it and resigns himself to the inevitability and finality of death. It is often assumed that a hope of recompense in a future life would have sustained Job and solved his problem. Certainly it would have mitigated the difficulty considerably. But whether the prospect of future bliss gives one the strength and consolation to bear present pain, a pain that is meaningless and unjustified, is questionable.

The famous passage, xix 25–27, has been commonly regarded as the climax of Job's quest. Unhappily, these lines are extremely difficult, the text having suffered irreparable damage.[99] It is clear that Job expects to be vindicated, but it is not certain whether he expects his vindication to come in the flesh or after his body has disintegrated. The traditional Christian understanding of the passage is based more on the interpretation of the Vulgate than on the Hebrew. Jerome thought that Job here prophesied the resurrection of the body but this is contradicted by xiv 12 and by several other passages (iii 11–22, vii 9–10, x 18–22, xvi 22, xvii 1, 13–16, xxi 23–26). Many critics, ancient and modern, have recognized

[97] Terrien, IB, III, pp. 900 f.
[98] Kramer, in WIANE, pp. 172–82.
[99] Cf. Rowley, BJRL 41 (1958), 203 ff.

that Job refers to his hope for vindication in the flesh (as expressed in xiii 15–16, xxiii 7, 10) and to his hope for restoration (as in ch. xxix). This passage has to be interpreted in the light of Job's other utterances, as well as of the immediate context. In spite of textual difficulties, it should be apparent that the vindicator on whom Job pins his hopes is not God, but the person elsewhere called an umpire (ix 33) and a witness (xvi 19, 21). This vindicator or redeemer, like the umpire or witness, would defend his case, acquit him of guilt, and restore him to favor with God. Job does not, as has been alleged, surrender all claim on God and put his trust in a sort of heavenly high priest.[100] Rather he continues to press his demand for vindication which must come sooner or later. In spite of all his protests and railings against God, Job never completely gives up his conviction that justice must somehow triumph. Even if his flesh rots away and his body turns to dust, in his mind's eye he sees his ultimate vindication and expects to be conscious of it when it comes, though it be beyond this life in the dust of the netherworld.

As a last resort, Job appeals to the ancient test of the oath. The taking of an oath was the last word in assertion of innocence, tantamount to acquittal, since it was assumed that the terror of the sanctions of the self-imprecations would deter anyone from swearing falsely.[101] After the oaths there is no more the friends can say. It is now up to God to strike down the blasphemer or acquit him.

Some scholars have assumed that the intent of the Dialogue is to refute once and for all the doctrine of exact individual retribution, or terrestrial eschatology, as it has been called, the doctrine that righteousness always brings prosperity and wickedness misfortune, in this life. The corollary of this doctrine is, of course, that prosperity is proof of divine favor and misfortune of sin. This dogma is doubtless a great comfort to the healthy and the prosperous, but a cruel taunt to the sick and the poor. This corollary doctrine is often expounded in the Old Testament, especially as applied to Israel and the nations (cf. Exod xxiii 20 ff.; Lev xxvi; Deut xxviii; Jer vii 5–7, xii 14–17), but also to the individual (cf. Pss i, xxxvii, xlix, lxxiii; Isa lviii 6–14; Jer xvii 5–8; Ezek xviii). This view has

100 Terrien, IB, III, p. 901b.

101 Cf. J. Pedersen, *Der Eid bei den Semiten,* 1914; S. H. Blank, "The Curse, Blasphemy, the Spell, and the Oath," HUCA 23 (1950–51), 73–95; M. H. Pope, "Oaths," in IDB, III, pp. 575–77.

been called "orthodox," with the implication that it is normative for the Old Testament. Now it must be admitted that there is considerable justification for the use of the term "orthodox" as applied to such statements as the famous utterance of Ps xxxvii 25,

> I was once young, and now have grown old;
> And I never saw a righteous man forsaken
> Or his offspring begging bread.

Righteousness certainly ought to be rewarded and wickedness punished and it sometimes happens thus. All too often, however, the very opposite seems to be the case, as Qoheleth observed (Eccles iii 16, viii 14). There ought to be no exceptions, and Job's comforters argue that there are in fact none. But Job refutes their doctrine thoroughly, not only with reference to his own case but to the world at large. The friends would have been well advised to maintain their discreet silence as they had in the Prologue, since the premise of their argument had already been nullified by the certification from the highest authority that Job was blameless. The author of the Dialogue could not allow either the victim or his miserable comforters to share this knowledge, else there would have been no basis for the disputation. The poet appears to give equally of his great talent to the rhetoric of both sides of the argument, but there can be no mistaking the fact that his sympathies are with Job and that the speeches of the friends are skillfully presented to show how wrongheaded traditional piety can be. The view of the friends was indeed venerable orthodoxy. The recovery of Mesopotamian Wisdom Literature now makes it clear that the position of the friends is essentially what was normative in Mesopotamian thought[102] for centuries before Israel emerged in history. This doctrine is certainly asserted many times in the Old Testament, but to take it alone as normative is to overlook a great deal that contradicts it. The fates of Abel, Uriah, and Naboth, for example, were not recounted to suggest that they got merely what they deserved.[103] Jeremiah, who is credited, along with Ezekiel, with refining the doctrine of individual retribution (Jer xxxi 30) complains of its lack of application to himself. The thorough refutation of the doctrine in Job and Ecclesiastes did not eradicate the fallacious dogma. It persisted and was confuted again by Jesus of Nazareth (cf. Luke xiii 1–5; John

[102] Cf. Lambert, BWL, pp. 15–20.
[103] Cf. Rowley, BJRL 41 (1958), 195 f.

ix 2) who urged men to love their enemies and pray for those who persecute them in order that they may be sons of the heavenly Father who makes his sun rise on the evil and the good, and sends rain on the just and the unjust (Matt v 43 ff.).

The contributions of the Elihu speeches, such as they are, have already been noted. It is hard to see how some critics can regard them so highly. Kaufmann[104] suggested that Elihu is a reflex of the poet himself, while Gordis[104a] goes further and regards the Elihu speeches not only as an integral part of the book but as the last and best word of the poet who in his later years put his more mature insights into the Elihu speeches and inserted them before the great climax of the divine speeches. (Gordis sees in the name Elihu a play on Eliyahu [Elijah] and an evocation of the theme of forerunner of the Lord, as in Mal iv 5–6. The appearance of Elihu just before the theophany in the whirlwind evokes for Gordis the theme of Elijah's assumption and its attendant messianic ideology.) As for Elihu's verbosity, Gordis notes that the history of literature offers many instances in which a writer's style grows more complex and difficult with advancing years, and he cites as examples Shakespeare's *Tempest,* Yeats's later poems, Joyce's *Finnegan's Wake,* and especially Goethe's *Faust,* which gestated over a period of some sixty years and was written over a period of thirty years. As for the substance of Elihu's argument, Gordis notes that Elihu denies the conclusions both of Job and the friends and declares that even though suffering may not be a penalty for sin, yet God's justice remains unassailable. A "virtually new" idea which Gordis finds in the Elihu speeches is one that had been advanced in another form by Deutero-Isaiah who maintained that national suffering was not the consequence of national sin, but, on the contrary, an integral element in the moral education of the human race. Elihu, however, goes substantially further, according to Gordis, and sees suffering as discipline and warning to the righteous, not only against sins actual and patent, but also against sins both potential and latent (xxxiii 16–30, xxxvi 9–12). This view of suffering as discipline, however, is not novel, and it had already been introduced by Eliphaz in his first speech, v 17 ff. It is hard to find anything new in Elihu's bombast. Whether composed by the author of the Dialogue, or by

[104] *The Religion of Israel,* p. 336.
[104a] *The Book of God and Man,* pp. 104–16.

someone else, the Elihu speeches seem to represent one more futile attempt to support the same discredited traditional view which the friends had asserted.

Either the book ends in magnificent anticlimax, or we must see the highlight in the divine speeches.[105] Job has silenced the friends with a series of terrible oaths affirming his innocence and has challenged God to answer. The content of the divine answer from the storm is something of a surprise and, on the face of it, a disappointment. The issue, as Job had posed it, is completely ignored. No explanation or excuse is offered for Job's suffering. As Job had expected, God refuses to submit to questioning. But, contrary to expectation, God does not crush him, or brush him away, or multiply his wounds. Rather he subjects Job to questioning. God's queries are ironical in the extreme, almost to the point of absurdity. Job had already expressed his awe and wonder at God's power in hymns among the most beautiful in the Old Testament. Man's finitude and helplessness Job had fully acknowledged. He had questioned not divine omnipotence but justice and mercy. The complete evasion of the issue as Job had posed it must be the poet's oblique way of admitting that there is no satisfactory answer available to man, apart from faith. God does not need the help or advice of impotent and ignorant men to control the world, any more than he needed such to create it. God cannot be summoned like a defendant and forced to bear witness against himself. No extreme of suffering gives mere man license to question God's wisdom or justice as Job had done. It is apparently on this very point that Job repents and recants (xlii 3b, c). Note that Job does not mention the question of his innocence and integrity which we may assume he would still maintain. It is noteworthy, too, that Yahweh makes no charge against Job except that he had spoken out of ignorance. Nothing is said that would imply that Job deserved his misery. The absence of any charge of guilt must be considered tantamount to vindication. This is at least part of what Job had sought to silence the friends who had argued that he must be guilty and would be proved so if God were to speak. The Prologue already informed us that Job was blameless. Here we have the complete refutation of the argument of the friends that suffering is itself proof of sin. This is perhaps the basis for the reprimand of the friends in the Epilogue, that they asserted a lie in the foolish belief that they had to defend God. (The only other way

[105] Cf. M. Burrows, JBL 47 (1928), 117–32.

to understand their rebuke is to assume that in the old folk tale the friends had taken quite a different attitude and, like Job's wife, had urged him to curse God and die.) The fundamental question, If not for sin, why then?, is completely ignored. The reason for this is not too difficult to understand, in view of the fact that virtually all the arguments the human mind can muster had already been thrashed out in the Dialogue. The problem still baffles the philosopher and theologian, and we are thrown back on faith. It is quite understandable that readers, critical or otherwise, are left with a feeling of chagrin at the seemingly magnificent irrelevance of much of the content of the divine speeches. Some critics resort to surgery in the attempt to improve the divine reply, but this leads to more and more drastic cutting till scarcely a torso is left.[106] The zoological as well as the meteorological marvels show the divine power and providence. Even the apparent stupidity of the ostrich testifies to the divine wisdom and providential care. The monsters Behemoth and Leviathan,[107] dread powers of evil from ancient pagan Semitic myths, subdued or slain in primeval conflicts before creation of the world, are the final proof of the divine power and providence. Given but a glimpse or a whisper of God's power and glory and loving care for his creation, Job realizes that he had spoken from ignorance and rashly. His resentment and rebellious attitude disappear.

The fact that the Epilogue upholds the discredited doctrine of exact retribution has already been noted. This was doubtless a feature of the ancient folk tale that could not be altered. It is hard to imagine how else the story could end. It would scarcely do to leave Job in his misery after he had been vindicated. Perhaps the most significant line in the Epilogue is xlii 10 which seems to put Job's restoration in a temporal and perhaps causal nexus with his intercessory prayer for his friends. After all the hard things they had said to him—for his own good, as they doubtless felt—it would not have been easy to forgive them and pray for them. The possible implication of this line may be related to the idea elaborated at the end of the famous eulogy of the Suffering Servant, Isa liii 10–12[108]:

[106] Cf. Rowley, BJRL 41 (1958), 192 ff.

[107] For a list of critics who reject the descriptions of Behemoth and Leviathan, cf. Rowley, BJRL 41 (1958), 190, n. 2.

[108] On the interpretation of this famous passage, cf. H. H. Rowley, "The Servant of the Lord in the Light of Three Decades of Criticism," *The Servant of the Lord and Other Essays on the Old Testament*, 1952, pp. 3–88.

Yahweh willed to crush and afflict him;
If his life were offered in expiation,
He will see progeny and prolong his life,
Yahweh's pleasure will prosper through him.
After travail of soul he will be satisfied
With the knowledge that he was righteous,
Though he bore the sins of many.
So will I allot him a share with the great,
With the mighty he will share the spoil;
Since he emptied himself to the death,
And was reckoned among the transgressors;
Yet he bore the sins of many
And for transgressors made intercession.

While the Job of the Dialogue apparently has no thought of suffering vicariously for the friends, or for anyone else, the Job of the Epilogue is placed in the line of development of the Christian doctrine of the Cross, though still a long way from it (cf. xxii 27–30).

A modern man reflecting on the Book of Job from the vantage point of two millennia of human experience must marvel at the religious insights to be found therein.

Viewed as a whole, the book presents profundities surpassing those that may be found in any of its parts. The issues raised are crucial for all men and the answers attempted are as good as have ever been offered. The hard facts of life cannot be ignored or denied. All worldly hopes vanish in time. The values men cherish, the little gods they worship—family, home, nation, race, sex, wealth, fame—all fade away. The one final reality appears to be the process by which things come into being, exist, and pass away. This ultimate Force, the Source and End of all things, is inexorable. Against it there is no defense. Any hope a man may put in anything other than this First and Last One is vain. There is nothing else that abides. This is God. He gives and takes away. From Him we come and to Him we return. Confidence in this One is the only value not subject to time.

But how can a man put his faith in such an One who is the Slayer of all? Faith in Him is not achieved without moral struggle and spiritual agony. The foundation of such a faith has to be laid in utter despair of reliance on any or all lesser causes and in resignation which has faced and accepted the worst and the best life can offer. Before this One no man is clean. To Him all human righteousness is as filthy rags. The transition from fear and hatred to trust and even love of this One—from God the Enemy to God the Friend and Companion—is the pilgrimage of every man of faith. Job's journey from despair to faith is the way each mortal must go. Almost invariably there must be initial shock and disappointment to bring a man to the realization of his predicament. Time and again it has happened, to individuals and to groups. A people that regarded itself as chosen by God and especially favored has suffered cruelly. The Son of Man who was obedient to death was put to the ultimate test. Here, as with Job, we are confronted in the most striking way with the apparently ruthless Slayer who brings to nought the life of even the most devoted servant. Only by faith can such seeming defeat be turned to victory and the anguished cry, "My God, why have you forsaken me?" give way to resignation and trust, "Father into your hands I commend my spirit." The scribal sage who altered Job's defiant protest "He may slay me, I'll not quaver" to read "Though he slay me, yet will I trust in him" did so advisedly in the knowledge that this was the attitude to which Job must be driven at last since there is no escape and no other refuge.[108a] The Psalmist (lxxiii 25–26) put it thus:

[108a] To the discussion must be added the recent treatments by Gordis, *The Book of God and Man*, and M. Tsevat, "The Meaning of the Book of Job," HUCA 37 (1966), 73–106. Gordis sees the poet's latest and best word in the Elihu speeches, but concedes that the problem of the meaning and relevance of the God speeches must be solved else Job has eluded us (p. 123). Granted that no justification for suffering is given in the God speeches, or elsewhere, Gordis nevertheless feels that the poet has shown "that it is possible for men to bear the shafts of evil that threaten their existence if they cultivate a sense of reverence for the miracle and mystery of life, seek to experience joy in the world, and discover intimations of meaning in its beauty" (p. 156). The ultimate message is clear to Gordis: "Not only *Ignoramus*, 'we do not know,' but *Ignorabimus*, 'we may never know,'" yet the poet "calls upon us *Gaudeamus*, 'let us rejoice,' in the beauty of the world though its pattern is only partially revealed to us. It is enough to know that the dark mystery encloses and in part discloses a bright and shining miracle" (p. 134). "The analogy of the natural order gives the believer in God grounds for facing the mystery with a courage born of faith in the essential rightness of things. What cannot be comprehended through reason must be embraced in love. For the author of Job, God is one and indivisible, the moral order is rooted in the natural world" (p. 156).

In Tsevat's view, "only the elimination of the principle of retribution can solve the problem of the book" (p. 98) and this, he maintains, is actually the solution offered. The message implicit in the divine speeches is that "no retribution is provided for in the blueprint of the world, nor does it exist any-

Whom (else) have I in heaven?
(When) with you, I care not for earth.
(Though) my flesh and mind waste away,
My mind's rock and my portion is God forever.

---

where in it. None is planned for the non-human world and none for the human world. Divine justice is not an element of reality" (p. 100). This doctrine "does more than demythologize the world; it also 'de-moralizes,' which is to say, makes it amoral" (p. 102). Since there is no retribution, "piety, whatever its other attributes, must be disinterested" (p. 103), and thus the Book of Job "presents the purest moral theory in the Bible" (p. 104).

SELECTED BIBLIOGRAPHY

A complete bibliography on the Book of Job is scarcely possible. The most complete listings are given by Kurt Kuhl, "Neuere Literaturkritik des Buches Hiob" and "Vom Hiobbuche und seinen Problemen," in *Theologische Rundschau* 21 (1953), 163–205, 257–317, and 22 (1954), 261–316. To attempt to bring these up to date would require space that would exceed the limits of this book. However, a few of the most important books and recent articles are cited.

Books

Barton, G. A., *The Book of Job* (The Bible for Home and School, ed. S. Matthews), 1911.

Blommerde, A. C. M., *Northwest Semitic Grammar and Job* (Biblica et Orientalia, 22), 1969.

Brooks, C., ed., *Tragic Themes in Western Literature,* 1960.

Buttenwieser, M., *The Book of Job,* 1922.

Crook, M. B., *The Cruel God: Job's Search for the Meaning of Suffering,* 1959.

Daniélou, J., *Holy Pagans in the Old Testament,* 1957. (Job, pp. 86–102.)

Davidson, A. B., *The Book of Job* (The Cambridge Bible), 1886.

Delitzsch, Franz, *The Book of Job,* tr. from the German by F. Bolton (Clark's Foreign Theological Library, X–XI), 1876.

Dhorme, É., *Le Livre de Job,* 1926.

Driver, S. R., and G. B. Gray, *A Critical and Exegetical Commentary on the Book of Job Together with a New Translation* (The International Critical Commentary), 2 vols., 1921. 2d ed., 1950.

Duhm, B., *Das Buch Hiob,* 1897.

Eerdmans, B. D., *Studies in Job,* 1939.

Fohrer, G., *Das Buch Hiob,* 1948.
———*Glaube und Welt im Alten Testament,* 1948.
———*Studien zum Buche Hiob,* 1963.
Freehof, S. B., *Book of Job* (The Jewish Commentary for Bible Readers), 1958.
Gese, H., *Lehre und Wirklichkeit in der alten Weisheit. Studien zu den Sprüchen Salomos und zu dem Buche Hiob,* 1958.
Glatzer, N. N., *The Dimensions of Job: A Study and Selected Readings,* 1969.
Gordis, R., *The Book of God and Man: A Study of Job,* 1965.
Guillaume, A., *Studies in the Book of Job,* 1968.
Hölscher, G., *Das Buch Hiob* (Handbuch zum Alten Testament), rev. ed., 1952.
Horst, F., *Hiob,* Lieferungen 1–4, 1960–63.
———*Hiob,* I. Teilband (chapters i–xix) (Biblischer Kommentar, XVI/1), 1968.
Jastrow, M., *The Book of Job,* 1920.
Jepsen, A., *Das Buch Hiob und seine Deutung* (Aufsätze und Vorträge zur Theologie und Religionswissenschaft, Heft 28), 1963.
Jung, C. G., *Antwort auf Hiob,* 1952.
Kallen, H. M., *The Book of Job as a Greek Tragedy Restored,* 1918.
King, A. R., *The Problem of Evil: Christian Concepts and the Book of Job,* 1952.
Kissane, E. J., *The Book of Job,* 1946.
Kraeling, E. G., *The Book of the Ways of God,* 1939.
Kramer, S. N., *Sumerian Mythology,* 1961.
Larcher, C. P., *Le livre de Job* (La Sainte Bible traduite en francais sous la direction de l'École Biblique de Jérusalem), 1950.
Möller, H., *Sinn und Aufbau des Buches Hiob,* 1955.
Noth, M., and D. W. Thomas, eds., *Wisdom in Israel and in the Ancient Near East* (abbr. WIANE). Presented to H. H. Rowley on his sixty-fifth birthday. VTS, III, 1955.
Paterson, J., *The Wisdom of Israel: Job and Proverbs* (Bible Guides, eds. W. Barclay and F. F. Bruce, No. 11), 1961.
Peake, A. S., *Job* (The New Century Bible), 1904.
———*The Problem of Suffering in the Old Testament,* 1904.
Pope, M. H., *El in the Ugaritic Texts* (abbr. EUT), 1955.

Pritchard, J. B., ed., *The Ancient Near East in Pictures* (abbr. ANEP), 1954.

———*Ancient Near Eastern Texts Relating to the Old Testament* (abbr. ANET), 2d ed., 1955.

Reichert, V. E., *Job: with Hebrew Text and English Translation,* Commentary (Soncino Books of the Bible, ed. A. Cohen), 1946.

Ringgren, H., *Word and Wisdom: Studies in the Hypostatization of Divine Qualities and Functions in the Ancient Near East,* 1947.

Robinson, H. W., *Suffering Human and Divine,* 1940.

———*The Cross in the Old Testament,* 1955.

Robinson, T. H., *Job and His Friends,* 1954.

Rowley, H. H., *Submission in Suffering and Other Essays,* 1951.

Sanders, J. A., *Suffering as Divine Discipline in the Old Testament and Post-Biblical Judaism* (Colgate Rochester Divinity School Bulletin 38, November 1955).

Sanders, P. S., ed., *Twentieth Century Interpretations of the Book of Job: A Collection of Critical Essays,* 1968.

Schärf, R. R., *Die Gestalt des Satans im Alten Testament,* 1948.

Scharbert, J., *Der Schmerz im Alten Testament* (Bonner Biblische Beiträge 8), 1955.

Sewall, R. B., *The Vision of Tragedy,* 1959.

Sockman, R. W., *The Meaning of Suffering,* 1961.

Steinmann, J., *Le Livre de Job,* 1955.

Stevenson, W. B., *The Poem of Job,* 1947.

———*Critical Notes on the Hebrew Text of the Poem of Job,* 1951.

Stewart, J., *The Message of Job,* 1959.

Stier, F., *Das Buch Ijjob.* Hebräisch und Deutsch, 1954.

Sutcliffe, E. F., *Providence and Suffering in the Old and New Testaments,* 1955.

Terrien, S., *The Book of Job. Introduction and Exegesis.* The Interpreter's Bible, III, 1954, pp. 877–1198.

———*Job, Poet of Existence,* 1957.

Tromp, N. J., *Primitive Conceptions of Death and the Nether World in the Old Testament* (Biblica et Orientalia, 21), 1969.

Tur-Sinai, N. H. (H. Torczyner), *The Book of Job: A New Commentary,* 1957.

Weiser, A., *Das Buch Hiob,* 2d ed., 1956.

Wright, G. E., ed., *The Bible and the Ancient Near East* (abbr. BANE). Studies presented to W. F. Albright, 1961.

Articles

Albright, W. F., "Some Canaanite-Phoenician Sources of Hebrew Wisdom," in WIANE, VTS, III, 1955, pp. 1–15.

Baker, J., "Commentaries on Job," *Theology* 66, No. 515 (May 1963), 179–85.

Caquot, A., "Traits royaux dans le personnage de Job," *maqqêl shâqêdh, Hommage à Wilhelm Vischer,* 1960, pp. 32–45.

Driver, G. R., "Mythical Monsters in the Old Testament," *Studi Orientalistici in onore di Giorgio Levi Della Vida* I, 1956, pp. 234–49.

Ginsberg, H. L., "Studies in the Book of Job" (Hebrew), *Leshonenu* 21 (1956), 259–64.

Gordis, R., "The Temptation of Job. Tradition versus Experience," *Judaism* 4 (1955), 195–208.

Guillaume, A., "The Arabic Background of the Book of Job," in *Promise and Fulfilment: Essays Presented to S. H. Hooke,* ed. F. F. Bruce, 1963, pp. 106–27.

Knight, H., "Job—Considered as a Contribution to Hebrew Theology," *Scottish Journal of Theology* 9 (1956), 63–76.

Kramer, S. N., "Man and his God: a Sumerian Variation on the 'Job' Motif," in WIANE, VTS, III, 1955, pp. 170–82.

———"Sumerian Theology and Ethics," HTR 49 (1956), 45–62.

Kuyper, L. J., "The Repentance of Job," VT 9 (1959), 91–94.

MacKenzie, R. A. F., "The Purpose of the Yahweh Speeches in the Book of Job," *Biblica* 40 (1959), 435–45.

Rowley, H. H., "The Book of Job and Its Meaning," BJRL 41 (1958), 167–207.

Sarna, N. M., "Epic Substratum in the Prose of Job," JBL 76 (1957), 13–25.

Shapiro, D. S., "The Problem of Evil and the Book of Job," *Judaism* 5 (1956), 46–52.

Skehan, P. W., "Strophic Patterns in the Book of Job," CBQ 23 (1961), 129–43.

Stockhammer, M., "The Righteousness of Job," *Judaism* 7 (1958), 64–71.

Taylor, W. S., "Theology and Therapy in Job," *Theology Today* 12 (1955–56), 451–63.

Tebbe, W., "Predigthilfe aus Kommentaren. Neuere Literatur zum Buche Hiob," *Monatsschrift für Pastoraltheologie* 43 (1954), 156–67.

Thompson, K. T., Jr., "Out of the Whirlwind. The Sense of Alienation in the Book of Job," *Interpretation* 14 (1960), 51–63.

Tsevat, Matitiahu, "The Meaning of the Book of Job," HUCA 37 (1966), 73–106.

Williams, R. J., "Theodicy in the Ancient Near East," *Canadian Journal of Theology* 2 (1956), 14–26.

JOB

1. THE TESTING OF JOB
(i 1–22)

I 1 A man there was in the land of Uz, Job was his name.
That man was blameless and upright, one who feared God and
shunned evil. 2 Seven sons and three daughters were born to
him. 3 His property was seven thousand sheep, three thousand
camels, five hundred yoke of oxen, five hundred she-asses, and
many servants, so that he was the wealthiest of all the Easterners. 4 His sons used to hold feasts, each in his house on his
day, and they would send and invite their three sisters to eat
and drink with them. 5 When the feast days were over, Job
would send and have them purified. He would get busy in the
morning and offer sacrifices for each of them, for he said,

> "Perhaps my sons have sinned,
> And cursed God in their mind."

This Job did regularly.
6 The day arrived when the gods come and present themselves before Yahweh, and the Satan also came with them.
7 Yahweh said to the Satan:

> "Where did you come from?"

The Satan answered Yahweh:

> "From roaming the earth,
> And strolling about in it."

8 Yahweh said to the Satan:

> "Have you marked my servant Job?
> There is none like him on earth,
> A blameless and upright man
> Who fears God and shuns evil."

9 The Satan answered Yahweh:

"Does Job fear God for nought?
10 Have you not hedged him round,
Him and his household
And everything he has?
His efforts you have blessed,
And his property has increased in the land.
11 Just reach out and strike what he has,
And he will curse you to your face."

12 Yahweh said to the Satan:

"Here, all he has is in your power,
But do not lay hand on him."

Then the Satan went out from Yahweh's presence.
13 There came a day when Job's sons and daughters were eating and drinking wine in the oldest brother's house.
14 A mes-
senger came to Job and said:

"The oxen were plowing,
The asses grazing beside them,
15 When the Sabeans attacked and took them.
The boys they put to the sword.
I alone escaped to tell you."

16 While he was still speaking, another came and said;

"Lightning fell from heaven
And burned the sheep and the boys and consumed
them.
I alone escaped to tell you."

17 While he was still speaking, another came and said:

"The Chaldeans formed three bands
And fell on the camels and took them.
The boys they put to the sword.
I alone escaped to tell you."

18 While he was still speaking, another came and said:

"Your sons and your daughters
Were eating and drinking wine
In the house of their oldest brother,
19 When, lo, a great wind came
From across the desert
And struck the four corners of the house.
It fell on the young folk and they died.
I alone escaped to tell you."

20 Then Job rose and tore his robe and shaved his head. He fell on the ground, and worshiped. 21 He said:

"Naked I came from my mother's womb,
And naked shall I return there.
Yahweh gave, Yahweh took away.
Blessed be Yahweh's name."

22 In all this Job did not sin, nor ascribe blame to God.

Notes

i 1. The book does not begin with the regular formula for historical narrative, which would have been *wayĕhî 'îš*, "there was a man," but rather with *'îš hāyāh*, "a man there was." This formula is used to indicate a clear-cut beginning without connection with any preceding event, like Nathan's parable, II Sam xii 1, and the story of Mordecai, Esther ii 5. The principal witnesses of LXX begin the Samuel story in this way, I Sam i 1, as against the MT which has the regular formula. This suggests that the Samuel story was once an independent narrative which was incorporated into the history by the Deuteronomic historian.

Uz. There are two conflicting lines of evidence for the location of Job's homeland. The one points to the Hauran and the other to Edom. Josephus (*Antiq*. I.6.4) says that Uz, one of the four sons of Aram (cf. Gen x 22, 23; I Chron i 17), founded Trachonitis and Damascus. Uz was also the name of the oldest son of Abraham's Aramean brother Nahor, Gen xxii 21, thus making the Aramean connections of the name very strong. Byzantine and Arab tradition place Job's homeland in the Hauran near Nawā and Sheikh Meskīn. According to Abulfeda (*Historia anteislam*, p. 26), the whole of Bethenije, a part of the province of Damascus, belonged to Job as his possession. The monastery Deir Ayyub near Damascus is another witness to this tradition. The appendix to

LXX places Job's homeland on the borders of Edom and Arabia and names his city as Dennaba, the modern Dhuneibeh between Dera' and Sheikh Meskīn. Etherius (ed. Geyer, p. 56) further identifies Job's city Dennaba with Carneas, i.e., Qarnayim (the Qarnini of the Assyrian records), mentioned in Amos vi 13. Qarnayim has been identified with the conspicuous mound Sheikh Sa'ad in the Hauran, about twenty-three miles east of the Sea of Galilee. Qarnayim was an important city in the first two millennia B.C. A badly weathered stela of Ramses II with a relief of a deity and a worshiper and a dedication in hieroglyphic to the Semitic deity Lord of Zaphon found at Sheikh Sa'ad became known as the Job Stone because of the Arab traditions connecting the patriarch Job with this place (cf. ANET, p. 249, n. 6).

The Edomite connections of Uz are equally strong. Dishan the Horite chief of Edom had a son named Uz, Gen xxxvi 28. Jeremiah mentions the kings of the land of Uz in connection with those of Egypt, Philistia, Edom, Moab, and Ammon, Jer xxv 19–20. Edom and the land of Uz are plainly identified in Lam iv 21. A. Musil has proposed identification of Uz with el-'Iṣ some three kilometers south southeast of eṭ-Ṭafīle (*Arabia Petraea,* II, 1907, book 1, pp. 337, 339, n. 6). The mention of the raid of the Sabeans, vs. 15, suggests a still more southerly location. Dhorme, however, would identify these Sabeans not with the great South Arabian kingdom whose celebrated queen paid a visit to Solomon but with the Sheba mentioned along with Tema in vi 19. Dhorme would find a reminiscence of this Sheba in the name of the wadi es-Saba in the territory of Medina. Tema is also mentioned in Jer xxv 23 along with Dedan and Buz. Dedan is identified with the oasis el-'Ula directly south of Medain Saliḥ and for Buz Dhorme suggests a location between Jauf and Tema, thus fixing the land of Uz in the vicinity of Edom and western Arabia. The location of Buz, however, is uncertain. Albright would place it on the east of the Arabian peninsula in the hinterland of the island of Dilmun, modern Bahrein (W. F. Albright, "Geschichte und Altes Testament," in *Festschrift A. Alt,* 1953, p. 8, n. 2).

It appears impossible to reconcile the conflicting evidences and opinions as to the exact location of Uz. Tur-Sinai's reminder that the names Aram and Edom may be confused in several places in the OT (because of the resemblance of the letters *dāleṯ* and *rēš* in various stages of the Hebrew-Aramaic script) does not help to solve the problem. Delitzsch suggests that the term *'uṣ/'iṣ* (the Arabic name of Esau is *el-'iṣ*) may have been applied collectively to the northern part of the Arabian desert, extending northeast from Edom to Syria. This covers a lot of territory, but one still not vast enough to encompass the widely separated locales proposed for Job's homeland. An inscription of Shalmaneser III mentions tribute from a certain Sasi, "a son of the land of Uṣṣa," (D. D. Luckenbill, ed., *Ancient Records of Assyria and Babylonia,* I, 1926–27, No. 585, p. 201) presumably our Uz, but unfortunately gives no indication of its location.

Job. The English form of the name, derived from Greek and Latin transcriptions, does not present a very accurate rendering of the Hebrew form of the name, which is *'Iyyôḇ*. The German form, Hiob, is somewhat closer to the Hebrew, but still rather inexact.

It has been thought that the name was constructed, *ad hoc,* to characterize the hero of the story. Accordingly, attempts have been made so to interpret it. The name has been assumed to be connected with the root *'yb* which carries the sense of "enmity, hostility." The common word for enemy in Hebrew is the simple active participle of this root, *'ôyēḇ*. The form of the name *'Iyyôḇ,* however, appears to correspond to the nominal pattern which in the Semitic languages regularly designates a profession, or a habitual or characteristic activity. Accordingly, the meaning would be "inveterate foe," or the like. This form of the root *'yb,* however, is otherwise unknown. If the name was understood as meaning "enemy," it may have been chosen to symbolize the principal's attitude toward God, his adverse reaction to the suffering inflicted on him. Some of the rabbis made puns on the name, connecting it with "enemy." According to Rabbah (TB, Baba Bathra 16a), or Raba (Niddah 52a), Job blasphemed when he used the term "tempest" in ix 17, meaning, "Perhaps a tempest passed before Thee which caused the confusion between Job (*'iyyôḇ*) and "enemy" (*'ôyēḇ*)." For some reason, the translator of the Wisdom of Jesus Ben Sira was subject to the same confusion in Ecclesiasticus xlix 8–9 where the Hebrew of the Cairo Genizah text reads "Ezekiel saw a vision and described the features of the chariot; he also mentioned Job, who maintained all [the ways of ri]ghteousness," but the translator rendered the latter verse, "For he remembers the enemies in rain, / To do good to those who made their ways straight." The idea of enmity has been taken in the passival sense, i.e., that the name is intended to designate one who is the object of enmity or persecution rather than the agent. This sense would be quite appropriate for the victim of such cruel treatment by God and unfair criticism by his friends. There is, however, very scant philological evidence to support this explanation of the name.

It has been suggested further that the name is to be explained by the Arabic root *'wb,* "return, repent." Accordingly, the meaning would be "the penitent one."

In recent decades it has become clear that the name *'Iyyôḇ* was not simply an invention of the author of the book. In one of the Amarna Letters (No. 256), dating from about 1350 B.C., the prince of Ashtaroth in Bashan bears the name *'Ayyāb,* an older form of the biblical name.

Still earlier, about 2000 B.C., in the Egyptian Execration Texts there is mention of a Palestinian chief named *'ybm,* which is almost certainly to be vocalized *Ay(y)abum* (with the nominative ending *-um* which was later dropped). The name *Ayyab-um* also appears in the Akkadian documents from Mari and Alalakh dating from the early second millennium B.C. W. F. Albright has explained the name *Ay(y)ab-um* as contracted from *'Ayya-'abu(m)*, "Where is (My) Father?" Similar names occur with other relatives in place of *'abu,* "father," such as *Ay(y)a-'aḫu,* "Where is (My) Brother?", and *Ay(y)a-ḫammu/ḫalu,* "Where is the Paternal/Maternal Clan?" The name Ayyab is apparently shortened from a longer form, such as we have attested in *Ayabi-sharri,* "Where is My Father, O King?", and *Ayabi-ilu,* "Where is My Father, O God?" Cf. W. F. Albright, "Northwest Semitic Names in a List of Egyptian Slaves from the Eighteenth Century B.C.," JAOS 74 (1954), 223–33. The Ugaritic version of the name also occurs in a list of personnel from the palace of Ugarit in the form *ayab* (*Mission de Ras Shamra* VII/*Le Palais Royal d'Ugarit* II, 1957, text 35 reverse, line 10). In the same text (obverse column II, line 6) occurs the name *ayḫ,* a variant of the fuller form *ayaḫ* (spelled in Akk. *a-ya-a-ḫi*), with the element *aḫ* "brother," rather than *ab,* "father," and exhibiting already the elision of the intervocalic glottal stop. The Ugaritic name thus might have been written *ayb* to reflect the pronunciation *'ay(y)ābu* from an original *'ayya-'abu.*

The name *Ayyāb*>*'Iyyôḇ* is thus well attested as a fairly common name among western Semites in the second millennium B.C. The name may have been chosen for the hero of the story simply because it was an ordinary name. It may be, however, that some ancient worthy bearing that name actually experienced reversals of fortune and became the model of the righteous sufferer. The mention of Job (Ezek xiv 14, 20) along with Noah and (the Ugaritic hero) Danel suggests a hero of great antiquity.

blameless and upright. The first word carries the sense of perfection in terms of completeness while the second is connected with the idea of straightness. The two roots occur in juxtaposition in Ps xxv 21 and in parallelism in Ps xxxvii 37. Taken together they indicate the peak of moral perfection.

feared God and shunned evil. Cf. 8, ii 3. Biblical Hebrew has no word corresponding exactly to our term "religion." The closest approximation is "fear of God/the Lord," which the orthodox sages equated with the beginning and the end of wisdom. The fear of the Lord gives one the intelligence to avoid evil, Prov iii 7, xiv 16, xvi 6.

2. The children are mentioned directly following Job's righteousness, for such is the Lord's reward, Pss cxxvii 3, cxxviii 6.

The ratio of seven sons to three daughters is apparently ideal and is retained when the lost children are replaced, xlii 13. (The same ratio between Job's sheep and camels, vs. 3, and between Solomon's wives and concubines, I Kings xi 3, has no apparent rationale.) Seven children, I Sam ii 5, or better seven sons, Ruth iv 15, are the ideal blessing.

In the Ugaritic myths the god Baal has three daughters and seven "boys" (67 v 8–9); cf. xlii 13.

3. *wealthiest.* Literally "greatest." The verb "be, become great" has the sense "becomes rich" in Gen xxvi 13.

Easterners. Literally "sons of the East (*qeḏem*)." The Semitic term *Qedem* (East) is used in the Egyptian Tale of Sinuhe in the second millennium B.C. as a vague designation of the region east of Byblos where lived semi-nomadic Semites. In Gen xxix 1 the term is applied to the Arameans along the northern Euphrates. In Isa xi 14 the term designates Israel's enemies on the east, the Edomites, Moabites, and Ammonites, as contrasted with the Philistines on the west. The term is applied particularly to the nomads who with the Midianites and Amalekites raided the Israelite borders in the period of the Judges, Judg vi 3, 33, vii 12, viii 10, and during the Babylonian Conquest, Jer xlix 28; Ezek xxv 4, 10. The Arabs of this region, according to Musil (*Arabia Petraea,* III, 1908, p. 22) occasionally use the term "people of the East" (*'ahāli eš-šerq*) to designate the inhabitants of the desert in contrast to the peasants. The wisdom of these people of the East rivaled that of Egypt, I Kings iv 30(v 10). The term is too general to locate Job's homeland accurately.

Job's wealth is made up of such property as a semi-nomadic chieftain might hold; cf. Gen xii 16, xiii 6, xxiv 35. The collective term *miqneh* usually designates sheep and cattle and does not include camels and asses which are the wealth of the nomad. The three thousand camels are not excessive, for Aristotle testifies (*De anim. hist.* ix.50, 5) that the Arabs sometimes owned such a number of camels. The female asses are mentioned because they exceeded the male asses in number and in value, because of their milk and their breeding. They are also better for riding than male asses. A small number of stud asses would suffice for a herd of five hundred. The ancient Semitic nomads were parasites first of the ass and later of the camel. A single term, *'ăḇuddāh,* as in Gen xxvi 14, designates the staff of male and female slaves who are usually mentioned separately.

4. *each in his house.* Cf. 13, 18. It is not clear whether the sons were married. Each had his own house, like David's sons Amnon and Absalom, II Sam xiii 7, xiv 28. The unmarried sisters probably stayed in the father's house, like David's daughters, II Sam xiii 7, 8, 20.

It is not to be assumed that since there were seven sons and seven days to the week that Job's sons and daughters engaged in incessant rounds of feasting. The feast was doubtless an annual affair, most likely the feast of ingathering at the year's end; cf. Exod xxxiv 22. The festival of booths, e.g., was observed with seven days of offerings, followed on the eighth day by a holy convocation and a solemn assembly with offerings by fire, Lev xxiii 36; Num xxix 35; II Chron vii 9.

5. Job's patriarchal dignity, apparently, did not permit him to visit his sons' houses, but he had them undergo purification for the sacrifices which he offered as head of the family.

The cult depicted here is primitive, without priesthood. The patriarch himself performs the sacrifices, as in the case of Balaam, Num xxiii 1, 14, 29. The prescribed sacrifices in xlii 8 are seven bulls and seven rams, as in the Balaam story. In Num xxix 36 the prescription is one bull, one ram, and seven male lambs.

get busy. This verb (*hškm*) is regularly rendered "rise early." The notion of earliness, however, does not appear to be intrinsic to its meaning. The implication of earliness comes from the frequent use of the phrase "in the morning" immediately after the verb. When the phrase "in the morning" is absent, and the context does not otherwise indicate a matinal setting, the word is used adverbially in the sense of quickly, eagerly, assiduously, persistently, urgently, or the like; cf. Jer vii 13, 25, xi 7, xxv 4, xxvi 5, xxix 19, xxxii 33, xxxv 14, 15, xliv 4; Hos vi 4; Zeph iii 7. The verb is apparently denominative, from the noun *šikm*, "shoulder," and perhaps originally had to do with the early morning activity of breaking camp which would involve the use of the shoulders of both man and beast, and no small degree of exertion.

cursed. Literally "blessed." A standard scribal euphemism. The same substitution occurs in i 11, ii 5, 9; I Kings xxi 10, 13; Ps x 3.

mind. Literally "heart." In the OT, "heart" rarely refers literally to the bodily organ. Nor does the term have quite the same range of meaning as in our figurative usage. It is more the seat of the intellect and the will than of the affections and emotions (which are more often located in the bowels, kidneys, or liver). Cf. Exod xxxi 6; Deut xxix 4(5); I Kings iii 9; Prov x 8. Hos vii 11 is a striking illustration of this meaning:

> Ephraim was like a dove,
> Silly, with no sense [literally heart].

One could sin in mind, even lying in bed, Ps iv 4(5); Eccles x 20. The Babylonian penitential psalms often express contrition for unknown and inadvertent sins.

6. *The day*. The Jerusalem Targum places this first heavenly assize on New Year's Day and the second (ii 1) on the Day of Atonement. This is an entirely natural understanding in accordance with Jewish tradition. New Year's Day is the time of the preliminary judgment, when the good are immediately inscribed in the book of life and the wicked are blotted out. For those who are in-between, neither good nor bad, there is a period of grace until the Day of Atonement and then in a final judgment those fates previously undecided are fixed in accordance with each one's repentance. It is not unlikely that the interpretation of the Jerusalem Targum has some basis. The Jewish New Year was undoubtedly influenced by the more ancient beliefs and practices of Mesopotamia and Canaan. It is not possible here to treat the recent lively literature relating to the alleged Israelite New Year's Festival. (For a judicious appraisal of the evidence, cf. R. de Vaux, *Ancient Israel,* 1961, pp. 502–4.) Whether on New Year's Day and the Day of Atonement, or on successive New Year's Days, or on some other days, the scenes depict two heavenly councils in which Job's fate is at stake. The Satan works very hard for an adverse decision, but each time Job is vindicated.

the gods. Literally "sons of the gods." These are lesser members of the ancient pagan pantheon who are retained in later monotheistic theology as angels; cf. xxxviii 7; Gen vi 2, 4; Pss xxix 1, lxxxix 7. In Ps lxxxii 1 they are called simply "gods." The Ugaritic mythological texts give us vivid glimpses of the meetings of the gods; cf. EUT, pp. 47–49. Yahweh as king of the gods holds court as in the vision of Micaiah ben Imlah, I Kings xxii 19–23, surrounded by his divine entourage of counselors and servants.

and present themselves. Literally "to station themselves" (*lĕhiṯyaṣṣēḇ*), as courtiers before the king, as in Prov xxii 29. The usual expression for this is "stand before," as David before Saul, I Sam xvi 21; cf. Jer lii 12. In Akkadian the term *manzaz pāni,* "one who stands before (the king)," is the designation of a royal official. The Satan is but one of the heavenly officials who come to report and receive orders. After presenting themselves before Yahweh, they go out to their various assignments; cf. Zech vi 5.

the Satan. Note the definite article, as in Zech iii 1–2, which shows that the term is a title and not yet a proper name. The figure here is not the fully developed character of the later Jewish and Christian Satan or Devil. It is not expedient here to attempt a detailed discussion of the origin and development of his Satanic majesty, but some comment is in order since here in the Prologue of Job we have one of the principal passages in the OT in which the Satan appears in a clear-cut role. The Satan is one of the members of the divine court and comes with other attendants to present himself at the celestial court and report on the fulfillment of his duties. The picture of the celestial court with Yahweh enthroned as king is presented in I Kings xxii 19; Isa vi; and Zech iii–iv. In Zech iv there is some rather bizarre symbolism. God is the lampstand and the seven lamps are his "eyes" which range through the whole earth, Zech iv 10b. Tur-Sinai has made the attractive suggestion that the figure and role of the Satan derives from the Persian secret service. Herodotus tells us that the royal secret police in Persia were called "the eyes and ears of the king." Both in the present passage and in Zech iv 10 the verb used for the action of the Satan and of the roving eyes is *šûṭ* "roam, rove," which is probably more than a mere wordplay. S. D. Luzatto has already suggested that the title Satan is derived from this root and that the Satan was a kind of spy roaming the earth and reporting to God on the evil he found therein. Since he must have appeared to men as their enemy and accuser, they renamed him *śāṭān* from a verb "to accuse"; cf. Tur-Sinai, p. 41, n. 1. (The shift from *š* to *ś*, or the reverse, presents no impediment since these are mere dialectal variants of a single consonant distinguished only by diacritical marks in the Masoretic system.) Tur-Sinai's idea was arrived at independently and carries greater conviction because of the specific connection with a mundane royal court. As a roving secret agent, the Satan stood ready to accuse and indict his victim and serve as prosecutor, as in Zech iii 1; cf. Ps cix 6. If the roving investigator found nothing to report, it might occur to him to assume the role of agent provocateur, as in I Chron xxi 1. Thus, the diabolical character of the figure finds rationale. The origin of the concept of the Satan from the analogy of the security system of the Persian Empire would quite naturally explain the later development of the concept of the Adversary and Tempter (cf. Tur-Sinai, pp. 38–45). The vast Persian Empire, as organized by the genius of Darius the Great, depended in great measure for its security on the well-developed system of highways and communications which linked the provincial capitals, and on an efficient intelligence agency which kept the powerful governors under surveillance to detect and prevent sedition and rebellion. Some of these inspectors or master spies were known as "The King's Eye" and "The King's Ear." "The Eye of the King" appears to have been an officer in constant attendance on the king (cf. W. W. How and J. Wells, *A Commentary on Herodotus*, 1928, I, p. 108). The effectiveness of this spy system is reflected in Xenophon's quotation of the proverbial saying, "The King has many ears and many eyes" (cf. A. J. Arberry, ed., *The Legacy of Persia*, 1953, p. 9). But certainly the Persians did not invent spying and secret police and informers which must have evolved very early in the prehistoric stage of politics. The Persian court may have contributed something to the idea of the Satan, but the background is much older, as reflected in the divine court scenes of more ancient Near Eastern mythological literature.

7b. *roaming.* A play on the word Satan, and perhaps the very root from which the title was originally derived. Cf. previous NOTE.

strolling. The common verb to walk, stroll, but perhaps used here in a technical sense of roaming around looking for trouble or an opportunity to do harm. In Akkadian, the participle of this root is applied to the evil eye and evil spirits that rove about seeking to do harm. In Prov xxiv 34 the participle (*miṯhallēḵ*) is used in parallelism with "an armed man" (*'îš māḡēn*) as the figure of the poverty which will suddenly seize the sluggard, perhaps like a sudden arrest by secret police. The description of the Devil in I Pet v 8 as strolling about like a roaring lion (*hos leōn ōruomenos peripatei*) seeking prey, preserves the figure of the rover. The term "Watcher" (*'îr*) applied to certain members of the heavenly court in Dan iv 13(10), 17(14), 23(20), may also reflect the royal spy system. In Dan iv 17 the Watchers and Holy Ones give the decree against Nebuchadnezzar, but it is made clear, Dan iv 24, that they are only acting as agents of the Most High. Here their function is not that of spies or vigilantes, but as prosecutors, as is the Satan in Zech iii 1; cf. Ps cix 6.

8. *marked.* Literally "set your mind upon," i.e., Have you paid attention and given thought to him? The question naturally arises, why all the concern about Job's integrity? Yahweh apparently knows that the Satan takes a dim view of mankind and is convinced that every man has his price or his breaking point. There is something of taunt and provocation in Yahweh's query; he appears confident that in Job he has a winner, one who will prove the Satan wrong. What would be the value of such a victory? Even if the Satan were proved wrong about Job, this exception would only confirm the general rule that each man is concerned only for his own skin. Perhaps there is more involved than is made explicit. Ezekiel vigorously opposed the notion (which must have been more or less normative) that a single righteous man, even Noah, Danel, or Job, could nullify the divine judgment against a whole community of sinners. Abraham raised the question whether a wicked city might be spared for the sake of a few righteous men who might be found in it (Gen xviii), but he stopped short at the minimum of ten. He did not dare to press his point to the ultimate: Suppose just one righteous man were found in the city? (Cf. D. Picard, "Réflexions sur l'interprétation chrétienne de trois récits de la Genèse," in *maqqél shâqédh, Hommage à Wilhelm Vischer,* 1960, pp. 181–97, especially pp. 181–83 on Gen xviii 22–23.) What Ezekiel and Jeremiah denied (Ezek xiv 14, 20, xviii; Jer xxxi 29) is apparently affirmed by Eliphaz (Job xxii 27–30) who comforts Job with the

thought that if he were restored to his former purity he could then intercede and save others, even the guilty. This doctrine of vicarious expiation and atonement so strikingly explicit in the famous Suffering Servant poem (Isa lii 13–liii 12) doubtless had a very ancient background of which we have only random bits in the OT.

my servant. Many other persons are designated servants of the Lord, e.g., Moses (Exod xiv 31; Num xii 7; Deut xxxiv 5); Caleb (Num xiv 24); David (II Sam vii 5, 8); Isaiah (Isa xx 3); Zerubbabel (Hag ii 23); and even Nebuchadnezzar (Jer xxv 9). The prophets are referred to as servants of the Lord in II Kings ix 7, xvii 13, 23, xxi 10, xxiv 2; Jer xxv 4, xxvi 5, xxix 19, xxxv 15, xliv 4; Amos iii 7; Zech i 6; Dan ix 6, 10; Ezra ix 11. C. Lindhagen, *The Servant Motif in the Old Testament,* 1950, has made an exhaustive study of the background of this OT term which designates the relation of the weaker partner to the stronger in a covenant.

9b. A rhetorical question. The Satan is confident that the answer is in the negative. Here is the crux of the issue, the question which provoked the cruel experiment.

10. *hedged.* With a thorny hedge (cf. Hos ii 6) protecting his property and welfare.

increased. Literally "burst out." The same verb (*prṣ*) is applied to Jacob's sudden increase in wealth, Gen xxx 30.

11. *to your face.* This expression occurs also in vi 28, xiii 15, xvi 8, xxi 31, with variations in the preposition. The expression is the same as that rendered "before me" in the First Commandment, Exod xx 3; Deut v 7, but the meaning is quite different here.

14. The use of the feminine plural participle, *ḥôrĕšôṯ,* with the masculine singular (collective) *bāqār,* "cattle," parallel to the mention of she-asses is interpreted by A. Guillaume as evidence that the plow animals were female. In the neighborhood of Tema and Dedan, according to Doughty, cows rather than oxen were put to the yoke. Guillaume's observations and inquiries on this point indicate that this practice is confined to the vicinity of Tema and that elsewhere in the Arabian peninsula the male is always used for plowing, except in unusual circumstances. This grammatical detail is thus for Guillaume an important bit of evidence for the setting of the book in Tema. No great weight can be accorded this point. Although *bāqār,* "cattle," and *ṣō'n,* "sheep/goats," are regularly construed as masculine, the latter word also occurs with a feminine plural adjective in Gen xxx 43. (The use of the feminine plural forms with *ṣō'n* in Ps cxliv 13b is not relevant to the present point since there the reference is to fertility of the flock, which is a function of the females.) Samson's complaint, Judg xiv 18, "If you had not plowed with my heifer, you would not have found out my riddle," has a possible bearing on the question of use of cows

for plowing, but it is not clear whether the implicit impropriety was in the use of any heifer or of a heifer not one's own.

15. *Sabeans.* Heb. *šĕḇā'*. To be kept distinct from the Sabeans (spelled *sĕḇā*) frequently mentioned in the OT (*Seba, Sheba:* Gen x 7; I Chron i 9; Ps lxxii 10; *Sheba:* Gen x 28; I Chron i 22; Gen xxv 3; I Chron i 32; I Kings x; Isa lx 6; Ps lxxii 15; Jer vi 20; Ezek xxvii 22, xxxviii 13; Job vi 19; Sabeans: Joel iii 8). Sheba was considered to be far distant, Jer vi 20; Joel iii 8. The homage of potentates from the distant land is cited to signal the far-reaching fame of Israel and enhance its prestige, I Kings x; Ps lxxii 10. The territory of these wealthy Sabeans was in the region now known as Yemen and their capital lay at the site of modern Marib. They attained a high degree of civilization as indicated by the remains of buildings, dams, and irrigation systems, and numerous inscriptions, many of which are still unpublished. The prosperity of the area earned it in classical times the name Arabia Felix as contrasted with Arabia Deserta; cf. Wendell Phillips, *Qataban and Sheba,* 1955; R. L. Bowen, *Archeological Discoveries in South Arabia,* 1958, pp. 215–86; G. W. van Beek, "South Arabian History and Archaeology," BANE, pp. 229–48. It is, however, unlikely that the Sabeans here intended were the distant South Arabians. In Job vi 19 Sheba is parallel to Tema. In Isa xxi 13 and Jer xxv 23 Tema is related to Dedan, while in Gen x 7 and xxv 3, Sheba is parallel to Dedan. Tema is identified as the oasis of that name northeast of Medain Saliḥ in the vicinity of Medina. Dedan is the oasis of el-'Ula. This North Arabian Sheba is thus to be located somewhere in the neighborhood of the other two known sites. *Wadi eš-Šaba* in the region of Medina may be a reminiscence of these earlier North Arabian Sabeans who are probably the *Saba* mentioned in the inscriptions of Tiglathpileser III and Sargon II as allies of the *Aribi* (Arabs), nomadic border raiders as here in Job. The North Arabian and the South Arabian Sabeans must be kept apart from a third group who lived in Africa. Isa xliii 3 mentions this Seba along with Ethiopia, and Isa xlv 14 speaks of their (exceptional) stature. One may think of some of the unusually tall African tribes like the Watusi. Josephus (*Antiq.* II.10.2) identifies this Seba with the kingdom of Meroë in Nubia. Guillaume takes the reference to the Sabeans here and to the Chaldeans in vs. 17 as confirmation of his theory that the book comes from the time of Nabonidus' operations in Tema.

I alone. The feature that only one escapes disaster is found several times in the OT. Elijah, I Kings xviii 22, laments, "I, even I only, am left a prophet of the Lord"; cf. Gen xliv 20; Josh xiii 12; II Sam xiii 32; Isa xlix 21; Ezek ix 8.

15b. Literally "and the boys they smote by the mouth of the sword."

As arrows may drink blood, so the sword may devour flesh, Deut xxxii 42; II Sam xi 25; Nah iii 15. It appears that the term "mouth of the sword" may be something more than a poetic figure. Swords have been found with the hilt shaped in the form of a lion's head with the blade coming forth from the mouth (T. J. Meek, BASOR 122 [1951], 31–33). In Rev i 16, ii 16, xix 15 the sword is figured as proceeding from the mouth of the avenging Messiah.

16a. *While he was still speaking.* Cf. Gen xxiv 15; I Kings i 42; Dan iv 31. This same striking literary device is used in the Ugaritic texts, e.g., in the Danel epic (1 Aqht 112–16):

> From his mouth the word had not come forth,
> From his lips the utterance,
> The wings of the eagles Baal broke,
> Baal broke their pinions,
> They fell beneath his feet.

16b. *Lightning.* Literally "fire of God." Thunder is the "voice of God." In the contest between Yahweh and Baal on Mount Carmel, I Kings xviii 38, the lightning is called "fire of Yahweh" to emphasize that it was not Baal, the Canaanite weather-god, who sent it. In II Kings i 12, in the Elijah story, it is again "fire of God." Cf. Num xi 1; Gen xix 24.

consumed. Literally "ate." Cf. xv 34, xx 26, xxii 20; Num xvi 35, xxvi 10.

16c. The extra verb translated "consumed" at the end makes the line overlong in comparison with adjacent lines and also adds a prosaic, pedestrian element to the style which is otherwise epic in character.

17. *Chaldeans.* The Chaldeans first appear in history in the ninth century B.C. in Assyrian records from the time of Ashurnasirpal II (884–859 B.C.) which represent a group of them known as Bit Yakin settled west of the Tigris. They several times gained control of Babylon in the late eighth century B.C. before Nabopolassar in 626 founded the Neo-Babylonian Empire to which the term Chaldean usually refers in the OT. Here in Job the Chaldeans appear as unsettled semi-nomadic marauders which would reflect their situation earlier than the seventh century B.C.

formed three bands. Literally "put three heads," i.e., made a three-pronged attack. This strategy of dividing forces is mentioned in Judg vii 16, 20, ix 34, 43–45; I Sam xi 11, xiii 17.

boys. As in many languages, words for "boy" in the OT often have the sense of "servant." Cf. iv 18.

18. *While.* MT here has *'ad*, "until," instead of *'ôḏ*, "still, yet," as in vss. 16 and 17 above. The reason for this difference is obscure. The defective spelling *'d*, instead of *'wd*, is the more archaic form (cf.

F. M. Cross, Jr., and D. N. Freedman, *Early Hebrew Orthography*, 1952, pp. 58–60) but the vocalization *'aḏ* for *'ôḏ* here is puzzling in view of the preceding *plene* spellings. Ugaritic used *'d* in the sense of "while," particularly in the cliché *'d lḥm šty ilm*, "while the gods ate and drank." The same usage is found in Song of Songs i 12a, "While (*'aḏ*) the king was at his banquet."

19. *From across the desert.* The desert wind is mentioned in Jer xiii 24. It was not simply the searing east wind that blows across the burning sands and brings the stifling heat and dust, the sirocco or khamsin, but apparently a sudden and violent wind. The violence and destructiveness of the wind of the ancient storm-gods is frequently mentioned in the literature of the Near East, often as the sanction to deter or punish the treaty breaker; cf. xxxviii 1b.

20. Tearing the garments was the customary gesture of grief; cf. Gen xxxvii 34; Josh vii 6; II Sam i 11, iii 31, xiii 31; Ezra ix 3, 5; Esther iv 1. Among other peoples the act had other meanings. Julius Caesar tore his garments after crossing the Rubicon. The robe is the outer mantle worn by the nobility; cf. I Sam xviii 4, xxiv 5, 12; Ezek xxvi 16.

Shaving the hair and beard was also a standard mourning rite (Isa xxii 12; Jer vii 29, xvi 6, xli 5, xlvii 5, xlviii 37; Ezek vii 18; Amos viii 10). Such rites are expressly forbidden in the Law, Lev xix 27–28; Deut xiv 1. In the Annals of Sargon it is said that Merodach-baladan threw himself on the ground, tore his clothing, and took the razor. In one of the Ugaritic myths we have vivid descriptions of violent mourning. When the chief god El received news of the death of Baal (67 VI 12–22),

> Thereupon Beneficent El Benign
> Descended the throne, sat on the footstool,
> From the footstool took seat on the ground.
> He strewed mourning straw on his head,
> Wallowing dust on his pate.
> Robe and loin cloth he ripped,
> Skin with stone he gashed,
> Incisions with stick he cut,
> Cheek and chin he furrowed,
> Upper arm he plowed,
> Like a garden his chest
> Like a valley he furrowed his back.

The Virgin 'Anat, Baal's spouse, went through similar rites when she discovered her consort's corpse (62: 2–7).

worshiped. The verb here used is the common term for obeisance before royalty or divinity and occasionally even before one's peers

(Gen xxiii 7, 12; Exod xviii 7; I Kings ii 19). The act consisted of falling down and touching the face to the ground. Even before a mortal it might be done three (I Sam xx 41) or seven times (Gen xxxiii 3). Vassals of the Pharaoh in the Amarna Letters speak of prostrating themselves seven times each way on belly and back. This verb occurs frequently in the Ugaritic texts from which its grammatical analysis is made clear. The root is not *šḥw*, as grammarians and lexicographers had previously thought, but *ḥwy* used in the Št conjugation, corresponding to the tenth form of Arabic.

21. This utterance is of a piece with other pessimistic observations on human fate, as Gen iii 19; Eccles v 14, xii 7; Ecclesiasticus xl 1.

naked. Cf. Eccles v 14; I Tim vi 7.

there. The passage cannot mean literally what it says, that Job will return to his human mother's womb; cf. John iii 4. The sense is clarified by Ecclesiasticus xl 1:

> Great hardship God has allotted,
> A heavy yoke upon Adam's sons,
> From the day he comes out his mother's womb
> To the day he returns to the mother of all life.

The body of man is formed in the entrails of the earth, Ps cxxxix 13, 15, and the dead thus return to the womb of Mother Earth. Classical literature contains many similar allusions to Mother Earth who bears all and finally receives all back to herself; cf. Dhorme ad loc. In Egyptian the expression "they who are there" (*ntjw 'im*) is a common circumlocution for the dead. Similarly in Greek *ekei,* "there," and *ekeise,* "thither," are common euphemisms for Hades, and *hoi ekei,* "they (who are) there," for the dead; cf. iii 17 and especially xl 20b where LXX renders *šām* as *en tō tartarō,* "in Tartarus."

Yahweh gave, . . . away. A formula of resignation; cf. I Sam iii 18. Musil (*Arabia Petraea,* III, p. 427) reports that among the Bedouin of Arabia Petraea, immediately after a death the next of kin recites the formula "His Lord gave him, his Lord has taken him away" (*Rabbu jābu, rabbu aḫaḏu*).

Blessed be Yahweh's name. This benediction recurs in Ps cxiii 2 with the addition of "now and forever."

The Satan is foiled, for he had predicted a curse, 11b.

22. *In all this.* LXX understood this phrase to refer to the circumstances just related, and this is the view of many eminent expositors. In ii 10 the addition of "with his lips" indicates that the author had in mind sinning in speech.

blame. The sense of the word *tiplāh* has been much discussed. The emendations usually suggested are to *'awlāh,* "wickedness," or *nĕbālāh,* "folly," or even to retain the consonants *tpl*(*h*) and vocalize *tĕpillāh* in the sense of "protest" rather than "prayer." But the reading is well established and the context is sufficiently clear to establish the general sense of the term. The word is doubtless to be connected with Ar. *tafala,* "expectorate," *tifl,* "spittle." Spitting is the reaction to anything disgusting or shameful. The sense of "reproach" or "blame" is indicated here. The expression "to ascribe *tip̄lāh* to God" is similar in construction to the common one "to ascribe glory (*kāḇôd*)" to God (I Sam vi 5; Jer xiii 16; Prov xxvi 8) and *tip̄lāh* here is very nearly an antonym to "glory."

2. MORE DRASTIC MEASURES
(ii 1–13)

II 1 The day arrived when the gods come to present themselves before Yahweh, and the Satan also came with them to present himself before Yahweh. 2 Said Yahweh to the Satan:

"Where did you come from?"

The Satan answered Yahweh:

"From roaming the earth
And strolling about in it."

3 Yahweh said to the Satan:

"Have you marked my servant Job?
There is none like him on earth,
A blameless and upright man,
Who fears God and shuns evil?
He still holds fast to his integrity,
Though you incited me against him
To destroy him without cause."

4 The Satan answered Yahweh:

"Skin after skin.
All that a man has
He will give for his life.
5 Reach out and strike him,
Touch his bone and flesh,
And he will curse you to your face."

6 Yahweh said to the Satan:

"Here, he is in your power;
Only spare his life."

7 The Satan went out from Yahweh's presence and afflicted Job
with a foul pox from sole to pate. 8 He took a potsherd to
scrape himself, and sat in the ashes.
9 His wife said to him:

> "Do you still maintain your integrity?
> Curse God and die."

10 Job said to her:

> "You talk like a foolish woman.
> Shall we accept good from God,
> And not accept evil?"

In spite of all this Job did not sin with his lips.
11 When Job's three friends heard of all the calamity that had
befallen him, they came each from his place, Eliphaz the
Temanite, Bildad the Shuhite, and Zophar the Naamathite.
They arranged to meet together to go and condole and comfort
him. 12 When they saw him from afar, they could not recognize
him, and they raised their voices and wept; each tore his robe
and sprinkled dust on his head [heavenward]. 13 They sat with
him on the ground seven days and seven nights, and no one
said a word to him, for they saw that his anguish was very great.

Notes

ii 1. The repetition of *lĕhiṯyaṣṣēḇ 'al-YHWH*, "to present oneself before Yahweh," is omitted by LXX and supplied from Aquila and Theodotion. It is difficult to judge whether it is a dittograph from i 6 or whether the omission was motivated by a concern to minimize the Satan's status in the divine council.

3. *holds fast.* The verb means literally to grasp and hold firmly. One may hold fast to deceit, Jer viii 5, or to anger, Mic vii 18. Job steadfastly maintains his integrity; cf. xxvii 6 where Job holds fast to his claim of innocence.

incited me. This verb is generally used in a derogatory sense, as here and in xxxvi 18; cf. Deut xiii 7; Josh xv 18; I Sam xxvi 19; II Sam xxiv 1. But it may also have a favorable sense, as in xxxvi 16 and II Chron xviii 31. Yahweh here gives the Satan credit for instigating the experiment.

destroy. Literally "swallow." The verb is often used in this sense; cf. x 8, xxxvii 20, and II Sam xx 20; Isa xlix 19; Hab i 13. In Sophocles' *Philoctetes* the Chorus says:

> But I know of no other, by hearsay, much less by sight, of all mankind whose destiny was more his enemy when he met it than Philoctetes', who wronged no one, nor killed but lived, just among the just, and fell in trouble past his deserts.

(*The Complete Greek Tragedies,* eds. D. Grene and R. Lattimore, 1959, II, p. 427, lines 680–85.)

4. *Skin after skin.* This is clearly a proverbial saying, but, like many such sayings, it is so terse that it is difficult to interpret of itself. Happily the general sense is given by the following line, "All that a man has, he will give for his life." One explanation is that the saying derives from barter, "a skin in exchange for a skin." However, one does not usually barter a commodity for another of the same kind. The sense of "value for value" would suit the context admirably. The preposition *ba'aḏ* does not have the primary sense of "for," "in exchange for," but means "after, beyond." It is used in its separative sense with verbs meaning "to protect," as in i 10 above; thus it developed the sense "on behalf of" with verbs "to pray," "pay ransom," and the like. The Targum, Rashi, and others understood the expression to mean that one will put forth a less important part of the body to protect a more important part, as one instinctively raises his arm to block a blow to the head. The suggestion (Schultens) that the sense is *cutis super cute* is attractive. Man has dermis under his epidermis, and Job's wounds have been only superficial thus far. Merx (*Das Gedicht von Hiob,* 1871) adduces as a parallel the German proverb: *das Hemd sitzt näher als der Rock,* "the undershirt is closer than the coat." Against this, however, is the fact that Job's person has not yet been touched; there is no skin off him as yet. Accordingly Thomas Aquinas and others understood the saying to mean that Job was willing to pay with the skin of others, his children and his cattle, rather than his own, *carnem alienam pro carne sua.* The interpretation of Tur-Sinai is inviting, and is the one implied by the translation "skin after skin." The wise men reflected on the wonders of the human body. The human heart is well protected, the most inaccessible part of man's body; only God can search the heart and probe man's inward parts, Jer xvii 9–10. Thus man's heart, the seat of his affections and inmost being, is protected by a series of walls, as the inner chamber of a labyrinth, "a chamber within a chamber," I Kings xx 30, xxii 25. Only the outer wall has been touched; cf. i 10. The Satan wants permission to get at Job himself to do more than scratch the surface, to penetrate his outer defenses and put his very being in

jeopardy. The Lord thus gives the Satan leave to get under Job's skin, to do anything to him short of extinguishing his life.

7. *foul pox.* Job's malady has had many diagnoses. The root *šḫn* occurs in Akkadian, Ugaritic, Aramaic, and Arabic and denotes heat, fever inflammation, and the like. In the OT the term *šĕḥîn* is applied to skin diseases. In Deut xxviii 27 the term is modified by the word for "Egypt" and has been taken to mean elephantiasis or leprosy which, according to Pliny (*Nat. hist.* xxv.7 f.) was especially connected with Egypt. In Deut xxviii 35 the disease is said to strike in the knees and legs, and, as in the present passage, to cover from sole to pate. The reference to knees and legs suggests a disease that causes buboes or the swelling of the lymph nodes of the groin. In the Ugaritic text designated BH (for Baal-Hadad [75 II CT]), the god Baal-Hadad falls victim to *šḫn* which burns his loins and leaves him prostrate. The term in the OT always denotes a severe skin inflammation. Leprosy begins with *šĕḥîn,* Lev xiii 18 ff., and *šĕḥîn,* "boil" or "botch," may break out in pustules, Exod ix 9. The malady in question may be an especially severe case of the skin infection common in the Near East and variously known as the "Baghdad Button" or "Jericho Rose," a boil which becomes ulcerous and leaves a deep scar.

A recent diagnosis of Job's illness by J. V. Kinnier-Wilson, "Leprosy in Ancient Mesopotamia," *Revue d'Assyriologie* 60 (1966), 47–58, makes it a combination of scurvy and pellagra. Both these diseases are connected with chronic malnutrition and vitamin deficiency which are rather unlikely for a man of substance like Job.

8. *potsherd.* It is not clear whether the potsherd scraper is used to scratch the itching skin as a counterirritant, or to lacerate the body as a sign of grief. The latter appears more likely; cf. Lev xix 28, xxi 5; Deut xiv 1; Jer xvi 6, xli 5, xlvii 5, xlviii 37. In Akkadian the term "place/mound of potsherds" appears to designate the realm of the dead; cf. K. Tallqvist, *Sumerisch-Akkadische Namen der Totenwelt,* 1934, p. 23.

ashes. LXX has "on the dunghill," *epi tēs koprias,* and adds "outside the city." This is in keeping with the traditional view of Job, smitten with leprosy, sitting on the dunghill beyond the city. The LXX "dunghill" recalls the description of Priam's mourning the death of Hector, *Iliad* xxii.414. The dunghill (Ar. *mazbalah*) of towns in the Near East corresponds roughly to our town dump. St. John Chrysostom declared that pilgrims came from the ends of the earth to Arabia to visit Job's dunghill.

9. *His wife said . . .* The role of the woman as temptress did not escape the notice of the churchmen. Augustine called Job's wife *diaboli adjutrix* and Calvin, *organum Satanae.* Chrysostom asked why the Devil left Job his wife and answered with the suggestion that he considered her a scourge by which to plague him more acutely than by any other

means. The rabbis note, however, that Job did not listen to his wife as did Adam (cf. Midrash Rabba Gen xix 12). Note the parallel with Tobit's wife Hanna, Tobit ii 11–14, which Jerome makes explicit.

Curse. The same euphemism as in i 5. Death is not necessarily the immediate consequence of cursing God. His wife, perhaps, meant to suggest that since he was not long for this world, he might as well give vent to his feelings, or hers, and curse God.

LXX adds:

> After a long time had passed his wife said to him: "How long will you endure and say, 'See, I will wait a bit longer, looking for the hope of my salvation.' Look, your memory is already blotted out from the earth [along with] the sons and daughters, the travail and pangs of my womb, whom I reared in toil for nothing. And you, you sit in wormy decay, passing the nights in the open, while I roam and drudge from place to place, and from house to house, waiting for the sun to go down, so that I may rest from my toils and the griefs which now grip me. Now, say some word against the Lord, and die." He, however, looked up and said to her, . . .

This addition is repeated in part in the apocryphal Testament of Job where the devotion of his wife is such that she makes the supreme sacrifice of selling her hair to buy bread.

10. The Koran xxxviii 43 alludes to Job's rebuke of his wife as follows:

> And [we said to him]: Take a bundle [of rushes?] in your hand, and strike [your wife?] with it; and do not break your oath.

This is explained on the supposition that Job, in a moment of anger, swore to give his wife a hundred stripes if he recovered. Muslim commentators are vague as to what the wife's offense may have been, some even suggesting that she may have stayed too long on an errand. In his note to Sura xxi 83, G. Sale (*The Koran,* 1889, pp. 247 f.) summarizes Muslim tradition about Job and his wife:

> that he was of the race of Esau and was blessed with a numerous family, and abundant riches; but that God proved him, by taking all that he had, even his children, who were killed by the fall of a house; notwithstanding which he continued to serve God, and to return thanks as usual: that he was then struck with a filthy disease, his body being full of worms, and so offensive, that as he lay on the dunghill none could bear to come near him: that his wife, however (whom some call Rahmat the daughter of Ephraim the son of Joseph, and others Makhir the daughter of Manasses), attended him with great patience, supporting him by what she earned by her

labour; but that the devil appeared to her one day, after having reminded her of her past prosperity, promised her that if she would worship him, he would restore all they had lost: whereupon she asked her husband's consent, who was so angry at the proposal, that he swore, if he recovered, to give his wife a hundred stripes: that Job having pronounced the prayer recorded in this passage ["Verily evil hath afflicted me: but thou art the most merciful of those who show mercy"], God sent Gabriel, who taking him by the hand raised him up; and at the same time a fountain sprang up at his feet, of which having drunk, the worms fell off his body, and washing therein he recovered his former health and beauty: that God then restored all to him double; his wife also becoming young and handsome again, and bearing him twenty-six sons: and that Job, to satisfy his oath, was directed by God to strike her one blow with a palm branch having a hundred leaves.

10. *a foolish woman.* The occurrence of the word "folly" (*nĕḇālāh*) here and in Gen xxxiv 7 suggested to Rabbi Abba ben Kahana that Job's wife was Dinah, Midrash Rabba Gen xix 12. Others identify Dinah as Job's second wife. As grandson of Esau and son-in-law of Jacob, Job would be doubly related to Israel; cf. L. Ginzberg, *Legends of the Jews,* II, 1910, pp. 225 f.

Shall we . . . Rabbinic exegesis apparently understood the plural subject of the verb as including Job's wife, hence the implication that she, too, was righteous. Cf. Soncino *Midrash Rabbah,* I, p. 157, n. 6, on Gen xix 12.

with his lips. Apparently a man was not regarded as culpable for his thoughts if they remained unexpressed in word or deed; cf. vi 30, xxvii 4; Ps xxxix 2. Targ. adds "but in his thoughts he already cherished sinful words."

11. *Eliphaz.* Meaning, possibly, "God is fine gold." According to the genealogies, Eliphaz was the first-born of Esau and the father of Teman, Gen xxxvi 11, 15, 42; I Chron i 36, 53.

Temanite. Teman, from a root *ymn* designating the right hand, means "southland" because when one faces the rising sun his right hand is to the south. Pliny (*Nat. hist.* vi.32, 14) connects the Temanites with the Nabateans. Eusebius in his *Onomasticon* (ed. Lagarde, 1887, p. 264) also places Teman in Nabatean territory about fifteen miles (Jerome says five miles) from Petra. The site has not been identified. Teman is always represented as one of the principal localities of Edom; cf. Jer xlix 7; Ezek xxv 13; Amos i 12 f.; Obad vs. 9. Edom, and particularly the Temanites, had a great reputation for wisdom; cf. Jer xlix 7; Baruch iii 22–23.

Bildad. Of uncertain analysis and meaning. Among the most likely suggestions are those of Speiser and Albright. The former explains the name as derived from Akk. *Bil Adad*, a form of *Apil Adad*, "Son of Hadad," the exact equivalent of the Aram. *Ben Hadad* (AfO 6 [1930], 23). Albright suggests derivation from the Amorite type name *Yabil-Dad(a)* (JBL 54 [1935], 174, n. 3). Others compare the names Eldad, Bedad, Medad and Akk. *Dadi-ilu* and see in the element *Bil* the name of Baal. Dhorme's explanation of the name as a *qitlal* form of the word *balad* "country," hence "countryman," or the like, appears most unlikely.

Shuhite. Shuah is mentioned as the son of Abraham and Qeturah, the brother of Midian and the uncle of Sheba and Dedan, Gen xxv 2; I Chron i 32. Cuneiform sources mention a country Suḫu, located on the Middle Euphrates below the mouth of the Ḫabur, the principal city in this area being ʻAnat, the present day ʻAnah. The OT connection with Dedan and Sheba, however, suggests a more southerly locale in Edom or Arabia.

Zophar. The name has the pattern *qawtal*, like Ar. *jawzal*, Heb. *gôzāl*, "young dove." As *ṣippôr* means "bird," so, possibly, *ṣôp̄ar* means "young bird." The name occurs only in Job, although LXX has it instead of Zepho/i in Gen xxxvi 11, 15; I Chron i 36.

Naamathite. Not, of course, the town Naʻamah in the foothills of Judah, Josh xv 41. The most likely suggestion is that of Jaussen and de Savignac (*Mission Archéologique en Arabie*, I, 1914, p. 64) who identify it with Jebel el Naʻāmeh, roughly forty miles east of Tebūk. For other suggestions, cf. F. M. Abel, *Géographie de la Palestine*, I, 1933, p. 287, n. 4.

LXX makes Job's friends kings and transposes the consonants of Naʻamah so that Zophar becomes king of the Mineans.

arranged to meet. Cf. Josh xi 5; Amos iii 3; Ps xlviii 5; Neh vi 2. According to Jewish legend the three friends entered Job's house simultaneously, though they lived three hundred miles apart. Each had a crown, or, according to another version, a tree on which were carved images of the others; and as soon as one suffered misfortune his image was altered. Thus the friends learned of Job's calamity; cf. TB, Baba Bathra 16a.

condole. The verb (*nûḏ*) means "to shake the head," as an expression of commiseration; cf. Isa li 19; Jer xv 5, xvi 5, xviii 16, xxii 10, xxxi 17, xlviii 17; Nah iii 7; Ps lxix 21. In Job xlii 11 the verb is used synonymously with *naḥ(ḥ)ēm*, "to comfort."

12. The sickness and suffering had disfigured Job beyond recognition, like the suffering servant of the Lord, Isa liii 3.

robe. Like Job, each of the sheikhs wore a robe as a badge of nobility; cf. i 20.

and sprinkled dust on his head. As a sign of extreme grief one tore his garments and sprinkled dust on his head, Josh vii 6; I Sam iv 12; II Sam xiii 19; Ezek xxvii 30; Lam ii 10; cf. i 20.

heavenward. Missing in LXX. Flinging dust in the air is a gesture of anger and disdain; cf. II Sam xvi 13; Acts xxii 23. Perhaps the reading "heavenward" may result from a misreading of *hašmēm,* "appalled," as *haššāmaymāh,* "heavenward."

13. *on the ground.* Omitted in LXX.

An impressive demonstration of sympathy and grief. Seven days and nights are devoted to mourning for the dead, Gen. l 10; I Sam xxxi 13; Ecclesiasticus xxii 12. Comforters are not permitted to say a word until the mourner opens the conversation; cf. TB, Moed Qatan 28b.

3. JOB'S PROTEST
(iii 1–11; 16; 12–15; 17–26)

III 1 After this Job opened his mouth and cursed his day.
2 Job spoke out and said:

3 "Damn the day I was born,
The night that said, 'A boy is begot.'
4 That day—let it be darkness.
God above ignore it,
No light break upon it,
5 Darkness and gloom claim it,
Cloud settle over it,
Eclipse terrify it.
6 That night—gloom seize it.
Include it not in the days of the year,
In the roll of the months let it not enter.
7 Yea, that night be sterile,
Let no joyful sound come in.
8 Let the Sea-cursers damn it,
Those skilled to stir Leviathan.
9 Its twilight stars be darkened,
Let it seek light in vain,
Nor see the eyes of dawn,
10 Since it closed not the womb's doors,
To hide trouble from my eyes.
11 Why did I not die at birth,
Emerge from the womb and expire?
16 Like a stillbirth would I were hidden,
Like babes that never saw light.
12 Why did knees receive me,
Or breasts give me suck?

13 For now would I be lying quiet;
I would be asleep and at rest,
14 With kings and counselors of the earth
Who built themselves ruins,
15 Or with princes who had gold,
Who filled their houses with silver.
17 There where knaves cease strife,
Where the weary are at rest,
18 Where prisoners take ease together,
Heedless of the slave driver's shout.
19 Small and great alike are there,
And slave is free from master.
20 Why gives he light to the wretched,
Life to the bitter of soul,
21 Who yearn in vain for death,
Seek it like a treasure-trove,
22 Glad to get to the grave,
Happy to find the tomb?
23 To a man whose way is hidden,
Whom God has fenced about?
24 Instead of my food come sighs,
Groans are poured me as water.
25 What I most feared has befallen me,
What I dreaded has o'ertaken me.
26 I have no rest, no quiet,
No repose, but continual agony."

Notes

iii 1. *After this.* After the seven days' silence. The style is classical; cf. Gen xv 14, xxiii 19, xxv 26. Similarly in the Ugaritic texts *aḫr* introduces the transition to a new episode.

opened his mouth. A literary device to draw attention to what follows, as in the introduction to the Sermon on the Mount, Matt v 2.

and cursed his day. "Day" has been taken here in the sense of "fate," but it is abundantly clear from vss. 3 ff. that Job curses the day of his birth, just as the prophet Jeremiah cursed the day of his birth, Jer xx 14–18. Jeremiah, mindful that it is futile to curse a day that is past, turns his imprecations on the man who brought the news of his birth to his father:

> Cursed be the day I was born,
> The day my mother bore me.
> (Let it not be blessed.)
> Cursed be the man who brought the news
> To my father, saying,
> "A son, a male, is born to you,"
> Making him very glad.
> Let that man be like the cities
> Yahweh destroyed unrelenting.
> Let him hear a cry in the morning,
> An alarm at noontime,
> Because he slew me not in the womb;
> That my mother might be my tomb,
> Her womb ever pregnant.
> Why did I emerge from the womb,
> To see trouble and toil,
> And spend my days in shame?

If vs. 1 had no connection with vss. 3 ff., it would be quite in order to take "day" in the sense of "fate," as in xxx 25. But vs. 1 is certainly the introduction to Job's soliloquy that follows. There is no incongruity, here, since it is Job's latter-day plight that leads him to rue the day he was born.

3. The curse is not simply against his birthday as such, but against a life now so embittered that he wishes it had never begun. The day of birth and the night of conception are distinct events, yet treated, for purposes of poetic parallelism, as one and the same. The fact that they are mentioned in reverse of the normal order is enough to show that one ought not to press the details too hard. The versions, except the Targ., interpret "the night in which one said." In poetic language, of course, day and night may speak, as in Ps xix 3–5. LXX reads "behold a man" (*hĕrê ḡaḇer*) for MT *hōrāh ḡaḇer,* "a man has been conceived," thus making the day or the night the time of birth without reference to conception. The night may be a witness to all that occurs in it, and, conceivably, may know the sex of the child conceived in it. Since the day and the night are again separately cursed in vss. 4–5, 6–10, it appears that the MT reference to conception is to be retained; cf. vs. 10. The report of a birth to the father is always a momentous occasion. In the Ugaritic myth "The Birth of the Beautiful and Gracious Gods" we have a striking poetic description of conception, birth, and the report to the father of the gods (52:49–53):

He bends, their lips he kisses.
Lo, their lips are sweet,
Sweet as grapes.
As he kisses, they conceive,
As he embraces, they become pregnant.
They go into labor and bear
Dawn and Dusk.
Word to El they bring,
"Thy wives, O El, have given birth!"
"What have they borne?"
"Two boys, Dawn and Dusk."

4–6. The translation suffers from the scarcity of different words for darkness in English. The Semitic languages have a wealth of words for darkness, since besides its literal sense it symbolized everything that was evil, as well as fearsome and mysterious; cf. xii 25; Exod xx 21(18); II Sam xxii 29; Isa v 20, lx 2; Ps lxxxii 5; Prov iv 19; Matt vi 23.

5c. *Eclipse.* As vocalized, the MT *kimrîrê yôm* would mean "like bitternesses of the day." The term *mĕrîrî* occurs in Deut xxxii 24 as applied to pestilence and Rashi and Ibn Ezra, taking the cue from Ps xci 6, understood *kimrîrê yôm* to mean "like demons which rule at noon." The expression *mry/wry ym* is found both in the Cairo Geniza text of Ecclesiasticus xi 4 (*'l tqls bmryry ywm,* "do not jeer at the embittered of day") and in a Thanksgiving Hymn (v 34) from Qumran (*wnpšy bmrwry ywm,* "and my soul by the bitterness of day"). In Amos viii 10 the term *yôm mar,* "bitter day," is associated with eclipse of the sun:

I will make the sun set at noon,
Darken the earth in broad daylight,
Turn your festivals to mourning,
All your ditties to dirges.
I will put sackcloth on all loins,
On every head baldness.
I will make it like mourning for an only son,
Its end like a bitter day.

In spite of the evidence that eclipse of the sun was associated with bitterness, it seems best in the present passage to take the initial letter of *kmryry* as radical, rather than as the comparative particle "like," and to connect the word with the Syriac cognate meaning "black, gloomy." This sense is confirmed by the variant of the expression in xv 23–24 where the parallelism and stichometry have been misunderstood. In the light of *yĕba'ăṯûhû kimrîrê yôm* we have to read in xv 23–24 *yôm ḥōsek̲ yĕba'ăṯēhû* (for MT *yĕb̲'ăṯûhû*), but it is clear that *kimrîrê yôm* and *yôm ḥōšek̲* are synonymous.

6b. *Include it not.* MT *'al yiḥad,* "rejoice not," but Gen xlix 6 suggests the reading *yēḥaḏ,* from the root *yḥd,* "be one," rather than *ḥdw,* "be joyful."

7. *sterile.* The word (*galmûḏ*) is explained from its Arabic cognate which is used of rock as infertile and unproductive; cf. xv 34 and xxx 3. It is found elsewhere in the OT only in Isa xlix 21 where it is used synonymously with childlessness instead of the usual word for barrenness (*'ăqārāh*).

8a. *Sea.* With Gunkel reading *yām* for MT *yôm,* "day"; cf. vii 12, ix 13, xxvi 12, 13. The MT reading has vexed commentators. Some understand the "day-cursers" to be magicians who can make a day good or bad by incantations. Others take it to refer to eclipse, the dragon (Leviathan) supposedly devouring the sun and moon, as many primitive peoples explain an eclipse. Dhorme understands this line to refer to Job's fellow sufferers who, like him, curse the day of their birth, but the next line he recognizes as a mythological allusion. The effort to interpret the line as reference to the wicked who prefer night to day (cf. xxiv 13–17, xxxviii 15) is quite mistaken. Both this line and the following are patent mythological allusions, as Gunkel demonstrated (*Schöpfung und Chaos,* 1895, pp. 59–61). The Ugaritic myths have confirmed the correctness of the main features of Gunkel's interpretation. The cursing of an enemy and use of magic and spells as an indispensable part of warfare is well nigh universal. In Baal's battle with Prince Sea in the Ugaritic myth, there is no reference to cursing, but the weapons by which Sea had been defeated were rendered effective by incantations tantamount to curses pronounced by the god Koshar who specialized in magic as well as metallurgy. Job here invokes the help of the master curser among the gods so that his conception and birth may be thoroughly cursed, even though retroactively. The importance of calling on an expert to provide curses or blessings is illustrated by the Balaam story, Numbers xxii–xxiv; cf. xli 4.

8b. *Leviathan.* Cf. NOTES on xli 1(xl 25H) and xli 12(4H).

9. *twilight.* The word (*nešep̄*) denotes either morning twilight, as here and in vii 4; Ps cxix 147, or evening twilight, as in xxiv 15; Prov vii 9. The reference here is to the morning stars Venus and Mercury which should have remained dark so that the day of Job's birth might never have dawned.

9c. *eyes.* The word *'ap̄'appayim* which occurs also in xvi 16, xli 18(10) has been generally supposed to designate the eyelids and the expression "the eyelids of dawn" has been assumed to be synonymous with the "wings of dawn", *kanp̄ê šaḥar,* Ps cxxxix 9. The eyelids or wings of dawn have thus been compared with the Homeric figure "rosy fingered Dawn" (*Iliad* vi.175; *Odyssey* ii.1). Ugar. *'p'p(m),* however, apparently refers to eyeballs rather than eyelids, as seen in Krt 147, 295 where the damsel's *'p'p* are described as bowls of some sort of semiprecious stone, *'p'ph sp ṯrml,* "her eyes are *ṯrml* bowls." The word also stands in apparent synonymous parallelism with the usual word for eyes in Prov iv 25, vi 4, xxx 13; Pss xi 4, cxxxii 4, and Jer ix 17. Dahood (*Psalms III,* fourth NOTE on Ps cxxxii 4) cites the Qumran text 4Q184:13 *w'p'ph bpḥz trym lr'wt,* "And she wantonly raises her *'p'p* to see" and observes that one does not see with the eyelids. Although the matter is not absolutely certain, it appears that *'p'p* designates eyes rather than eyelids.

10a. *the womb's doors.* Literally "doors of my womb/belly." Certainly not Job's, but his mother's womb. This line tends to support the MT reference to the night of conception in vs. 3b above, as against the interpretation of LXX; cf. I Sam i 5; Gen xxix 31, xxx 22; Isa xxxvii 3, lxvi 9a.

11. Cf. x 18–19.

16. This verse fits better between vss. 11 and 12 than in its present position. Cf. Ps lviii 9(8); Eccles vi 3. An aborted foetus would be carefully buried as everything connected with childbirth was beset with fear of evil spirits. LXX renders 16a somewhat freely, "Or like an abortion coming out from a mother's womb."

would I were. MT has the negative *lô'* which we take as the precative *lû'* in keeping with the context. If the negative is retained, it is necessary to turn the line into a question, "Could I not be/have been?"

12. *knees.* It is not clear whether the knees are those of the father or the mother. It may be that, as among the Romans where the father had the right to accept or reject the newborn child, the knees of the father or grandfather received the child as a token of legitimation. Joseph's grandchildren, it is said, were born upon his knees, Gen l 23.

In the Hebrew of Ecclesiasticus xv 2a, although the word "knees" is not expressed, the same verb (*qdm*) as here is used of the mother's reception of the child. Bedouin women receive their newborn on the knees (cf. B. Stade, ZAW 16 [1886], 153). The child, of course, sits on the mother's lap or knees to nurse, even as a royal child was said to nurse a double-breasted goddess: "You were weak, Ashurbanipal. You were seated on the knees of the goddess of Nineveh; of four nipples which were placed near your mouth, you sucked two and hid your face in the other two" (cf. M. Streck, *Assurbanipal und die letzten assyrischen Könige bis zum Untergang Niniveh's,* 1916, p. 348).

14b. *ruins.* The word *ḥŏrāḇôṯ* has been much emended, e.g., to "squares" (*rĕḥōḇôṯ*), "fortresses" (*'armānôṯ*), "palaces" (*hêḵālôṯ*), "eternal tombs" (*qiḇrôṯ 'ôlām*), "mausolea" (*ḥărāmôṯ*). Since the book is supposed to have Egyptian connections, some critics relate the word to Ar. *hirām* or *'ahrām,* "pyramid," but the origin and etymology of this word are uncertain and the laryngeal does not suit either the word in the present text nor that of the Coptic word *XPAM*. It seems best to retain the MT in the sense of ruins, desolation. The objection that kings do not usually achieve fame by rebuilding ruined sites (ICC) overlooks the fact that the Mesopotamian kings frequently boasted of their accomplishments in restoring and rebuilding ancient ruins. The building or rebuilding of ruins is mentioned by the Second (or Third?) Isaiah, Isa lviii 12, lxi 4.

15. Commentators generally regard this as alluding to the treasure-filled tombs of the wealthy. It seems more likely that the reference is to the former earthly prosperity of the now defunct potentates; cf. xxii 18a, which varies only slightly from iii 15b and clearly refers to earthly riches. Emphasis on magnificent tombs richly furnished would make little sense in this context where the point is that rich and poor, prince and slave, are now equal.

17. *There.* Again, possibly a euphemism for the netherworld; cf. i 21. *strife.* More exactly, "agitation."

19a. *alike.* The pronoun *hû'*, "he," is used in this sense in Isa xli 4, xliii 10, 13, xlvi 4, xlviii 12; Ps cii 28.

20a. *gives.* So MT. All the versions, however, construe the verb as passive. The omission of the subject may be due partly to reverence and partly to reluctance to make charges against God. But note the expressed subject in 23b. Under the goading of his "comforters," Job later makes his charges direct and specific.

20b. *bitter of soul.* Cf. Judg xviii 25; I Sam i 10, xxii 2, xxx 6; II Sam xvii 8. Sophocles makes Philoctetes cry:

> Death, death, how is it that I can call on you, always, day in, day out, and you cannot come to me?

(*Complete Greek Tragedies,* II, p. 432, lines 797–98.)

21. W. M. Thomson (*The Land and the Book,* new ed., 1913, p. 112) considers this the most vivid comparison within the whole compass of human actions. Thomson had heard of treasure hunters who got so excited that they fainted when they found a single coin and dug frantically all night till exhausted. The copper scroll from Qumran listing fabulous buried treasure reflects the long-time interest in buried treasure. Archaeologists know the fever that seizes their workers when there is rumor of treasure.

22a. MT has "who rejoice unto exultation." This bizarre expression "unto exultation" occurs in Hos ix 1, but there the text is certainly corrupt and RSV corrects it on the basis of LXX. With Graetz, Beer, and Duhm, on the basis of the Syriac and one Hebrew manuscript, we read *gal* for *gîl.* The sense "burial heap" is not attested for *gal* alone, and *gal 'ăḇānîm,* "heap of stones," Josh vii 26, viii 29; II Sam xviii 17, does not refer to ordinary graves. Guillaume ("The Arabic Background of the Book of Job," in *Promise and Fulfilment,* p. 110) has found the desiderated parallel to *qeḇer* in Ar. *jāl,* "the inner side of a grave."

23a. The path of the fortunate man is illumined, xxii 28, and level and smooth, Isa xxvi 7; Prov xv 19, but that of the unfortunate, and thus presumably wicked, is the opposite; cf. xvii 9.

23b. Cf. xix 8–10.

24. Cf. Pss xlii 4(3), lxxx 6(5). A similar figure is found in Ugaritic. The sun goddess while assisting 'Anat in the recovery and burial of Baal's corpse is sated with weeping and "She drank tears like wine" (62:10).

24a. *Instead.* The expression "to the face of," *lip̄nê,* is difficult here, but usually understood as meaning "instead of." The meaning "like, as, for, instead" is seen in iv 19c, where the context dictates the rendering "quick as," and most clearly in I Sam i 16 where Hannah says "Do not take your maidservant for a bad woman."

24b. *Groans.* Literally "my groans."

26. *continual agony.* Literally "agitation comes" (and keeps on coming).

4. ELIPHAZ REMONSTRATES
(iv 1–21)

IV 1 Eliphaz the Temanite then spoke:

2 "Should one dare a word, could you bear it?
But who could be silent now?
3 Look, you have instructed many,
Feeble hands you strengthened,
4 Your words encouraged the faint,
Braced tottering knees.
5 But it befalls you and you falter;
It strikes you, and you are aghast.
6 Is not your piety your assurance,
Your hope your perfect conduct?
7 Consider, what innocent ever perished,
Or where have the righteous been destroyed?
8 I have observed that they who plow evil
And sow trouble reap the same.
9 At a breath of God they perish,
A blast of His anger, and they vanish.
10 The lion may roar, the old lion growl,
But the young lion's teeth are broken.
11 The lion perishes, robbed of prey,
The lioness' whelps are scattered.
12 Now a word came to me quietly,
Just a whisper caught my ear.
13 In a nightmare, in a trance,
When slumber falls upon men,
14 Terror seized me, and trembling,
All my members shuddered.

15 A breath passed over my face,
The hair of my body bristled.
16 It paused, but I could not discern it,
Just a form before my eyes.
A hush, then a voice I heard:
17 'Can mortal be just before God?
A man pure to his Maker?
18 Even his servants he distrusts,
Charges his angels with error.
19 What then of those who dwell in clay houses,
Whose foundations are in the dust,
Who are crushed quick as a moth,
20 'Twixt morning and evening shattered?
They perish forever nameless,
21 Their tent cord pulled up,
They die and not with wisdom.'

Notes

iv 1. Eliphaz takes the initiative, probably because of seniority.

2a. He starts with a note of apology for presuming to lecture his friend in such a state of misery. But since Job has broken the silence, he now feels free to speak; cf. ii 13.

could you bear it? Literally "would you be weary?" Eliphaz wants to know whether Job is physically and emotionally able to listen. In Sophocles' *The Women of Trachis,* Hyllus says to Heracles:

> Ah! It is wrong to argue with a sick man, yet how can one stand to see him with such thoughts as these?

(*Complete Greek Tragedies,* II, p. 323, lines 1230 f.)

2b. *silent.* Literally "hold back with words." Eliphaz is somewhat like Elihu in xxxii 18–20, but much more restrained.

3a. *instructed.* The word (*ysr*) carries connotations of chastisement, correction, discipline, admonition; cf. xxvi 2–4.

many. Or possibly "the aged" as suggested by M. Dahood, *Biblica* 48 (1967), 425; cf. xxxii 9a where the term (*rabbîm*) is rendered "seniors."

3b, 4b. Cf. xxix 15; Isa xxxv 3; Heb xii 12.

5. Kissane quotes Terence (*The Lady of Andros,* Act II, line 9),

Facile omnes, quum valemus, recta consilia aegrotis damus; tu, si hi hic sis, aliter sentias (It is quite easy, when we're well, to give sound advice to a sick man; but, if you are thus, you feel differently).

6. Eliphaz appears to concede that Job's piety and conduct have been exemplary. Job, thus, should have confidence and hope that God will deal with him accordingly. Eliphaz is about to get himself involved in a contradiction, so he quickly withdraws from consideration of Job's particular case and turns to generalizations. It is not quite true, as Kissane asserts, that Bildad (viii 5) and Zophar (xi 4–5) admit that Job is not to be classed with the wicked. To concede that Job was innocent would wreck their argument completely. What Bildad says is conditional: if Job were innocent, God would restore him. Zophar is sure that God must have something against Job and could make it known if he cared to speak about it.

6a. *piety*. Literally "fear," i.e., fear of God; cf. i 8.

6b. On the construction with "pleonastic *w*-" cf. M. Pope, JAOS 73 (1953), 97, and Blommerde, pp. 29, 40.

7. The general truth of this doctrine is turned to vicious falsehood by the insistence, as in Ps xxxvii 25, that there are no exceptions; cf. Prov xii 21; Ecclesiasticus ii 10. The suggestion (Kissane) that since Job's life has been spared, he does not belong in the category of the wicked, is casuistry surpassing that of the friends. Job considered death preferable to his present state. We must, however, appreciate the dilemma of Job's comforters. They were genuinely concerned for his welfare and wished to see him restored to health and prosperity. Since he is still alive, there is hope. And that hope is to confess his guilt and repent and seek God's mercy. The approach of modern practitioners of mental and spiritual healing is not so radically different. The practical value of self-purgation by confession has been clinically proved, but the solution of the problem of theodicy is not thereby furthered. The very ancient answer that no man is clean in God's sight does not eliminate the question of degree of guilt or explain why some are singled out for severe punishment while others escape.

8. Cf. Hos viii 7, x 13; Prov xxii 8; Gal vi 7–9.

9. Cf. Hos xiii 15; Isa xl 7.

10–11. The figure of the lion and lioness is common in the Wisdom Literature; cf. Pss xvii 12, xxii 14, 21(22), xxxiv 10(11); Prov xxviii 15.

12 ff. Cf. xxxiii 15. The description is of the terrifying effect of a dream or nightmare.

This passage is one of the most uncanny in the OT. The poet toys in poetic fancy with the dread effect of contact with the divine; cf. E. Robertson, BJRL 42, 2 (March 1960), 417. Elihu regards dreams as warnings; cf. xxxiii 15.

13a. *nightmare*. The word (*śĕʿippîm*) occurs in the Bible only here and in xx 2, although a derived form with epenthetic *r* (*śarʿappîm*) occurs in Pss xciv 19, cxxxix 23. The Arabic cognate has the sense "be disquieted."

15a. *breath.* Or "wind," or "spirit." The movement of the air is often taken as a token of supernatural presence; cf. II Sam v 24.

15b. *hair.* Others take the word *ś'rt* to mean "storm" rather than "hair." Gordis, e.g., rendered "a storm made my skin bristle." Cf. Blommerde, pp. 40 f.

16b. "form." Heb. *těmûnāh.* The word *rûaḥ,* "spirit," is never used of an apparition in the OT, but here the spirit is given a semblance of form.

16c. *hush.* Cf. I Kings xix 12 f. where the word (*děmāmāh*) applied adjectivally to "voice, sound" (*qôl*) is traditionally rendered "still small voice." The basic meaning of the word is "stillness, silence." In Ps cvii 29 it is used of the calm after the storm. In the present passage the word may be construed as a *casus pendens* with adverbial sense, "in a hush."

17. Cf. xiv 4, xv 14, xxv 4–6; Ps cxliii 2.

before God . . . to his Maker. KJ renders "more just than God," "more pure than his Maker," which is the meaning ordinarily conveyed by this construction, the normal device for expressing the comparative sense. It is obvious, however, that this is not the sense intended. The preposition "from" is used in this same way—in the sense of "before"—in Num xxxii 22 and Jer li 5b.

18. *servants.* The lesser gods who with the development of monotheism became angels. II Pet ii 4 alludes to the myth of the punishment of the rebellious angels. In the Ugaritic myths, the major deities have special divine lackies who serve mostly as messengers and who are regularly referred to as "boys" (*ġlmm*), the same word as Heb. *'elem,* "boy," (the feminine form *'almāh,* "girl," erroneously rendered "virgin" in Isa vii 14). The Ugaritic pantheon also featured divine slave girls, designated by a term frequently used in the OT for human slave girls, and concubines; cf. Gen xxi 12. These divine slave girls were sometimes guilty of gross misbehavior. At one of the divine banquets they did something—just what we are not told—which so disgusted Baal that he rose and spat in the midst of the assembled gods; cf. xxxi 11a.

18b. *error.* This word (*tohŏlāh*) is unique in the OT. It may be related to Ethiopic *tahala,* "wander." Many critics emend to *tip̄lāh,* "folly"; cf. i 22.

19. *clay . . . dust.* Cf. x 9, xxxiii 6; Gen ii 7, iii 19; I Cor xv 47.

houses. As a figure for the body; cf. Wisdom of Solomon ix 15, "earthen tent" (*geōdes skēnos*); II Cor v 1; II Pet i 14.

foundations. Cf. xxii 16; Prov x 25; Matt vii 24–27.

If even the angels who surround God are deemed impure, how much more man whose body is clay. This same argument is repeated in xv 15–16. Because of man's impurity, Paul (I Cor xv 42–54) insisted there must be in the resurrection a change from the earthy and corruptible mortal body to a pure and incorruptible spiritual body.

19c. *quick as.* Literally "before" (*lip̄nê*); cf. iii 24a.

moth. The word *'āš* has been regarded as suspect here. Delitzsch connected it with Akk. *ašāšu,* "nest of reeds," and Herz proposed emendation to *'ôśām,* "their Maker." Dhorme noted that the understanding of the meaning of *lip̄nê* here frees us from the necessity of resorting to the subtleties of modern commentators who insist that a moth is a creature which devours and accordingly translated "as by a moth." Dhorme's dictum is cogent: "When the text presents itself to us with normal and simple meaning, it is unnecessary to complicate it." The moth is one of the easiest of insects to catch and crush. Elsewhere in the Bible, the moth or its larvae is proverbial for its own destructive power; cf. xiii 28; Isa li 8; Matt vi 19, 20; James v 2. A different meaning of *'āš* is found in xxvii 18a.

20b. *nameless.* Reading *mibbĕlî-m šēm* for the enigmatic *mibbĕlî mēśîm* of MT, following a suggestion of M. Dahood (NWSPJ, p. 55). The reading *šēm* for *mēśîm* was suggested long ago by N. Herz (ZAW 20 [1900], 160), but has not been regarded with favor because it left the superfluous *m* unexplained. The Ugaritic evidence neatly removes this objection: the extra *m* may be added to the preceding word as the enclitic emphatic particle. Cf. xxx 8 where the expression occurs without preposition or enclitic *-m.*

21. *tent cord.* Targ., Vulg., and Syr. take the word *yeṯer* in the sense of "excellence," which makes no sense in this context. LXX has "He blows upon them and they are withered" which is reminiscent of Isa xl 24, but bears no relation to MT. The objections of commentators to the meaning "tent cord" and the consequent interpretation are groundless. The meaning "cord" is certain because of its use in the sense of bowstring, as in Ps xi 2. In xxx 11 we have what appears to be a variant form of the same idiom. Though it is possible that the "cord" there is a bowstring, it appears more likely that a tent cord is to be understood. Isa xxxiii 20 and xxxviii 12 offer excellent parallels to the present passage:

You will see Jerusalem,
A quiet home, an immovable tent,
Whose pegs will never be plucked up,
Nor its ropes be broken.

My abode is plucked up,
Removed like a shepherd's tent;
My life wound up like a web,
Cut off from the thrum,
Finished in a single day.

The verb (*ns'*) used in all three passages is a technical term for pulling up stakes and ropes and moving on. Cf. vi 9 and vii 6 where the figure is of the weaver's thread, as in the latter half of Isa xxxviii 12.

21b. Since the immediate context deals with the contrast between men and angels, vis-à-vis God, and not merely with the fate of the wicked, Eliphaz's words carry a note of bitterness and frustration. Man as a finite and ephemeral creature of clay, subject to sudden catastrophe, scarcely lives long enough to acquire wisdom. The mood is reminiscent of Ps xc.

5. ELIPHAZ'S DISCOURSE (*continued*)
(v 1–27)

V 1 "Call now, will any answer you?
To which of the holy ones will you turn?
2 Impatience kills the fool,
Passion slays the simpleton.
3 I have seen the fool strike root,
Then his abode suddenly accursed,
4 His children abandoned helpless,
Crushed in the gate, defenseless.
5 His harvest the hungry consume,
Snatching it among the thorns,
While the thirsty pant for their wealth.
6 Verily, sorrow springs from the soil,
From the ground trouble sprouts;
7 Man, indeed, is born for trouble,
And Resheph's sons wing high.
8 Still would I resort to God,
To God I would commit my cause;
9 Doer of great deeds inscrutable,
Marvels beyond number,
10 Who gives rain to the earth,
Sends water on the face of the field,
11 Who exalts the lowly on high,
Lifts the forlorn to safety.
12 He thwarts the plots of the crafty,
So their hands attain no gain,
13 Catches the clever in their contrivances,
And their wily schemes collapse.
14 By day they meet with darkness,
Groping at noon as 'twere night.

15 Thus he saves the simple from the sword,
The poor from the clutch of the strong,
16 So that the humble have hope,
And evil's mouth is stopped.
17 Fortunate the man whom God corrects.
Spurn not Shaddai's discipline.
18 He makes a bruise, but he dresses it;
He wounds but his hand also heals.
19 In six disasters he will save you,
In seven no harm will befall you.
20 In famine he will save you from death,
In war from the stroke of the sword.
21 From scourge of tongue you'll be hidden,
Nor fear a demon when he comes.
22 You may laugh at plunder and famine;
Wild beasts you need not fear.
23 You will have a pact with the field-sprites,
Savage beasts will make peace with you.
24 You will know that your tent is secure,
Inspect your fold and miss nothing.
25 You will know a numerous progeny,
Offspring like the grass of the ground.
26 You will come in full vigor to the grave,
Like a sheaf of corn in its season.
27 This we have probed: 'tis true.
Now hear it and know it yourself."

NOTES

v 1b. *holy ones*. Cf. xv 15. These "holy ones" (*qĕḏôšîm*) are the same divine beings as the "servants" and "angels" of iv 18. They are mentioned also in Hos xi 12(xii 1); Zech xiv 5; Dan iv 10, 14, 20, viii 13; Ps lxxxix 7(8). Eliphaz appears to be taunting Job with the suggestion that it is hopeless to appeal to any of these lesser divine beings in the hope of finding an intercessor with God. This then would be a sort of polemic against the Mesopotamian idea of a personal god on whom a man could rely to make his appeal heard in the assembly of the great gods; cf. ix 33, xvi 19, 21, xxxiii 23–24.

2. This verse has all the earmarks of a proverbial saying; cf. Prov xiv 30. In the present context, it may be intended to advise Job not to let himself get too excited about life's mishaps, since only fools vex themselves unduly about matters that cannot be helped.

3–5. Here Eliphaz gets to the point which he and the friends will reassert repeatedly throughout the Dialogue—that the seeming prosperity of the fool and the wicked (to the wise men they are synonymous) is only illusory and momentary.

3a. *root.* The figure of the tree and roots is common in Job, viz., viii 16, xiv 7–9, xv 32, xviii 16, xix 10, xxiv 20, as in the OT generally; cf. Pss i 3, lii 8(10), xcii 12(13); Prov xii 3, 12; Isa v 24; Hos ix 16; II Kings xix 30.

3b. *accursed.* MT has "I cursed." With LXX, it seems best to construe the verb as passive, reading *wayyûqab̲* for *wā'eqqōb̲*.

4b. *gate.* The city gate was the administrative center where justice was dispensed and other legal matters and general business carried on, Gen xxiii 10, 18; Deut xxi 18–21, xxii 13–21; Ruth iv 1–11; I Kings xxii 10; II Kings vii 1; Amos v 15. A helpless person without family or patron to take his part was not likely to receive much consideration in the gate; cf. xxxi 2.

5b, c. As they stand, these two lines are impossible and the various emendations not much better. The translation above is, perforce, somewhat free. Literally rendered, 5b says "And unto from thorns he takes it," while 5c reads "And he pants [snares] thirsty ones their wealth." The general sense is clear, that the wealth of the wicked becomes prey to others, especially the desperate destitute ones, perhaps the Bedouin who lurk on the edge of the cultivated land and seize whatever they can.

6. If the particle *l'* is taken as the negative (*lô*), the sense, which is given clearly in 7a, calls for a rhetorical question, as rendered in previous editions of this work. On reconsideration, it seems preferable to take the particle as asseverative (*lû'*). Man is born to hardship, and a hostile ground is his heritage; cf. Gen iii 17–19.

7b. *Resheph.* This Northwest Semitic god has long been known from inscriptions of North Syria and Cyprus. Bilingual texts from Cyprus identify him with Apollo. A recently discovered Ugaritic list of gods known as the "Ugaritic Pantheon" equates Resheph with the Mesopotamian Nergal, the god of pestilence and the netherworld. This equation accords with the OT use of the word in the sense of pestilence, Deut xxxii 24; Hab iii 5. The plural of the word is used of flames, of lightning, Ps lxxviii 48, and of love, Sing of Songs viii 6. In Ps lxxvi 4 *rišpê qešet*, "flames of the bow," is used of arrows. In a Ugaritic text (1001:3) Resheph is called "Lord of the arrow" (*b'l ḥẓ ršp*). This may be enough to indicate that it is problematic whether "Resheph's sons" in the present passage is a poetic image for flames or sparks, or a more direct allusion to the god of pestilence. The translation, however, is not entirely non-committal on this point, since the word is rendered as the proper name of the god. Just as Death had a first-born, xviii 13, so the various forms of pestilence may have been thought of as Resheph's children. Still it is possible to interpret the expression, literally rendered above, as referring to flames. Either sense is appropriate to the context. "Man is born for trouble, as surely as sparks fly up," and Resheph's children fly up from the netherworld to plague mankind. It is interesting to note that Resheph is a god of fertility and well-being, as well as of pestilence. An Egyptian prayer of the thirteenth century B.C. beseeches Resheph to grant life, prosperity, and health, while in inscriptions from Zenjirli and Karatepe, Resheph is one of the patron deities of the king. The ambivalent nature of the god is understandable from the principle of polarity which associates opposites. Moreover, it would be expedient to pray to the god of pestilence for protection from the same; cf. M. Dahood, "Le antiche divinitá semitiche," in *Studi Semitici,* I, ed. S. Moscati, 1958, pp. 83–87.

8 ff. Eliphaz, having admitted that trouble and suffering are inescapable, still advises Job to resort to God who can deliver him.

8. *God . . . God.* The two words are different in the Hebrew (*'ēl* and *'ĕlôhîm*). What one would expect here in the place of *'ĕlôhîm* is the name Shaddai which is regularly used in parallelism with *'ēl* and *'ĕlôah;* cf. v 17, vi 4, viii 3, xiii 3, xxii 2, 3, xxvii 10, xxxi 2. The word *'ĕlôhîm* is rare in the Dialogue, occurring only in v 8, xxviii 23, and once in the Elihu speeches, xxxiv 9.

9. Repeated almost verbatim by Job, ix 10; cf. Pss cxxxvi 4, cxlv 3; Ecclesiasticus xliii 32.

10. Cf. xxxvi 27 ff., xxxviii 25 ff.; Pss civ 11, cxlvii 8; Ecclesiasticus xliii 22.

11. Cf. xxxvi 7b; I Sam ii 8; Ps cxiii 7.

12. Cf. Isa xxxii 7; Mic iii 1–3, vii 3.

12b. *gain.* The etymology of this word (*tûšiyyāh*) is obscure. It is used only in poetic and didactic passages in the sense of "sound wisdom" and "effective action," Isa xxviii 29; Prov ii 7, iii 21, viii 14, xviii 1; Mic vi 9. The word is used also in Job vi 13, xi 6, xii 16, xxvi 3, and xxx 22b, but in the latter passage it is apparently a mistake for a similar word with different meaning. The word is used in the Ugaritic myth of 'Anat ('nt II 27) in reference to the victorious gloating of the violent goddess as she slaughters mankind and wades hip deep in blood and gore, bedecking herself with a necklace of severed heads and a girdle of severed hands. The general connotation of the word is apparently "success, victory" without regard to moral quality.

13a. Cited by Paul in I Cor iii 19, and not in accordance with LXX. The figure is that of the wicked caught in their own trap; cf. xviii 7–10; Pss vii 15, xxxv 8, lvii 7(6); Prov xxvi 27, xxviii 10.

13b. Literally "And the counsel of the twisted one is carried headlong."

14. Cf. xii 24 f.; Deut xxviii 29; Isa xix 14, lix 10.

15a. MT reads "He saves from the(ir) sword from their mouth" which is manifestly corrupt. The context requires a word parallel to "the poor" in the companion line. The most likely emendation is the change of *mippîhem*, "from their mouth," to *pĕṯāyîm*, "simple ones." This emendation leaves a superfluous *m* which may be attached to the preceding word as the enclitic emphatic particle.

16a. On hope and the lack of hope, cf. viii 13, xi 18, xiv 7; Jer xxxi 17; Ezek xxxvii 11; Prov xix 18; Ruth i 12; Lam iii 29.

16b. Almost identical with Ps cvii 42b. Cf. Isa lii 15.

17 ff. Eliphaz suggests that suffering is a form of divine discipline. This is usually pointed up as Elihu's chief contributon to the problem; cf. xxxiii 19 f. Cf. Prov iii 11–12 which is quoted in Heb xii 5 f.

17b. *Shaddai.* This divine name is generally rendered by LXX and Vulg. as *pantokratōr* and *omnipotens* (although here Vulg. renders *Domini*), whence the traditional English rendering "the Almighty." It occurs in the OT some forty-eight times, mostly in Job, and ten times in the NT as *pantokratōr*. KJ once renders "omnipotent," Rev xix 6. The etymology of the name is obscure, and diverse interpretations have been offered. Many moderns incline to a connection with Akk. *šadū*, "mountain" (=Heb. *śāḏeh*, "field"). F. M. Cross, Jr., suggests connection with the Semitic word for "breast"; cf. HTR 55 (1962), 246, n. 98. The wordplay in Isa xiii 6, *šōḏ miššadday*, suggests that the word may come from the root *šdd*, "devastate." The rabbinic analysis of the word as a compound *še-day*, "the one who is (self-)sufficient," is reflected in Aquila's and Symmachus' rendering *hikanos*. A number of other etymologies have been proposed, but none is satisfactory. Accordingly, we transliterate the word as a proper name without interpretation. The name harks back to the patriarchal period; cf. Gen xvii 1; Exod vi 3. Whether it is a studied use of archaism by the poet, or a genuine token of patriarchal religion, depends on the vexed question of dating the component parts of the book. The use of the word *'ēl* along with Shaddai as the designation of deity has all the earmarks of authentic early terminology. On *'ēl* as the proper name of God, cf. Eissfeldt, EUP; Pope, EUT; D. N. Freedman, BANE, pp. 205 f.; "The Name of the God of Moses," JBL 79 (1960), 151–56.

18. Cf. Deut xxxii 39; Isa xxx 26b; Hos vi 1.

19. *six . . . seven.* The graded numerical idiom, the collocation of a numeral with its sequel, is common in Hebrew poetry; cf. Amos i 3–13,

ii 1–6; Mic v 4; Prov vi 16, xxx 15, 18, 29; Eccles xi 2; Ecclesiasticus xxv 7. It is especially characteristic of the Ugaritic myths and epics:

> Two feasts Baal hates,
> Three the Cloud Rider (51 III 17–18).

> He smites him twice on the pate,
> Thrice on the ear (1 Aqht 79).

> Double I will give in silver,
> Treble in gold (Krt 205–6).

A favorite combination in Ugaritic is seven-eight:

> Seven years may Baal fail,
> Eight the Cloud Rider (1 Aqht 42–44).

> El answers in the seven chambers.
> From within the eight crypts ('nt v 34–35).

This pair is used in the OT in Mic v 5(4) and Eccles xi 2. Nine-ten occurs once in Ecclesiasticus xxv 7, but is not found in Ugaritic. Note the sequence 12-13-14 in Gen xiv 4–5. Ugaritic also uses ascending multiples of eleven:

> Sixty-six cities he takes,
> Seventy-seven towns (51 VII 8–10).

> He lies with her seventy-seven times,
> She lets him mount eighty-eight (67 v 19–21).

A related use of the multiple of seven and eleven occurs in the Song of Lamech, Gen iv 24, and in Jesus' answer to Peter's query, Matt xviii 22, which has been mistakenly rendered "seventy times seven." It is patent that the numbers in these expressions are not intended to be specific or exact, but are used for rhetorical effect; cf. W. M. W. Roth, "Numerical Sayings in the OT," in VTS, XIII, 1965.

21a. For the tongue as a weapon, cf. Isa liv 17; Jer xviii 18; Pss xii 3–5, xxxi 21; Jas iii 5–6.

21b. *demon.* Reading *šēḏ* for MT *šōḏ*, "devastation." The "scourge of tongue" in the preceding line suggests that the reference is to incantations and use of black magic, hence "demon" appears to be a better parallel than "devastation." The word *šōḏ* occurs in the next verse in conjunction with "famine," with which it is quite congruous, and thus is rendered "plunder."

23a. *field-sprites.* MT "stones of the field" is difficult. Stones are, indeed, especially troublesome in agriculture (cf. Isa v 2; II Kings iii 19, 25), but the idea of making a covenant with them is very strange.

What would the stones do as their part of the agreement? K. Köhler, "Das Erdmännlein" (ARW 7 [1910], 75–79), suggested the reading "lords of the field," *'ădônê haśśāḏeh,* instead of *'aḇnê haśśāḏeh.* This reading was mentioned by Rashi as a variant to Sifra from Lev xi 27 and Köhler found it as a variant in an Oxford fragment of Midrash Tanḥuma. G. Beer (ZAW 35 [1915], 63 f.) similarly proposed reading *bĕnê haśśāḏeh,* "sons of the field." These "sons/lords of the field" are understood as the spirits who inhabit the soil and have to be placated by the farmer. The Arabs call them *'ahl el-'arḍ,* "earth folk," and they are believed to cause malignity of the soil (cf. C. M. Doughty, *Arabia Deserta,* I, 1921, p. 136). These earth demons are probably related to the "satyrs" (*śĕ'îrîm*) which the Israelites were wont to placate with bloody sacrifices in the fields; cf. Lev xvii 5–7.

23b. A peace pact with marauding beasts is a messianic motif, a feature of the paradise of the past or of that to come; cf. Isa xi 6–8; Hos ii 20. A Sumerian Paradise Myth published by S. N. Kramer (BASOR, Suppl. Studies 1, 1945) depicts the ancient paradise of the pure land of Dilmun as a place where

> The lion kills not,
> The wolf snatches not the lamb, . . .

24a. Job describes the prosperity of the wicked in similar fashion in xxi 7 ff. Cf. iv 21.

24b. *miss nothing.* The verb *ḥṭ',* "sin, offend, miss the mark," is used in the latter sense in Isa lxv 20 of an old man who yet fails to reach his full quota of years, in Prov viii 36 of failing to make contact with wisdom, and in Prov xix 2 of missing the path in haste; cf. Jer xxiii 2–4 for the figure of the divine shepherd taking stock of his fold.

25. Cf. Isa liii 10.

25a. Literally "You will know that your seed will be many."

25b. Cf. xlii 16; Ps lxxii 16.

26a. *full vigor.* The word *kelaḥ* occurs only here and in xxx 2. The guess that the word means "old age" suits the context but is not greatly enhanced by resort to Gematria, since the sum of the letters, including the preposition (*b-klḥ*) amounts to a scant threescore. Ar. *kalaḥa* in the sense of "be or appear hard or stern," used of the countenance or of a time of dearth or famine, does not offer satisfactory meaning. The supposed Syriac word *klḥ* with the suitable sense of "health, soundness," is based on an error of Castel in interpreting a gloss of Bar-Bahlul, as pointed out by Gesenius. Connection of the root with *kly,* reflected in some of the versions, and adopted by some moderns, is impossible. The sense that suits both occurrences is "vigor," or the like. The quality, here assured to the righteous, is in xxx 2 lost to the dregs of humanity who mock at Job in his misfortune. There the word is parallel to *kōaḥ* "strength." Some modern critics (Merx, Hontheim, Budde, Cheyne) have related the word to *lēaḥ*, used of Moses' virility at the age of 120, Deut xxxiv 7. This interpretation may gain support from the possible use of this word as a verb in Ugaritic; cf. W. F. Albright, "The Natural Force of Moses in the Light of Ugaritic," BASOR 94 (1944), 32–35. For a different analysis of the Ugaritic word in question (apparently accepted by Albright, "The Psalm of Habakkuk," in *Studies in Old Testament Prophecy*, ed. H. H. Rowley, 1950, p. 4, n. 17), cf. H. L. Ginsberg, "The North-Canaanite Myth of Anath and Aqhat," BASOR 98 (1945), 17, n. 32a. M. Dahood (*Gregorianum* 43 [1962], 66), followed by J. Bright, *Jeremiah* (The Anchor Bible, vol. 21), finds the word in Jer xi 19 (see textual note [h–h]).

6. JOB'S REPLY TO ELIPHAZ
(vi 1–30)

VI 1 Job answered:

2 "Could my anguish but be weighed,
My misery heaped on the balances,
3 'Twere heavier than the sands of the sea;
Therefore are my words vehement.
4 For Shaddai's barbs pierce me,
My soul sucks in their venom;
God's terrors beset me.
5 Does the ass bray over his grass?
The bull bellow over his fodder?
6 Can flat food be eaten unsalted?
Is there flavor in slimy cream cheese?
7 My soul disdains to touch such;
They are putrid as my flesh.
8 O that my entreaty might be granted,
That God might reward my hope:
9 That it please God to crush me,
Loose his hand and snip me.
10 That would even be my comfort;
I would revel in the racking pain;
For I have not denied the Holy One's words.
11 What strength have I to endure?
What prospects to bolster my spirit?
12 Is my strength that of stones?
Or is my flesh bronze?
13 Have I any help within me,
Since success has deserted me?

14 A sick man should have loyalty from his friend,
Though he forsake fear of Shaddai.
15 My friends have betrayed me like a wadi.
Like wadi channels they overflow;
16 They run turbid with ice,
Darkened with snow.
17 When they should flow, they fade;
Comes the heat and they vanish away.
18 Caravans change their course,
Go off in the desert and perish.
19 Caravans from Tema look,
The trains of Sheba yearn.
20 They are tricked that trusted;
They come and are confounded.
21 Thus you have been to me.
You see a fright and are panicked.
22 Have I said: 'Give me something'?
'Ransom me with your wealth'?
23 'Rescue me from an enemy'?
'Redeem me from brigands'?
24 Teach me, and I will be quiet;
Show me where I have erred.
25 How pleasant are honest words!
But what does your arguing prove?
26 You think to reprove me with words,
But count as wind my words of despair?
27 You would cast lots for an orphan,
Barter over your friend.
28 Try now to look at me;
Surely I would not lie to your face.
29 No more, have done with injustice.
Relent, for my cause is just.
30 Is there iniquity on my tongue?
Can my palate not discriminate words?

NOTES

vi 2b. *My misery.* Reading *hawwāṯî*, as in xxx 13b, for MT *hayyātî*. The basic sense of the root is apparently "happen," hence the development of the meaning "accident," "misfortune."

3a. Cf. Prov xxvii 3.

4. Cf. v 7b and Dahood, *Psalms I*, first NOTE on Ps xxxviii 3, on Resheph as archer. Cf. xvi 13. The figure of God as an archer is frequent in the OT; cf. Deut xxxii 23; Ezek v 16; Lam iii 12–13; Pss vii 13, xxxviii 2(3), lxiv 7(8). The lightning is represented as God's arrows in Ps cxliv 6. The present passage plainly refers to poisoned arrows, which are not mentioned elsewhere in the OT. The word rendered "venom" is the same as that used of the deaf adder in Ps lviii 4(5). Fiery arrows were used in war, and arrowheads have been found with perforations for threading oil-soaked tow. Paul mentions the flaming darts of Satan which can be quenched with the shield of faith, Eph vi 16.

4a. *pierce.* Literally "(are) with me"; cf. xxviii 14 where the prepositions *b* and *'im* are parallel.

4c. Cf. x 16–17, xvi 12–14; Ps lxxxviii 17.

5. As it is natural and instinctive for a hungry ass or ox to bray and bellow, so a man in pain will cry out. This is apparently a proverbial saying, by which Job means to convey that he has ample cause to complain.

6. This statement in context would seem to refer to Job's afflictions. But to say that he finds them unappetizing is worse than insipid. The figure of taste, however, is commonplace for reason and sense and would be most appropriate as applied to Job's reaction to Eliphaz's argument. Perhaps the text has been disarranged, or some lines have disappeared which would have made it clear that Job has reference to the insipidity of Eliphaz's logic. For the respects paid to one another's argument, cf. viii 2, xi 2, xiii 3–5, xv 2–3, xvi 3, xix 5, xx 2–3. These not so polite exchanges are reminiscent of more elegant and courteously sarcastic insults swapped by the participants in the Babylonian Theodicy (cited from Lambert, BWL):

> Where is the wise man of your calibre?
> Where is the scholar who can compete with you? (p. 71.)
>
> My reliable fellow, holder of knowledge,
> your thoughts are perverse (p. 77).
>
> You have let your subtle mind go astray.
> [———] you have ousted wisdom (p. 83).

O wise one, O savant, who masters knowledge,
In your anguish you blaspheme the god (p. 87).

6a. *flat food*. The word (*tāpēl*) occurs elsewhere only in Lam ii 14 where it is used of the false and deceptive visions which the false prophets have divined. AT renders, paraphrastically but aptly, "stuff and nonsense." This usage accords with the interpretation suggested above, that Job has reference to the content of Eliphaz's discourse. Cf. i 22 on *tiplāh*, which is formed from the same root as *tāpēl*.

6b. *slimy*. Literally "spittle (of)," but obviously referring to the viscous juice of some insipid substance.

cream cheese. The nature of this tasteless substance is uncertain. Targ. guesses at "the white of an egg," which offers the consistency and insipidity suggested but is doubtful since there is nothing to indicate that the enigmatic word has anything to do with eggs or albumen. Many moderns assume that the reference is to the bland juice of some plant, AT, RSV "slime of purslane," JPS "the juice of mallows." Tur-Sinai's "the saliva of the dreams," in the sense of LXX's "empty words," is insipid. A. S. Yahuda (JQR 15 [1903], 702) suggested that the unique Hebrew word *ḥallāmûṯ* is to be related to Ar. *ḥalūm*, or *ḥallūm* (cf. *Lisān el 'Arab*, XV.38.6 f.) designating a kind of soft cheese which, for want of a special term, we render "cream cheese." The consonants of the Arabic word correspond exactly to those of the Hebrew word and the nature of the substance designated suits the context admirably. The word also occurs in Coptic; cf. W. E. Crum, *A Coptic Dictionary*, 1939, p. 170a. In its raw state, cream cheese is about half water and exudes a milky liquid. It is quite bland and has at least to be salted, and usually other flavor and condiments added, before it is at all palatable.

7a. Job rejects Eliphaz's arguments as his appetite would reject insipid food. For "soul" as appetite, cf. Deut xiv 26; Isa xxix 8; Mic vii 1; Prov xxiii 2.

7b. Literally "They are like the sickness of my meat." The word *leḥem* which usually means "bread" in Hebrew has in Arabic the meaning "meat." In xx 23 and Zeph i 17 the word has, as here, reference to human flesh and not to bread. Because there is no clear antecedent for the pronoun "they," many interpreters emend the text. Dhorme, e.g., reads *zihămāh kĕḇôḏî* for *hēmāh kiḏwê*, and renders, "mon coeur a été degoûté de mon pain." Kissane changes the reading to *hāmāh biddĕwā lĕḥûmî*, "It is agitated by the sickness of my flesh." There is no warrant whatever for emending the text. The pronoun "they" refers to Eliphaz's words or arguments. The condition of Job's flesh, like Eliphaz's argument, is putrid; cf. vii 5, xviii 13, xxx 30.

8. *entreaty . . . hope*. That he be allowed to die; cf. iii 11.

9a. Note again the parallel with Isa liii 10.

9b. *snip me.* Cf. iv 21, vii 6, xxvii 8; Isa xxxviii 12. A technical term of the weaver.

10b. *revel.* The verb *sld* is hapax and often emended. Dhorme suggested that the word may be related to the Indo-European root *sal,* Lat. *salire,* Gr. *hallomai,* "jump." In post-biblical Hebrew *sld* is used of jumping back to avoid danger. LXX *hēllomēn,* "I jumped," and Targ. *'bw',* "I will exult," together support the retention of the MT, according to Dhorme.

racking. Literally "(which) does not spare."

pain. This feminine form of the word (*ḥîlāh*) occurs only here. Elsewhere the masculine form *ḥîl* refers to the pain and writhing of childbirth.

10c. This line is suspect, but if original it would seem to suggest that God owes Job the favor of quickly putting him out of his misery, since he, Job, had always been an obedient servant.

the Holy One. Cf. Isa xl 25; Hab iii 3. "The Holy One of Israel" is a favorite term of the Second Isaiah who uses it some twenty-five times as compared with seven occurrences elsewhere.

11b. Literally "And what is my end that I should prolong my soul?"

12. M. Held, "Rhetorical Questions in Ugaritic and Biblical Hebrew," *Eretz-Israel,* IX, 1969, pp. 73 f., considers the text in error, in the sequence *'im–'im,* contaminated by the *ha'im* of vs. 13, and proposes to alter the first *'im* to the interrogative particle *ha-*. Amos iii 6, which also presents the sequence *'im–'im,* Held likewise considers corrupt.

13b. *success.* Cf. v 12b.

14. It seems impossible to reproduce the sense of this first line with the terseness of the original which consists of three words, "For the fainting—from his friend—loyalty." The great difficulties commentators find in this line are of their own making. It is a straightforward and simple statement. The word *ḥeseḏ* here carries the sense of both "loyalty" and "sympathy," and there is no reason for invoking the Aramaic sense of "shame, reproach," with Hitzig: "If reproach comes to one who is in despair, he will forsake the fear of the Almighty." Ewald supposed that two lines had dropped out and he composed a neat little homily:

> Kindness is (due) from his friend to him that is in despair [and compassion from his brother to him that is afflicted of God; that he succumb not to the pain of his heart,] and forsake the fear of the Almighty; cf. ICC, II, p. 40.

What Job says is that his friend(s) should remain loyal, even if he, as Eliphaz already has begun to insinuate, had turned from God; cf. xvii 5, xix 21–22. Held (cf. vs. 12 above) chides the writer for failure to discern a difficulty here. This stricture is in part merited since there should have been a note on the nature of the supposed difficulty and the solution which is implicit in the translation. The crux is the word *lammās* for which the context suggests some such meaning as "unfortunate," hence the Talmudic connection with Gr. *limós,* "hungry dog." Guillaume construes the *l* as the Arabic asseverative and interprets *mās* as cognate with Ar. *'ašima,* "he despaired." The *l* is merely dative, "to/for," and Ar. *mss* affords the meaning desiderated, in the passive, "be seized with madness, possessed with a demon." The noun *mass* denotes a misfortune or calamity, attack or fit (of a disease).

15–20. But Job's friends have betrayed him like the wadies which run dry, or the dry oasis (or mirage?) which diverts the caravan and lures it to its doom. Jeremiah in like manner accused Yahweh of being false to him as a deceitful brook, or waters that fail, Jer xv 18.

15–17. The wadies of Syria-Palestine may be surging torrents in the rainy season and are usually bone-dry in the summer when water is most needed. The reference to the thaw suggests the region of the Lebanons where in the spring the melting ice and snow sends down floods of dark and roaring waters, but in the heat of summer the stream beds may look as if they had never known a drop of water.

16. In previous editions of this work, this verse was rendered:

> They run turbid with the thaw,
> Covered by the melted snow.

Other translations and treatments were discussed briefly and it was argued that there is no need to emend 16b since the snow is not the subject of the verb, but the accusative of material. The snow does not cover or hide itself, but it is the wadi channels which are covered with the floodwaters from the melting ice and snow. This new note reaffirms the previous interpretation, but with a significant modification. The verb *yiṯ'allēm* does not mean "covered," but "darkened." Thus the parallelism is synonymous between the verbs *qdr* and *'lm,* "be dark," and between the nouns *qeraḥ,* "ice," and *šeleḡ,* "snow." The connection of *'lm* with darkness is certified by the variant of the expression *mî zeh maḥšîḵ 'ēṣāh,* "Who is this who obscures counsel?" xxxviii 2a, which in xlii 3a substitutes *ma'lîm* for *maḥšîḵ* (cf. M. Dahood, *Biblica* 33 [1952], 206). Other passages where *'lm* is related to darkness have been discussed by Dahood, notably Eccles iii 11 (*Biblica* 43 [1962], 65), Job xxii 15 (NWSPJ, p. 65), and Pss xxvi 4 (*Psalms I,* second NOTE ad loc.) and lv 2 (*Psalms II,* second NOTE ad loc.). It is clear that *'lm* in the sense of "be dark" is cognate with Ugar. *ġlm,* Proto-Semitic *ẓlm.* Original *ẓ* is similarly represented by *ġ* in several other Ugaritic words, e.g. *ġr,* "mountain," *ġm',* "be thirsty," and *nġr,* "guard." The Arabic cognate *ẓlm,* "be dark," is actually used of a wadi in flood, *ẓalama al-wādī* meaning "the wadi overflowed (its banks and reached a peak beyond what was usual)." Job's friends are like the wadis which overflow in the spring thaw, turbid with ice, snow, and silt sediment, but when the need is greatest, in the heat of summer, they fail. The suggestion of "covering" is supplied by *'ālêmô,* "upon them," but is omitted in the translation in the interest of brevity.

17a. *flow.* This verb *yĕzōrĕḇû* is hapax and is usually emended to *yiṣṣārĕḇû,* from *ṣrb,* "burn," "scorch." In Arabic, however, *zrb* has the meaning "flow" and *mizrab* designates "canal," "gutter." Aramaic and Syriac also use *zrb* in connection with flowing water, *naḥlā zĕrīḇa* designating a wadi in flood. I am indebted to Mr. Bruce Zuckerman for this observation. The friends are unreliable like a wadi which fades at the very time it should flow.

18a. *Caravans.* The word might be rendered "paths," as referring to the wadi beds, for this is what wadies do—they wind their way into the desert and disappear. JPS renders,

> The paths of their way do wind,
> They go up into the waste, and are lost.

In vs. 19a, however, the same word obviously refers to caravans. The vocalization should be *'ôrĕḥôṯ* in both cases, rather than *'orḥôṯ;* cf. Gen xxxvii 25; Isa xxi 13.

19. *Tema . . . Sheba.* Cf. i 15; cf. W. F. Albright, BASOR 163 (1961), 41, n. 24.

20. The mention of caravans from the south suggests that the figure has suddenly shifted from dry wadi beds to dry oases. A caravan might also follow a dry wadi in the hope of finding water, but the prospects would be very poor. In any case, the figure is the same. Job's fair-weather friends have failed like a wadi in summer or a dried up oasis.

21a. Reading *kēn,* "thus" for MT *kî,* "for," and *lî,* "to me" for MT *lô'/lô* (the Western reading is *lô,* "to him," while the Eastern reading is *lô',* "not," with the Qere *lô,* "to him"). KJ renders "For now ye are nothing." JPS has "For now ye are become His." The rendering of LXX suggests that the final word is a mistake or an abbreviation for the word "cruel," but this is a desperate guess and interpreters who accept it (e.g., Kissane) are then forced to transpose the verse to a more suitable context between 23 and 24.

21b. The Hebrew has a wordplay on "you see" (*tir'û*) and "you fear" (*tîrĕ'û*) which is impossible to capture in translation; cf. II Sam x 19 for a similar collocation of "see" and "fear." The sight of Job in his horrible physical condition has scared the friends out of their wits and made them forget their obligation of loyalty.

22. Job had asked nothing from them but friendship. Lending and borrowing among friends was a sure way to spoil friendship long before

Shakespeare put the famous observation in the mouth of Polonius. Jeremiah said "I have not lent or borrowed, yet everyone curses me," Jer xv 10.

This allusion to ransom and bribery Guillaume understood as Job's personal experience at the hands of the ruthless Chaldeans under Nabonidus. Job's property was plundered by the invaders (i 17) and he himself escaped slavery and possible death by paying a ransom.

23. Cf. Jer xv 21.

24. Eliphaz has insinuated that Job must have merited his woes, for this is the clear corollary of his doctrine that the wicked are always punished. Job does not categorically deny the possibility that he may have committed some minor or inadvertent errors, but he would like to know what he has done to deserve such calamity; cf. xiii 26. For inadvertent and presumptuous sins, cf. Lev iv; Num xv 22–29; Ps xix 13.

25. *pleasant.* The usual meaning of the word *nimraṣ* is "grievous, sore" (sickened), as in Mic ii 10; Jer xiv 17; I Kings ii 8. The opposite sense, however, is indicated in the present context. On the basis of Ps cxix 103 *nimrĕṣû* is often amended to *nimlĕṣû,* "smooth, pleasant." It may be, however, that no emendation is necessary since *l* and *r* may interchange in dialects, as in *ḥlṣ/ḥrṣ,* "hip."

26. The verb "think, reckon, consider" (*ḥšb*) applies to both lines. It is rendered "think" in the first line where it is expressed and "count" in the second where it is to be understood as extending its force. "Words" (*millîm*) is used adverbially as the instrument with which they argue. Though Eliphaz resorts to rhetoric, he regards Job's words, which rise out of personal experience of pain, as so much wind; cf. viii 2, xi 3, xv 2.

27a. Cf. Ps xxii 19; Matt xxvii 35. In II Kings iv 1 we have the picture of a creditor coming to take a widow's two children as slaves. If there were more than one creditor, they might gamble to see who would take the orphans. Job's friends are as heartless as this.

27b. *Barter.* Cf. xl 30 where the same verb is used of fishmongers (wholesalers) haggling over a big fish (Leviathan). The same verb (*kry*) is used in Deut ii 6 and Hos iii 2 (of Hosea's purchase of a harlot on the slave market).

28. His friends had turned from him unable to bear either his appearance or what they considered his blasphemous ranting. He challenges them to look him in the face and read therein his honest anguish. He can look them in the eye and declare that he is innocent. Similarly, Heracles says in Sophocles' *The Women of Trachis:*

> Come close to me, stand by your father and look well at my misfortune, see what I suffer. I shall take off the coverings and show you. Look, all of you, do you behold this poor body? Can you see how miserable, how pitiful I am?

(*Complete Greek Tragedies,* II, p. 317, lines 1076–80.)

29. *No more . . . Relent.* The same word, *šûḇû,* "return you." The injustice is the unfair assumption that Job must be guilty.

30a. Job asserts his own integrity and sincerity of utterance, which, in the next line, he contrasts with his appraisal of Eliphaz's hypocritical arguments.

30b. *words.* The word *hawwôṯ* here does not mean "destruction, disaster," as in vi 2b above and xxx 13b. It is not in parallelism with *'awlāh,* "iniquity," and if it were would not be apposite. The word is unquestionably the same as one so common in the Ugaritic texts in the sense of "word, utterance," *hwt,* which is cognate with Akk. *awat*^{um}; cf. xii 11 which expresses the same idea in similar terms. Syr. caught the sense with the rendering "truth." Job, here as elsewhere, reminds his interlocutors that he still has intelligence and can recognize nonsense and falsehood when it is dished out; cf. xii 2–3.

7. JOB'S REPLY (*continued*)
(vii 1–21)

VII 1 "Has not man hardship on earth?
Are not his days like those of a hireling?
2 Like a slave that gasps for the shade,
Like a hireling that longs for his wage;
3 Thus I am allotted empty months,
Weary nights are appointed me.
4 When I lie down, I say,
'When may I rise?'
But the night drags on,
And I am surfeited with tossing till dawn.
5 My flesh is clad with worms and dust;
My skin cracks and oozes.
6 My days go swifter than a shuttle;
They run out without hope.
7 Remember my life is mere wind;
My eye will not again see good.
8 The eye that looks will not spy me.
Your eye will be on me, and I'll be gone.
9 A cloud evaporates and vanishes,
So he that goes down to Sheol does not come up;
10 He returns to his house no more,
His home never sees him again.
11 Therefore I'll not restrain my mouth;
I will speak in anguish of spirit,
Complain in the bitterness of my soul.
12 Am I the Sea or the Dragon,
That you set a guard over me?

13 If I say, 'My couch will comfort me,
My bed will ease my complaint,'
14 Then you dismay me with dreams,
Terrify me with nightmares,
15 Till my throat would choose strangling,
My bones death.
16 I loathe [it]; I would not live forever.
Hold off, for my days are a breath.
17 Why do you rear man at all,
Or pay any mind to him?
18 Inspect him every morning,
Test him every moment?
19 Will you never look away from me?
Leave me be till I swallow my spittle?
20 What have I done to you, man watcher?
Why have you made me your target?
Why am I a burden to you?
21 Why not pardon my fault,
Forgive my iniquity,
That I might now lie in the dust,
And you seek me but I would not be?"

NOTES

vii 1a. *hardship.* Literally "army/warfare," in reference to life as comparable to onerous compulsory military service; cf. xiv 14; Isa xl 2. Saul apparently inaugurated a sort of haphazard conscription by drafting any likely specimen he happened to see; cf. I Sam xiv 52. Solomon developed systematic conscription and built up a large standing army quartered in garrison towns; cf. I Kings ix 19, x 26. Solomon also initiated forced labor with permanent enslavement of non-Israelite minority groups, I Kings ix 15–22. Uzziah had a large conscripted army with a secretary to look after the muster, II Chron xxvi 11. The soldier's life is in some respects like that of a slave (cf. Luke vii 8) and it was natural that Christians should adopt the figure of willing slaves and soldiers of Christ, cf. I Cor ix 7; Philip ii 25; II Tim ii 3, 4; Philem i 2.

1b. *hireling.* The term used for any person or thing hired for a wage or fee, an animal, Exod xxii 14, a razor, Isa vii 20, mercenary soldiers,

Jer xlvi 21, but especially, for ordinary menial day laborers, Deut xxiv 15; Matt xx 8, 12. It might also apply to the indentured laborer; cf. Isa xvi 14.

2a. *slave.* On slavery in the ancient Near East, cf. de Vaux, *Ancient Israel,* pp. 80–90 with the excellent bibliography, p. 525, to which should be added the exhaustive study by Lindhagen, *The Servant Motif in the Old Testament.* In ancient Mesopotamia it was assumed that man was created as slave and servant of the gods. A Sumerian myth tells how in days of yore, before earth and sky and day and night had been differentiated, the gods had to work with their hands and earn their bread with sweat, which they found most unpleasant. When, at the suggestion of Enki, the intellectual among the gods, man was created to do the work, the gods celebrated with a feast. In the course of the drunken revelry, they became involved in a game of creating human oddities and deformities to see what could be done with them. The game ended in a quarrel when the ultimate in divine mischief was produced: an old man with eyes diseased, inwards in pain, hands atremble, too weak to grasp a piece of bread; cf. Kramer, *Sumerian Mythology,* pp. 68–72; T. Jacobsen, in *Before Philosophy,* 1949, pp. 175–79.

shade. The work day was long and hot and the weary worker who had "borne the burden of the day and the scorching heat" (Matt xx 12) longed for the decline of the day and the lengthening evening shadows, Jer vi 4.

2b. The hireling customarily received his wages at the end of each day, Deut xxiv 15, and this was his incentive to endure. To withhold the hireling's wage was prohibited as cruel; cf. Lev xix 13; Mal iii 5; Rom iv 4; I Cor iii 8; I Tim v 18; James v 4.

3a. *allotted.* Literally "I am caused to inherit."

empty. The word (*šāw'*) denotes what is unsubstantial, unreal, empty, worthless, etc., either materially or morally.

months. Apparently an allusion to the term of an indentured servant; cf. Gen xxix 18; Isa xvi 14. From this allusion to months, Rabbi Aqiba assumed that Job's affliction, like the Deluge, lasted a year (Mishnah, 'Eduyot ii 10). The Testament of Job v 9 reckons the time as seven years.

4. Cf. Deut xxviii 67. The Chorus in Sophocles' *Philoctetes* sings:

The sleep of a sick man has keen eyes. It is a sleep unsleeping.

(*Complete Greek Tragedies,* II, p. 434, lines 847–48.)

5. In one rabbinic tradition, the worms boring holes in Job's body began to quarrel. Job placed each worm in its own hole, with the

comment, "It is my flesh, yet you quarrel about it." (*Pirqe Abot de Rabbi Natan*, ed. Schechter, p. 164.) Cf. Sophocles' *Philoctetes:*

> —the raging, bleeding sore, running, in his maggot-rotten foot.

(*Complete Greek Tragedies*, II, p. 428, lines 699–700.)

6. Cf. iv 21.

6b. *hope*. A wordplay on *tiqwāh* in the sense of "hope" and "thread." Cf. Josh ii 18, 21 where the same word is used of the scarlet thread identifying Rahab's house. As a weaver's shuttle runs out of thread, so Job's life has run out of hope. Cf. Browning's line, "Swift as a weaver's shuttle fleet our days" in "The Bishop Orders His Tomb." Sophocles has Electra say:

> But for me already the most of my life has gone by without hope.
> And I have no strength any more.

(*Complete Greek Tragedies*, II, p. 339, lines 183–85.)

7–21. As often in the course of the argument, Job turns from his human tormentors to address God directly.

7a. *mere wind*. Wind symbolizes what is transient and unsubstantial, vain and empty; cf. Ps lxxviii 39; Isa xli 29; Jer v 13; Eccles i 14.

7b. *good*. Cf. ix 25, xxi 13, 25, xxxvi 11; Pss iv 6(7), xxxiv 13. To see or taste good means to experience and enjoy prosperity and happiness.

8. Job is apparently speaking to God rather than the friends. Time is short and there will be no more opportunity for restoration.

9–10. Cf. x 21, xiv 7–22, xvi 22; II Sam xii 23; Ps lxxxviii 11–12. The netherworld was called in Akkadian "the land-of-no-return." Peake quotes Mallock's paraphrase of Lucretius *On Life and Death* (p. 26):

> Never shalt thou behold thy dear ones more,
> Never thy wife await thee at the door,
> Never again thy little climbing boy
> A father's kindness in thine eyes explore.

11. Cf. vi 3b. Job now lodges his complaint directly against God. The rabbis were more considerate of Job's plight than the friends, in accordance with the principle that "A man may not be held responsible for what he does in his anguish" (TB, Baba Bathra 16a–16b). Sophocles makes Philoctetes say:

> It is no occasion for anger when a man crazy with storms of sorrow
> speaks against his better judgment.

(*Complete Greek Tragedies*, II, p. 447, lines 1193–95.)

12a. Before the recovery of the Ugaritic myths, comparison was quite naturally made with the sea-monster Tiamat in the Babylonian cosmogony. The West Semitic Ugaritic myths, however, are much closer to the biblical mythological allusions in every way. This verse clearly refers to a form of the myth corresponding to that in the Ugaritic texts (68, 129, 137) which relate the development and consummation of the conflict between the sea-god Yamm and the weather-god Baal, with the result that Prince Sea is soundly defeated and effectively neutralized. There is, however, no motif of creation in connection with the conquest of the Sea in the extant Ugaritic texts, as there is in the Babylonian myth; see iii 8, ix 13, xxvi 12, xl 25 f.; Pss lxv 8, lxxiv 13–14, lxxvii 17, lxxxix 10–11, xciii 3–4, cxlviii 7; Isa xxvii 1, li 9. The most recent study of this motif is by O. Kaiser, "Die mythische Bedeutung des Meeres in Ägypten, Ugarit und Israel," BZAW 78 (1959); cf. review by J. Greenfield, JBL 80 (1961), 91 f.

the Dragon. Cf. xl 25.

12b. *guard*. M. Dahood (JBL 80 [1961], 270 f.) suggests that the word *mišmār* here has the meaning "muzzle." He is certainly right in his brilliant recognition of the corrupted reference to the muzzling of the Sea in Ps lxviii 23b where the meaningless reading "I will bring back from the depths of the sea" (*'šyb mmṣlwt ym*) is to be read "I muzzled the deep sea" (*'šbm mṣlwt ym*). According to Dahood, Job in the present passage asks God if he is trying to silence him by putting a muzzle on him as he did to Yamm and Tannin, the Sea and the Dragon. Pss xxxix 2b and cxli 3, which speak of muzzling and guarding the mouth from blasphemy, certainly offer strong support for Dahood's proposal. The consideration which deters the present writer from accepting this interpretation here is the impression that it does not suit the context. There is nothing to suggest that God is attempting to silence Job. What Job complains of is the constant harassment and surveillance which God maintains (cf. vss. 18–20) and this accords perfectly with the normal meaning of *mišmār* as "guard, watch." Jer v 22 and Ps civ 9 mention the confinement of the sea within bounds, as in xxxviii 8–11. Unfortunately, the Ugaritic text which tells of the defeat and final disposition of Prince Sea is fragmentary at this very point. There is, however, mention of captivity of Prince Sea. Just as Baal was about to dispatch his fallen enemy, 'Ashtart intervenes (68:28–30):

By name 'Ashtart rebukes him:
"Be ashamed, O Mighty Baal,
Be ashamed, O Cloud Rider.
For our captive is Prince Sea,
Our captive is Chief River."

And Baal is ashamed and apparently relents, but the following text is so fragmentary that we are left largely to our imagination. We may safely assume that Prince Sea was not annihilated, but, as OT tradition attests, made captive and kept under guard. Dahood's restoration of Ps lxviii 23b would indicate that in some versions of the myth the Sea was muzzled as well as the Dragon, since the verb restored (*šbm*) is the same that 'Anat used in her boast of having muzzled the Dragon. The details of the myths are so variable that it is impossible to reconstruct a canonical version.

13–15. Cf. Eliphaz's description of a disturbing dream, iv 12–16.

15. Though Job longs for death, he does not for a moment contemplate suicide. The case of Ahitophel, II Sam xvii 23, is the only bona fide example of suicide in the OT. The two instances of warriors resorting to this means to escape dishonor, Judg ix 54; I Sam xxxi 4, are not quite the same as deliberate and premeditated suicide.

15a. The word *nep̄eš* here has the primitive sense "throat," as indicated by the reference to strangulation.

15b. MT has "Death from my bones," i.e., "rather than my bones." The Ugaritic usage of the enclitic *-m* has supplied a plausible solution to the difficulty of this line. As suggested by N. Sarna, "Some Instances of Enclitic *-m* in Job," JJS 6 (1955), 109, the *m* prefixed to the word "my bones," *'aṣmôṯāy,* taken as the preposition "from," is to be attached to the end of the preceding word *māweṯ,* "death," as the emphatic enclitic particle. Cf. Dahood, *Psalms I,* NOTE on Ps xxii 21.

16a. *I loathe* [*it*]. The verb *mā'astî* is troublesome. The missing object is generally supplied as "my life." Perhaps the simplest device is to ignore it as a gloss. For a different solution, cf. the first two editions of this volume.

16b. *breath.* Cf. vii 7a where "wind" (*rûaḥ*) is used instead of the present word *heḇel* which means "exhalation, breath." Cf. Isa lvii 13 where *heḇel* and *rûaḥ* stand in synonymous parallelism in the sense of "wind."

17–18. What in happier circumstances would be regarded as providential care (cf. Pss viii, cxliv 3) is here ironically presented as overbearing inquisitiveness and unrelenting surveillance. If what he has received is divine providence, Job would prefer to be spared such. These two verses are often regarded as a bitter parody of Ps viii. The Psalmist asks how God could care for a creature like man and so exalt him, Job asks why not leave him alone.

19b. A figurative expression for a mere moment, as in Arabic "Let me swallow my spittle" (*'abli'nī rīqī*), i.e., "Wait, or leave me be for a moment."

20a. The line is too long for one colon and too short for two. The most likely expedient is to drop the first word of the line, "I have sinned," as unnecessary. Elihu apparently is thinking of this argument of Job's in xxxv 2 ff.

20b. Cf. xvi 12c.

20c. *burden.* This word *maśśā'* in its known meanings, "burden," "oracle," does not seem appropriate to the context. What seems desiderated is a synonym for target, but it is difficult to see how *maśśā'* could have such a meaning.

to you. Reading with LXX. MT "to me," according to Masoretic tradition, is one of the "Emendations of the Scribes." Here the motive was clearly to eliminate the impious imputation; cf. xxxii 3.

8. BILDAD'S FIRST DISCOURSE
(viii 1–22)

VIII 1 Bildad the Shuhite answered:

2 "How long will you prate so?
Your speech is so much wind.
3 Does God pervert justice?
Does Shaddai distort the right?
4 Your children sinned against him,
And he paid them for their sin.
5 If you will but look to God
And implore the mercy of Shaddai,
6 If you are pure and upright,
He will bestir himself for you
And restore your righteous estate.
7 Then your past will be as nothing,
And your future will prosper greatly.
8 Only ask the past generation,
Consider the experience of their fathers.
9 We are ephemeral and know nothing,
For our days on earth are a shadow.
10 Will they not teach you and tell you,
And bring forth words from their minds?
11 Can papyrus grow without marsh?
Rushes flourish without water?
12 While still fresh and uncut,
'Twould wither quicker than grass.
13 Such is the fate of all who forget God;
The hope of the impious will perish.
14 His confidence gossamer,
His trust a spider's house.

15 He leans on his house, it does not stand;
He grasps it, but it will not hold.
16 Moist is he in the sunlight,
His roots spread over his garden.
17 Round a rock pile his tendrils twist;
A house of stone they grasp.
18 When his place swallows him,
It disowns him: 'I never saw you.'
19 Lo, this is the joy of his way,
And from the dust another sprouts.
20 God will not reject the upright,
Nor grasp the hand of evildoers.
21 He will yet fill your mouth with laughter,
Your lips with shouting.
22 Your enemies will be clothed with shame,
The tent of the wicked be no more."

NOTES

viii 2. Cf. xvi 3.

3. *pervert//distort.* The same verb, *yĕʿawwēṯ,* is used in both lines. LXX, Vulg. and Targ. use different verbs. Dhorme suggested the readings *yĕʿwwēṯ* and *yĕʿawweh,* similar verbs with virtually identical meaning. Cf. xxxiv 10–12; Deut xxxii 4.

4. This verse connects the Dialogue and Prologue, indicating that the two are not independent compositions.

5–7. Job is advised that even if he is innocent, he may regain his former happy condition only by appealing to God's mercy.

6a. Dhorme regards this line as a gloss; cf. iv 6.

6c. *your righteous estate.* Literally "the abode of thy righteousness," i.e., Job's former estate which was the proper reward of his piety; cf. Prov iii 33. The term is applied to the temple in Jer xxxi 23.

7. Cf. v 23–26, xi 13–19, xlii 12.

8, 10. Cf. xv 18; Deut iv 32; Ecclesiasticus viii 9. Bildad's assertion that the wisdom of the ancients is in accord with his doctrine and counsel is quite correct, as confirmed by much of Mesopotamian Wisdom Literature; cf. Lambert, BWL, pp. 10–20.

8b. *Consider.* The reading *bônēn* for MT *kônēn* adopted in previous editions appears to have been mistaken in view of the association of *šal* and *knn* in Ugaritic, UT 1161:5–9; cf. M. Dahood, *Biblica* 46 (1965), 329.

experience. Literally "searching out," i.e., the results of investigation and experience.

The suggestion that the final *-m* of *'ābôṯām* is the enclitic emphatic particle is herewith retracted in favor of the possessive suffix which refers to the past generation. The proposal of Fitzmyer and Albright to read *'ōḇôṯām,* "their ghosts," seems unlikely in the light of xv 18 and Ecclesiasticus viii 9; cf. W. F. Albright, *Yahweh and the Gods of Canaan,* 1968, p. 142, n. 85.

9. *ephemeral.* Literally "of yesterday." The brief and transitory character of life is a common theme of Wisdom Literature; cf. xiv 2; Pss xc 9–10, cii 3(4), 11(12), cxliv 4; Eccles vi 12, viii 13. Life is so short that one individual cannot by himself acquire any considerable knowledge or wisdom without recourse to the experience of past generations.

11. *papyrus . . . Rushes.* Both words (*gōme'* and *'āḥû*) are apparently of Egyptian origin, but do not necessarily indicate Egyptian background for the present passage. In Ugaritic the latter word (*aḫ*) is applied to the marshlands of Lake Samak (Huleh) (76 I 9); cf. xl 15a, 23b.

11–13. The law of retribution is as sure as physical law. The wicked will perish in the midst of their prosperity, as plants wither when deprived of water; cf. xv 32.

12b. *quicker than.* Literally "before all."

13a. *fate.* Reading with LXX (*ta eschata='aḥărîṯ*) instead of MT "paths" (*'orḥôṯ*); cf. xv 20–35, xx 5–29, xxiv 19–24, xxxvi 6, 13 f. B. S. Childs, *Isaiah and the Assyrian Crisis* (Studies in Biblical Theology, Second Series, No. 3, 1967), pp. 128 ff., aptly terms this, and similar expressions in xviii 21, xx 29, and xxvii 13, a "summary appraisal form."

14a. *gossamer.* MT *'ăšer yāqôṭ* is questionable on two counts: first the relative particle *'ăšer* is unusual in poetry and secondly the form *yāqôṭ* is hapax and suspect. The clue to the meaning may be found in the parallel "a spider's house," *beṯ 'akkāḇîš.* Saadia already perceived this and rendered *ḥabl eš-šams,* "sun thread(s)," a poetic term for gossamer. The hint of thread may have already been introduced in 13b with the word *tiqwāh* which means both "thread" and "hope"; cf. vii 6b. The term gossamer (Dutch *zomerdraden,* Swedish *sommartrâd,* German *Sommerfäden*) designates the filaments secreted from the spider's spinneret which are wafted by the breeze and settle on shrubs and stubble in late summer and early autumn. The hapax *yāqôṭ* has accordingly been emended to *qayiṣ* or *qayiṭ,* "summer," preceded by a word for "thread"; e.g. Bickell proposed the reading *ḥûṭ qayiṣ* and Budde *qûrê qayiṭ,* "summer thread(s)," for MT *'ăšer yāqôṯ.* Tur-Sinai related *yaqôṭ* to

Ar. *waqṭ* or *waqiṭ*, "a hole which collects rainwater," and thus translated "Whose hope shall be a water hole." Dhorme changed *yāqôṭ* to *yalqûṭ*, which denotes a shepherd's scrip, and rendered "He whose trust lies in a *bag*" with the explanation that an empty bag would be the symbol of something unstable and futile. It seems best here to rely on synonymous parallelism, or what Dahood terms "congruity of metaphor," leaning on the flimsy "spider's house" rather than a water hole or empty bag. With the change of a couple of letters and slight revision of the word division we get *qiš(û)rê qayiṭ*, "summer strands," or gossamer; cf. KB, 398a.

15. Cf. xxvii 18.

16–17. Cf. xv 30–33, xviii 16–19; Ecclesiasticus xl 15; Matt xiii 4–9.

17b. *grasp*. Reading *yôḥĕzû* for MT *yeḥĕzeh*, "he sees." LXX reads "he lives," but the parallelism favors the emendation adopted; cf. xxix 19.

18a. MT "When he/it swallows him from his place." Following Sarna, JJS 6 (1955), 109 f., the preposition *m* is detached from the word "place" and attached to the end of the preceding verb as the enclitic emphatic particle.

19a. Admittedly, the text makes little sense. The versions vary and offer nothing better than MT. Many emendations have been proposed, but all are dubious. Perhaps the most attractive suggestion is that of Kissane who changes *mĕśôś*, "joy," to *miššemeš*, "by the sun," and *darkô*, "his way," to *ḥōrak*, "he is parched." Tur-Sinai, in keeping with his translation theory, assumed that the Hebrew translator mistook an original Aram. *ḥdt'*, "renewal," for *ḥdwt'*, "joy," and thus rendered *mĕśôś*. But the result of this ingenious suggestion, "Behold, he will renew his way," makes scant improvement on the MT. For want of anything better, we follow the MT, although it is probably corrupt.

19b. The subject and the verb in Hebrew are incongruent in number, the subject being singular and the verb plural. The usual expedient is to make the subject agree with the verb, but the inverse process appears to make better sense. Perhaps the *-û* ending of the verbal form represents not the third person masculine plural ending of the imperfect or present-future tense, but the old indicative modal ending *-u*.

20. Cf. xxxvi 5; Ps li 17b(19b).

For the expression "grasp the hand" cf. Isa xlii 6, li 18. The Sumerian ruler Gudea refers to himself as one "whose hand was grasped by (the goddess) Nindar." The Hittite king Hattusilis in his Apology claims divine election and guidance. "And my Lady Ishtar took me by the hand; and she guided me."

21. *yet*. Reading *'ôḏ* for MT *'aḏ*. Cf. Ps cxxvi 2.

22. Cf. Pss xxxv 4, 26, cix 29, cxxxii 18.

9. JOB'S REPLY TO BILDAD
(ix 1–35)

IX 1 Job answered:

2 "Indeed, I know that this is so.
But how can man be acquitted before God?
3 If he deigned to litigate with him,
Could he answer him one in a thousand?
4 Be he clever or mighty,
Who could defy him unharmed?
5 Who moves mountains before one knows it,
Overturns them in his anger;
6 Who shakes the earth from its place,
And her pillars tremble;
7 Commands the sun that it rise not,
Seals up the stars from sight.
8 Alone he stretched out the heavens,
Trod on the back of Sea;
9 Maker of the Bear, Orion,
The Pleiades and the Chambers of the South;
10 Doer of great deeds inscrutable,
Marvels beyond number.
11 He passes by and I cannot see him;
Moves on and I cannot perceive him.
12 He despoils and who can restrain him?
Or say to him, 'What are you doing?'
13 A god could not turn back his anger;
The cohorts of Rahab groveled 'neath him.
14 How then could I answer him,
Or match my words with him?

15 Though in the right, I could not answer;
I would have to entreat my opponent.
16 If I summoned and he answered,
I do not believe he would heed me.
17 He would crush me for a hair
And multiply my wounds without cause.
18 He would not let me draw my breath,
But would sate me with bitterness.
19 Be it power, he is strongest;
Or litigation, who could arraign him?
20 Though I be righteous, my mouth would condemn me;
Though guiltless, he would declare me perverse.
21 I am innocent;
I care not for myself;
I loathe my life.
22 'Tis all the same. Therefore I say,
'Guiltless as well as wicked he destroys.'
23 When the scourge slays suddenly,
He mocks the despair of the innocent.
24 Earth is given to the control of the wicked.
The faces of her judges he covers.
If not he, then who?
25 My days go swifter than a courier;
They flee, they see no good.
26 They pass like reed boats,
As an eagle stoops on prey.
27 If I say, 'I will forget my trouble,
Fix my face and be cheerful,'
28 I am appalled at my agony.
I know you will not release me.
29 I am already found guilty;
Why should I struggle in vain?
30 Were I to scrub myself with soapwort,
Cleanse my hands with lye,
31 You would douse me in filth,
And my clothes would abhor me.

32 He is not, like me, a man whom I could challenge,
'Let us go to court together.'
33 Would there were an umpire between us
To lay his hand on us both.
34 Let him put aside his club,
Let his terror not dismay me,
35 Then I would speak and not fear him.
But I am not so with him.

Notes

ix 2b. Cf. iv 17.

3b. For similar odds, cf. Deut xxxii 30; Josh xxiii 10, Eccles vii 28.

4b. *defy*. Literally "hardened" (the heart/spirit/neck); cf. Deut ii 30, x 16; II Kings xvii 14; Jer vii 26; Ps xcv 8; Prov xxviii 14, xxix 1.

6. Cf. Ps xviii 7; Isa xiii 10, 13; Joel ii 10, iii 16(H iv 16). The earth was thought to be supported on massive pillars, xxxviii 4, 6; I Sam ii 8; Pss lxxv 3, civ 5.

7. The allusion may include both astronomical and meteorological phenomena, including the planets and stars periodically hidden, as well as instances of obscuration by storm clouds, sandstorms, etc.

8b. *back*. Not "high places," or "waves," as regularly understood, but a reference to the myth of the victory of Baal over the sea-god Yamm and the trampling of the body of the fallen foe. The cognate word in the Ugaritic texts always designates the "back" of an animal or a god. In Deut xxxiii 29 the same expression refers to the trampling of the backs of the defeated enemy and not to marching on elevated terrain, as recognized by F. M. Cross, Jr., and D. N. Freedman, JBL 67 (1948), 196 and 210, n. 93. In Amos iv 13 and Mic i 3 the picture of Yahweh treading on the "high places" of the earth represents the victorious avenger trampling the backs of the wicked of the earth, as in Isa lxiii 3. In the Babylonian Creation Epic, Marduk trampled the body of the vanquished Tiamat and, splitting her carcass like a shellfish, used one half of it to form the sky (Tablet IV, lines 104, 129, 136–40; cf. ANET, p. 67). The mention here in parallel lines of stretching out the heavens and trampling the back of the Sea (-god) reflects a version of the myth which, like the Mesopotamian account, connects the defeat of the sea-god and the creation of heaven and earth; cf. iii 8.

9. The order and identity of these constellations varies. LXX renders Pleiades, Hesperus, Arcturus. Vulg. has Arcturus, Orion, and Hyades;

cf. xxxviii 31–32 and Amos v 8. The first constellation, *'āš,* or in xxxviii 32 *'ayiš,* is probably Ursa Major. The second, *kĕsîl,* "fool," is to be identified with Orion, in myth the brash young hunter who offended the goddess of the chase and was done to death for his impudence. Targ. translates *kĕsîl* here and in xxxviii 32 as *nĕp̄îlā',* "the fallen one" (cf. the Nephilim, "Fallen Ones," of Gen vi 4) and Syr. as *gabbārā',* "giant." In Arabic the constellation Orion is called *al-jabbār,* "the Giant." Astral legend identifies Orion with the giant Nimrod transported to the sky; cf. T. H. Gaster, *Thespis,* 1961, pp. 65, 263–66. The third constellation, *kîmāh,* is commonly taken to be the Pleiades. The "Chambers of the South" are not identified and it seems unlikely that the term refers to a constellation. In xxxvii 9 there is reference to the "Chamber" as the source of the tempest. The reference may thus be to "the Chambers of the Southwind," for *têmān,* "south," is used of the south wind in Ps lxxviii 26; Song of Songs iv 16.

10. Note the identical words in the mouth of Eliphaz, v 9.

12. Cf. xi 10, xxiii 13; II Sam xvi 10; Eccles viii 4; Dan iv 35.

12a. *despoils.* The verb *yaḥtōp̄* is hapax, but the general sense is established by the Akkadian and Arabic cognates. M. Dahood (*Biblica* 38 [1957], 310), followed by Blommerde, took the final *p* of *yaḥtōp̄* as the particle *p* and construed the verb *yaḥaṯ* as an apocopate form of *ḥth, hēn yaḥat pā mî yĕšibennû,* "If he should snatch away who could resist him?"

13b. Rahab is one of the marine monsters slain by Yahweh in the course of his defeat of the sea-god; cf. xxvi 12; Ps lxxxix 11; Isa li 9. We learn here that Rahab had helpers, just as in the Babylonian Creation Epic, Tiamat had her cohorts. In the Ugaritic version of the myth which describes the battle between Baal and Prince Sea, there is no mention of Sea's allies. The goddess 'Anat, however, as Baal's ally, boasts in another myth of having defeated a series of monsters along with Prince Sea ('nt III 34–44); cf. xl 25. The root of the name Rahab has the sense of "be excited, agitated," and is thus an appropriate title for a marine monster. In Isa xxx 7 and Ps lxxxvii 4 the name is used as a symbolic designation of Egypt.

Guillaume thinks it strange to find Babylonian mythology appearing so suddenly in what he takes to be an Arabian story and he wonders whether this may be a thinly veiled reference to Nabonidus and his allies.

14a. The verb *'ānāh,* "answer, speak up," is often used as a juridical term, as in 16a below.

14b. Job recognizes the futility of attempting to argue his case in the face of God's power. Since God is both judge and executioner, the ordinary rules of legal procedure cannot be enforced.

15. Even though innocent, he cannot expect justice but can only throw himself on the mercy of his adversary who is also the judge.

15a. The unpoetic relative particle *'ăšer* is omitted as metrically superfluous.

15b. *opponent.* Reading with MT *měšôpěṭî* (participle of the *qôṭala* conjugation, corresponding to the third form of Arabic, connoting conation and a measure of reciprocity) instead of the common emendation to *mišpāṭî,* "my right." A similar form, *mělôšēn,* "calumniator," occurs in Ps ci 5.

16–18. Even if God were to consent to come into court, he could not be required to testify. He would crush the plaintiff or intensify the unjust affliction.

17a. *hair.* Reading with Targ. and Syr. *běśa'rāh* rather than with MT *bis'ārāh,* "with a storm," the latter word being spelled with *s* instead of *ś,* except in Nah i 3. The verb *š(w)p,* "crush," is not suitable to the action of a storm, and "hair," i.e., a trifle, comports with the parallel *ḥinnām,* gratis, without cause.

18b. *with bitterness.* The peculiar reading *mamměrōrîm* was intended to suggest that it should be *bamměrōrîm,* on the basis of Lam iii 15, the only other place where the noun *měrōrîm* is used with the verb *śb',* "be sated." Dahood (*Biblica* 48 [1967], 427), followed by Blommerde, suggested that the initial *m* be attached to the preceding verb as the enclitic particle, *yaśbi'anî-m,* with *měrōrîm* as accusative of material. Another possibility is to read simply *mimměrōrîm.* The meaning is unchanged in any case.

19. Since God is supreme in power and subject to no court, man has no grounds on which to contend with him. *Kōaḥ,* "power," here in parallelism with *mišpāṭ,* "judgment," or litigation, apparently has in this context the sense of "legal authority," as in Mishnaic and modern Hebrew; cf. xxiii 6, xxx 18.

19a. The anomalous ending of the line, *hinnēh,* "behold," needs only the slight change to *hinnēhû,* "behold him." Another alternative is to read *hû'* instead of *hinnēh.*

19b. *arraign him.* The verb has the suffix of the first person, "me," but it seems likely that it was changed to remove even the suggestion that man might call God to account. The alteration is slight in either direction, *yô'îḏēnî/yô'îḏennû.*

20a. In the first edition of this commentary it was proposed to read *pîw,* "his mouth," following Olshausen, Merx, Hoffman, Ehrlich, Fohrer, et al. In the second edition, the suggestion of Dahood (*Biblica* 38 [1957], 311) that MT *pî,* "my mouth," be taken as the resumptive conjuction *pa,* with deletion of the *mater lectiones y* as a scribal error, was tentatively adopted. According to Blommerde, Dahood has since abandoned this suggestion in favor of construing the final *y* as the third masculine suffix, as in Phoenician, citing as parallel the Arslan Tash incantation, line 16 (KAI, 27:16), *ḥwrn 'š tm py,* "Hawron whose mouth is blameless." The possibility that the third masculine suffix may be represented by *y* in Ugaritic and Hebrew, as in Phoenician, is not to be rejected categorically, but the matter is still moot, and it may be expedient to revert to the previous view that final *w* has been lost or confused with *y*. There is also the possibility that the MT is correct and that Job complains that though innocent he is forced to plead guilty with his own mouth. It is not unknown in human legal processes that a sovereign power can coerce an innocent defendant to plead guilty and testify falsely against himself. Whether it is Job's own mouth, or God's, that asserts the guilt, Job denies it.

21. Job will gladly forfeit his miserable life, but he will not relinquish his integrity and claim of innocence. The form of this verse is unusual. It consists of three short clauses which are too long for one poetic line and too brief for two. It seems best to divide them naturally into a tricolon. The effect is striking and this may have been the original intent of the skilled poet—to suggest the intensity of Job's emotion.

21b. *care not.* Literally "know not." Cf. Gen xxxix 6; Deut xxxiii 9 where the verb "know" has similar meaning, as in our expression "to neither know nor care"; cf. vii 16.

22. Job here explicitly denies any moral order in the universe. God is simply indifferent to good or evil.

23a. The "scourge" (*šôṭ*) apparently refers to calamities in general (war, famine, plague, earthquake, etc.) which take their victims indiscriminately; cf. Isa x 26, xxviii 15, 18.

23b. Rashi, unwilling to believe Job would make such a charge, suggests that the reference is to Satan.

24. "Earth" is here undetermined by the definite article. It seems best to take it in the universal sense rather than as referring to any specific land or even empire. The "orthodox" view is that the pious will possess the earth/land (cf. Ps xxxvii 9; Prov ii 21, x 30; Matt v 5), but Job asserts that the opposite is true. Ideally, rulers should administer justice under the guidance of divine wisdom (Prov viii 15–16), but God makes them blind to justice.

24c. Literally the Hebrew says "If (this is) not (so), then who is he?" This may be, as Ibn Ezra and other commentators have held, a truncation of the expression, "If this is not so, who will prove me a liar?", as in xxiv 25. In any case, it is God whom Job holds solely responsible. There is no Satan, or anyone else, to whom the blame may be shifted.

25–26. From this glance at the world's moral disorder, Job returns to his own sad plight. His life is fast running out with no good in sight;

cf. vii 7. The "courier" presumably refers to the swift runner of the royal messenger service; cf. II Sam xviii 21–33; Isa xli 27, lii 7.

26a. *reed.* The word *'ēḇeh* occurs in Scripture only here, but it has cognates in Akk. *abu/apu* and Ar. *'abā,* "reed(s)." Pliny noted that the Egyptians used papyrus reeds for the construction of boats (*Nat. hist.* xxiii.22) and Isa xviii 1–2 refers to the dispatch of reed vessels, *kĕlê gōme',*

> Ha, land of buzzing wings
> Beyond the rivers of Cush,
> That sends couriers by sea
> In reed vessels over the water.
> Go, swift couriers . . .

The speed of these light boats may be referred to in xxiv 18a. Cf. ANEP, p. 33, pl. 109, for representation of the Egyptian reed boat and Thor Heyerdahl's *The Ra Expeditions* (1971) for modern experimentation with such craft.

26b. *stoops.* The verb (*ṭ*(*w*)*ś* is hapax, but the Aramaic cognate is used of the flight of a bird, often with explicit emphasis on speed. The term "stoop" is the technical designation in falconry for the swift swoop of the bird on its prey. The falcon in its stoop reaches a speed in excess of 150 miles per hour. Among biblical references to the eagle's flight and stoop, cf. xxxix 27–30; Deut xxviii 49; II Sam i 23; Prov xxiii 5; Jer iv 13; Hab i 8; Lam iv 19. In the Ugaritic myth of Baal's battle with Prince Sea, Baal strikes down his opponents with weapons that swoop like eagles (68:14–27). In the Aqhat Legend, the goddess 'Anat places the assassin Yaṭpan like an eagle in her girdle and, as she hovers over the young hero, releases the murderer to strike the hapless hero on the head (3 Aqht obv. 17–37). Dr. Walter L. Michel has suggested (in an unpublished dissertation, "The Ugaritic Texts and the Mythological Expressions in the Book of Job," University of Wisconsin, 1970) that the Ugaritic references cited above reflect familiarity with falconry.

prey. The term here is *'ōkel,* "food." TEV for reasons obscure renders "rabbit," "as fast as an eagle swooping down on a rabbit."

27–28. No amount of resolve to ignore his troubles, or to "grin and bear it," can keep Job from despair when he fears that God will not acquit him of guilt.

27b. *Fix.* The verb *'zb* has usually been taken here in the sense of "leave," "abandon," "forsake," thus JPS and RSV "I will put off my sad countenance." Driver (VTS, III, p. 76) related the word to Ar. *'ḏb* which in the causative (iv) stem may mean "make agreeable," and translated "I will make pleasant my countenance." Ugar. *'db,* "make, prepare, set," offers new possibilities and Dahood (JBL 78 [1959], 303–9) has applied this sense of *'zb* II to the present passage (and also to x 1, xviii 4, xx 19, xxxix 14), "I shall arrange my face," meaning "I shall wash and anoint my face." The rendering "fix" seems suitable here as including the cleansing and cosmetic processes as well as the psychic effort to change the mood and countenance and put on a happy face.

29. He has been found guilty in advance of a trial, so that his efforts to clear himself are futile.

30a. *soapwort.* Reading with the Kethib *bĕmô šeleḡ,* rather than the Qere *bĕmê šeleḡ,* "with snow water." J. Preuss (*Biblisch-talmudische Medizin,* 1923, p. 431) correctly interpreted the word *šeleḡ* here in parallelism with "lye" as designating not snow but soapwort. Even though cleanness and purity may be compared to snow, as in Isa i 16, 18, one would hardly seek to cleanse himself with snow water. The roots of the plant *Leontopetalon* used for soap is called in the Mishnah *'ešlāḡ* and in the Gemara *šalgā'*. The term, although attested elsewhere only in post-biblical literature, is not an evidence of late vocabulary. On the contrary, it is derived from Sumerian through Akkadian; cf. W. von Soden, *Akkadisches Handwörterbuch,* 1959, p. 81, s.v. *ašlāku.*

30b. *lye.* The word *bōr* here stands for *bōrîṯ,* as in Mal iii 2, designating the fuller's lye soap.

31a. *filth.* The word (*šaḥaṯ*) regularly designates the netherworld; cf. xvii 14, xxxiii 22, 28. The context, however, suggests the sense of "filth," and LXX and Vulg. render *en 'rupō* and *sordibus.* Many moderns therefore, emend *šaḥaṯ* to *suḥôṯ* or *suḥāh* "refuse," on the basis of Isa v 25 and Lam iii 45. There is, however, no evidence that this word denotes liquid filth. The watery character of the netherworld is, of course, well attested; cf. xxxiii 22; Tromp, pp. 59–67. But its putrescent nature is not generally recognized. Philo of Byblos, however, mentions in connection with the abode of the god *Mouth,* Death, a similar word *Mōt* which he explained as designating mud or slime (*'ilus*), or a putrescent watery mixture. Several Semitic etymologies are possible. W. F. Albright, JBL 60 (1941), 211, suggested connection with Heb. *m(w)ṭ,* "shake, quiver," in the sense of "a quivering jelly." The present writer's proposal of Ar. *māṯa,* JBL 83 (1964), 276, should be retracted in favor of the roots *m(w)ṯ* or *mṯṯ* which have in Arabic the requisite connection with repulsive matter and slime. Cf. D. Hillers, *Interpretation* 19 (1965), 468. Dahood now finds this word *môṯ* in the sense of Quagmire as a designation of the netherworld in Pss lxvi 9 and cxxi 3; cf. *Psalms I, 1–50,* NOTE on Ps xiii 5, *when I stumble.* The watery and putrescent character of the netherworld is noted in the description of the abode of Mot in the Ugaritic myths.

31b. Unimaginative critics make this line unduly difficult. If Job were doused in filth, his clothing would absorb more of the stench than he, and would have no right to abhor him. The supposed difficulty is clarified by reference to Zech iii 3–5. The allusion is to the practice of clothing an acquitted defendant in clean garments. Job's meaning is that even though he were clean (innocent), God would dunk him in muck so that he would be unfit for the clean garments given to the acquitted. The personification of clothing is not strange in poetry.

32a. *challenge.* Literally "speak out, answer."

33a. *umpire.* Since his case is prejudiced by God's arbitrary power, Job wishes for an umpire or arbiter (*môḵîaḥ*) who could mediate and decide the dispute with equity; cf. the use of the verb *ykḥ* in Gen xxxi 37; Isa ii 4. This person would have to be superior in authority to either party, one who could reprove or rebuke either or both contenders. For the expession "lay hand on," cf. Ps cxxxix 5. The translation of the word *môḵîaḥ* by "umpire" (from Lat. *non-par*) is thus justified in this context. Job's wish, however, is futile for there is no such person. Accordingly, he introduces his wish with the particle *lû* which indicates condition contrary to fact. In ancient Sumerian theology each man had a personal god who acted as his advocate in the council of the gods and pleaded his cause before the great gods who were too busy to give much attention to individual cases. This idea may be in the background of Job's thought, but he rejects it as unreal or unsatisfactory.

34. The word *šēḇeṭ*, here rendered "club," is the generic term for any implement for striking or beating, the tool, weapon, symbol of authority. It is the word rendered "rod" in Ps xxiii 4, but Job does not find it a comfort. Job asks merely that God dispense with violence and affliction and allow him to plead his cause without being intimidated or coerced.

35b. MT has "For I am not so with me." These words have generally been taken to refer to Job's conscience or mental state. Ibn Ezra thought Job meant to say, "In my own soul, I am not as you think," and similarly Gesenius, *non ego sic sum* (as Terence often) *apud me,* "I am not so constituted with myself," "I am not so at heart." This is far from convincing. LXX reads "For I do not think myself unjust with him." This reading is certainly more in keeping with Job's attitude and clear conscience; cf. xxvii 6. It would appear simple to read instead of *'immāḏî,* "with me," *'immāḏô,* "with him," but the latter form is not attested so that to obtain the sense indicated we would have to read *'immô.* It would be a still greater improvement in the sense if the subject pronoun "I" were changed to the third person singular, "But he (God) is not thus/just with me." The word *kēn* could be taken either in the sense of "thus/so" or "right/honest." Thus Job would say either "God does not deal thus with me" (i.e., he declines to put aside force and terror), or "He is not honest with me." If this were the original reading, it is easy to see how it would very quickly be altered to obscure or eliminate the blasphemy. This is perhaps too bold a change to dare make, so we take the less drastic measure of following the LXX reading "with him." Blommerde rendered "though I am not just before him", taking *lô' kēn* in the sense of "not steady," "unjust," and construing the final *î* of *'immādî* as the suffix of the third person masculine.

10. JOB'S REPLY (*continued*)
(x 1–22)

X

1 "My soul is sick of life;
I will give vent to my complaint;
I will speak in the bitterness of my soul.
2 I will say to God: 'Don't condemn me;
Let me know your case against me.
3 Is it good for you to oppress,
To despise your own hands' labor,
While on the counsel of the wicked you beam?
4 Do you have eyes of flesh?
Do you see as humans see?
5 Are your days as the days of a mortal?
Your years as men's years?
6 That you seek out my iniquity,
And search for my sin?
7 Though you know that I am not guilty,
There is no escape from your hand.
8 Your hands molded and made me,
And then turned to destroy me.
9 Remember, it was of mud you made me;
And back to dust will you return me?
10 Did you not pour me out as milk,
Curdle me like cheese,
11 Clothe me with skin and flesh,
Knit me with bones and sinews?
12 Life and love you granted me,
And your providence guarded my spirit.
13 Yet these things you hid in your mind;
I know this is what you did.

14 If I should sin, you are watching me,
And would not acquit me of guilt.
15 If I am guilty, woe is me!
Or innocent, I may not lift my head.
Sated with shame,
Drenched in misery.
16 Bold as a lion you stalk me,
Repeat your exploits against me,
17 Renew hostility against me,
Multiply anger against me,
Incessant hardship for me.
18 Why did you bring me from the womb?
I could have expired unseen,
19 Could be as if I had not been,
Carried from womb to tomb.
20 Few are my days, let me be.
Hold off, let me smile awhile
21 Before I go, never to return,
To a land of darkness and gloom,
22 A land of utter darkness,
Of gloom without order,
Which shines like darkness.' "

NOTES

x 1. Some critics wish to delete one or the other lines of this tricolon. Line 1a is a variation of ix 21c and 1c of vii 11b. If, however, every verse that resembles or echoes some other verse in the book were deleted, the size of the work would be considerably reduced. Since tricola are not uncommon in Ugaritic poetry, there is no good reason to suspect them here unless one of the cola is discrepant with the sense of the others, and even then it may be that the line has been corrupted rather than augmented.

1a. Blommerde (p. 58) takes the final *y* of *ḥayyāy* as the third masculine singular possessive suffix, "my soul is sick of its life."

1b. *give vent to.* The expression *'e'ezḇāh 'ālay* literally translated would be something like "Let me put (forth) upon me." Dahood rendered "I shall prepare on my behalf my complaint" (JBL 78 [1959], 305), but later (*Psalms I*, first NOTE on Ps xlii 5) preferred to construe the final letter of *'ly* as representing the third person masculine suffix, "I shall set my complaint before him." The former analysis seems preferable here.

2b. Blommerde takes *'l* here not as the preposition but as the divine name *'ēl*, "Most High," in the vocative case. This is plausible in view of the divine name in the preceding line, but the case is not so strong here as in other instances.

3. Job here charges God with oppression of the righteous and favoritism for the wicked. The question "Is it good?" may mean either, "Do you like it?", "Is it advantageous?", or "Is it proper?", "Can there be any justification for such a state of affairs?"

4. The question is not so much whether God has human limitations, but whether he can really understand and sympathize with man's predicament. Job certainly conceived of God's knowledge as infinitely greater than man's; cf. I Sam xvi 7. But he wonders whether God can really put himself in man's place.

7b. Cf. Blommerde, pp. 59 f., on the construction here with *waw apodoseos.*

8b. Reading with LXX *'aḥar sabbôṯā* for MT *yaḥad sāḇîḇ*, "together 'round about."

9a. The figure of the potter and the clay is one of the Bible's most striking illustrations of God's sovereignty; cf. Isa xlv 9; Jer xviii 5–12; Rom ix 20–25.

9b. Cf. Gen iii 19; Ps xc 3.

10–11. The marvelous mystery of man's conception and prenatal development is metaphorically depicted here. Semen, poured like milk into the womb, is coagulated like cheese, and finally bones and muscles are formed; cf. Ps cxxxix 13–16; Eccles xi 5; Wisdom of Solomon vii 2. In Pirqe Abot iii 1, man is said to come from a fetid drop. The prophet Muhammad frequently cited the marvel of man's creation from a drop of semen or a clot (of blood), Koran xxii 5, xxxvi 76, lxxx 19, xcvi 2.

12. These lines probably refer not to the miracle of gestation and birth, but to God's providential care of Job in his earlier years, before the calamities befell him.

13. Job's later fate convinces him that all the time of his prosperity God had concealed the sinister plan to reduce him to misery. This is a switch on the idea that behind a frowning providence God hides a smiling face, an idea to which the doctrines of divine prescience and predestination lead inevitably. Calvin (*Institutes* III.23.7) admitted that the decree is horrible (*Decretum quidem horrible, fateor*), "and yet it is impossible to deny that God foreknew what the end of man was to be

before He made him, and foreknew, because He had so ordained by His decree."

13b. Literally the line says, "I know that this [is what was] with you," meaning, as in the preceding line, "what you had in mind."

14. God is alert to catch Job in any misstep and to hold him guilty for even the most trivial fault; cf. vii 18–20.

15a, b. Cf. ix 15–24, 29.

15c, d. This may be taken as a single line, with four stressed words, or as two short lines with two stresses each. It may be that the text has suffered damage, or the line may have been interpolated by someone unsympathetic to Job's attitude. But Job could very well say this of himself, for it is an obvious fact that he is sated with shame and misery. The question is whether he merited his misfortune.

15d. *Drenched.* Reading *ūrwēh* for MT *ūr'ēh,* "and see thou."

16. It may be that Job's shocking accusation against God has contributed to the obfuscation of the simple sense of this line. Instead of *yiḡ'eh,* "he is proud/bold," we read *gē'eh,* "proud, bold." This seems preferable to the assumption that the unexpressed subject of the verb is Job's head: "[my head] rises, and you hunt me like a lion." Job here speaks in bitter irony. God shows his marvelous power and heroism by assaulting a helpless mortal.

17a. The Hebrew says "you renew your witnesses against me." But the context here refers not to the judicial process but to the lion's attack on his prey and God's assault on Job. Of the various interpretations that have been proposed, that of A. B. Ehrlich (*Randglossen zur hebräischen Bibel*) is by far the best. Instead of "your witnesses," the meaning is "your hostility," connecting the word with Ar. *'dy,* "be hostile." Dahood (*Psalms I,* fourth NOTE on Ps xxxii 9) would relate the word to Ar. *ġadda,* "swell up," "be irritated"; cf. Blommerde, p. 60.

17c. The text says, literally, "successions and hardship." The word *ṣāḇā'* here rendered "hardship" also means "army, warfare" and some interpreters take the expression to mean "fresh troops." In either case, the sense is essentially the same, whether God's treatment of Job is represented as a series of assaults by fresh troops or successive and incessant hardships; cf. vii 1, xiv 14.

18–19. Job returns to the question of his opening discourse.

20a. *let me be.* With Targ. according to the Qere *waḥăḏāl* rather than Vulg. which followed the Ketib *yeḥdāl.* The reading *yĕmê ḥeldî,* "the days of my life," reflected by LXX and Syr., seems unlikely since imperative *waḥăḏāl* comports with the imperative of the following line *wĕšîṯ,* again following the Qere rather than Ketib.

21. Cf. vii 9–10, xiv 7–22.

22. This verse is a tricolon and some critics accordingly delete a line, but this is quite unwarranted. The LXX reading differs markedly from

the Hebrew—"to a land of eternal darkness, where there is no light nor sight of life of mortals." Four different words for darkness are used in vss. 21–22; cf. iii 4–6. The sense of this verse is paraphrased by Milton (*Paradise Lost,* Book I, line 63), "No light, but rather darkness visible."

11. ZOPHAR'S FIRST DISCOURSE
(xi 1–20)

XI 1 Zophar the Naamathite answered:

2 "Shall this spate of words go unanswered?
Shall the glib one be acquitted?
3 Shall your babbling silence men?
Shall you mock and none rebuke?
4 You say, 'My doctrine is pure.'
You are clean in your own eyes.
5 But would that God might speak,
Might open his lips against you.
6 He would tell you what is hidden,
For there are two sides to wisdom.
God even forgets part of your guilt.
7 Can you fathom the depth of God,
Find the limits of Shaddai?
8 The heights of heaven, what can you do?
Deeper than Sheol, how can you know?
9 Longer than earth in measure,
Broader than the sea.
10 If he overlook, or shut up,
Or condemn, who can restrain him?
11 For he knows false men;
He sees and ponders evil.
12 The inane man will get sense,
When a wild ass is born tame.
13 If you would order your mind,
And stretch out your hand toward him,
14 If guilt be in your hand, remove it;
Let not evil dwell in your tent.

15 Then could you lift up a face unblemished;
You might be steadfast and undaunted.
16 Trouble you would then forget,
As water gone by you would remember it.
17 Life would rise brighter than noon,
Darkness become as morning.
18 You would trust because there is hope,
Look about and recline in confidence.
19 You would lie down and none disturb.
Many would court your favor.
20 But the eyes of the wicked will dim;
Refuge will fail them,
Their hope an expiring breath."

NOTES

xi 2. *glib one*. Literally "man of lips."

3. *babbling*. This word in Hebrew usually denotes idle talk and boasting. In the Ugaritic myths, however, it is used of singing; cf. xli 4.

4a. On the basis of the LXX reading (*tois ergois*), it is tempting to emend MT *liqḥî*, "my doctrine/discourse," to *leḵtî*, "my conduct." But this is probably unnecessary, since the friends object primarily to what Job has been saying, viz., that he is innocent and therefore God is unjust.

4b. MT has "I am pure in your eyes." LXX reads "before him" and RSV follows this with the rendering "and I am clean in God's eyes." Now this scarcely accords with what Job has actually been saying. The Job of the Dialogue does not know that God reckons him as just; this is his complaint, that God treats him as the wicked ought to be (and often are not) treated. Perhaps the simplest way out of this difficulty is to change one vowel, *hāyîṯî*, "I am," to *hāyîṯā*, "you are."

5. Zophar knows that Job must be guilty and if God would speak this would be made clear.

6. While it is risky to emend the text *metri causa*, we have ventured to delete the word *ḥoḵmāh* in 6a, taking it as an explanatory gloss to the rare and difficult word *tûšiyyāh* in 6b. RSV renders 6b "For he is manifold in understanding" and in a note characterizes the Hebrew as obscure. The word *kip̄layim*, however, does not mean "manifold," but "double, duplex." We take the sense to be that God knows both sides of every matter, the manifest as well as the hidden, and it is the hidden

side that he would reveal if he were to speak to Job's challenge. The last line of the tricolon, 6c, says "Know that God forgets for you some of your iniquity." The line is a good deal longer than the other two and is somewhat awkwardly worded, but the sense is clear. Far from punishing Job unjustly, God gives him less than he deserves. This is in keeping with the attitude of the "friends" and we retain the line as genuine, though some critics reject it.

7a. KJ's "Canst thou by searching find out God?" mistakes the sense. The word *ḥēqer* is not in the adverbial case, but stands in construct relation with the following word. JPS and RSV thus interpret correctly, "Can you find out the deep things of God?" (RSV). It is not that man cannot find God, but that his greatness is beyond human comprehension.

7b. KJ's "Canst thou find out the Almighty unto perfection?" approximates the sense. The word *taḵlîṯ*, however, does not mean "perfection," but "boundary, limit"; cf. xxvi 10, xxviii 3. The JPS rendering, "purpose," is inappropriate to the context. This post-biblical meaning of the word is not attested in the OT.

8–9. The height and depth, the length and breadth of God are beyond human comprehension; cf. Isa vii 11. In the Ugaritic poem called "The Birth of the Beautiful and Gracious Gods" (52:33–34) it is said that the hand of God (El) is long as the sea. (It is, however, possible that "hand" is a euphemism in this Ugaritic text which depicts a divine love scene; cf. EUT, p. 39.) Cf. Lam ii 13 where Jerusalem's devastation is compared to the vastness of the sea.

8. As it stands, the text reads "the heights of heaven . . . deeper than Sheol." The usual expedient is to make the first line conform to the second, "higher than heaven." Dahood (NWSPJ, pp. 57 f.) adjusts the second line to the first by shifting the proclitic element *m*, "from/than," from the word Sheol to the end of the preceding word where it would serve merely as the enclitic emphatic particle.

10. This verse echoes Job's words in ix 11–12 and some scholars regard it as a misplaced interpolation. It can hardly be said that Zophar takes up Job's words and turns them back at him, for Job has acknowledged God's power and man's inability to oppose him; cf. ix 2 ff.

10a. *overlook.* Literally "pass on," i.e., choose to ignore some human action.

10b. *condemn.* Literally "call an assembly," for the purpose of condemning a culprit; cf. Ezek xvi 40, xxiii 46; Prov v 14. The emendation of "call an assembly" (*yaqhîl*) to "execute" (*yaqṭîl*) is unwarranted.

11. Zophar, by implication, charges that Job is wicked and God knows it, even though man may not be aware of it. The second half of the verse says literally, "He sees iniquity and does not consider it," which can hardly be what Zophar intended to say. To take the last part of the line as a question yields suitable sense, "He sees iniquity, and

will he not consider it?" Such a rhetorical question is equivalent to asseveration, so it seems legitimate to render it as a declaration. The suggestion that the latter part of the line means "though he himself is unperceived" seems rather improbable. Blommerde interpreted the abstract *'āwen,* "iniquity," as a concrete noun, "sinners," because of the parallelism with *mĕṯê šāw',* "false men," in the preceding line, and rendered "and sees sinners, but considers them nothing," construing the negative *lô'* substantively.

12. The meaning of this verse is problematic. It appears to be a proverbial saying and, indeed, a very artful one, to judge from the alliteration and assonance:

wĕ'îš nāḇûḇ yillāḇēḇ
wĕ'ayir pere' 'āḏām yiwwālēḏ.

The crux of the problem is the syntactic relation of the words *'ayir pere' 'āḏām.* There is no warrant for construing *'ayir* as being in construct relation with *pere'* (so KJ, AT, RSV) in the sense of "a wild ass's colt." The word *'ayir* does not designate a colt. The familiar rendering of the word as "colt" in Zech ix 9, "on a colt the foal of an ass," is misleading since the text says literally and simply "on a he-ass, son of a she-ass." The word *'ayir* designates the male of the domesticated ass, whereas *pere'* applies to the wild ass, or onager. It would make scant sense to put the two terms in construct relation, "a (male) (domesticated) ass of a (male) wild ass." Moreover, Gen xvi 12 shows that *pere' 'āḏām* is a unit. M. Dahood (CBQ 25 [1963], 123–24) has shown that *'āḏām* is sometimes equivalent to *'ăḏāmāh,* "ground." Accordingly, *pere' 'āḏām* would mean "a wild ass of the steppe" and not "a wild ass of a man"; cf. xxxvi 28. Thus, the sense of Job xi 12b could hardly be "when a wild ass's colt is born a man." The contrast and implicit comparison is between the inane man and the sensible man and the wild ass and the domesticated ass, the thought being that a stupid man may be expected to become intelligent when and if a wild ass were born tame, or could be made so. The emendation of *yiwwālēḏ,* "be born," to *yillāmēḏ,* "be taught," improves the alliteration with *yillāḇēḇ* of the preceding line and perhaps also makes better sense. But the fact that the verb *lmd* is never used in the Nif'al militates against this emendation.

14b. *tent.* The form is plural. Cf. Dahood, UHP 13.37, p. 37, and Blommerde, p. 61.

15b. *steadfast.* Literally "poured," i.e., cast like metal, hence "hard, solid, firm"; cf. xxxvii 10, 18, xxxviii 38.

17a. *Life.* The word *ḥeleḏ* is connected with durability and survival, continuing health and vigor in advanced age. MT says literally, "More than noon shall rise *ḥeleḏ*." Tur-Sinai renders, "Brighter than noon shall keep eternal light," on the basis of his reading of the last line of the Arslan Tash Incantation as *ḥld ḥld* which he renders "the morning shines." Other scholars read, however, *ḥl wld,* "travail and give birth," and there is thus no reliable evidence for any basic relation of the word to light, apart from the association with noon and contrast with darkness in the present instance. The implication of light here derives from the term *ṣohŏrayim,* "zenith, noon," rather than from *ḥeleḏ*.

19a. This expression recurs verbatim in Isa xvii 2; Zeph iii 13. The verb *rbṣ,* used properly of quadrupeds, is applied figuratively to human beings, as in Ps xxiii 2.

19b. Literally "many would make sweet your face." For this idiom applied to God, cf. Exod xxxii 11; Jer xxvi 19; Mal i 9; and to man, Prov xix 6; Ps xlv 13.

12. JOB'S REPLY TO ZOPHAR
(xii 1–25)

XII 1 Job answered:

2 "No doubt you are gentry,
And with you wisdom will die.
3 But I have a mind as well as you;
I am not inferior to you.
Who does not know such things?
4 A derision to his neighbor I am become,
One whom God answered when he called,
The just and perfect a derision.
5 The comfortable hold calamity in contempt,
Fitting for those whose feet slip.
6 Robbers' households prosper,
God-provokers are secure,
One who carries God in his hand.
7 Now ask the beasts, they will teach you;
The birds of the sky will tell you;
8 Or speak to the earth, it will teach you;
The fish of the sea will tell you.
9 Who does not know all these things,
That God's hand has done this?
10 In his hand is every living soul,
The breath of all human flesh.
11 Does not the ear test words,
The palate taste its food?
12 Do the aged have wisdom,
The long-lived understanding?
13 With him is wisdom and might;
His are counsel and understanding.

14 If he tear down, there is no rebuilding.
If he imprison, there is no release.
15 If he withholds the waters, there is drought;
Or lets them go, they engulf the earth.
16 With him are power and victory;
Pervert and perverter are his.
17 Earth's counselors he makes foolish;
Judges he makes mad.
18 He loosens the belt of kings,
And binds a rag on their loins.
19 He makes priests go bare,
Overturns the well-established.
20 The confident he deprives of speech,
Takes away the reason of elders,
21 Pours contempt on princes,
Loosens the girdle of nobles,
22 Reveals from darkness mysteries,
Brings forth dense darkness to light,
23 Makes nations great then destroys them,
Expands nations and leads them away,
24 Deprives leaders of intelligence,
Makes them wander in a pathless waste.
25 They grope in darkness with no light.
He makes them stagger like a sot.

Notes

xii. Job's third speech, chapters xii–xiv, like the previous ones, is addressed in part to the friends, xii 2–xiii 19, and in part to God, xiii 20–xiv 22.

2a. *gentry*. Cf. xxxiv 20. The word "people" (*'am*) is here taken in a sense similar to that of the technical term "people of the land," i.e., the effective male citizenry, the upper-class landowners who rank next below royalty and priesthood. As Job uses the term here, the sense is somewhat like that of "gentry" in British English, the people of wealth, breeding, and education who rank next below the nobility. There is no need to add any modifier, such as "prudent, clever, knowledgeable," or the like. The LXX addition of "alone" (*monoi*) followed by the Vulg. (*soli*) is not a sure indication than an additional word (supposedly *lĕḇaḏ,* as an error for *lēḇāḇ,* "heart, mind") stood in the Hebrew which the Greek translator had before him. He may have felt that the text needed something to modify "people."

Dahood, *Psalms I,* first NOTE on Ps xviii 28, assumes the existence of a root *'mm,* "to be strong, wise," and renders the present verse "You no doubt are the Strong/Wise One and with you will wisdom die."

3. This may be in reply to Zophar's implicit comparison of Job with a wild ass, xi 12. Some scholars would delete 3b which occurs again in xiii 2, but there is no warrant for this.

3c. Literally "with whom (are) not (things) like these." Job here refers, presumably, to what Zophar had said of God's power in xi 7–10. This Job acknowledges. However, if this line refers to Zophar's affirmation of retributive justice, then Job's statement is intended ironically, for this is exactly what he knows to be untrue, in spite of repeated affirmations by the friends.

4–6. These verses break the train of thought between 2–3 and 7 ff. and many critics regard them as an interpolation. LXX omits 4a, b and differs from the Hebrew in 4c, 5. While there is nothing to indicate that the friends have laughed at Job, it is not unfair to say that they have not been entirely sympathetic. They have assumed that Job must be guilty and have offered the only counsel they knew. From Job's point of view, their attitude leaves much to be desired and it is not unthinkable that he should feel himself the butt of their derision since they have already reached the stage of swapping insults; cf. xi 2, 12.

4a. *derision.* KJ and RSV "laughingstock"; cf. Jer xx 7; Lam iii 14.

5a. This is another difficult line, which may be read in at least two different ways, neither of which gives very clear sense. It may be read "a contemptible torch to the thought of one at ease," or "for misfortune there is contempt in the thought of one at ease." Vulg. took the former sense, *lampas contempta,* as did Rashi who explains that "the fire of hell (*Gehinnom*) stands against him who is at ease in his thoughts, saying 'I shall have peace.'" Ibn Ezra took it in the latter sense, reading *la(p)pîḏ,* "for misfortune," rather than *lappîḏ,* "torch."

6c. This vexed line may be rendered, as literally as possible, "Whom God brings in his hand," or "To him who brings God in his hand." The difficulties are evaded or glossed over in the versions. The clue to the sense must be sought in the similar expression *yēš lĕ'ēl yāḏî* which occurs in Gen xxxi 29 and with variations in Deut xxviii 32; Mic ii 1; Neh v 5; Ecclesiasticus xiv 11, with the meaning "it is in my power"; cf. EUT, p. 17. Virgil's *dextra mihi deus* (*Aeneid* x.773) seems to be related to this expression. Buttenwieser's "they whose god is their fist" and Moffatt's "who make a god of their own power" seem the best interpretations. Guillaume applies this line to Nabonidus' bringing of his patron deity, the moon-god Sin, with him to Tema, which was an offense and provocation to the already beleaguered Jewish community.

7–10. The irony with which Job began is resumed. The profound wisdom which the friends have been giving out is knowledge common to the lowliest of creatures.

8a. With slight alteration, the text could be read "Or the shrubs of the earth, and they will teach you." RSV adopts this sense and relegates the more exact rendering to the margin. AT translates boldly "Or speak to the earth and let it teach you." The usual objection to both these renderings is that neither the earth nor the non-sentient shrubs of the earth seem likely candidates for interrogation. The parallelism with the "beasts" and "the fish of the sea" suggests something like "creeping things of the earth," as in Gen vii 21; Lev xi 29, 41. Duhm's emendation to *zôḥălê 'ereṣ* as in Mic vii 17 (cf. Deut xxxii 24) is widely accepted; cf. Moffatt, CCD, and the BJ's "Les reptiles du sol." Dahood has removed the difficulty by pointing out that *'ereṣ* here refers to the netherworld, as in x 21, 22, xv 29 (NWSPJ, p. 58). Thus we see reflected the quadripartite division of the universe: earth, sky, netherworld, and sea. Dahood cites as a parallel the Ugaritic passage ('nt III 19–22):

rgm 'ṣ wlḫšt abn	Speech of wood, whisper of stone
tant šmm 'm arṣ	converse of heaven with earth,
thmt 'mn kbkbm	the deep(s) with the stars.

The (chiastic) parallelism of heaven/stars and deep(s)/earth indicates that "earth" here has reference to the nether regions.

9a. *all these things.* Buttenwieser argues that the prevailing interpretation (which takes this to refer to the knowledge that God is creator and ruler of the universe) cannot be maintained. Rather he understands the meaning to be quite the opposite—what every animal knows is the brutal and unjust system which God allows to prevail, the law of the jungle.

9b. *God.* The text has Yahweh, but this name is found nowhere else in the Dialogue, except in xxviii 28 which is almost universally recognized as no part of the original poem. Some manuscripts have God (*'ĕlôah*) instead of Yahweh. This verse is almost identical with Isa xli 20. Duhm regarded it as extracted from that source. Gordis makes this a major point in this argument that Job is dependent on Deutero-Isaiah; see Introduction, pp. XXXVIII f.

10b. *all human flesh.* A strange expression not elsewhere attested. The common expression "all flesh" usually refers to humanity, but not necessarily exclusively. The suggestion that the word *'îš*, "man," here individualizes the expression "every individual human being" is attractive. LXX omits "all flesh," but this would make the Hebrew line much too short. Cf. the expression "God of all flesh," Jer xxxii 27, and "God of the spirits of all flesh," Num xvi 22, xxvii 16. Dahood (UHP 8.19, p. 16) would read *'ôš* in place of MT *'îš* and relate it to Ar. *'aws* and Ugar. *ušn,* "gift," "and the spirit in all flesh is his gift"; cf. Blommerde, p. 62.

11. This expression recurs in xxxiv 3 and may be a proverbial saying. In several of the Semitic languages, notably Akkadian, Hebrew, Aramaic, the verb "taste" is used figuratively of mental processes. The noun may mean "decision, decree," as in Jon iii 7; Dan iii 10, 29, iv 3, vi 27; Ezra iv 21, v 3, vi 1, 3, 12, ix 13; or "reason, understanding, discernment," Prov xxvi 16; Dan ii 14; or "mind," Dan iii 12, vi 14. When David feigned insanity, I Sam xxi 14, the expression is "he changed his 'taste.'" The import of the saying is that as the palate tastes its food, so the mind assesses the validity of ideas, and the implication is that the ideas of the friends are insipid or downright repellent; cf. vi 6.

12. Taken as a declaration, so KJ and RSV, the sense of this verse is out of keeping with the context. Taken as a question, as in JPS, with the negative answer implicit, the sense comports with Job's attitude toward his friends. They are, to his mind, living proof that wisdom does not necessarily come with years; cf. xxxii 9. W. Quintens in an unpublished dissertation (cf. Blommerde, p. 62) takes *yĕšîšîm* and *'ōreḵ yāmîm* as divine epithets, "the Old One" and "the Long-lived." Similarly it is suggested that Ps xciii 5, *Yhwh lᵉ'ōrek yāmîm* means "Yahweh, O magne dierum." Quintens reportedly based the interpretation of *'ōreḵ yāmîm* as a divine title on the Ugaritic text UT 1018:20 *urk ym* (the reading is erroneously cited as *urk ymm*) regarded as a title of El supposedly parallel to *il.mṣrm* in line 22 of the same text. The interpretation is quite mistaken. Although the Ugaritic text is fragmentary, it is clear from what is preserved, as well as from epistolary parallels, that the writer wishes the Egyptian monarch long life, ". . . and length of days of my Lord before Amon and before the (other) gods of Egypt who guard the life of the Sun, the Great King, My Lord." Although xii 13 ff., clearly affirm God's wisdom and power, the preceding verse applies to human wisdom which may be and often is defective despite age and experience; cf. xxxii 9.

13. *wisdom and might.* Cf. II Kings xviii 20 for a variant of the phrase. To the proposition that wisdom comes with senility, Job replies that God (only?) has wisdom and power. The friends, of course, have not asserted that wisdom resides only with old men. Neither does Job mean that God keeps wisdom entirely to himself and does not impart it to man. Perhaps the main point of the line is that God has power

as well as wisdom. The word "wise" (*ḥākām*) had originally the sense "intelligent, shrewd, crafty," without ethical connotation, as illustrated by its application to Jonadab in II Sam xiii 3.

14–25. Job shows that God is the author of both weal and woe. All human efforts he frustrates and human institutions he destroys. There is no escape from his power, 14b, and no moral purpose is discernible in his violence, 16b. There is no suggestion here that the victims of the violence are the wicked. The passage has affinities with Ps cvii and Isa xliv 24–28. Verses 21a, 24b agree verbatim with Ps cvii 40; 14b is reminiscent of Ps cvii 16; 15 of Ps cvii 33–36; 18, 22b of Ps cvii 14; 23, 24b, 25b of Ps cvii 4, 7. Verse 15a is similar to Isa xliv 27, and 17 to Isa xliv 25. In Ps cvii and Isa xliv 24–28, God's power may be applied with justice and beneficence, but Job sees only violence without meaning.

14a. The object of God's destructiveness is not specified, but because the second half of the verse speaks of building, the reference presumably is to cities; it may include any human endeavor and human life itself which God may wreck or destroy.

14b. The imprisonment may be both literal and figurative; cf. Exod xiv 3.

15. The two extremes of drought and flood, which affect all alike, without regard to moral condition, shows the divine power to be amoral.

16a. *victory*. It hardly suits the context to render the word *tûšiyyāh* as "wisdom" or "sound counsel" in the present lines. Here, as in v 12b, the word is used in a sense like that found in Ugaritic where it is applied to the goddess 'Anat's exultation and gloating over her wanton slaughter of mankind ('nt II 5–31).

16b. All erring humanity fall into one category or the other, the misled or the misleader. In the light of the succeeding verses, the author may have particularly in mind the leaders of nations and the masses of the people who suffer alike from error in policy. Moral error is not necessarily excluded, but is not primarily intended.

17–25. There is no reason to take these allusions to the destruction of nations and the humiliation and exile of kings, priests, and nobles as a specific reference to the fate of Israel or Judah. Other nations, both before and after, suffered similar fates.

17a. MT has "He makes counselors go stripped," but this disturbs the parallelism with the following line and also is repeated in 19a. On the basis of LXX, and in keeping with the companion line, we read with Duhm *yô'ăṣê 'ereṣ yĕsakkēl*.

18. The Hebrew of 18a has *mûsar*, "discipline," which could be read *môsēr*, "band/bond," as with the Targ. and Vulg. The idiom "loose the bonds" occurs in Isa lii 2 and Ps cxvi 16 and refers to the liberation of prisoners. In xxxix 5 the expression is applied to the

wild ass's freedom from restraint. The present context, however, has to do with the reversal of the fortunes of the great and contrast between their former glory and latter humiliation. It does not seem likely that the figure here is of the liberation of captive kings and the restoration of their honor by having a girdle placed on their loins. The opposite seems the more likely, that kings are stripped of their royal robes and led away naked or with only a loincloth to cover them. Blommerde changes *wayye'sōr* to *wayyĕ'assēr,* construed as a privative Pi'ēl, "and loosens the girdle from their loins."

19. The word rendered "well-established" (*'êṯānîm*) means "perpetual" and is usually applied to streams of water that never run dry. Here, in parallelism with priests, it must mean "nobles," those of inherited status whose position is as secure as human contrivance can make it. The hereditary priesthood is an example of this sort of guaranteed status, but the word probably refers to classes other than the priesthood. Vulg. renders here *optimates.* The word is not used in this sense elsewhere. In Jer v 15 the term is applied to an ancient nation of conquerors.

20a. The "confident" may refer to royal counselors who need to be ever ready with some word of advice. Dahood (*Psalms II,* first NOTE on Ps lviii 2) would read, instead of *lĕne'ĕmānîm, ln 'ămûnîm* and connect the form with the *ammounēis,* "learned priests," mentioned by Philo of Byblos. The resultant form of the preposition *ln* has a parallel in Ugaritic; cf. UHP 10.11, p. 30.

speech. Literally "lip," as in Gen xi 1; Isa xix 18.

21a. Ps cvii 40a coincides verbatim with 21a and Ps cvii 40b is verbatim with 24b. The combination of 21a and 24b would make good sense in the present context and 24b could very well be spared where it now stands.

21b. On the problems of this verse occasioned by the usual meaning of *'ăp̄îqîm,* "water channels," cf. the NOTE in previous editions of this work. A. Guillaume (p. 91) has dispelled the difficulty by relating the word to Ar. *'afiqa,* "excellent" (cited already in BDB) and *'ufuq,* "noble qualities," thus offering an excellent parallel to the preceding *nĕḏîḇîm,* "princes."

22. This verse is obviously misplaced. Some critics would insert it after xi 9, but it does not fit very well there. Those who would retain it take it to refer to conspiracies which God suddenly unmasks. It seems clear that the verse refers to God's control of darkness and the netherworld and perhaps alludes to some cosmic myth.

24–25. Guillaume refers these verses to the depredations of the Chaldean troops of Nabonidus against the inhabitants of Tema during his sojourn there, 552–542 B.C. The author of the book, in Guillaume's view, was a victim as well as a witness of the maltreatment described here.

24a. *leaders.* Literally "chiefs of the people of the land." LXX, however, omits "people" which reduces the excess length of the line without changing the sense; cf. xii 2a on the term "people of the land."

24b. Cf. xii 21b. The word here rendered "waste," *tōhû,* is in Gen i 2 applied to primeval chaos, but in Deut xxxii 10 is used of the desert. Here it could mean either "confusion" or "desert."

25. Cf. v 14; Ps cvii 27; Isa xix 14, xxiv 20.

13. JOB'S REPLY (*continued*)
(xiii 1–27)

XIII 1 "Lo, my eye has seen all this,
My ear has heard and understood it.
2 I know as much as you know;
I am not inferior to you.
3 Rather would I speak with Shaddai,
I wish to remonstrate with God.
4 But you are daubers of deceit,
Quack healers, all of you.
5 I wish you would keep strictly silent.
That would be wisdom for you.
6 Hear, now, my argument,
The plea of my lips attend.
7 Is it for God's sake you speak evil,
For him that you utter deceit?
8 Will you show partiality for him,
Will you contend for God?
9 Will it be well when he probes you?
Can you trick him as men are tricked?
10 He will rebuke you severely,
If you covertly curry favor.
11 Will not his fear overwhelm you,
And his dread fall upon you?
12 Your maxims are ashen aphorisms,
Defenses of clay your defenses.
13 Be silent before me that I may speak,
Then come upon me what may.
14 I take my flesh in my teeth,
My throat I put in my hand.

15 He may slay me, I'll not quaver.
I will defend my conduct to his face.
16 This might even be my salvation,
For no impious man would face him.
17 Listen closely to my speech,
My declaration be in your ears.
18 See, now, I set forth my case.
I know I will be acquitted.
19 Who will contend with me?
I would then be silent and expire.
20 Two things only do not do to me,
Then I will not hide from your face.
21 Remove your pressure from me,
Let your dread not dismay me.
22 Then challenge and I will answer;
Or let me speak and you reply.
23 How many are my iniquities and sins?
Tell me my offense and my sin.
24 Why do you hide your face,
And treat me as a foe?
25 Will you harry a driven leaf?
Will you chase withered chaff?
26 That you write bitter things against me,
Make me inherit the iniquities of my youth,
27 Put my feet in fetters,
Make prints on the soles of my feet,
To mark all my paths."

Notes

xiii 1a. *all this*. The Hebrew has "all" and LXX has "these (things)." The original reading may have been "all this."

2b. A repetition of xii 3b.

3. The word rendered "remonstrate" is a juridical term meaning to "reason, argue, reprove," etc.; cf. xxiii 7 and Isa i 18.

4. Cf. Ps cxix 69. Tur-Sinai would derive the word *šeqer*, "falsehood,

deceit," from an original meaning "paint." Instead of curing the patient, the quack doctor smears on red (?) paint to simulate the glow of health. In Isa iii 16 the belles of Jerusalem are condemned for walking about with their eyes *mĕśaqqĕrôṯ* which is usually taken to mean "glancing wantonly," or the like. It may be, as Tur-Sinai suggests, that the meaning is rather "with painted eyes." The word *mascara* may be derived from this Semitic root; cf. Syr. *sĕqar*, "smear paint." In any case, Job's meaning is clear. The "friends" are glossing over the ugly truth, trying, as it were, to whitewash God.

5. Job rebukes his hecklers with an adage which has analogues in many languages; cf. Prov xvii 28,

> The silent fool is deemed wise,
> who keeps his mouth shut, intelligent.

Si tacuisses, philosophus mansisses.

6–19. Before he turns to plead his case with God, Job has a few more words to say to his "friends." They are doing God no service in lying to defend him. They should beware lest their attempt to cajole and curry favor with God should cause him to turn on them. He asks his hecklers to keep quiet and listen attentively to his plea to God. He is willing to risk his life and stake his case on his integrity, confident that God will recognize his sincerity.

6. The word rendered "argument," *tôḵaḥaṯ*, is from the same root as the verb rendered "remonstrate" in vs. 3. LXX adds in 6a "of my mouth" which makes perfect parallelism with "of my lips" in the following line, but this is hardly the original reading. It is usually the second line that expands or contracts the parallel for artistic variation. The word rendered "plea," *rîḇôṯ*, is also a juridical term; cf. Deut xvii 8.

8. *show partiality*. The Hebrew idiom is literally "lift up the face." The phrase has often the sinister implication of showing partiality in consideration of a *quid pro quo*, such as a bribe, Deut x 17; Prov xviii 5, or desire to curry favor, xxxii 21, xxxiv 19. The expression is also used of divine partiality, as in xlii 8 and Gen iv 7 (with omission of "face").

10. The idiom here rendered "curry favor" is the same as "show partiality" in vs. 8a.

11a. *fear*. The word *śĕ'ēṯ* is usually interpreted as "majesty, excellence" from the verb *nāśā'*, "lift, carry," but context and parallelism here and elsewhere indicate the sense of "fear, terror"; cf. xxxi 23, xli 17. The word is apparently related to *šô'āh* in the same sense in Ps xxxv 8; Prov iii 25. It may be, as Tur-Sinai suggests, that the word is to be derived from a root *š'y* meaning "to fear." Ibn Ezra understood the word to mean "fire" on the basis of the similar word apparently meaning "fire/smoke signal" in Judg xx 40.

12. *maxims.* The word *zikrôn* usually has the meaning of "memorial," or the like. Here, however, it seems to refer to the arguments which the friends have put forth, time-honored, but bankrupt notions. The word rendered "defenses," *gab*(*b*), means "protuberances," or the like, and in xv 26 is used of the bosses of a shield, hence the common interpretation. In Rabbinic literature, however, the verb *gābab* is used of raking leaves and straw. In the Talmud, Yoma 76a, it is said in an argument, "How long will you rake up (*mĕgabbēb*) trifles?" Accordingly, A. Cohen (AJSL 40 [1923–24], 165) renders, "Like useless bits of clay is your array of arguments." Another possibility is to relate the word to Ar. *j*(*w*)*b,* "answer," as with Guillaume, "Your replies are dusty answers." In any case, it is clear from the context that the reference is to argumentation.

13a. Again, as in vs. 5, Job asks his hecklers to keep silent.

13b. Cf. II Sam xviii 22.

14a. The verse is introduced by the words *'al-māh,* "Upon what? . . . Why?" These words, however, are clearly dittography of the last two words of the preceding verse and are generally expunged or ignored. Dahood, NWPSJ, p. 58, retained the *'al-māh,* construing it as *'ôlām* plus the adverbial *āh,* "Forever will I take my flesh in my teeth, And put my life in my hand." The expression "take one's flesh in one's teeth" does not occur elsewhere and its meaning can only be guessed at. Rashi understood it to mean "to afflict myself and force myself to silence." Tur-Sinai also interprets it in this way, taking "flesh" here to mean "tongue." Some commentators see here the metaphor of a wild beast at bay that takes its prey in its teeth. The expression is taken to mean simply to risk one's life: this is supported by the parallel line which is a well-attested idiom, Judg xii 3; I Sam xix 5, xxviii 21; Ps cxix 109.

14b. The expression may be related to the Akkadian terms *napištam lapātum,* "to touch the throat," and *lipit napištim,* "touching of the throat," used in the Mari Letters in connection with treaties. Cf. J. M Munn-Rankin, "Diplomacy in Western Asia in the Early Second Millennium B.C.," *Iraq* 18 (1956), 68–110. It is not clear whether the act of touching the throat symbolized strangulation or cutting the throat, but it is best understood as a symbolic act representing the jeopardy of one's life as sanction in an oath.

15a. The KJ rendering of this verse is one of the most famous lines of the OT and countless sermons have been based on this text "Though he slay me, yet will I trust in him." This utterance has been hailed as the quintessence of the Hebrew spirit of faith as contrasted with the sullen acquiescence of the pagan philosophers. This sort of blind faith in God is expressed in some of the Psalms, notably lxxiii 25–26, but there is no real basis for it in these words of Job. This interpretation derives from an ingenious emendation by the Masoretes who suggest that the reading should be *lô* spelled with the vocalic consonant *wāw*, rather than *'ālep̄* which stands in the text. According to Rashi, the sense is "though he slay me, I will not be separated from him, but will constantly hope for him." Both the consonantal text and the context support the opposite sense.

At the risk of death, which is what he hopes for, or expects anyhow, Job will defend, argue, plead his innocence before God. His concern is not with his life, to be delivered from his suffering or restored to prosperity, but to maintain his integrity and be vindicated before God and man.

Dahood, *Psalms I*, fourth NOTE on Ps xxii 30, takes *l'* in this passage and elsewhere as *lē'*, a stative participle from the root *l'y*, meaning "victor," and would render the present verse, "If the Victor should slay me, I will yet hope; indeed, I will defend my conduct to his face." The LXX reading *ho dynastēs* appears to support Dahood's interpretation of *l'* as a divine title.

16. Job takes hope for a moment in the thought that his very boldness in confronting God might be the means of salvation for him. God would surely know that no hypocrite would have the courage to face him.

17. Again Job calls on his opponents to pay close attention to his oration. The imperative is emphasized by the infinitive absolute, hence the various renderings, "diligently, carefully," "hear, O hear." Job appears to be preparing his interlocutors for the direct plea to God which comes in vss. 20 ff. The noun rendered "declaration" is an apparent Aramaism not found elsewhere in the OT, as Ibn Ezra noted, although the verb is used in xv 17, xxxii 6, 10, 17, xxxvi 2, and Ps xix 3.

18a. The verb here rendered "set forth" is usually applied to the arranging of objects, as wood on an altar, Gen xxii 9, food on a table, Ps xxiii 5, and frequently of military array. Its use in reference to an argument, a word battle, as it were, is found only in Job, here and in xxiii 4, xxxii 14, xxxiii 5 and xxxvii 19, with omission of the implied object in xxxiii 5 and xxxvii 19.

18b. *acquitted.* Cf. xi 2; Isa xliii 9, 26. Job pleads again for a fair hearing and trial, although he realizes that it is not possible to bring his opponent into court or to arbitration; cf. ix 16, 33.

19a. *Who will contend with me?* This may be the opening formula of a plaintiff; cf. the almost identical words in Isa l 8 where the servant of Yahweh challenges his adversary to come into court.

19b. The exact import of this line is uncertain. It has usually been taken to mean that if his guilt were proved in a fair trial, he would be content to accept the verdict and expire in silent resignation.

20. In the rest of the speech Job addresses God directly. He has, however, two requests to make at the outset in order to make it possible for him to face God.

21. *pressure.* MT has here "your hand," *kappĕḵā,* and in the following line the corresponding element is *'ēmāṯĕkā,* "your dread/terror." Dahood, on the basis of parallelism, would change the word *'ēmāh,* "terror," to *'ammāh,* "arm" (cf. *Psalms II,* fifth NOTE on Ps xci 4). Rashi found it difficult to accept MT *kappĕḵā* here since the word *kap̄* is used only in a beneficent sense, as in Exod xxxiii 22. Accordingly, Rashi read *'aḵpĕḵā,* "your pressure," on the basis of xxxiii 7b, *'aḵpî,* "my pressure." In xxxiii 7, Elihu actually paraphrases Job's words in the present passage and explicitly reminds Job of other similar things he had heard him say. The verb *'kp* is used in Prov xvi 26 of the pressure of hunger that drives a man to work. In the Talmud *'aḵpā* is used in the sense of "weight," or "load," as of stones used to protect sheaves from blowing away, and the term is also applied to a contrivance for carrying a load. In Syriac the word has the sense of urgency, care, necessity, again a sort of pressure. Ar. *'ikāf* designates a saddle. With Rashi, one should read *'aḵpĕḵā* instead of *kappĕḵā,* and to retain MT *'ammāṯĕḵā* to comport with *kappĕḵā.* The word *'ammāh,* "forearm, cubit, ell," is used in the Bible only as a measurement of length, but Ugar. *amt* is used of the cubit and also a couple of times of the forearm or elbow, with reference to ritual handwashing up to the elbow or shoulder; it is not attested as designating the instrument of power in either Ugaritic or the Bible. In post-biblical usage *'ammāh* is applied to the arm-pit and is also used as a euphemism for the penis. If the word *'ammāh* originally stood in Ps xci 4c, it is easy to see why it would have been changed; the mere change of vocalization, however, does not prevent the carnal-minded from seeing the possibility of a pun.

22. Job offers his divine opponent the choice of roles and determination of procedure. God may choose to be either appellant or respondent, it makes no difference to Job, so long as he agrees to come into court. The expression "call and I will answer" is used again in xiv 15a, but in a very different context and sense; cf. Isa lviii 9. In xxxviii 3 it is Yahweh who arraigns Job and does not give him the choice of role; cf. also xlii 4, which is out of place.

23. In the absence of a response from God, Job takes the initiative. He challenges God to bring a bill of indictment against him, with charges and specifications.

24a. The idiom "hide the face," as indicated by the parallelism of the following line, means to be unfriendly, hostile; cf. Deut xxxi

17; Pss xxvii 9, xxx 8(7), xliv 25, lxxxviii 15, civ 29; Isa liv 8, lvii 17.

24b. Cf. xxxiii 10.

25. Job accuses God of brutal harassment of a helpless creature. The verb rendered "harry," *'rṣ*, carries a connotation of ruthless violence. The withering leaf is often used of the destruction of the wicked, Isa i 30, xxxiv 4, lxiv 5(6); Jer viii 13; Ezek xlvii 12; Ps i 3, and so also wind-driven chaff, Pss i 4, lxxxiii 14, but the use of both leaf and chaff in the sense of a helpless and insignificant victim of such overwhelming power occurs nowhere else in the OT. By implication, Job taunts God with using irresistible power against a victim incapable of resistance.

26. *bitter things.* Both Rashi and Ibn Ezra take the word *mĕrôrôṯ* in the sense of rebelliousness rather than bitterness. It has been suggested that the figure is that of the prescription of bitter medicine. While we have no evidence of written prescriptions for individual cases among the Hebrews, we have Egyptian medical texts with diagnoses and standard prescriptions, and from Ugarit we have texts of standard prescriptions for ailing horses. It is not a matter of medicine for healing, in any case. One may think of the curses which the priest wrote and dissolved in bitter liquid and administered to the suspected adulteress, Num v 23–24. Tur-Sinai assumes that the translator of the original Aramaic mistook the word *mērĕṯā'*, "inheritance," for *mārāṯā'*, "bitter things," and takes the line to mean "For thou assignest to me an inheritance." He then takes 26b to refer to the sins of Job's children rather than the sins of his own youth. Ingenious as this interpretation is, it is quite unconvincing. Job's children may have sinned, as Job feared they might (cf. i 5), and Bildad even suggested that their fate was merited (viii 4); but even Bildad did not suggest that Job's punishment was for his children's sins. The usual interpretation seems the most likely one, that Job here admits of some youthful indiscretions (cf. Ps xxv 7), but does not think it fair for God to go back so far to find cause against him. Surely the sins of his youth were not serious enough to merit such punishment now. Dahood (NWSPJ, pp. 59–60), followed by Blommerde, took the word here to designate "acts of violence" and understood the metaphor as commercial, "For you write against my account acts of violence."

27a. The word for "fetters" here is not the same as in Jer xx 2 f., xxix 26; II Chron xvi 10. The word here (*saḏ*) occurs elsewhere in the OT only in Elihu's citation of Job's words, xxxiii 11. The Aramaic form of the word occurs in the Talmud with the meaning of "stocks."

27b. If Job's feet were in fetters, he would make no tracks to be watched. The suggestion that "lime," *sîḏ*, be read instead of *saḏ*, "fetters," is on the assumption, presumably, that the victim's tracks would then be easy to follow. The word "paths" may mean here, as elsewhere, "conduct, behavior."

27c. Slaves were identified by markings on various parts of the body, sometimes on the forehead, usually on the hands (cf. Isa xliv 5, xlix 16) and also apparently on the soles of the feet. A design on the soles of the feet would make tracking of a runaway slave easier. Perhaps 27b should be read after 27c, as a final (purpose) clause.

[Verse xiii 28 is transposed after xiv 2 (Sec. 14). See NOTE ad loc.]

14. JOB'S REPLY (*concluded*)
(xiv 1–2; xiii 28; xiv 3–22)

XIV 1 "Man born of woman,
Short-lived and sated with strife.
2 Like a flower he comes forth, then withers;
Like a shadow he flits never staying.
[XIII 28 He withers like a rotten thing,
Like a moth-eaten garment.]
XIV 3 And on such would you turn your gaze,
Bring me into judgment with yourself?
4 [Who can produce clean from unclean? No one.]
5 His days indeed are determined;
The sum of his months you control.
You have set him limits he cannot exceed.
6 Look away from him, relent;
Let him enjoy his hireling day.
7 A tree, though cut down, has hope;
It may continue and its suckers not cease.
8 Though its root grow old in the ground,
And its stump die in the dust,
9 At the scent of water it will sprout
And put forth shoots like a seedling.
10 But man dies and is helpless;
A human expires and where is he?
11 Water fails from a lake,
A river parches and dries up,
12 And man lies down and never rises.
They wake not till the heavens decay;
They rouse not from their sleep.

13 O that you would hide me in Sheol,
Conceal me till your anger pass,
Then set me a time and remember me.
14 If a man dies, may he live again?
All my weary days I would endure,
Till my relief come.
15 You would call me and I would answer;
You would care for the work of your hands.
16 Then you would [not] count my steps,
Nor be alert for my sins.
17 My guilt would be sealed in a bundle,
You would coat over my iniquity.
18 But mountains topple and crumble,
Rock moves from its place.
19 Water wears away stone,
Torrents sweep away earth's soil,
And you destroy man's hope.
20 You overwhelm him forever and he passes;
You change his visage and send him away.
21 His sons achieve honor, but he never knows;
They are disgraced, but he perceives not.
22 Only his own flesh pains him,
And his own soul mourns itself."

NOTES

xiv. This passage is sometimes regarded as an independent poem. It is similar in tone to chapter vii, but there the emphasis is on human misery and here on the brevity of human life. In vss. 1–13 Job laments the condition of humanity in general, identifying his personal misfortune with that of all mankind. In vss. 14–17 he turns momentarily to his concern for himself, but then in the remainder of the poem generalizes on the fate of humanity at large.

1a. There is here a note of both contempt and pity for man's condition. Conception and birth often arouse mixed feelings of wonder (cf. x 10) and disgust (cf. Pirqe Abot iii 1). The conception of man from a malodorous drop of semen in the heat of passion and birth with its blood and messiness gives man a taint of uncleanness from the start; cf. xv 14, xxv 4b; Ps li 7. Christian exegetes have seen in this passage an allusion to original sin, but the concern is perhaps more with physical and ritual uncleanness.

1b. Even the longest life (cf. xlii 16; Gen xxxv 29, xlvii 28) is all too brief; cf. Ps xc 9–10.

strife. Cf. iii 17, 26 where the same word (*rōḡez*) occurs.

2a. *Like a flower*. Cf. Pss xxxvii 2, xc 6, ciii 15; Isa xxviii 1, 4, xl 6; James i 10, 11; I Pet i 24.

comes forth. Dahood (NWSPJ, p. 60) related the verb to *wḍ'*, "shine," in order to create a wordplay with *ṣîṣ*, "flower," "blossom," which is related to the root *ṣ(w)ṣ*, "shine," setting up a contrast with "shadow" in the following colon.

2b. *Like a shadow*. Cf. viii 9; Ps cxliv 4; Eccles vi 12. A common figure in literature—"Life's but a walking shadow" (*Macbeth*); ". . . what shadows we are, and what shadows we pursue" (Burke); "And I myself the shadow of a dream" (Tennyson, "The Princess").

xiii 28. This verse is obviously out of place. It fits fairly well after xiv 2 and so I venture to transpose it.

rotten thing. The noun *rāqāḇ* designates "decay" or "rot," as applied to bone rot in Prov xii 4, xiv 30; Hab iii 16. In Hos v 12 the word stands in parallelism with *'āš*, "moth." The verb is applied to wood in Isa xl 20. In Aramaic *ruqbā* designates a leather bottle and Syr. used that word here; similarly LXX, *isa askō*. Guillaume rendered "like a wine skin that wears out" and cited a double connection with Arabic, *muraqqab* as applied to a piece of hide such as would make a wine skin, and *raqbat* as designating a skin tied at the neck with strips of skin. Wine skins, of course, rot and tear, and may be mended (cf. Josh ix 4), but the use of old skins is unwise (cf. Matt ix 17). It may be that the poet intended the specific sense "wine skin" as parallel to a moth-eaten garment, or at least to suggest the wordplay on *ruqb*, "wine skin," and *rāqāb*, "decay." It seems best, with Targ. and Vulg., to follow MT *rāqāḇ*, "rot," rather than to read *rōqeḇ*, "wine skin."

xiv 3. It is unworthy of God to concern himself with such a frail, ephemeral, and insignificant creature who has no means of defense; cf. Ps cxliii 2.

4. This verse, if genuine, is out of place. Some scholars regard it as a marginal comment mistakenly introduced into the text. It is apropos of vs. 1 that from an unclean thing (woman) no clean thing can be expected. The second part of the line, with only two short words, literally "not one," is entirely too short. Targ. adds, "except God." Vulg. takes a similar line, "Is it not you alone?", i.e., God. The various modern emendations are scarcely worthy of serious notice. It seems better to delete

or bracket the verse. Blommerde read the negative *lô'* as the alleged divine title *lē'* which Dahood translates as "the Victor" (cf. *Psalms II,* pp. xxiii, second NOTE on Ps lxxv 7, first NOTE on Ps lxxxv 7) and Blommerde as "the Mighty One,"

Who can make the impure clean?
The Mighty One alone.

This interpretation was suggested to Blommerde by Vulg., *Nonne tu qui solus est,* and Targ. "none except God."

5a. The line is a trifle short and some slight addition seems to be called for. LXX adds "on earth."

5b. *you control.* Literally "are with you."

6a. Cf. vii 19, x 20. The received text has "that he may cease," but it seems better to take the form as imperative, with God understood as subject, as does the Qere of x 20a. Blommerde takes his cue from P. Calderone's treatment of the verb *ḥdl* II, "to be fat, fill oneself with food, to be prosperous" (CBQ 23 [1961], 451–60; 24 [1962], 412–19) and construes the preposition *'d* as a noun *'ōḏ,* "lifetime," to which he adds the possessive suffix *-y,* "his," and rearranges the lines to produce the following:

Look away from him
that he may enjoy his lifetime
that he may be pleased with his day like a labourer.

The supposed improvement scarcely repays the effort.

6b. *enjoy.* Hardly the appropriate word for the hireling's lot; cf. vii 1. The sense is that he should be allowed to make the best of his short life without having it made more difficult by God's constant surveillance. Unlike Milton who resolved to live "as ever in my great Taskmaster's eye," Job wishes God would simply leave him alone.

7–9. Wetzstein reported that east of the Jordan and especially around Damascus dying trees were renewed by cutting them off close to the ground so that in the following year new shoots would sprout from the stump and subsequently bear fruit (F. Delitzsch, *Das Buch Hiob,* 1876, I, p. 245).

10–12. Again, as in vii 7–10, Job expresses the standard OT view, shared by his friends. There is no afterlife worthy of the name. The torpor of the shades in the netherworld cannot be regarded as life.

10a. *helpless.* The verb *ḥlš* is used transitively in Exod xvii 13, Isa xiv 12, of weakening or defeating, but here intransitively, of being weak or helpless. The noun in the pattern of nomen profession, *ḥallāš,* "weakling," in contrast to *gibbôr,* "strong man, hero." In Exod xxxii 18 the passive participle *ḥălûšāh,* "defeat," is used as the antonym of *gĕbûrāh,* "victory." I. Eitan (*A Contribution to Biblical Lexicography,* Columbia University

Press, 1924, pp. 42 ff.) related *ḥlš* to Ar. *ḥalaša*, "reap with a sickle," but the normal permutation of the sibilant militates against this. There is no real difficulty here, since the three verbs in sequence *yāmûṯ, wayyeḥĕlāš, wayyigwa'* all refer to the act of dying.

11. The second line of this verse is identical with Isa xix 5b, but the contexts of the two passages are altogether different.

12b. Cf. Pss lxxii 5, 7, 17, lxxxix 30, 37, cii 27; Isa xxxiv 4, li 6. In Sophocles' *Electra* the Chorus sings:

> But from the all-receptive lake of Death you shall not raise him,
> groan and pray as you will.

(*Complete Greek Tragedies*, II, p. 337, lines 138 f.)

wake. The verbs which precede and follow *yāqîṣû* suggest that it is to be connected with the root **yqẓ*, "be awake." The form is perfect, to be read *yāqēṣû*, since the imperfect would be *yîqāṣû*. G. R. Driver (VTS, III [1960], p. 77) appealed to Ar. *q(w)ḍ*, "burst," "so long as the heavens do not burst." The following line Driver then had to reject as a gloss provoked by the glossator's misunderstanding of the double negations *biltî* and *lô'*. The misunderstanding, however, lies elsewhere. The subject of the plural verbs is not the heavens but man(kind). There is, accordingly, no need to construe the verbs as singular and explain the *u* endings of *yāqîṣû* and *yē'ōrû* as the old indicative modal endings, as does Blommerde.

decay. Reading with the versions (except Targ.) *bĕlōṯ*, "wasting away," instead of the negative particle *biltî*.

12c. Blommerde construed the verbs, *yāqîṣû* and *yĕ'ōrû* as singular and thus had to get rid of the plural suffix of *miššĕnātām*, "from their sleep," by taking it as the enclitic *-m*, "from sleep."

13–15. Job here gropes toward the idea of an afterlife. If only God would grant him asylum in the netherworld, safe from the wrath which now besets him, and then appoint him a time for a new and sympathetic hearing, he would be willing to wait or even to endure the present evil.

13. Isa xxvi 20 calls ironically on the people of Judah to hide in their chambers till Yahweh's wrath be past, and Amos ix 2 ff. pictures the wicked as trying vainly to hide in Sheol, heaven, Mount Carmel, the bottom of the sea.

14a. *again*. There is no explicit element representing the idea "again," but it is implicit in the situation.

14b. *my weary days*. Literally "days of my warfare"; cf. vii 1.

14c. *relief*. The word here in Hebrew is cognate with the term "caliphate," and has the meanings "change, exchange, alteration, succession." The renderings "relief" or "release" are quite appropriate to this context.

Job is thinking of relief or release from his troubles as a soldier or slave might think of release from his service.

15b. God's attitude would be different from that which Job charges he had hitherto displayed toward the creature of his hands; cf. x 3, 9–13. The verb rendered "care" has the sense "be or become pale" (the color of silver) from desire or longing, Gen xxxi 30; Ps lxxxiv 3(2), or shame, Zeph ii 1 (cf. Isa xxix 22). In Ps xvii 12 it is used of a lion longing to pounce on its prey.

16. The two halves of this verse are not congruent. The almost identical verse in xxxi 4 shows that both lines have to agree, that one cannot be positive and the other negative. The context indicates that Job is still referring to the future which he hopes will bring a change in God's attitude. Thus it seems preferable, following the Syriac reading, to insert the negative particle in 16a to make the two lines agree in sense. Job has complained in vii 12, 19 of God's constant surveillance. Now, he hopes for less vigilance and more leniency.

17. The reference in this and the preceding verse is clearly to the recording, registration, and accounting of Job's transgressions. The "bundle" Tur-Sinai understood as relating to the tying and sealing of papyrus documents. Instruments thus bound and sealed were legally inaccessible to persons unauthorized to break the seal, and the content of the document could not be known until it was opened; cf. Dan vii 10. The "bundle" (of the living), I Sam xxv 29, would thus be the equivalent of the "book(s)" in the celestial accounting; cf. Exod xxxii 32; Isa iv 3; Mal iii 16; Ps lxix 29; Dan xii 1; Luke x 20; Heb xii 23; Rev iii 5, xiii 8, xvii 8, xx 12, xxi 27.

New light on ancient methods of accounting has been shed by the cuneiform documents excavated at Kerkuk, ancient Nuzi. A. Leo Oppenheim, "On an Operational Device in Mesopotamian Bureaucracy," JNES 18 (1959), 121–28, has plausibly explained allusions to stones representing sheep and goats in Nuzi documents as reflecting a system of accounting. One such document, so far unique, is an ovoid clay pouch with an inscription on the outside listing stones referring to forty-eight sheep and goats of various kinds and conditions. When originally discovered, the pouch contained forty-eight small pebbles. The purpose of the instrument, apparently, was to transfer the items listed to different accounts, the tally stones being accompanied by written instructions as to their distribution. Oppenheim's study of the terminology applied to the stones referring to sheep and goats in the Nuzi documents indicates that the stones were "deposited," "removed," or "transferred" in, from, or to various receptacles to represent the actual movements or change in status of the animals in question. A series of receptacles must have been kept for pebbles representing every category of animals, so that when an animal died, was lost, or stolen, used for food, sacrifice, or transferred for shearing, pebbles representing each animal could be added, removed, or transferred to the appropriate containers. When young were born, pebbles would be added to appropriate containers for lambs/kids, male/female. By this simple operational device a constant and instant inventory would be available on the state and distribution of flocks. This system has some advantages even over written records and may be used in conjunction with written accounts. Various uses of this device still persist in the Near East. P. Delougaz recalled an instance that occurred at Kerkuk about the time of the discovery of the aforementioned clay receptacle. A servant of the Nuzi expedition was sent to the market to buy chickens and when the chickens he bought in town were accidentally mixed with those kept in the expedition courtyard, he was able to sort out the fowl and the finances by pebbles he had used to represent each purchase (Oppenheim, JNES 18 (1959), 123). The present writer observed a similar device employed by a gateman in Jerusalem who kept account of the guests attending social functions by dropping a pebble in his pocket for each guest. An elaborate system of this sort was used in the West African kingdom of Dahomey in the eighteenth and nineteenth centuries for census records, pebbles in different sacks indicating the number, sex, age group, births, deaths, change of status from boy to man, etc. Even the British exchequer reportedly used tally sticks along with its pen, ink, and paper bookkeeping as late as the early nineteenth century.

O. Eissfeldt, "Der Beutel der Lebendigen, alttestamentliche Erzählungs und Dichtungsmotive in Lichte neuer Nuzi-texte" (*Berichte über die Verhandlungen der Sächsischen Akademie der Wissenschaften zu Leipzig,* Philologisch-historische Klasse, Band 105, Heft 6, Berlin, 1960), has related the Mesopotamian evidence adduced by Oppenheim to the OT allusions to the "bundle of the living." While there is no trace in the OT of the use of counting stones kept in a bag, the words of Abigail to David, I Sam xxv 29, imply that the "bundle of the living" was thought of as containing stones which represented the living, or those destined for life: "If men rise up to pursue you and seek your life, the life of my lord shall be bound in the bundle of the living [which is] with Yahweh your god; but the life of your enemies he will sling out [as it were] from the hollow of a sling." The figure is not of a bag of slingstones which are collected only to be hurled away, or of lot stones to be shaken out, but rather of tally stones for accounting. The removal of stones from the bundle of the living, casting them violently away as with a sling, is the equivalent of blotting names from the book of the living, Ps lxix 29.

It is not clear whether Job's transgressions are represented as tallied by means of pebbles in a receptacle or bundle, or written on papyrus or leather, or whether they are sealed in order to be hidden away and forgotten, or filed for future reference (cf. Isa viii 16). The question depends in part on the interpretation of the preceding verse, but no matter what the recording system, Job does not admit guilt commensurate with his suffering and he hopes for a fair accounting eventually.

19b. *torrents.* Whether reading with MT *sĕp̄îḥehā* or emending to *sĕḥipāh,* on the basis of Ar. *saḥîfah,* "rainstorm," and Akk. *saḫāpu,* "overturn," "devastate," the sense is clear. The versions do not reflect the possessive suffix on the word, and Blommerde, on the ground that there is no clear antecedent for the suffix, reads *sĕp̄îaḥ-yāh,* construing *yāh* as the "intensifying element," "a mighty torrent." The present writer remains dubious about the existence of this element, even in the case of *šalhebetyāh* of Song of Songs viii 6.

20a. *forever.* D. W. Thomas (JSS 1 [1956], 107) interpreted *nēṣaḥ* here as superlative, "thou prevailest utterly against him." It is not clear whether it relates to the verb which precedes or follows and the translation retains deliberately the word order of the original. In the nature of the case, the action is superlative, extreme and permanent.

passes. The general verb for going is here used as a euphemistic substitute for dying. The destination is the netherworld, the land of no return; cf. x 21; II Sam xii 23; Eccles i 4, iii 20; Ps xxxix 13(14).

20b. *change his visage.* Ibn Ezra understood this to refer to *rigor mortis.* Tur-Sinai's radical reinterpretation, "his yearly contract hath expired and thou dismisseth him," can itself be dismissed.

21. The dead in the netherworld have no knowledge; cf. Eccles ix 5. Job generalizes on the fate of mankind which he is to share. The reference to children is not inconsistent with the Prologue, i 9, for Job is not thinking of his own children but of other men's.

22. Although man is deprived of knowledge by death, he is still subject to pain. The flesh is gnawed by Death's first-born, xviii 13. The worm and fire ravage the body, Isa lxvi 24, and the victims feel it and wail forever, Judith xvi 16.

15. ELIPHAZ'S SECOND DISCOURSE
(xv 1–35)

XV 1 Eliphaz the Temanite answered:

2 "Ought a wise man to answer with wind,
Fill his belly with sirocco?
3 Argue with useless talk,
With words utterly worthless?
4 You even subvert religion,
And deprecate devotion toward God.
5 Your guilt prompts your mouth,
You choose a crafty tongue.
6 Your own mouth condemns you—not I;
Your own lips testify against you.
7 Are you the first man ever born,
Were you brought forth before the hills?
8 Do you eavesdrop on the divine council,
Do you hold a monopoly on wisdom?
9 What do you know that we do not know,
Or understand, and not we too?
10 We have the grayheaded and aged with us,
Older even than your father.
11 Are God's consolations too little for you,
The word that treats you gently?
12 What has taken from you your mind,
Why have your eyes become dim,
13 That you vent your ire 'gainst God,
Spouting words from vour mouth?
14 How can man be innocent,
One born of woman, righteous?

15 Even his angels he distrusts,
The heavens are not pure in his sight.
16 How then one loathsome and foul,
Man who gulps evil like water?
17 I will tell you, listen to me;
What I have seen I will declare,
18 What the sages have said,
What their fathers did not conceal.
19 [To whom alone the land was given,
And no alien passed among them.]
20 The wicked is tormented all his days,
Few years are in store for the oppressor.
21 Terror sounds in his ears,
While at peace the spoiler may assail him.
22 He despairs of return from darkness;
He is sought out for the sword.
23 He wanders as food for vultures,
He knows that his ruin is sure.
24 The dark day terrifies him,
Distress and anguish overwhelm him
Like a king set for attack,
25 Because he lifted his hand against God,
Vaunted himself 'gainst Shaddai.
26 He charges at him with hauberk,
With his thick-bossed shield.
27 He puffed his face with fat,
Bloated his loins with blubber.
28 He will dwell in ruined cities,
Tenantless houses will be his,
Which are ready to go to heaps.
29 He will not be rich, nor his wealth endure,
Nor his possessions reach the netherworld.
30 He will not escape from darkness,
His shoots the flame will wither,
He will pass away by the breath of his mouth.
31 [Let him not confide in vanity, being misled;
For it will be vanity.]

32 His palm withers before its time,
His frond no more flourishes.
33 Like a vine stripped of green grapes,
As an olive tree casts its blossoms.
34 For an impious gang is impotent,
Fire devours the tents of the briber.
35 Pregnant with pain, he gives birth to evil;
Their womb nurtures disappointment."

Notes

xv. Eliphaz's second speech opens the second cycle of the Dialogue. He is much less courteous and less conciliatory than in his previous speech. He now accuses Job of mouthing a lot of hot air and nonsense. He charges him with subversion of piety. He even practices a bit of psychoanalysis, suggesting that Job's protestations are really prompted by (feelings of) guilt. Job's claim to wisdom and his deprecation of the traditions of the ancient sages are deemed sheer arrogance. Whereas, Eliphaz regarded Job at first as an essentially pious man only temporarily and lightly chastised by God, he now sees him as a hardened sinner and rebel against God.

2. A wise man, such as Job claims to be, xii 3, xiii 2, ought to have better arguments. The east wind, the searing sirocco which blows from the desert, would be roughly the equivalent of our expression "hot air." It may also designate what is useless or harmful, Hos xii 1(2). Bildad, viii 2, also characterized Job's word as wind and Zophar meant the same, xi 2, although he does not use the word "wind." "Fill his belly" was understood by Ewald to refer to speeches which come from the belly, the seat of unruly passion, rather than from the heart. The more likely meaning is simply that Eliphaz calls Job a bag of hot air; cf. Virgil's *ventosa lingua* (*Aeneid* xi.390).

3. Cf. xiii 3, 6.

4a. *subvert.* The word in Hebrew means to "frustrate, annul, destroy," or the like. In v 12 I translate "thwart."

religion. Literally "fear." The Hebrew term which most nearly corresponds to what we mean by our term "religion" is "fear [of the Lord]."

4b. *devotion.* The word *śîḥāh* usually means "musing, meditation," as in Ps cxix 97, 99, but with reference to God it has something of the sense of our term devotion as applied to a religious exercise.

5a. *prompts.* This sentence can be read more than one way, as comparison of the versions, ancient and modern, will show. It could be rendered, "your mouth teaches your guilt," or "your guilt teaches your mouth." In accordance with the parallelism of 5b, the latter sense seems preferable. Eliphaz uses a device very popular in our time, that of attempting to discredit an opponent by psychoanalyzing him rather than speaking to his arguments.

Dahood (*Biblica* 44 [1963], 294) construed the verb *yĕ'allēp̄* as denominative from the numeral *'elep̄,* "thousand," and Blommerde rendered accordingly, "For your mouth increases your guilt a thousand fold." It seems better to retain the usual sense "teach," as in xxxiii 33 and xxxv 11.

5b. Job's protestations of innocence, Eliphaz insinuates, are only attempts to hide his guilt.

6. Nothing Job has yet said, except possibly his admission of youthful sins, xiii 26, could be construed as overt admission of guilt. Job, however, has charged that God could and would coerce him into a false confession of guilt, ix 20. Eliphaz's meaning is, apparently, that Job's protests and charges against God are in themselves sinful and tantamount to self-incrimination; cf. II Sam i 16.

7a. The word rendered "man" is *'āḏām,* and some interpreters see here an allusion to the myth of the Primeval Man, known in later Jewish literature as *'āḏām haq-quaḏmôn.* This Primeval Man supposedly eavesdropped on the divine council and appropriated divine wisdom (cf. vs. 8) as Prometheus stole fire from the gods.

7b. Cf. Prov viii 25; Ps xc 2.

8. The idea of the council of the gods goes back to Mesopotamian and Canaanite antecedents. The word here used, *sôḏ,* is one of several designations of the assembly of the gods. Its primary sense is that of intimate, confidential conversation. RSV renders the word "friendship" in Ps xxv 14. Jeremiah (Jer xxiii 18, 22) derides the false prophets who act as if they had stood in the council of Yahweh to hear his word, but actually have no authentic mission or divine word; cf. Ps lxxxix 7(8).

9. Job has made no claim to superior knowledge. He merely criticized the friends' pretensions that they knew God's mind. He denies any inferiority to them in respect to knowledge, xii 3, xiii 2.

10. Eliphaz affirms what he had accused Job of claiming, superiority in wisdom by virtue of seniority. Eliphaz, doubtless referring to himself, asserts that his side boasts members older than Job's father. Job already, xii 12, had denied any necessary connection between senility and sagacity; cf. Wisdom of Solomon iv 8–9. The graybeard Eliphaz is appalled at this damnable heresy.

11. *God's consolations.* What God has done to Job could scarcely be termed consolation. Eliphaz apparently has reference to his attempt to console Job with the doctrine that suffering is never unmerited. This defense of God, to Eliphaz's mind, is as true as if God spoke for himself. Job, however, is far from consoled by the doctrine of the friends

and feels that God himself does not appreciate their effort to defend him at the expense of truth; cf. xiii 7–12 and xvi 2.

12b. The verb used here, *rzm,* does not occur elsewhere in the OT. It is usually connected by metathesis with a root *rmz* which means "to wink or flash the eyes." Some scholars would substitute the verb *r*(*w*)*m,* "be high," "Why are your eyes so lofty?"; cf. Prov vi 17, xxx 13. The interpretation of Tur-Sinai is adopted provisionally, connecting the verb with its Arabic cognate in the sense of "dwindle away, become weak." The failure of eyesight represents loss of perceptiveness.

13. *vent your ire.* Literally "turn your wind/spirit." Cf. Prov xvi 32, xxv 28, xxix 11 for the use of wind/spirit in the sense of anger.

14. Cf. iv 17, ix 2b, xxv 4.

15. *angels.* Literally "holy beings." The angels are conceived as celestial bodies, the astral deities of the pagan cults, degraded to mere members of the heavenly army; cf. iv 18, xxv 5, 6, xxxviii 7; Isa xl 25–26. Eliphaz reverts to the point made in his first speech that even the angels are not without fault before God and how much less can man claim to be innocent. The allusion to the culpability of the angels may refer to the myth of a theomachy in which the defeated gods are punished; cf. II Pet ii 4.

16a. *foul.* This word in Arabic is used of souring of milk, but in the OT is applied only in the moral sense, occurring elsewhere only in Pss xiv 3, liii 3(4).

16b. Man's propensity for sin is as natural as taking a drink of water. This is probably a proverbial saying, but Eliphaz certainly intends it to apply to Job in particular; cf. xxxiv 7.

17–35. Eliphaz expatiates on his favorite theme, the fate of the wicked.

18b. The *m* before *'ā̲b̲ô̲ṯ̲ām,* "their fathers," is to be attached to the end of the preceding verb as the enclitic emphatic particle. The final *-m* of *'āḇôṯām,* which in the previous editions was taken as enclitic emphatic, may better be construed as the possessive suffix; cf. viii 8.

19. This verse has been seized on as a clue to the date of the poem. If the land in question is Canaan, the reference must be to a time when Israel had undisputed control of the land and was supposedly free from foreigners. The event that ended the ancient era has been taken to be either the Fall of Samaria or the Exile of Judah. There is, however, no indication that the poet had either of these events in mind, nor is there any clue as to the period of time that has elapsed. Delitzsch was possibly right in the assumption that Eliphaz has reference to his own land and tribe. Cf. Joel iii(iv) 17 which describes the idyllic future in the same terms as Eliphaz describes the idyllic past.

20. This may be Eliphaz's answer to Job's assertion that robbers prosper, xii 6. Eliphaz claims that in reality the wicked are constantly

in torment (cf. Isa lvii 20–21), and he goes on to describe the tortures of the guilty conscience.

20b. *Few*. Blommerde, following Dahood (*Biblica* 48 [1967], 428 f.) reads *missappēr,* "beyond numbering," for MT *mispar,* "a number," i.e., a few. Blommerde renders:

> The wicked trembles all his days
> for beyond number are the years in store for the oppressor.

It does not help the cause of justice to refer the innumerable days to the netherworld, since no differentiation is made there between the righteous and the wicked. The argument of the friends is that the difference is made on earth, that the wicked are short-lived and miserable, but the days of the righteous are many and happy.

21. The terror that dins in the ears of the wicked man is the product of his own imagination. The wicked flee when no one pursues, Prov xxviii 1. Even in apparent peace and prosperity the wicked man is haunted with forebodings of disaster.

22. *darkness.* Figuratively of misfortune, as in vss. 23, 30, and xix 8. Three of the five words in this verse, exclusive of particles, belong, according to Guillaume, to "an Arabic sphere of influence." The word *ḥōšeḵ,* "darkness," e.g., he says is no real parallel to the "sword" and he suspects that it must mean something else. Accordingly, he cites Ar. *ḥasak* which means "an instrument of iron or wood with sharp points like the prickles of thorns or thistles which was thrown round an encampment in the way of horses or camels." His translation of the verse, however, does not reflect the alleged Arabic influence. The form *ṣāp̄û* is acceptable as it stands as a passive participle of the root *ṣpy,* like *'āsû* in xli 25. There is no need to appeal to Ar. *ṣaffa,* "reserve," "set apart," which would yield the form *ṣāpûp̄.*

23a. The Masoretes vocalized the text so as to yield the sense "He wanders for bread. Where is it?" The rendering there follows LXX which reads *'ayyāh,* "kite/vulture," instead of *'ayyēh,* "where."

23b. Emending *bĕyāḏô,* "in his hand," to *pîḏô,* "his ruin," and, with the LXX, taking the final phrase, "dark day," as the beginning of the following line. The change from *b* to *p* is very slight in the classic Hebrew script and these two letters remain similar throughout the history of the script. The similarity in sound also enhances the possibility of a *memoriter* error.

24. The Masoretic stichometry gives acceptable sense, but 24b is too long for a single line and too short for a double. Taking "dark day" from the preceding verse, and balancing the length of the lines, we get a tricolon which makes excellent sense. Cf. iii 5c.

The word rendered "attack," *kîḏôr,* is not used elsewhere in the OT, but is explained from its Arabic cognate which is applied to the swooping attack of the hawk. The word occurs in Ugaritic (23:10) in association with the generic term for bird, *'ṣr;* cf. xxxix 27b.

25. From a description of the wicked man's apprehension that a divine assault is imminent, Eliphaz switches suddenly to the figure of an attack on God. This is, indeed, a bold metaphor. Tur-Sinai suggests that the reference is to a rebellion and attack by a primeval titan and not to any contemporary evildoer. Be that as it may, Eliphaz's intention is to suggest that this is what Job is doing, rebelling against, and assailing God.

26. *hauberk.* Literally "with neck" which is usually taken to mean with a stiff neck, i.e., insolently, stubbornly. It is also possible to take it in the sense of "headlong." The parallelism of neck and shield, however, suggest a technical term for neck armor and we adopt Tur-Sinai's rendering "hauberk."

27. Literally:

> For he covered his face with his fat
> And made weight [?] upon [the] hip[s].

The accumulation of fat leads to a rebellious spirit; cf. Deut xxxii 15; Jer v 28; Pss lxxiii 7, cxix 70. Tur-Sinai, following through on his understanding that the assailant is a titan or primeval hero who fought with the sea-god against the God of heaven, understands the text as referring to the smearing of grease on a swimmer to shed water! The word here rendered "blubber" (*pîmāh*) is unique in the OT. Whether it is related to the unit of weight called a "pim," I Sam xiii 21, is uncertain. It is very likely related to the Akkadian word *piāmu,* meaning "robust," and Ar. *fa'ama,* "fill."

28. The meaning of this verse is not altogether clear. Rashi took it to mean that the wicked choose ruined cities to rebuild and dwell in them. This is reminiscent of iii 14. The ruins of cities were objects of dread and were avoided, especially at night (cf. Isa xiii 20 ff., xxxiv 10 ff.), perhaps because they had been put under the ban. To rebuild a devoted city was to incur the displeasure of the deity; cf. Josh vi 26; I Kings xvi 34. Ibn Ezra supposed that the wicked concealed themselves in ruined cities from which they raided passers-by.

29a. LXX connects this line with 28c and gives the sense "What he has acquired, others will take away / neither will his substance endure."

29b. *minlām,* the last word of this line, is hapax and its meaning uncertain. LXX reads "He shall not cast a shadow on the earth." Vulg. reads *nec mittet in terram radicem suam,* apparently reflecting *'eṣlām* instead of the enigmatic *minlām,* and this interpretation is adopted by AT and RSV. Saadia compared the word with Ar. *manāl,* "acquisition," which in Hebrew would have the form *mānôl.* We follow Dahood

(NWSPJ, pp. 60 f.) in connecting the word with Ar. *manāl* and construing the final *-m* as enclitic. The possessive suffix "his" would be sandwiched in between the end of the word and the enclitic *-m* and its vocalization is problematic. (Dahood vocalizes the form *mĕnōlem* without explanation.) The meaning "property, possessions," or the like comports very well with "be rich" and "wealth" in the preceding line. The word "earth," parallel to "darkness" in the succeeding line, refers to the netherworld, as pointed out by Dahood. Cf. Ps xlix 18.

30a. A variant of 22a and perhaps to be deleted since it does not fit the figure of the blasted plant.

30c. In previous editions of this commentary the final word of this line, *pyw*, "his mouth," was emended to *pryw*, "his fruit," to produce the *pis aller* "His fruit will be carried off by the wind." LXX has simply "And his flower will fall." Dahood (*Biblica* 50 [1969], p. 343) proposed to read, for MT *rûaḥ* "breath, wind," *rewaḥ* "expanse," and to relate the wide mouth to the netherworld:

> He will not escape from the Darkness,
> His shoots the Flame will wither,
> Nor will he escape from its massive mouth.

The negative *lô'* with the verb *yāsûr* in 30a, according to Dahood, serves double-duty and applies also to the same verb here in 30c. This would be easier to accept if the two cola followed one another directly, since it is difficult to believe that the double-duty negative would skip over the intervening positive colon 30b. Another minor emendation may be suggested, viz. the addition of an ' before *pyw* to produce *'appāyw*, "his nostrils," or "his anger," but this is also unconvincing. Though the meaning is by no means clear, it seems best to attempt to translate MT as closely as possible without elaboration.

31. This verse is incongruous with the series of figures of plant life, 29b, 30b, c, 32, 33, and may be misplaced. Tur-Sinai supplies the botanical reference by vocalizing the last word of 31b as "his palm tree" (*timmôrāṯô*) rather than "his recompense" (*tĕmûrāṯô*). Perhaps a better device is to take "his palm [tree]" as the beginning of the next verse. With or without the palm tree, this verse is out of touch with its context. Perhaps the best solution is to see most of this verse as a prosaic gloss on vs. 30, a view which finds support in the repetition of the word *šāw'*, "vanity," apparently suggested by the phrase "the breath of his mouth."

32a. Taking over the last word of the preceding verse in the sense of "palm" and reading the verb as *timmāl*, "wither," rather than *timmālē'*, "be filled."

33a. *stripped.* Literally "he does violence"; cf. Isa xviii 5.

33b. The olive tree blossoms profusely and sheds its blossoms with great prodigality like snowflakes. Only a very small proportion of the blossoms comes to maturity.

34a. *impious.* Cf. xiii 6b, xvii 8, xx 5, xxvii 8, xxxiv 30, xxxvi 13,

gang. Literally "congregation," but here in a derogatory sense. The word is used of a "swarm" of bees in Judg xiv 8.

impotent. The same word is rendered "sterile" in iii 7.

35a. Cf. Ps vii 14 which is almost identical with this verse. Apparently it was a proverbial expression.

16. JOB'S REPLY TO ELIPHAZ
(xvi 1–22)

XVI 1 Job answered:

2 "I have heard plenty of this;
Galling comforters are you all.
3 Have windy words a limit?
What moves you to prattle on?
4 I, too, could talk like you,
If you were in my place.
I could harangue you with words,
Could shake my head at you.
5 I could strengthen you with my mouth,
My quivering lips would soothe.
6 If I speak my pain is not lessened,
If I desist, it does not leave me.
7 But now he has weakened and dazed me;
All my woe 8 has wizened me.
As a witness it has risen against me;
My leanness testifies to my face.
9 His anger rips and rages against me;
He gnashes at me with his teeth;
My enemy whets his eye against me.
10 They gape at me with their mouth,
They slap my face in scorn,
Together they mass against me.
11 God puts me in custody of the vicious,
Tosses me into the hand of the wicked.
12 I was at ease and he crushed me,
Grabbed me by the neck and mangled me.
He sets me up as his target,

13 His archers ring me round.
He stabs my vitals without pity,
Pours out my guts on the ground.
14 He rends me rift on rift,
Rushes at me like a warrior.
15 Sack I have sewed on my hide,
I have thrust my horn in the dust.
16 My face is flushed with weeping,
Upon my eyes is darkness,
17 Although there is no violence in my hands
And my prayer is pure.
18 O earth, cover not my blood,
That there be no tomb for my plaint.
19 Even now my witness is in heaven,
My guarantor is on high,
20 Interpreter of my thoughts to God,
Toward whom my eye drips
21 While he pleads for a man with God,
As a fellow does for his friend.
22 The innumerable years come,
The way of no return I go.

Notes

xvi 2. Job has had enough of pious platitudes. In this context the translation "wearisome" is hardly strong enough for the word *'āmāl*. It is the very opposite of comfort that Eliphaz and the friends have given him. They rub salt in his open wounds.

3. This perhaps in reply to xv 2.

4c. J. J. Finkelstein (JBL 75 [1956], 328–31) has shown that the root *ḥbr* here and in Deut xviii 11; Ps lviii 6; Prov xxi 9, xxv 24 is to be connected with an original *ḫbr* with the basic meaning "sound, noise" rather than with *ḥbr* in the sense of Ar. *ḥabara,* "beautify, adorn" (KB interprets this line as meaning "I could be brilliant in words against you"), or the Hebrew sense of "join, associate" (RSV, "I could join words together against you"). The translation here is that suggested by Finkelstein. Cf. also O. Loretz, CBQ 23 (1961), 293 f., who suggests the rendering, "I could also speak to you with mere noise."

4d. The shaking of the head is elsewhere associated with mockery and derision, II Kings xix 21; Isa xxxvii 22; Pss xxii 8, cix 25; Lam ii 15; Ecclesiasticus xii 18; Matt xxvii 39, and in the present context it may connote feigned or mock sympathy. In Jer xviii 16 a different verb is applied to the shaking of the head in derision, from the same "root," *n(w)d*, used of consolation or condolence in ii 11 and xlii 11, but without expression of the presumed object, head. A gesture could have different meanings according to circumstances.

6. The transition is rather abrupt from rebuke of his friends to consideration of his suffering.

6b. Reading *māh* as the negative rather than interrogative, as in xxxi 1. The negative use of *mā*, "what?", as in Arabic, is found also in I Kings xii 16; cf. II Sam xx 1.

7. The difficulties of this verse and the following are apparently due to faulty stichometry. Line 7a is too short and, with many critics, I borrow the first word of 7b and make it agree in person with the preceding verb. The word *'ăḏāṯî*, "my company," then has to be emended to *rā'āṯî*, "my calamity/woe." This expedient, dubious as it may be, seems preferable to the futile effort of torturing suitable sense from the text as it stands.

9c. Probably best taken with 10a. The opponent here is not Satan, as Rashi piously suggested, nor is it God. Rather it is human adversaries who gloat over his misfortune.

Dahood (*Psalms I*, third NOTE on Ps vii 13; *II*, third NOTE on Ps lxxxix 44) reads instead of *ṣārî*, "my enemy," *ṣūrî*, "his blade" (from *ṣūr*, "knife of flint," with the suffix construed as third rather than first person). "He (namely Yahweh) sharpens his blade." The Ugar. *ḥrb lṭšt*, "a sharpened sword" (137:32), is cited in support. Blommerde renders the entire line, "He sharpens his blade, his eyes are fixed on me." Examination of the Ugaritic passage, however, suggests that the "whetted sword" is a figure for the hostile eyes. The fierce messengers of Prince Sea so intimidate the divine assembly that they put their heads on top of their knees as they sat on their lordly thrones. The mien of the fearsome messengers is thus described: *išt ištm yitmr ḥrb lṭšt* [']*nhm*, "A fire, two fires are seen, a whetted sword their [e]yes." While the reading "eyes" is not entirely certain because of the small lacuna, it seems most plausible, especially in view of the preceding reference to "two fires" which presumably designate their flashing eyes.

10a. Omitted by LXX. Cf. Ps xxii 14(13); Isa lvii 4.

10b. Cf. I Kings xxii 24; Lam iii 30; Mic v 1(iv 14); Matt v 39; Luke vi 29.

12c. This line makes a couplet with 13a, both featuring the figure of archer and target; cf. vi 4; Ps lxiv 7(8); Lam iii 12. God is not the archer, but the field commander who directs the volleys of the archers; cf. xix 12 where God as commander directs a siege against Job.

13b. *vitals.* Literally "kidneys," but used metaphorically for the sensitive inwards, as in Lam iii 13 where RSV renders "heart"; cf. Prov vii 23, "until an arrow pierce his liver."

13c. *my guts.* Literally "my gall bladder." In the same sense as "kidneys," above. Cf. Lam ii 11, "my liver is poured on the ground," and II Sam xx 10, "and he poured out his guts on the ground." In xx 25 the word is used in the same sense as here and should be vocalized *mĕrērāh,* "gall bladder," rather than *mĕrôrāh,* "gall," as in xx 14.

14. Dahood (*Psalms I,* NOTE on Ps xl 14, second NOTE on Ps xlviii 14, NOTE on Ps l 10) would take the second breach, *pāreṣ* as the conjunction *pa* plus the infinitive absolute *rōṣ* and connects it with the following verb *yārûṣ, pa-rōṣ yārûṣ,*

He breaches me with a breach in front
And charging he charges me like a warrior.

14a. The figure is that of attack on a fortified city and breach of its walls; cf. xxx 14; Isa v 5; Amos iv 3; Pss lxxx 12(13), lxxxix 40(41).

14b. Cf. xv 26; Joel ii 7.

15a. The sewing of sackcloth is not mentioned elsewhere. It has been thought that the reference is to the wearing of sackcloth under ordinary clothes, since it is said to be next to the skin, like a hair shirt; cf. II Kings vi 30.

15b. *horn.* The horn is the symbol of power, pride, and dignity, Pss lxxv 5, lxxxix 17, 24, xcii 10, cxii 9. As the wounded bull droops its head and sinks its horn in the dust, so Job is felled by his misfortunes.

16a. Involuntary weeping is a symptom of leprosy, but Job has trouble enough to account for his weeping without attributing it to leprosy or elephantiasis.

16b. Progressive loss of vision is also a concomitant of leprosy. Excessive weeping could also be said to dim the eyes. The word *ṣalmāweṯ* does not mean "shadow of death" and there is no allusion to death here or in Ps xxiii 4. Possibly the darkness refers to the blackness around the eyes of the sick man.

17. Job again categorically denies his guilt. His suffering is without any justification; cf. Isa liii 9.

18. Spilled blood cries out from the ground for vengeance, Gen iv 10, hence the attempt to cover it over with dust, Gen xxxvii 26; Isa xxvi 21; Ezek xxiv 8. Job wishes his blood to remain uncovered as a permanent protest and appeal for vindication.

18b. *tomb.* Dahood (NWSPJ, pp. 61 f.) argues that the word *māqôm,* "place," here means "tomb," as in Ezek xxxix 11 and in the inscriptions of Panamuwa and Eshmunazar. The final *-î* of *za'ăqāṯî*

Dahood construes as the suffix of the third person rather than the first, so that the blood is represented as crying; cf. Gen iv 10,

> O earth, cover not my blood,
> And let its cry have no burial place.

19. Many exegetes take the heavenly witness here to be God himself, the God of justice and steadfast love, to whom Job appeals against the God of wrath. As the Koran (ix 119) puts it, "There is no refuge from God but unto Him." Ibn Gabirol expresses a similar thought (in Israel Abraham's paraphrase):

> When all within is dark,
> And Thy just angers rise,
> From Thee I turn to Thee
> And find love in Thine eyes.

A similar thought is expressed in Tennyson's "Despair,"

> Ah yet—I have had some glimmer, at times, in my gloomiest woe,
> Of a God behind all—after all—the great God for aught that I know;
> But the God of Love and of Hell together—they cannot be thought,
> If there be such a God, may the Great God curse him and bring him to nought!

In this context, however, the heavenly witness, guarantor, friend can scarcely be God who is already Accuser, Judge, and Executioner. Verse 21 shows clearly that the witness is an intermediary, an intercessor who will testify on Job's behalf and plead for him with God as a man pleads for his friend. This witness for the defense is to serve a purpose similar to that of the umpire of ix 33 and the vindicator of xix 25; cf. xxxiii 23–24.

20. The text has suffered some damage and none of the efforts to emend it or to interpret it as it stands can be regarded as satisfactory. With only two words, the line 20a presents several possibilities: "My interpreter[s]/scorner[s] [is/are] my friend[s]/thought[s]/shepherd[s]." It is, however, clear from the context that the proper sense of the first word (*mēlîṣ*) is "interpreter." The word is used in this sense in xxxiii 23 and Gen xlii 23, and in two fourth century Phoenician Inscriptions from Cyprus (CIS, I, 44, 88). But further progress in interpretation of the line is balked until its deficiency is restored. LXX renders "May my prayer come to (the) Lord, toward him my eye drips." While it is difficult to connect the two words of the Hebrew of 20a with this inter-

pretative rendering, the stichometry offers a clue to the solution of the difficulty. The words "to God" (*'el-'ĕlôah*) are to be taken with 20a to fill out the defective line. This leaves 20b short, but LXX (*enanti de autou*) supplies the remedy. Because of the similarity with the preceding phrase "to God" (*'l 'lwh*), the word "to him" (*'lyw*) was lost by haplography. The line as restored then reads:

mĕlîṣ rē'ay 'el-'ĕlôah
'ēlāyw dālĕpāh 'ênî

The interpreter to whom Job appeals is the same figure as the witness and guarantor of the preceding verse and the umpire and vindicator of ix 33 and xix 25.

22a. *innumerable.* Reading *missappēr* for MT *mispār,* following Dahood, *Biblica* 48 (1967), 429.

22b. Cf. x 21b.

17. JOB'S REPLY (*continued*)
(xvii 1–16)

XVII

1 "My spirit is broken,
My days are spent;
It is the grave for me.
2 The Mounds loom before me,
On the Slime-Pits my eye dwells.
3 O take my pledge with you!
Who will shake my hand?
4 Since you have closed their mind to reason,
You will not, therefore, exalt them.
5 Who denounces friends for reward,
The eyes of his children should fail.
6 He has made me a popular byword,
One in whose face they spit.
7 My eye is dimmed with anguish,
My limbs are all like a shadow.
8 [The righteous are astonished at this,
The innocent are aroused against the impious.
9 But the righteous retains his force,
The clean-handed grows in strength.]
10 But come back, you all, come on;
I shall not find a wise man among you.
11 My days are done,
My plans shattered,
My heart's desires.
12 They turn night to day;
'Light is near,' in the face of darkness.
13 If I await Sheol as my home,
Spread my couch in darkness,

[14] Say to the pit, 'You are my father,'
To the maggot, 'My mother and sister,'
[15] Then where, O where, is my hope?
My happiness, who can see it?
[16] Will it go down to Sheol with me?
Shall we descend to the dust together?"

NOTES

xvii 1. The verse falls naturally into three short lines and it seems best to take it thus rather than to augment it in some way to yield two longer lines. The word for "grave" in the last line is construed as singular with the enclitic emphatic particle *-m*.

2. This verse is difficult and probably corrupt, but the various emendations that have been proposed do not improve matters greatly. Cf. Dahood, *Psalms I*, NOTE on Ps xlvi 3, *jaws of the nether world*, for the basis of this interpretation. It is not necessary, however, to construe the word rendered "the Mounds" (*htlym*) as a dual form (*hatillēm*) nor "the Slime-Pits" (*hmrwtm*) as "the twin miry deeps" (*hămîrôṯēm*) since *htlym* suggests the plural form and the final *-m* of *hmrwtm* may be the enclitic emphatic particle. On the Slime-Pits or muck, cf. NOTE on ix 31a.

3a. As the MT is vocalized, God is asked to give (a pledge) and to be a pledge with himself for Job. With a very slight change in the vocalization of one word, reading *'erḇônî*, "my pledge," instead of *'orḇēnî*, "be surety for me," we get a more acceptable sense. Job offers his pledge or surety to God and in the following line wishes that God would accept or ratify a mutual pledge. The giving and taking of pledges was common commercial and juridical practice; cf. Gen xxxviii 17–20; Exod xxii 26(25); Deut xxiv 6–17; Neh v 3. The risk of a third party becoming surety without collateral was very grave and the sages warned against it, Prov vi 1, xi 15, xvii 18, xxii 26; Ecclesiasticus xxix 14–20.

3b. The gesture of striking (or shaking?) the hand ratified the giving of a pledge, as seen from Prov vi 1, xvii 18. Job's words here would seem to be an open invitation or challenge to anyone to make a pledge with him, but there can be little doubt that the words are directed to God, as most interpreters have understood.

4. This verse is difficult. The suffix "their" attached to the word "heart/mind" indicates that Job is referring to the friends. He appeals to God not to let their unreasonable argument prevail. In the Psalter

it is a common prayer of the innocent sufferer that his foes not be allowed to triumph over him; cf. Pss xiii 3–5, xxx 2, xxxviii 19(20), xli 11.

5. This verse also is difficult. Some scholars regard it as a marginal comment and others give it up as hopelessly corrupt. All attempts to explain it place a strain either on the text or on the comprehension of the reader. According to the usual sense of the words, the text seems to say, "For a portion he tells his friends, and the eyes of his children fail." The older Jewish commentators understand the word *ḥēleq* in the sense of "flattery," from the root "be smooth," and so KJ rendered "He that speaketh flattery to his friends," and JPS "He that denounceth his friends for the sake of flattering." Peake and Buttenwieser take it as a proverbial saying, "One invites friends to share (one's table), while his own children's eyes fail." RSV spells out its interpretation, "He who informs against his friends to get a share of their property," using more than a dozen words to render three words of the Hebrew. In spite of the prolixity, the RSV interpretation seems the most likely of any offered. This sense would comport with the estimate of the friends which Job has already given in vi 27 and xiii 7–11.

6a. Ibn Ezra understood the subject of the verb to be the pain. Others think Eliphaz is the one who has made Job an object of ridicule. Such are merely pious efforts to shield God from Job's charges. The reading *limšal* instead of MT *limšōl* is generally accepted. Blommerde read, instead of *'ammîm,* "peoples," *ammay-m,* "my relatives," with enclitic *-m* after the possessive suffix. Dahood (*Psalms II,* first NOTE on Ps lxxi 7) interprets *māšāl* as meaning "butt," parallel to *tōp̄eṯ* in the succeeding line which is taken as a by-form of *mōp̄eṯ* in the sense of "target." "He has made me the butt of peoples, and I have become a target before them."

6b. Targ. took the word *tōp̄eṯ* to refer to Gehenna. Rashi understood it as equivalent to *tōp̄,* "drum," and this error was followed by KJ, "tabret." The word has here its primary meaning of "spitting," and *lĕp̄ānîm* does not mean "formerly, aforetime," but rather "to (in) the face." Spitting in the face or in the presence of someone was the extreme insult and expression of contempt; cf. xxx 10; Deut xxv 9; Isa l 6; Matt xxvi 67, xxvii 30; Mark x 34, xiv 65, xv 19. Blommerde ascribed to *tōp̄eṯ* the sense "shame" and interpreted *pānîm* here as meaning "those who are before, ancestors":

> And he has made me a proverb for my relatives
> and a shame for my ancestors I have become.

7a. Cf. xvi 16; Ps vi 8(7).

7b. Cf. xvi 8. The word rendered "limbs" occurs only here. Both

Rashi and Ibn Ezra understood it in this sense. Job is a mere shadow of his former self. N. Sarna (JJS 6 [1955], 108–10) proposed to read instead of MT *kullām*, "all of them," *kālû* plus enclitic *-m*. Blommerde rendered accordingly:

> My eye is dimmed with anguish
> my limbs fail like a shadow.

8–10. These verses are impossible to integrate into the rest of Job's speech. Attempts to explain the text as it is or to alter it to agree with Job's viewpoint are eminently unsatisfactory.

8b. It has been suggested that the sentence be altered to read, "And the godless shall stir himself up against the innocent," but this is of scant help in clarifying the immediate context.

9. Some interpreters have seen here a highlight of the book. Delitzsch regarded this verse as "a rocket which shoots above the tragic darkness of the book, lighting it up suddenly, although only for a short time," while Davidson considered the passage as "perhaps the most surprising and lofty in the book." It is indeed surprising in the mouth of Job, for it smacks of the view of the friends and is quite the opposite of what Job has been saying and continued to say. It appears to be Job's argument by confusion.

9a. *force*. Following Blommerde who noted here the parallelism between *dereḵ* and *'ōmeṣ*. (For bibliography and notes on *dereḵ* and *darkāh* in the sense of "power, strength," cf. Dahood, *Psalms I*, third NOTE on Ps i 1; *II*, first NOTE on Ps ci 2, third NOTE on Ps cii 24, second NOTE on Ps cxix 37, first NOTE on Ps cxxxviii 4, fourth NOTE on Ps cxlvi 9.) Blommerde argues for the integrity of this verse within Job's speech, explaining it thus: "Because of the misery which has befallen the just Job, the righteous are astonished, this is against all rules; they have to cling to their force, to defend themselves against this trial of their faith."

10. This sounds like Job taunting the friends, but it may be out of place.

11. This verse continues the description of Job's sad state which was interrupted by vss. 8–10. The stichometry is problematic. LXX divides the verse into two parts, "My days have passed on the run / Broken are the joints of my heart." But this cannot be made to fit the present Hebrew text exactly. If the MT is made into a bicolon there is need for an additional verb in the second element, thus: "My days are done, my plans shattered, / My heart's desires destroyed." To avoid emendation of the text, wherever possible, I divide the line into three short cola. This is the same arrangement as in xvii 1 and appears to be the poet's way of expressing heightening of the emotions.

12. This verse is quite incompatible with the context. The usual ex-

planation is that Job charges his friends with trying to cheer him with predictions of a brighter day to come. This they did to some extent in the first round of speeches, v 17–26, viii 20–22, xi 13–19, and Zophar actually promised that Job's darkness would become like morning, xi 17. But Eliphaz has said nothing of the sort in his second speech to which Job now replies. The best expedient is to regard the verse as misplaced. It would fit very well in a context such as xiii 7 where Job charges the friends with falsification. Cf. Isa v 20.

13–16. These verses are clear and virtually free of difficulty. Job is resigned to death and sees no glimmer of hope.

14. Cf. Prov. vii 4.

15. *hope . . . happiness.* MT has "hope" in both cases but on the basis of the LXX reading "my good" it may be permissible to emend the latter instance to *ṭôḇaṯî.*

16a. The word *baddê* is ignored in the translation, but deserves comment. It certainly does not mean "parts of" in this context. RSV's "bars of Sheol" is a poor guess. Dahood (NWSPJ, pp. 62 f.) has explained the word as a contraction of *ba-yadê,* "in the hands (power) of," as with Ugaritic *bd* and Amarna *badiu* (contracted from *ba-yadi-hu*). Note the expression "hands/power of Sheol," in Ps xlix 16(15). The verb *tēraḏnā,* "they shall go down" is perhaps mistakenly vocalized for an original *tērēdanna,* "it will go down," the *n* representing the *modus energicus* which is so common in Ugaritic.

16b. Reading with LXX, *nēḥaṯ,* "we will descend" for MT *nāḥaṯ* "[at] rest," but turning the phrase into a question.

18. BILDAD'S SECOND DISCOURSE
(xviii 1–21)

XVIII 1 Bildad the Shuhite answered:

2 "How long will you set word snares?
Be sensible and then we may talk.
3 Why are we counted as cattle,
Deemed dull in your eyes,
4 One who tears himself in his anger?
Shall the earth be abandoned for your sake,
The rock be moved from its place?
5 The light of the wicked is put out,
The flame of his fire does not shine.
6 The light in his tent grows dark,
His lamp above him goes out.
7 His mighty strides are narrowed,
His own schemes trip him.
8 He is thrown by his feet in the net,
He steps upon the webbing.
9 The snare seizes him by the heel,
The bands tighten on him.
10 His noose is hid on the ground,
His trap upon the path.
11 Round about terrors affright him,
And harry him at every step.
12 The Ravenous One confronts him,
Calamity ready at his side.
13 He eats his skin with two hands,
First-born Death with both his hands.
14 He is snatched from his comfortable tent
And marched before the King of Terrors.

15 Fire is set in his tent,
On his abode is scattered brimstone.
16 His roots dry up below,
And above his branch withers.
17 His memory perishes from the earth,
He has no name abroad.
18 Driven from light into darkness,
Chased out of the world.
19 No kith or kin 'mongst his people,
Nor survivor in his old haunts.
20 At his fate westerners are appalled,
Easterners seized with dismay.
21 Surely these were the dwellings of an evil man,
This the place of one who knew not God."

NOTES

xviii 2a. Bildad addresses Job in the plural. This detail is obscured in modern English by the use of "you" for both singular and plural. It has been suggested that Bildad's intent is to ignore Job as an individual and address him as belonging to the class of the impious. LXX, however, renders the verbs in the singular. The line is a bit long and some critics delete the first two words as introduced on the analogy of xix 2. This is hardly necessary. The word rendered "snares" (*qinṣê*) is not found elsewhere in the OT. The Jewish commentators Rashi, Gersonides, Joseph Qimḥi, and Ibn Ezra took the word as a form of *qēṣ*, "end," and so KJ. The word, however, is to be explained from Ar. *qanaṣa*, "hunt," and from Akk. *qinṣu*, "trap." On the use of the "construct" form *qinṣê* before the preposition, cf. GKC, 130.

2b. LXX reads, "Leave off, that we may speak," meaning that Job has held forth long enough and should give an opportunity for rebuttal. The Hebrew enjoins Job to show some intelligence as a requisite for continuation of the dialogue.

3a. Cf. xl 15a; Ps lxxiii 22.

3b. The meaning of the verb is uncertain. Some interpreters connect it with the root meaning "to be unclean," but it is better connected with an Aramaic root meaning "stupid." Blommerde reads *niṭmannû* for MT *niṭmînû* and renders "must we hide from your sight?" This does not seem appropriate to the sense of the preceding line. The plural possessive suffix on the word for "your eyes," *'ênêḵem*, Blommerde changes to the singular, *'ênêḵā,* and takes the final *-m* as the enclitic particle, this because Bildad is addressing Job.

4a. Some critics think a line has been lost here. Duhm transposes xvii 10a just before this line. It seems preferable, however, to take 4a as forming a tricolon with the preceding verse.

4b, c. Because "rock" is often an epithet of God, Rashi so understood it here, but wrongly. Bildad suggests, with sarcasm, that Job thinks the whole world hangs on his fate, or that for his sake the order of nature should be altered. Connecting this verse with what follows, the implication is that the law of retribution is firm as the rock and built into the order of the world.

5–6. The dogma is reaffirmed, but Job still does not accept it; cf. xxi 17. "The light/lamp of the wicked" is a common proverbial expression, Prov xiii 9, xx 20, xxiv 20.

7. The fortunes of the wicked fail like the strength of an aging man whose once mighty stride (cf. Ps xviii 36; Prov iv 12) is reduced to a feeble hobble; he is trapped by his own devices.

8a. The evil man's own feet lead him into the trap, just as in 7b his own wiles bring about his downfall. G. Gerleman, JSS 4 (1958), 252–54, interprets *bĕraḡlāyw,* "with his feet," as an idiomatic phrase meaning "on the spot," "instantly," as also in Judg v 15.

8b. *webbing.* The word designates things interwoven, such as a woman's hair net, a window lattice, or grating. It is not clear whether the reference here is to a net, as indicated by the parallel in 8a, or to a grill or trapdoor over a pit.

9–10. Intrigued by the figure of the wicked snared in his own trap, Bildad elaborates with about every term available to him; cf. Isa viii 14; Jer xlviii 44; Pss cxxiv 7, cxl 6(5); Prov v 22.

11. Cf. xxii 10 where snares and sudden dread are parallel. Whether the terrors that dog the steps of the wicked here are physical hazards or some sort of demons is not clear. The latter seems more likely. Cf. vs. 14 below and xv 21, xxiv 17, xxvii 20, xxx 15; Isa xvii 14; Ps lxxiii 19; Ezek xxvi 21, xxvii 36, xxviii 19.

11b. *harry him.* This form, *wehĕp̄îṣûhû,* "and they disperse him," was related by G. R. Driver (ZAW 64 [1953], 259 f.) to the causative (IVth) form of Ar. *fâṣa(y), (urinam) jaculando emisit.* NEB accordingly rendered:

> The terrors of death suddenly beset him
> and make him piss over his feet.

12a. MT appears to say "Let his strength/wealth be hungry." In the earlier editions the suggestion of Dhorme was adopted, assuming omission of the preposition *bĕ-* before *'ônô,* by haplography of the final letter of the preceding word, "With his wealth he is famished." It was noted, however, that the parallelism favors the sense of Moffatt's paraphrase, "ruin is ravenous for him." The suggestion of Dahood is now accepted, that *rāēḇ,* the "Hungry One," is an epithet of Mot (Death), as in Ps xxxiii 19, and that *'ônô* is derived from the verb *'ny* III, "to meet," with the accusative suffix; cf. Dahood, *Psalms I, 1–50,* NOTE on Ps xxxviii 18.

12b. *at his side.* Literally "to/for his rib," which Targ. renders "for his wife," on the basis of Gen ii 21. Tur-Sinai accordingly rendered "rib," meaning "wife."

13a. In previous editions of this commentary, the troublesome *baddê* was emended to *biḏway,* "with disease," to produce "His skin in gnawed by disease." N. Sarna suggested (JBL 82 [1963], 317) that *baddê* here means "with two hands" and *baddāyw* in the following stich means "with his two hands." The latter was rendered in the previous editions "on his limbs." Sarna cited the Ugaritic passage (67 I 19–20) in which Môt boasts *bklat ydy ilḥm,* "With both my hands I eat" (the element *hm* which Sarna read as the object suffix "them," *ilḥm, hm,* "I shall eat them," is an asseverative particle beginning the following stich). The present verse, Sarna suggested, might well be translated, "The first-born of Môt will devour his skin with two hands, yea with his two hands he will devour (him)." This translation implies some juggling of the word order of the MT, but the general sense seems suitable in the light of the Ugaritic parallel.

13b. *First-born Death.* The expression *bĕḵōr māweṯ* has been much discussed and bizarre interpretations have been offered. Tur-Sinai, e.g., explained that the evildoer's starving first-born will grow his own skin—"the starving first-born shall eat his own flesh strips." The view commonly held is that the expression is a metaphor for a deadly disease, or for the specific malady that afflicts Job. This is probably correct. Now, however, we are in a position to understand the metaphor since we know the god Death (Mot) from the Ugaritic texts. While there is no reference to any of Mot's children in the Ugaritic myths, it is understandable that any death-dealing force like disease or pestilence might be regarded as his offspring. Michel (in his unpublished dissertation, "The Ugaritic Texts and the Mythological Expressions in the Book of Job") proposed that First-born and Death may be taken in apposition rather than as a construct, "the First-born, Death." This suggestion is very attractive and is adopted with a slight modification. The rights of primogeniture make the first-born son the prime heir and hence in a royal family the crown prince. The use of *bĕḵōr,* first-born, as a royal title is seen in Ps lxxxix 28,

> I will make him first-born,
> Highest of the kings of earth.

(This latter suggestion comes orally from Mr. Bruce Zuckerman.)

14b. *marched.* The difficult form *wĕtaṣʿiḏēhû* was explained by Sarna (JBL 82 [1963], 317 f.) as masculine singular corresponding to the Amarna Canaanite forms with *t-* preformative instead of *y-*. Sarna understood "that Môt, king of the netherworld, sends his first-born as his emissary to slay the unrighteous one and to march him off to the infernal regions." More likely is the analysis of W. Moran (*Biblica* 45 [1964], 82, n. 1) who saw the form as third masculine plural, to be vocalized *wĕtaṣʿidûhû,* "and they march him," with the subject unidentified and thus equivalent to the passive, "he is marched."

King of Terrors. Doubtless an epithet of Mot, the god of death and of the netherworld, corresponding to the Mesopotamian Nergal and the Greek Pluto. The title may be taken to imply that Mot is ruler over a host of infernal spirits who seize the victim and hustle him into the presence of their king. Rashi understood it, more or less correctly, as a designation of the chief of demons. The god Mot is termed the shepherd of the denizens of the netherworld in Ps xlix 14, shepherd being an ancient royal title.

15. We follow Dahood (*Biblica* 38 [1957], 312 ff.) who has brilliantly restored this corrupted verse in the light of Ugaritic. The crux of the difficulty was the meaningless jumble of words *mibbĕlî lô,* "from without to him," which Dahood recognized from the parallelism as the corruption of a word meaning "fire," having cognates in Akkadian and Ugaritic. Thus we read with Dahood:

toškān bĕʾōhĕlô mabbēl
lîzōreh ʿal-nāwēhû gop̄rîṯ

The extra *l* of *mibbĕlî lô* is added to the following verb as the *lamedh* of emphasis, cf. *Biblica* 37 (1956), 339.

16. Destruction root and branch, or root and fruit (cf. Amos ii 9) is proverbial; cf. vs. 19 below which makes it clear that the reference is to progeny and posterity. The author is fond of figures drawn from plant life, viii 16 f., xiv 2, 7, xv 30, xix 10.

17. Cf. Pss ix 6, xxxiv 17; Prov x 7.

18. The verbs are vocalized as third person plurals, which in Aramaic is the common mode of expressing the equivalent of the passive, the agent being undesignated, "they shall drive him," i.e., "he shall be driven." The consonantal text, however, would normally be read "he shall drive him," in which case the subject would be understood to be God. This reading may have been avoided as offensively anthropomorphic.

19. Cf. Ps xxxvii 28. The extinction of a family line was a fate much feared. The Ugaritic epics of Danel and Keret, like the stories of Abraham, Samson, Samuel, John the Baptist, feature the concern for lack of progeny. Levirate marriage and adoption were devices to prevent

this from happening. Polygamy and concubinage also were in part motivated by the desire to ensure progeny and posterity.

20. *fate.* Literally "day," i.e., his final day; cf. I Sam xxvi 10; Jer l 27; Ezek xxi 29(30); Ps xxxvii 13.

westerners . . . Easterners. Literally those "behind" and "before." The terms could mean "latter" and "former," in the sense of followers and predecessors. Ibn Ezra understood it thus, explaining that the former were the villain's contemporaries. This is a strange way to express such an idea. It seems preferable to take the terms as geographical, or directional, designating the inhabitants of the earth from one end to the other. A similar usage occurs in the Ugaritic myth about the violent goddess 'Anat who goes on a bloody rampage and smites the people of the sunrise and the seashore, i.e., east and west, meaning all humanity ('nt II 7–8).

21. Bildad clinches his argument. The application to Job is patent. What has happened to Job is irrefutable proof that he is an evil and godless man.

19. JOB'S REPLY TO BILDAD
(xix 1–29)

XIX 1 Job answered:

2 "How long will you torment me,
Crush me with words?
3 These ten times you have taunted me,
Shamelessly abused me.
4 If, indeed, I have erred,
Does the error lodge with me?
5 You vaunt yourselves against me,
And argue my disgrace against me.
6 But know 'tis God who has subverted me,
Has thrown his net around me.
7 I cry 'Violence,' but am not answered;
I shout for help, but there is no redress.
8 He has blocked my way so I cannot pass,
He puts darkness upon my path.
9 He has stripped my honor from me,
Removed the crown from my head.
10 He has demolished me, I am ruined;
He has uprooted my hope like a tree.
11 He has kindled his anger against me;
He counts me as his enemy.
12 His troops come massed against me,
Set siege against me,
Camp round about my tent.
13 My kin have abandoned me,
My acquaintances are alienated from me.
14 My relatives and intimates have deserted,
The inmates of my house have forgotten me.

15 My slave girls treat me as a stranger,
To them I have become an alien.
16 I call my slave but he doesn't answer,
Though I entreat him humbly.
17 My breath is offensive to my wife,
My stench to my own children.
18 Even urchins despise me;
I rise up and they revile me.
19 All my bosom friends detest me,
Those I love turn against me.
20 My flesh rots on my bones,
My teeth drop from my gums.
21 Pity me, pity me, my friends,
For the hand of God has struck me.
22 Why do you pursue me like God?
Are you not satisfied with my flesh?
23 O that my words were written,
Were engraved on a stela,
24 With iron stylus and lead,
Carved in rock forever.
25 I know my vindicator lives,
A guarantor upon the dust will stand;
26 Even after my skin is flayed,
Without my flesh I shall see God.
27 I will see him on my side,
My own eyes will see him no stranger.
My heart faints within me.
28 [If you say, 'How we will persecute him!'
And 'The root of the matter is found in me,'
29 Then beware of the sword,
For wrath will destroy iniquity,
That you may know Shaddayan."]

Notes

xix 2a. *torment*. With RSV, as against KJ's "vex my soul." In contemporary usage "vex" has too much of the connotation of trifling annoyance and Job's "comforters" do more than merely annoy. In Isa li 23 the same verb (*wgy*) is used of Israel's tormentors who say, "Fall down and let us walk over you." In Lam i 5, 12 the word is used of suffering which Yahweh inflicted on Israel.

2b. *Crush*. This verb (*dk'*) is used of the contrite or penitent in Isa lvii 15, but here it refers to the devastating effect of the friends' cruel insinuations.

3a. *ten times*. Rashi took the number to refer to the speeches thus far, five by Job and five by the friends. The figure is merely a round number, as in Gen xxxi 7, 41; Num xiv 22.

4a. It is not clear whether Job here admits error or denies it. We may be sure, from all else that he says, that he does not admit sin of such magnitude as to merit his woes.

4b. Whether taken as a declaration or question, this line is capable of several differing interpretations. The implication may be: granting or supposing I have erred, it is no business of yours; or, I keep it to myself (and how can you know about it?); or, I should be conscious of it (and I am not). If the words are directed to God rather than the friends, the line would agree with vii 20 where the question is raised as to what harm man can do to God. Taken as a question, it might mean, "Is my error to remain with me?", i.e., Must the punishment continue? Or, it could mean, "Does the fault lodge with me?" In the light of Job's charges against God in his previous speeches, and particularly below in vss. 6 ff., the charge that it is all God's fault seems most likely.

LXX here adds a couplet not found in the Hebrew:

> I have spoken vain words,
> My talk has been ignorant error.

Some interpreters regard these lines as original, considering it appropriate for Job to concede that he has been intemperate in speech. The admission of a minor error, it is argued, adds strength to his main tenet: that he has done nothing to warrant such drastic punishment; cf. xiii 26. These words, however, sound too much like a final recantation and were probably added on that basis.

5. Some scholars take this verse as a question, but here it makes no

real difference in sense. If it is a rhetorical question, the answer is positive, for this is exactly what the friends have been doing, arguing from the effect to the cause, that Job's humiliation is proof of his guilt.

6. According to Bildad, viii 3, and Elihu, xxxiv 12, it is unthinkable that God would pervert or distort justice, which is what Job asserts he has done. For Job, God's arbitrary act, and no sin of his own, accounts for his cruel sufferings. This verse supports the interpretation of 4b above, that it is all God's fault. Bildad had asserted that the evil man is caught in his own net, xviii 8, but Job declares it is, in his case at least, a matter of God's willful injustice.

6b. In the "Net Cylinder" of Entemena (Yale Babylonian Collection), the oldest peace treaty known, among the sanctions against the possible violator of the treaty is the threat that the god Ningirsu will cast his great net over the culprit (G. A. Barton, *Royal Inscriptions of Sumer and Akkad,* 1929, p. 65). In the Babylonian Creation Epic, Marduk spread out his net to enfold the monster Tiamat (ANET, p. 67, line 95).

7. Cf. Isa lviii 9; Jer xx 8; Mic iii 4; Hab i 2. Elihu has an explanation of Job's failure to get an answer, xxxv 12.

8. Cf. i 10, iii 23; Hos ii 6(8); Lam iii 7.

9. The word rendered "honor," *kāḇôḏ,* could also mean "riches, wealth" and it may well be that this is the sense intended. At any rate, Job has been bereft both of his material possessions and the prestige he once enjoyed by virtue of his reputation for righteousness. Honor and shame are often figured as garments that may be put on or stripped off; cf. xxix 14; Isa lxi 3; Ezek xvi 39, xxiii 26.

crown. Cf. xxxi 36; Jer xiii 18; Lam v 16.

10a. *demolished.* This verb is regularly used of the destruction of houses, walls, altars, ovens, etc. Tur-Sinai is probably right in viewing the expression here, and in Ps lii 5(7), as a laconism meaning "he has destroyed (my house)." The verb translated "ruined" is the ordinary word to go, *hālaḵ,* which in Arabic has the sense "perish," as here.

10b. Cf. xiv 7.

11. Cf. xiii 24. MT reads "his enemies," but the versions have the singular.

12. Military expressions, as in x 17, xvi 14, xxx 12.

13. Cf. Pss xxxviii 12, lxix 9, lxxxviii 9, 19.

14–15. The Masoretic stichometry is faulty. The last word of vs. 14 and the first two words of 15 make one line.

16. The slave, the lowliest of humanity, whose every concern is the slightest whim of the master (cf. Ps cxxiii 2), now ignores his call and even his abject entreaty. Whether the entreaty is effective or not is no matter; the humiliation is already complete when the slave is supplicated

rather than commanded. The attitude toward the slave here is quite different from that expressed in xxxi 13–15.

17. Job's halitosis along with his other symptoms—eruption and itching of the skin, ii 7, 8; marked change in appearance, ii 12; skin lesions and putrefaction of the flesh, vii 5; nightmares, vii 14; weeping and loss of vision, xvi 16; emaciation, xix 20; osteitis, xxx 17; discoloration and peeling of the skin, xxx 30—have been seized on as clues for diagnosis of the ailment. Probably the poet had no particular disease in mind. Halitosis may result from many conditions. LXX omits the first two words of 17a "my breath is offensive," but Vulg. renders the Hebrew exactly, *halitum meum exhorruit uxor mea.* The word rendered "offensive," is probably to be connected with an Arabic root having this sense rather than the Hebrew sense "be strange" (KJ). The first word of 17b is probably not a verb "I entreated" (KJ), but a noun with the possessive suffix of the first person singular, parallel to "my breath." "My supplication" (RV) is hardly apposite to "my breath." Tur-Sinai takes "my breath" in the sense of "my sigh" and the parallel word as meaning "my groaning." Arabic and Syriac, however, have a similar word with the sense "feel bad, be stinking," or the like, and this sense suits the context admirably. Duhm's suggested emendation of the word on the basis of Joel ii 20 is unnecessary.

my own children. Literally "the children of my womb/body," remains a *crux interpretum.* The connection with Ar. *baṭn* in the sense of "clan" seems unlikely here. It has been taken to refer to Job's uterine brothers and sisters; cf. Gen xliii 29; Judg viii 19. "My womb/body" can also refer to the male's part in procreation as seen from Deut xxviii 53; Ps cxxxii 11; and Mic vi 7. The children thus could be Job's own, but to this it is objected that Job's children have already been annihilated, as the author of the poetic dialogues well knows; cf. viii 4 and xxix 5. The dodge that they might be his children by concubines, or his grandchildren, is carrying the issue too far, although Blake in his Third Illustration assumes that the sons are married. It seems best to agree with Duhm that the poet here did not trouble himself with the details of the prose account. It seems likely that the complaint of the sick man that he is alienated even from wife and children is the sort of thing that would become a standard feature and cliché in a lament of this sort.

18. Such juvenile disrespect for elders was apparently not infrequent, but it was regarded as meriting drastic punishment; cf. II Kings ii 23.

revile. Literally "speak against," as in Pss l 20, lxxviii 19.

19. *bosom friends.* Literally "men of my intimate group"; cf. Gen xlix 6; Jer vi 11, xv 17, xxiii 18; Pss xxv 14, lv 15(14).

20. Both halves of this verse are notoriously difficult. The Hebrew of 20a says "To my skin and to my flesh my bone clings." The usual

expedient is to strike out "my flesh" and invert the order, "my skin clings to my bones." Ps cii 6, however, also speaks of the bones clinging to the flesh. LXX has a somewhat better reading in the first half of the verse, but it is doubtful whether the second line is any improvement over the Hebrew:

> In my skin the flesh is rotten,
> My bones are held in the teeth.

The verb in the first line is read as from *rqb* instead of *dbq* and "my bones" is taken with the following line. Note also the omission of "with the skin [of]" in the second line. Some critics emend the second line to read "my teeth are falling out." In BJ Larcher renders "et mes os se dénudent comme des dents." It is quite hopeless to arrive at any certainty as to the correct text and the exact sense of the verse. Rashi and Gersonides understood the meaning to be that all Job's flesh was putrefied except his gums and similarly Szold explained that Job was able to survive only by the little food he could masticate with his gums. KJ's "I am escaped with the skin of my teeth" has become proverbial for a narrow escape, but the context offers no support for this idea. It is certain only that Job refers to his poor physical condition.

22a. *like God.* Dahood would render "Why do you pursue me like a ram?" Cf. *Psalms I, 1–50,* second NOTE on Ps ii 5.

22b. This expression is generally explained by the idiom "eat the flesh of someone" in the sense of slander, calumniate, which is found in Akkadian, Aramaic, and Arabic and occurs in Ps xxvii 2; Dan iii 8, vi 24(25). But there is no reference here to calumny. Tur-Sinai may be right in his view that the metaphor "to be sated with another's flesh" derives from the ancient practice of sexual abuse of captives of war and other helpless persons. See NOTE on xxxi 31.

23. *stela.* The word *sēpēr* usually means "book" or "scroll." The verb *ḥqq,* however, means to "engrave," thus the material can scarcely be leather or papyrus. It would be possible to take *sēpēr* in the more general sense of "record" or "document" without regard to the material on which it is written. The word may, however, be related to the Akk. *siparru,* "copper." The use of bronze and copper for writing material was not uncommon in antiquity. (Cf. D. Diringer, *The Alphabet: A Key to the History of Mankind,* 2d ed. rev., 1953, pp. 158, 164, and G. R. Driver, *Semitic Writing,* 1954, p. 92.) The now famous copper treasure scroll from Qumran may be an illustration of what Job had in mind, a record for posterity. In former editions of this work, *sēpēr* was rendered "copper." It now seems preferable to take the cue from the Phoenician usage of the term with reference to inscriptions on stone and from

Targ. *piṯqā',* "(stone) tablet," or "stela." Ar. *sufrat* in the sense of "tableboard, table" suggests that the word could very well designate a tablet or stela of considerable size. W. H. Brownlee ("Philistine manuscripts from Palestine?—a supplementary note," *Kadmos* 10 [1971], 173), opposed the translation of *sēp̄er* as "copper," and proposed instead "parchment." By this rendering Brownlee obtained a climactic progression from the softer to the harder material for engraving, from "parchment" to "lead" to "rock." His translation takes some liberties with the text on behalf of his theory:

> O that my worlds were written,
>   were engraved in parchment,
> or with an iron stylus on lead,
>   or carved in rock for all times.

The supposedly Philistine manuscripts engraved on parchment appear on closer examination to be camel leather of no great antiquity (as reported by Brownlee at the 1971 meeting of the Society of Biblical Literature in Atlanta) and a group of symbols repeated several times bears striking resemblance to the initial word of the Siloam Tunnel Inscription. The authenticity of the documents is thus highly suspect and their relevance for the interpretation of the present passage is questionable.

24a. Since a lead stylus would make no impression on even the softest rock, it has been supposed that the reference is to the use of an iron implement for incising the letters with the lead being used to fill the incisions. This was suggested already by Rashi. In the previous editions of this work it was asserted erroneously that the techniques of inlaying incised letters of an inscription with lead is not otherwise attested in antiquity. At least one case is known. George Cameron in a reexamination of the inscription of Darius at Behistun in 1948–49 found in the small inscription above the head of the king that the symbols spelling the king's name had been inlaid with lead (cf. *Life* magazine of June 1949, pp. 48 f.; E. Weidner, AfO 15 [1945–51], 146–47; J. J. Stamm, ZAW 65 [1953], 302; K. Galling, WO 2 [1954], 3–6). Driver and Gray (ICC) suggest that "lead" is parallel with "rock" as the material on which the writing is to be inscribed. The Greek and Latin versions appear to lean to this understanding and Luther rendered "mit einem eisernen Griffel auf Blei." There is no need to depart from the literal translation as was done in the earlier editions of this work. "With iron stylus and lead" is like the expression "with pen and paper," the preposition with the first noun serves also the second.

Lead tablets (*molubdinoi chartai, tabulae plumbae*) were used by the Greeks and Romans. An inscription of the third–second centuries B.C.

found in the necropolis of Duimes at Carthage in 1899 is inscribed on a small sheet of lead and contains an imprecation against the writer's enemies who exulted over him in a monetary dispute which he claims to have settled in full. This tablet was apparently intended, like the Greek and Roman *tabellae devotionis,* as a missive to the gods of the netherworld. These lead tablets were rolled up and dropped through a tube into the sepulcher—the same tube used for libations—to the infernal gods. (Cf. G. A. Cooke, *North-Semitic Inscriptions,* 1903, No. 50, pp. 135 f.) Hittite hieroglyphic texts on lead have also been found. (Cf. Driver, *Semitic Writing,* pp. 15, n. 8, and 84, n. 11.) It is not entirely certain that the word *'ōp̄eret̠* designates "lead." In Akkadian, Aramaic, and Arabic the term for "lead" is *'br.* There is no problem with the interchange of *b* and *p,* but the loss of ' without effect on the adjacent vowels in the Akkadian form *abāru* would be strange. The Sumerian logograms are A.LÙ and A.BÁR. The word may well be non-Semitic. There is a Ugaritic word *ġprt* attested in a list of garments (1106:7, 24) and which Gordon (UT 19:1980) took as a designation of some kind of garment. It should be noted, however, that this fragmentary text mentions in connection with the various garments *iqnu,* "lapis lazuli" (1106:6, 7, 12, 16, 31, 39) and that there is also reference (1106:10) to three hundred *abn ṣrp,* "smelted or shiny stones" (on *ṣurrupu ša abni,* smelting stone, or melting glass[?], cf. CAD, XVI, s.v. *ṣarāpu* A, lexical section). It is thus not clear whether *ġprt* represents a garment, precious stone, or a metal. It is clear from Ezek xxii 20 that *'ōp̄eret̠* designates a metal that can be smelted. It seems unlikely that in the present instance *'ōp̄eret̠* designates the hard material of the point of the stylus, as in Jer xvii 1 *bĕ'ēṭ barzel bĕṣippōren šāmîr,* "with iron stylus, with diamond(?)/emery point."

24b. *forever.* Another possibility is to read with Theodotion *lĕ'ēd̠,* "as witness/testimony", instead of MT *lā'ad̠.* The parallel with Isa xxx 8 is striking:

> Now go, write it,
> On a tablet *cut* (it),
> On a stela grave it.
> Let it be for a latter day,
> As witness to eternity.

(The meaningless *'ittām,* "with them," is conjecturally read as the imperative of *'tm,* "cut," a sense attested in Arabic. The word *sēp̄er* is here rendered "stela" rather than "book," "inscription," or "copper," because of the parallelism with *lûaḥ,* "tablet," and because of the verb *ḥqq,* "engrave." The reading *lĕ'ēd̠,* "as witness," here seems definitely preferable to MT *lā'ad̠.*)

25a. *vindicator.* It is difficult to find an adequate translation of the term *gô'ēl.* It designates the nearest kinsman who was obligated to exact vengeance in a blood feud (Deut xix 6–12; II Sam xiv 11) or otherwise look after the interests of his kinsman by redeeming him from slavery (Lev xxv 48) or regaining the family property (Lev xxv 25), including the decedent's widow in order to provide him an heir by proxy (Ruth iv 4–6). Thus the *gô'ēl* is the defender of the widow and orphan, the champion of the oppressed (Prov xxiii 10–11). The term is often applied to Yahweh as deliverer of Israel from bondage in Egypt (Exod vi 6, xv 13) or from exile (Jer l 34) and dispersion (Isa xliii 1, xliv 6, 24, xlviii 20, lii 9). It is also applied to Yahweh's deliverance of the individual from imminent death (Ps ciii 4; Lam iii 58). It is not clear here whether Job has in mind a human agent who will act as his vindicator. The strongest point in favor of taking the vindicator and guarantor as God is the specific reference to seeing God in 26b. Dahood (*Biblica* 52 [1971], 346) rendered *'aḥărôn* here as "the Ultimate." The application of the term *gô'ēl* to God in this context is questionable since elsewhere in Job's complaint it is God himself who is Job's adversary rather than defender. The difficulty may be alleviated by understanding the term *gô'ēl* here to refer to the agent elsewhere termed an umpire (ix 33) and a witness (xvi 19) who is to serve the same function as the personal god of Sumerian theology, i.e., act as his advocate and defender in the assembly of the gods; cf. xxxiii 23.

25b. The word *'aḥărôn* has generally been construed here as adverbial, "at last." It may also be taken substantively as parallel to *gô'ēl.* Second Isaiah uses the term as a divine epithet, "First and Last," and in Isa xliv 6 it stands in virtual parallelism with *gô'ēl.* If *'aḥărôn* is parallel to *gô'ēl* one may appeal to the Mishnaic and Talmudic term *'aḥăra'y* in the sense of "guarantor."

upon the dust. Cf. v 6, viii 19, xiv 8, xli 25. On *'āpār* as a designation of the netherworld, cf. Dahood, *Psalms I,* fourth NOTE on Ps vii 6, third NOTE on Ps xxii 16, second NOTE on Ps xxx 10, and N. J. Tromp, *Primitive Conceptions of Death and the Nether World in the Old Testament* (Rome, 1969), pp. 32–34, 85–91.

will stand. A juridical term meaning to rise (stand) as a witness in a trial; cf. xvi 8, xxxi 14 and Deut xix 16. Dahood (*Biblica* 52 [1971], 346) suggests that one may consider here the possibility of reading *yiqqôm,* "he will take vengeance," for unexplained MT *yāqûm,* "he will arise," and offers the following translation of xix 25:

> For I know that my Redeemer lives,
> And that the Ultimate will take
> vengeance upon the Slime.

Dahood sees here another allusion to the motif of Yahweh's victory over Sheol; cf. *Biblica* 52 (1971), 346.

26. This verse is notoriously difficult. The ancient versions all differ and no reliance can be placed in any of them. Various emendations have been proposed, but are scarcely worth discussing. Many Christian interpreters since Origen have tried to read here an affirmation of immortality or resurrection, but without success: Chrysostom quite correctly refuted this interpretation with the citation of xiv 12 ff. If one sticks to the text as received, the given translation appears to fit the context as well as any, though many problems persist. Cf. J. Speer, ZAW 25 (1905), 47–140. Dahood (*Psalms II*, second NOTE on Ps lxxiii 26) offers a novel and provocative interpretation of the famous enigma *mibbĕśārî* which he would read *mĕbuśśārî*, construing the form as Pu'al participle with the suffix representing the third person rather than the first and functioning as the dative of agency, "Refleshed by him, I will gaze upon God." Thus Dahood finds here expression of "the doctrine of the creation of a new body for the afterlife." This interpretation, if it could be validated, would have considerable interest as anticipating the climax of Paul's famous discourse on the topic in I Cor xv.

27a. *on my side.* Literally "to/for me."

27c. Literally "my kidneys wear out in my bosom." The bowels and kidneys were regarded as the seat of the emotions, as was the heart of thought. This line, while befitting Job's disturbed condition, stands alone and seems a rather limp conclusion to what precedes.

28–29. These lines are a jumble of verbiage and possibly the text is damaged or misplaced. As far as any sense can be made in the present context, Job appears to charge the friends with prejudice and a desire to persecute him. (Cf. vi 14–30, xiii 7–11, xvii 4–5, xix 1–5.) He warns them of divine judgment. Verse 29 appears to smack of the argument of the friends rather than of Job.

Targ. and many Hebrew manuscripts have in 28b "in him" instead of "in me," but this does not clarify the situation.

29c. *Shaddayan.* MT *šdyn,* remains difficult. LXX's *ischus* relates the word to the root *šdd* in the sense of "violence, power." Vulg. apparently took the *š* as a particle and rendered *dyn* as *judicum.* Similarly Targ. rendered "that you may know that the Supreme Judge is a Righteous Judge." Most moderns follow a similar line, usually emending to *yēš dayyân.* L. R. Fisher, VT 11 (1961), 342–43, suggests that the word is merely an archaic variant of the name Shaddai. The name *šdyn* occurs several times in the alphabetic texts from Ugaritic and is attested also in Akkadian as *šadû-ya-nu,* a variant of the form *ša-du-ya.* While there is no evidence that the form *šdyn* is a divine name, it may very well be that the name Shaddai had a variant form with the *ân/ôn* afformative just as the ancient divine name 'Elyon appears to have had a short form 'Aliy; cf. EUT, p. 58, n. 20. (Even though the names *'ly* and *'lyn* may have never been applied to the same deities, the two forms cannot be separated.) Cf. xxxvi 30a, 33a. We follow Fisher's suggestion here, although with some misgivings.

20. ZOPHAR'S SECOND DISCOURSE
(xx 1–29)

XX 1 Zophar the Naamathite answered:

2 "My dismay gives me answer,
Because of the agitation within me.
3 I listen to your shameful rebuke,
And the spirit of my frame gives me answer.
4 Are you aware of this from of old,
Since man was placed on the earth,
5 That the mirth of the wicked is brief?
The joy of the impious but a moment?
6 Though his pride mount up to heaven,
And his head touch the clouds,
7 He shall perish utterly like dung;
They who saw him will say, 'Where is he?'
8 Like a dream he flies, none can find him,
Dispelled like a phantom of the night.
9 The eye that spied him no more will,
His place never sees him again.
10 His children must redress the poor,
His hands give back his wealth.
11 His bones full of youth
Lie with him in the dust.
12 Though evil is sweet in his mouth,
And he hide it under his tongue,
13 He relishes it, will not let it go,
Retains it under his palate,
14 The food in his bowels is changed
To viper's venom within him.

15 The riches he gorged he vomits;
God expels them from his gut.
16 He shall suck the poison of asps,
The viper's fangs shall slay him.
17 He shall see no streams of oil,
No torrents of honey or curd.
18 He shall restore his gain unused,
His massed wealth he shall not enjoy.
19 For he oppressed and forsook the poor,
Robbed houses he never built.
20 He knew no quiet in his belly,
In his greed he let nothing escape.
21 Nothing survived his ravening;
Therefore his prosperity will not endure.
22 At the peak of plenty stricken,
Every misery will befall him.
23 He shall have his belly full.
He shall send on him his fierce anger,
Rain on him the fire of his wrath.
24 Should he escape the iron weapon,
The bronze bow will overtake him.
25 The shaft will come out his back,
The gleaming point from his gall.
Terrors shall come upon him,
26 Total darkness is in store for him,
An unfanned flame shall consume him.
Who is left in his tent will fare ill.
27 The heavens shall reveal his guilt,
The earth rise up against him.
28 Flood shall roll away his house,
Torrents on the day of wrath.
29 This the fate of a wicked man,
The heritage appointed him by God."

Notes

xx 2–3. Zophar explodes with exasperation at Job's charges against God and his friends. The "shameful rebuke" may have special reference to xix 22 where Job used an offensive figure of speech derived from the practice of homosexual abuse of prisoners; see NOTES on xix 22b and xxxi 31.

3b. *frame*. MT reads *mibbînāṯî*, "from my intellect." Dahood (*Biblica* 38 [1957], 315 f.) proposed the emendation to *bênôṯay*, "within me," transferring the initial *m* to the end of the preceding word as the enclitic emphatic particle. More recently Dahood (NWSPJ, pp. 63 f.) has offered a simpler and better suggestion reading *maḇnîtî*, "my frame." This word occurs in a similar usage in a Thanksgiving Hymn from Qumran (1Q Hodayot VII 4), *wyrw'w kwl 'wšy mbnynty w'ṣmy yprdw*, "all the foundations of my frame were shattered, my bones disjointed."

4 ff. Zophar returns to harp on the same string as his two colleagues: the prosperity of the wicked is only momentary and their downfall will be swift, sure, and ignominious. The worldly success of the wicked in contrast to the sufferings of the righteous was, and is, a vexatious problem to the thinking and feeling man and is a major concern of the biblical wisdom literature. Zophar here elaborates the standard answer; cf. Pss xxxvii and lxxiii.

5b. The Qumran Targum preserves two words from the end of this verse, *l'b' t'd'*, "suddenly it [i.e. joy] passes away." The adverbial phrase *l'wb'*, "suddenly," occurs also in the Genesis Apocryphon xx 9; cf. P. Grelot, "On the Root *'bq/'bṣ* in Ancient Aramaic and in Ugaritic," JSS 1 (1956), 202–5; "Complementary Note on the Semitic Root *'bq-'bṣ*," JSS 2 (1957), 195. On the Ugaritic cognate *'bṣ*, cf. M. Pope, JCS 6 (1952), 135.

6. Cf. Ps xxxvii 35. Some interpreters see here an allusion to the myths of the theomachy and titanomachy, the unsuccessful attempt of displaced or rebellious gods to storm heaven and unseat the high god; cf. Isa xiv 13–14; Ezek xxviii 2, 17, xxxi 6–10. For a discussion of these passages in connection with older forms of the myth, see EUT, pp. 27–32, 92–104.

8. Cf. Ps lxxiii 20 and Isa xxix 8.

9. Cf. vii 8, 10, viii 18; Pss i 4, ciii 16.

11. A premature death is the lot of the wicked; cf. Ps lv 23.

12–14. Evil is likened to a tasty tidbit that turns to poison within the body; cf. Prov xx 17.

15. This figure is independent of the preceding. God does not admin-

ister an emetic to rid the evil man of the poison, rather the greedy man is forced to disgorge his ill-gotten gains.

16a. Cf. Deut xxxii 33.

16b. *fangs*. Literally "tongue." The serpent's darting tongue was apparently thought to carry the poison.

17. The parallelism of the couplet has been marred. The first line is too short and a word for "oil" is to be expected. Therefore, I follow Klostermann in supplying *yiṣhār* or perhaps *šemen;* cf. Mic vi 7. The second line has a surplus with two words for streams and two words (honey and curd) for the material with which the streams flow. I have taken what appears the simplest expedient, adding a word for "oil" in the first line and deleting one of the words for "streams" in the second.

Cf. xxix 6. Oil, butter, milk, and honey were for the symbols and substance of plenty, Exod iii 8, 17, etc. In the Ugaritic myth of Baal the return of the god to life and the restoration of the fertility of the earth is hailed thus (49 III 4–9):

> In a dream of Beneficent El Benign,
> In a vision of the Creator of Creatures,
> The heavens rain oil,
> The wadies flow with honey,
> And I know that Mighty Baal lives,
> That the Prince, Lord of Earth, exists.

Blommerde, following a suggestion of H. P. Chajes, retains the reading *nhry* instead of emending it to *yiṣhar,* on the ground that the root *nhr* means "shine," as does the root of *yiṣhar,* and thus *nhry,* which he vocalizes *nǎhārî,* can also mean "oil." The translation "see" for the idiom *r'y b-* Blommerde considers too weak and he renders "He shall not enjoy streams of oil."

19a. *forsook*. Dahood (JBL 78 [1959], 306), following Ehrlich, took *'zb* here as a noun parallel to "house" in the succeeding line, connecting it with the Mishnaic and modern Hebrew *ma'ăzîḇāh* which designates "a floor built of branches and covered with clay, roof plastering, ceiling." The preceding verb *rṣs* Ehrlich emended to *ntṣ* and translated "Weil er die Lehmhütten der Armen niedergerissen hat." Dahood retained the verb *rṣṣ,* pointing out that the roofs of the huts of the poor are often made of reeds plastered with mud and that the verb *rṣṣ* is used in the famous expression "a bruised reed" (Isa xlii 3). Thus Dahood rendered, "For he crushed the huts of the poor, He has sacked a house which he did not build."

22. *Every misery*. Literally "every miserable hand." "Hand" here is used in the sense of "force, power," so that the meaning is not "the hand

of every one that is in misery," but "the force of every misery, every miserable force."

23b. *He.* I.e., God.

23c. MT "And he shall rain on him in his flesh." Following Dahood (*Biblica* 38 [1957], 314 f.) we read *wĕyamṭēr 'ālāw mabbēl ḥammô.*

24. *bronze bow.* Since bronze is not a practical material for construction of a bow, it has been argued that "bow" is here synecdoche for "arrow" (cf. G. R. Driver, VTS, III [1960], 82). Iron and bronze are elsewhere used as symbols of strength, as in xl 18 of Behemoth's bones; cf. Deut xxxiii 25; Jer xv 12; Amos i 3. Dahood (*Psalms I,* second NOTE ad loc.) interpreted the *qešeṯ nĕḥûšāh* of Ps xviii 35 and II Sam xxii 35 as "the miraculous bow," taking *nĕḥûšāh* from *nḥš* in the sense of "practice divination, to charm, enchant," and relating it to the episode of the bow (allegedly miraculous) crafted by the artisan god Kothar in the Aqhat legend (2 Aqht v 9–13). The "marvelous bow" of Ps xviii 35, however, must be distinguished from the homonymous "bronze bow" of the present passage, according to Dahood. The meaning here is simply that if the wicked escape one disaster, an equal or worse one will befall him. Cf. Isa xxiv 18; Amos v 19; and the Arabic proverb "He ran from the bear and fell in the well" (*harab min al-dubb, waqa' fil-jubb*).

25a. Reading *šelaḥ* for MT *šālap̄,* "he drew," on the basis of LXX (*belos*).

25b. *The gleaming point.* Literally "lightning." Cf. Deut xxxii 41 where "the lightning of my sword" means "my glittering sword," and Nah iii 3; Hab iii 11. Cf. xvi 13c.

26a. Cf. xv 22.

26b. *An unfanned flame.* Literally "a fire not blown (by man)," presumably lightning which in i 16 and II Kings i 12 is called "fire of God."

27. Cf. Deut xxxii 1; Isa i 2. Heaven and earth will testify against the wicked man. The invocation of heaven and earth as sanctioning witnesses apparently goes back to an ancient form of a treaty or covenant oath; cf. the sanctions of the Hittite treaties, ANET, pp. 202–6. Heaven may be a collective representation of all the gods of heaven, and earth a term for the gods of the netherworld, like the Anunnaki and Igigi of Sumerian theology.

28a. According to the Masoretic vocalization vs. 28a says "the increase of his house shall depart/go into exile." The translation above is based on a very slight change in vocalization (*yāḡōl* instead of *yiḡel*) and accords with the LXX understanding of the passage. Vulg. rendering is somewhat different and dubious: "The offspring of his house shall be exposed; he shall be pulled down on the day of God's wrath."

The parallelism shows that *yĕḇûl* does not have here the meaning "produce," but rather "flood," Ar. *wabl, wubul,* Akk. *bubbula, bibbulu.*

Whether the vocalization of the noun is correct in this instance is uncertain, but it is clear that the meaning is the same as the usual Hebrew form *mabbûl*.

28b. The meaning "torrents" for the word *niggārôṯ* is supported by II Sam xiv 14.

29a. Omitting the final word *mē'ĕlôhîm*, "from God." Cf. viii 13, xxvii 13.

29b. *appointed him.* Some critics find the reading *'imrô* unacceptable. On the assumption that it represents a synonymous parallel to the preceding "wicked man," *'aḏām rāšā'*, Eitan related the form to the root *mr'*, "be rebellious," and took it to mean "a violent man, an oppressor." Tur-Sinai, following his hypothesis of mistranslation from Aramaic, assumed that the translator mistook an original *mamrēh*, "rebel," for *mēmĕrēh*, "his word", and accordingly rendered *'imrô*. Fohrer emended to *'îš mĕrî*, "obstinate man." There is no problem whatever with the expression *naḥălaṯ 'imrô mē'ēl*, "the heritage of his command from God," i.e. the heritage appointed him by God. The antecedent of the suffix of the verbal noun *'imrô* is "the wicked man" of the preceding line and the recognition of this simple fact dispels the need to seek for a parallel phrase through ingenious emendation.

21. JOB'S REPLY TO ZOPHAR
(xxi 1–34)

XXI 1 Job answered:

2 "Hear my word attentively,
Let this be the solace you give.
3 Bear with me, let me speak.
When I have spoken, mock on.
4 Is my complaint against man?
Why should I not be impatient?
5 Look at me, and be dismayed,
Clap your hand over your mouth.
6 When I think of it, I am appalled,
Horror lays hold of my flesh.
7 Why do the wicked go on living,
Grow old, even get richer?
8 Their progeny secure with them,
Their offspring in their presence.
9 Their homes free from fear,
No scourge of God upon them.
10 His bull sires without fail,
His cow calves with no loss.
11 They produce a flock of infants,
Their children dance about.
12 They sing to the timbrel and harp,
Revel to the tune of the flute.
13 They pass their days in prosperity,
And quickly go to Sheol.
14 Though they said to God, 'Be gone!
We care not to know your ways.
15 What is Shaddai that we should serve him,
What use for us to entreat him?'

16 [Their prosperity is not in their control,
I am far from agreement with the wicked.]
17 How often is the wicked's lamp snuffed,
Or destruction come upon them?
Or he apportion them pains in his anger?
18 That they become as straw in the wind,
Like chaff the storm snatches away?
19 God stores up misery for his children?
He should pay him so he would know it.
20 Let his own eye see his calamity,
Let him drink the wrath of Shaddai.
21 What cares he for his family after him,
When his quota of months is spent?
22 [Will he teach God knowledge,
Will he judge even the Exalted?]
23 One dies in full vigor,
Wholly at ease and contented,
24 His haunches full and plump,
His bones supple with marrow.
25 Another dies with bitter soul,
Having never tasted happiness.
26 Together they lie in the dust,
And worms crawl over them.
27 Look, I know your thoughts,
The wiles you plot against me.
28 You say, 'Where is the tyrant's house,
Where the dwelling of the wicked?'
29 Have you not asked the wayfarer,
Do you not find their tales strange,
30 That the wicked is spared the day of disaster,
They are delivered from the day of wrath?
31 Who will tell him what he is to his face?
Who will pay him for what he has done?
32 He is borne to the grave,
And over him the tomb keeps watch.

33 Sweet to him are the clods of the valley.
After him all men will follow,
As before him numberless ones.
34 Why then offer me vain comfort?
Your answers remain sheer fraud."

Notes

xxi 2b. *the solace you give.* Literally "your consolations." The literal rendering would be ambiguous, since in English consolation more often refers to what is received rather than given. Job asks nothing of his miserable comforters except the courtesy of discreet silence and an attentive hearing.

3b. *mock on.* The verbs preceding are all plural, but this one is singular. A single Hebrew manuscript has the plural form as does the Syr., Vulg., and LXX. If the singular form is authentic, Job directs this verse specifically to Zophar who has just ended a discourse on the fate of the wicked with the pointed implication that Job falls in this category.

4. Held, *Eretz-Israel,* IX, p. 78, n. 67, admits that the above translation is smooth but charges that it ignores a difficulty. In striving for beauty and terseness, it seemed best to omit the wooden rendition of the elliptical *wĕ'im,* "and if [that be the case]." Admittedly, there should have been a Note. Comparison of the treatments of Dhorme and Tur-Sinai will make it clear that the above sense is in agreement with both. Held's restoration, "Is my complaint to man, or (my vexation to a mortal)?" does not seem justified.

4b. Cf. vi 3, 26, xvi 4–6.

5b. The gesture of awe and stupefaction; cf. xxix 9, xl 4; Mic vii 16. This gesture is graphically represented on a Mesopotamian seal cylinder of the late third millennium B.C. depicting Etana mounting heavenward on eagle's wings while one of the gaping onlookers holds his hand to his mouth; cf. ANEP, 695, p. 333.

6. For MT *bĕśārî,* "my flesh," the Qumran Targum has simply *ly* "me," *wtmh' 'ḥd ly,* "amazement seizes me." Perhaps the change was motivated by the desire to avoid the sexual suggestiveness associated with the term *bāśār,* "flesh"; cf. xxxi 31b.

7. Cf. Jer xii 1–2; Pss lviii 1–5, lxxiii 3 ff.; Mal iii 15.

8 ff. Job flatly contradicts Bildad's view of the fate of the wicked so graphically detailed in xviii 5–21. The first statement contrasts by

implication the case of Job and his ill-fated offspring with the prosperity of the wicked and his progeny. Blommerde, following Dahood (*Biblica* 47 [1966], 411), made this verse a tricolon by construing *lip̄nêhem*, "before them, in their presence," as meaning "ancestors, forefathers," and translated thus:

> Their line is stable;
> their fathers are with them
> and their offspring are before their eyes.

11–13. Job's children also led a joyful life, but they were cut off in youth.

12. Cf. Isa v 12 and Amos vi 5 for similar descriptions of the lyrical revelry of the wicked, probably in the service or cult of Baal. The same mode of expression was used in the worship of Yahweh. The versions confirm the reading *bĕṯōp̄*, "to the timbrel," against the MT *kĕṯōp̄*. Dahood proposed, howbeit "with due reserve," that the reading *ktp* preserves an allusion to the sword dance about which much has been written in connection with Song of Songs vii 1. (On *ktp* as a sword, cf. R. T. O'Callaghan, "The Word *ktp* in Ugaritic and Egypto-Canaanite Mythology," in *Orientalia* 21 [1952], 37–46). Dahood (NWSPJ, p. 65) thus translated xxi 11–12,

> They send forth their young like sheep,
> And their children dance.
> They take up the sword and harp,
> And make merry to the sound of the flute.

Suffice it to note here that no sword is mentioned in connection with "the dance of the two camps" of the Canticle and utmost reserve should be exercised in introducing one in the present context.

13b. *quickly*. Literally "in a moment." Rashi rightly explained this as meaning that the wicked enjoy happy, festive lives and die quietly in old age, spared the pangs of prolonged illness.

14–15. The righteous man desires above all to know God's ways, Ps xxv 4, and to follow the path that brings life, Ps xvi 11. The perverse willfully reject God, yet they continue to prosper.

16. This verse makes excellent sense of itself, but attempts to fit it into the context without twisting the translation have been eminently unsuccessful. The CCD rendering may serve to illustrate:

> If their happiness is not in their hands
> and if the counsel of the wicked is repulsive
> to God,
> How often is the lamp of the wicked put out?

It may be that the verse is misplaced (cf. xxii 18), but if not it may be best to regard it as the pious protest of someone who was scandalized at the idea that the attitude of the wicked might be condoned. Blommerde offered two attempts to make sense of this verse:

> Is not from his hands their prosperity?
> Still, the council of the wicked is far
> from him.

Or:

> Behold, the Mighty One, from his hands
> is their prosperity,
> the council of the wicked is far from him.

(Blommerde read in both cases *bĕyādēm,* instead of MT *bĕyādām,* and construed the suffix as third singular, with enclitic *-m* presumably, and *mennî* as meaning "from him" rather than "from me." In the second alternative the negative *lô'* is read as *lē',* "the Mighty One.")

17. An echo of xviii 5–6; cf. xviii 10 ff., xx 7, 22, 26–28, xxvii 20 ff.; Ps i 4. Job, by implication, admits that things may sometimes happen as the friends claim, but not often enough to make it the rule.

19–21. Job is citing an ancient view that a man's sins are visited on his children, even to the third and fourth generations; cf. Exod xxxiv 7; Deut v 9. This, he objects, if true, is not just. The Deuteronomic Code forbade the application of this principle in law, Deut xxiv 16, and Jeremiah (xxxi 29) and Ezekiel (xviii) received prophetic oracles repudiating the notion that God acts thus. Jesus likewise rejected the imputation that a man's blindness might be punishment for the sin of his parents, John ix 1–3. The mob at the crucifixion, however, is represented as willing that guilt be passed on to their offspring, Matt xxvii 25. Job already has answered the present argument with the denial that the dead in the netherworld either know or care what happens to their descendants (xiv 21–22); cf. Eccles ix 5.

20a. *his calamity.* In previous editions of this work, Dahood's suggestion (*Biblica* 38 [1957], 316) was adopted and the hapax *kîdô* was changed to *kaddô,* "his pitcher." Dahood pointed out that the Ugaritic texts use the word *krpn* (Akk. *karpu, karpatu,* "jar, pitcher") in parallelism with the word *ks* (Heb. *kôs,* "cup") as the vessel from which the gods drink. Thus "pitcher, jar" is an ancient poetic synonym for cup. The allusion thus would be to the cup of fate and divine wrath; cf. Pss xvi 5, lxxv 9; Isa li 17; Jer xxv 15; Rev xvi 19. The reference to drinking in the parallel line may be taken to support this emendation. Dhorme emended *kîdô* to *pîdô,* "his calamity," rejecting Ar. *kayd* in the sense of "fraud, trickery," as unsuitable. Ar. *kayd,* however, also has the meaning "punishment" and *kayd 'allāh* refers to divine punishment for perfidy which is exactly the sense indicated by the present context. The Qumran Targum is very fragmentary here, but enough is preserved to support the retention of MT *kîdô,* [. . .']*nwhy bmplth,* "his eyes [will look] on his downfall."

21a. MT may be woodenly rendered, "For what is his concern with his house after him?" The Qumran Targum referred the suffix of *ḥep̄ṣô,* "his concern," to God, . . .] *ṣbw l'lh' bbyth,* . . .] "interest for God in his house."

22. This verse, like 16 above, seems out of place in Job's mouth. Some interpreters regard it as an ironical thrust of Job against the friends. Others see it as Job's musing to himself. It seems more likely that it is misplaced from one of the discourses of the friends, or that some scandalized scribe has added it as a marginal protest against Job's blasphemous accusations against God. The Qumran Targum, however, preserves the beginning of the verse, *hl'*[*lh'* . . . , "Is it to God . . . ?", and the second half verse in its entirety, in the order of MT. Blommerde noted that *rāmîm* may be a plural of majesty rather than *rāmî-* plus enclitic *-m.* The translation "Most High" employed by both Dahood and Blommerde and adopted in the former editions of this work is here abandoned in favor of "the Exalted," since "Most High" has long been pre-empted for *'elyôn* under the influence of the Greek rendering *hypsistos.*

22b. *Exalted.* Dahood (*Biblica* 38 [1957], 316f.) suggested that *rāmîm,* "high ones," does not refer to the angels but to God himself and should be read *rām* or *rōm* with the enclitic emphatic *-m*(*a*). This line is preserved in the Qumran Targum, [*w*]*hw' rmy' mdyn,* "And he judges the High Ones." S. Kaufman notes that Heb. *špṭ* is usually translated by the *Pĕ'al* of *dyn* in the Targums, but the present form *mdyn* can only be the *Pa'ēl* participle. The *Pa'ēl* normally means "to argue" in Western Aramaic as in Rabbinic Hebrew, but is used in the sense "to judge" in TB and Mandaic, according to Kaufman.

23–26. The time and manner of one's death appear to have no relation to the quality of life involved, and in the netherworld all are equal; cf. iii 19; Eccles ii 14–16, iii 19–30; Ecclesiasticus xli 1–3.

23b. *at ease.* This unique form, *šal'ănān* has generally been taken as a scribal error for *sa'ănān.* Blommerde (p. 12) explains it as "congeneric assimilation" of *šālēw* and *ša'ănan.* Guillaume regarded the word as "a pure Arabism," comparing the "intrusive" *l* with forms like *jalmūd,* "rock" in both Arabic and Hebrew, and Ar. *dahmat* and *dalham,* "blackness." There is no need to regard the form as an Arabism since analogous forms with insertion of a liquid are common in Semitic, e.g. Akk. *algamešu,* Ugar. *algbṯ, krpn, ḫnzr, grdš.*

24a. *haunches.* The first word of the line is hapax and has never been satisfactorily explained. In post-biblical Hebrew the root is connected with oil pressed from olives, in Arabic the connection is with a watering place where camels kneel. The ancient versions shrewdly guess that the reference is to a part of the body. LXX and Vulg. took it to mean "intestines" (*'égkata*), *viscera;* the Targ., "teats." JPS renders "His pails are full of milk." The change of a letter, *n* to *m,* would give the Aramaic word for "bones," but against this is the use of the Hebrew cognate in the parallel line 24b. The same change would also give a plausible meaning "flanks, haunches"; cf. Akk. *eṣmu,* Aram. *'iṭmā'*. This I adopt as a *pis aller.* The Qumran Targum preserves two letters of the beginning of this line, *'b,* presumably part of the word which renders the hapax *'āṭîn.* Mr. Bruce Zuckerman suggested a plausible restoration *'b*[*wz*], a word which is also hapax in TB (Erubin 53b) as a euphemism for "buttocks." Another possibility is *'k*[*wz*], also meaning "buttocks."

full and plump. Literally "full of fat," reading *ḥēleḇ* for MT *ḥālāḇ,* "milk."

24b. Cf. Prov iii 8 where moist bones are a figure of health and prosperity.

25. Cf. iii 20.

26b. Cf. xvii 14; Isa xiv 11b.

27. Job lets his opponents know that the thrust of their argument is not lost on him: The wicked are ruined; Job is ruined; Job is therefore wicked. Cf. iv 7.

28. Cf. viii 15, xv 34, xviii 15, 21.

29. Any wayfarer (Lam i 12, ii 15; Pss lxxx 13, lxxxix 42[41]; Prov ix 15), not necessarily a world traveler, could tell them that their assertions are not consonant with everyday experience.

29b. *tales.* Literally "signs, tokens, monuments."

30. This verse is difficult. Certainly Job is denying what the friends have asserted in xv 22–24, xviii 14–15, 18, xx 11, 22, 25, that the wicked always suffer. In order to make the sense suit the context, it is necessary to take the preposition *lĕ* in both lines in the sense of "from" rather than "to/for." The prepositions *b* and *l* frequently have separative force in Ugaritic, and C. H. Gordon has pointed out several passages in the OT where this seems to be the case (cf. UH 10.1).

30b. *delivered.* Literally "brought" (away from). On the day of wrath, cf. xx 28; Deut xxxii 35; Isa xxvi 20; Jer xviii 17; Ezek vii 19; Zeph i 15, 18; Prov xi 4.

31a. *what he is.* Literally "his way," i.e., his conduct and way of life. Ibn Ezra and Rashi suggested that the allusion may be to God, but it seems more likely that the reference is to the human despot who comes to his end without anyone ever having dared to oppose him or tell him to his face his true character.

32. Contrary to what the friends assert, the wicked usually die in peace and have a grand funeral and their body is guarded by a mausoleum, perhaps with curses engraved to ward off grave robbers.

33a. Burial was often in a valley or ravine; cf. Deut xxxiv 6.

clods. Guillaume argues that the meaning "stones" is required here since the winter rains would sweep clods away and destroy all traces of the grave. In xxxviii 38 the meaning "clods" is clearly demanded by the context, but Guillaume explained that the poet used *regeḇ,* "stone," in the sense of "clod" because after the rain clods became hard as stones in the heat of the sun. It seems best to render "clods" in both places.

33b. It is uncertain whether the reference is to the masses who follow in the funeral procession, or to those who imitate the defunct one's mode of life.

33c. Larcher in BJ understands this line as a gloss, added by someone who understood "after him" of the preceding line in the temporal sense, and accordingly he omits the line.

34. Cf. xvi 2. This speech of Job completes the second cycle.

22. ELIPHAZ'S THIRD DISCOURSE
(xxii 1–30)

XXII 1 Eliphaz the Temanite answered:

2 "Can a man benefit God,
Even a sage benefit him?
3 What good to Shaddai if you are just?
What gain if your conduct be perfect?
4 Is it for your piety he reproves you,
Enters into judgment with you?
5 Is not your wickedness great?
Are not your iniquities endless?
6 You have taken your brothers' pledge unjustly,
And stripped the clothing of the naked.
7 You gave the weary no water,
You withheld bread from the hungry.
8 A mighty man who owns the earth,
A privileged inhabitant of it!
9 Widows you sent away empty,
Orphans' arms you broke.
10 Therefore snares surround you,
And sudden dread dismays you,
11 Darkness where you cannot see,
The streaming water covers you.
12 Is not God in the height of heaven?
See the topmost stars, how high!
13 And you say, 'What does God know?
Can he judge through the dark cloud?
14 Clouds hide him, he cannot see.
He walks the rim of heaven.'
15 Do you mark the dark path
The way worthless men have trod,

16 Who were snatched untimely away,
Their foundation swept by the torrent?
17 They said to God, 'Let us be!
What can Shaddai do for us?'
18 [Though he filled their houses with good—
Far from me be the attitude of the impious.]
19 The righteous see and rejoice,
The innocent deride them:
20 'Surely their substance is cut off,
Their surplus the fire burns.'
21 Yield to him, submit;
Thereby good will come to you.
22 Accept instruction from his mouth,
Take his words to your heart.
23 If you return to Shaddai you will be healed.
Put iniquity far from your tent,
24 Lay your gold in the dust,
Ophir among the pebbles of the brook.
25 Let Shaddai be your gold,
Silver piled high for you;
26 Then, shall you delight in Shaddai,
And lift your face to God.
27 When you pray, he will hear you,
And your vows you will fulfill.
28 You will decree and it will happen.
Light will shine on your path.
29 When they abase, you may order exaltation;
And the lowly of man he will save.
30 He will deliver one not innocent,
Who may escape by your clean hands."

Notes

xxii 2–3. Cf. xxxv 7 where Elihu expresses the same thought. The point of the argument seems to be that God can have no ulterior motive in dealing with Job, since there is nothing Job can do to benefit Him. As Milton put it, "God doth not need / Either man's work or his own gifts." Job has already (vii 20) used this argument in quite a different way: What harm can man do God? Why then should God care what man does? Why not leave him alone?

6. The Law required that a garment taken in pledge be returned before sundown. Exod xxii 26; Deut xxiv 10–13; cf. Amos ii 8; Ezek xviii 12.

6b. The text reads: "And the clothing-of-the-naked you have stripped." We cannot press the poet to be more precise. The victims are, of course, naked *after* they have been stripped.

7. Cf. Isa lviii 7, 10; Matt xxv 35, 42.

8. *mighty man.* Literally "man of arm." Cf. Isa v 8. Apparently an oblique reference to Job as an arrogant land-grabber who dispossessed his weaker neighbors. Some critics have suspected the verse as out of place, since elsewhere in the discourse Eliphaz addresses Job directly. R. Gordis, in accordance with his views on "The Use of Quotations in Job" (ch. xiii of his commentary, pp. 169–89), introduced this verse with the explanatory addition *For you believe* (p. 180 italicized but not so delineated as an addition in the translation; cf. M. Pope, JBL 85 [1966], 529). The Qumrân Targum preserves of this verse only the introductory addition *w'mrt,* "And you say." S. Kaufman opined that this targumic addition lends support to Gordis' theories on the use of quotations in Job. This is a striking coincidence, but it proves no more than that the Targumist anticipated Gordis in one instance, and both could be mistaken. Of several other places where Gordis also supplied introductory formulae, no confirmation is found in what is preserved of the Qumran Targum.

9. The widow and the orphan were objects of particular concern; cf. Exod xxii 21; Deut xxiv 17; Isa i 17. The Code of Hammurabi required that the widow and orphan be treated fairly. In the Ugaritic epics of Danel and Keret, the sage Danel is one who judges the cause of the widow and adjudicates the case of the orphan (2 Aqht v 7–8) and the ailing King Keret is accused by his son of neglecting this very duty (127:41–52); cf. NOTE on xxxvi 17.

10. What Bildad (xviii 8–11) had predicated of the wicked in general, Eliphaz here applies specifically to Job; cf. also xix 6.

11a. Contrast Isa lviii 10–11.

11b. This line in Hebrew is verbatim with xxxviii 34b, but the contexts are quite different. Water and mire, like darkness, are standard figures for the perils of death and the netherworld; cf. Ps lxix 2–3; Jon ii 3–6. On the watery, miry, and putrescent character of the netherworld, cf. ix 31a.

12–14. God's transcendence could be regarded in opposite ways. The impious man might think that God did not even exist, or at least was not concerned with man, Pss x 4, lxxiii 11; Isa xxix 15.

The pious man could view God's exalted position as a vantage point from which all man's doings are observed; cf. Ps xxxiii 13; Isa xl 22, 26–27. Eliphaz's insinuation that Job thinks God does not see is contradicted by Job's own words; cf. vii 19, x 6, 14, xiv 3, 6. Dahood (*Orientalia* 34 [1965], 171, and *Psalms I,* second NOTE on Ps x 4) saw here two divine titles in chiastic parallelism, *gōḇah šāmayim,* "the Lofty One of Heaven", and *rô'eh,* "the One Who Sees" (reading as the participle instead of MT's imperative), and rendered:

> Is not God the Lofty One of Heaven,
> and the One Who Sees the tops of the stars
> though they are high?
> And yet you say, "What does El know?
> Can he govern through the heavy cloud?"

14b. *rim.* Literally "circle." The reference is to the dome or vault of heaven; cf. Isa xl 22 where "the circle of the earth" refers to the horizon above which God sits, and Prov viii 27 where the "circle on the face of the deep" describes the ground plan for the creation of heaven and earth.

15. *the dark path.* MT reads the "old way." In Jer vi 16 "the ancient paths" refers to the good way. The evil way is doubtless as old as the good, but one may wonder whether it would be dignified by the title "ancient." Tur-Sinai suggested connection of the word with the root *'wl,* "wicked," rather than *'lm,* "old." The final *-m* of *'wlm* might then be either the masculine plural ending or the enclitic emphatic particle used as a "ballast variant" to add a syllable to the line. Dahood (NWSPJ, pp. 65 f.) offers a better suggestion, connecting the word with Ugaritic *ġlm,* "grow dark." The word is used in xlii 3 *ma'lîm 'ēṣāh,* "darkening counsel," a variant of the term *maḥšîḵ 'ēṣāh*. The noun occurs in Eccles iii 11, "darkness," or "ignorance," hardly "eternity." References to walking in darkness are too numerous to be listed; cf. Eccles ii 14; Prov ii 13.

15b. *The way.* Instead of MT's vocalization as the relative particle *'ăšer,* read *'āšûr.*

16b. Many interpreters incorrectly take this line to refer to the Flood. The thought is only of the sudden destruction of the wicked, exactly as in Jesus' parable of the man who built his house on sand, Matt vii 26.

17b. Cf. xxi 14b, 15a. "For us" or "to us," rather than "them," with LXX and Syr. Dahood (*Biblica* 46 [1965], 324; 47 [1966], 409) assumes a new morpheme in consonantal *lmw,* "for us," rather than a scribal error. The Qumran Targum preserves two words of this line *ln' 'lh*['], the *ln',* "for us," corresponding to MT *lmw* and *'lh*['] to *šadday.*

18b. Cf. xxi 16b.

19a. Almost verbatim with Ps cvii 41a; cf. also Ps lxix 33.

20a. Reading with LXX (*hypostasis autōn*) *yĕqûmām* for the improbable MT *qîmānû*. The parallel *yitṯrām* in the next line confirms the sense of the word and the person of the possessive suffix. Guillaume related the word *qîmānû* to Ar. *qiwām*, "sustenance," and *qiyām*, "subsistence," and opined that though the suffix *ānû* is hard to explain, there is no need to emend.

21a. The verb here rendered "yield" (*haskēn*) occurs twice elsewhere in somewhat different senses, Num xxii 30 and Ps cxxxix 3. The usage here is virtually identical in form and sense with an occurrence in the Ugaritic myth of Baal (*šskn*). LXX *genou dē sklēros* is difficult to understand. Vulg. reads *acquiesce* and Syr. *'štwy*, "agree," Targ. *'ălep̄ kĕḏûn*, "learn now." The Qumran Targum reads *hstkl*, "reflect, become wise." The Ugaritic use of the term (51 I 21) is in connection with an entreaty:

ap mṯn rgmm argmk
šskn m' mgn rbt aṯrt ym
mġẓ qnyt ilm

A further word I would tell you.
Pray agree to entreat Dame Aṯirat of the Sea,
To beseech the Creatrix of the Gods.

Vulg. *acquiesce* seems most suitable to the context.

submit. Literally "be at peace." The sense here is very similar to the usage in Islam. The Muslim is he who attains peace by submission to God. Eliphaz here repeats the advice he offered in his first speech, v 8, 17–27. This is essentially the same as the ancient Sumerian view, that a man in straits like Job had no recourse or hope except to bow to his fate and importune the god to reverse his fortunes. Cf. Kramer, WIANE, pp. 170 ff.; HTR 49 (1956), 59 f.

21b. Literally, "through them your income [will be] good." Blommerde takes the feminine nominal form *ṭôḇāh* as a divine title, "the Good One," "then your gain will be the Good One," and similarly in Pss xvi 2 and lxxxvi 17; cf. Dahood, *Psalms II*, second NOTE on Ps lxxxvi 17, and *III*, second NOTE on Ps cxix 122.

22b. Dahood (*Biblica* 47 [1966], 108 f.) suggested that the underlying figure here is that of a scribe taking dictation; cf. *Psalms II*, fourth NOTE on Ps lvi 9.

23a. *healed.* Literally "you will be built [up]." LXX reads "humbly" which RSV adopts. The passive of the verb *bny*, "build," is used of persons rendered prosperous in Jer xii 16; Mal iii 15. In the Ugaritic epic of Aqhat, or Danel (1 Aqht 119), *bny* is used of the restoration of the eagle's broken wing. It is, therefore, not too remote to take the word here in the sense of "heal, restore," as tentatively suggested by Dahood (NWSPJ, p. 66).

24b. Cf. xxxi 24. Ophir, the name of the land, is here used for its famous product. Solomon sent ships from Ezion-geber to fetch gold from Ophir (I Kings ix 26–28, x 11) and Jehoshaphat tried unsuccessfully to do the same (I Kings xxii 48). Ophir has not been located. India, South Arabia, and East and South Africa have been suggested sites.

25. *piled high.* A conjecture since the word in question (*tô'ăpôṯ*) has never been satisfactorily explained. Cf. Num xxiii 22, xxiv 8 where it is applied to the horns or humps of the wild ox (cf. W. F. Albright, JBL 63 [1944], 215, n. 47) and Ps xcv 4 to the mountain heights.

26. Cf. xxvii 10; Isa lviii 14. Lifting the head in confidence, as in x 15, xi 15.

27. Cf. Isa lviii 8–9.

28a. Literally "You will decree a thing and it will stand for you."

28–30. The idea that a righteous man, a *ṣaddîq,* or saint, had great influence with God, even to the point of nullifying a divine decree, or saving the wicked out of consideration for the righteous, is implicit in the story of Abraham's plea on behalf of Sodom, Gen xviii 21–33. The three ancient worthies Danel, Noah, and Job were apparently credited with the ability to save others through their own transcendent righteousness, Ezek xiv 14, 20, though this notion is emphatically rejected by Ezekiel (Ezek xiv 12 ff., xviii) and Jeremiah (Jer xxxi 29–30). This idea is explicit in a saying in TB, Moed Qatan 16b. "The Holy One, blessed be He, said, 'I rule over man, but who rules over Me? The Saint, for when I issue a decree, he sets it aside.'" This notion is reflected in the popular belief in the thirty-six saints by whose righteousness the sinful world was preserved from ruin. "The world could not do with less than thirty-six saints who greet the Divine Presence (Shekinah) daily," TB, Sukkah 45b. The Rabbinic concept of Zekut Abot, by which the ordinary Israelite could draw on the supererogatory merits of the patriarchs, is another expression of the same idea; cf. R. Gordis, JNES 4 (1945), 54–55. Cf. Matt. vi 19 f. and H. L. Strack and P. Billerbeck, *Kommentar zum Neuen Testament aus Talmud und Midraschim,* I, 1922, pp. 429 ff.

30a. This verse has been a vexation to exegetes. Targ. took *'î nāqî* to be an abbreviation for *'îš nāqî,* "an innocent man," and so RSV. LXX, Vulg., and Syr. simply omit the offending element *'î.* KJ's "island of the innocent" derives from Ibn Ezra and is given a different twist by Tur-Sinai who takes it to mean "the innocent man delivereth the (is)land." N. M. Sarna (JNES 15 [1956], 118–19) would connect the element *'î* with the indefinite pronoun *'ayyu,* as did Samuel Lee in 1837 (*The Book of the Patriarch Job,* p. 366).

The sense, according to Sarna, is "He delivers whoever is innocent." Actually there is no warrant for scouting the natural negative sense of the particle *'î*, as it occurs in Phoenician (cf. Z. S. Harris, *A Grammar of the Phoenician Language,* 1936, p. 76) and elsewhere in Hebrew. Verse 30b clinches the negative sense of 30a, since if a man were already innocent he would not need Job's clean hands to effect his deliverance. Cf. R. Gordis, JNES 4 (1945), 54–55.

23. JOB'S REPLY TO ELIPHAZ
(xxiii 1–17)

XXIII 1 Job answered:

2 "Even today my speech is defiance.
His hand is heavy despite my groaning.
3 O that I knew where to find him,
That I might come to his tribune.
4 I would lay my case before him,
Would fill my mouth with arguments.
5 I want to know what words he would answer me,
To consider what he would say to me.
6 Through an attorney would he sue me?
Nay, he himself should give heed to me.
7 There the upright could reason with him;
I could bring justice to successful birth.
8 Lo, I go forward, and he is not there;
Backward, and I cannot perceive him;
9 Left I turn and cannot see him;
I turn right and do not spy him.
10 But he knows the way I take;
When he tests me, I shall emerge as gold.
11 My foot has held to his path,
I have kept his way unerring.
12 The commands of his lips I have not neglected;
In my bosom I treasured the words of his mouth.
13 He chooses and who can turn him?
What he wishes, he does.
14 He will execute my sentence;
Many such things he has in store.

15 Therefore I am dismayed before him;
I think of it, and recoil from him.
16 God has made my heart weak,
Shaddai has terrified me.
17 Would that I could vanish in darkness,
And thick gloom cover my face.

Notes

xxiii 2a. This literal (?) translation is not very satisfactory, but neither are any of the various emendations based in part or in the whole on the LXX reading "And now surely I know that from my hand is the blame." "Even today" has been taken as an indication that the debate lasted several days, the sequel being held over to the following day to heighten the interest, as in the Arabian Nights and modern serial melodrama. This, presumably, would be the third day of debate. The text, however, is very difficult and may be corrupt.

2b. This line also is difficult. The text says "My hand is heavy upon my groaning." With LXX, Syr., and RSV, we read "his hand." The difference between the letters which represent the two suffixes is very slight in late forms of the script, and in the Dead Sea scrolls the two letters (*w* and *y*) are often indistinguishable. Dahood (NWSPJ, p. 62; *Psalms II,* sixth Note on Ps lxxvii 3), followed by Blommerde, construed the final *-y* of *ydy* as representing the third masculine suffix. The preposition *'al,* "upon," may denote opposition and is here taken in that sense, but it is something of a strain to get any likely meaning from this part of the line. The line is strikingly similar to the beginning of the third tablet of *Ludlul Bēl Nēmeqi,* "His hand was heavy (upon me). I was not able to bear it." Lambert (BWL, p. 23) considers this line of great importance for the understanding of the Akkadian poem. The Mesopotamian writer avoids using the name of the god in his protest and refers to him obliquely with the suffix of the third person singular. "The almighty Marduk was at the root of the trouble, and although the pious hero dare not openly expostulate with him, he cannot leave the subject without a guarded allusion to the cause of his suffering." Job, in contrast, has no scruples against making his charges directly and explicitly against God.

3. Cf. xiii 3.

4a. Cf. xiii 18a.

4b. Cf. ix 14–17, xiii 6; Ps xxxviii 15.

6–7. If only he could argue his case before God in a fair trial, Job is confident of his vindication.

6. *attorney*. Tur-Sinai has shown rather convincingly that the term *kōaḥ* in this context means "legal power" and that *raḇ-kōaḥ* is a technical term for "plenipotentiary," one given power of attorney; cf. ix 19 where "strength" (*kōaḥ*) is parallel to "judgment" (*mišpāṭ*).

7b. As vocalized, the MT has to be rendered "And I would escape successfully/forever from my judge." A slight change in the vocalization of the last word gives the sense above. The verb here is used in xxi 10b of a cow giving birth. The idiom is the same as in Hab i 4, though different verbs are used. The figure is that of justice escaping or emerging as it were from the womb, successfully, or in Hab i 4, unsuccessfully and distorted.

8–9. Forward, backward, left, right, *or* east, west, north, south. Forward (*qeḏem*) often means "east" and "behind, backward," may also mean "west"; cf. Isa ix 11 "from before" and "from behind" meaning "on the east" and "on the west." Rashi and Ibn Ezra understood the words to refer to the four cardinal directions and certainly it amounts to just that.

9a. "Where/when he doth work" (KJ and JPS) makes little sense. The best suggestions (I. Eitan and D. Yellin) have been to connect the word with Arabic verbs meaning either "go/turn" or "cover." Either sense would suit the parallel verb of 9b which may mean "cover," as in Pss lxv 14, lxxiii 6, or in Syriac and Arabic "turn, turn back." The Syr. and Vulg. reading "I turn" are followed here; cf. Ps cxxxix 7–10.

10a. *the way I take*. Literally "the way (that is) with me." A strange way of saying "the way I go." Probably the text is corrupt. Cf. Ps cxxxix 1–6; Jer xi 20.

10b. Cf. Ps xvii 3.

emerge. Or possibly "shine." That the verb *yṣ'* sometimes has the sense "shine" (related to Ar. *waḍu'a*, "be clean, fair," and *ḍa'a*, "shine") has long been recognized. Perhaps the best examples are Isa lxii 1; Jer xlviii 9; Hos vi 5; Ps xxxvii 6; cf. Dahood, NWSPJ, p. 67, n. 65.

11. Cf. Ps xvii 5.

12a. It has been suggested that the poet here betrays his Israelite-Jewish background in the use of the word "commandment" (*miṣwāh*), but in itself the use of this word is not conclusive evidence.

12b. Reading with LXX "in my bosom," rather than MT "more than my prescribed portion"; cf. xxii 22 and Ps cxix 11. On the locative sense of the preposition *min*, cf. Dahood, *Biblica* 48 (1967), 427.

13. *chooses*. The emendation involves a very slight change, from *b'ḥd* to *bḥr*, and is virtually confirmed by the parallelism; cf. Ps

cxxxii 13 where the same two verbs, choose/wish, occur as parallel synonyms. Dahood (NWSPJ, p. 67) retains the reading *bĕ'eḥād* and explains it as meaning "only ruler," on the basis of Ugar. *aḥdy dymlk 'l ilm*, "I alone will rule over the gods" (UT, 51 VII 49 f.) and similar expressions in Akkadian, such as *edišs̆iya*, "I alone," and *edišša ṣirat*, "she alone is mighty." The preposition *b-* Dahood explains as "an emphasizing particle, a kind of exponential strengthening of the substantive." There is yet another way to retain and explain MT *bĕ'eḥād*, viz. to take *'eḥad*, "one," as the indefinite pronoun, "anyone"; the line might thus be rendered, "Were He against one, who could turn him back?" It seems best to take the cue from the verb *'wy* of 13b and read *bḥr* instead of *b'ḥd*.

14. This verse is omitted in manuscripts of LXX, but this is not necessarily an indication that it was missing from the original. The divine decree is immutable; cf. Isa xlv 23, lv 10–11.

14a. *my sentence*. Syr. and Vulg. read the third person rather than the first person suffix. Dahood (*Orientalia* 32 [1963], 499), followed by Blommerde, suggested that the final *î* of *ḥuqqî* represents the third person suffix, as in Phoenician. On the term *ḥōq*, cf. Dahood, *Psalms I*, first NOTE on Ps ii 7.

14b. *in store*. Literally "with him." It is not clear whether Job means that God has still more calamity reserved for him or for others, or both.

17a. MT reads "Because I was not cut off/did not become extinct from before darkness." One manuscript omits the negative and RSV follows this reading, but the sense is still unsatisfactory. The best expedient seems that taken by CCD, reading the precative *lû'*, "O would that," instead of the negative *lô'*, "not."

24. JOB'S REPLY (*continued*)
(xxiv 1–3; 9; 21; 4–8; 10–14b; 15; 14c; 16–17)

XXIV

1 "Why are times not set by Shaddai,
And his friends never see his days?
2 The wicked remove landmarks;
They seize flock and shepherd.
3 Orphans' asses they drive away;
They take the widow's ox for a pledge.
9 They snatch the orphan from the breast,
The suckling of the poor they seize.
21 [He feeds on the childless woman,
He does no good to the widow.]
4 They push the needy from the path;
The poor of the earth are driven into hiding.
5 Like an onager in the steppe they go
To their task of finding food;
The desert yields bread for their young.
6 In the field of the villain they reap,
In the vineyard of the wicked they glean.
7 Naked they sleep, without clothing,
With no cover against the cold.
8 Wet with the mountain rains,
For shelter hugging the rocks.
10 Naked they go without clothing,
Hungry, they carry the sheaves.
11 Between the millstones they press oil,
The presses they tread, but thirst.
12 From the city the dying groan,
The throats of the wounded cry;
Yet God thinks nothing amiss.

13 They are rebels against the light
Who do not know its way,
Nor remain in its paths.
14 At twilight the murderer rises
To slay the poor and the needy.
15 The adulterer waits for dusk,
Thinking, 'No eye will see me.'
He puts a cover over his face,
14c At night he becomes like a thief.
16 In the dark he breaks into houses.
They shut themselves in by day;
They do not know the light.
17 Morning to them is darkness;
Well they know the terrors of darkness."

NOTES

xxiv 1. *times*. RSV adds "of judgment," by way of interpretation. The times or days are apparently the same as depicted in the Prologue, i 6, ii 1, the days of decision.

friends. Literally "his knowers," i.e., "those who know him"; cf. xviii 21 and Ps xxxvi 11.

2a. Supplying the subject "the wicked," following LXX. The line is too short and the need for an explicit subject is variously supplied by the versions. Targ. refers to "the generation of the Flood." Saadia supplies "people" (*qawm*); cf. Deut xix 14, xxvii 17; Prov xxiii 10.

2b. *and shepherd*. Following LXX. MT has "and they feed (them)." If MT is correct, the meaning is apparently that the wicked are so brazen as to publicly flaunt their plunder of the helpless.

3. Cf. xxii 6, 9; Num xvi 15; I Sam xii 3. The Code of Hammurabi (No. 241) imposes a fine on a man who takes the ox of one in distress. The spoliation of the widow and orphan is doubly heinous.

9. This couplet is out of place and is perhaps best inserted here.

9b. Reading with LXX *'ul*, "suckling," rather than MT *'al*, "upon."

21. This verse also fits better here than in its traditional position.

21a. *the childless woman*. Literally "the sterile female who does not produce children," a redundant or *idem per idem* construction, similarly

Isa liv 1. Cf. II Sam xiv 5, "I am a widow and my husband is dead"; Gen. xxiv 16, "a virgin and no man had known her."

4. This passage makes it clear that the almost identical passage in Amos ii 7 should be rendered "and turn aside the afflicted from the way" rather than "and turn aside the way of the afflicted," even though the preposition is missing; cf. Amos v 12 and Isa x 2 where prepositions are used in analogous expressions. On this grammatical feature, cf. M. Pope, "Ugaritic Enclitic *-m*," JCS 5 (1951), 123–28.

5a. It is not necessary to assume the omission of the comparative particle *k*, or that *hēn* is a corruption of *hêḵ*, in order to get the sense required by the context. As in Hos viii 9, the word *pere'* is used adverbially to indicate mode or manner. Possibly the word *pere'* is to be construed here as singular, as in Hos viii 9, and the final *-m* would thus be the enclitic poetic "ballast variant" so common in the Ugaritic texts. The plural verb in 5b has no bearing on this question since the subject is not the word "onager/s." The unexpressed subject has changed from the oppressors of vss. 2–4 to the oppressed, "the poor of the earth/land" mentioned in 4b. Cf. xxx 2–8, where the condition of the destitute and outcast is described vividly but unsympathetically. The verb *yāṣĕ'û*, "they go (out)," is read as the last word of the first stich rather than as the first word of the second.

5c. *The desert.* The word *'rbh* may be taken in several different senses here and the versions disagree: cf. Dhorme. The context suggests either "evening" or "desert." Dhorme opted for the sense "evening," but indicated his uncertainty with italics:

Although they work until the evening,
No bread for the children!

The word *miḏbār* "steppe(land)," in 5a is taken as the cure for the rendering "desert." Dhorme discusses several other difficulties in this passage and comments: "A spirit of arbitrariness seems to have presided over the various attempts to restore this unfortunate verse."

6. The parallelism of this couplet would be perfect were it not for the second word of the first line which, as it now stands, means "his mixed fodder." The same consonantal text is reflected by LXX, Vulg., and Targ., but the word is divided in two: *bly/lw*, "not his." Following the suggestion of Houbigant, many modern exegetes read *blylh*, "at night," but this is not much better. Taking the cue from "the wicked" of the second member of the bicolon, we emend to *bly'l*, "worthless person, villain," with Larcher. Guillaume related the word *rāšā'* to Ar. *rassaġa*, "he provided handsomely for his family," and rendered vs. 6 thus:

They cut their provender in the field;
And they glean the vintage of the rich.

7a. *sleep.* Literally "pass the night." The redundant "without clothing" is the same sort of construction as in xxiv 21a.

8b. *For shelter.* Literally "from (*being*) without shelter."

10a. This line is almost verbatim with 7a and would appear to be a misplaced variant except for the parallelism of 10b. Tur-Sinai suggested that the translator-redactor here mistook the Aram. *'zl,* "spin," for *'zl,* "go," and accordingly mistranslated *hlk.* Those who spin or weave remain naked, as those who reap are hungry (10b) and they who tread the wine press thirsty (11). This is one of the most striking of Tur-Sinai's many ingenious proposals, but it is difficult to accept the theory of translation on which it is based.

11a. The difficulties of this line are formidable and one can only guess at the meaning, assuming the text to be correct. The verb is generally taken as denominative from *yiṣhār,* "oil," in the sense of "produce, or press out oil." It might also be connected with the noun *ṣōhar,* "zenith," in the sense of "do [something] at high noon." The text then seems to say "between their walls/rows they press out oil/spend the noon." Emendation of "their walls" to "their songs" or "their cows" does not help. The clue to the sense is furnished by the parallel line; accordingly Dhorme's suggestion (reading *šûrôṯayim* for *šûrôṯām* and giving it the sense of "two mills") seems the best yet offered and is here adopted as a *pis aller.* Tur-Sinai's emendation and rendering "They pass the noonday between deceptive palm trees" is no better than the "vain juniper bushes" he rejects as not fitting the context! The form *šwrtm* is explained by Dahood (NWSPJ, p. 68; *Psalms I,* fifth NOTE on Ps xvi 4) as a Canaanite or Northern Israelite spelling of the dual feminine, to be vocalized *šûrôṯēm.*

12. LXX apparently mistook the verb *yin'āqû,* "they groan," for a form of the root *q(y)',* "vomit," to arrive at the interpretation:

Who cast out from (the) city
and their own houses.

The Qumran Targum preserves of this verse only the words *mn qryhwn,* "from their city."

12a. Reading *mēṯîm,* "dead, i.e., dying" instead of *mĕṯîm,* "men," as parallel to "wounded (mortally)." The reference is to earthly suffering and there is no warrant for emending "city" (*'îr*) to *'āpār,* "dust," i.e., the netherworld.

12b. The word *nepeš* is taken here in its primitive sense of "throat" rather than the derived senses "appetite, élan, soul." The word rendered "wounded" (*ḥălālîm*) designates mortally wounded and is often rendered "slain." The verb here used often refers to a cry for help, but the sound from the throat of the mortally wounded might range from screams to groans to the death rattle.

12c. Syr. and two Heb. manuscripts read *tĕp̄illāh,* "prayer," instead of *tip̄lāh,* on which word, see NOTE on i 22. The meaning then would be "But God does not regard [their] prayer." In either case, the implication is the same—that God does nothing about human misery because either he does not know or does not care.

13–17. Ibn Ezra and others understood light here to refer to God as the light of the world. It seems clear, however, that the meaning is literally daylight, but with the full implication of the figurative meaning of light as good and darkness as evil. The breakers of the Sixth, Seventh, and Eighth Commandments, the murderer, adulterer, and burglar prefer to operate in the dark; cf. John iii 20; Eph v 8; I Thess v 4.

13–14. The interpretation of "those who rebelled against the light" as an allusion to a primeval theomachy, of a titan king in the netherworld who rose up against the light as a murderer (Tur-Sinai) is wholly fanciful here.

14. The LXX rendering of this verse is entirely at variance with MT. Verses 14–18a, moreover, were missing from the old LXX and were supplied by Theodotion.

14a. The context requires darkness and the reading *lā'ôr,* "for the light," thus appears to be the very opposite of what is expected. The difficulty may be solved by taking the preposition *lĕ* in the separative sense "from," as frequently in the Ugaritic texts, or one may appeal to the usage in Mishnaic Hebrew where *'ôr lĕyôm* designates the evening.

14b. On the assumption that there would be no motive or profit in murder of the poor, Duhm emended the text to "his enemy" and "his adversary." The wicked, however, are elsewhere charged with killing the poor and the helpless; cf. Pss x 8, 9, xxxvii 14.

15a. *waits.* Literally "The eye of the adulterer watches (for) the twilight." Cf. Prov vii 9 on the nocturnal habits of the adulteress.

15b. *Thinking.* Literally "saying" (to himself).

15c. The adulterer seeks double protection, of darkness and concealment or disguise. It has been suggested that the libertine disguises and veils himself as a woman so as to slip unnoticed into the harem. It is scarcely necessary to press the disguise so far, since the ample, all-purpose garment could serve to conceal the face of a man or a woman; cf. Ruth iii 14.

14c. This line seems best transposed between 15c and 16a, thus avoiding the inference in 14a–b that the murderer also operates nights as a thief. The Qumran Targum preserves the last word of 14b and part of the first word of 14c; *wmskn wbly*[*ly'*], ". . . and (the) poor and at ni[ght] . . ." As usual, the Qumran Targum agrees with the order of MT.

16a. *breaks.* Literally "digs." The thief gained access to a house by digging through the (mud) wall. Exod xxii 2 uses the same root (*ḥtr*) for housebreaking; cf. Ezek viii 8, xii 5, 7, 12 where this verb is used of breaching a wall. In the Code of Hammurabi (No. 21) also digging (*ḫapāru*) is the burglar's mode of entry.

17a. The words *"kî yaḥdāw,"* "for it is the same," at the beginning of the line anticipate the following statement and make the line too long. Accordingly, we omit the phrase as a marginal comment.

[Verses 18–20, 22–25 are transposed after xxvii 23 (Sec. 26). On the reasons for this transfer, cf. Introduction, pp. XIX–XX.]

25. BILDAD'S THIRD DISCOURSE
(xxv 1–6; xxvi 5–14)

XXV 1 Bildad the Shuhite answered:

2 "Dominion and reverence are his;
He imposes peace in his heights.
3 Is there any numbering his troops?
On whom does his light not rise?
4 How can a man be just before God,
One born of woman be clean?
5 Even the moon is not bright,
Nor the stars clean in his sight;
6 How much less man, a maggot,
The son of man, a worm!
XXVI 5 The Shades beneath writhe,
Terrified are the Waters and their denizens.
6 Naked is Sheol before him,
Perdition has no cover.
7 He stretches Zaphon over the void,
Suspends the earth on nothing.
8 He binds the waters in nimbus,
But the clouds burst not with the burden.
9 He obscures the face of the full moon,
Spreading his cloud over it.
10 He marks a circle on the surface of the water
As the boundary of light and darkness.
11 The pillars of heaven tremble,
Stunned at his rebuke.
12 By his power he quelled the Sea,
By his cunning he smote Rahab.

13 By his wind he bagged the Sea,
His hand pierced the fleeting serpent.
14 Lo, these are but bits of his power;
What a faint whisper we hear of him!
Who could attend his mighty roar?"

Notes

xxv 2b. Perhaps an oblique allusion to some version of a mythical theomachy; cf. ix 13. The "peace" here is in the nature of retribution and revenge, pacification and punishment of the rebel gods, often equated with the earthly powers of evil in eschatological passages like Isa xxiv 21 ff., xxxiv 5, li 9; Ps lxxxix 10; Rev xii 7–12. The Qumran Targum preserves the first half of this verse nearly complete, but only the beginning and end of the second half:

š]*lṭn wrbw 'm 'lh'*
'[*bd šlm bmrw*]*mh*

[Do]minion and grandeur are with God,
He ma[kes peace in his h]eights.

The suffix of MT *'immô,* "with him," is made specific, "with God."

3a. The innumerable celestial army is composed of mighty astral deities under most rigid discipline; cf. Isa xl 26; Ecclesiasticus xliii 10.

3b. The LXX rendering "And against whom does his ambush not rise up?" (reading *'orbô* for *'ôrēhû*) is scarcely preferable to MT. The Qumran Targum preserves most of the verse, but with losses at the ends of each verse:

h'yty rḥṣn lhš[*hyh?*]
'w 'l mn l' tqwm [ ]

The editors conjecturally restored the end of the first half verse and rendered:

y a-t-il de l'espoir à ce qu'on re[mette . . . . .
ou sur qui ne se lève pas [. . . . . .]?

The word *rḥṣn* was explained as an addition "pour nuancer la question de Bildad." B. Zuckerman and S. Kaufman suggested that *rḥṣn* corresponds to LXX *parelkusis.* The word, as Kaufman remarked, does not mean "hope," but rather "trust, security, safety." The remnant of the word at the end of the first half verse *lhš*[ ], was taken by the editors to correspond to LXX *parelkusis* and Van der Woude proposed the restoration of the word as the Hap̄'ēl of *šh'*, "remettre," *lhš[hyh]*, hence the translation "à ce qu'on re[mette . . .]." Zuckerman and Kaufman, however, noted that the vestigial *lh-* must translate MT *liḡḏûḏāyw*. It is, however, difficult to find a suitable noun beginning with *h* and approximating the meanings of Heb. *gĕḏûḏîm*. In the second half of the verse Kaufman suggested the reading *tqwm [kmnh]*, "a trap will rise." LXX apparently read *'orbô,* "his snare," for MT *'ôrēhû,* "his light," and interpreted the verse as follows:

> Let one not think that there is respite for robbers;
> and on whom will there not come a snare from him?

Kaufman's perceptive restoration *kĕmānēh,* "his snare," gains support from the use of that word to translate MT *ma'rāḇ* in Targ. of Judg ix 35 and Ps x 8 and LXX rendering with the verb *enedreuō* in the former instance and in the latter with the noun *enedra,* as in the present verse, *enedra par autou,* "a snare from him." It thus appears that the Qumran Targum of this verse accords with LXX:

> Is there security for r[obbers],
> Or on whom will not rise [(his) trap]?

The editors of the Qumran Targum note that the space occupied by this verse is about one and a half times larger than that of the adjacent vss. 2, 4, 5, 6 and this leads to the supposition that the translator elaborated more than usual on the ideas of MT, or that his Hebrew text may have been longer (a hemistich or more?).

4–6. A repetition of Eliphaz's argument in iv 17 and xv 14–16, the point having been freely admitted by Job in ix 2, xiv 4. This sentiment echoes the rhetorical question asked in the more ancient Mesopotamian wrestlings with the problem of theodicy: "Was ever sinless mortal born?" Cf. Eccles vii 20.

5. Cf. iv 17, xv 15. The sun is omitted here as in Ps viii 3–4.

5a. *bright.* The form of the verb is unique, but has been correctly understood as a Hip̄'îl of the root *hll,* "shine, be bright," as the versions agree. The normal form *yāhēl* is attested in xxxi 26 and Dhorme observed that the true vocalization has been distorted by the use of the *matres lectionis,* i.e. *y'hyl* was intended to be vocalized *yāhēl* rather than *ya'ăhîl.* The remainder of this verse in the Qumran Targum . . .]*zky wkwkby' l'*[. . . suggests that *zky* is the rendering of MT *y'hyl* even though the same root is used in the second hemistich of MT.

6. *maggot . . . worm.* Cf. Isa xli 14; Ps xxii 6.

[xxvi 5–14 is inserted here. See Introduction, p. xx.]

xxvi 5a *Shades.* Heb. *rĕp̄ā'îm,* inhabitants of the netherworld; cf. Isa xiv 9, xxvi 14; Ps lxxxviii 10; Prov ii 18, ix 18, xxi 16. They are mentioned also in Phoenician funerary inscriptions (Tabnith and Eshmunazar) and in a group of fragmentary and obscure Ugaritic mythological texts (*rpum, rpim*). In Gen xiv 5, xv 20; Deut ii 10, 11, 20, 21, iii 11; Josh xii 4, 5, xiii 12; I Chron xx 4 the name is attached to extinct gigantic aborigines in the Transjordanian area. The megalithic dolmens in Transjordan may have suggested the connection of the ancient inhabitants with a defunct race of giants; cf. Deut iii 11.

5b. *Terrified.* MT *mittaḥaṯ*, "from beneath." Dhorme proposed to attach *mittaḥaṯ* to the preceding line and add *yēḥattû*, "they are terrified," before the word *mayim*, "Waters." Blommerde attached the *m of mtḥt* to the end of the preceding line as the enclitic particle, *yĕhôlālû-m*, and parsed the remaining *tḥt* as the Nip̄'al of *ḥtt*, "to crush," *tēḥaṯ*, third feminine singular followed by a plural collective subject. The translation would be essentially the same with either arrangement, except that "terrified" here seems preferable to "crushed." This arrangement puts the verbs and their subjects in chiastic order.

Commentators invariably have taken the allusion to the inhabitants of the waters to mean fishes, marine monsters, and other denizens of the deep. The netherworld, however, was a watery abyss; cf. II Sam xxii 5; Jon ii; Pss xlii 7, lxxxviii 3–7. The earth rested on a watery foundation, Pss civ 6, cxxiv 5, cxxxvi 6. Accordingly, in keeping with the parallelism, the reference is to the inhabitants of the netherworld.

6. Cf. Prov xv 11; Ps cxxxix 8; Amos ix 2.

6b. *Perdition.* Heb. *'ăḇaddôn*, meaning "destruction, ruin," from *'bd*, "perish," another designation of the netherworld; cf. xxviii 22, xxxi 12; Ps lxxxviii 11; Prov xv 11, xxvii 20. In Rev ix 11 the word is transliterated into Greek.

7a. *Zaphon.* Originally the name of the sacred mountain of Hadad or Baal, the Syrian Weather-God. Mount Zaphon, the Mount Ḫazzi of the Hittite texts, Mons Casius the storied Syrian Olympus of later classical sources, is identified (Eissfeldt) with Jebel el 'Aqra, Bald Mountain, on the Syrian coast opposite the finger of Cyprus, some thirty miles north of Ras Shamra, ancient Ugarit, whence have come the mythological texts which tell of the Baal-Hadad's construction of his marvelous dwelling on the heights of Mount Zaphon. We now see why Zaphon means "north" in the OT: the mountain lay directly north of Palestine. Before the discovery of the Ugaritic myths, exegetes could only guess that the reference is to the celestial or terrestrial north. The Ugaritic myths about Baal and his holy Mount Zaphon make it clear that the allusion here is to that storied mountain of the gods, the Mount of Assembly, as in Isa xiv 13. Tur-Sinai's connection of Zaphon with the root *ṣûp̄*, "float," the earth being here represented as a "floating island," is bizarre.

7b. It does not seem likely, as suggested by Buttenwieser, that the author of Job shared Pythagoras' advanced astronomical knowledge of "the obliquity of the ecliptic and of the earth's being a sphere freely poised in space." The question in xxxviii 6–7 hardly suggests that the author rejected such primitive notions of cosmography.

8b. *with the burden.* Literally "under them," i.e., under the weight of the water.

9a. *obscures.* The verb *'ḥz,* "grasp, hold," is used of barring gates in Neh vii 3 and its cognate in Syriac often has the sense of shutting, closing in, as in Matt vi 6. "Full moon," reading *kese'* instead of *kissē',* "throne"; cf. Ps lxxxi 4; Prov vii 20.

9b. The quadriliteral verb *paršēz* is hapax and abnormal. Either *prz* or *prś* would give the sense required by the context, but *pršz* is unexplained.

over it. Perhaps the ancient name of the weather-god 'Aliy is here hidden by the preposition *'ālāyw.* Cf. xxxvi 30, 33.

10. Cf. xxii 14; Gen i 4, 7, 14. The circle is apparently the horizon of the primeval ocean mentioned in Prov viii 27. The Qumran Targum preserves only the end of this verse which the editors read as]'-[*s*]*ypy ḥswk* and render "aux bords de la limite." The last word read as *ḥswk* was taken as the correspondent of MT *tklyt.* The term *ḥswk,* from *hśk,* "withhold," could hardly mean "la limite" and S. Kaufman suggested the reading *ḥšwk,* "darkness," which would accord with the ending of MT.

11. Cf. II Sam xxii 8, "foundations of the heavens," and the parallel Ps xviii 8, "foundations of the mountains"; cf. also Isa xiii 13; Joel ii 10. Modern interpreters generally understand these pillars or foundations of heaven to refer to the distant mountains which appear to support the dome of heaven.

11a. *tremble.* The hapax *yerôp̄ēp̄û* is usually related to Ar. *raffa,* "quiver." A similar verb *trp,* attested in Aramaic and post-biblical Hebrew in the sense of "perish, decay," is applied to the heavens in Ugaritic in a context similar to the present. The god Mot, Death, instructing Baal's messengers to deliver a dinner invitation to Baal, a meal at which Baal is to be both guest and food, alludes to Baal's victory over Leviathan (an exploit of which 'Anat boasts in 'nt III 35 ff.):

> When you smote Lotan, the swift serpent,
> Destroyed the serpent Twisty,
> The Tyrant with seven heads,
> The heavens parched and withered (67 I 1–4).

W. F. Albright (BASOR 83 [1941], 40, n. 10) called attention to the parallel with the present passage and suggested that the verbs *trp* and *rpp* are cognate.

The Qumran Targum presents instead of the plural verb *yĕrôp̄ēp̄û* of MT a singular from [*y*]*zy',* either a Pa'ēl or Hap̄'ēl form, "he makes tremble," the subject being God, presumably.

12. Cf. vii 12 and ix 13.

12a. *quelled.* The verb *rg‘* has commonly been taken in the sense of "disturb, stir up," but it can also have the opposite sense of "still" as noted by RV margin. This is the sense required by the proper understanding of the context. In both the Mesopotamian version of the battle between Marduk and Tiamat and in the Ugaritic version of Baal's battle with Prince Sea the quietus is put on the sea. There is no warrant for emending *rg‘* to *g‘r,* "rebuke," or any need to appeal to Ar. *rajja‘a* in the sense of "cause to return, retreat." Admittedly in Isa li 15 and Jer xxxi 35 the verb *rg‘* seems at first glance to have the sense of "stir up," but perusal of the context makes it clear that the message of comfort to Israel is drawn from the appeal to Yahweh's creative power and his defeat and control of the boisterous sea.

12b. *By his cunning.* The clever stratagems by which Marduk defeated Tiamat are described at length in the Mesopotamian Cosmogony Enuma Elish; (cf. ANET, pp. 66 f.). In the Ugaritic myth, Baal-Hadad strikes down Prince Sea by means of wonder weapons supplied to him by the artisan god Koshar, who pronounced incantations over the weapons to render them effective.

The Qumran Targum preserves only the final two letters of the first hemistich, but the second is complete:

[. . . . . *d*]*nḥ*
ḥllt ydh tnyn ‘rq

[. . . . . shi]nes;
His hand pierced the fleeing dragon.

The restoration [*d*]*nḥ,* "shine," cognate with Heb. *zrḥ* (**ḏrḥ*), is plausible and confirms MT *šip̄rāh.* Nevertheless, the two halves of the bicolon are incongruous and it is obviously the first half which calls for some sort of alteration to harmonize with the second.

13a. MT reads "By his wind/spirit the heavens are brightness [*šip̄rāh*]." LXX has "The bars of heaven feared him." MT has usually been taken to refer to the clearing of the skies after a storm. And, accordingly, the following line is explained as an allusion to the defeat of a mythical serpent who was supposed to cause eclipse by swallowing the sun! The serpent is slain and light is restored. It is clear, however, that 13b is, like Isa xxvii 1, li 9, an allusion to the defeat of the sea-god and his monster cohorts. In the Mesopotamian Creation Epic, Marduk subdued the sea monster Tiamat by means of a mighty wind. He also used a net to ensnare her; (cf. ANET, p. 67, lines 94–100). The Akkadian word for "net" (*saparu*) is similar to the obscure last word of 13a (*šip̄rāh*). This word occurs in Ps lvi 9 in the sense of "bag" or "skin bottle," as a receptacle for tears. We follow Tur-Sinai in taking the word in this sense and in dividing the word *šmym,* "heavens," into two words *śm ym,* "he put Sea." Thus, "By his wind he put Sea (in) a bag."

13b. Cf. iii 8, xl 25; Isa xxvii 1; Rev xii 3.

14a. *power.* Not "ways." Dahood (*Biblica* 38 [1957], 306–20) has shown that in this passage, as in xl 19, and a few other places in the OT, the word *dereḵ,* has the meaning "power," just as *drkt* in the Ugaritic mythological texts means "dominion," or the like.

14b. *faint whisper.* Tur-Sinai took *šemeṣ* here, as in iv 12b, to mean "fear," "and how dreadful is what we have heard of it!" The Qumran Targum renders *šemeṣ dāḇār* as *'ṭr ml',* apparently in the sense "vapor of a word."

14c. *attend.* Literally "understand, contemplate." The shock of thunder is such that man cannot withstand or leisurely contemplate and understand it; cf. xxxvii 2, 5.

26. JOB'S REPLY TO BILDAD; ZOPHAR'S THIRD DISCOURSE

(xxvii 1; xxvi 1–4; xxvii 2–23; xxiv 18–20; 22–25)

XXVII 1 Job continued his poem.

XXVI 1 Job answered:

2 "How you have helped the powerless,
Aided the arm that had no strength!
3 How you have counseled the unwise,
Offered advice in profusion!
4 With whose help have you uttered words,
Whose breath came forth from you?
XXVII 2 As God lives, who withholds my right,
Shaddai who has embittered my soul,
3 While I have life in me,
God's breath in my nostrils,
4 My lips will not speak falsehood,
Nor my tongue utter deceit.
5 Far be it from me to declare you right;
Till I die I will not renounce my integrity.
6 My innocence I maintain, I will not relinquish it;
My conscience gives no reproach my lifelong.
7 May my enemy be as the wicked,
And my opponent as the unjust."

[Zophar the Naamathite answered:]

8 "What hope has the impious when he is cut off,
When God takes away his life?
9 Will God hear his cry,
When trouble comes upon him?
10 Will he delight in Shaddai,
And call on God at all times?

11 I will teach you of God's power,
What Shaddai has I will not conceal.
12 Behold, you all have seen it,
Why then do you speak utter vanity?
13 This is the wicked's portion from God,
The tyrant's inheritance from Shaddai:
14 If his children increase, it is for the sword;
His offspring will not have food enough.
15 His posterity will not be buried in a tomb;
His widows will not weep.
16 Though he heap silver like dust,
And lay up stacks of raiment,
17 What he stored the righteous will wear,
The innocent will divide the silver.
18 He builds his house like a watchman
Like a hut the guard makes.
19 Rich he lies down his last,
Opens his eyes and is no more.
20 Terrors overwhelm him by day,
By night the tempest carries him off.
21 The east wind takes him away,
Sweeps him from his place.
22 It pounces on him without sparing,
From its power he fain would flee.
23 It claps its hand at him,
And hisses him from his place.

XXIV 18 Swift is he on the surface of the water;
Their portion is accursed in the land.
He turns not toward the vineyards.
19 Heat consumes the snow,
Sheol those who have sinned.
20 The womb forgets him,
The worm sucks sweetly on him.
He is remembered no more;
The evil man is broken like a tree.

22 He lures the mighty with his power.
He rises and he trusts in life.
23 He gives him security on which he relies,
But his eye is on their conduct.
24 They are exalted a moment, and are gone,
Laid low and gathered up like grass,
Like heads of grain they wither.
25 If not, who can confute me,
Or prove my words worthless?"

Notes

xxvii 1. *continued.* Literally "added to lift up," i.e., "took up again." This remark was felt to be needed after the order of parts of the preceding discourses had been jumbled; cf. Introduction p. xx. The same note is added in xxix 1 after the disjunction caused by the long extraneous poem (xxviii) on the elusive character of wisdom.

poem. It is difficult to find an appropriate rendering for this literary term *māšāl.* LXX here uses *prooimion* and Vulg. *parabola.* RSV's "discourse" and CCD's "theme" are not entirely satisfactory. On etymological grounds, the term should mean "similitude" and many of the *mĕšālîm* (the term applied to the collections in the Book of Proverbs) are pithy comparisons, e.g.,

A cripple's shanks flop,
And (so does) a *māšāl* in fools' mouths (Prov xxvi 7)

As the cur comes back to his puke,
The fool repeats his folly (Prov xxvi 11).

The terse bits of popular wit and wisdom in I Sam x 12, xxiv 14; Ezek xii 2, xviii 2 are designated by this term, as well as longer poems, Num xxiii, xxiv; Isa xiv. Not infrequently the term is used in association or parallelism with the term *ḥîḏāh,* variously rendered, "riddle," "dark saying," "mystery," as in Ezek xvii 2, xxiv 3; Hab ii 6; Pss xlix 5, lxxviii 2. In a number of instances the word is associated with terms of derision, disgust, and horror; cf. Deut xxviii 37; I Sam x 12; I Kings ix 7; Isa xiv 4; Jer xxiv 9; Ps lxix 11; II Chron vii 20. In Isa xiv 4; Jer xxiv 9; and Hab ii 6, RSV renders the word as "taunt," in Job xvii 6 and Ps lxix 11 as "byword," and in II Chron vii 20 as "proverb." It is clear that the term covers a wide variety of literary composition, but it is also patent that in every case it denotes poetic composition. Since parallelism is the very heart of ancient Near Eastern poetics, and every comparison or contrast involves a juxtaposition, the term *māšāl* is about as near as we come—leaving aside the words that denote song or musical accompaniment—to the range of meaning carried by our word "poem." There is in Job's and the friends' (poetic) dialogue too much variety to be characterized by a single specific term, but the terms "discourse" and "theme" are too general. The flexibility of the word "poem" will cover the parts and the whole. It is, as Emerson put it, "meter-making argument that makes a poem," and a poem, like a *māšāl,* can be long or short as "even one lone verse sometimes makes a perfect poem" (Ben Jonson). For discussion and bibliography on the term *māšāl,* cf. G. Rinaldi, "Alcuni termini ebraici relativi alla letteratura," *Biblica* 40 (1959), 267–89. The idiom "take up one's *māšāl*" is found also in Num xxiii 7, 18, xxiv 3, 15, 20, 21, 23; Isa xiv 4; and Hab ii 6.

xxvi 2–4. These lines are typical ironical exordium, similar to viii 2, xi 2 f., xii 2 f., xv 2 f., xvi 2 f., xviii 2 ff., and they connect very well with xxvii 5–14 after xxvi 5–14 is transposed to Bildad's preceding discourse.

xxvii 2–6. Job affirms his innocence in a solemn oath by an ancient god El. On the connection and equation of El with the Israelite deity Yahweh, cf. the writer's study EUT, pp. 12–15, 104. The paradoxical fact that Job swears his innocence by the same god whom he accuses of having wronged him was noted by the rabbis. From this Rabbi Joshua deduced that Job served God out of Love (TB, Sotah 27b).

2a. Cf. xxxiv 5 (and antithetically xxxvi 6).

2b. Cf. vii 11, x 1, xxi 25; Ruth i 20.

3a. *life.* Literally "my breath." It seems preferable, on stylistic grounds, to avoid repetition of the word "breath" in the parallel lines, since different words are used in the original; cf. xxxiii 4; Gen ii 7, vii 22. The word in the second line is *rûaḥ,* which seems best rendered as "breath" here, since it does not seem appropriate to say "the spirit of God is in my nostrils." Blommerde rendered:

> For as long as his breath is in me
> and God's spirit in my nose.

taking the final *î* of *nišmātî* as the third person suffix.

6a. Cf. ii 9.

6b. *conscience.* Literally "heart." The heart is the seat of intelligence, reason, and to some extent of the emotions; cf. I Sam xxiv 6, "David's heart smote him," i.e., he felt remorse. Job here denies any consciousness of sins such as his "friends" had charged to him; cf. xxii 6–9.

gives no reproach. Guillaume related the verb *yeḥĕrap̄* to Ar. *ḥarafa* in the sense of "change" and rendered "My mind will not change as long as I live."

7. This malediction implies that the wicked are punished, whereas Job has argued that the wicked often prosper. It may be that this is merely a stereotype curse which Job uses to pay his respects to the friends who assert the doctrine that the wicked are always punished.

8–23. These verses present the point of view of the friends and cannot be attributed to Job. We take them as part of Zophar's missing speech and accordingly supply the introductory formula. The speech thus has a rather abrupt beginning which might be relieved by inserting a few verses from the beginnings of other speeches of the friends. It is, however, difficult to find lines that cry out to be transposed to this spot. The conclusion to Zophar's speech may be found in xxiv 18–20, 22–25, which I venture to transpose after xxvii 23.

13a. *from God.* The context clearly indicates that the sense of the preposition *'im* is here "from" rather than "with." In previous editions *'im-'ēl* was emended to *mē'ēl* on the supposition that the ' resulted from dittography of the final consonant of the preceding work *raša'*. In agreement with Dahood (UHP, p. 32), this expedient was "ill advised" in view of the Ugaritic example (2065:14–17): *[i]rš 'my mnm irštk dḫsrt w ank aštn liḫy,* "Ask of me whatever you wish that is lacking and I will send it to my brother." This lone Ugaritic example of *'m* meaning "from" is sufficient warrant for retaining *'im* as the counterpart of *min* in the parallel line, *'im 'ēl // miššaday,* as Dahood advised. Cf. viii 13, xx 29. The Qumran Targum preserves only the end of the second hemistich, [. . . *mn*] *qdmwhy ynswn,* "[. . . from] before him they get." The divine name Shaddai was apparently omitted in the second hemistich but some divine title must have been used in the first as antecedent for the suffix.

14. The Qumran Targum preserves of 14a only the first word and the last letter of the final word of MT, and a larger part of 14b:

hn[*ḥr*]*b ypṣwn wl' yšb'wn*

The editors comment that *ypṣwn* corresponds to MT *wṣ'ṣ'yw,* but with different sense, *pṣ'* meaning "to open the mouth," as in Job xxxv 16. It is, however, only the position of the verb *ypṣwn* which corresponds to the MT noun *wṣ'ṣ'yw,* "and his offspring," assuming that the *b* which precedes is the final letter of the word *ḥrb,* "sword." It is not entirely clear whether *ypṣwn* goes with the first or the second half of the verse. It could belong to the first hemistich as the verb relating to the action of the sword, from the root *p(w)ṣ* or *pṣṣ,* "break, shatter, scatter." It seems more likely, however, that it is to be taken with the second hemistich:

They will open the mouth, but will not be sated. . . .

Perhaps there was a word for "food" in the following lacuna. In any case, there is no connection between MT *wṣ'ṣ'yw,* "and his offspring," and the verb *ypṣwn.*

15. The Qumran Targum preserves only two words of this verse, *w'rmlth l',* "and his widows (will) not . . ."

15a. MT has "His survivors will be buried in death/by Death," but the parallel line 15b, as well as the context, indicates that it is a matter of a disgraceful death, as befits the wicked. Not to be buried (cf. II Kings ix 10; Jer viii 2, xiv 6, xxii 19) or mourned (cf. Ps lxxviii 64: Jer xxii 10) was a great calamity. Accordingly, what is expected in 15a is a statement that his posterity will lack burial. JPS and RSV attempt to solve the difficulty by taking "death" in the sense of "pestilence," but it is doubtful if "death" is ever to be thus translated. In Jer xv 2, xviii 21 where RSV also renders "death" as "pestilence" it is probable that the word is intended as the proper name of the infernal god Mot, long known from Philo of Byblos and now vividly depicted for us in the Ugaritic myths. It would be tempting to see the name Mot here also, but it does not suit the context. It would make no better sense to say that one is buried "by Death" than "in death." The solution may lie in reading *bmwt* as *bāmôṯ,* a cultic term for tomb or funerary monument (cf. De Vaux, *Ancient Israel,* p. 287), rather than *bammāweṯ,* "in/by d/Death." The Qumran Isaiah scroll contains this word in the famous crux Isa liii 9 which removes the difficulty in a simple and convincing manner; the words *qeḇer,* "grave," and *bāmāh,* "tomb," standing in synonymous parallelism:

> They made his grave with the wicked,
> And with the rich [evil?] his tomb.

Ezek xliii 7 also uses *bāmāh* in this sense. It is still necessary to supply the negative in order to obtain sense. Cf. xxi 32 where Job points out that the wicked (usually) have a grand funeral.

16b. The Qumran Targum preserves something of the end of the first and the beginning of the second half of the verse:

> . . . *zwzy' kṭyn' ysg'* . . .
>
> (like dust) money like mud he increases (raiment)

17. The first half of this verse is missing in the Qumran Targum, but the second is partially preserved:

> *[m]m[wn]h qšyṭ' yplg*
>
> His wealth a true one will divide.

18a. *watchman.* MT *'āš* is usually taken to mean "moth"; "He builds his house like the moth." LXX rendered "like a moth and like a spider," apparently reading *kā'aš* and *kā'akkaḇîš*. Delitzsch, Ehrlich, and Driver related *'āš* here to Akk. *ašāšu* which occurs in lexical lists among terms for a bird's nest; cf. CAD A II, p. 422b, s.v. *ašāšu* A. NEB rendered, "The house he builds is flimsy as a bird's nest/or a shelter put up by a watchman." A bird's nest is perhaps a little better than a moth's cocoon as a parallel to the flimsy shelter (*sukkāh*) set up by a watchman, but still somewhat incongruous. It is unlikely, moreover, that Akk. *ašāšu* can be connected with *'āš* because the laryngal ' would have affected the adjacent vowels to produce *ešēšu*. Arabic *'ās*, "night watchman," participle of *'ass*, "keep night-watch," offers a precise parallel to *nôṣēr* "guard," and thus gives chiastic parallelism between (night-)watchman//guard and house//hut. The poetic structure corresponds to the commonest pattern in Ugaritic poetry, with the verb expressed in the first line and omitted in the second:

> He builds like a watchman his house,
> Like a hut (which) the guard makes.

The verb *'āśāh*, "he makes," in the second line is not parallel to *bānāh*, "he builds," in the preceding line but belongs to the asyndetic relative clause, "(which) the guard makes," i.e. made by a guard or watchman. The watchman's hut, or booth (*sukkāh*), is a flimsy, temporary shelter. (In the Festival of Booths a shelter that partakes of a permanent nature or gives the appearance of permanence is invalid.) The paronomasia between *'āš* and *'āśāh* is noteworthy, but more striking is the poet's play on the word *'āš* which he uses elsewhere with reference to a moth iv 19. The reader would naturally think first of the moth and his house as being similar to the flimsy spider's web, and it is only with recognition of the parallelism between *'āš* and *nôṣēr* and *bêṯ* and *sukkāh* that the meaning of *'āš* as "night watchman" is divined.

The Qumran Targum preserves a single word of this verse *kqṭwt'*, which corresponds to MT *ūksukkāh*, "and like a hut." The editors relate the word to *qĕṭûṭā'*, "branch," and suggest that it could have the sense of hut ("cabane") made of branches and leaves. S. Kaufman suggests that the word is rather to be connected with Mishnaic Hebrew *q(y)ṭwn*, plural *qyṭwnt*, Syr. *qayṭōnā*, a loan word from Gr. *koitōn*, "bedroom" (*koitē*, "bed," *koitazō*, "put to bed"), a word twice used of a part of a *sukkāh* (TB Sukkāh 3a). The spelling *qṭwt'*, Kaufman suggests, may be an error for *qṭwn'* (*wn* read as *t*) or it may represent assimilation of *ôntā* to *ôttā*.

19a. *his last.* Reading with LXX and Syr. *yôsîp̄* in the sense of "do (something) again," instead of MT *yē'āsēp̄*, "and he shall not be gathered." Blommerde took the negative *lô'* as the divine title *lē'*, "the Mighty

One," and interpreted the verb *'sp* in the sense of "snatch away," as in Ps xxvi 9, and rendered:

Rich he lies down, but the Mighty One takes him away.

From the little that is preserved of this verse in the Qumran Targum it is clear that the element *l'* was not construed as a divine title:

yš]kb wl' 'ytḥd

he lies down and is not seized

On the word *'ytḥd* Kaufman comments: "Due to the unusual spelling of the prefix and the distorting effect of the worn fragment edge, the correct reading of this word must remain in doubt. Note, however, that the assimilation of the root-initial *aleph* apparently occurs already in Elephantine Aramaic."

20. MT has *kammayim,* "like water," but the parallel "by night" suggests that the meaning should be "by day." This could be achieved with minimum change in the consonantal text, reading *kĕmô yôm* as a variant of the familiar *kayyôm,* "today, now," as in Gen xxv 31, 33; I Sam ii 16; Isa lviii 4. The sense "by day" would be a bit forced in this reading and I prefer the more drastic change to *yômām* which yields exactly the meaning required. Dahood (*Biblica* 50 [1969], 342) retains the MT and renders: "Terrors will overtake him like a flood, Night will kidnap him like a tempest." Both Terrors and Night are taken as names for the netherworld. The Qumran Targum preserves of this verse the letters *kmyn b'š[t']*, "like evil waters," confirming MT *kammayim.* If the *km ym,* "by day," was mistaken for *kmym,* "like waters," as proposed, the error antedates the Qumran Targum.

23. The ambiguities of this verse may be pointed up by a comparison of KJ, JPS, and RSV, and especially RSV's footnotes. The unexpressed subject of the verbs of vss. 22–23 may be either "God," "the east wind," or an indefinite "one, men." With RSV I take the subject to be the east (wind) mentioned in vs. 21. For clapping the hands in anger cf. Num xxiv 10, and in derision Lam ii 15. Hissing is a gesture of horror, Jer xlix 17, and derision, Ezek xxvii 36; Lam ii 15; Zeph ii 15. The ambiguities are compounded in vs. 23b which says "and he will hiss against him from his place." KJ's and JPS's supplying of the indefinite subject "men" is unlikely on both logical and grammatical grounds. Being driven from one's place by the hissing derision of men does not suit the context which speaks of tempests and terrible violence. It is the (hissing, howling) storm wind which sweeps away the wicked; cf. vs. 21, xxi 18; Ps i 4; Isa xl 7; Prov x 25. Now if one construes *'ālāyw,* "at/against him," as indirect object, then it appears necessary to understand "from his

place" to refer to the wind which hisses from its place rather than to the object of the hissing which is swept away. This is insipid and much too tame for the context. KJ and JPS boldly take *'ālāyw* as direct object, "and shall hiss him out of his place." I prefer this sense also, in spite of the grammatical difficulty. A still bolder expedient is to take *'ālāyw* as a corruption of *'Aliy,* an ancient cognomen of the storm-god. Cf. xxxvi 30, 33.

xxiv 18–20, 22–25. These corrupt and obscure lines, as far as they are at all intelligible, present the view of Job's opponents, that the wicked always suffer eventually and that suffering is of itself proof that the victim deserved it. The difficulty cannot be overcome by translating in the optative mood, as attempted by the versions. Neither is it convincing to argue that Job is parroting the views of his opponents in order to ridicule or refute them. We must assume that the verses have been misplaced, perhaps deliberately, from one of the discourses of the friends. For want of a more appropriate place, they are transposed to the reconstituted third speech of Zophar, after xxvii 23.

18a. Cf. ix 26 "like reed boats" and Hos x 7 "like a chip on the water."

18c. The import of this line is obscure. The implication apparently is that the wicked man will have no vineyard to enjoy.

19. Omitting one each of the redundant synonyms drought/heat and water/snow of 19a. Many emendations of this verse are occasioned by misapprehension of the simple sense—the netherworld snatches away the wicked as the hot sun consumes the snow.

20a, b. The greater part of this verse has no counterpart in LXX. Vulg. and Targ. take *reḥem,* "womb," in the sense of "pity." Syr. interprets "womb" in the sense of "from the womb," i.e., "from birth." Emendation of *reḥem* to *rĕḥôḇ,* "city square," and *rimmāh,* "worm," to *šĕmām,* "their name" (RSV), is dubious. It seems best to translate the text as it stands and divide it into two short lines rather than a single overlong one.

22a. *lures.* Literally "draws."

22b. *rises.* Or perhaps "raises, establishes," reading *yāqîm* instead of *yāqûm.*

he trusts. Omitting the negative or else taking it as asseverative.

24b. *like grass.* MT "like all," but the parallelism requires some sort of vegetation and this is supplied by the LXX *molochē* which transcribes the Heb. *mallûaḥ,* "saltwort; cf. xxx 4. On the complexities presented by the readings of other versions, cf. Dhorme. The Qumran Targum reads *kybl',* i.e., *kĕyaḇlā',* "like dog grass." The plant is identified by I. Löw (*Aramäische Pflanzennamen* [Leipzig, 1881], p. 183) as the *cynodon dactylum.* The form *yaḇlîṯ* (which according to Jastrow designates a pulp made of cynodon leaves and used for lining large water vessels) is applied in modern Hebrew, along with *yab̲lāh,* to couch grass or crab grass.

25. The Qumran Targum preserves most of the first half of the verse and a couple of letters of the second half:

> . . . *m*]*n 'pw ytybnny ptgm*
> *wy*[
>
> . . . who then will answer me a word,
> and. . . .

27. POEM ON THE INACCESSIBILITY OF WISDOM (xxviii 1–28)

[XXVIII

1 "There is a smelter for silver,
A place where gold is refined.
2 Iron is taken from the dust,
Copper is smelted from stone.
3 Man puts an end to darkness,
Every recess he searches.
Through dark and gloomy rock
4 He sinks a shaft far from habitation.
Forgotten by the foot of man,
Suspended remote from men they sway.
5 The earth, from which comes food,
Below is changed as by fire.
6 Its stones are the source of sapphire,
And its dust contains gold.
7 The path no bird of prey knows,
No falcon's eye has seen.
8 The proud beasts have not trodden it,
No serpent passed over it.
9 He puts his hand to the flint,
Overturns mountains at the base.
10 In the rocks he hews out channels,
His eye sees every precious thing.
11 The sources of the rivers he probes,
Brings hidden things to light.
12 But wisdom, where can it be found?
Where is the place of understanding?
13 Man knows not its abode,
'Tis not found in the land of the living.

14 Deep says, 'It is not in me.'
Sea says, 'Not with me.'
15 It cannot be got for bullion,
Nor can silver be weighed as its price.
16 It cannot be bought for gold of Ophir,
With precious onyx or sapphire.
17 Gold or glass cannot match it,
Nor vessels of fine gold be its barter.
18 Coral or crystal are not to be mentioned;
Wisdom's value surpasses rubies.
19 The topaz of Ethiopia cannot equal it,
It cannot be bought with pure gold.
20 Wisdom, whence does it come?
Where is the place of understanding?
21 It is concealed from the eyes of all living,
Even hid from the birds of the air.
22 Perdition and Death say,
'We have heard a rumor of it.'
23 God knows the way to it,
He is familiar with its place.
24 When he looked to the ends of the earth,
Surveyed all under the heavens,
25 When he allotted weight to the wind,
Meted out the waters by measure,
26 When he made a groove for the rain,
A path for the thundershower;
27 Then he saw it and appraised it,
Discerned and tested it.
28 And he said to man,
'Behold, the fear of the Lord that is wisdom;
To turn from evil is understanding.' "]

NOTES

xxviii. On the extraneous character of this poem, cf. Introduction, p. xx. Column xii of the Qumran Targum preserves of this chapter only vestiges of the beginnings and endings of nine lines covering vss. 4–13 of MT. Column xiii preserves considerably more of vss. 20–28, but no single stich is entirely preserved.

1a. *smelter*. The word *môṣā'*, "place of coming forth," is used of water, II Kings ii 21; Isa xli 18, lviii 11; Ps cvii 33; II Chron xxxii 30, and of the sunrise, Pss lxv 9, lxxv 7, and in the sense of "gate, exit" in Ezek xlii 11, xliii 11. The meaning "mine" is regularly assumed in the present passage, although this sense is not attested elsewhere. P. Joüon (*Biblica* 11 [1930], 323) proposed emendation to *mimṣā'* which would mean "a place where something is found." Dahood (NWSPJ, p. 67), taking his cue from the parallelism, suggests the meaning "smelter," a synonym of *marṣēp̄* in Prov xvii 3 (xxvii 21),

The smelter for silver,
The furnace for gold,
But the tester of hearts is Yahweh.

The meaning "smelter" for *môṣā'* would derive from the root *wḏ'*, "be clean"; cf. xxiii 10b.

Silver was not mined in Palestine but was imported from Tarshish; cf. Jer x 9; Ezek xxvii 12. The word "Tarshish" is derived from an Akkadian word meaning "refinery" or "smelter" and was applied by the Phoenicians to their mining colonies in Spain and North Africa and on the island of Sardinia. The Tarshish of the Bible is probably Tartessus in Spain (cf. Herodotus iv.152) and the "ships of Tarshish" have been understood as craft plying between Spain and Syrian ports. W. F. Albright has suggested (BASOR 83 [1941], 21 f.) that the "ships of Tarshish" may be rendered "refinery fleet," i.e., ships bringing metals from the refinery to the market ports.

1b. Gold was not plentiful in Palestine, but was imported from the distant lands of Ophir (Isa xiii 12; I Kings x 11; I Chron xxix 4) and Sheba (Ps lxxii 15; I Kings x 2).

refined. Not "washed." Cf. Mal iii 3 where it is clear that fire is used in connection with the process. Where this verb is used of liquids (wine in Isa xxv 6, and water in Job xxxvi 27), it must be in a secondary sense. The primary meaning of the word is seen in

Akk. *zaqāqu,* "blow," whence *zaqīqu* and *ziqziqqu,* "wind." The Ar. *ziqq,* "sack," is applied especially to the bellows of the forge.

2a. Iron was first known from meteorites, as indicated by the name "heavenly metal" applied to it both in Egypt and Mesopotamia. The earliest beaten-iron ornaments found in prehistoric tombs are of meteoric origin, as indicated by the high nickel content. Iron derived from terrestrial ore, here called "dust," was known in small quantities as early as the third millennium B.C., but did not become common till the thirteenth century B.C. The description of the Promised Land as one "whose stones are iron," Deut viii 9, is not altogether hyperbolic. Deposits of very high grade ore are found in the plateau east of the Jordan Valley. The scarcity of iron among the Israelites in Saul's day and the monopoly held by the Philistines (cf. I Sam xiii 19–22, xvii 7) may have been due to lack of technical skills on the part of the Israelites rather than Philistine control of the supply. In David's time iron became plentiful. The source of supply is uncertain. The expression in Jer xv 12 "iron from the north," refers to the mettle of the weapons of the foe from the north rather than the provenience of Israel's iron supply.

2b. *is smelted.* MT *yāṣûq* is difficult and critics correct it to *yiṣqû,* "they smelt," or *yiṣṣôq,* "one smelts," or *yûṣoq,* "it is smelted." Dhorme construed *yāṣûq* as a passive participle with the meaning "hard," the usually feminine noun *'eben,* "stone," being taken as feminine, "And a hard stone becomes copper." Blommerde proposed to read *yṣwq* as the infinitive construct, *yĕṣôq,* "and from stone is the smelting of copper." Cf. Deut viii 9. Copper was plentiful in this part of the world and was smelted very early. The major mines were on Cyprus, in Edom, and in the Sinai Peninsula. Solomon had refineries at Eziongeber; cf. N. Glueck, BA 1 (1938), 13–16; 2 (1939), 37–41; 4 (1940), 51–55; BASOR 71 (1938), 3–17; 75 (1939), 8–22; 79 (1940), 2–18. The apertures which Glueck thought to be airducts (facing the prevailing winds for forced draft) now appear to have been caused by burning or decay of horizontal wooden beams; cf. N. Glueck, BA 28 (1965), 70–87.

3. The subject of the verb is not expressed. The reference is presumably to the use of artificial light in the mine shafts. Diodorus Siculus (late first century B.C.) in his description of operations in the gold mines at Eskhuranib in Nubia (iii.11 ff.) mentions the lamps used by the workers.

4a. The phrase *mē'im-gār* (literally "from with a dweller") is awkward, but the proposed emendations are unconvincing. The neatest suggestion is that of Graetz who with a simple change of the word division and vocalization to *pāraṣ nĕḥālîm 'am-gār* obtains the sense "alien people break shafts." The use of foreign slaves and war prisoners in such perilous and difficult work was common. There is, however, no hint of concern for the miners. The parallelism indicates that the interest is in the remoteness of these operations from the centers of human habitation; cf. vss. 7–8 below. Though there is no thought here of the sufferings endured by the wretched slaves who worked the mines, the imagination can scarcely exaggerate their misery. Diodorus Siculus relates that children accompanied the gold miners to carry off the pieces of ore to be crushed by women and old men.

4c. The allusion is to the suspension of the miners by ropes and perhaps the lowering of them in baskets or cages.

5. The surface of the earth produces food, but in its depths there is a transformation of its substance as if by fire. Some critics have taken this to refer to a mode of blasting or the use of fire to split the rocks by heating and dousing with cold water. St. Jerome apparently understood 5b in this way, as reflected by the rendering *in loco suo igni subversa est.* Diodorus Siculus mentions that in the gold mines in Nubia the stone was made brittle by fire so that it could be dug out with iron picks. It seems more likely, however, that the reference is to the appearance of the rocks in which precious stones are found. The knowledge of volcanoes and igneous rock, of meteorites, and the effect of heat on ore in the smelting process would naturally give rise to the idea that fire has played a part in the formation of certain rocks. In Ezek xxviii 14 the term "stones of fire" seems to be a generic term for the various precious stones mentioned in the preceding verse, Ezek xxviii 13. The term "stone of fire," *aban išāti,* occurs in an Akkadian lexical text, but its exact meaning is not clear. In the Ugaritic myth relating the building of Baal's splendiferous palace out of gold and silver and sapphire (lapis lazuli) the term applied to the material is "stone(s) of lightning," *abn brq,* which recalls the term *brqt* in Exod xxviii 17, xxxix 10 and Ezek xxviii 13; cf. Pope, EUT, pp. 99 f. Tur-Sinai has given a highly fanciful explanation of Ezek xxviii 13–14 in which the cherub who guarded Eden's jewels (which he claims the ancient Israelites regarded as burning stones) tried to smuggle some out in his mouth but got burned.

7–8. These verses agree with vs. 4 above in stressing the remoteness and inaccessibility of the mines. The ancient gold mines worked by the Egyptians in Nubia were seven or eight days' journey into the rocky and burning desert. The turquoise mines at Serabit el Khadem in the Sinaitic peninsula were also remote and difficult of access.

8a. *proud beasts.* Literally "sons of pride." This expression occurs elsewhere only in xli 26 where it is applied to the mythological monster Leviathan. Sigmund Mowinckel (in *Hebrew and Semitic Studies Presented to Godfrey Rolles Driver in Celebration of His 70th Birthday, 20*

August 1962, eds. D. W. Thomas and W. D. McHardy, 1963, p. 97) suggests that the term belongs not as much to zoology as to mythology. The mythological connections are clear in xli 26, but not in the present passage.

8b. *serpent*. The word *šaḥal* regularly means "lion," as is clear in iv 10 f.; Hos v 14, xiii 7; Prov xxvi 13. In the present passage, however, it seems rather odd to say that no lion has even traversed the secret haunt of wisdom. The preceding verse speaks of far-sighted birds of prey that can see what man cannot and yet cannot see the remote abode of Wisdom. One would expect the word *šaḥal* then to refer to a creature that could enter places inaccessible to man. More than forty years ago, Mowinckel translated the word *šaḥal* in the present passage and in Ps xci 13 as "lizard" (Norwegian *ögle*) and only recently has presented in some detail his reasons for so doing. There are apparent cognates in Semitic which mean "lion" in one dialect and "serpent" in another, such as Heb. *nāḥāš*, "serpent," which may, as Mowinckel suggests (there is no phonological impediment), be cognate with Akk. *nêšu* which means "lion." The word *nêšu*, however, is applied to the serpent in the term *nêš qaqqari*, "lion of the earth," used of the serpent that stole the plant of life in the Gilgamesh Epic. Although this is obviously a metaphorical expression, it suggests some sort of connection between the lion and the serpent. There is also Ethiopic *'arwē*, "serpent," which may be cognate with Heb. *'aryeh*, *'ărî*, "lion." The place where lion and serpent meet and mingle is, of course, in mythopoetic fancy and Mowinckel points to the Mesopotamian *mušruššu* represented on the Ishtar Gate at Babylon, the serpent griffin of Marduk's temple at Nippur, and the figures which flank the caduceus on Gudea's famous vase, to show the blending of leonine and serpentine features. He suggests that originally *šaḥal* may have designated the serpent dragon, the mythical *Lindwurm*, and that in Job xxviii 8 the poet was aware of this. Mowinckel's suggestion is adopted here, though not with full confidence.

9–11. These lines, like vss. 3–4 above, stress man's dauntless efforts in search of treasure. The tunnel of the mines at Serabit el Khadem was driven through a great ridge of rock.

10a. The word rendered "channels" (*yĕ'ôrîm*) is the plural of the designation of the Nile (*ye'ôr* < Eg. *yrw*) which is used a number of times in the plural in reference to the branches of the river in the Delta which in ancient times formed seven main branches where now are only two flowing into the sea at Rosetta and Damietta. The use of the term here is unique. Some take it to refer to mine shafts or galleries, others to drainage channels.

11. LXX and Vulg. rendered 11a more or less correctly (*bathē de*

potamōn anekalupsen and *profunda quoque pluviorum scrutatus est*). In spite of this, most modern renderings have missed the sense completely, e.g., KJ, "He bindeth the floods from overflowing." The Ugaritic mythological texts now confirm the rendering of the older versions. The term *mbk nhrm* of the Ugaritic myths is identical in meaning and virtually identical in form with the hitherto unique expression *mibbĕkê nĕhārôṯ*. In the Ugaritic texts this term is one of the regular designations of the watery abode of the god El, father of gods and men and erstwhile head of the pantheon. Visits to El by other gods are described thus (51 IV 20–24):

idk lttn pnm	Forthwith she sets face
'm il mbk nhrm	Towards El at the springs of the (two) rivers,
qrb apq thmtm	Midst the Channels of the (two) deeps.
tgly ḏd il wtbu	She penetrates the domain of El and enters
qrš mlk ab šnm	The pavilion of the King, Father of Exalted ones.

The location of El's abode is thus at the juncture of the two subterranean seas, as the present writer has demonstrated in detail; cf. EUT, pp. 61–81. The mythological term is used here in Job merely as a poetic designation of the subterranean regions which man has the temerity to explore. The emendation of the verb *ḥbš*, "bind," to *ḥpš*, "search," is suggested by the sense, but is not necessary as *b* and *p* frequently interchange in Semitic dialects. This line has nothing to do with the prevention of flooding in the mine. The parallel line completes the sense admirably: man searches the watery depths and brings hidden treasures to the light.

12, 20. *Wisdom* and *understanding* are regular synonyms in the poetic parallelism of the Wisdom Literature. Cf. Prov i 2, iv 5, 7, ix 10, xvi 16.

13a. *abode*. In previous editions of this work, *'erkāh* was emended to *darkāh*, "its path," on the basis of LXX, since the presumed meaning of MT *'erkāh*, "its price," seemed inappropriate. It may be, however, that the emendation was misguided. Dahood (*Biblica* 50 [1969], 355) called attention to the apparent parallelism of the word *'rk* with *bt*, "house," in text 12:3–4 of Ugaritica V, *b'lt bhtm*, "Mistress of the Palace(s)," and *b'l 'rkm*, "Lord of the House(s)," and proposed that the word means something like "house, temple." This meaning Dahood would also apply to the Nabatean phrase *'rkwt' wbty'* (CIS II, 350:2) which would thus mean "buildings and houses."

13b. *land of the living*. As opposed to the netherworld mentioned in vs. 22 (cf. Isa xxxviii 11, liii 8; Jer xi 19; Ezek xxvi 20).

14. *Deep* and *Sea*. The primeval oceans which have their sources in the depths of the earth; cf. NOTES on iii 8, vii 12, ix 13. Though

man may explore even the watery abyss, as he does in search of gold and jewels (cf. vs. 11), wisdom will not be found there.

15. *bullion.* I.e., "gold bullion." The word *sĕgôr* stands for *zāhāḇ sāgûr,* corresponding to Akk. *ḫurâṣu sagru.* Cf. I Kings vi 20, vii 49, x 21; II Chron iv 20, 22, ix 20 where the term in each instance apparently refers to the quality of the gold.

weighed. Cf. Gen xxiii 16; Zech xi 12.

16a. The word for "gold" here (*keṯem*) is derived from the Egyptian designation of the land from which gold was obtained, presumably Nubia. From the Twentieth Dynasty on the expression *nb-n-ktm,* "gold of Ktm," is common.

Ophir. Cf. xxii 24.

16b. *onyx.* Heb. *šōham,* Akk. *sāmu.* The identity of the precious stone is conjectural. Carnelian has also been suggested; cf. Gen ii 12; Exod xxxix 13; Ezek xxviii 13.

17a. *glass.* KJ "crystal." The Syriac and Arabic cognates of the word *zĕḵûḵîṯ* designate glass. Glass was made in Egypt as early as the fourth millennium B.C. and later in Phoenicia. This opaque glass was used for ornamentation. Glass vessels did not become common in Palestine till the Roman period.

18. *Coral* (*rā'môṯ*). A guess. The red coral of the Mediterranean and Red Sea was used for ornamentation and jewelry. Ezek xxvii 16 lists this commodity among the wares traded by Edom for Tyrian goods. The word occurs in the Ugaritic myths as *rimt* and refers to some sort of pectoral ornamentation.

crystal. The word (*gāḇîš*) occurs only here. Ar. *jibs,* "gypsum," and Heb. *kāpîs,* "stucco," "plaster" (Hab ii 11) may be related, but do not designate the same material. The word here is apparently shortened from *'elgāḇîš* (Akk. *algamešu,* Eg. *'a-ar-qa-bi-sa*), used of hailstones, Ezek xiii 11, 13, xxxviii 22.

18b. *rubies* [?] (*pĕnînîm*). RSV variously renders this word "pearls," "jewels," "costly stones," "coral." In Lam iv 7 we get the only clue to the color of this gem as being reddish. Like wisdom, the worthy wife is to be valued beyond these jewels, Prov xxxi 10.

19. *topaz* (*piṭdāh*). Cf. Exod xxviii 17, xxxix 10; Ezek xxviii 13; Rev xxi 20. The Gr. *topazion* apparently derives from the Sanscrit *tapas,* "heat, fire"; cf. above vs. 5. The OT term probably designates yellow chrysolite. Chrysolite was obtained mainly from the island of Zabarqad off the Egyptian coast, called by Pliny (*Nat. hist.* xxxvii.9) Topaz Island.

20. Almost identical with vs. 12, perhaps a refrain.

21b. It is not likely that the birds are singled out to represent the celestial sphere, although the earth, sea, and netherworld are mentioned in vss. 13, 14, 22. The aerial view of the birds gives them advantage in reconnaissance, but even they cannot locate the hiding place of wisdom.

22a. Cf. xxvi 6b.

Death. Cf. xviii 13 f. Targ. has "The Angel of Death" in recognition of the personification of the dread power.

22b. Cf. II Sam vii 22; Ps xliv 2 and the similar expression in Job xlii 5. To "hear with the ears" apparently connotes secondhand, hearsay evidence. The netherworld has only vague rumor as to the location of wisdom's abode.

24. Cf. xxxvii 3, xli 3; Isa xl 28, xli 5, 9. The heavens and earth were created by wisdom and understanding, Prov iii 19.

25. By wisdom God regulates the force of the wind and measures the waters; cf. v 10, xxxvi 27–33, xxxviii 26–27; Isa xl 12. As Rashi observes, some lands are parched and need much rain, while other lands do not require so much. Cf., however, xii 15 for apparent lapses in this providence.

26a. *groove.* The word *ḥōq* here does not mean "decree," but is used in the sense of "bound, limit," as in Jer v 22; Ps cxlviii 6; Prov viii 29. The basic meaning of the root is "to engrave," hence as applied to the rain, rather than the sea, "groove" may be an appropriate rendering. Cf. xxxviii 25a where the word *tĕʻālāh,* "trench, conduit," is used instead of *ḥōq* in a variant of this line.

26b. *path.* The path, *dereḵ,* corresponds to the groove of the preceding line. On the path of the rain, cf. E. F. Sutcliffe, "The Clouds as Water Carriers in Hebrew Thought," VT 3 (1953), 99–103. The figure of the conduit for the rain recurs in xxxviii 25b.

thundershower. The phrase *ḥăzîz qôlôṯ* has occasioned difficulty from of old. Syriac rendered "visions of the voices," reading *ḥzywn* for MT *ḥzyz;* Vulg. translated *procellis sonantibus.* Dhorme opined that the exact meaning is "rumble of thunder," relating *ḥăzîz* to Ar. *ḥazîz,* "rumble," and explaining that by extension "rumble of thunder" will acquire the meaning "storm." In modern Hebrew *ḥāzîz* is used both for lightning and thundercloud. In post-biblical Hebrew and Aramaic the word is used of the cumulonimbus clouds which bring the rain. Jastrow explained *ḥāzîz* as designating a cloud with uneven surface (like scabs or swollen lumps) and cited the answer to the question, "What are *ḥăzîzîm?*" (TB Taʻnit 9b) viz. that they are *pôrĕḥôṯ,* i.e. "eruptions." This would suggest connection with Ar. *ḫaḏḏ,* "suppurate, fester," *ḫaḏîḏ,* "suppuration" (and possibly also with *ḫinḏîḏ* applied to a poet, a mountain, or a stallion, and as an adjective in the senses "long and thick, able, apt, heroic"). In the Targum to the Song of Songs ii 9 the word is used of clouds in an expression recalling the Ugaritic epithet of Baal as "Cloud Rider." "Said the congregation of Israel at the time the Glory of Yahweh was revealed against Egypt on the night of Passover and killed all the firstborn: 'He was mounted on the swift cloud (*rĕḵīḇ ʿal ḥăzîzā' qallîlā'*) and ran like a gazelle or an antelope. . . .'" It is clear, however, from Zech x 1, where the word stands in association and parallelism with three other words for rain, that it can also mean "rain":

> Ask rain of Yahweh
> In the time of the latter-rains,
> Yahweh who makes the rains (*ḥăzîzîm*),
> Who gives rain showers to them,
> For man grass in the field.

The meaning "rain" is patent in Ugaritic which puts the word in parallelism with *yr* (Heb. *yôreh*), "(early) rain." The sortie of the innumerable army of King Keret is compared to the showers (*ḫḏḏ*) and the rain (*yr*), (Krt 92–93, 180–81):

hlk lalpm ḫḏḏ	They went by the thousands (like) showers
wbrbt km yr	By the myriads like rain.

27. *appraised.* The verb (*spr*) in the factitive stem may have the sense "count, number, evaluate" (cf. xxxviii 37; Ps xxii 18), as in the simple stem (cf. xiv 16).

Discerned. Reading *hĕḇînāh* instead of *hĕḵînāh.*

tested. This verb gives the clue to the understanding of the two verbs preceding. In the process of creation, God gave wisdom a searching and thorough trial.

28. This verse is suspect on several grounds. The introductory formula "And he said to man" is too short to constitute a poetic line and is obviously an editorial splice. The form of the divine name used here—spelled with the consonants *'dny*—is found nowhere else in the entire book. After the poetic elaboration of the point that wisdom is inaccessible to man, the definition of an entirely different kind of wisdom seems rather abrupt. The divine wisdom by which God created and regulates the cosmos is beyond man's grasp and ken. For man there is only the practical wisdom of piety. This is a standard affirmation and formulation of the conservative school (cf. Prov i 7, iii 7, ix 10; Ps cxi 10) which is appended as an antidote to the agnostic tenor of the preceding poem. The Qumran Targum preserves a vestige of this verse, with the introductory formula "And he said to the sons of . . . and to turn . . ."

28. JOB'S PERORATION
(xxix 1–10; 21–25; 11–20)

XXIX 1 Job resumed his poem:

2 "O that I were as in months past,
In the days when God watched over me;
3 When his lamp shone over my head,
By his light I walked through darkness;
4 As I was in the prime of my life,
When 'Aliy founded my family,
5 When Shaddai was still with me,
My young ones round about me;
6 When my steps were bathed in cream,
The rock flowed streams of oil!
7 When I went out the city gate,
Took my seat in the square,
8 The young men saw me and hid,
The old men rose and stood,
9 Princes stopped speaking,
Put their hand on their mouth;
10 The voices of chieftains were hushed,
Their tongues stuck to their palates.
21 They listened to me and waited,
Keeping silent for my counsel.
22 When I had spoken, they said no more;
My speech dropped on them;
23 They waited for me like the rain,
They spread their mouths as for the late rain.
24 I smiled on them and they scarce believed,
The light of my face they let not fall.

25 I chose their course and sat as chief,
I dwelt as a king with his troops.
Wherever I guided they were led.
11 When the ear heard, it blessed me,
When the eye saw, it commended me;
12 For I rescued the poor who cried,
The orphan who had no helper.
13 The blessing of the destitute came to me,
The widow's heart I made joyful.
14 I was clothed with righteousness and it with me;
Like robe and turban was my justice.
15 Eyes I was to the blind,
Feet to the lame was I.
16 I was a father to the poor,
The cause of the stranger I championed.
17 I broke the jaws of the wicked,
Plucked the prey from his teeth.
18 I thought, 'In ripe age I shall expire,
Like sand I shall multiply days,
19 My root spread out to the water,
The dew lodged on my branches,
20 My glory fresh within me,
My bow renewed in my hand.'

NOTES

xxix 1. The same formula as in xxvii 1.

2b. Cf. Num vi 24; Pss xvi 1, xci 11, cxxi 7 f.

3. Cf. Pss xviii 28, xxxvi 9, xcvii 11, cxii 4; Isa 1 10; Mic vii 8. Blommerde cited a couple of passages from Ugaritic letters which speak of the shining of the king's face: "and the face of the king shone upon me" (117:17–18, *wpn mlk nr bn*), and "the face of the sun (i.e. the king) shone very much upon me" (1015:9–10, *pn špš nr by mid*).

4a. *prime.* The rendering "in the autumn of my life" in previous editions of this work was mistaken. The explanation that autumn was the season of harvest, symbolizing maturity and prosperity rather than the decline of life, as in our usage, is misleading. The basic meaning of *ḥrp* is "be early, young," as applied in Akkadian to green olives, or in Arabic to spring lamb. Rashi cited the rabbinic use (Ta'nit 3b, Niddah 65b) of the term for early clouds as contrasted with late clouds. The meaning "autumn" developed with the change from the primitive calendar which began the year with the paschal rites of spring (cf. Exod xiii 2, 18) to the calendar in which the year began in the fall. Vulg. *adolescentiae meae* and Theodotion's and Symmachus' rendering *neotātós mou,* Luther and KJ are thus correct, as against the RSV. AT's choice of "prime" for *ḥōrep̄* is accepted as most felicitous. (This revised NOTE was written on the basis of a discussion with M. Dahood before seeing the treatment of the passage by A. C. M. Blommerde, *Northwest Semitic Grammar and Job,* 1969, p. 109.)

4b. *'Aliy.* The preposition *'ly,* "upon," as Dhorme noted, "does not suit the context," and the phrase *bĕsôḏ 'ălê* is "oddly constructed." The idiom *yāsaḏ 'al,* as in Amos ix 6, requires an indication of place upon which something can be founded or established. The difficulty is relieved simply by taking *'ly* as the divine name. It seems better to delete *'ĕlôah* as a variant rather than a compound, "'Aliy God." As noted in the earlier editions, there is no need to amend *sôḏ* to *sôḵ* on the basis of LXX in order to get the sense "protect," if that were really desiderated. It seems preferable to construe *bswd* as the preposition plus the infinitive *yĕsôḏ,* i.e., *bîsôḏ.*

family. Literally "tent," but in the sense of household, "family," as in xxxi 31.

5a. Cf. Gen xxviii 20, xxxi 5; Pss xxiii 4, xlvi 7.

5b. Cf. i 2, 4, 19, viii 4. Cf. II Sam xviii 29 where *na'ar* is used of the mature Absalom. Numerous progeny was regarded as the sure token of divine favor, Pss cxxvii 3–5, cxxviii 3–4.

6. Cf. xx 17; Song of Songs v 12. In the Ugaritic myth of Baal the resurrection of the dead god becomes known by the fact that fertility returns to the barren earth (49 III 6–9):

> The heavens rain oil,
> The wadies run honey.
> Thus I know that Mighty Baal lives,
> That the Prince Lord of Earth exists.

For honey and oil from the rock, cf. Deut xxxii 13; Ps lxxxi 16b, and feet bathed in oil, Deut xxxiii 24. The term "bath oil" (*šmn rḥs*) occurs in the Samaria ostraca. Here, however, the oil is not for toiletry, but a symbol of plenty.

7. Cf. v 4. The city gate and square were the scene of judicial proceedings and public business, Deut xxii 15; Ruth iv 1; II Chron

xxxii 6; Neh viii 1. The "square," or broad open place (*rĕḥôḇ*), also called "threshing floor" (*gōren*), stood at the entrance of the city gate; cf. I Kings xxii 10 (=II Chron xviii 9). That it was outside the gate is seen from the comparison of II Sam xxi 12 and I Sam xxxi 12 and from Neh viii 1, 3. Thus the preposition *'ălê* here has the meaning "from," as does *'l* in Moabite, Phoenician, and possibly in Ugaritic; cf. Dahood, NWSPJ, p. 68.

7a. LXX has instead of "gate" *orthios,* "morning," apparently having read *šḥr* instead of MT *š'r.* The Qumran Targum, however, reads . . . *ṣpryn btr'y qry',* ". . . morning(s) in the gates of the city," with both the words "morning" and "gate." This reading is puzzling since an extra word for morning would make the original line metrically overweighted.

8. Cf. Isa xlix 7.

9. The Qumran Targum preserves 9a virtually complete and part of 9b:

> [*w*]*rbrbyn ḥšw mll'*
> *wkp yšwn*[ ]
>
> [And] nobles become silent of speech,
> And put hand [to their mouth].

S. Kaufman suggests that, since the root *ḥš',* "be silent," is intransitive, the word *mll'* cannot be a direct object, but can only be the Pa'ēl infinitive of *mll,* perhaps as haplography for *mlmll'.* The noun *mll',* however, is attested in the Targ. of xv 15 where it renders MT *dāḇār.* Since MT in the present passage uses a cognate form with a preposition, *bĕmillîn,* it may be that the Qumran Targum *mll'* is to be construed as a noun in the adverbial accusative, "with respect to speech," rather than a scribal error.

9–10. Cf. Wisdom of Solomon viii 12b and Isa lii 15.

10a. *were hushed.* The same form *neḥbā'û* is used at the end of vs. 8, "and (they) hid (themselves)." Guillaume saw here a fine example of the rhetorical device which the Arabs called *jinās,* the use of the same word with different meanings. Guillaume appealed to Ar. *ḫb'* in the sense of "become extinct," *ḫabi'a* = "(the fire) died out," explaining that the voice of the nobles became mute like a dead fire. Dhorme took note of a similar suggestion by Chajes (cited by Gesenius-Buhl, *Handwörterbuch,* s.v. *ḥb'*), but appealed to the sense "be veiled," as suggested by the noun *ḥeḇyôn,* "veil." The basic meaning of the root *ḫb',* "be hidden," could provide the sense "be hushed." In the preceding line, 9b, the speech was stopped by the putting of the hand to the mouth, either to muffle the sound or to stop it abruptly; the former method could be viewed as a mode of concealment, and perhaps also the latter. Translators have been slightly bothered by the apparent grammatical incongruity of the singular subject, *qôl nĕḡîḏîm,* "voice of chieftains," and the plural verb *neḥbā'û.*

Syr. added the relative particle, "the voices of the chieftains who were hidden," while Vulg. and Targ. made the chieftains rather than the voice(s) the subject of the verb. The Qumran Targum translates MT exactly, *ql sgnyn hṭmrw*, "(the) voice(s) of grandees were hidden."

21–25. These verses are out of place where they now stand in MT and appear to fit better between vss. 10 and 11. Thus transposed, there is a smoother transition to the description of Job's changed social status in the first part of chapter xxx.

21. Cf. Ps xxxvii 7 and Lam iii 26 where similar expression is used of quiet waiting for God.

22b–23a. Cf. Deut xxxii 2; Prov xvi 15; Hos vi 3. The word of God, king, or charismatic person is like the rain which is so vital to the land and to life; cf. Deut xi 14.

23b. Cf. Ps cxix 131 which is understood in the light of this verse. The pious man pants with open mouth, as with thirst, for the divine word. The Ugaritic epic of King Keret gives a vivid poetic description of the anxious farmers waiting for rain on the parched earth (cf. James v 7):

Sweet to the earth is Baal's rain,
To the fields the rain of 'Aliy,
Sweet to the wheat in the furrows,
In the tilth to the spelt.

———

The plowmen lift their heads,
Upwards the corn-growers,
For food is spent in their bins,
Spent the wine in their skins,
The oil in——

24. Comparison of the several modern versions reveal diverse understandings or misunderstandings of this couplet. There is no need here to discuss all possible and improbable renderings and emendations. There is no good reason to reject the most natural and literal interpretation. The idiom *śḥq 'l* does not mean "laugh at," which is expressed by *śḥq l* (cf. v 22, xxxix 7, 18, 22, xli 21) and *śḥq 'l* (xxx 1), but "smile upon." A smile from Job was regarded by his loyal retainers as such an unmerited and unexpected favor that they could hardly believe their good fortune. The light of the countenance, the glow or halo that proceeds from the face of a god or king, was regarded as beneficent; cf. Num vi 25; Pss iv 7, xliv 3; Prov xvi 15. Job's subjects were eager to catch the light of his countenance and let none of it be lost.

25a. *their course.* The Qumran Targum reads "my way," *'rḥy,* instead of MT *darkām,* "their way." Cf. Pss xxv 12, cxix 30.

25b. *troops.* Cf. xix 12, xxv 3, and for the similar term "captain(s)/chief(s) of troops," II Sam iv 2; I Kings xi 24; I Chron xii 18.

25c. The MT *ka'ăšer 'ăḇēlîm yĕnaḥēm,* "according as mourners he comforts," is awkward syntactically and the sense is inappropriate to the context. Rather than reject the line, it seems best to adopt, with minor modifications, the emendation suggested by Herz (ZAW 20 [1900], 163) *ba'ăšer 'ôḇîlām yinnāḥû.* Since the root *nḥy* is not attested in the Nip̄'al, it seems better to construe it as Hop̄'al, *yonḥû.* The final *-m* of *ynḥm* may be retained and regarded as the enclitic element so common in Ugaritic poetry, *yonḥû -ma.* The same sense could be obtained by reading *yanḥûm,* "they would lead them."

11. Cf. Prov xxxi 28; Song of Songs vi 9.

12. Cf. Ps lxxii 12. Here Job gives the lie to Eliphaz's charge in xxii 6–9. It was the prime duty of a ruler to protect the poor, widows, and orphans. The sage Danel of the Ugaritic epic of Aqhat "judges the cause of the widow, adjudicates the case of the orphan." In the Keret epic, the king's son Yaṣṣib charges his father with dereliction of duty, suggests that his illness is a result of this neglect, and recommends that the father abdicate in his favor:

> You have not judged the cause of the widow,
> Adjudicated the case of the wretched.
> Thus thou art taken to the sickbed,
> Prostrated on the couch of disease.
> Descend from rule, that I may reign;
> From thy dominion, that I may sit.

13a. *destitute.* Literally "one perishing," *'ôḇēḏ;* cf. xxxi 19.

came to me. Literally "entered upon me," i.e., came before me/into my presence. The preposition *'al* often has this sense with verbs meaning "arrive," "enter," or the like; cf. II Sam xv 4; II Kings xxv 20. In the equivalent expression in biblical Aramaic, the variants *'al 'al* (Dan ii 24) and *'al qŏḏām* (Dan iv 5) show the sense of the preposition *'al* to be the same as *qŏḏām,* "before, in the presence of." The same idiom is used in Ugaritic, *'l abh y'rb,* "in the presence of his father he entered." The same expression, "enter upon," sometimes denotes sexual contact, Gen xix 31; Deut xxv 5, or contact with a corpse, Gen xxxiv 27a.

13b. LXX reads "the widow's mouth praised me," which presents a closer parallel to the preceding line than does MT. The Qumran Targum agrees with LXX [*bp*]*wm 'rmlh hwyt lṣlw*[*t'*], "in the widow's mouth I was for pray[er]."

14. Righteousness, salvation, honor, shame, etc., are often represented metaphorically as a garment; cf. xix 9; Ps cxxxii 9, 16, 18; Isa lix 17. Just as Job was, as it were, clothed with righteousness, it was clothed with him; cf. Judg vi 34 where the spirit of the Lord was clothed with Gideon. Blommerde rendered:

> I put on justice and it clothed me;
> my robe and my tartan was my justice.

The suffix of the verb *wayyilbāšēnî* Blommerde made to serve also for *mĕ'il*, "my robe," and *sānîp̄*, "my tartan." More questionable is the rendering "and it clothed me." In order to get this meaning, the verb would have to be read as the causative *wayyalbîšēnî* because the simple stem is stative and means "be clothed." The stuff with which one is clothed is supplied as the accusative of material, thus *wayyilbāšēnî* means "it was clothed with me." The transitive causative form *yalbîšēnî*, "it clothed me," would take extra accusatives for the identification of the clothing. It would be possible to read the verb *wylbšny* as causative transitive with *mišpāṭî* as its subject, "and my justice clothed me like a robe and a turban," but this goes against the Masoretic punctuation and metrical balance.

15. Cf. Jer xxxi 8. The blind, the lame, and the pregnant needed special protection.

16a. Cf. Ps lxviii 6; Isa xxii 21; I Maccabees ii 65. The righteous king protects the helpless as a father his child. Hammurabi in the epilogue of his Code of laws represents himself as "a ruler who is to the people like the father who bore (them)"; cf. ANET, p. 178 (rev. xxv, lines 20 f.). King Kilamuwa of Y'dy (Zenjirli), in an inscription dating from the ninth century B.C., boasts of his fidelity to his royal duty, "I to some was father, and to some I was mother" (*w'nk lmy kt 'b wlmy kt 'm*); cf. ANET, p. 500.

16b. Literally "the dispute of him I did not know I searched." The meaning is not that Job investigated thoroughly the issues of every dispute, but that he went out of his way to help the hapless stranger. Solicitude for the stranger, as for the widow and orphan, is enjoined in the Law, Exod xxii 21 f.

17. Cf. iv 10; Pss iii 8, lviii 7, cxxiv 6–7.

18a. We follow the clue of LXX, *hē helikia mou gērasei*, which reflects the reading *zqny*, "my old age," rather than *qny*, "my nest." MT "with my nest" doubtless suggested the connection with the fabulous phoenix in the following line. The other versions give no real help here.

Syr. translates (?) twice, "poor people I will save," and "I shall end like a reed." Targ. renders "in my nest" (*bšrkpy*). Some interpreters retain "my nest" as applied to Job's children (cf. Deut xxxii 11; Isa xvi 2), but drop the figure in the following line. If "nest" is retained here, one should probably, on the basis of parallelism, choose the "phoenix" rather than "sand" in the next line.

18b. The *crux interpretum* of this verse lies in the word *ḥôl* and the well-attested meaning "sand" is chosen rather than the fabulous "phoenix." (The rabbis of Nehardea read *ḥûl* rather than *ḥôl*, but the reason is not clear.) This choice dictates the emendation of *qny*, "my nest," to *zqny*, "my old age," in the preceding line. LXX *hōsper stelechos foinikos* may suggest obliquely the phoenix legend, but the word *stelechos* indicates the sense "palm tree" for *foinix*, as with the Vulg. *sicut palma.* How the word *ḥôl*, "sand," could be taken to refer to the palm tree is unintelligible apart from the phoenix fable. The representation of the phoenix which Herodotus saw in Egypt (ii.73.1) was probably the hieroglyphic symbol of the benu bird, a kind of stork. The confusion of phoenix and palm tree may have something to do with the similarity of the words in Egyptian (*bnw*, "phoenix," and *bnr*, "date," *bnr.t*, "date palm"). In the tree cult at Heliopolis, the sacred tree, however, was the *išd* (cf. H. Bonnet, *Reallexikon der ägyptischen Religionsgeschichte,* 1952, s.v. "Baumkult," p. 82). Pliny (*Nat. hist.* xiii.4) tells us, "The bird phoenix is supposed to have taken that name of this date tree (called in Greek *foinix*); for it was assured me that this bird died with the tree, and revived of itself as the tree sprung again."

The palm tree symbolizes eternal youth in Ps xcii 12–14:

> The righteous shall flourish like the palm.
>
> ———
>
> They shall bear fruit even in old age,
> Ever succulent and green.

The figure of the eagle as symbolizing the renewal of youth, Ps ciii 5, Isa xl 31, may be related to some myth or legend similar to that of the phoenix and may have influenced the interpretation of the present passage in the light of the phoenix legend. The fabled phoenix at the end of its life-span (500, 600, or 1461 years) burned itself in its nest and from its ashes sprang another of its kind. In Jewish legend, the phoenix alone of all birds refused to partake of the forbidden fruit and was rewarded with eternal life; cf. Midrash Rabba Gen xix 5; TB, Sanhedrin 108b.

Dahood (*Biblica* 48 [1967], 542–44) has argued for the phoenix and its nest in the present passage. Support for the rabbinic appeal to the fable of the phoenix is adduced from an alleged allusion to the phoenix in Ugaritic. The word *ḥl* in the Keret Epic was related to the phoenix myth by the late lamented W. F. Albright and one cannot dissent from the view of so great a scholar without attempting to show cause (cf. M. Pope, JBL 85 [1966], 400 ff.). The passage in question (125 I 5–9) Albright ("Baal Zephon," in *Festschrift für Alfred Bertholet*, pp. 1–14) arranged and translated as follows:

bd aṯt ab	The women will chant, O my father,
ṣrry / tbkyk ab	The co-wives will mourn thee, my father:
ġr bʿl / ṣpn ḥlm qdš /	"O mountain, Baal-zephon, O holy phoenix,
any ḥlm adr	O bark, 'Glorious Phoenix,'
ḥl / rḥb mknpt	Phoenix wide of wings!"

The content of the women's dirge for the ailing Keret thus consists entirely of an invocation of Baal's holy mountain as a ship and as the phoenix. This interpretation is supported with prodigious erudition and would be overwhelmingly convincing but for an oversight which undermines it completely. Attention to the variations in the parallel passages (125 I 2–11a, 11b–23, 98b–111) reveals that the stichometry of Albright's arrangement is insupportable and the interpretation depends on the stichometry. Comparison of lines 5–6, 19–20, 104–5 makes it quite clear that the word *ṣrry* must begin new lines. Thus the words *bd att ab ṣrry* form a single line and Ginsberg's arrangement and interpretation (ANET, p. 147) must be supported. Ginsberg's rendering and implied arrangement are as follows:

Wilt thou die, then, father like mortals,	*ap ab ik mtm tmtn*
or thy joy change to mourning,	*u ḫštk lntn ʿtq*
(to) a woman's dirge, O father, my song?	*bd aṯt ab ṣrry*
For thee, father, weeps the mount of Baal,	*tbkyk ab ġr bʿl*
Zaphon the sacred circuit,	*ṣpn ḥlm qdš*
The mighty circuit laments,	*any ḥlm adr*
The circuit broad of span.	*ḥl rḥb mknpt*

Ginsberg indicated some uncertainty about the meaning of *ṣrry* which he conjecturally rendered "my song." The word may be related to Ar. *ṣarīr*, "cry, shriek," which sense is quite suitable to the context. Since *bd* is used in Ugaritic only of joyful song, it seems preferable to render *bd aṯt* as "a woman's song" rather than "a woman's dirge." A slight improvement may be made by rendering *bd aṯt ab ṣrry* as "A woman's song, O father (change to) a shriek?" With the correction of the stichometry, the parallelism necessarily shifts so that the subject of the verb *bky* is not *ṣrry* but *ġr bʿl*, "the mount of Baal," and *ḥl-m qdš* is in apposition with *ṣpn* and parallel to *ġr bʿl;* the word *any* is thus not a noun meaning "ship," but a verb meaning "lament," and is parallel to *bky*, "weep." The words *bʿl* and *ṣpn* fall in successive poetic lines and do not form here the compound *Baal-Ṣapān*. Accordingly, the word *ḥl* in Ugaritic has nothing to do with the phoenix and no positive bearing on the present passage in Job. The question whether *ḥôl* here means "sand" or "phoenix" remains moot.

19. Cf. viii 16, xviii 16; Ps i 3; Jer xvii 8; Ezek xxxi 7.

20b. *My bow*. Cf. Gen xlix 24. To break one's bow reduced him to impotence, Hos i 5; Jer xlix 35.

29. JOB'S PERORATION (*continued*)
(xxx 1–31)

XXX

1 "But now they deride me,
Men younger than I,
Whose fathers I had disdained
To put with the dogs of my flock.
2 What to me the strength of their hands?
From them all vigor had perished;
3 With want and famine gaunt,
Gnawing the dry ground,
By night in desolate waste,
4 Plucking saltwort among the scrub,
Broom roots for warmth,
5 Driven from the community,
Shouted at like a thief.
6 In the wadi gullies to dwell,
Holes in the ground and rocks.
7 Among the bushes they bray,
Under the nettles they huddle.
8 An ignoble, nameless brood,
Scourged out of the land.
9 And now I am their jest,
I have become to them a gibe.
10 They detest me and stand aloof;
From my face they spare no spit.
11 My cord they loose and afflict me,
Cast off restraint before me.
12 On the right a vile brood
Rise and trip my feet,
Rear roads of ruin for me,

13 Break up my path to destroy me;
They attack with none to stay them.
14 As through a wide breach they come;
Amid a tempest they roll on.
15 Terrors are turned on me,
Dispelling my dignity like the wind,
Like a cloud gone my prosperity.
16 My soul within me is emptied;
Days of affliction seize me.
17 Night rives my bones away,
My torturers never relax.
18 With violence he grasps my garment,
Seizes me by the coat collar.
19 God casts me into the mire,
I become as dust and ashes.
20 I cry to you, but you do not answer;
You stand and look at me.
21 You are changed to a tyrant toward me;
With your strong hand you assail me.
22 You lift me up and mount me on the wind,
You toss me about with a tempest.
23 I know that you will return me to Death,
To the meetinghouse of all the living.
24 One does not turn his hand against the needy,
When in his distress he cries for help.
25 Did I not weep for the hapless,
My soul grieve for the poor?
26 Yet when I expected good, came evil;
I hoped for light, but darkness came.
27 My bowels boil unceasing;
Days of affliction confront me.
28 In gloom I go, with no sun;
I stand in the crowd and cry for help.
29 I have become the jackal's brother,
The ostrich's companion.

30 My skin blackens and peels,
My bones are scorched with heat.
31 My harp is turned to mourning,
My flute to the sound of weepers.

Notes

xxx 1a. Cf. xix 18, xxix 8.

1b. Cf. xv 10.

1c, d. Probably an adaptation of a popular expression of contempt. The dog was despised by the ancient Semites as a filthy and vicious scavenger (Exod xxii 31; I Kings xiv 11, xxi 19, 23; Jer xv 3; Ps lxviii 23; Prov xxvi 11) and the epithet *kalb* was a grievous insult (I Sam xvii 43; II Sam iii 8, xvi 9) or an extreme form of self-abasement (I Sam xxiv 14; II Sam ix 8; II Kings viii 13). In the Amarna Letters the Semitic vassal appealing to the Pharaoh abases himself as a dog. In the NT, cf. Matt vii 6, xv 26; Philip iii 2. Greedy dogs and careless shepherds are mentioned together in Isa lvi 10–11.

2b. Reading, with Budde, *kl-lḥ* for *klḥ;* cf. v 26. Blommerde suggests that *klḥ* is formed by "congeneric assimilation" of *kō'aḥ* and *lēaḥ*.

3a. *famine*. The translation of *kāpān* as "hunger" in the previous editions is here changed to "famine" (cf. v 22a) in accordance with Guillaume's observation that the parallel here with *ḥeser* shows that the meaning is not so much hunger as poverty of diet. Instead of Ar. *kafana,* "shrouded, wrapped" (with which meaning the LXX translator of Ezek xvii 7 may have been familiar, as Guillaume surmised), one could appeal to Ar. *kbn* which in the XIth stem means "be shrunk, contracted" and is the nominal form *kubunn,* "miser, niggard."

3. *gaunt*. Cf. iii 7, xv 34.

3b. *gnawing*. The word *'rq* which occurs only here and in vs. 17 below may also mean "go away, flee," or the like. Either sense would be acceptable here, e.g., "Roaming the arid steppe" as with the Targ. (*'rqyn ršy'y' b'r'' ṣhyy'*). The line is too short; the simplest expedient is to assume the omission of a word, possibly *'ereṣ,* "earth." Duhm proposed to restore *yĕraq* supposedly lost after *h'rqm,* to which Dhorme objected that the "verdure of the steppe" is not a thing that one gnaws at. Interestingly enough, the Qumran Targum reads [*k*]*pn r'yn hw' yrq d*[ ] which the editors translate ["Dans (leur f]aim (leur) désir était la verdure du d[esert] . . ."

3c. This line has been troublesome, as standard commentaries will show. Taking all three words as adverbial accusatives, as in the above translation, obviates the necessity of giving the word *'emeš*, "[last] night," the sense of "darkness," which is not elsewhere attested. The alliteration in this line (*'emeš šô'āh ûmšô'āh*) is too striking to be emended away; cf. xxxviii 27.

4a. *saltwort*. Heb. *mallûaḥ*, probably derived from *melaḥ* (*milḥ*), "salt." The Talmud (Qiddushin 66a) mentions this plant as food for the poor. It is commonly identified as *atriplex halimus*, the foliage of which is edible but has a sour taste and would be eaten only in dire extremity.

4b. *Broom roots*. These yielded good charcoal; cf. Ps cxx 4. On the basis of Isa xlvii 14, we may take *laḥmām* to mean "to warm (oneself)" rather than "their food." The roots of the broom or desert furze are not edible; cf. Immanuel Löw, *Flora* II, 1924, pp. 470 f.

5. Dahood (*Biblica* 38 [1957], 318 f.) suggested that in the obscure phrase *min gēw* there may well be the frequently occurring Ugaritic word *g* "voice." The expression *min gēw*, Dahood explained as the equivalent of *miqqôl* (Isa vi 4, xxx 31, xxxiii 3; Jer viii 19) and translated the present passage as follows:

> With a shout they are driven forth.
> they raise a hue against them as against a thief.

5a. *community*. This sense is attested for the word *gēw*, "interior, midst," in Syriac commonly and once in a Phoenician inscription from Piraeus (Cooke, *North Semitic Inscriptions*, 1903, 33:2). Although the line is too short, no emendation is necessary to make sense.

7a. *bray*. The root *nhq* occurs in the OT only in Job (twice), but is known from Aramaic and Arabic and now attested in Ugaritic. It does not seem likely that the braying is intended to suggest lust, like the neigh of the stallion in Jer v 8. Braying may also be a sign of hunger; cf. vi 5.

7b. There is no indication that the verb here rendered "huddle" has sexual connotation, as Peake suggested. Not that the miserable rabble would be averse to alfresco copulation, but, if I have interpreted vs. 2b above correctly, they are represented as too debilitated. The exact nature of the plant (*ḥārûl*) rendered "nettles" is uncertain. In Prov xxiv 31 it is parallel to "thorns"; in other Semitic dialects it refers to certain leguminous plants.

8a. Literally "sons of a fool, also sons of no name."

9. Harking back to vs. 1.

jest. Literally "song"; cf. Ps lxix 12; Lam iii 14.

gibe. Literally "word."

10. Cf. xix 13, 19; Isa l 6.

11a. Whether one follows the Kethib ("his cord") or the Qere ("my cord") it is necessary to change the two verbs to plurals or else transfer the line to a suitable context in which Job lists God's assaults on him, as in xvi 9–14 or xix 6–12 or vss. 18–22 below. It seems best to follow the Qere and emend the verbs to plurals, although the metaphor remains obscure. Whether the "cord" is a bowstring or tent cord is uncertain. It is clear only from the context that the rabble seek to undo him.

11b. *restraint.* Literally "bridle."

12a. *vile brood.* The word (*pirḥāḥ*) occurs only here and the meaning is conjectural. It is generally explained from the root *prḥ* meaning "break forth (from the womb), sprout, etc."; cf. Ps lxxxiv 4 (*'eprōaḥ*). In Arabic *farḫ* is used of a base or abject person and in the Mishnah (Middot i 8, Yoma i 7) *peraḥ* is used of young men of the priesthood, but without suggestion of contempt. The duplication of the final consonant is a bit odd in this word and it may be that the syllable *ḥāḥ* hides the word *ḫaḫḫu,* attested in Akkadian and Ugaritic in the sense of "spittle, filth, unseemly conduct," or the like—i.e., *prḫ ḫḫ,* "a vile brood."

12b. Taking the verb *yāqûmû* with this line rather than the preceding one.

12c. *roads of ruin.* Siegework; cf. xix 12.

13a. Taking *lĕhawwāṯî,* "for my destruction," i.e., "to destroy me," with this line rather than the following. The verb *nts,* here rendered "break up," is hapax and commonly connected with *ntṣ,* "pull down, break down." The root *nts,* however, may be attested in Ugaritic in Baal's boast of what he will do to his enemy Prince Sea (68:4) *ṯm ḥrbm its,* "there with (two?) sword(s) will I shatter (him)."

13b. *stay.* The change of *'ôzēr* to *'ôṣēr,* after S. R. Driver, which was accepted in the previous editions of the work, is here abandoned, not because *z* and *ṣ* are interchangeable as Guillaume asserted, but because Ar. *'zr* is used in the opposite senses of "help" and "hinder."

The symmetry of this bicolon is deceptive in the translation because in the original the second line is about twice as long as the first. Blommerde's arrangement as a tricolon may be better:

> They break up my path,
> They further my undoing;
> there is none to help me against them.

14b. *tempest.* Cf. Prov i 27; Ezek xxxviii 9 where the word *šô'āh* is used in this sense. The figure is not entirely clear. It may be that the word denotes here the crash of the breached masonry. The versions give no help on this line. The Qumran Targum adds to the vexations of this verse addition puzzlement:

> *btqp šḥny ytwn*
> [*tḥwt*] *b'yšh 'tkppt*

The editors render:

> Lorsque mon ulcer(?) est terrible, ils viennent,
> j'ai été courbé [sous] le mal.

The *ḥ* of *šḥny* is uncertain. The word *šiḥnā'* developed the sense of "burden" from the sore caused by pressure of the load on the camel's back. MT *pereṣ* "breach, rupture," may have suggested skin lesions.

15b. *dignity*. LXX has *elpis,* "hope," and Vulg. *desiderium,* "desire." KJ renders "soul," JPS, AT, and RSV, "honor." Moffatt paraphrases, "my happiness is blown away." With CCD, we prefer "dignity" in this context. Cf. Isa xxxii 8 where the word designates the quality of character and deeds of a "liberal" (KJ) or "noble" man (Moffatt, AT, RSV).

like the wind. Cf. xxi 18; Ps i 4.

15c. *Like a cloud.* Cf. Hos vi 4; Isa li 5; Ps lxviii 3.

prosperity. This word (*yĕšû'āh*) is often rendered "salvation," but its basic meaning has to do with material and physical welfare and never exclusively with spiritual well-being.

16. This verse is largely preserved in the Qumran Targum, but there are some uncertainties. The editors read and translated thus:

> *wk'n 'ly tt'šd [npšy]*
> *[wy]wmy tšbr' y'qpwny*
>
> Et maintenant [mon âme] s'épanche sur moi,
> [et des j]ours d'oppression m'entourent.

The form *tšbr'* was related by the editors to the root **ṯbr,* in spite of the anomalous orthography. S. Kaufman, however, suggested that the correct reading is *tškr',* related to Syr. *škr,* "to insult, disgrace." The verbal form *y'qpwny* is also problematic, and Kaufman rejected the editors' analysis as an *'ap'ēl* imperfect of the root *nqp* and commented: "Apparently the Ap̄'ēl *'aqqep̄* was incorrectly analyzed as a Pa'ēl of **'qp,* yielding the imperfect *y^{e}'aqqep̄.*" The sense of the Qumran Targum's rendering, we may surmise, is approximately as follows:

> And now for me [my soul] is spent,
> And days of disgrace beset me.

16a. *soul.* The term (*nep̄eš*) has a wide range of meaning, including breath, life, appetite, emotion, and the whole person. The idea of the soul as a separate entity from the body is unbiblical. One pours out the "soul," I Sam i 15; Ps xlii 5, as one's heart (mind) is poured out, Lam ii 19, in sorrowful supplication before God. The meaning here is apparently that the emotional strain caused by suffering has drained Job of all zest for life.

17a. *away.* Dahood (*Psalms I,* second NOTE on Ps xii 7) took MT *mēʿālay*, "from upon me," to mean "than a caldron," relating *ʿly* to Ar. *ġly*, "seethe, boil," and rendered the present line "At night my bones are hotter than a caldron." A similar treatment was accorded vs. 30 below.

17b. Literally "My gnawers do not lie down (i.e., to sleep)." LXX has "my sinews" (*ta neura mou*); cf. Ar. *ʿurūq*, "veins" and Aram. *ʿarqā*, "ligament."

18. This verse is so beset with difficulties that some interpreters do not attempt a translation. KJ renders literally except for the addition of the italicized words, "By great force *of my disease* is my garment changed: it bindeth me about as the collar of my coat." RSV follows LXX which read a form of the verb *tpś*, "seize," instead of *ḥpś*. This, however, leaves the two lines inapposite and it seems best to emend also the verb of the second line from *'zr*, "gird," to *'ḥz*, "grasp." The implied subject of the verbs thus emended would be none other than God and this may explain the textual corruption as a pious attempt to obscure Job's blasphemous charges.

19a. Cf. ix 31. This line is too brief, consisting only of two short words. We follow Moffatt and RSV in supplying the unexpressed subject as "God." LXX, Vulg., and Targ. all make this line agree with 19b, *comparatus sum luto*.

20a. Cf. xix 7.

20b. Reading with the Syr. rather than MT "I stand."

21a. Cf. xvi 9–14; Isa lxiii 10.

22a. Cf. ix 17, xxvii 21. Yahweh, as supplanter of the Canaanite storm-god Baal-Hadad, is depicted as riding on the wind, Ps xviii 11, but for a frail mortal the storm wind represents destruction and terror.

22b. *tempest*. The word is vocalized by the Masoretes as *tûšiyyāh* which has the meaning "wisdom, success, victory" or the like; cf. xi 6. There can be little doubt that the consonantal text is to be preferred, with the vocalization *tĕšû(')āh*, "noise," in the sense of "tempest."

23a. *Death*. Probably to be taken as the proper name of the ruler of the infernal region, Mot. There is no reason to evade the clear implication of this line by rendering "bring," instead of "bring back, return"; cf. NOTE on i 21.

24. *needy*. Reading *ʿānî* instead of *ʿî*, "heap, ruin." Job is, indeed, a wreck, but a heap crying for help is a bizarre metaphor. This verse has been regarded as one of the most difficult in the entire poem. Except for the problem of the emended word, which makes no sense in any case, the major difficulty disappears when the idiom *šlḥ yd b-*, "send the hand against," is taken in its regular hostile sense. By implication, Job accuses God of assaulting him while he is helpless and imploring help.

25. *hapless*. Literally "the hard of day."

27. Cf. Lam i 20, ii 11.

28a. *gloom*. The word *qdr* has the primary sense "be/become dark," used of the sun, moon, and heavens, Joel ii 10, iv 15; Jer iv 28; Mic iii 6; and also of mourning, Jer viii 21, xiv 2; Pss xxxv 14, xlii 9, xliii 2. Ps xxxviii 7 has the identical expression *qôḏēr hillaḵtî*, rendered by RSV "I go about mourning," but here "I go about blackened." The word *ḥammāh*, "sun," as in Isa xxiv 23, xxx 26; Song of Songs vi 10, may also mean "heat," as in Ps xix 7. It seems unlikely, however, that the darkness here refers to Job's skin, which turns black from disease rather than the sun; (cf. vs. 30 below).

29. Cf. Mic i 8. The mournful howl of the jackal still disturbs the desert night in the Near East. The ostrich, too, inhabited the desert, Isa xiii 21, xxxiv 13. The ostrich reportedly has considerable vocal versatility, including hissing, cackling, and a hideous, doleful moaning.

30. Cf. vii 5, xviii 13, xxx 31; Ps cii 3; Lam iv 8.

30a. *peels*. Literally "from upon me," *mē'ālay*. Dahood, as in vs. 17a above, took *'ly* as a noun meaning "caldron" and rendered this verse: "My skin is blacker than a caldron, and my bones are hotter than a scorching wind."

31. Cf. xxi 12; Ps cl 4; Lam v 15. The harp (*kinnôr*) is often mentioned in connection with religious celebrations. The "flute" (*'ûḡāḇ*), KJ "organ," RSV "pipe," is probably the single pipe or true flute, as opposed to the double pipe (*ḥālîl*).

30. JOB'S FINAL OATH
(xxxi 1–8; 38–40b; 9–14; 23; 15–22; 24–37; 40c)

XXXI

1 "I put a ban on my eyes
That I would not look upon folly.
2 What is God's allotment from above,
Shaddai's heritage from on high?
3 Is it not disaster for the evil,
Woe for the workers of wickedness?
4 Does he not see my way,
Count all my steps?
5 If I have walked toward vanity,
My foot hustled to deceit;
6 Let him weigh me in just scales,
And let God know my innocence.
7 If my steps have strayed from the way,
Or my heart followed my eyes,
Or spot stuck to my hands;
8 May I sow and another eat,
And my offspring be uprooted.
38 If my land cried out against me,
Or its furrows wept together;
39 If I ate its yield without paying,
Or snuffed out the life of the tenants;
40 Instead of wheat let thistles grow,
Instead of barley, weeds.
9 If my heart has been lured by a woman,
If I lurked at my neighbor's door,
10 Let my wife grind for another,
And others bend over her.
11 For that were licentiousness,
Criminal iniquity,

12 A fire that devours to Perdition,
Destroying all my income.
13 If I despised the claim of my slave,
Or my slave girl, when they complained;
14 What could I do if God should arise,
Or answer if he took me to task?
23 For God's calamity is a dread to me;
I could not withstand its terror.
15 Did not he who made me in the belly make him?
The same One fashion us in the womb?
16 If I refused any need of the poor,
Or made the widow's eye to pine,
17 While I ate my food alone,
And the orphan shared none of it;
18 Nay from my youth I reared him like a father,
From infancy I guided her;
19 If I saw one dying for lack of clothing,
A poor man with nothing to cover him;
20 If his loins did not bless me,
Warmed by the fleece of my sheep;
21 If I raised my hand against the orphan,
When I had the advantage in the gate;
22 Let my shoulder drop from its socket,
My arm be wrenched off above the elbow.
24 If I put my confidence in gold,
Called fine gold my security;
25 If I gloated when my wealth was great,
When my hand had acquired riches;
26 If I looked at the shining light,
Or the moon marching in splendor,
27 And my mind was secretly seduced,
And my hand kissed my mouth;
28 That were perfidious sin,
I had betrayed God on high.
29 If I rejoiced at my foe's misfortune,
Exulted when trouble befell him,

30 Or let my mouth offend,
Seeking his life with a curse;
31 If males of my household ever said,
'O that we might sate ourselves with his flesh.'
32 The stranger did not sleep in the street;
My door I opened to the traveler.
33 If I hid my transgressions like Adam,
Concealing my guilt in a covert;
34 Though I feared the rabble clamor,
And the scorn of the clan terrified me,
I brought no man out the door.
35 O that someone would listen to me!
Behold my signature, let Shaddai answer me.
Let my opponent write a document.
36 I would wear it on my shoulder,
I would bind it on like a crown.
37 I would tell him the number of my steps;
I would approach him like a prince."

40c Job's words are ended.

Notes

xxxi. In this final apology, Job rests his case on a series of oaths of clearance. The oaths are in some cases complete, with the sanction of self-imprecation fully expressed (cf. Num v 20–22). The moralizing comments following some of the oaths are perhaps best understood as additions by pietists who could not resist the urge to drive home the point that the conduct Job repudiates is thoroughly reprehensible. Belief in the efficacy of the oath made it the ultimate test of probity; cf. Exod xxii 9–10; I Kings viii 31–32. Job's repudiation of evil here has been compared to the negative confession in the Egyptian Book of the Dead in which the deceased facing the final judgment before Osiris enumerates a long list of sins he has not committed; cf. ANET, p. 34. The similarities are striking, but not sufficient to indicate direct interdependence. Both catalogues of sins reflect high ideals of social ethics. The Egyptian list is a mixture of ethical and ritual concerns, while Job's, with one exception (vss. 26–28), is entirely ethical.

1a. *put a ban on.* Literally "cut a covenant for." The preposition "for" (*lĕ*), in place of the usual "with" (*'im* or *'ēṯ*), designates conditions imposed by the superior on the inferior party in a treaty; cf. I Sam xi 2; II Sam v 3; II Kings xi 4. Job, as master of his senses and his emotions, laid an interdict on his eyes.

1b. The particle *māh* is here to be construed as the negative rather than as the interrogative "How?", as in xvi 6b.

folly. Reading with Peake, *nĕḇālāh* for MT *bĕṯûlāh,* "virgin." The received reading is very intriguing, but fraught with difficulty and critics who retain the reading have to transfer the verse to the section that treats of relations with women, after vs. 12. Transfer of this verse, however, leaves the succeeding vss. 2–4 without connection with what precedes or follows. The reading "virgin" recalls Ben Sira's warning (Ecclesiasticus ix 5): "At a virgin do not look, / Lest you be trapped into sin with her." Ben Sira goes on to elaborate his warning:

Don't look around in the city gate;
Don't roam about in the streets.
Avert your eyes from a pretty woman;
Don't gaze at beauty that is not for you.
By a woman's beauty many have been destroyed;
Her lovers she burns with fire.
Don't eat with a married woman,
Don't take liquor with her;
Lest she draw (your) heart to her
And in bloodshed you go to Perdition.

(The translation is from the Hebrew text of the Cairo Genizah.) Rashi quotes Pirqe Abot de Rabbi Nathan to the effect that Job's piety was such that he would not even look at an unmarried woman, for fear that when she was married he might feel attracted to her. Abraham is alleged to have exceeded even Job in this respect, since he had not even looked at his own wife before the episode related in Gen xii 11 when he said, "Behold, now I know that you are a beautiful woman" (TB, Baba Bathra 16a). The implication is that heretofore Abram had been unaware of Sarai's beauty. (TB, Baba Bathra 16a.) This goes beyond the NT condemnation of ocular adultery, Matt v 28. The normative Jewish attitude toward feminine beauty, and beauty of every sort, regarded it as one of God's favors to the world which should elicit from man a grateful response whenever seen, "Blessed art thou, O Lord, our God, ruler of the universe, who hast such as these in the world"; (cf. TB, Berakot 58b). It is with some reluctance that I emend away the reference to Job's modesty in respect to virgins, but the context calls for some more comprehensive term for evil; cf. the description of the righteous man in Isa xxxiii 15,

> Who shakes his hands, lest they hold a bribe,
> Stops his ears against hearing of bloodshed,
> Shuts his eyes against looking at evil.

Cf. Matt xviii 8.

Dr. Walter Michel directed the writer's attention to the suggestion made in 1928 by G. Jeshurun (in the *Journal of the Society of Oriental Research,* Toronto, p. 153) that "virgin" here refers to the notorious *virgo coelestis,* the goddess Ishtar. The title Virgin, *btlt* is the regular epithet of 'Anat in the Ugaritic mythological texts. The worship of the great goddess as the Venus Star, Queen of Heaven was still popular in Jeremiah's day when the children gathered the wood, the fathers kindled the fire, and the women kneaded dough to make cakes for the Queen of Heaven (Jer vii 18). Jeremiah's condemnation of this worship was answered with a bold affirmation: "As for the word you have spoken to us in the name of Yahweh, we will not heed you. Indeed we will certainly do everything we promised to do, burn incense to the Queen of Heaven, pour libations to her, as our ancestors, our kings, and our princes have done in the cities of Judah and the streets of Jerusalem. We had plenty of food, we prospered and experienced no disaster. But from the time we stopped offering incense to the Queen of Heaven and pouring libations to her, we have lacked everything and have been consumed by sword and famine. So we burn incense to the Queen of Heaven and pour libations to her. Was it without our husbands that we made cakes for her in her image and poured libations to her?" (Jer xliv 16–19). If the virgin in question here is the Queen of Heaven whose licentious worship Job has forsworn, vowing not to look at her even as he avoided looking to the sun and moon as objects of worship, then the difficulties considered at the beginning of this note vanish.

2. This expression appears to be an adaptation of the cry of secession as in II Sam xx 1; I Kings xii 16. Here, however, the particle *māh/meh* has the interrogative sense "What?" rather than negative force as in xvi 6b and 1b above; cf. xx 29.

4. Cf. xiv 16.

5–6. Job begins his series of oaths repudiating evil with a general denial of any sort of sinful conduct. There is nothing here to indicate that the vanity and deceit refer specifically to commercial dishonesty. The sanction invoked is not properly a self-imprecation, but a challenge to God to judge justly and thus exonerate him.

5. Dahood (UHP, p. 31) makes the nature of the offense specific by rendering the words *šāw'* and *mirmāh* as "an idol" and "a fraud": "If I went to an idol, or my foot hastened to a fraud."

5a. *toward.* The preposition *'im* here parallel with *'al* has directional meaning, as in Ugaritic; cf. Dahood, UHP, 10.14, p. 32; *Psalms II*, NOTE on Ps lxxviii 37.

6a. False scales and weights are often condemned; cf. Prov xi 1, xx 10, 23. For the figure of judgment as weighing, cf. vi 2; Dan v 27; Matt vii 2. Among the Egyptians, the heart of the deceased was represented as weighed against the feather of Truth.

6b. *my innocence.* M. Dahood (VTS, XVI [1967], 47) suggested that congruity of the metaphor here requires that *tummāṯî* be rendered "my full weight," not "my innocence." "Job is not himself a fraud; if weighed he will be found full weight." The quest for congruity can be pushed too hard. One's avoirdupois has nothing to do with integrity or innocence. Cf. xxvii 4–6.

7a. Cf. xxiii 11.

7b. Cf. Num xv 39; Prov iv 25–27; Matt vi 22; II Pet ii 14; I John ii 16.

7c. *spot.* The Oriental Kethib, Syr., and Targ. represent *mĕ'ûmāh*, "anything," instead of *mûm* (wrongly spelled *mĕ'ûm*), "spot, blemish," probably as a reminiscence of Deut xiii 18. Clean hands (cf. ix 30, xvii 9) go with a clean heart (i.e., "mind"), Ps xxiv 4.

8a. Cf. v 5, xxvii 17; Lev xxvi 16; Mic vi 15; Isa lxv 22.

8b. *offspring.* Some interpreters take the word (*ṣe'ĕṣā'îm*) here to refer to produce of the earth rather than human progeny, citing Isa xxxiv 1 and xlii 5 as examples of this meaning. In these, and other cases, the context and the parallelism indicate that the reference is to human progeny. Therefore, I incline to that understanding here (cf. JBL 80 [1961], 196). Human beings may be "uprooted" as well as plants; cf. Ps lii 5(7) and Job xxxi 12b.

38–40. These verses provide a rather weak ending to Job's eloquent deposition and markedly weaken the rhetorical effect. Accordingly, with many critics, I transfer them to follow vs. 8 where they appear to fit better.

38. The very soil may protest injustice, as Abel's blood cried from the ground (Gen iv 10), or the walls and beams of a house cry out against a ruthless tenant, Hab ii 11.

39b. *tenants.* Not "owners," but "workers." The reference is certainly not to independent owners but rather to serfs or share croppers. As M. Dahood has pointed out (*Gregorianum* 43 [1962], 75), there is no need to emend *b'l* to *p'l* to get the required sense of "workers" rather than "owners." The dialectical form *b'l* for *p'l* is attested in Ugaritic (*yb'l qšt lk*, "he will make a bow for you"). Whether this meaning for *b'l* obtains in Isa liv 5 (where *bĕ'ālayiḵ*, "your husband/maker," stands in juxtaposition with *'ôsayik̲*, "your maker") is less certain because the larger context several times uses the figure of marital relations.

40. Cf. Gen iii 17–18, iv 12; Hos x 4, 8; Jer xii 13.

9. Cf. xxiv 15; Prov vii 6–27; Exod xx 17.

10. *grind.* Some interpreters understand this verb in the literal sense, i.e., may my wife become a drudge, "the slave girl behind the mill," Exod xi 5; cf. Isa xlvii 2. In later Jewish tradition something like this happened to Job's wife. In the Testament of Job, while Job sat on the dunghill his wife Sitis had to work as a water carrier to earn bread for the two of them and was even reduced to the humiliating experience of having to sell her hair (to Satan in disguise) in order to get bread. The versions and the rabbis recognized the sexual connotations of the verb "grind." A Talmudic dictum (Soṭah 10a) asserts that the word *ṭḥn* refers to (carnal) violation or trespass (*ăb̲ērāh*) and this view is cited by Jerome in connection with Samson, Judg xvi 21, and reflected in the rendering of Lam v 13b, *adolescentibus impudice abusi sunt.*

10b. Rashi's comment on the preceding line, "Our sages interpreted this in the sense of sexual intercourse," is validated by this line. The verb *kr'* is used of kneeling to rest, to pray, to give birth, of physical exhaustion, and submission. In Arabic the word is used of the woman's sexual acquiescence, *kara'at al-marāt ilā arrajul, curvat se mulier ad virum.* The self-imprecation, the accused adulterer asking to be repaid in kind, recalls the common truncated oath formula, "May Yahweh/God do thus to . . . , and worse, if . . ." (Ruth i 17; I Sam iii 17, xx 13, xxv 22; II Sam iii 9, xix 13; II Kings vi 31). Here, as generally in this series of oaths, the sanction invoked is specified. To have one's betrothed ravished by another man is one of the most repugnant of curses; cf. Deut xxviii 30.

11a. *licentiousness.* This word (*zimmāh*) is used regularly of lewdness, indecent and disgusting sexual conduct. A cognate of this word *tdmmt* is used in Ugaritic in reference to some shameful misdeed committed by the slave girls at a divine feast, an act so repulsive that Baal himself stood up and spat in the midst of the assembly of the gods!

> [. . . . .] Mighty Baal,
> [. . . . .] the Cloud Rider.
> [. . .] he rose and heaved,
> He stood and spat
> Amid the assembly of gods.
> [Dishonor] have I drunk at my table,
> Insult I drank from a cup.
> Two banquets Baal hates,
> Three the Cloud Rider:
> A banquet of shame, a banquet of baseness,

And a banquet of wenches' lewdness (*tdmmt*).
For therein shame is seen,
And therein is wenches' lewdness (*tdmmt*) (51 II 10–22).

Dahood (UHP 1072, p. 60; *Psalms I*, second NOTE ad loc.) takes *zimmāh* in Ps xxvi 10 to mean "idols" and he rendered:

In whose left hand are idols,
and whose right hand is full of bribes.

The balance with concrete *šōḥad*, "bribes," led Dahood to assume a concrete signification for *zimmāh*. It seems best to maintain the abstract sense, "lewdness," "licentiousness," as a metaphor for idolatry rather than real idols; cf. Pope, JBL 85 (1966), 458.

11b. Literally "judicial iniquity," i.e., iniquity deserving of judicial condemnation, reading *pĕlîlî*, as in vs. 28, and regarding the final *-m* as the enclitic emphatic particle which is so common in Ugaritic and is being recognized with ever-increasing frequency in OT poetry. This whole verse, however, is suspect as a pious, moralizing comment. Dhorme omits it as a gloss.

12. This verse is co-ordinate with the preceding, and thus also suspect. It appears to be an echo of Deut xxxii 22:

For a fire is kindled in my nostrils,
That burns to the depths of Sheol,
Devours the earth and its produce,
Kindles the bases of the mountains.

The sure punishment for adultery is likened to deadly fire, Prov vi 27–29:

Can a man take fire to his bosom,
And his clothes be not burned?
Can he walk on hot coals,
And his feet be not scorched?
So with one who goes into his neighbor's wife;
He will not go unpunished, who touches her.

Cf. Ecclesiasticus ix 8b, "Her lovers she burns with fire"; cf. NOTE on 1b.

12a. Cf xxvi 6.

12b. *income*. Though this rendering may seem objectionable because of its modern connotation, it is the most exact and literal translation possible for the word *tĕḇû'āh*, from the root *bw'*, "arrive, come in."

13. The caesura (*'aṯnaḥ*) after "my slave girl" in MT unbalances the two lines. The lot of slaves in the ancient world was hard. The Mosaic Law attempted to mitigate their harsh treatment, especially of Israelite

slaves, appealing to the fact that they once were a nation of slaves; cf. Exod xxi 2–11; Lev xxv 39–55; Deut v 14. The manumission of Hebrew slaves after six years' service was apparently more honored in the breach than in the observance; cf. Jer xxxiv 8–22. Cf. I. Mendelsohn, *Slavery in the Ancient Near East,* 1949, and R. de Vaux, *Ancient Israel,* pp. 80–90.

14. Perfidy in dealing with slaves was interpreted by Jeremiah as a factor in Yahweh's condemnation of the southern kingdom to destruction by the Babylonians, Jer xxxiv 15–22.

arise. Dahood (*Biblica* 52 [1971], 346) suggests that *yiqqôm,* "take vengeance," is to be read here, as in xix 25b. LXX *ean etasin mou poiēsetai,* "when he prepares my trial," may be taken as support for this reading.

23. A number of critics transpose this verse after 14 and offer various emendations. We may strike a balance by leaving the text unaltered but placing it after vs. 14.

23b. *terror.* Cf. xiii 11a, xli 17a.

15. This passage is as close to expressing the full implication of the doctrine of the universal fatherhood of God and its corollary, the brotherhood of all mankind, as anything in the OT. The passage in Mal ii 10, "Have we not all one Father? Did not one God create us?", is limited by the context to concern for the nation. Job here accords, at least in theory, to the lowliest of human beings respect as a child of God with equal claim for justice. Cf. Prov xvii 5a, "One who mocks the poor insults his Maker," and xxii 2, "Rich and poor have this in common: Yahweh is the maker of them all." Paul in his letter to Christian masters and slaves at Ephesus can say no more on this score, that both master and slave have a common heavenly Master who shows no partiality, Eph vi 9.

16–17. Cf. xxii 7–9. Eliphaz's charges Job denies under oath.

17. Cf. Isa lviii 7; Prov xxii 9; Tobit iv 6–11, 16–17; Matt xxv 35.

18. As it stands the MT would have to be rendered, "For from my youth he grew up (with) me as a father / And from the womb of my mother I guided her." Of several expedients, the simplest appears to be the alteration of the first verb *gĕḏēlanî* to *'ăgaddĕlennû,* "I reared him." The picture of the infant Job rearing orphans and guiding widows is something of a hyperbole. What he intends to affirm is lifelong concern for the unfortunate; cf. xxix 12–13; Matt xix 20.

18b. *infancy.* Literally "my mother's womb."

her. The widow; cf. James i 27, "Pure and undefiled religion to God the Father is this: to look after orphans and widows, and keep oneself unstained from the world."

19. Cf. xxiv 7; Isa lviii 7.

20. The loins once aching from the cold bespeak blessing on him who supplied them warmth, even as one's bones may praise God, Ps xxxv 10; cf. above vs. 38.

21a. *raised.* Swing or wave the hand to strike or menace; cf. Isa xi 15, xix 16; Zech ii 13. The poor, the widow, and orphan had no hope for justice or redress of wrong unless some powerful citizen was willing to support their cause; cf. v 4, xxix 12; Prov xxii 2.

21b. *advantage.* Literally "saw my help." This may refer to the custom of parties to a dispute having an escort to shout down, or, if necessary, beat down the opposition.

22a. The words rendered "shoulder" and "socket" both mean shoulder. Tur-Sinai's notion that the meaning is "let my (one) shoulder fall from the other" seems unlikely. We cannot press the terms too hard for anatomical distinctions. In poetry there may be disconcerting freedom in the use of terms, e.g., in the Ugaritic epic of King Keret (Krt 157–58) we have,

> He washed his hands to the elbow,
> His fingers up to the shoulder.

22b. The word here rendered "elbow" actually means "reed," and is used in several senses in the OT, as a unit of measure (whence is derived the term "canon"), in the sense of stalk, shaft, or the arm of a balance. In post-biblical Hebrew the word is used of the *radius,* as distinct from the *ulna.* KJ and JPS here rendered "bone," Moffatt "collarbone," AT and RSV "socket." Its occurrence in Ugaritic makes it fairly clear that it refers to part of the arm, probably the upper arm, and presumably included the flesh. The passage in question describes the violent mourning rites such as proscribed in the Mosaic Law (Lev xix 28, xxi 5). The goddess 'Anat is mourning for her dead brother and consort Baal (62:2–5):

> Skin with stone she scraped,
> Chest with stick she lacerated.
> Cheek and chin she furrowed,
> Her upper arm she plowed,
> Like a garden her chest,
> Like a valley she furrowed her back.

While it would be possible here to translate the Ugaritic *qn ḏr'h tḥrṯ* as "to the bone her arm she plows," it seems more probable that the word *qn* is in construct relation with *ḏr'h,* "her arm," and designates a part of the arm, presumably the upper part. Thus the line in Job would mean "May my lower arm be broken off from the upper arm." Cf. A. Herdner, RES (1942–43), 49.

24–25. Cf. iv 6, viii 14; Pss xl 4, xlix 10–13, lxxi 5, lxxviii 7; Prov xi 28; Jer xvii 7; Ecclesiasticus xxxi 5–10; Matt vi 24.

26. *light.* The light par excellence (Gen i 16) just as Homer used *faos* of the sun. Similarly xxxvii 21 and Hab iii 4; cf. Deut iv 19; Jer viii 2; Ezek viii 16; II Kings xxi 5, xxiii 5, 11. Worship of the sun, moon, and stars (the army of heaven) was as severely condemned by the prophets as it was avidly practiced by the majority of the people.

27b. The line is translated literally. The reading is not "and my mouth kissed my hand," but "and my hand kissed [to] my mouth." Tur-Sinai's suggestion that the reading should be *tiśśaq,* "rose" (from *nśq-slq*), "and my hand hath risen up to my mouth," is worthy of consideration in the light of the well-attested usage of placing the hand on the mouth as a token of reverent silence; cf. xxix 9, xl 4; Mic vii 16; Isa lii 15. The kiss is an ancient form of adoration. Idols were kissed by worshipers in the pagan fertility cult, Hos xiii 2; I Kings xix 18. Because the celestial bodies themselves were inaccessible, the worshipers may have thrown them a kiss. Pliny (*Nat. hist.* xviii.2, 5) mentions such a gesture: *Inter adorandum dexteram ad osculum referimus et totum corpus circumagimus.* This gesture is apparently represented by the beautiful statuette of bronze and gold (7⅝ inches high) from Larsa, representing the kneeling worshiper Awil-Nannar who dedicated the object for the life of Hammurabi, King of Babylon. The worshiper's hand is before his mouth, but a few inches away. A. Parrot suggests that this is the "gesture familiar to anyone who has lived in the East, where it occurs whenever one man tries to convince another in the course of an argument"; cf. *The Arts of Mankind: Sumer,* ed. A. Malraux and G. Salles, translated by S. Gilbert and J. Emmons, 1960, p. 284, fig. 350. Perhaps the gesture made by Awil-Nannar is that designated by the Akkadian verb *šukênu* which some scholars interpret as a gesture performed with the hand; cf. A. Goetze, JNES 4 (1945), 248, n. 12, and the literature there cited, especially B. Meissner, "Der Kuss im Alten Orient." If the line under discussion actually refers to the "wafting" of a kiss with the hand, the grammatical difficulty is easily solved by taking the preposition *l-* in the sense of "from" rather than "to," "my hand kissed from my mouth."

28. *perfidious sin.* The same phrase is rendered "criminal iniquity" in vs. 11 above.

29. Rejoicing at the calamity of an enemy is all too common and natural in Holy Writ and even unto this day; cf. viii 22, xii 5, xxvii 7. The imprecatory Psalms (e.g., lviii, cix, cxxxvii), even interpreted as directed

against the heathen collectively, are full of vengeful malevolence. The opposite attitude is enjoined in Exod xxiii 4–5; Lev xix 18; Prov xx 22, xxiv 17–18, xxv 21–22; and radically in Matt v 43–48; Rom xii 14. After vs. 29 the Qumran Targum has vestiges of three or four hemistichs, or a couple of verses, which are lacking in MT and the versions and are too fragmentary to be restored.

30a. Reading *lû'*, for condition contrary to fact, rather than the negative *lô'*. Cf. Eccles v 5 for the almost identical expression used of rash vows.

30b. Cf. I Kings iii 11.

31a. This truncated or incomplete oath is introduced by "if not" (*'im lô'*) which would require that we understand it as the equivalent of an asseveration that the men of Job's tent did indeed say "O that we might be sated with his flesh." This, as will appear below, is exactly what Job asserts that his men did not say and were not permitted to carry out, i.e., the homosexual abuse of strangers. The grammatical difficulty may be solved by deleting either *'im* or *lô'*. If *lô'* is retained, it should be vocalized *lû*, the conditional particle designating unfulfilled action. (Cf. GKC, 159 1.)

household. Literally "tent."

31b. The import of this and succeeding lines has been missed by all interpreters, save Tur-Sinai. Certainly it is a matter of hospitality, as Rashi and Ibn Ezra note. The argument that the men of Job's tent are represented as expressing the wish that they could find anyone who had not yet been filled from Job's rich table does violence both to the text and to common sense. The expression "eat the flesh of some one" is well attested in Semitic in the sense of "to slander," Akk. *akālu qarṣi* (cf. Dan iii 8, vi 24[25]), and Ar. *akala laḥmahu,* "he ate his meat." This sense might be argued in the context of xix 22, but is entirely incongruous here in xxxi 31. There is no reference to eating, but to being sated and one may be sated with anything—food, drink, life, or love. The range of meaning of the word "flesh" is well known. In Ezek xvi 26, xxiii 20 the word clearly means *phallus,* and this is certainly also the sense in Lev xv 2–15 which deals with *gonorrhea benigna.* If the expression itself were not suggestive of sexual connotation, we find an almost identical term in a Ugaritic passage which, although fragmentary, has been recognized by interpreters as having sexual implication. The violent goddess 'Anat, mistress of Baal, devotee of love, war, and the chase, covets the marvelous composite bow which the artisan god Koshar had bestowed on Danel's son Aqhat. After attempting unsuccessfully to get it from him with an offer of immortality, she threatens him with violence, and goes to visit her aged father El and threatens to batter his gray head to a bloody pulp unless he permits her to carry out her intention to get the bow by any means. She returns to Aqhat and says (3 Aqht rev. 23–25):

> Hear, O hero, Aqhat,
> Thou art (my) brother and I [thy sis]ter.
> ——with satiety of thy flesh——
> ——

The rest of the passage is too badly broken to get any connected sense, though there may be reference to going hunting and an offer by the goddess to teach the young hero something, perhaps how to hunt. (In the previous encounter, the hero had scoffed at the idea that a female could use a bow and hunt.) The Venus and Adonis motif here is not quite the same as in the encounter of Ishtar and Gilgamesh, or the late classical development of this theme, or Shakespeare's elaboration of it, but the terms "brother" and "sister" are reminiscent of the Song of Songs iv 9–12, v 1 f. and of the relationship of Baal and 'Anat. It is almost certain that the goddess offers her love to the young hero in return for the coveted bow and is again rebuffed. The fragmentary phrase "with satiety of thy flesh" (*b.šb' ṯirk*) might refer to the game which the hero would kill with his bow, but more likely it expresses the (feigned) sexual desire of the goddess for the young hero.

The famous homosexual abuse of Horus by Seth in Egyptian mythology has been treated recently by J. Gwyn Griffiths (*The Conflict of Horus and Seth,* Liverpool, 1960, "The Homosexual Episode," pp. 41–46) and it is thus unnecessary to enter here into the details of this unsavory affair. For our present purpose the problems raised by the elaboration of this motif in the Egyptian myth and the numerous allusions to it in Egyptian religious literature do not have to be solved. Whether or not it was a form of humiliation inflicted on a defeated enemy, the Egyptian texts make it clear that it was an abominable deed, not only for the ignominy inflicted on the victim but also for the shame attached to the act itself. Biblical disapproval is even stronger; cf. Gen xix 7; Judg xix 23. The depravity of Sodom and Gomorrah brought on their merited destruction. The story in Judg xix indicates that episodes of this sort persisted down to the period of the Judges at least. Job's disavowal indicates that it was not unheard of in his day, whenever that may have been. For a classic modern account, see T. E. Lawrence, *The Seven Pillars of Wisdom,* Ch. LXXX.

32. The situation envisaged here is exactly that elaborated in Gen xix and Judg xix; cf. especially Gen xix 2 and Judg xix 20. To sleep in the street would have been a sure invitation to abuse by the local degenerates. Job, like Lot and the hospitable old sojourner in Gibeah, made special effort to spare the stranger this outrage by offering the protection of hospitality.

33a. *like Adam.* With KJ, rather than "after the manner of man," JPS, or emending with RSV, "from men"; cf. Gen iii 8, 10. Blommerde translated this verse:

> If I concealed my rebellious acts as in my hands
> hiding my guilt in my bosom.

For MT *kĕ'āḏām* he read *kĕ'āḏēm,* explaining the form as a Northern dual of *'āḏ=yāḏ,* "hand." The suffix was omitted from *'āḏēm,* according to Blommerde, either because that of *ḥubbî,* "my bosom," may do duty also for *'āḏēm,* "(my) two hands," or because *'āḏ* is a part of the body.

33b. *covert.* This word occurs in the OT only here and is usually explained from Aram. and Ar. *ḥubbā, 'ubbā, 'ubb,* used of the space between the chest and the shirt, a sort of shirt pocket, hence "bosom." It seems best, with Rashi and Ibn Ezra, to connect the word with the root *ḥby,* "to hide."

34a. Cf. Gen xix 4, 9; Judg xix 22.

34c. *man.* Reading *'āḏām* for *'eddōm,* "I kept silent."

I brought . . . out. Reading *'ôṣî* for *'ēṣē,* "I went out." In spite of the threat of violence, Job did not give over his guest to the mob; cf. Gen xix 6–11; Judg xix 22–26.

35a. Literally "Who would give me a hearer." All along Job has been pleading for a hearing (cf. xiii 22–23, xix 23–24, xxiii 4) and now he concludes his deposition of innocence under oath, which is tantamount to acquittal, unless the curses fall upon him as invoked.

35b. *signature.* Literally "mark," the final letter of the alphabet, *tāw,* which had the ancient form of a cross-mark (× or +). Perhaps the symbol was used as a signature by illiterates. In any case, Job would be willing to validate his oath by signature.

35c. *my opponent.* Literally "man of my controversy," i.e., God as his accuser.

document. It is not clear whether Job has in view a writ of indictment or of acquittal, but in the light of the following verses the latter appears more likely.

36. What Job would wear on his shoulder and head is not immediately clear. The natural antecedent is the aforementioned document. To wear or carry something on the shoulder is to display it proudly; cf. Isa ix 5(6) (perhaps the symbol of authority) and Isa xxii 22 ("the key of the house of David"). Something inscribed or bound on the hand or forehead, Exod xiii 16; Deut vi 8, xi 18, or worn around the neck, Prov vi 21, could serve both as a reminder to the wearer and an advertisement to the spectator. Acquittal of an accused was marked by exchange of dirty clothes for clean, Zech iii 2–6. Moreover, in some cases, certifications of acquittal were apparently inscribed, Zech iii 8–9. Perhaps the figure

is deliberately mixed to imply both the display of the document of acquittal and the clean clothes and turban of righteousness; cf. xxix 14.

37a. Cf. xiv 16.

40c. Cf. Ps lxxii 20; Jer li 64. Presumably, an editorial note, but LXX took it with the following chapter.

31. ELIHU INTERVENES
(xxxii 1–22)

XXXII 1 Then these three men ceased answering Job because
in his own opinion he was righteous. 2 But the anger of Elihu,
son of Barachel the Buzite of the clan of Ram, flared up against
Job, because he held himself to be righteous rather than God.
3 And against his three companions his anger also flared because
they had not found an answer and so had made God guilty.
4 Elihu had waited while they spoke because these men were
years older than he. 5 But when Elihu saw that the three had no
answer in their mouth, his anger flared up. 6 So Elihu, son of
Barachel the Buzite, spoke out and said:

"I am young in years,
And you are venerable men;
So I recoiled and was afraid
To declare my view to you.
7 I thought, 'Days should speak,
Many years ought to teach wisdom.'
8 But it is a spirit in man,
The breath of Shaddai gives insight.
9 Seniors may not be sage,
Nor elders understand aright.
10 So I say, 'Listen to me,
I too will speak my speech.'
11 I waited for you to speak,
I gave ear to your arguments
While you tested words.
12 I paid close attention to you,
But none of you confuted Job.
None of you answered his words.

13 Can you say, 'We found wisdom.
Let God rebuke him, not man'?
14 He has not matched words with me;
I would not answer him as you did.
15 Dismayed, they answer no more;
Words have forsaken them.
16 Should I wait when they cannot speak,
When they stop and answer no more?
17 I will now say my piece;
I will speak my speech.
18 For I am brimming with words,
Wind bloats my belly.
19 My belly is like unvented wine,
Like new wine-skins ready to burst.
20 I must speak and get relief,
Open my lips and reply.
21 Let me be partial to no one,
Nor flatter any man.
22 I know not how to flatter,
Else would my Maker soon dispatch me.

Notes

xxxii 1. Note the change in terminology, from "friends" (ii 11, xix 21, xlii 10) to "men," one of several indications of diverse authorship, hardly to be understood as indicating alienation by reason of the harsh words that have been spoken. LXX, however, reads "friends" here and MT returns to this usage in vs. 3.

in his own opinion. Literally "in his [own] eyes." LXX, Syr., and one Hebrew manuscript read "their eyes" which reading is adopted by some critics with the understanding that the three friends are now convinced of Job's innocence after his series of oaths of clearance.

2. *Elihu, . . . Ram.* The author of the Elihu speeches gives the father's name (cf. Isa i 1; Jer i 1; Ezek i 2) and even adds the name of the clan, in contrast to the usage of the Prologue. The name Elihu was apparently fairly common in the time of David, since four different persons of that name are mentioned, including a brother of David: I Sam i 1; I Chron xii 20(21), xxvi 7, xxvii 18. The meaning of the

name, "He is my God," may have influenced the author's choice. The name of Elihu's father, Barachel, "God has blessed," is not found elsewhere in the OT but is attested in Akkadian documents as *Barik-ilu/i* and is borne by several persons (presumably Jewish) mentioned in the business documents of the firm Murashu sons from the fifth century B.C. in Babylon.

the Buzite. Buz, the eponymous ancestor of this Aramaean tribe, is represented as Abraham's nephew, Gen xxii 20, 21, and brother of Uz, the presumed founder of Job's tribe; cf. Gen x 22, 23. Jeremiah (Jer xxv 23) mentions Buz along with Dedan and Tema, "all who cut the corners of their hair; all the kings of Arabia and all the mixed tribes that dwell in the desert" (RSV). (Cf. Jer ix 25, xlix 32.) Inscriptions of Esarhaddon mention Bazu which has been located in the hinterland of the island of Dilmun, modern Bahrein on the Persian Gulf.

Ram. Some manuscripts of LXX read *Aram.* Symmachus has *Syrias,* Targ. *Abraham.* Elsewhere the name Ram has Judahite connections (I Chron ii 9, 25, 27; Ruth iv 19). As ancestor of David and of Jesus Christ, the Judahite Ram of Ruth iv 19 is erroneously called Aram in some NT manuscripts in Matt i 3; Luke iii 33; cf. KJ, RSV. The Qumran Targum reads *rwm'*[*h*] for MT *rm.* The editors note that a town Rumah (*rwmh*) is mentioned in II Kings xxiii 36 as the home of King Jehoiachim's mother.

3. *God.* According to Jewish tradition, this is one of the eighteen "Emendations of the Scribes." The original reading, it is alleged, was "God" rather than "Job." The three friends, having found no answer (to Job), had thereby made God guilty. Blommerde retained MT *'iyyôḇ* and construed the *w* of the verb *wayyaršî'û* as *waw- explicativum* to produce the sense "because they had found no answer by which they could prove Job guilty."

4. *while they spoke.* Reading *bĕḏabbĕrām* rather than *biḏḇārîm* and omitting *'eṯ-'iyyôḇ,* "with Job," as dittography from the preceding line.

these men were years older. Elihu lays great stress on his youthful modesty in the next few verses.

8. *it.* I.e., Wisdom.

spirit (*rûaḥ*). The spirit of God gives both life, xxvii 3, xxxiii 4; Gen ii 7, and wisdom, or any special ability, Gen xli 38; Exod xxxi 3; Num xxvii 18; Isa xi 2; Dan v 12–13. Wisdom is not necessarily a concomitant of old age, xii 12, xv 10; Ecclesiasticus xxv 2–6. Piety is prerequisite for the recipient of true wisdom, since wisdom comes from God, Prov i 7, ii 6, x 31, xv 33; Wisdom of Solomon i 5–7, vii 22–23, ix 17; I Cor ii 6. Young Elihu, like the Psalmist (Ps cxix 99) feels he has more understanding than his elders, since it is God who inspires him.

9. *Seniors.* Following Moffatt's wording. LXX, Syr., and Vulg. readings suggest the emendation of *rabbîm* to *rabbê yāmîm,* but this is

unnecessary since the term is now proven to have a sense roughly synonymous with its parallel in this verse, elders (*zĕqēnîm*), by its use in the Essene Manual of Discipline as a designation of the senior members of the order. Cf. iv 3a.

10. *Listen.* In most Hebrew manuscripts the imperative is in the singular, and accordingly would be addressed to Job. Actually, Elihu is speaking to both parties, though he may switch from one to the other. In the next chapter, he addresses himself directly to Job.

10b. *my speech.* In previous editions of this work the line was translated, "I too will state my view", while in 17b below the same expression was rendered "I will declare what I know." The revision is occasioned by the Qumran Targum.

H. L. Ginsberg (BASOR, Suppls. 2–3 [1946], 42 f.) expressed doubt that the forms *dēʿî* here and in xxxvi 3a, *dēʿôt* in xxxvi 4b, and *dēʿîm* in xxxvii 16b are from the root *ydʿ*, "know." "The word in question," Ginsberg suggested, "is far more probably from the root *dʿw*, 'to call' [cf. Arab.] and means simply 'word,' 'speech,' or 'utterance.'" This is most obvious in xxxvi 3–4, according to Ginsberg. Unfortunately, the Qumran Targum is not preserved in xxxvi 3–4. In xxxii 10b and 17b, however, Ginsberg's suggestion is supported by the readings *mly*, "my words." On the Qumran Targum's treatment of xxxvii 16b, see below.

11. On the textual complexities of this verse cf. Dhorme's detailed treatment. Syr., as noted by Beer, appears to have read in 11b *tklytkm* "your completion," for MT *tbwntykm*, "your arguments." This sense is supported by the Qumran Targum [*ʿd*] *tsypwn*, "[until] you (would) finish."

11b. *gave ear.* Dahood (PNWSP, p. 38) connected the present form *'āzîn*, as well as *mēzîn* in Prov xvii 4, to the root *wzn*, "weigh," instead of the usual analysis of *'āzîn* as contracted from *'ā'ăzîn*, causative denominative from *'ōzen*, "ear," hence "give ear."

13. Perhaps Elihu means that the friends were unjustified in dropping the argument, as if there were no human answer to be given.

14a. The line could also be rendered, "Would he had directed his words to me," reading *lû'* (precative) instead of *lô'* (negative). Dahood (NWSPJ, p. 70) took the *l* of *wl'* as the emphatic particle and attached the ' to the following verb to produce *ūl'aʿărōḵ*, "I will indeed prepare," and translated the verse thus:

> I will indeed prepare my own discourse
> and not with your arguments will I answer him.

14b. *as you did.* Literally "with your words."

17b. Cf. 10b above.

18–20. Elihu is flatulent with words. Cf. Matt ix 17 for the figure of bursting wine-skins. The wine, as well as the skin, is new and threatens to split the skin unless vented; cf. Jer xx 9.

21a. *be partial.* Literally "lift up the face"; cf. xiii 8.

21b. *flatter.* The verb (*kny*) means "to give an honorific title"; cf. Isa xliv 5, xlv 4. There has been little in the preceding dialogues that could be called flattery. Perhaps Elihu means that the "friends" have been too polite to Job. In the Babylonian Theodicy the parties address one another with lofty titles and epithets, but then proceed to trade hard verbal blows; cf. vi 6.

22b. *dispatch.* Literally "lift me up," i.e., carry him away as with a tempest; cf. xxx 22. This sample of Elihu's rhetoric may strike the modern reader as ridiculously pompous and verbose. There is, however, no ground for supposing that this effect was intended by the author. Rather, the author puts his best literary effort into what he feels is a divinely inspired defense of God's justice.

32. ELIHU ATTEMPTS TO REFUTE JOB
(xxxiii 1–33)

XXXIII

1 "Hear now, Job, my speech,
Give ear to my every word.
2 See, I open my mouth,
My tongue forms words on my palate.
3 My words are from an upright heart,
My lips utter knowledge in purity.
4 God's spirit made me,
Shaddai's breath gives me life.
5 If you are able, answer me;
Prepare, take [your] stand before me.
6 By God, I am just like you,
I, too, was nipped from clay.
7 My terror should not dismay you,
Nor my pressure be heavy on you.
8 You have said in my hearing,
I heard the very words,
9 'I am pure and sinless,
Innocent, and without guilt.
10 But he finds pretexts against me,
Counts me as his enemy,
11 Puts my feet in fetters,
Watches my every step.'
12 You are not right in this, I tell you,
For God is greater than man.
13 Why do you charge him
That he answers none of your words?
14 God may speak in one way,
Or another, and one not perceive it.

15 In a dream, a vision of the night,
When slumber falls on men,
As they sleep upon their bed,
16 Then he opens men's ears,
Terrifies them with warning
17 To deter man from evil,
To keep man from pride,
18 To spare his soul from the Pit,
His life from crossing the Channel;
19 Or one may be chastened on a bed of pain,
With ceaseless agony in his bones,
20 Till his soul loathes food,
His appetite, choice dishes.
21 His flesh wastes from sight,
And his bare bones are seen.
22 His soul draws near the Pit,
His life to waters of Death.
23 Unless he have by him an angel,
A spokesman, one out of the thousand,
To tell of the man's uprightness,
24 To have pity on him and say,
'Spare him from going down to the Pit,
I have found him a ransom.'
25 His flesh becomes plump as a boy's,
He returns to the days of his youth.
26 He prays to God and he accepts him,
He sees his face with joy.
He announces to men his salvation,
27 He sings before men and says,
'I sinned and perverted the right,
Yet, he did not fully requite me.
28 He saved my soul from the Pit,
And my life sees the light.'
29 All these things God does,
Twice or thrice over with a man,
30 To turn back his soul from the Pit,
To light him with light of life.

31 Heed me, Job, listen to me.
Be silent and I will speak.
32 If you have something to say, answer me;
Speak, I want you to show your righteousness.
33 And if not, then listen to me;
Be silent, let me teach you wisdom."

Notes

xxxiii 1. In the Dialogue the friends never address Job by name. This greater familiarity on the part of Elihu is scarcely to be attributed to closer ties of consanguinity between Job and Elihu than between Job and the three friends. It is in the nature of Elihu's temperament, or rather in that of the author of these speeches.

3a. Literally "Uprightness of heart are my words"; cf. vi 25a; Deut ix 5; Ps cxix 7; I Chron xxix 17.

3b. Cf. Zeph iii 9.

4. Cf. xxxii 8. Elihu apparently means to suggest that he has the charismatic gift of divine wisdom which was deficient in his elders who were unable to confute Job successfully.

5b. *Prepare.* The unexpressed object may be either "words," as in xxxii 14, or "a legal case," as in xiii 18, xxiii 4, or "battle array," as is most frequently the case.

take [*your*] *stand.* In a military sense, I Sam xvii 16; II Sam xxiii 12; cf. i 6 for the juridical sense.

6a. *By God.* Literally "to God" (*lā'ēl*). Most interpreters have understood the meaning to be "I (belong) like you to God." The emendation to *lô' 'ēl,* "Behold, I, like you, am no god/not God," is worthy of consideration. It seems best, however, to understand "to God" here in a sense similar to that in Jon iii 3, "Now Nineveh was a great city to God," or as one would say in modern colloquial speech, "a hell of a big city." This asseverative and superlative use of the divine name finds its most natural explanation in the oath, as the modern Arabs say *wallāhi,* "by God," scarcely realizing that they are using an old oath formula. This example is overlooked by D. Winton Thomas in his interesting study, "A Consideration of Some Unusual Ways of Expressing the Superlative in Hebrew," VT 3 (1953), 209–24, and he fails to note that in Jon iii 3 "to God" might be regarded as an oath formula. Elihu means only to assure Job that he, Elihu, is merely a mortal whom Job need not fear.

just like you. Blommerde read *kĕp̄îk̠ā,* "like your mouth," i.e. "like you," as *kĕp̄îk̠,* "like a little jar," relating *p̄îk̠* to Heb. *pak̠,* Ugar. *bk,* and Gr. *bîkos,* "flask, pitcher, jar." The *y* in *pyk,* in contrast to the normal *pk,* may indicate, according to Blommerde, the diminutive. The *l* of *lā'ĕl* he construed as the preposition with the meaning "from." Thus he arrived at the translation:

> Behold I am like a little jar from God;
> from clay I too have been pinched off.

It seems preferable to retain the MT and the usual analysis of the expression *kĕp̄îk̠ā,* "like your mouth," i.e. "like you." The metaphorical use of *peh,* "mouth," to indicate relationship is well established in Hebrew (cf. KB s.v. *peh* 7, p. 753b). Akkadian also employs the same expression "like the mouth of," *kī pī,* to comparative relationships (cf. C. Brockelmann, *Grundriss der vergleichenden Grammatik der semitischen Sprachen,* II, pp. 390 f., and É. Dhorme, *L'Emploi métaphorique des noms de parties du corps en hébreu et en akkadien,* 1923, p. 85).

6b. *nipped.* The same verb (*qrṣ*) is used in the Gilgamesh Epic of the creation of Eabani from clay.

7. Elihu alludes to Job's charges that God intimidates him with violence and terror, ix 34, xiii 21. With what is intended as clever irony, Elihu assures Job that this charge cannot be made in the present situation since his opponent now is mere mortal.

7a. *terror.* Dahood (*Psalms II,* fifth NOTE on Ps xci 4) would read *'ammāh,* "arm," instead of *'êmāh,* "terror," as in ix 34 and xiii 21. The Qumran Targum *ḥrgty* reflects MT *'ymty.*

7b. *pressure.* Cf. xiii 21a. In previous editions of this work, the word *'ak̠pî,* "my pressure," was emended to *kappî,* "my hand," or the basis of xiii 21a. On reflection, it seems better to retain the MT here and emend in xiii 21a. Dahood (*Psalms II,* third NOTE on Ps li 9) prefers to regard *'ᵊk̠ep̄* as *kap̄,* "hand," with prothetic *aleph.*

8b. *the very words.* Literally "a sound of words."

9. Cf. ix 21, x 7, xvi 17, xxiii 10, xxvii 5–6, and ch. xxxi. Elihu's quotations are substantially correct, but there is an unfair twist. Job has admitted minor human failings; cf. vii 21, xiii 26. The point of Job's complaint is that he never committed sins grave enough to merit such drastic punishment.

10. *pretexts.* Reading *tō'ănôt,* "occasions" or "opportunities" (for hostility), as in Judg xiv 4; Prov xviii 1, rather than MT *tĕnû'ôt* which occurs elsewhere only in Num xiv 34 in the sense of "alienation, displeasure," which is less appropriate here. Elihu apparently has in mind passages such as xiii 24, xix 6, 11.

11. Cf. xiii 27.

Watches. For MT *yišmōr* the Qumran Targum reads *wskr,* "and he obstructs," offering a closer parallel to the preceding line. It is interesting to note that Ar. *šmr* is used in connection with varying modes of ambulation, both nimble and impeded, e.g. "to walk with drawn sinews," "walk with a light step and elegantly," and also in the sense of "draw together, contract." The identical expression occurs in xiii 27b, except for a difference in the person of the verb, but the Qumran Targum is not preserved there.

12. That God is greater than man, Job certainly had not denied. Indeed, Job had extolled God's power in some of the most magnificent hymns in Scripture; cf. ix 1–13, xii 13–25. If Elihu's point is that because God is mightier, man cannot argue with him (cf. Eccles vi 10), Job had already said this very forcefully, ix 14–20, 32, xiii 13–16.

12b. LXX rendered this hemistich as "Eternal is he who is above mortals." The Qumran Targum reflects MT virtually verbatim, *'rw rb 'lh' mn 'nš',* "Behold God is greater than man."

13a. MT literally rendered is "Why against him contentions?" The Qumran Targum here has for MT *rîḇôṯ,* "contentions," a meaningless form *rbbrn* followed by the verb *tmll,* "you speak." This is manifestly a scribal error for *rbrbn,* "great things" (as in Dan vii 8, 20; cf. Ps xii 4 and Rev xiii 5), "great things you speak."

13b. *your words.* Literally "his words." Syr. reads "my words"; cf. LXX and Vulg. If "his words" is the correct reading, the antecedent is presumably "man" in the preceding verse. The difference in reading is of no importance, since Job in complaining that God gives him no answer (cf. xxiii 5) speaks for any and every man who asks and receives no answer.

14. Elihu adds the qualification, since Job had apparently failed to recognize the divine word. Blommerde emended the negative *lô'* to *lē',* as parallel to *'ēl,* and translated:

> For a first time God speaks
> and a second time the Mighty One appears.

15–16. Elihu expresses what is implicit in most of the material relating to dreams in the Bible and in the literatures of the ancient world, viz., that they may be a communication from the divine. The meaning of the communiqué, however, was usually veiled and required interpretation; cf. Gen xli 11, 12; Num xii 6; Judg vii 13, 15; Dan ii, iv, vii. Elihu refers specifically to dreams intended as warnings and deterrents from sin. For warning dreams, cf. Gen xx 3, xxxi 24, xli 1; Dan iv;

Matt ii 13, xxvii 19. On the terrifying aspect of dreams, cf. iv 12–15, vii 14. A critical and skeptical attitude toward dreams and dreamers is recommended, Deut xiii 1–5; Jer xxiii 28.

15a. *a vision.* LXX appears to have read *hegyôn,* "meditation," for MT *ḥezyôn.* The Qumran Targum reads for "of the night" *bhdydy lyl',* "during the night."

16a. *opens.* Literally "uncovers." The expression "uncover the ear" is used always of conveying information of vital concern to a person, I Sam ix 15, xx 2, 12, xxii 8, 17; II Sam vii 27; Ruth iv 4; cf. xxxvi 10, 15.

16b. Reading with LXX *mar'îm,* "visions," instead of the ambiguous MT *mōsārām,* "their bond," or their "chastisement," and vocalizing the verb form *yĕḥittēm,* "he terrifies them," rather than MT *yaḥtōm,* "he seals"; cf. iv 12–15, vii 14. Dahood (*Biblica* 49 [1968], 360) related this verb to the root *nḥt,* "descend," and translated vss. 16–17 accordingly, "Then he opens the ears of men, and for their instruction descends to teach them, to teach man his work, his voice to man disclose."

17a. *from evil.* Reading *mē'awlāh* instead of MT *ma'ăśeh,* "deed." MT says, literally, "To remove man deed."

17b. Literally "And pride from man he covers." Some interpreters connect the verb with *kss,* "cut," rather than *ksy,* "cover."

18a. Cf. ix 31a.

18b. *Channel.* Cf. Dhorme, "Et sa vie de passer par le Canal." In some contexts the word *šelaḥ* designates a weapon, "missile, dart"; cf. II Sam xviii 14. Here, however, the parallelism makes it clear that the reference is to the netherworld (cf. Moffatt, CCD, and J. M. P. Smith in AT) and not to perishing by the sword (so KJ, JPS, RSV). The Akkadian cognates *šalḫu* and *šiliḫtu* designate a water conduit or channel, and this sense may be seen in Neh iii 15, "the Pool of Shelah," and in the regular form *šilôaḥ,* the pool and tunnel of Siloam. The Channel is the infernal stream, the river Ḫubur of Mesopotamian mythology and the Styx of the Greeks. The element *šelaḥ* also appears as the theophoric element in the proper name Methushelah (*mutu-šelaḥ,* Man of Šelaḥ, i.e., worshiper of Šelaḥ) and in the Phoenician name *'bšlḥ,* "Šelaḥ is Father." Cf. M. Tsevat, "The Canaanite God Šälaḥ," VT 4 (1954), 41–49. Cf. xxxiii 18b.

19a. *a bed of pain.* Literally "with pain upon his bed"; cf. Deut viii 5; Prov iii 12; Ps xxxviii. Eliphaz has said this already in v 17.

19b. *agony.* Following the Kethib, *rîḇ,* rather than Qere, *rōḇ,* "multitude." The context favors the sense given above rather than the alternate possibility, "While the multitude of his bones are firm."

20a. *soul.* Literally "life" in the sense of "appetite," as in xxxviii 39; cf. Ps cvii 17. Loss or regaining of appetite is a sure sign of illness or recovery. In the Ugaritic epic of Keret, the ailing king is healed of his distemper by someone called Š'tqt who bathes away the sweat and opens his appetite (*npšh*) for food, his zest (*brlth*) for meat (127:10–12).

21b. Literally "And his bones which were not seen are laid bare."

22b. The MT *měmîṯîm,* "killers," recalls the Akkadian term for infernal demons, *mušmîtûti.* However, the parallelism with the Pit (*šaḥaṯ*) indicates that the reference is to the abode of the dead, or of the god Death, Mot. LXX has "Hades," Syr. and Targ. "death." The line is short and possibly a word has fallen out. It may be lengthened slightly by reading *lěmô mēṯîm,* instead of MT *laměmîṯîm.* If the MT is retained, the allusion would be to the destroying angels (cf. II Sam xxiv 16; II Kings xix 35; I Chron xxi 15; Ps lxxviii 49), a motif elaborated in later Jewish literature. I venture a new and quite simple emendation, reading *lěmê -māweṯ-mô,* "to the waters of Death," with the enclitic emphatic particle at the end. The watery nature of the netherworld is well attested; cf. ix 31a; II Sam xxii 5, "the waves of Death." (On the basis of F. M. Cross, Jr.'s, and D. N. Freedman's study, *Early Hebrew Orthography,* 1952, there would be no emendation since both would be written *lmmtm.*)

23–24. Mediation by an angel is not an original idea of Elihu's (so Larcher), but has its background in more ancient religious thought. The Mesopotamian belief in a personal god who looked after the interest of his mortal client in the divine assembly is clearly related to the concept of guardian angels and interceding saints; cf. Ps xci 11–13; Tobit v 4, xii 15; Matt xviii 10; Acts xii 15; Rev viii 3. Eliphaz alludes to this same idea in v 1, the "holy ones" being lesser gods among whom a man might have or find a defender. Job apparently had this in mind when he appealed for an arbiter, ix 33, a witness, an interpreter, xvi 19–21, and a vindicator, xix 25–27. This concept is apparently related to the doctrine of intercession by righteous men (cf. xxii 28–30, xlii 8; II Maccabees iii 31 ff.), and of vicarious expiation (cf. Isa lii 13–liii 12). On the Mesopotamian concept of a "personal god," cf. Kramer, WIANE, p. 171 and HTR 49 (1956), 59.

23b. The heavenly court was a numerous body; cf. I Kings xxii 19; Dan vii 10; Rev v 11. Out of the great number of the divine retinue, a man could hope for just one to intercede for him before the king of the gods.

24. The sense required of the imperative here is clear, but no known meaning of either the root *pd'* or *pr'* (the reading of a couple of manuscripts) offers suitable sense. Guillaume's connection of the form with Ar. *wada'* preceded by the particle *p,* Ar. *fa,* appears to be the correct analysis. But there is no need to regard either the particle or the verb as exclusively Arabic. Guillaume noted that the Arabic conjunction *fa* is irrepressible, to be found in Aramaic, Nabatean and Palmyrene in-

scriptions. He should have noted that it is also attested several times in Ugaritic and thus cannot be considered a characteristic of Arabic.

24c. *ransom*. This was something no man could give for himself; cf. Ps xlix 7–9; Matt xvi 26, xx 28; I Tim ii 6; Rev v 9.

25a. *plump*. The emendation of the hapax form *ruṭāpaš* to *yiṭpaš*, adopted in previous editions of this work, may not be advisable. Dhorme's emendation to *yirṭab*, on the basis of xxiv 8, is also questionable. Perles' connection of the word with Akk. *ritpāšu*, "wide open, receptive," was properly rejected by Dhorme. The form is manifestly an infix *-t-* adjective from *rapāšu*, "be wide." Guillaume declared the form to be an Arabic quadriliteral verb formed by affixing *š*. The word is thus related to Heb. *rāṭōḇ* and Ar. *raṭuba*, "was soft, tender," according to Guillaume, and the final *š* is the equivalent of the *s* affixed to some verbs in Arabic, e.g. *ḫalbasa*, "deceived with soft words."

25b. Cf. Isa xl 31; Pss ciii 5, cx 3, cxliv 12; Eccles xi 9.

26a. Cf. xxii 27; Isa lviii 8–9.

26b. To see the face of a king or god meant to be admitted to his presence to seek favor, or as the result of restoration to royal or divine favor; cf. Gen xxxii 20, xliv 23, 26; II Sam iii 13, xiv 24, 28, 32; Ps xi 7. Prayer is the seeking of admission to God's presence, Pss xxiv 6, xxvii 8, cv 4; Hos v 15. To seek the face may also be used of pursuit of other sorts of intercourse, Prov vii 15.

with joy. The noise of joyous shouting and/or music; cf. Ps xxxiii 3.

26c. *announces*. Reading *yĕḇaśśēr* instead of MT *wayyāšeḇ*.

his salvation. Literally "his righteousness," i.e., God's righteous act of acquittal; cf. Pss xxii 22–31, xxx, lxvi, cxvi.

27a. Reading *yāšîr* for MT *yāšōr*. The Qumran Targum omits the clause "He sings before men," but preserves "and he say[s]" (*wy'm*[*r*]).

before. The idiom "sings before" occurs also in Prov xxv 20, "One who sings songs before a sad heart . . . ," and in Ugaritic,

yšr ġzr ṭb ql	He sings, does the sweet voiced hero,
'l b'l bṣrrt ṣpn	before Baal in the fastness of Zaphon.

Dahood (NWSPJ, pp. 29 f.) alone has recognized the exact sense of the preposition in the Ugaritic passage above; cf. xxix 13a. The Abbé le Hir, however, recognized the proper sense of the expression in the present passage in Job and rendered it "alors il chante devant les hommes."

27c. Reading *šiwwāh* for MT *šāwāh*.

30b. *light . . . life*. Cf. iii 20. Dahood (*Psalms I*, third NOTE on Ps xxxvi 10) included Job xxxiii 30 among several texts wherein he would see allusions to the Elysian Fields. Taking the noun *'wr* as meaning "field" (the vocable *ur* occurs in Ugaritic in the phrase *byġl ur* which may mean "in the foliage of the field," 1 Aqht 66, 73), Dahood proposed to translate the present verse thus: "To turn back his soul from the pit, that he might be resplendent in the field of life."

31b–33. LXX omits these last five lines thus reducing Elihu's wordiness slightly.

33. ELIHU'S SECOND SPEECH
(xxxiv 1–37)

XXXIV 1 Elihu continued:

2 "Hear, you wise ones, my words,
You savants, give ear to me;
3 For the ear tests words
As the palate tastes by eating.
4 Let us choose for ourselves what is just,
Let us decide between us what is good.
5 Now Job has said, 'I am righteous,
And God has robbed me of my right.
6 Concerning my case he lies,
Wounded with his darts, yet sinless.'
7 Was ever a fellow like Job?
He gulps mockery like water,
8 Keeps company with evil doers,
Consorts with wicked men.
9 For he says, 'It profits man nothing
When he is pleasing to God.'
10 So, you sensible men, hear me.
Far be it from God to do evil,
From Shaddai to do wrong.
11 Nay, he pays a man for his work,
Brings home a man's conduct to him.
12 Surely God would not do evil,
Nor Shaddai pervert justice.
13 Who entrusted the earth to him?
Who assigned [him] the whole world?
14 If he took it in his mind
To take back his spirit and breath,

15 All flesh would expire together,
And man return to the dust.
16 Now, if you have intelligence, hear this;
Give ear to the sound of my words.
17 Can one who hates justice govern?
Will you condemn the Just and Mighty One?
18 Does one say to a king, 'Scoundrel'?
'Criminal' to nobles?
19 He pays no respect to princes,
Nor favors rich over poor.
They are all the work of his hands.
20 In a moment they die, at midnight;
Gentry are shaken and pass away,
The mighty are removed without hand.
21 For his eyes are on man's conduct,
He sees his every step.
22 There is no darkness, no shadow
Where evil doers can hide.
23 For he sets no man a date
To come before God in judgment.
24 He shatters the mighty without inquiry,
And sets others in their stead.
25 Because he knows their deeds,
He overthrows them in a night and they are crushed.
26 As criminals he strikes them down
In the public place,
27 Because they turned away from him
And heeded none of his ways,
28 To bring the cry of the poor before him
That the complaint of the afflicted he may hear.
29 If he keep quiet, who can condemn?
If he hide his face, who can see him?
Be it nation or man, 'tis the same;
30 Lest the impious man rule,
Lest snares of the people——
31 Has he said to God,
'I was mistaken, I will offend no more;

32 That I may see, teach me;
If I have done evil, I will no more'?
33 Shall he requite on your terms since you object?
Shall you choose and not he?
What do you know? Speak!
34 Sensible men will say to me,
Any wise man who hears me,
35 'Job speaks without knowledge,
His words make no sense.
36 Job ought to be tried to the limit
For answering like impious men.
37 For he adds to his sin,
Denies his transgression among us,
Multiplies his words against God.' "

NOTES

xxxiv 3. An almost verbatim citation of xii 11, except for a slight variation of the construction.

4. In other words, let us decide which is the correct view, Job's or the traditional attitude toward the question of theodicy.

5. As in xxxiii 9 above, Elihu again quotes Job, referring this time to xxvii 2a.

6a. Following LXX "he lies" instead of MT "I lie." It appears likely that this form was changed to obscure the blasphemy of calling God a liar. Job could scarcely be accused of saying that he had lied or been made to lie (the Pi'ēl of this verb always means "to lie" and never "to be counted a liar"), since throughout he insists on his innocence. By implication, as the friends saw it, this is tantamount to making God a liar and they urged Job to recant and confess his sin.

6b. *his darts.* MT "my darts." Blommerde suggested that the final *-y* of *ḥṣy* may be the suffix of the third person and he vocalized it *ḥiṣṣay* instead of MT *ḥiṣṣî.*

7b. An adaptation of xv 16.

8. Cf. xi 11, xxii 15, xxxi 5; Ps i 1.

9. Cf. ix 22, x 3, xxi 7. Mal iii 13–14 expresses more clearly the sentiment which Elihu correctly attributes to Job. Elihu attempts to refute this view in his next discourse, xxxv 5 ff.

9a. *he says.* LXX reads *mē gar eipēs,* "you should not say," and Syr. *d'mrt,* "since you have said."

It profits. The versions vary in the interpretation of MT *l'yskn gbr.* LXX *ouk estai episkopē andros,* Symm. *ouchi sothēsetai,* Syr. *l' zk',* "he is not pure," Vulg. *non placebit.* Targ. presents a double translation *l' y'lp,* "he does not learn(?)," and *l' ystkn,* "he is not in danger."

The Qumran Targum renders MT *yskn* as *yšn',* but the sense intended is uncertain because of a lacuna in the middle of the verse, *'rw 'mr l' yšn' gbr my*[. . . . . *b*]*ṯr 'lh'*. The editors translate:

> Car il dit: L'homme ne change pas
> par [. . . . . ap]rès Dieu.

10a. *sensible men.* Literally "men of heart."

10b, c. Cf. viii 3; Gen xviii 25.

11a. Cf. iv 8; Ps lxii 13; Prov xxiv 12; Ecclesiasticus xvi 14; Matt xvi 27; Rom ii 6; Gal vi 7–10.

11b. Literally "And according to the path of a man he makes him find it."

12. Cf. vs. 10 and viii 3.

Surely. The Qumran Targum renders this line as a rhetorical question, *hk'n ṣd' 'lh' yšqr,* which the editors translate: "Eh bien, Dieu fera-t-il vraiment ce qui est faux?" MT *'omnām* is rendered by *ṣd'* which occurs in Dan iii 14 with the interrogative particle *hṣd'*. For discussion of *ṣd'* cf. J. A. Montgomery, *A Commentary on Daniel,* (ICC), p. 207; H. H. Rowley, *The Aramaic of the Old Testament,* 1929, p. 132; W. Baumgartner, ZAW 45 (1933), 89.

13. God rules the earth and is answerable to no one for his action, as Elihu says again in xxxvi 23. This fact Job has already asserted emphatically, ix 12. Job's point is that God as sovereign is ultimately responsible for evil, ix 24.

14–15. Cf. Gen ii 7, iii 19; Isa xlii 5; Ps civ 29; Eccles xii 7.

16. Cf. xxxiii 31, 33.

17b. *the Just and Mighty One.* In previous editions of this work, the word *ṣaddîq* was emended to *maṣdîq,* repeating the *m* from the preceding word, to produce the sense, "Will you condemn him who judges the mighty?" It seems advisable to abandon this expedient and retain the MT. Dahood (*Psalms II,* p. XXIV) suggested that *ṣaddîq 'attîq* of Ps xxxi 19, which he rendered "the Ancient Just One," clarifies Job xxxiv 17 for which he offered the translation, "Shall the enemy of justice conduct the inquiry, or will you pronounce the Venerable Just One guilty?"

18. Elihu's reasoning that God must be just because he rules does not obtain necessarily in the human sphere. Fools may be set in high places, Eccles x 5, and be addressed with noble titles, Isa xxxii 5. The lowly subject fears to curse the king or the rich, even in secret or in thought, Eccles x 20. Mortal royalty and nobility cannot thus intimidate God.

Again Elihu's argument is stale, for Job had already expatiated on God's humiliation of the mighty, xii 17–21.

18a. *Scoundrel.* Heb. *bĕliyya'al,* "worthlessness." A term applied to various kinds of base conduct, such as greed (Deut xv 9; I Sam xxv 25, xxx 22), sexual perversion (Judg xix 22), perjury (I Kings xxi 10; Prov xix 28).

19. God is impartial in respect to all his creatures; cf. Deut x 17; Prov xxii 2; II Chron xix 7; Wisdom of Solomon vi 7; Acts x 34–35; Rom ii 11; Eph vi 9; Col iii 25; I Pet i 17.

20. This verse is a bit awkward, but emendation may be scouted. The word *'am,* "people," is taken in the sense of gentry, as in xii 2. Targ. applied the first line to the men of Sodom and the second to the Egyptians, apparently taking the cue from Lam iv 6.

without hand. Cf. Lam iv 6; Dan ii 34, viii 25; Isa xl 23–24.

21a. An almost verbatim citation of xxiv 23b and xxxi 4; cf. Ecclesiasticus xxiii 19.

21b. Cf. xiv 16.

22. Cf. Ps cxxxix 11–12; Jer xxiii 24; Amos ix 2–3; Matt vi 4.

23. *date.* Reading *mô'ēḏ* for MT *'ôḏ.* Again the loss of the *m* is explained as haplography of the final letter of the preceding verb. This same expression "to set a date" occurs in Exod ix 5. Job had asked to come into an impartial court with God, ix 32, and pleaded for an appointment for a hearing, xiv 13; cf. xxiv 1.

24. The similarity of this verse to ix 10 appears to have confused ancient translators.

He shatters. LXX has for MT's Aramaism *yārōa'* (= *rṣṣ,* **rḍḍ,* "shatter") *ho gar Kurios pantas ephora,* "For the Lord looks down upon all." Targ. related *the mighty, kabbîrîm,* to "the mighty waters," *mayim kabbîrîm,* of Isa xvii 12b. LXX rendered MT *lô' ḥēqer* as *anexichniasta,* "unsearchable things," which is identical with its rendering of *'ad-'ên ḥēqer* in ix 10 where it is parallel to *'ên mispār,* "without number." Thus LXX took the whole verse to say, "For the Lord looks upon all men, he who comprehends unsearchable things, even glorious and excellent things without number." Syr. *'kḥd',* "together," reflects the reading *'ḥd* for MT *'ăḥērîm,* "others." The Qumran Targum is not completely preserved here, yet it gives important witness to MT:

> . . . . . *r]brbyn dy l' swp*
> *wyqym '[ḥrnyn* . . . . .
>
> . . . . . g]reat ones without end
> And sets up o[thers . . . . .

The reading *dy l' swp* for MT *l' ḥqr* accords with Syr. *dl' sk,* influenced wrongly by xxxvi 26 where *lô' ḥēqer* is associated with number and ix 10 where *'aḏ-'ên ḥēqer* is balanced by *'ên mispār,* "innumerable." The context indicates that *ḥēqer* here has the sense of search, inquiry, inquisition.

24–25. Elihu's answer to Job's request for his day in court is to point out that God sees all, vs. 21, and there is no need for an inquiry. Retribution is dispensed directly. The Qumran Targum preserves a final letter of vs. 25a and omits entirely 25b and the first two words of 26a.

25a. *he knows.* Guillaume rendered *yakkîr* as "he takes knowledge of," but in a note suggested a possible derivation from Ar. *ankara,* "disapproved of," so that the verse could be translated: "Therefore he disapproves of their way of life and overthrows them in a night."

26a. Literally "among criminals" or "in the place of/for criminals," the preposition *taḥaṯ,* "under," having the sense of "among" or "in the place of," as in xl 12. This same sense is attested in Ugaritic, "He . . . sat . . . among (*tḥt*) the dignitaries."

26b. Literally "in the place of spectators," i.e., like criminals at a public execution. The Qumran Targum reads here *wyrm' hmwn b't[r . . .* , "and he throws them in the pla[ce of . . .".

27. Only the last two letters of 27a are preserved in the Qumran Targum, . . . *]ḥh,* and these suggest the restoration *[mn 'r]ḥh,* "from his way," at variance with MT *m'ḥryw,* "from after him." It is tempting to adopt the reading of the Qumran Targum here on the basis of the parallelism with *dĕrāḵāyw* in 27b, but MT is quite acceptable and perhaps even preferable to the rigid congruity of paths // ways. The parallel line 27b is almost completely preserved in the Qumran Targum and reflects the MT precisely, *wbkl šbylwhy l' hstk[lw].*

27. Cf. xxiv 13.

28–33. The following verses, 28–33, are replete with difficulty. LXX originally omitted them entirely. Modern critics have emended freely, with imagination and originality.

28. The connection of this verse with the preceding is indicated by the use of the infinitive "to bring." The sense appears to be that the cry of the oppressed attracts God's attention to the oppressor so that divine wrath might be visited on the tyrant.

29a. The meaning of this line is vague. The sense intended may be that man has no right to condemn God for apparent failure to answer or act on a complaint of injustice.

29b. Cf. xiii 24, xxiii 9; Pss x 1, xliv 24, lxxxviii 14, civ 29; Isa xlv 15. The Qumran Targum reads *[wyst]r 'npwhy mn ytybnh,* "[and should he hid]e his face, who could make him return." The puzzling reading reflects a Hebrew verb *yĕšîḇennû* instead of MT *yĕšûrennû.* This recalls the reading of *yĕšîḇennû* for *yĕšûrennû* in a couple of MSS at xxxiii 14 which several critics accepted (cf. Dhorme, ad loc. and BDB, s.v. *šwr* II 2, p. 1003). Unfortunately, the Qumran Targum does not preserve the second half of xxxiii 14.

29c. *the same.* The word *yaḥaḏ* here has been emended in ways too numerous to catalogue, none of which carries conviction. Dahood (*Biblica* 45 [1964], 407–8; *Psalms I,* NOTE on Ps xxxiii 15, second NOTE on Ps xlix 11) explained the *yḥd* as a dialectical form of *ḥzy,* "see." Blommerde rendered accordingly,

> Upon nation and man he gazes.

30a. Literally "from the ruling of an impious man."

30b. *Lest.* Literally "from," as above, 30a. The line is short and the meaning highly conjectural.

31b. *I was mistaken.* Reading *niššē'tî* for MT *nāśā'tî,* "I have borne," and taking the word with the following rather than the preceding line. Dittography offers a plausible solution to the difficulties of the rest of this line and the beginning of the next. The word *'ôḏ,* "again," desiderated at the end of this line is taken from the meaningless *bil'āḏê* of the following line, the *bl* regarded as dittography of the end of the verb *'eḥbōl.* The Qumran Targum in place MT *lô' 'eḥbōl* reads *lh 'yḥl* which recalls the MT Qere of xiii 15a. According to the editors *'yḥl* is a typical Hebrew word that until now has not been found in Aramaic dialects. The translation offered is "en lui j'espère." The connection between *ḥbl* and *yḥl* is, however, furnished by Syriac which uses the Aphel of *yḥl* in the sense of "be remiss" which approximates the sense of *ḥbl* in the present context.

32a. *That.* Reading *'ăḏê,* "until," for MT *bil'ăḏê.* Job had indeed challenged both the friends and God to show the nature of his offense; cf. vi 24, x 2, xiii 23. Elihu's argument is the same as the friends', that Job should admit guilt as the preliminary step. The Qumran Targum here supports MT *bl'dy* with the reading *blḥwdwhy.* The editors suggest, however, that the translator may have understood the word as the end of the preceding verse.

33a. *on your terms.* Literally "from with thee."

33b. *he.* Hebrew has "I." Sudden alternation in person is common in the OT; cf., e.g., the switch from "he" to "thou" in Ps xxiii. Elihu accuses Job of arrogating to himself the divine prerogative of choice, of attempting to set the terms under which God must operate. The Qumran Targum preserves the beginning and the end of this verse. At the beginning the MT interrogative particle *h* is rendered by *'rw,* "behold." The end of the verse reflects MT precisely, *tb]ḥr wl' 'nh.*

34a. Cf. vs. 10a.

35. Cf. xxxv 16, xxxviii 2, xlii 3.

36a. *ought.* Taking *'ăḇî* as expressing wish or entreaty, in accordance with Wetzstein's elucidation from the usage of the Arabs of the Hauran (cf. Delitzsch, II, pp. 261–66). Certainly the word does not mean "my father" (so Vulg.) here and probably not in I Sam xxiv 12 and II Kings v 13. Cf. A. M. Honeyman (JAOS 64 [1944], 81–82) on "Some Developments of the Semitic Root *'by.*"

36b. Cf. xxii 15.

37b. With Dhorme, taking *peša',* "transgression," with this line rather than the preceding and reading *yaspîq,* instead of MT *yispōq,* in the sense attested in Aramaic of "doubt," or in the causative "put in doubt."

34. ELIHU'S THIRD SPEECH
(xxxv 1–16)

XXXV 1 Elihu went on to say:

2 "Do you think this according to justice?
You say, 'It is my right from God.'
3 You say, 'What does it profit you,
What should my sin get me?'
4 I will answer you on that,
You and your friends with you.
5 Look to the heavens and see,
Mark the clouds how high above you.
6 If you have sinned, what do you to him?
If your transgressions are many, what do you to him?
7 If you are righteous, what do you give him?
Or what does he get from your hand?
8 Your wickedness concerns man like yourself,
Your righteousness only human beings.
9 In great oppression they cry out,
Call for help against the arm of the mighty.
10 One says not, 'Where is God, my Maker,
Who gives strength in the night,
11 Who teaches us by the beasts of the field,
Makes us wise by the birds of the heavens?'
12 There they cry, but he does not answer,
Because of the pride of evil men.
13 God does not listen to deceit,
Shaddai takes no notice of it.
14 You say you cannot see him.
The case is before him, wait for him.

[15] But that his anger does not punish,
That he does not mark transgression well,
[16] Job opens his mouth with vanity,
Without knowledge multiplies words."

Notes

xxxv 3b. Literally "What do I gain from my sin?" The usual rendering of "from my sin" is "more than if I had sinned." Job, of course, does not admit that he has sinned—at least not seriously enough to warrant such drastic punishment; cf. xxxii 2. Elihu, like the friends, could not admit that Job had not sinned, for this would impugn divine justice. Job's attitude at times had been that it wouldn't matter whether he sinned or not, since justice appears to be abortive in the world. The literal rendering above is amenable to each of these viewpoints; cf. xxxiv 9.

4b. Elihu lumps Job and the friends together, and probably means to include all who have any sympathy for Job's position. As Dhorme aptly remarks, Elihu is speaking to the gallery; cf. xxxiv 2–4, 10–15, 34–37.

5. Cf. xi 7–9, xxii 12. Job had expressed similar and even more lofty thoughts about God's transcendence; cf. ix 8–11.

6–7. Essentially a repetition of xxii 2–4. Job has adduced this argument too, vii 20. Cf. Luke xvii 10; Rom xi 35.

8. Man's good or evil affects only man, and cannot benefit or harm God. So also man's wisdom or folly affects only himself, Prov ix 12.

9–10. Elihu is not accusing Job of being an oppressor, nor of failing to come to the aid of the oppressed (so Kissane). Tur-Sinai is on the right track when he says this is Job's, not Elihu's, viewpoint. Job had dwelt at length on the magnitude of human misery caused by oppression and social injustice, xxiv 2–17, and had noted that God does not seem to think anything is wrong, xxiv 12c. To this Elihu seems to say that those who cry out in oppression do not, like Job, complain that God does not appear to be on duty (10a). If Elihu is addressing himself to the question "Why does God ignore the cries of the oppressed?", he does not offer a very substantial answer. With Peake, the question rises naturally, "But if God's rule is righteous, why the cry of the oppressed?" Job already had raised this question by implication, xxiv 12c.

10b. *strength.* This word (*zĕmîrôṯ*) is usually rendered "songs." Critics explain that in the night of distress God gives help which fills the recipient with gratitude and causes him to break forth in songs of joy and praise. In several passages in which this form of the word occurs, Exod xv 2; II Sam xxiii 1; Isa xii 2, xxv 5; Ps cxviii 14, the context and parallelism favor the sense "strength," "protection," or the like. The word is to be connected not with *zmr*, "make music," but with the root attested in Arabic as *ḏmr*, "violent, courageous, mighty." This root is common in early Northwest Semitic proper names, in old South Arabic, and in the OT (Zimri, Zimran). It appears also in Ugaritic as a cognomen of Baal, *dmrn*, which Cassuto correctly equated with the title of Zeus, Demarous (genitive Demarountos); cf. U. Cassuto in *Sefer Dinaburg*, 1949, pp. 65–67. Cf. Dahood (*Psalms II*, third NOTE ad loc.) for *zmr*=*ḏmr* in Ps lix 18b, with bibliographical references on other likely occurrences. The Qumran Targum reads *lnṣbtn'* "(our) strength, firmness" for *zĕmîrôṯ*. The editors misunderstood *lnṣbtn'* and translated "pour notre plantation, dans la nuit?" In a footnote (p. 63, n. 5) it is asserted that the expression *lnṣbtn'*, "à notre plantation," has no correspondence in the MT and was added by the translator. The sect of Qumran liked to call itself a "plantation" (cf. 1QS VIII 5, XI 8; 1QH VIII 10, etc.), an expression found already in Isa lxi 3 where Israel is called a *mṭ' YHWH* (cf. Enoch x 6). The term applied to the community, however, is *mṭ'* and not *nṣbtn'*. The *n'* ending of *lnṣbtn'* may not be the first plural suffix, but could be the afformative *ān* plus the post-positive article *ā*. The sense of *nṣbtn'* of the Qumran Targum is thus equivalent to *niṣbĕṯā'* of Dan ii 41, "strength." Syr. has the form with both *t* and *ān* afformative, *neṣbĕṯānāyā*, applied to innate powers, vegetative and intellectual.

11. *teaches us*. MT *mallĕpēnû* results from contraction of *mĕ'allĕpēnû*, as confirmed by Targ. which preserves the ', *dm'lp*. Syr. *mn qdm*, "from before," also confirms the consonantism of MT by the erroneous reading of *mlpnw* as a preposition instead of a verb. LXX presents a sense at variance with MT, "who makes me differ from the quadrupeds of the earth, and from the birds of the sky." Dhorme suggested that LXX *ho diorizōn me* harmonizes with *ho porēsas me* of vs. 10b above, in the translation of *'ôśāy*, "my Maker." The Qumran Targum sheds light on the LXX rendering. MT *mlpnw* is translated by *prsn'* which can mean both "separate" and "explain." The text of the Qumran Targum is fairly well preserved and the gap is easily restored:

dy pršn' mn b'[*yr' 'r' '*]
[*wmn*] *ṣpry' ḥkmnh*

The editors translate:

Qui nous a distingués des bê[tes *de la terre*
et] nous a faits [plus] intelligents [que]
les oiseaux?

The source of the difficulty for the Targumist was the preposition *min* which he apparently understood in its usual separative sense rather than as equivalent to *b-* and thus chose to render *m(')lp* by the ambiguous *prš*.

by. The preposition *min* is usually interpreted as the comparative here, "more than the beasts/birds." To say that man knows more than the beasts and birds is too banal even for Elihu. That man may learn and derive wisdom from observation of the natural world is a commonplace in popular wisdom. Solomon's sapiential productivity dealt in large measure with the beasts, birds, reptiles, fish, I Kings iv 33, and many of the biblical proverbs draw wisdom from the animal world; cf., e.g., Prov vi 6, xxvi 2, 11, xxx 24–31. A large part of Yahweh's speech from the storm, xxxviii–xli, consists of nature poems for Job's instruction. The idea that special information may be conveyed by the beasts and birds is also commonplace; cf. xii 7; Eccles x 20. What the animals are supposed to teach in this case is not clear. Perhaps Elihu intends to suggest that since even the animals in their need and distress cry to God (cf. Pss civ 21, cxlvii 9; Joel i 20), Job should emulate them rather than rail against God.

LXX omits the verb in the second line, "and from the birds of the sky." The Qumran Targum, however, preserves the verb which is needed to balance the length of the lines, [*wmn*] *ṣpry' ḥkmnh*, "[and from] the birds he makes us wise."

12–13. These verses appear to hark back to vs. 9 above.

13. Cf. Hab i 13.

14a. Cf. xiii 24, xxiii 8–9, xxiv 1b, xxx 20.

14b. Job has argued his case like a lawyer (cf. xiii 18, xxiii 4), and Elihu reminds him that it depends on the judge.

case. The reading *dîn* as a noun has been questioned because the ancient versions suggest a verbal form. B. Jacob (ZAW 32 [1912], 287) proposed connection with Ar. *dāna*, "stoop, submit," and the same proposal has been put forward again by G. R. Driver (WO I [1947–52], 408; VTS, III [1960], 89) and by A. Guillaume who rendered, "Submit yourself to him and wait for him." Jacob's proposal was noted and rejected by Dhorme and there is no good reason to revive it.

15. The text is awkward and probably has suffered damage. The translation follows Dhorme.

15b. *transgression*. Reading *peša'* for the unique *paš*. The appeal to Ar. *fašša*, "emit wind, belch, utter calumny," appears to be ruled out by the congruity of the sibilants. Ar. *fasīs*, "weak," while phonologically acceptable, is inappropriate semantically.

35. ELIHU'S FOURTH AND FINAL SPEECH
(xxxvi 1–28; 31; 29–30; 32–33)

XXXVI 1 Again Elihu spoke:

2 "Wait a bit, and I will show you
That there are still more words for God.
3 I will fetch my speech from afar,
I will ascribe righteousness to my Maker.
4 Truly, my word is no lie;
One perfect of utterance is with you.
5 Lo, God is mighty in power,
But he despises not the pure-minded.
6 He will not keep the wicked alive.
He gives justice to the oppressed.
7 He does not withdraw his eyes from the righteous.
With kings on the throne he seats them.
Forever they are exalted.
8 But if they be bound in fetters,
Held in the cords of affliction,
9 He tells them what they have done,
Their sin, that they were insolent.
10 He opens their ear to discipline,
Commands them to turn from evil.
11 If they obey and serve him,
They end their days in prosperity,
Their years in pleasure.
12 If they obey not, they cross the Channel;
They die without knowing.
13 But the impious-minded harbor anger;
They cry not when he chastises them.

14 Their soul dies in youth,
Their life among the sodomites.
15 He saves the afflicted by affliction,
Opens their ear with tribulation.
16 He lured you out of distress,
In unconfined expanse he set you.
Your table was loaded with rich food.
17 But the case of the wicked you did not judge,
The orphan's justice you belied.
18 Beware, lest he entice by abundance,
Let not a great bribe seduce you.
19 Will your opulence avail with him in trouble,
All the power of your wealth?
20 Pant not for the night,
When peoples vanish in their place.
21 Beware, lest you turn to evil,
For to this end you were tested by affliction.
22 Behold, God is sublime in power.
Who is a teacher like him?
23 Who prescribes for him his conduct?
Who can say, 'You have done wrong'?
24 Remember to extol his work,
Of which men have sung.
25 All mankind have seen it;
Man beholds it from afar.
26 Lo, God is greater than we know;
Innumerable are his years and beyond comprehension.
27 He draws the waterdrops
That distill rain from the flood,
28 That trickle from the clouds,
Pour on the ground in showers.
31 For with them he nourishes nations,
Gives them food in abundance.
29 Can one understand the spreading clouds,
The thundering from his pavilion?
30 Lo, 'Aliy spreads his light,
The roots of the sea are his throne.

32 On his palms the lightning prances,
He directs it with sure aim.
33 'Aliy speaks with his thunder,
Venting his wrath against evil.

Notes

xxxvi 2a. *Wait.* The verb *ktr* is common in Aramaic, especially in Syriac, in this sense, while elsewhere in the OT it has the sense "surround, congregate around a person." The two meanings are so closely connected that it is scarcely necessary to consider it an Aramaism here. Blommerde took *kattar* in the sense of "surround" and *zĕ'îr* as "a young man," Elihu's reference to himself, and translated:

> Form a circle around me, a young man, and I will show you,
> that I have still more words from God.

The preposition *l-* with *'ĕlôah,* "God," Blommerde took to mean "from," as in 3b below, *ūlpô'ălî,* "and from my Maker."

3a. Ibn Ezra understood this to refer to God and it appears that he may have been right; cf. xxxii 10b and xxxvii 26b. Elihu apparently regards himself as spokesman for God and his words as inerrant.

3b. Dahood (VTS, XVI [1967], 41, n. 4) took the preposition of *lĕpô'ălî* to mean "from" and Blommerde followed:

> I shall fetch my knowledge from afar
> and report the truth from my Maker.

4b. *perfect of utterance.* Cf. xxxii 10b and xxxvii 16b.

5. MT "Lo, God is mighty and does not despise, mighty in strength of heart," is almost certainly corrupt. LXX supplies the missing object of the verb in 5a as "the innocent" (*ton akakon*). Of the several emendations proposed, the most likely appears to be that adopted by Dhorme, transposing *kōaḥ* of 5b after *kabbîr* in 5a and reading *bĕḇar* for *kabbîr,* 5b. On the interpretation of this verse in rabbinic tradition, see S. Esh, VT 7 (1957), 190 f. Dahood (*Psalms II,* second Note on Ps lxxv 7) proposed to read the negative *lô'* as *lē',* "the Victor," and to take *kabbîr* also as a divine epithet, "the Old One," and rendered, "Though El is the Old One, he is still the Victor; the Old One detests stubbornness."

6a. Elihu contradicts Job's assertion of xxi 7.

7b, c. The translation disregards the Masoretic punctuation which divides the lines symmetrically but contrary to the sense. This leaves the second line too short, but avoids the necessity for emendation. Cf. v 11; I Sam ii 8; Ps cxiii 7; Luke i 52.

8–11. Elihu here makes his major contribution to the problem in the suggestion that affliction may be disciplinary, to keep man from pride and from sin. Eliphaz, however, broached this idea in his first speech, v 17.

10a. *their ear.* Blommerde suggested that MT *'oznām,* "their ear," be vocalized *'oznēm* "as a contracted northern dual." The suffix may be omitted, Blommerde noted, since "ear" is a part of the body.

discipline. For a detailed study of this word (*mûsār*) in connection with affliction, cf. J. A. Sanders, *Suffering as Divine Discipline in the Old Testament and Post-Biblical Judaism,* Colgate Rochester Divinity School Bulletin 38 (1955). On the biblical teachings in general, cf. Sutcliffe, *Providence and Suffering in the Old and New Testaments.*

11–12. Cf. Isa i 19–20.

11a. *obey.* Literally "hear."

11c. *in pleasure.* The Qumran Targum renders MT *banně'îmîm,* "in pleasure(s)," as "in honor and pleasure," *byqr w'dnn.* The latter word has strong connotations of sensual and sexual pleasure, as seen in the cognate *'ednāh* in Gen xviii 12 and the association of this root with the name of the lost Paradise, *gan 'ēḏen,* "Garden of Delight"; cf. E. A. Speiser, AB, vol. 1, NOTE on Gen ii 8.

12b. Cf. xxxiii 18. The Qumran Targum is not preserved in xxxiii 18b where the expression *'br bšlḥ* is used. It is, however, preserved for 12b where it offers the traditional interpretation, *bḥrb' yplwn,* "by the sword they will fall." In spite of this earliest witness to the traditional understanding, the interpretation offered in the NOTE on xxxiii 18b is maintained. The translation "fall" for *'br,* "cross over," was dictated by the misunderstanding of *šelaḥ.*

13a. *impious-minded.* Literally "impious of heart" (*ḥanpê-lēḇ*). The same expression occurs in the Ugaritic epic of Aqhat (*ḥnp lb*), applied to the ruthless goddess 'Anat when she plots to rob the young hero Aqhat of his magnificent bow.

13b. *chastises.* Reading *yissěrām* instead of MT *'ăsārām,* "he binds them."

14b. *sodomites.* Literally "holy males," the consecrated prostitutes of the Canaanite fertility cult; cf. Deut xxiii 17; I Kings xiv 24, xv 12, xxii 47; II Kings xxiii 7. The usual explanation is that the orgiastic excesses imposed on the hierodules so debilitated them that their predisposition to early mortality became proverbial. The parallelism with "youth" in 14a has led some interpreters to ascribe this sense to the term *qěḏēšîm* here, but there is no other evidence to support this view. LXX read *qěḏôšîm* and rendered "angels." Jerome rendered *inter effeminatos.* RSV paraphrases "and their life ends in shame," but gives in the footnote the more exact rendering "among the cult prostitutes." The LXX interpretation "and their life wounded by the angels" appears to have support in the Qumran Targum which reads *bmmtyn*, "by the killers," i.e. the angels (of death). (The word which precedes *bmmtyn* may be only partially preserved and the editors restore [*m*]*dynthwn* and render "et] leur [v]ille (périt) par les destructeurs." If the restoration is correct, the reading might be explained by reference to the destruction of Sodom and Gomorrah (Gen xix) for the attempted homosexual assault on the angels.) Targ. confirms the interpretation of *qĕḏēšîm* as male prostitutes with the rendering *hêḵ mārê zĕnû*, "like masters of prostitution."

15a. Elihu puts in a nutshell the argument of his first speech, xxxiii 16–30. Affliction accepted in humility may purge and save a man from perdition. Elihu puts it paradoxically as if it were a sort of homeopathic therapy.

15b. Cf. xxxiii 16a.

16–20. These verses are so difficult that many critics omit them in despair. CCD leaves a blank and gives in the notes a translation of the Vulg. which makes scarcely more sense than the MT. With the reader warned of the uncertainty, we attempt a translation omitting elaborate discussion of detail.

16a. *distress*. Literally "from the mouth of distress."

16b. Construing *rōḥaḇ*, "expanse," adverbially and reading *nĕḥāṯĕḵā*, "he set you," for MT *taḥtêhā*, "in her stead." Cf. Pss xviii 19, xxxi 8.

16c. Deleting *wĕnaḥaṯ* as a dittography from *nĕḥāṯĕḵā* as emended above.

rich food. Literally "fatness."

17. MT has "And of wicked judgment thou art full / Judgment and justice take hold." This can be twisted to make some semblance of sense in the context, although the wording is awkward. As Tur-Sinai has noted, it appears too striking to be accidental that the consonantal text *wdynrš'ml'tdynwmšpṭytmkw* may be divided quite differently, and more naturally, to produce "And the case of the wicked thou didst not judge / The justice of the orphan. . . ." The missing verb of the second line may then be reconstituted conjecturally from the extra letters at the end of this line and the beginning of the next. The parallelism and sense suggest something like "pervert, deny, falsify," hence in approximate consonance with the vestigial letters I suggest *kizzaḇtā*, "thou hast falsified." Cf. vi 27, xxii 9, xxiv 3, 9, xxxi 17, 21; Deut x 18; Isa i 17, 23, ix 17, x 2; Jer v 28; Ezek xxii 7; Mal iii 5; Pss x 14, 18, lxviii 5. In the Ugaritic epic of King Keret, the king's son Yaṣṣib attributes his father's misfortunes to dereliction of duty in respect to social justice:

The youth Yaṣṣib departed,
In his father's presence he entered,
He lifted his voice and cried:
"Hear, O noble Keret,
Listen and lend ear
. . . . .
You did not judge the cause of the widow,
Adjudicate the case of the wretched,
Nor put down the oppressor of the poor.
You did not feed the orphan before you,
Nor the widow behind your back.
So you are brother to the sickbed,
Companion to the bed of disease" (127:39–52).

Guillaume found here in the two occurrences of *dîn* an obvious case of the rhetorical device which the Arabs call *tauriyat*, i.e., a concealed double meaning. The first occurrence of *dîn* Guillaume took to mean "food," cognate with Ar. *zuwān*, while the second he understood in the usual meaning "judgment." Guillaume translated accordingly:

But you are full of a rich man's food;
Judgment and justice take hold of you.

The meaning "rich" for *rāšā'* Guillaume derived from Ar. *rassaġa*, as in xxiv 6b.

18a. *Beware.* Reading *ḥămēh*, "see thou," for MT *ḥēmāh*, "wrath," and regarding the conjunction *kî* as a corrupted vestige of the missing verb of the preceding line. Or, with Delitzsch and Dhorme, the word may be related to Ar. *ḥmy*, "defend, protect, keep safe," again in the sense of "beware" as befits the present context.

abundance. Connecting the word (*śep̄eq*) with the root meaning "suffice, abound" rather than the one meaning "clap the hands."

19a. Critics have found great difficulty in this line. The rendering above is based on the slightest of emendations, reading *lô*, "to him," for MT *lô'*, "not." The verb *'rk*, "arrange, set in order," is used of military disposition of troops (cf., e.g., I Sam iv 2) and of juridical presentation (cf. xiii 18, xxiii 4; Ps l 21). The juridical sense suits the context best. Wealth and bribery cannot influence the divine judge.

20a. The night is the time of catastrophe; cf. xxxiv 20, 25; Dan v 30; Luke xii 20. Job is admonished not to be eager for the divine judgment.

20b. *vanish.* Literally "go up," i.e., like dust; cf. Isa v 24. Cf. Ps cii 24 where "cause to go up" is used of cutting off a man in the middle of his life.

in their place. Suddenly and without warning. Elihu admonishes Job not to be too eager for the divine judgment which may annihilate him along with others, even whole nations; cf. Ps vii 8.

21. MT, woodenly rendered, has "For upon this thou hast chosen from affliction." Syr. solves the difficulty happily by construing the verb as passive with the sense of "test, prove," as commonly in Aramaic. Accordingly, the MT *bāḥartā* is to be vocalized *bōḥartā,* equivalent to *bōḥantā,* "thou hast been tested." The sense now is in accord with Elihu's main point, that suffering may be disciplinary, to warn and turn a man from evil.

22b. *teacher.* The word *môreh* is used of God in Isa xxx 20. A favorite figure of Elihu, xxxiv 32, xxxv 11. LXX interprets "teacher" as "ruler," *dynastēs.* Dahood (*Psalms III,* seventh NOTE on Ps cii 24) took the word *môreh* here as a by-form of the root *mrr,* "to be powerful," and translated *môreh* as "puissant." The present verse and the succeeding one he rendered: "Look, El is supreme in his strength, and who is puissant like him? Who entrusted him with his power? And who can say, 'You have done wrong?' " The final *w* of *kḥw,* "his strength," Dahood repeats as the conjunction before *mî,* "who," so that both cola perfectly balance with seven syllables each. It may be questioned whether the balance thus achieved is significant, since two following cola have seven and nine syllables, respectively.

23a. Cf. xxxiv 13; Isa xl 13; Dan iv 35; Rom xi 34. In spite of the words for strength and power in these two verses, as emphasized by Dahood's translation cited above, and the acceptance of the meaning "power" for *dereḵ* in some contexts, it seems preferable to render *darkô* as "his conduct" because the parallel line 23b speaks of wrongdoing. Perhaps the poet intended to suggest both meanings, "power" and "conduct."

23b. Cf. ix 12, xxi 31.

24b. *sung.* Rashi, Ibn Ezra, and Tur-Sinai derive the verb from the root *šûr,* "see," as in Num xxiv 17, rather than *šîr,* "sing." This might appear to be favored by the two verbs meaning "to see" in the next verse, except that three is a bit too much. This Pô'lēl form of the verb occurs about thirty times, usually the participle, in the sense of "sing." Men have always hymned the praises of deity; cf. Ps civ 33.

26. The Qumran Targum elaborates somewhat on MT, *h' 'lh' rb hw' wywmwhy sgy'* [*l' n*]*d' wmnyn šnwhy dy l' swp.*

> Lo God is great,
> And his numerous days we know not,
> And the number of his years are endless.

26b. *Innumerable.* Reading *missappēr* for Mt *mispār,* as in xvi 22a. Cf. Ps cii 28.

27a. *draws.* The verb *gr'* appears to have the basic sense of "diminish, deduct," or the like. It is used of clipping the beard in mourning, Isa xv 2; Jer xlviii 37, of reducing a wife's allowance of food, clothing, and sexual intercourse, Exod xxi 10. In Arabic the meaning is "to swallow (water)," as from a water skin, hence the noun *jur'a,* "a draught, drink." Tur-Sinai suggests that the figure is that of a bottle with a strainer in the mouth which explains why rain comes down in drops.

27b. *flood.* This word (*'ēḏ*) occurs in the OT only here and in Gen ii 6. The conjectured meaning "mist" is certainly erroneous. W. F. Albright (JBL 58 [1939], 102 f., n. 25) properly connected the word in Gen ii 6 with the Sum. *ID,* Akk. *edû,* as a designation of the subterranean waters. This subterranean cosmic reservoir was the source of moisture before there was rain, Gen ii 6. E. A. Speiser (BASOR 140 [1955], 9–11) has noted that the Akk. *edû* as a loan word in Hebrew should have resulted in *'ēḏê* in Hebrew, with *'ēḏ* as an alloform. In the light of Speiser's suggestion, it may be that the ending of the form *'ēḏô* is not the possessive suffix "his" but the modification of the Akkadian form *edû.* It is not necessary to change the verb from plural to singular, as many critics do, for the subject of the verb is not "God" but the "waterdrops" of the preceding line. Neither is it necessary to emend *lĕ'ēḏô* to *mē'ēḏô* (Duhm) in order to secure the appropriate sense "from," because the preposition *l,* as C. H. Gordon has shown, frequently has the meaning "from" in Hebrew as it has in Ugaritic. Duhm's idea—that the author of the Elihu speeches here exhibits more advanced meteorological knowledge than is reflected in the divine speeches—that he understands how clouds are formed by evaporation from the sea, and thus must have gained such knowledge of physics from Greek sources—is quite fanciful. What we have here in brief is the same idea as in the biblical flood story, that the rain comes from the cosmic reservoirs, whether below or above the earth, or both.

The Qumran Targum presents some differences from MT.

'rw 'nn[yn . . . . .]
wzyqy mṭr yhkn

Behold clouds . . . . .
And storms of rain he prepares.

The translation of the verb *gr'* in the first line is presumably lost in the lacuna. The verb of the second line appears as a noun of the same root and an auxiliary verb *yhkn* is supplied. The element *lĕ'ēḏô* is apparently ignored.

28a. *from the clouds.* The verb *nzl* in the simple stem is intransitive.

When an apparent object is expressed, it must be construed as the accusative of material, as in Isa xlv 8 clouds trickle righteousness, in Jer ix 17 eyelids trickle water, in Prov iii 20 the clouds drip dew. Here the unmentioned material is the waterdrops of 27a. There is a choice of construing either the clouds or the waterdrops as the subject of the verb, "with which (waterdrops) the clouds trickle," or, as above, "which trickle from the clouds," taking clouds as an adverbial accusative.

28b. *in showers.* MT *'āḏām rāḇ* does not mean "many men" since *'āḏām* means mankind generically and collectively. The rain falls on all, good and bad, Matt v 45. Neither can *rāḇ* be construed as an adverb, "abundantly." G. H. B. Wright (*The Book of Job,* 1883) was correct in taking this word as a by-form of *rĕḇîḇîm,* "showers," as in Deut xxxii 2. Moffatt rendered "dropping in showers on man." This has been proven right by the occurrence of *rb* and *rbb* as "showers" in the Ugaritic poems. Dahood (CBQ 25 [1963], 123–24) has shown that *'āḏām* here and in several other instances (Zech ix 1, xiii 5; Prov xxx 14b; Jer xxxii 20) has the same meaning as *'ăḏāmāh,* "ground." Thus the showers drop on the ground which is thereby rendered productive. It is tempting to see here in the preposition *'ălê* before *'āḏām* the ancient name of the weather-god 'Aliy, as in 30a below. The meteorological context is suited to the use of this name.

The Qumran Targum interprets MT *šĕḥāqîm* as "clouds" and construes it as the subject of the verb. The phrase *'āḏām rāḇ* is rendered *'m sgy',* "numerous people":

> *w'nnwhy y^{n}ḥtwn ṭ[ypyn 'l] 'm sgy'*
>
> And his clouds made d[rops] descend [upon]
> numerous people.

It may be that the verb corresponding to MT *yr'pw* is lost in the lacuna. The word *rb* was interpreted according to MT and not as a term for rain showers, as proposed above.

31. This verse is out of place where it stands, but fits very well after vs. 28. MT has "he judges" (*yāḏîn*) which makes no acceptable sense. God does not judge either with lightning or rain. The parallel line 31b shows that it is a matter of God's providing food for all mankind by means of the rain. The emendation to *yāzûn,* "he feeds, nourishes," makes the two lines apposite, but is not necessary since *yāḏîn* may be a dialectical form equivalent to *yāzîn.*

29b. *thundering.* The word denotes loud noises, such as the roar of the storm, xxx 22, shouting of a crowd, xxxix 7; Isa xxii 2; Zech iv 7. The meteorological context would thus indicate "thunder." The emendation to *taświṯ*, "bed, carpet," or the like, is accepted by CCD, "Lo! he spreads the clouds in layers / as the carpeting of his tent."

pavilion. "Covert, booth," *sukkāh,* as in Ps xviii 12. The dark clouds are the dwelling of the storm-god.

30a. *light.* The senseless LXX reading *ōdē,* "ode, song," derived from Theodotion's transcription *ēdō,* serves as the basis for the common emendation to *'ēḏô,* "his mist." But *'ēḏ* nowhere means "mist." The MT reading *'ôrô,* "his light," is to be retained in the sense of "lightning," as in xxxvii 3, 11b, 15b. I venture to see here in the preposition *'ālāyw,* "upon it," the ancient divine name, *'Aliy,* which was discovered by H. S. Nyberg in several OT passages, with other occurrences in Pss vii 9, lvii 3 pointed out by M. Dahood after the name was recognized by H. L. Ginsberg as a title of Baal in the Ugaritic epic of King Keret; cf. EUT, p. 58, n. 20. Blommerde suggested that the final *w* on *'lyw* represents the nominative case ending *u,* to be read therefore *'elyû.* It seems more likely that the *w* was added when the name was mistaken for the preposition.

30b. The MT "And the roots of the sea he covers" makes no sense. On the basis of Ps xviii 16 the verb "cover" (*ksy*) is often emended to the passival form of *gly,* "uncover, reveal." Duhm's emendation of "roots of the sea" (*šoršê hayyām*) to "tops of the mountains" (*rā'šê he-hārîm*) derives from the mistaken emendation of *'ôrô,* "his light," in the preceding line and the notion that the figure is that of clouds covering the mountain tops. Kissane's emendation to *šemeš bayyôm,* "He covereth the sun by day," is simple and ingenious, but also predicated on the preceding erroneous emendation. The emendation proposed by St. J. Marshall, of *kissāh,* "he covers," to *kis'ô,* "his throne," "and the roots of the sea are his throne," is very striking in view of the present writer's demonstration that the erstwhile head of the Ugaritic pantheon dwelt at the confluence of the subterranean seas; cf. EUT, pp. 61–81. The description here is of a storm-god whose dwelling was naturally on a mountain, as Baal's was on Mount Zaphon, but it is possible that incongruous features of El and Baal are mixed in Yahweh who absorbed elements of both. As a *pis aller,* Marshall's emendation is adopted, although it is not entirely suitable to the context.

32a. How KJ arrived at "With clouds he covereth the light" is a puzzle. MT has "Upon hands he covers light." It is generally agreed that the figure has to do with lightning but the various emendations are far from satisfactory. The crux appears to lie in the verb *kissāh,* "he covers." Dhorme emends to *nissāh,* as an auditory error for *niśśā',* "he lifts." One may think also of the root *nss,* Akk. *nasāsu,* which means "move to and fro, vibrate," or the like. In Ps lx

6 the root is used in some obscure connection with shooting a bow and in Zech ix 16 of the glittering of jewels. In Isa x 18, the context deals with the divine wrath as a consuming fire, so that the rendering of the difficult *kimsōs nôsēs* "as when a sick man wastes away" (AT, RSV) is most unlikely. In view of the connection of the root *nss* with fire, the glistening of jewelry, and the shooting of a bow, I venture an adaptation of Dhorme's emendation to apply to this root rather than *nś'*, "lift." I propose to read *nassāh* as describing the flickering action of cloud-to-cloud lightning which may seem to the imaginative to prance on the palms of the storm-god before he sends it earthward. The feminine form of the verb as emended agrees with the suffix of the preposition ("upon her"—in Hebrew text, but omitted in translation) of the following line which supports the view that "light/lightning" is the subject of the verb. The word *'ôr*, "light," is construed as feminine in Jer xiii 16 and its Akkadian cognate *urru* is regularly feminine.

32b. *with sure aim.* Retaining MT *map̄gîa'* instead of the usual emendation to *mip̄gā'*, "target, mark," as in vii 20, and following the interpretation of Delitzsch.

Vss. 29–32 are fragmentary and confused in the Qumran Targum and the problems of correlation with MT are too complex to be considered in detail. It is interesting to note that the difficult *'al kappayim* of 32a seems to be represented by *'l m'mrh*, "by his word," which would furnish a parallel to the verb of 32b *wayyĕṣaw*, "he commands." In xxxix 27a the Qumran Targum renders MT *'im 'al-pîḵā* as *'w 'l m'mrh*. This suggests that *'l kpym* may be an error for *'l pyw*, "by his command." The word *m'mrh* is followed by the letter *m* which might be the preformative of a participle. It is risky to overhaul the MT on the basis of vestigial remains of a translation, nevertheless the reading *'l m'mrh*, in the light of the treatment of xxxix 27a, favors the reading *'l pyw* instead of MT *'l kpym*. Unfortunately too little is preserved of the remainder of the verse to provide any reliable reconstitution of the whole. The suggestion that *'l m'mrh* reflects an original *'l pyw* is one of the numerous acute observations offered by Mr. Bruce Zuckerman.

33. This verse is notoriously difficult. Peake, more than half a century ago, noted that more than thirty explanations had been offered. JPS renders, as usual, as literally as possible, "The noise thereof telleth concerning it, / The cattle also concerning the storm that cometh up," supplying "the storm" in explanation of the participle. This is supposed to reflect the ancient observation that cattle appear to have a presentiment of an approaching storm. Accordingly, Dhorme emended *rē'ô*, "his noise," to *rô'ô*, "his shepherd (son pasteur)," *'ap̄*, "moreover," to *šô'ēp̄*, "panting," and *'al-'ôleh*, "concerning that which comes up,"

to *'al'ôlāh,* "tempest," to get "Il en avertit son 'pasteur,' / Le troupeau 'qui flaire' la 'tempête.'" The translation above is based on minimal alteration of the text, reading the preposition *'alāyw* as the ancient name of the storm-god 'Aliy, and changing *miqneh,* "cattle," to *maqnî',* "one who incites passion," and reading *'awlāh,* "evil," for *'ôleh,* "one who rises."

36. ELIHU'S FINAL SPEECH (*continued*)
(xxxvii 1–18; 21; 19–20; 22–24)

XXXVII

1 "At this my heart trembles,
Leaps out of its place.
2 Hear his thunderous voice,
The rumble that comes from his mouth.
3 Beneath the whole heaven he flashes it,
His lightning to the corners of the earth.
4 After it growls his voice,
Crashing with majestic roar.
Men stay not when his voice is heard.
5 God thunders with his voice wondrously,
Does great things we cannot comprehend.
6 To the snow he says, 'Fall earthward,'
To the downpour of rain, 'Be strong.'
7 Every man he shuts in,
That all men may know his work.
8 Then the beast enters its lair,
Lies down in its den.
9 From the Chamber comes the tempest,
From the Scatter-winds the cold.
10 From the breath of God comes ice,
The wide waters are congealed.
11 He hurls lightning from the nimbus,
Scatters his light from the clouds.
12 It changes direction as he wills,
Doing whatever he commands
All over his inhabited earth.
13 Whether for discipline, or for grace,
Or for mercy, he makes it find its mark.

14 Give ear to this, O Job,
Stop and consider the wonders of God.
15 Do you know how God commands them,
Makes lightning appear in his clouds?
16 Do you know about the cloud banks,
The wonders of one perfect in knowledge,
17 You, who swelter in your garments
When the earth is becalmed from the south?
18 Can you spread out the sky with him,
Strong as a molten mirror?
21 They cannot look at the light,
Bright as it is in the skies,
When the wind has passed and cleared them.
19 Tell us what we should say to him;
We cannot argue from ignorance.
20 Should he be told I wish to speak?
Does a man ask to be devoured?
22 From Zaphon comes gold;
Around God is awful majesty.
23 Shaddai we cannot reach;
Pre-eminent in power and judgment,
Great in justice, he does not oppress.
24 Therefore men should fear him;
He respects no clever mind."

Notes

xxxvii 1–5. The thunder is God's voice, Ps xviii 13, and the violence of the thunderstorm a weapon against the wicked, Exod ix 22–35, xix 16; I Sam vii 10; Ps lxxvii 17–18; Isa xxx 30. In like manner the storm-god Baal-Hadad in the Ugaritic myth strikes terror in his enemies and puts them to flight (51 VII 29–36):

> Baal uttered his holy voice,
> Echoed the issue of his lips,
> His holy voice rocked the earth,
> . . . . .
> The high places of the earth shook;
> Baal's enemies took to the woods,
> Hadad's foes to the hillsides.

The striking similarities between this Ugaritic passage and Ps xxix were noted by H. L. Ginsberg in 1936 (*Kitḇê Ugārit,* pp. 129 ff.) and have since been much discussed. Cf. T. H. Gaster, JQR 37 (1946–47), 54–67; F. M. Cross, Jr., BASOR 117 (1950), 19–21.

3a. *he flashes it.* In previous editions of this work, the verb *yišrēhû* was rendered "it flashes" and no mention was made of the Ugaritic parallel. In the myth dealing with the building of Baal's house (text 51), the goddess Asherah commends El's wisdom in assenting to Baal's desire for a house and assures El that Baal can now be relied upon to give his rain in due season (51 IV 68–71):

> Now the time of his rain Baal will keep,
> The time of showers with snow(?)
> He will utter his voice in the clouds,
> Flash lightnings to earth.
> (*šrh larṣ brqm*)

It seems likely, as Gordon suggested (UT 19:2484), that the verb *šrh* is transitive. It is also probably transitive in the present instance. Blommerde proposed that the final *u* of *yišrēhû* represents the indicative modal ending. It seems better, as the revised translation indicates, to construe it as the object suffix anticipating the object expressed in the following line. The intervocalic *h* of the suffix *hû* would probably be elided following the *h* of the root, *yišrĕhēhû* becoming *yišrēhû.*

4c. *stay not.* The ending of the verb *yĕʻaqqēḇēm* construed as the object suffix "them" presents such difficulty that some interpreters emend; cf., e.g., RSV which, following Budde, substitutes *bĕrāqîm,* "lightnings," for the suffix, "and he does not restrain the lightnings when his voice is heard." Surely this line intends to convey something other than the observation that lightning accompanies thunder. Verse 4a reveals awareness that the flash precedes the crash. It seems preferable to construe the ending of the verb as the enclitic emphatic particle, as in Akkadian and Ugaritic. The verb *ʻqb* is used in the sense which it has in Aramaic, "stop, hold back." The subject then is not God, but the one who hears his terrifying voice, as in the description of the panic of Baal's foes above.

5. Cf. v 9, ix 10.

6a. *Fall.* This use of *hwy* in the sense "fall" is unique in the OT and has to be explained from Arabic. This does not mean that it is to be regarded as an Arabism since the nominal cognates *hawwāh* and *hōwāh,* "destruction, disaster," occur about fifteen times in the OT.

6b. MT has repetition of "downpour of rain(s)." The word here translated "downpour" is usually rendered "shower," but it refers to the prolonged heavy rain of the Syrian-Palestinian winter and not to sudden summer showers.

7a. MT has "With the hand of every man he seals." On the basis of ix 7, the emendation of *bĕyad̲* to *ba'ad̲* is virtually certain; cf. Gen vii 16 where the preposition *ba'ad̲* is also used with a synonymous verb meaning "shut, seal." As the wild beasts are forced to hibernate (cf. vs. 8), so the peasant has to suspend work and shut himself in against the wintry weather. Homer (*Iliad* xvii.549 f.) speaks of the chill storm that makes men cease their work on earth.

7b. MT has "For the knowledge of all men of his work," which JPS renders "That all men whom he hath made may know it." The awkwardness is remedied by reading either *'ĕnôš* or *'ănāšîm* for MT *'anšê*. Perhaps the *m* was omitted by haplography, since the following word begins with that letter.

8. Cf. xxxviii 40 where the same words are used of the animals' abode, but in a different context.

9a. *Chamber.* Whether this is an abbreviation of the term "Chambers of the South(wind)," ix 9, is uncertain. Ps cxxxv 7 mentions the bringing forth of the wind from storehouses, and treasures of snow and hail are mentioned in xxxviii 22. It is worthy of note that the term "chamber" (*ḥed̲er*) is used of the subterranean abode of El in the Ugaritic mythological texts. El is ensconced in a complex of seven (or eight, for purposes of poetic parallelism) chambers or enclosures:

> El answers from the seven chambers (*ḥdrm*),
> From the eight enclosures.

Whether these seven chambers were the storehouses of the seven winds of ancient Mesopotamian cosmology is an intriguing question that merits investigation. On the seven winds, cf. H. and J. Lewy, HUCA 17 (1943), 8–10, 15–21, n. 229, 52 f.

9b. *Scatter-winds.* The unique word *mĕzārîm* is taken by some to be a variant form of *mazzārôt̲* in xxxviii 32. The versions are at odds. The Koran (li 1) uses the term *d̲āriyāt,* "scatterers" of the cold north winds and Qimḥi similarly explained *mĕzārîm* as "winds that blow and scatter" (*rûḥôt̲ nôšĕb̲îm ûmĕzārîm*). In the light of the Arabic word, it is likely that the root of *mĕzārîm* is *zry* "scatter, disperse, winnow," whereas *mazzārôt̲* is probably a dialectical variant of *mazzālôt̲,* "constellations," II Kings xxiii 5, from Akk. *manzaztu*>*manzaltu,* "station, phase of the moon," from *nazāzu,* "stand," ultimately from a root *d̲wd̲* (cf. M. Pope, "Ugaritic *ndd/ydd,*" JCS 1 [1947], 337–41). The parallelism of *ḥed̲er* and *mĕzārîm* suggests that the latter word may be a term for storehouse. Tur-Sinai related the word to the root *zrr* in the sense of "squeeze, press," and explained that *mĕzārîm* "is thus God's press, wherein he squeezes rain, snow and hail out of the clouds." A meaning such as "magazine, storehouse, treasury" may be indicated. Ar.

mzr in the sense of "fill entirely" might be invoked, but dubiously. It seems for the present preferable to retain the traditional interpretation of the word pending more convincing explanation.

10a. *breath of God*. Cf. iv 9, xxxii 8; Isa xl 7, a poetic expression for wind which may be either hot or cold.

comes. Literally "he/it gives," perhaps to be emended to *yuttan*, "is given."

ice. For the suggestion that the abode of El (God) in the Ugaritic texts may have been icy, cf. EUT, p. 67.

10b. On the face of it, merely a description of freezing of water. But "wide waters" is suggestive of more than a puddle, pond, or lake. From Plutarch (*Peri tou prosōpou tēs selēnēs*, ed. P. Raingeard, 1934, 941b, p. 40) we learn that the sea of Kronos, i.e., the watery abode of El-Kronos, was frozen. This line may thus contain an indirect allusion to this mythological motif.

11a. *lightning*. MT *bĕrî* is otherwise unknown. Those who retain this reading have to construe it as a contraction of *rĕwî*, "saturation, moisture," plus the preposition *bĕ*, "with." The versions make various guesses, "grain, a chosen one, purity." Modern emendations favor *bārāḏ*, "hail," or *bārāq*, "lightning." Parallelism favors lightning, which is adopted above. The verb (*ṭrḥ*) also is hapax in the OT, although apparently cognate nominal forms occur in Deut i 12; Isa i 14 in the sense of "burden." In Arabic the verb means "throw" and this sense goes better with the lightning than the post-biblical Hebrew sense of "load."

The Qumran Targum reads for 11a *'p bhwn ymrq 'nn[yn]* which the editors translated thus:

Par eux aussi il fait briller le[s] nuage[s].

There is nothing corresponding to MT *bĕrî*, unless it be *bhwn*, "with them." The verb *mrq* which corresponds to MT *yaṭrîaḥ* has the meaning "cleanse, polish, purify," in Aramaic. The editors speculate that the Targumist may have read some form of *ṭhr*, "be clean." In Arabic *mrq* has among its several meanings the sense "shoot, pierce," which is not too far from the sense conjectured for *yaṭrîaḥ*. The word *'āḇ* is taken as the direct object of the verb, but in the parallel line 11b MT *'ānān* is construed as an adverbial accusative *mn 'nn nwrh*, "and he brings forth from the cloud his light(ning)."

from the nimbus. Taking *'āḇ* as adverbial accusative rather than as subject of the verb, and similarly in the following parallel line.

11b. MT reads "He scatters the cloud of his light." With most moderns, I read the absolute form *'ānān* rather than the construct *'ănan*, but construe it as adverbial accusative, "from the clouds," rather than subject. Dahood (*Psalms I*, second NOTE on Ps xix 9), followed by

Blommerde, took the word *bry* of 11a to refer to the sun (as suggested by Ehrlich) and construed the final *y* as the third person suffix parallel to *'ôrô* in 11b, and translated thus: "And his shining one dispels the mist, and his sun scatters the clouds." The context, however, seems to the present writer to suggest lightning rather than the dispersal of clouds by the sun. As a manifestation of divine power, the lightning is more spectacular than evaporation of clouds by the sun.

12a. The line is too long for a single colon and too short for a bicolon. The alternatives are to add or to delete something. Dhorme makes two lines by adding another verb. It appears simplest to drop the difficult word *mĕsibbôṯ* as possibly a gloss to *miṯhappēḵ*, "changing direction."

12b. The third person masculine plural suffixes on both verbal forms in this line disturb modern critics because there is no antecedent of this gender and number. Dhorme's suggestion that the poet has in mind both thunder and lightning, or meteorological phenomena in general, is plausible. In the light of Ugaritic usage, however, I prefer to regard the suffix as the emphatic particle.

12c. MT has "Upon the face of the habitable world eastward." In the light of Prov viii 31, the only other occurrence of this phrase, it could scarcely be termed an emendation to read *'arṣāh*, "earthward," as *'arṣôh*, "his earth." This whole verse conveys the thought that though the lightning may appear capricious, darting in all directions, yet every movement is by divine plan and guidance.

The Qumran Targum reads *whw' 'mr yšm'wn lh w'zlyn l'bdyhwn 'l kl dy br' ypqdnwn 'l 'npy tbl*, "And (when) he speaks, they listen to him and go to their works over all which he created. He commissions them over the surface of the earth." It is interesting to note that there is nothing in this rendering which corresponds to *mĕsibbôṯ*. It appears that *miṯhappeḵ* was read *miṯhalleḵ* and rendered by *'zlyn*, "they go." The two words *bĕtaḥbûlôṯāw* and *lĕp̄o'ŏlām* appear to be rendered by a single term *l'bdyhwn*, "to their works," which suggests that one of these terms is an explanatory gloss for the other. MT *yĕṣawwēm*, "he commands them" is rendered *ypqdnwn*, "he commissions them." The doublet *tēḇēl 'arṣāh* is represented by the single term *tbl*.

13a. *discipline*. Literally "the rod"; cf. xxi 9.

grace. MT *lĕ'arṣô* appears to mean "for his earth" which makes little sense in this context. Between "discipline" and "love" (*ḥeseḏ*) one would expect some comparable theological term. The "root" *rṣw* furnishes the sense desiderated. The prefixed ' makes the word appear identical with "his earth" (*'rṣw*) and it may be that the vocalization was identical, or nearly so. Nouns with prefix ' (such as *'aḥăwāh*, xiii 17) are not uncommon in Semitic. The name of the Palmyrene deity *'rṣw* presents the same apparent form as the noun in this passage and the sense of "favor, grace," or the like, is quite suitable as the designation of a deity. Cf. NWSPJ, p. 72.

13b. *mark.* Literally "he causes (something) to find it." God must be the implied subject of the verb and the lightning which he directs and commands must be the agent he makes to find something. The object represented by the suffix would then be the mark which the lightning strikes. The difficulty of this eminently logical analysis is that it is hard to see how the lightning can be regarded as an instrument of God's love or mercy (*ḥesed*). It could be, of course, argued that the love or mercy is for those the lightning misses. I Cor iv 21 appears to be a reminiscence of this verse.

The Qumran Targum's interpretation of this verse is replete with interesting problems: *hn lmktš hn l'r'' hn lkpn wḥsrnh whn ptgm* [ ]*b lhw' 'lyh,* "Whether for affliction, whether for pleasure/the earth, whether for famine and want, and whether a word of [ ] will be upon it." The editors have great difficulty with *l'r''* which they relate to the root *r''* (= Heb. *rṣṣ*), "break." It appears that they failed to consider the possibility of the root *rḍw,* "have pleasure." In the place of MT *heṣed,* "steadfast love," there are two terms, *kpn,* "famine," and *ḥsrnh,* "want," the latter apparently the result of reading *ḥeser* instead of MT *ḥesed.* Following *piṯgam* there is a trace of a short word of two or three letters for which the editors suggest either *ṭb,* "good," or *rîḇ,* "litigation." It may be that the clue to the solution of this muddle lies in the conjecture that the original reading juxtaposed pairs of apposites, punishment (*šbṭ*) and favor (*'rṣw*), want (*ḥeser*) and mercy (*ḥesed*). This would dictate the restoration *ṭb* rather than *ryb* after *ptgm* in order to balance *kpn* and *ḥsrnh,* "famine and want" as the double rendering of *ḥeser.* The phrase *ptgm* [*ṭb*], "a word of favor," would then be taken as the translation of *ḥesed.* The final verb *yamṣî'ēhû* of MT is not reflected in the rendering of the Qumran Targum, a detail unnoticed by the editors. The reconstitution of this verse will require more meticulous attention than the hasty observations here offered. On the interpretation of MT *l'rṣw* as "grace, favor," cf. Dahood's *Psalms II,* third NOTE on Ps lviii 3.

15–18. Elihu anticipates the divine challenge out of the storm with the same sort of ironical questions which Yahweh poses to Job, xxxviii. If Job cannot understand or control the physical world, how can he presume to question God's justice?

The Qumran Targum presents some interesting congruities and incongruities with MT in vss. 14–17:

(14) *hṣt d' 'ywb wqwm hstkl bgbwrt 'lh'*
(15) [*ht*]*nd' m' šwy' 'lh' 'lhw*[*n whw*]*p' nhwr 'nnh*
(16) [*htn*]*d' lhlbš' 'nnh gb*[*wrt'*
(17) *b*]*dyl dy lbwšk . . . .*

14 Hear this Job and stand,
Consider the powers of God.
15 Do you know what God imposed on them,
And (how) he made shine the light of his cloud?
16[a] Do you know how to clothe his cloud with power,
17[a] Because your garment . . .

Remnants of 16b and 17b follow. Most interesting is the reading *lhlbšh*, "to clothe," for MT *'l mplśy* which LXX rendered, *diakrisin*, "divisions."

15a. *commands.* Literally "puts upon them," i.e., lays charge upon them, presumably upon the clouds.

16a. *banks.* The work *mip̄lāś* occurs only here, but the context is so much like xxxvi 29 where *mip̄rāś* is used that it is tempting to regard the two words merely as variants of the same word. Most interpreters take the word here to mean "balancings," referring to the marvelous suspension of the clouds without visible means of support.

16b. Cf. xxxvi 4b where Elihu uses this same expression as applied to himself rather than God. Blommerde read *'al* of 16a as *'ēl* and took the expression *těmîm dē'im* as a divine appellative parallel to *'ēl*, and rendered:

> Do you recognize the Most High by his outspread cloud,
> by his wonderful acts, the Perfect in Knowledge?

Whether the element *'l* represents the divine title or not, it is clear that *těmîm dē'îm* relates to the deity and may be regarded as a divine appellative. As noted above, xxxii 10b, *dī'a* and *dē'āh*, as Ginsberg suggested, are probably not to be related to *yd'*, "know," but to a root *d'w*, "speak," and thus *těmîm dē'îm* may better be rendered "Perfect in Utterance," or the like. This recalls the epithet of the god Hawrōn in the incantation from Arslan Tash (KAI 27, line 16) *hwrn 'š tm py*, "Hawrōn whose mouth is perfect," and the Akkadian parallel, "Marduk whose speech is pure" (*[d]Marduk ša tūšu ellet;* cf. L. W. King, *The Seven Tablets of Creation*, II, pl. 61 II 27). Cf. ix 20a.

17a. Literally "who your garments are hot." The sultry air from the desert makes one feel as if he were about to suffocate in his clothing.

17b. W. M. Thomson (*The Land and the Book*, new ed., 1913, p. 536) gives a striking description of the effects of the sultry air:

> We can testify that the garments are not only warm, but hot. This sensation of dry hot clothes is only experienced during the siroccos; and on such a day, too, one understands the other things mentioned by the prophet—bringing down the noise and quieting the earth. There is no living thing abroad to make a noise. The birds hide in

thickest shades, the fowls pant under the walls with open mouth and drooping wings, the flocks and herds take shelter in caves and under great rocks, and labourers retire from the fields and close the windows and doors of their houses. No one has energy enough to make a noise, and the very air is too weak and languid to stir the pendant leaves even of the tall poplars. Such a south wind with the heat of a cloud does indeed bring down the noise and quiet the earth.

18. Mirrors in antiquity were made of polished bronze; cf. Exod xxxviii 8. The sky was thought to be a solid dome (firmament) separating the two primeval reservoirs, Gen i 6. In Deut xxviii 23 the sky in time of drought is likened to bronze.

21. This verse seems out of place in its present position. If the "light" refers to the sun, as in xxxi 26, then the sense is fairly suitable to the context of vss. 17–18. Though the sun is not mentioned in vss. 17–18, it is certainly intended to be in the picture. The blazing sun above the dust clouds which obscure it makes the sky like a brazen molten mirror. When the wind clears the sky, the sun is too bright for the eye to behold. These lines are reminiscent of Ben Sira's description of the sun (Ecclesiasticus xliii 2–4).

19b. *argue.* Draw up and present one's case in an orderly fashion; cf. xiii 18, xxiii 4, xxxii 14, xxxiii 5.

ignorance. Literally "darkness"; cf. Eccles ii 14.

20. Elihu intimates that he has more sense than to do what Job has done, to challenge God to an argument. To do such a thing is madness, tantamount to seeking self-destruction.

22. The supposed difficulties of this verse are dispelled by reference to the Ugaritic myths. Zaphon here is not simply the direction "north," but the name of the holy mountain of Baal; cf. xxvi 7. Many critics object to the MT reading "gold." LXX *nephē chrysagounta,* however, attests to the reading and reflects the same doubts that beset modern interpreters. The traditional English rendering "golden splendor" attempts to meet the problem in a fashion similar to that of the Greek translator. In keeping with this understanding, many critics, following Graetz, emend *zāhāḇ,* "gold," to *zōhar,* "brightness." Delitzsch suggested that the gold refers to the color of the sun after the passing of the clouds that had obscured it (cf. vs. 21c). Oriental and classical literatures, Delitzsch pointed out, furnish many instances of reference to the sunshine as golden, e.g., Abulola's words *eš-šamsu bi-tibrin,* "the sun is gold." The northerly origin of this golden sunlight Delitzsch does not attempt to explain. Driver supposed that "the allusion may

be to the Aurora Borealis, the streaming rays of which, mysteriously blazing forth in the northern heavens, may well have been supposed to be an effulgence from the presence of God Himself." Delitzsch was closer to the truth when he pursued the interpretation of "gold" in the literal sense, alluding to Herodotus' and Pliny's references to the north as the source of gold. With the recovery of the Ugaritic mythological texts, we are now in a better position to understand this verse which connects gold and Zaphon. A major motif of the Baal cycle of myths is the building of a splendiferous palace of gold, silver, and lapis lazuli on the height of Mount Zaphon. The rendering "golden splendor" may be appropriate as suggesting the glow of the lightning which comes from the mythical golden palace of the storm-god on Mount Zaphon. For an elaboration of this notion, cf. EUT, pp. 99–102.

Around. Blommerde took *'l* not as the preposition, but as a divine title *'ēl* which he combined with *'ĕlôah* as "The Most High God." The translation offered by Blommerde suggests that the problem remains:

> From Zaphon comes gold,
> The Most High God, awful in majesty.

23. The lines of this verse are both overlong, but fall nicely into a tricolon.

23a. Cf. xi 7, xxiii 8–9.

23b, c. Elihu denies Job's charge (ix 20–24) that God oppresses or otherwise acts unjustly.

24b. Literally "He will not see all the wise of heart." LXX and Syr. make "all the wise of heart" the subject of the verb. Thus even the wisest cannot see God. It seems more likely that God is to be understood as the subject of the verb. The wise of heart, the clever minded, those wise in their own conceit—as Elihu considers Job—God does not regard with favor; cf. ix 4.

37. THE THEOPHANY: YAHWEH'S FIRST DISCOURSE (xxxviii 1–41)

XXXVIII 1 Then Yahweh answered Job
From out of the storm, and said:

2 "Who is this that obscures counsel
With words void of knowledge?
3 Gird your loins like a hero,
I will ask you, and you tell me.
4 Where were you when I founded the earth?
Tell me, if you know so much.
5 Who drafted its dimensions? Surely you know?
Who stretched the line over it?
6 On what are its sockets sunk,
Who laid its cornerstone,
7 While the morning stars sang together,
And all the gods exulted?
8 Who shut the sea within doors,
When it came gushing from the womb;
9 When I made the cloud its garment,
Dark mist its swaddling bands,
10 When I put bounds upon it,
Set up bars and doors,
11 Saying, 'Thus far come, but no more.
Here your wild waves halt'?
12 Did you ever command a morning,
Post Dawn in his place,
13 Snatch off Earth's skirts,
Shaking the wicked out of it?
14 It changes like sealing clay,
Tinted like a garment.

15 The wicked are robbed of their light,
The upraised arm is broken.
16 Have your entered the springs of the sea,
Walked in the recesses of the deep?
17 Have Death's Gates been revealed to you,
Have you seen the Dark Portals?
18 Have you examined earth's expanse?
Tell, if you know all this.
19 Where is the way to light's dwelling,
Darkness, where its abode,
20 That you may guide it to its bourne,
Show it the way to go home?
21 You know, for you were then born,
The sum of your days is great!
22 Have you entered the snow stores,
Or seen the hoards of hail
23 Which I reserve for troublous times,
For the day of attack and war?
24 By what power is the flood divided,
The east [wind] spread over the earth?
25 Who cleft a channel for the downpour,
A path for the thundershower,
26 To bring rain on no-man's land,
The wilderness with no man in it,
27 To sate the desolate desert,
Make the thirsty land sprout verdure?
28 Does the rain have a father,
Who sired the dew drops?
29 From whose womb comes the ice,
The hoarfrost of heaven, who bore it,
30 When water hardens like stone,
The surface of the deep imprisoned?
31 Can you tie Pleiades' fetters,
Or loose Orion's bands?
32 Can you lead out Mazzarot on time,
Guide the Bear with her cubs?

33 Do you know the celestial statutes,
Can you determine his rule on earth?
34 Can you raise your voice in the clouds,
And let the streaming water cover you?
35 Can you send lightning scurrying,
To say to you, 'Here we are'?
36 Who put wisdom in Thoth?
Who gave Sekwi understanding?
37 Who counts the clouds in wisdom,
Tilts the water jars of heaven,
38 When the dust fuses to lumps,
And the clods cleave together?
39 Can you hunt prey for the lioness,
Appease the appetite of her cubs,
40 When they crouch in their den,
Lie in wait in their lair?
41 Who provides the raven prey,
When its fledglings cry to God,
Frantic for lack of food?

Notes

xxxviii 1a. *Yahweh.* The divine name here, as in xl 1, 3, 6, xlii 1, is that used in the Prologue and Epilogue, but not in the Dialogue or the Elihu speeches.

Job. Yahweh passes over Elihu and speaks directly to Job who had challenged him to answer, xxxi 35. This, in the view of most critics, is one of several indications that the Elihu speeches are interpolated.

1b. *storm.* A storm or other meteorological phenomena usually accompanies a theophany; cf. Pss xviii 8–16, l 3, lxviii 8–9, 14; Hab iii 5–6; Nah i 3; Ezek i 4; Zech ix 14; Exod xiii 22, xix 16. This feature is doubtless derived from the ancient cult of the weather-god. The storm appears to have been anticipated by Elihu (cf. xxxvii 2), and critics who accept or reject the Elihu speeches both appeal to this point in support of their opposite views. Severe storms, while not common, are not unknown in Syria-Palestine; cf. D. Nir, "Whirlwinds in Israel in the Winters 1954/55 and 1955/56," IEJ 7 (1957), 109–17. Y. Levy-Tokatly, "Easterly Storms in November 1958," IEJ 10

(1960), 112–17, reports on two wind storms strong enough to damage light structures and trees.

2a. Cf. vi 16, xlii 3a. In the previous editions of this work, this line was rendered "Who is this that denies Providence" and it was argued that *'ēṣāh,* "counsel, design, plan, scheme, purpose," as applied to God's control of the world (cf. Ps xxxiii 11; Prov xix 21; Isa xix 17, xlvi 10) justifies the rendering "Providence." Moffatt paraphrased "Who darkens my design with a cloud of thoughtless words?" The participle *maḥšîḵ* was thus rendered "denies" rather than "darkens." In keeping with the revised rendering of vi 16b, it seems best to revert to the traditional literal translation of *maḥšîk 'ēsāh* so that the synonymy of *ḥšk* and *'lm* may be confirmed by comparison of vi 16b, xxxv 2a, and xlii 3a.

2b. Elihu also charged Job with speaking out of ignorance, xxxiv 35.

3a. Cf. xl 7. Girding the loins is used figuratively of preparation for any strenuous or difficult undertaking; cf. Exod xii 11; I Kings xviii 46; Isa xi 5; Jer i 17. The origin of the term is usually seen in the girding on the sword; cf. Ps xlv 4, "Gird your sword upon the thigh, O hero." C. H. Gordon and others see here an allusion to the ancient ordeal of belt-wrestling to decide an issue. In a legal document from Nuzi we have a description of the process. "Matteshub took hold of Gurpazaḫ and fastened his own girdle to his girdle, and in the contest Gurpazaḫ won"; cf. C. H. Gordon, HUCA 23, I (1950–51), 131 ff., and N. H. Tur-Sinai, *Halashon Wehasepher* 3 (1955), 140–47. H. L. Ginsberg (JAOS 70 [1950], 158) averred that wrestling-belts are never mentioned in the Bible and doubted that they are so much as alluded to there. According to Ginsberg, the allusion here and in xl 7, is far more likely to be the belt of a warrior who is hampered in his movements when his kilt is loose.

3b. Job had demanded to argue his case with God (ix 32, xiii 3, 15) but the present turn is not quite what he had requested (except momentarily in xiii 22). But God declines to submit to questioning. However, instead of levying charges and specifications, as Job had challenged him to do (xiii 23, xxxi 35), God assails Job with questions he cannot answer about the wonders of nature and the control of the world. The purpose is to bring home to Job his ignorance and his folly in impugning God's wisdom and justice.

4a. Eliphaz had asked Job similar ironic questions, xv 7–8, as had Elihu in xxxvii 18.

4b. Literally "Tell, if you know understanding." The Qumran Targum reads *ḥkmh,* "wisdom," for MT *bînāh,* "understanding." Dahood (*Psalms III,* NOTE ad loc.), on the basis of the personification of Wisdom and Understanding in Prov viii, personified *tĕbûnāh* in Ps cxxxvi 5 and *bînāh* in the present instance rendered, "Where were you when I founded the earth? Tell if you are acquainted with Understanding." The questions, according to Dahood, imply that Understanding was present with God when the earth was created.

5a. *Surely*. Here, as noted by Dahood (*Psalms III*, second NOTE on Ps cxxviii 2), the emphatic *kî* with postposition of the verb is employed as in Ugaritic. The Qumran Targum reads *hn*, "if," for MT *ky: hn tnd'*, "if you know." The text is perfectly preserved here and the translation is quite precise:

mn šm mšḥth hn tnd'
mn ngd 'lyh ḥwṭ'

Who set its measure(s), if you know?
Who stretched over it the line?

6a. Cf. xxvi 7; Ps xxiv 2.

4–6. The earth was conceived as a building set on foundations, 4a (cf. Pss xxiv 2, lxxxix 12, cii 26, civ 5; Prov iii 19; Isa xlviii 13, li 13, 16; Zech xii 1), built according to plans and specifications, 5a (cf. Ezek xl 3–xliii 17; Zech i 16), with use of the measuring line, 5b (cf. Isa xxxiv 11; Jer xxxi 39), with its pillars set in sockets.

6b. Cf. Isa xxviii 16; Jer li 26; Ps cxviii 22. The cornerstone may refer either to a foundation stone or the capstone.

7. The laying of the foundation, Ezra iii 10–11, or the capstone of a building, Zech iv 7, was an occasion for rejoicing and music. The song of the morning stars is not merely a poetic figure. The stars were mighty gods in the pagan cults (cf. II Kings xvii 16, xxi 3; Deut iv 19), but were relegated to subservience in the celestial army of Yahweh (cf. Isa xl 26). The ancient pagan conception of the king of the gods enthroned with his court ranged around him, as in the Ugaritic myths, is reflected in I Kings xxii 19. The celestial army also functioned as a choir to hymn the praises of the king, Pss xix 2, xxix 2, cxlviii 2–3. The morning stars certainly include the planet Venus, the brilliant morning and evening "star"; cf. Isa xiv 12; II Pet i 19. The Ugaritic poem "The Birth of the Beautiful and Gracious Gods" celebrates the birth of the astral deities Dawn and Dusk, perhaps the Venus star regarded, as among the Romans, as the morning star (Lucifer) and the evening star (Hesperus).

This famous verse is almost completely preserved in the Qumran Targum which reads:

bmzhr kḥd' kwkby ṣpr
wyz'q[w]n kḥd' kl ml'ky 'lh'

When the morning stars shone together,
And all the angels of God shouted together.

The editors of the Qumran Targum suggest that the change of the verb *rnn*, "sing, jubilate," to *zhr*, "shine," was motivated by the desire to avoid saying that the stars, inanimate beings created by God but worshiped by the pagans, "jubilate." (LXX and Syr. apparently read *br'*, "create," for MT *brn*, "when sang.") For a similar reason, MT's "sons of God" was changed to "angels of God."

7b. *gods*. Cf. NOTE on i 6.

8a. *Who shut*. Vulg. *quis conclusit*, LXX *ephraxa de*, "and I shut," reflects a reading *w'sk*. Blommerde read *wayyussaḵ* (from *nsk*, "pour") for MT *wayyāseḵ* and translated: "When the sea poured out of the two doors, when it went forth, erupting from the womb." The reference of 8a, however, is to the containment of the sea, while 8b gives the temporal setting. Driver-Gray proposed to read instead of MT *bdltym*, "with (two) doors," *bĕhulledeṯ yām*, "when the sea was born," and remarked that "it is less easy to recover the beginning of the line, which should contain a question."

The Qumran Targum reads *htswg bdšyn ym'*, with the interrogative particle before the second person verbal form, "Did you shut the Sea within doors?"

8–11. Cf. vii 12, ix 13, xxvi 12. In the Mesopotamian Creation Epic, Marduk, after slaying the sea dragon Tiamat, created therefrom the primeval seas and placed a bar and guard to keep back the waters (cf. ANET, p. 67, lines 139–40). In the Ugaritic myth relating Baal's defeat of the sea-god Yamm we cannot tell what the victorious Baal did to his fallen opponent for the text breaks off, but there is mention of making him captive (cf. ANET, p. 131, line 30). The present allusion presents an otherwise unknown motif, the birth of the sea-god and the use of swaddling bands to restrain the violent infant. In the Ugaritic Text BH (75 I 18–19) there is mention of swaddling-bands in the birth of the bovine monsters called Eaters and Devourers; cf. xl 15a.

The Qumran Targum preserves most of vss. 8–11:

(8) *htswg bdšyn ym'*
b[hn]gḥwth mn rḥm thwm' lmpq
(9) *bšwyt 'nnyn [lbw]šh*
w'rplyn ḥwtlwhy
(10) *wtšwh lh tḥwmyn wdt*
[. . . . . .]*yn w*[ ]
(11) *w'mrt 'd tn' wl' twsp*
[*g*]*ll*[*yk*]

Did you shut the Sea within doors?
When it gushed from the womb of the deep, to come out
When I made the clouds its garment

The dark clouds its swaddling-bands
Did you set him a limit and a law?
. . . .
And I said, "Up to here and you will not exceed
. . . . [your wa]ves."

The womb from which the Sea emerged is here identified as the cosmic abyss.

10a. *put.* Various emendations have been offered for the verb *'ešbōr.* Dhorme transposed the two verbs, "I shattered" and "I imposed." F. Perles (*Analekten*) postulated the meaning "trace, mark out" for *šbr* and similarly Gaster (*Thespis,* p. 456), connecting it with Ar. *sbr,* "prescribe boundaries." Guillaume related the word to Ar. *šabara,* "spanned," and averred that "The view that Hebrew Shin must equal Arabic Sin and *vice versa* is antiquated and untenable." The Qumran Targum reads *wtšwh lh tḥwmyn wdt*[ ], "and you set for it bounds and law [ ]." It is not clear from this rendering exactly what the original wording was, but it is possible that *šwy tḥwmyn,* "set bounds," translates the verb *šbr* in the sense postulated by Perles and Gaster. Unfortunately, the verb of the second colon is not preserved in the Qumran Targum.

bounds. Dahood (*Psalms I,* second NOTE on Ps xvi 6) construed the suffix of *ḥuqqî* as third singular and rendered thus: "And I traced out its limits, and set bars and two doors."

11b. *halt.* The versions, as Dhorme remarked, have been embarrassed by *yšyt bg'wn.* LXX apparently took *bg'wn* as *b-gw-k,* "in your midst," and rendered, "but your waves will be confined within you." Vulg., *et hic confringes tumentes fluctus tuos,* may reflect the verb *šbr.* Targ. reads *tšwy,* "you will put," and Syr. *tktr,* "you will remain." The Qumran Targum does not preserve the verb of this hemistich. Blommerde proposed to read *yišatab* for MT *yāšîṯ b-* and construed the verb thus concocted as an infixed *-t-* form of a root *šbb,* Ugar. *ṯbb* which he would find in 1 Aqht 108, 123 (*yṯb*) and in Gen xlix 24 (*wtšb*); Hos viii 6 (*šbbym*); Lam i 7d (*mšbth*); Ps lxxxix 45 (*hšbt*), meaning "to break." The existence of such a root in Ugaritic or Hebrew is doubtful. Arabic has a root *ṯbb,* "sit firm, be completed," but that meaning is unsuitable here. Overlooked by Blommerde is the interesting fact that in the myth of Baal's defeat of Prince Sea, at the very point that the coup de grâce is administered, one of the verbs is identical in consonantism to the problematic verb of the present verse (68:27): *yqṯ b'l wyšt ym,* "Baal cut down and—Sea," *ykly ṯpṭ nhr,* "He annihilated Chief River." There are several possible etymologies for the Ugaritic *wyšt,* e.g. *štt* and *šty* which in Arabic mean "scatter, disperse," and *šty,* "drink." Whatever the meaning of *wyšt* in the Ugaritic passage cited, it should be taken as a warning against emendation of the MT *yš*(*y*)*t* in the present line.

12a. *ever.* Literally "from your days?", i.e., "Did you ever in your life?"

12b. *Post.* Literally "cause(d) to know," i.e., Did you ever tell Dawn to get to his post? Dawn (*šaḥar*) is the same name as that used in the Ugaritic poem about "The Birth of the Beautiful and Gracious Gods," Dawn (*šḥr*) and Dusk (*šlm*). On this divine pair, cf. M. Pope in *Wörterbuch der Mythologie,* ed. H. W. Haussig, 1961, pp. 306 f. Each day is ordained by divine decree; Dawn is given its assignment daily.

13. Night cloaks the earth like a garment and under its cover the wicked carry out their crimes; cf. xxiv 13–17. But Dawn, as it were, snatches off the covering and shakes the wicked out as one would shake out dust or vermin from his clothing.

13a. The Qumran Targum preserves only vestiges of the phrase "Earth's skirts," *knp*[*y*] *'r*[' '], and the rest of verse is lost.

13b. *the wicked.* The letter ' of the word *rĕšā'îm* is suspended above the line here and in 15a, indicating a subsequent addition. If the original reading here were *ršym,* several possible derivations could be found to designate things that could be shaken out of a garment. G. R. Driver (JTS 4 [1953], 208–12) has argued that the wicked ones here are the evil stars or constellations, especially the Dog-star whose heliacic rising is associated with sickness and pestilence. Driver further discussed the possibility of relating *rš'ym* to *š'rym,* "hairy ones" (cf. Gr. *komētai*) in the light of the Arabic name for the Dog-star Sirius, *ši'ra,* "the hairy one," and Canis Major and Canis Minor as the "two hairy ones," *ši'rayān,* and concluded that these are the stars indicated by *rš'ym* here, whether the text is retained or emended.

14a. *It changes.* The subject is apparently the feminine noun Earth of 13a.

The usual interpretation of this line is that as a seal stamps form and design on an amorphous piece of clay, so the light of dawn causes the indistinct shapes of the night to stand out in sharp relief. Dhorme, however, took the phrase *ḥōmer ḥôṯām,* "clay of (the) seal," as designating the same material as the Ar. *ṭin maḫtūm, terra sigillata,* the sealing clay colored by minium or vermilion. The dawn causes the earth to take on such a reddish hue. Tur-Sinai related *ḥwtm* to Ar. *ḥawiyyat,* "reservoir, cistern," and read *ḥawwāṯām* (the approximate pronunciation), to arrive at the translation "—Their pool was turned as clay and they stood as in a garment—."

14b. *Tinted.* Reading *wĕtiṣṣāḇa',* "and it is dyed," for MT *wĕyiṯyaṣṣĕḇû,* "and they take their stand." Emendations are always hazardous, but standing like a garment, or even "as in a garment" (Tur-Sinai), makes little sense.

15a. The "light" of the wicked is darkness; cf. xxiv 13–17.

15b. *the upraised arm.* This expression, *zĕrô'a rāmāh,* "high arm," seems readily understandable as a metaphor for high-handed wickedness. G. R. Driver, however, in connection with the *rš'ym* of 13b above, appealed to Arabic astral idiom in which "arm" is applied to the extension of the constellation Leo, a band of visible stars (Sirius, Procyon, Castor, and Pollux) coinciding almost entirely with "the Navigator's Line." "In other words," Driver explained, "the clusters of stars are in a fashion shaken out of the heavens . . . as locusts out of a garment or leaves off a tree . . . and, at the same time, their light disappears and the line of stars by which sailors learn to steer their vessels, some of the brightest stars in the heavens, seem to be broken up as one star after another fades away before the oncoming light" (JTS 4 (1953), 211 f.).

NEB reveals in 12–15, as elsewhere, the influence of the erudition of Sir Godfrey Rolles Driver (cf. above on 13b and 15a):

12 In all your life have you ever called up the dawn
or shown the morning to its place?
13 Have you taught it to grasp the fringes of the earth
and shake the Dog-star from its place;
14 to bring up the horizon in relief as clay under a seal,
until all things stand out like the folds of a cloak,
15 when the light of the Dog-star is dimmed
and the stars of the Navigator's Line go out one by one?

16. Cf. xxviii 11.

17. Cf. xviii 13, xxviii 22; Pss ix 14, cvii 18; Isa xxxviii 10; Wisdom of Solomon xvi 13. The abode of Death (Mot) is the Netherworld; cf. vii 9, x 21–22, xi 8, xxvi 5, xxxiii 18; Ps lxxxviii 13; Ezek xxxii 18. In the Mesopotamian myth of the Descent of Ishtar into the Netherworld, the goddess has to pass seven gates; cf. ANET, p. 107.

18a. Cf. xxxiv 13.

19. Light and darkness were separated on the first day of Creation, Gen i 6, and thus have different abodes.

20. After light and darkness have completed their day's or night's work, they go home as does a laborer. The challenge is sarcastically put to Job to direct light and darkness to their respective homes.

21. The sarcasm and irony become sharper. Job must surely know these secrets, since, like the personification of Wisdom in Prov viii 22 f., he was born before creation and was an observer of the arrangements; cf. xv 7.

22. Cf. xxxvii 9; Deut xxviii 12; Jer x 13; Enoch xli 4, lx 11–21.

23. Cf. Ecclesiasticus xxxix 29, "In his storehouse, kept for the proper time, are fire, hail, famine, disease." Cf. Exod ix 22–26; Josh x 11; Isa xxviii 17, xxx 30; Ezek xiii 13; Hag ii 17. This verse is largely preserved in the Qumran Targum:

d[*y*] *l'dn* '[*qt*]'
lym qrb w'štdw[*r*]

Which [ ] for the time of t[roubl]e,
For a day of war and rebellion.

24a. *power.* The word *derek* may mean either "way" or "power," as in xxvi 14a, xl 19. Here it may be that both meanings are intended, including both the place or way as well as the power by which the division was performed.

flood. Noting the inapposite character of the parallelism of "light," *'ôr,* and *qāḏîm,* "east [wind?]," critics have made various emendations to rectify the situation, changing "light" to "wind," or on the basis of LXX reading *pachnē*—used also to translate the word *kĕpōr,* "hoar-frost," in vs. 29 below—changing *'ôr* to *kĕpōr* and *qāḏîm,* to *qārîm,* "cold." LXX also uses the word *pachnē* to translate *qîṭôr,* "smoke," in Ps cxix 83 and Beer, accordingly, proposed the change of *'ôr* to *qîṭôr.* It is clear that the Greek translator did not read *'ôr,* "light," and that he was guessing at the meaning of the word he did read. Since his guess was in the area of vapor, smoke, or the like, it seems probable (following Hoffmann, Bickell, Duhm, and Hontheim) that the original reading was *'ēḏ,* as in xxxvi 27. We have seen above that this word does not mean "mist" but designates the cosmic water reservoir. These waters were divided in the creation; cf. Gen i 6. NEB by reason of the parallelism of *'ôr* and *qāḏîm,* "(hot) east (wind)," rendered:

By what paths is the heat spread abroad
or the east wind carried far and wide over the earth?

divided. Dahood (*Psalms III,* first NOTE on Ps cxix 57) would interpret *ḥlq* here in the sense of "create," Ar. *ḫalaqa,* rather than "divide." This meaning has been recognized in Ecclesiasticus xxxi 13 and xxxviii 1 and Dahood adduces other possible instances, the most striking and convincing being Jer x 16 (= li 19) where *ḥlq* and *yṣr* stand in parallelism. In the present instance, however, *ḥlq* stands in parallelism with *p*(*w*)*ṣ,* "be dispersed, scattered," hence it seems best to take *ḥlq* in the sense of "divide." It is not unlikely that the ambiguity was intentional on the part of the poet.

24b. *east* [*wind*]. Without the word for "wind," as in xv 2, xxvii 21; Gen xli 6, 23, 27; Ps lxxviii 26; Isa xxvii 8; Hos xii 2, xiii 15.

The beginning of vs. 24 is lost in the Qumran Targum and the preserved part differs from MT:

. . . . . . *hyk' ypq*

wtšwb qdmwhy 'l 'r''

. . . . . . how it goes forth,
And blows before him over the earth.

MT's *qādîm*, "the (searing) east (wind)," is construed as the preposition *qŏḏām*, "before," but the lost portion must have included a word for wind as subject of the verb *tšwb* (from *nšb*, "blow").

25a. *channel*. The word (*tĕʻālāh*) is that used elsewhere of a trench around an altar, I Kings xviii 32, 35, or of conduits or aqueducts, Isa vii 3, xxxvi 2; Ezek xxxi 4. Cf. xxviii 26a which uses *ḥōq*, "groove," in a variant of this line.

downpour. Cf. Nah i 8; Ps xxxii 6; Dan ix 26 where this word (*šeṭep̄*) is used of flood waters. The verb of this root is fairly common in the OT in the sense of washing, rinsing, or overflowing of a stream. In Egyptian the apparent cognate *śtf* is used of the careful pouring in the preparation of medicinal concoctions.

25b. This line is identical with xxviii 26b.

Vs. 25 is perfectly preserved in the Qumran Targum:

mn šwy' lmṭr' zmn
w'rḥ l'nnyn qlylyn

Who set for the rain a time,
And a path for the swift clouds.

The word *tĕʻālāh*, "channel," is rendered as *zĕman*, "time." The time of the rain was of greater concern than the conduit through which it came. This reference to the time of the rain is reminiscent of the Ugaritic allusion to Baal's appointing the time for his rain in return for the permission to construct a house, quoted apropos of xxxvii 3a. On the "swift clouds," cf. xxviii 26.

26. Some interpreters consider this verse an important point in the poet's answer to Job's doubts about the goodness of God. The beneficent rains fall beyond the areas of human habitation, hence God cares also for his sub-human creatures, even the denizens of the desert. Job had imputed to the beasts, birds, and fish knowledge that God is responsible for injustice in the world, xii 6–10. He had also given a description of the misery of human beings forced to subsist in the wilderness, xxiv 4b–5, xxx 2–8. Peake charges Job with being self-centered and failing to see beyond his own misery and that of mankind in general to a Providence that extends beyond mankind. The Egyptian hymn to the solar deity Amon-Re attributes to that god providential care for all living things: the gods, cattle, mankind, and the lesser creatures, snails, gnats, worms, flies, and the mice in their holes (cf. ANET, p. 366b, vi).

27b. Reading *ṣāmē'*, "thirsty (land)," as in Isa xliv 3, for MT *môṣā'*, "place of issue," which is difficult here. Another attractive emendation is *miṣṣiyyāh*, "from the dry (ground)."

Vss. 26–27 are perfectly preserved in the Qumran Targum:

(26) *lhnḥth ʿl ʾrʿ mdbr dy lʾ ʾnš bh*
(27) *lhsbʿh šytʾ wšbyqh*
wlhnpqh ṣmḥy dtʾh

To make (it) descend on the desert land which has no man,
To drench shrub and scrub,
And to bring forth the sprouts of verdure.

Verse 26a, b is consolidated into a single line by combining the phrases *ʾrṣ lʾ ʾyš*, "land-of-no-man," and *mdbr lʾ ʾdm lw*, "desert which has no man in it." The MT *šʾh wmšʾh* is rendered by *šytʾ wšbyqh*, "thorn-bush and scrub," the former word being attested in Isa v 6; vii 23, 24, 25; ix 17; xxvii 4, and the latter found in the Targum Jonathan on Lev xxv 5 as the rendering of MT *sĕpîaḥ* (explained by Jastrow as "abandoned, spontaneous growth." The word *šyt* also occurs in the Sefîre Treaty (II 5), *wš]bʿ šnn šyt*, "and (for) seven years thorns . . ." The editors rendered "ronce et arbustes agristes."

28. Some critics have rejected this striking verse for reasons too absurd to discuss. The title "Father of Rain," used of the southwest wind of Arabia, is not really a parallel to this rhetorical question. J. T. Milik, *Rivista Biblica* 6 (1958), 252–54, suggests connection of this verse with the Ugaritic goddess Pidray.

28b. *drops*. This word (*ʾēḡel*) is unique in the OT, but the context leaves no question as to its meaning. The apparent cognate in Arabic is used of confining or restraining (cattle) and in the factitive stem of the collecting of water, as in a pool. Drops of water may be regarded as small confined collections.

The Qumran Targum reflects MT precisely in vss. 28–29:

hʾyty lmṭrʾ ʾb
ʾw mn yld [ʿ]nny ṭlʾ
wmn bṭn mn npq glydʾ
wšyqw[ʿ šmyʾ] m[n yld]h

Has the rain a father?
Or who bore the dew [c]louds?
And from whose womb came the ice?
And the hoar-fr[ost of heaven] wh[o bore]it?

30a. *hardens*. MT has "they (the waters) hide themselves/are hidden." Apparently the best way out of this difficulty is to regard the form *yiṯḥabbĕʾû* as a dialectical form of *yiṯḥammĕʾû*, meaning "harden," Ar. *ḥamaʾa;* cf. xxxvii 10.

The Qumran Targum preserves the greater part of vs. 30:

kʾ[bn] myn htqrmw mnh
wʾnpy mbl[ʾ . . . . .

Like stone waters are encrusted by it,
And the surface of [the] flood [ ]

The translation of MT *yiṯḥabbĕʼû* by *htqrmw* tends to support the conjecture offered above. The verb *qrm* is used in Ezek xxxvii 6, 8 of covering bones with skin and in post-biblical Hebrew and Aramaic it is applied to various covering and encrustations, the crust which forms on the rim of a cooking pot and on the surface of the liquid, the crust on bread in an oven, and the membrane around an egg. It is thus appropriate for the freezing of water which begins with a surface layer or crust.

31a. KJ's "sweet influences of the Pleiades" goes back to interpretations of Nachmanides and Gersonides of the thirteenth and fourteenth centuries, taken over by Christian exegetes of succeeding centuries. Sebastian Munster rendered, *"Numquid tu ligabis suaves influentias Pleiadum."* These suave influences were understood as astrological forces which produce the pleasant flowers and fruits in the springtime. The enigmatic wording of the KJ has given rise to other bizarre notions, even to the suggestion of a pre-Newtonian allusion to the forces of gravity. The crux of the difficulty is the meaning of *maʻăḏannôṯ* which occurs elsewhere only in I Sam xv 32. What appears to be the masculine plural form of the same word (*maʻăḏannîm*) is used in Gen xlix 20 and Lam iv 5 of fine foods, "dainties." The root of this form is obviously *ʻdn* which denotes various sorts of physical delights, including sexual pleasure, Gen xviii 12 (*ʻeḏnāh*). This is the hypothetical etymology behind the rendering "sweet influences." In I Sam xv 32 *maʻăḏannôṯ* is used of the manner of Agag's approach to Samuel. KJ's "delicately" and RSV's "cheerfully" reflect the same etymology. Moffatt's "with tottering steps" and AT's "trembling" derive the form from *mʻd,* "shake, totter." The only clue we have to Agag's emotional condition is his remark, "Surely the bitterness of death is past." This does not suggest that Agag was either cheerful or fearful. Perhaps he was insolent. In any case, he was resigned to death, and expected no mercy from Samuel. The sense "insolence, obstinacy," or the like, could be supported from the Ar. *ʻnd.* In the present passage, however, the form stands in apparent parallelism with a word which clearly means "bands." The verb *ʻnd* is used in xxxi 36 and Prov vi 21 with the meaning "bind." Though the parallelism may not be synonymous, this appears to be the best guess. If *maʻăḏannoṯ* here means "fetters," or the like, it might mean the same in the case of Agag, "And Agag came to him in fetters"; cf. S. R. Driver, *Notes on the Hebrew Text of the Books of Samuel,* 1913, pp. 129 f.

31b. Cf. NOTE on ix 9.

Only the end of 31a and the beginning of 31b are preserved in the Qumran Targum, [ ] *kymʼ ʼw syg npylʼ t*[ ]. For the Pleiades, the designation of the MT is used, but for Orion, *kĕsîl*, "the Fool," is rendered by *npyl'*, "the Giant." The word *syg* used for MT *môšĕkôṯ*, "bands," is interesting. In Song of Songs vii 3d the lady's waist is bound with a lotus girdle, *sûḡāh baššôšānnîm* (Syr. reads *dsyg' bšwšn'*).

32a. The word *mazzārôṯ* occurs only here and its identification is uncertain. The Vulg. renders *Lucifer* and some interpreters follow this lead, regarding the word as a designation of Venus as the morning and evening star. Others suggest the Hyades, whose rising at sunset was regarded as marking the beginning of the rainy season. Dhorme proposed the Corona Borealis. The form *mazzārôṯ*, however, may be merely a dialectical variant of *mazzālôṯ*, "constellations," II Kings xxiii 5, and as such might refer to some or all of the southern constellations of the zodiac.

32b. The identity of the constellation in question is uncertain. The word here used (*'ayiš*, in ix 9 *'āš*) is apparently cognate with Ar. *'ay(y)ūṯ*, "lion," which designates the constellation Leo which encroaches on Cancer. The Arabs see four of Virgo's stars as dogs barking after the lion. In spite of the confusion in zoological terms, most critics see here a reference to the Great Bear and "her children" as the Little Bear. KJ's "Arcturus with his sons" designates the constellation Boötes which appears to follow the Great Bear. For more recent discussion of the identity of these constellations, cf. G. R. Driver, JTS 4 (1953), 208–12 and JTS 7 (1956), 1–11. NEB renders "the cluster of the Pleiades," "Orion's belt," "the signs of the zodiac," and "Aldebaran and its train."

The Qumran Targum preserves only the end of 32b, . . .' *'l bnyh ty'š*. The verb *y'š*, cognate with Ar. *ya'isa*, "be in despair," is used in the Nip̄'al in Isa lvii 10; Jer ii 25, xviii 12; and once in the Pi'ēl, Eccles ii 20, "make despair," where Targ. uses the corresponding Aramaic form. It appears that the Qumran Targumist mistook MT *tanḥēm*, a Hip̄'îl form of *nḥy* plus the object suffix, for a Pi'ēl of *nḥm*, in the sense of "comfort, cause relaxation." This detail was not noted by the editors of the Qumran Targum and was called to the writer's attention by Mr. Bruce Zuckerman. The comment of Dhorme, in rejecting the proposal of Merx, Hitzig, et al. to read *tĕnaḥēm*, "will you console," applies to the rendering of the Qumran Targum: "It is difficult to see what astro-mythological legend would be alluded to by the idea of consolation offered to the Bear for the loss of its little ones."

33b. *rule.* The word *mišṭār* is hapax in the OT but cognate with Akk. *mašṭāru*, "writing." The starry sky in Akkadian is termed *šiṭir šamē* or *šiṭirtu šamāmi*, "heavenly writing." The participle of this root is applied to Egyptian foremen, Exod v 6 ff., and in II Chron xxvi 11 is associated with *sôp̄ēr*, "scribe," and elsewhere is parallel with words meaning chief, ruler, elder, prince, and the like, Num xi 16; Deut i 15, xvi 18, xx 5; Prov vi 7. In parallelism with the word "statutes" (*ḥuqqôṯ*), the sense "rule" appears most likely. Tur-Sinai has given an involved interpretation of this line in relation to Ps xix (*Archiv Orientální* 17, 2 [1949], 419–33).

34a. Cf. xxxvi 29b, 33a, xxxvii 2, 4.

34b. This line in Hebrew is verbatim with xxii 11b, but the contexts are different.

35. Cf. Baruch iii 33, 35.

36. The two words transliterated are very uncertain. The first occurs in Ps li 8 in parallelism with *sāṯûm,* "hidden," and lends some support to the guess that it means "inward parts," hence the Vulg. rendered *Qui posuit in visceribus hominis sapientiam?* The second word provoked some discussion among the Jewish sages. Rabbi Levi (Talmud Yerushalmi, Berakot ix 2) averred that at Rome the cock is thus called. Simeon-ben-Laqish was informed that this was the case in the region of Gennesaret (TB, Rosh-ha-Shanah 26a). The Jewish benediction "Blessed art thou, O Lord, our God, King of the World, who gives the cock (*śeḵwî*) intelligence to distinguish between day and night" derives from this verse. The supposed meaning "cock" suggests the possibility that the parallel word represents a bird noted for wisdom, and Dhorme took the word to refer to Thoth's bird, the ibis, which like the cock was renowned for wisdom. The ibis was thought to announce the rising of the Nile, as the cock in popular lore was believed to presage the rain; cf. J. A. Jaussen, "Le coq et la pluie dans la tradition palestinienne," RB 33 (1924), 574–82. Some critics, taking the cue from other meteorological items in the immediate context, conjecture that the words may refer to cloud and mist (so RSV), but the effort to find philological support for this interpretation is rather strained. J. G. E. Hoffmann was probably right in taking *ṭḥwt* to refer to the god Thoth himself. The consonantal orthography corresponds rather closely to the form of the name which prevailed in the Eighteenth Dynasty (*ḏḥwty*) when the worship of Thoth was at its peak and spread into Phoenicia; cf. W. F. Albright's review of P. Boylan's *Thoth, the Hermes of Egypt* in JPOS 2 (1922), 190–98, and especially p. 192. Philo of Byblos gives the Phoenician pronunciation as *Taaut(os)* which would reflect the form *ṯāḥûṯ,* with softening of the laryngeal; cf. the Neo-Babylonian form Tiḫut. On this Taautos in the light of the Ugaritic data, cf. O. Eissfeldt, *Taautos und Sanchunjaton* (Sitzungsberichte der Deutschen Akademie der Wissenschaften zu Berlin, Klasse für Sprachen, Literatur und Kunst, 1952, No. 1). The suggestion of Hoffmann as to *śeḵwî,* connecting it with the Coptic name of the planet Mercury (*souchi*), seems preferable to the dubious connection with the "cock." The all-knowing, clever minded Thoth-Taautos, inventor of the alphabet and founder of all knowledge, was identified with the Hermes-Mercury of the Greeks and Romans under the title Hermes Trismegistos/Trimaximus.

TEV offers a delightful interpretation:

> Who tells the ibis when the Nile will flood,
> or who tells the rooster that the rain will fall?

37b. Cf. Ps xxxiii 7.

38. Whether this verse applies to the state of the soil before or after the rain is disputed. The former condition seems more likely; cf. Deut xxviii 23; Lev xxvi 19. In the Ugaritic myth which treats of the death and resurrection of Baal, the furrows of the fields are described as "cracked" because of the lack of Baal's life-giving rains:

> Aloud cried El to the Virgin 'Anat,
> "Hear, O Virgin 'Anat,
> Tell the Lamp of the Gods Shapash:
> 'Cracked are the furrows of the field, O Shapash,
> Cracked the furrows of the vast fields.'
> Let Baal provide for [?] the furrows of the tilth.
> Where is the Mighty Baal?
> Where the Prince, Lord of Earth?" (49 III 22–49 IV 29.)

39. Cf. Ps civ 21.
40. Cf. xxxvii 8.
41. Cf. Ps cxlvii 9.

38. YAHWEH'S FIRST DISCOURSE (*continued*)
(xxxix 1–30)

XXXIX

1 "Do you know the birth season of the ibex,
Do you watch the calving of the hind,
2 Do you count the months they fulfill,
Mark the time they give birth?
3 They crouch and squeeze out their young,
Expel their foetus in the field.
4 Their offspring thrive, they grow;
They leave and do not return.
5 Who set the wild ass free,
Loosed the onager from his bonds?
6 His home I made the wilderness,
His dwelling the salt flats.
7 He scorns the city's tumult;
He hears no driver's shout.
8 He roams the hills for pasture,
Seeks any bit of green.
9 Will the buffalo deign to serve you,
Will he stay beside your crib?
10 Can you hold him in the furrow with rope,
Will he harrow the valley after you?
11 Can you rely on his great strength,
Can you leave your labor to him?
12 Can you trust him to return
And gather the grain of your threshing floor?
13 The ostrich's wings flap wildly,
Though her pinions lack feathers.
14 She lays her eggs on the ground,
Lets them be warmed in the dust.

15 Heedless that foot may crush them,
Some beast trample upon them.
16 Her young she harshly rejects,
Caring not if her labor be vain;
17 For God deprived her of wisdom,
Apportioned her no understanding.
18 When up she spreads her plumes,
She laughs at horse and rider.
19 Do you give the horse strength,
Clothe his neck with mane?
20 Do you make him leap like a locust,
His majestic snort a terror?
21 He paws violently, exults mightily;
He rushes to meet the fray.
22 He laughs at fear, undaunted;
He shies not from the sword.
23 About him rattles the quiver,
Flash spear and sword.
24 Mid rattle and roar he races,
Unchecked by trumpet sound.
25 At the trumpet call he says, 'Aha!'
He scents the battle from afar,
The roar of the captains and shouting.
26 Does the hawk soar by your wisdom,
Spread his wings to the south?
27 Does the eagle mount at your command,
The falcon make his nest on high?
28 On the cliff he dwells and lodges,
The rocky crag his stronghold.
29 Thence he spies out the prey,
His eyes see it from afar.
30 His young ones extract blood;
Where the slain are, there is he."

NOTES

xxxix 1a. *ibex.* Literally "wild goats of the rock." The ibex is still found in the rocky wilderness of the vicinity of Khirbet Qumran and En Gedi, as in David's time, I Sam xxiv 1, 2. The species is identified with the *Capra walu* or *Capra nubiana.* It inhabits the inaccessible cliffs, but still God's providence reaches it; cf. Ps civ 18. On efforts to preserve the species, cf. Herbert Weiner, *The Wild Goats of Ein Gedi,* 1963.

1b. *hind.* Before the denudation of the Palestinian woodlands in the present century, deer still survived. In earlier times, they were apparently abundant; cf. Gen xlix 21; Deut xii 15, xiv 5; II Sam xxii 34; I Kings iv 23; Ps xviii 33; Prov v 19.

2a. *count the months.* In the Ugarit epic of Aqhat the same expression is used of Danel who after being restored to virility and having impregnated his wife, sat down to count months. Because of lacunae in the text, it is not clear whether he was waiting for the birth or for the child to grow up. The same expression is used elsewhere of longevity and immortality. The goddess 'Anat offers immortality to the young hero Aqhat in exchange for his bow (2 Aqht vi 26–29):

> Ask for life, O Hero Aqhat,
> Ask for life and I will give it,
> Immortality and I will bestow it.
> I will make you count years with Baal,
> With El's sons you will count months.

3a. *crouch.* The same term is used of human accouchement, I Sam iv 19.

3b. *foetus.* The word *ḥēḇel* is used here in the sense of Ar. *ḥabal.* Because this word in Hebrew usually designates the pains of childbirth, this line has been misunderstood as depicting painful delivery rather than the easy and rapid parturition normal for wild animals.

in the field. Reading *babbār* of 4a with this line.

For this half verse the Qumran Targum has only two words:

wḥblyhn twšr

The editors render this as a question, "et fais-tu sortir leurs portées?" The verb *twšr* which renders MT *těšallaḥnāh,* "they send (forth)," is apparently a Hap̄'ēl form of *yšr,* "be straight, firm, healthy," but this verb is also attested in the Hap̄'ēl with the meaning "send forth," which sense is chosen by the editors as comporting with the meaning of the verb in MT. Apart from the context offered by MT, it would be very difficult for a translator to make sense of this line. LXX took the line to mean "and will you loosen their pangs?"

In the Qumran Targum there is no indication of MT *babbār* in either vss. 3 or 4. Vs. 4 reads:

yqšn bnyhn wypqn
npqw wl' tbw' 'lyhn

Their children mature and go forth,
They go forth and do not return to them.

5. Cf. vi 5, xi 12, xxiv 5; Gen xvi 12; Hos viii 9; Isa xxxii 14.
6a. Cf. Jer ii 24; Dan v 21; Ecclesiasticus xiii 19.
6b. *salt flats*. Cf. Jer xvii 6; Ps cvii 34.
The Qumran Targum renders MT precisely:

dy šwyt dḥšt byth
wmdrh b'r' mlyḥh

Whose house I have made the desert,
His dwelling in the salt land.

The word *dḥšt* used to render MT *'ărāḇāh* is not otherwise attested in Aramaic and the editors point out that it is a Persian loanword having the form *dašt* in modern Persian, but preserving the *ḥ* in Sogdian, *daxšt*.

8. *He roams*. The vocalization of MT *yĕṯûr* is odd and it has been taken as a noun, e.g., KJ JPS, "the range," but RSV "he ranges." The reduction of the vowel of the preformative, rather than pretonic lengthening, may be regarded as an Aramaism. Targ. reads *yĕ'allēl*, "he goes around, searches." The Qumran Targum reads:

wybḥr lh ṭwryn lm[ ]
[*w*]*btr kl yrwq yrdp*

And he chooses for himself every mountain for [pasture]
[And] after any greens he chases.

The verb *rdp*, "pursue," is used for MT *drš*, "seek."

9a. *buffalo*. KJ's "unicorn" (cf. Num xxiii 22, xxiv 8; Pss xxii 21, xxix 6, xcii 10; Isa xxxiv 7) derives from the LXX rendering *monokeros*. Vulg. has *rhinoceros*. The legend of the unicorn may have arisen from representation in profile showing only a single horn. That the beast (*rĕ'ēm, rêm*) had more than a single horn is clear from Deut xxxiii 17. The animal in question is the *Bos primigenius* which roamed Syria in ancient times. In one of the Ugaritic myths of Baal (IV AB), the god takes his bow and goes hunting among the marshes of Samak (Lake Huleh) which teem with buffalo (*tk aḫ šmk mlat rumm*). Hunting this dangerous beast was a favorite sport of royalty. Tiglathpileser I killed a *rîmu* in Syria and Shalmaneser III had the beast portrayed among the items of tribute on his famous Black Obelisk. The great Ishtar Gateway of Babylon depicts the mighty beast in glaze. In Akkadian metaphor, as in the OT, the *rîmu* represents power (cf. Num xxiii 22, xxiv 8; Pss xxii 21, xxix 6, xcii 10; Isa xxxiv 7). Cf. A. H. Godbey, "The Unicorn in the Old Testament," AJSL 56 [1939], 256–96.

9b. Cf. Isa i 3.

10–12. Cf. Prov xiv 4.

10a. With LXX omitting *rêm* as unnecessary and possibly a scribal plus.

10b. *after you.* Apparently in harrowing, as opposed to plowing, the animal was led.

12a. Following the Kethib *yāšûḇ* instead of Qere *yāšîḇ*.

12b. Placing the caesura after *yāšûḇ* in the preceding colon, and reading *wĕzera' gornĕkā* for MT *zar'eḵā wĕgornĕḵā*.

13–18. This description of the ostrich was omitted in the original LXX and is rejected as an interpolation by some critics. Certainly the ostrich is a remarkable bird and its bizarre and grotesque appearance and behavior is bound to impress anyone who sees it. The seeming stupidity of this creature proves the wisdom and providential care of its Creator.

13a. *The ostrich's.* In spite of the confusion of the versions (on which cf. Dhorme), it is now generally agreed that the creature designated by the unique term *rĕnānîm* is the female ostrich, so named because of her cries which are less shrill than those of the male. Dhorme noted that in 1737 Schultens had already counted as many as twenty different interpretations of this verse, and added a few more recent ones. The list could be greatly enlarged from modern free translations, of which a couple of samples may suffice. NEB rendered:

> The wings of the ostrich are stunted;
> her pinions and plumage are so scant.

TEV translated:

> How fast the wings of an ostrich beat!
> But no ostrich can fly like a stork.

and added a note that "Verse 13 in Hebrew is unclear."

flap wildly. Literally "rejoice." The root here used (*'ls*) is found elsewhere only in xx 18 and Prov vii 18, although a similar root (*'lṣ*) with the same sense occurs several times.

13b. This line as it stands is a jumble of words—"If wing stork and feathers (?)." The apparent mention of the stork (*ḥăsîḏāh*, "devoted one [?]") suggests a contrast between the parental instincts of the two birds, but this is unsupported by any further reference to the stork. The most attractive emendation is the change of *ḥăsîḏāh,* "stork," to *ḥăsērāh,* "lacks." The word *nôṣāh* occurs in the sense of "feathers, plumage" in Lev i 16; Ezek xvii 3, 7, cognate with Akk. *nâṣu* in the same sense. The ostrich's wings, though absurdly small, are beautifully plumed.

14a. *lays.* We accept the suggestion of Dahood (JBL 78 [1959], 303–9) that the verb *'zb* here means "put, place," cognate with Ugaritic *'db*. The ostrich does not really abandon its nest. The hen and the cock take regular turns brooding, the cock taking his turn at sundown and during the night when his darker plumage makes him less conspicuous than the hen; cf. Mrs. Annie Martin, *Home Life on an Ostrich Farm* (1890), p. 117.

14b. In the Physiologus (an allegorical natural history which originated in Egypt in the second century B.C.) we are told that the ostrich lays her eggs in the sand and goes away and forgets them and the heat of the sun hatches them. This notion that the ostrich depends on the heat of the sun to hatch the eggs might naturally arise from the observation that the ostrich scatters many eggs outside the nest. The Arab author Kazwini, (thirteenth century A.D.) in his Cosmography tells us that the ostrich divides her eggs (usually twenty or more) into three groups and hatches only one third. When the chicks are hatched, she breaks one group of eggs to feed them. Later when they are larger she breaks the other group and the young feed on the vermin which collect on the broken eggs. Cf. B. Laufer, "Ostrich Egg-shell Cups of Mesopotamia and the Ostrich in Ancient and Modern Times," Field Museum of Natural History, Chicago, Anthropology Leaflet 23 (1926), 9–14. Mrs. Martin (*Home Life . . . ,* p. 123) reports that during the short time the hen is off the nest she is careful to cover the eggs with a good pinch of sand to protect them from the sun.

15. The observations relayed to Delitzsch by Wetzstein from the Arab ostrich hunters (Delitzsch, II, pp. 339–43) are extremely interesting and some are relevant to the present context. The eggs are barely covered and easily become prey to jackals and other predators. Wetzstein was told that when the ostrich observes that its nest is discovered, it tramples on its own eggs and makes its nest elsewhere. Mrs. Martin (*Home Life . . . ,* p. 128) reported a case of a cock deliberately trampling all the eggs in the nest in a fit of temper after his favorite hen had been removed.

16. The alleged cruelty of the ostrich to its young is mentioned also in Lam iv 3:

> Even the jackals offer the breast
> And give suck to their young,
> But my people's daughters are cruel
> Like ostriches in the desert.

There appears to be no reliable evidence to support this notion. On the contrary, the ostrich in the wild state is reported to display great solicitude and devotion for its young and to defend them in case of danger; cf. Laufer, "Ostrich Egg-shell Cups . . . ," p. 12. Captivity, however, has undermined the bird's parental instincts and it is reported that the old birds have no regard for incubator chicks and will attack them (*ibid.*, p. 49).

16b. *Caring not.* Literally, "At the emptiness of her toil with fear." Dahood (NWSPJ, p. 74) related the word *paḥaḏ* to Ugar. *pḫd,* "flock," and translated: "In vain is her toil—without a flock."

17. This judgment on the ostrich's intelligence is understandable, even if not entirely fair in comparison with other creatures. Pliny thought the bird silly because it imagined that when its head was thrust in a bush, the whole body was concealed. Diodorus Siculus (II 50.6), however, regarded this as wisdom in that the bird was protecting its weakest part. Seneca (Moral Essays, *On Firmness* xvii.1) relates an incident in which the insult of being called an ostrich, and a bare one at that (*struthocamelum depilatum*) so enraged the victim (one Cornelius Fido) that he wept. Among the Arabs the stupidity of the ostrich is proverbial *'aḥmaq min en-na'āme,* "more stupid than the ostrich." (Cf. Laufer, "Ostrich Egg-shell Cups . . . ," pp. 26 f.; F. Rosenthal, *A History of Muslim Historiography,* 1952, p. 254.) The peculiarities of this amazing bird are elaborated in order to suggest that, in spite of its stupidity, God looks after it and gives it speed greater even than that of a horse.

18a. The unique verbal form, as Wetzstein suggested, appears to be a hunting expression. Explanation of the word from an Arabic verb meaning to "strike the ground [of hooves]" is unsatisfactory. Tur-Sinai appears on the right track when he suggests connection with the hapax *mur'āh* in Lev i 16. The expression *mur'āṯô bĕnôṣāṯāh* refers to the protuberance above the anus with the feathers which are cut off and tossed in the refuse. The use of the Hip̄'îl which commentators find difficult (cf. Dhorme) is quite natural with a denominative verb. The spread of the ostrich's plumes as she flees impressed the Arab poets. Wetzstein cites the poet Rashid "And the head [of the bride with its loosened locks] resembles the [soft and black] feathers of the ostrich-hen, when she spreads them out. They saw the hunter coming upon them where there was no hiding place, / And stretched their legs as they fled." According to Wetzstein, the hunters reported that if the ostrich has the wind behind, it spreads its tail feathers like a sail and uses its wings for steering.

18b. "Swifter than the ostrich" is an Arab expression for the acme of speed. Xenophon (*Anabasis* I.v.2) relates an encounter with ostriches and how they outdistanced the horses. Mrs. Martin (*Home Life . . . ,*

p. 113) tells of pursuit of horse and rider by an ostrich which was able to deliver an occasional well-placed kick to the speeding horse.

19b. *mane*. The word *ra'māh* in the sense of "thunder" is not very appropriate to a horse's neck. The versions guess wildly (LXX *phobon*, "fear[?]"; Vulg. *hinnitum*, "neighing"; Targ. *tuqpā'*, "power"; Syr. *zînā'*, "armor"). What clothes a horse's neck is the mane. Bochart already in his *Hierozoicon* interpreted the word in this sense, and so too Gesenius (later rejected by Buhl) explained the word as "a trembling, quivering, shuddering," poetically for the mane of a horse and compared the Gr. *phobē*, "mane," from *phobos*, "fear." KB (p. 901) cites the Arabic designation of the hyena *umm ri'm*, "mother of the mane," which should remove all doubt as to the meaning of the word in the present context. The poet doubtless intended a play on words.

20a. Cf. Joel ii 4 f.; Rev ix 7.

LXX does not translate MT of this line, but appears to paraphrase the preceding half verse 19b, "And have you clad him in panopoly?" The Qumran Targum preserves only a fragment of 20a, *htzy'nh btqp*, "Can you make him leap with power . . . ?"

20b. LXX made this line approximate the sense of 19b, "And have you made his breast glorious with courage?" Syr. rendered "And do you terrify him with fear?" The Qumran Targum reads *bsḥrwhy 'ymh wdḥlh* "With his snorting terror and fear." The term *sḥr* used for MT *nḥr* is cognate with Ar. *šḫr*, "neigh, bray."

21a. *paws*. Literally "digs." The final *w* of MT *yḥprw* is to be deleted or transposed to the beginning of the verb.

violently. Here *bĕ'ēmeq* does not mean "in the valley," but "with force," exactly synonymous with *bĕḵōaḥ*, "with strength," i.e., "mightily." The word *'mq* in Akkadian has the meanings "deep, strong, wise" and is used in the Ugaritic texts both in the sense of "valley" and "strength." In Jer xlvii 5, "remnant of their valley" (KJ) probably means "remnant of their power"; cf. Albright, WIANE, p. 14; Dahood, *Biblica* 40 (1959), 166.

The Qumran Targum reads:

> *wḥpr bbq' wyrwṭ wyḥd'*
> *wbḥyl ynpq l'npy ḥrb*
>
> And he paws in the valley and runs and rejoices,
> And with might he goes against the sword.

The change of MT *b'mq* to *bbq'* makes it clear that the translator did not recognize *'mq* in the sense of "power." LXX reads "in the plain" in both lines, either a double translation of *b'mq* or reflection of a text with *b'mq* in one line and *bbq'* in the other.

23a. *rattles*. The verb form *tirneh* is hapax and puzzling. The vocalization *tārōnnā,* suggested by Dahood (NWSPJ, p. 74), as in Prov i 20, viii 3, appears likely, the ending *-nna* being "energic."

The Qumran Targum reads:

> *'lwhy ytlh šlṭ šnn*
> *wnzk wḥrp syp*

The editors translate:

> Au-dessus de lui est levée la lance aiguë,
> et le javelot et l'épée tranchante.

The term *šlṭ* used to translate Mt *'ašpāh,* "quiver," in Syriac usually means "a quiver," but also designates a weapon, according to Bar Bahlûl. The term occurs in the Qumran War Scroll (1QM VI 2) in association with the word *zrq,* and is counted among seven *zrqwt* which are to be inscribed with appropriate messages of divine wrath and hurled at the sinful foe. Y. Yadin (*The Scroll of the War of the Sons of Light against the Sons of Darkness,* 1962, p. 284) translates *šlṭ* as simply "weapon," "on the second weapon they shall write 'Sparks of blood to fell the slain by the anger of God,' on the third dart they shall write 'Glitter of a sword devouring the sinful slain by the judgement of God.'" It is not clear which word of MT is reflected in the term *nzk,* a word which the editors note is not otherwise attested in Aramaic or Hebrew but is manifestly related to the Arabic verb *nzk,* "pierce with a spear," denominative from the Persian loanword *naizak,* "short lance." The final word of MT, *kîḏôn,* has been taken as designating a spear or dart. From the uses of the term in the Qumran War Scroll, Y. Yadin (ibid., pp. 129–32) concluded that the implement in question is a kind of sword rather than a spear or lance. G. Molin (JSS 1 [1956] 334–37) equated the *kîḏôn* with the so-called sickle sword. Y. Yadin (*The Art of Warfare in Biblical Lands* [1963], p. 172) asserts that this peculiar weapon developed from the ax, as a cutting, rather than a thrusting, weapon. The present writer inclines to the view that the "sickle-sword" was not used in ordinary warfare, but was a divine weapon wielded by deities and used by kings for sacrifice of captives and carried as an emblem; the argument for this tentative view will be presented elsewhere. The editors of the Qumran Targum do not comment on the two words *wḥrp syp* which appear to be the translation of MT *kîḏôn* and which they render "et l'épée tranchante." The verb *ḥpr* has the meanings "grind, sharpen," and the noun *ḥarpā* or *ḥcrpā* in Syriac designates a blade, or sword. The term *syp* is used in post-biblical Hebrew, Aramaic, and Arabic for "sword," presumably related to the factitive stem of the verb *s(w)p,* "come to an end," *lĕsayyēp,* "to exterminate," and in neo-Hebrew "to fence," *siyyûp̄,* "swordplay." In the light of the Qumran Targum's use of two terms suggestive of the meaning "sword," it seems advisable to change the previous rendering "javelin" to "sword."

24a. *races.* Literally "swallows ground." Cf. the Arabic expression "the horse swallows up the ground," *iltaḥama-l-farasu-l-arḍa.*

24b. *Unchecked.* If the text is correct, it is difficult to see how the verb can have its usual meaning, "believe"—"he does not believe that/when it is the sound of the trumpet," i.e., he is so overjoyed that he can scarcely believe the battle call has sounded. Most moderns take the verb in the sense of "show firmness," i.e., "remain still." This is admittedly far from satisfactory, but the emendations so far suggested are no better. The Qumran Targum omits this verse, except for an overlapping of the end of 24b and the beginning of 25a, *qôl šôp̄ār* and *bĕd̠ê šôp̄ār* being rendered by *wlql qrn',* "and the sound of the horn," which has to go with vs. 25 since there is no trace of the MT clause *lô' ya'ămîn kî* which precedes *qôl šôp̄ār.*

25a. *call.* The word *bĕd̠ê,* as indicated by the Masoretic vocalization, is construed as composed of the preposition *bĕ* (the *b pretii*) and the word *day, dê,* "sufficiency," equivalent to the more common form *kĕd̠ê,* "according to the sufficiency of. . . ." Hence JPS renders "as oft as," RSV "when." It is possible, and perhaps preferable, to connect the word with the Ugaritic *bd,* "song," and to construe it as adverbial, "at the call of the trumpet," reading *bad̠* or *baddê.* Cf. xi 3, xli 4.

Aha. Heb. *he'āh.* A cry of joy; cf. Isa xliv 16; Ezek xxv 3.

The Qumran Targum reads:

> *wlql qrn' y'mr h'ḥ*
> *wmn rḥyq yryḥ qrbh*
> *wlnqšt zyn wz'qt 'štdwr yḥdh*
>
> And at the sound of the horn he says, 'Aha!'
> And from afar he sniffs the battle,
> And at the clash of arms and the clamor of war he rejoices.

The addition of the verb *yḥdh,* "he rejoices," was probably prompted by a feeling that the latter line is incomplete. This pattern, however, is the usual one in Ugaritic poetry and is also common in biblical poetry, the verb of the first line serving also for the second.

26b. *to the south.* It is not clear whether the reference is to seasonal migration (cf. Jer viii 7), or whether south (*têmān*) here means the (strong) south-wind, as in Ps lxxviii 26; Song of Songs iv 16. The preposition (*lĕ*) is imprecise.

The Qumran Targum reads:

> *hmn ḥkmtk yst'r nṣ'*
> *wyprws knpwh[y] lrwḥyn*

Is it by your wisdom that the hawk soars,
And spreads his wings to the winds?

The MT hapax *ya'ăḇer* is rendered by the reflexive form of *s'r* and the editors suggest that it may be a denominative from Heb. *s'rh,* "tempest." The south-wind is changed to the general term for winds.

27a. *eagle.* Cf. ix 26 and NOTE; Prov xxx 18–19. The term (*nešer*) in the OT designates both eagles and vultures, including the golden eagle and the carrion vulture.

27b. *falcon.* MT reads *kî,* "that." LXX has *gups,* "vulture," in chiastic parallelism with *aetos,* "eagle." J. Reider (VT 4 [1954], 294) related MT *ky* to Ar. *ky,* "pelican," and cited further a Syriac source which explained *ky* as the ibis, "the type of bird that inhabits rocky cliffs, on the ledges of which it builds its nest." Reider in translating the verse prudently eschewed both pelican and ibis and chose LXX's vulture: "This interpretation raises at once a weak verse to a high level of perfection: 'Does the eagle mount up at thy command, and does the vulture make her nest on high?' " The Qumran Targum is almost complete in this verse and accords with LXX:

'w 'l m'mrk ytgb[*h*] *nš*[*r'*]
w'wz' yrm qnh

Or is it by your word the eagle mounts,
And the falcon makes its nest on high?

The editors render *'wz'* as "l'aigle noir," apparently on the basis of the Targ. on Lev xi 13 and Deut xiv 12 which renders *'ozniyyāh* as *'ûzyā.* In any event, some poetic synonym for *nešer* stood in chiastic parallelism in the *Vorlage* used by the Qumran Targumist. The letters *ky* of MT provoke speculation that they might be the remnant of a poetic name for a high flyer, a lofty nester. Just such a word is found in *kîḏôr,* employed in xv 24b in a metaphor which may be derived from falconry, or at least from observation of such birds of prey.

28. Cf. Jer xlix 16.

29. Cf. Deut xxviii 49; Jer xlviii 40, xlix 22; Ezek xvii 3; Hab i 8.

30a. Cf. Prov xxx 17.

extract. The verb *yĕ'al*(*lĕ*)*'û* is hapax and efforts to explain it without emendation have not been convincing. Tur-Sinai suggested that it is an "enlarged form" of '(*w*)*l,* "suck (mother's) milk," and that perhaps we should read *yĕ'al'ălû.* The usual expedient is to lop off the offending ' at the beginning and relate it to Syr. *l*(*w*)', "lap up, lick up," and Ar. *wlġ,* with the same sense. Dhorme emended to *yālō'û,* "they lap up," and suggested that the superfluous ' is perhaps a *mater lectionis.* Dhorme cited Aelianus (*De nat. anim.* x.14) for the datum that the young of the eagle eat flesh and drink blood. Nevertheless, sipping or sucking does not seem appropriate to the action of an eagle whose beak is scarcely suited to the task. There is an Arabic verb *'lḍ* which could be connected with *'l'* viewed as an Aramaism with the final ' representing an original *ḍ* which might be written with either ' or *q*. The meaning of Ar. *'lḍ* is given as "shake a thing (in order) to pull it out" which seems more appropriate to the action of a bird of prey picking at bloody flesh than does a verb meaning to suck, sip, or lap. It is difficult to find a suitable poetic term for this method of ingesting blood but it seems that "extract" may be the best choice.

30b. A proverbial saying. Cf. Matt xxiv 28; Luke xvii 37, "Where there is a corpse, the eagles/vultures will flock."

39. JOB CHALLENGED; YAHWEH'S SECOND DISCOURSE
(xl 1–24; xli 1–8)

XL 1 Yahweh answered Job and said:

2 "Will the contender with Shaddai yield?
He who reproves God, let him answer for it."

3 Job answered Yahweh and said:

4 "Lo, I am small, how can I answer you?
My hand I lay on my mouth;
5 I have spoken once, I will not reply;
Twice, but I will say no more."

6 Then Yahweh answered Job
From out of the storm and said:

7 "Gird your loins like a hero;
I will ask you, and you tell me.
8 Would you annul my judgment,
Condemn me that you may be justified?
9 Have you an arm like God,
Can you thunder with a voice like his?
10 Deck now yourself with grandeur and majesty;
Be arrayed in glory and splendor.
11 Let loose your furious wrath;
Glance at every proud one and humble him.
12 Glance at every proud one and abase him;
Tread down the wicked where they stand.
13 Bury them in the dust together;
Bind them in the infernal crypt.

14 Then I will acknowledge to you
That your own right hand can save you.
15 Behold now Behemoth,
Which I made as well as you;
Grass he eats like an ox.
16 See the strength in his loins,
The power in his massive belly.
17 His tail arches like a cedar;
The thews of his thighs intertwine.
18 His bones are tubes of bronze,
His gristles like iron bars.
19 He is a primordial production of God;
His maker may bring near his sword.
20 The beasts of the steppe relax;
All the creatures of the wild play there.
21 Under the lotus he lies,
In covert of reed and fen.
22 The lotus gives him shade,
The wadi willows surround him.
23 Unperturbed though the river rage,
Though the torrent surge to his mouth.
24 Who would grasp him by his eyes?
Pierce his nose with barbs?

XLI 1 Can you draw out Leviathan with a hook, [xl 25]*
Press down his tongue with a cord?
2 Put a cord through his nose, [26]
Pierce his jaw with a hook?
3 Will he make long pleas to you, [27]
Cajole you with tender words?
4 Will he make a covenant with you, [28]
Will you take him as eternal slave?
5 Play with him like a bird, [29]
Leash him for your girls?
6 Will mongers haggle over him, [30]
Divide him among the hucksters?

* Verse numbers in Hebrew Bible.

7 Will you fill his hide with harpoons, [31]
His head with fishing spears?
8 Just lay your hand on him; [32]
Remember the battle, don't try again.

Notes

xl 1–5. Critics find great difficulty with these lines in their present position. Nevertheless, if they are retained, they fit better as the conclusion to Yahweh's first speech than in any other place. Vulg. makes this connection by including these verses with ch. xxxix.

1. This verse is missing in LXX.

2a. Reading the participial form *rāḇ* for the infinitival form *rōḇ* of MT, thus making it the subject rather than the main verb, and changing the unique nominal form *yissôr,* "professional disciplinarian, faultfinder [?]," to *yāsûr,* "he will turn aside, yield." This comports with the structure of the parallel line and with the interpretations given by the versions.

4b. Cf. xxi 5b, xxix 9.

5. Cf. xxxiii 14; Ps lxii 12. Only a vestige of this verse is preserved in the Qumran Targum, the letters *swp* apparently reflecting the final verb of MT *'wsyp.* The entire verse, however, is repeated between xlii 4 and 5 and the verb there is written *'wsp.*

6. Identical with xxxviii 1 (except for omission of the article before *sĕ'ārāh,* "storm"), introducing a second speech of Yahweh from the storm. Many critics assume that originally there was a single speech by Yahweh (xxxviii 2–xxxix 30, xl 2) and a single submissive reply by Job (xl 4–5, xlii 2–6).

7. Identical with xxxviii 3.

8. Job had indeed denied divine justice in his own case and even in the world at large; cf., e.g., ix 22. His outbursts were considered blasphemous by the rabbis, but excusable under the circumstances since "No man is taken to account for what he speaks in distress; Job spoke as he did because of his dire afflictions" (TB, Baba Bathra 16b).

9a. *arm.* Symbol of power, human and divine; cf. xxii 8; Exod xv 16; Pss lxxvii 15, lxxxix 13, xcviii 1; Isa xl 10, li 5, lix 16, etc.

9b. Cf. xxxvii 2–5. The logic of the argument here is similar to that used by Elihu. Since man has not God's power, he has no right to question God's justice; cf. xxxiii 12, xxxvi 22–23.

10. In effect, Job is invited to assume the royal attributes of divine office; cf. Pss xxi 6, xlv 4, civ 1.

11a. *Let loose.* Literally "scatter," as in xxxvii 11. The divine wrath which Job is challenged to loose is figured as the lightning.

11b, 12a. These lines are identical except for the synonymous verbs "humble" and "abase." If not accidental preservation of a variant, the repetition must be for emphasis.

13a. *the dust.* The netherworld as in x 9, xxxiv 15. Cf. Gen iii 19; Isa xxix 4; Ps xxii 29; Eccles iii 20. Cf. the expression "covered with the dust of the nether world" in Inanna's Descent to the Netherworld, ANET, p. 53, line 44.

13b. *them.* Literally "their faces," i.e., their persons; cf. II Sam xvii 11; Pss xlii 5, 11, xliii 5; Prov vii 15.

the infernal crypt. Literally "the hidden (place)," a circumlocution for the netherworld. On this term and similar ones for the netherworld, cf. Tromp, p. 46.

The Qumran Targum is well-preserved in vss. 6–12 and part of 13 and is given here with interlinear translation:

(6) *'n' 'lh' l'ywb*
God answered Job
[Mn rwḥ'] w'nn' w'mr lh
[From the wind] and the cloud and said to him
(7) *'sr n' kgbr ḥlsyk*
Gird now like a man your loins
'š'lnk whtybny ptgm
I will ask you and you answer me
(8) *h'p t'd' dynh*
Will you set aside judgment
wtḥybnny 'l dbrt dy tzk'
And make me guilty so that you may be clean?
(9) *'w h' dr' k'lh 'yty lk*
Or have you an arm like God?
'w bql kwth tr'm
Or with voice like his can you thunder?
(10) *h'dy n' gwh wrm rwḥ*
Remove now pride and haughty spirit
wzwy whdr wyqr tlbš
And with splendor, glory, and honor be clothed
(11) *h'dy n' ḥmt rgzk*
Remove now the venom of your anger
wḥz' kl g'h whšplh
And see every proud one and abase him
(12) *wkl rmt rwḥ ttbr*
And every haughty one of spirit do you break
whṭpy ršy'[yn tḥ]tyhwn
Snuff out the wicked on the spot

(13) *wṭmr [yt]hwn b'pr kḥ[d']*
And hide them in the dust together
[ ]*ṭm tksh*
cover

A few observations may be offered where there is significant deviation from MT. MT *'ăḏēh* in 10a, "deck, adorn," (*'dh* II) is mistakenly read as the Hap'ēl of *'dh* I, "remove," conforming to the translation of *hāp̄ēṣ* in 11a. In 12b the hapax *hăḏōḵ* is rendered by the Hap̄'ēl imperative of *ṭpy*. There is no need to change the verb to a noun *hôḏěḵā*, "your splendor" (cf. M. Dahood, *Biblica* 49 [1968], 509–10, and *Psalms III*, p. XXIX, n. 15). As Guillaume noted, Ar. *hadaka*, "demolish," offers a very satisfactory sense.

In 13b MT *ḥbš* appears to have been rendered by *ksh*, "cover," thus supporting the translation of Guillaume, "Veil their faces in the grave," with relation of the verb to Ar. *ḥabasa* which has both the senses "bind" and "veil."

14b. Cf. Judg vii 2; I Sam xxv 26, 33; Pss xliv 3, xcviii 1; Isa lix 16, lxiii 5. If Job could do what he charges God has neglected to do, then he could save himself.

15a. *Behemoth*. An apparent plural of the common noun *běhēmāh*, "beast, cattle." The verbs used with the noun in this passage are third person masculine singular thus indicating that a single beast is intended and that the plural form here must be the so-called intensive plural or plural of majesty, The Beast, par excellence. LXX renders *thēria*, "animals," and similarly Targ., but Vulg. and Syr. transliterate the word and take it to refer to a single animal. Some interpreters have understood the term to apply to the elephant. However, since Bochart most modern critics have identified the animal in question as the hippopotamus. It has been suggested that the word Behemoth itself is derived from a hypothetical Egyptian compound *p'-iḥ-mw*, "the ox of the water," but no such word has yet been found in Coptic or Egyptian and no known Egyptian designation of the hippopotamus bears any close resemblance to the word Behemoth. The descriptions of Behemoth and Leviathan (cf. xl 25 ff.) are indeed vivid and detailed enough to convince most moderns that the creatures are the two most impressive of Egypt's numerous fauna, the ponderous hippopotamus and the extremely fierce and dangerous crocodile. If this were the case, one might wonder why less puzzling terms were not used. Actually there are considerations which militate against the view that the animals described are creatures from the natural world. Both the hippopotamus and the crocodile were killed and captured by the Egyptians, whereas Leviathan at least is represented as too powerful and ferocious for mere man to dare to come to grips with it. (Cf. T. Säve-Söderburgh, *On Egyptian Representations of Hippopotamus*

Hunting as a Religious Motive, Horae Soederblomianae, III, 1953.) This point, of course, should not be pressed for Egyptian texts also speak of the crocodile as too terrible to approach. In view of the long recognized mythological and supernatural character of Leviathan (cf. Cheyne, *Job and Solomon,* 1887, p. 56; *Encyclopaedia Biblica,* s.v. "Behemoth" and "Leviathan"; Toy, *Judaism and Christianity,* 1891, pp. 162 f.; Gunkel, *Schöpfung und Chaos,* pp. 57, 61 ff.), now clearly established by the Ugaritic myths, it is in order to question again the interpretation of Behemoth as the hippopotamus. The plural form *bĕhēmôṯ* occurs elsewhere in the OT in Pss viii 8, l 10, lxxiii 22; Joel i 20, ii 22; Hab ii 17 without hint of mythological implications. In Enoch lx 7–9, however, we are informed that Behemoth and Leviathan were separated, the one to dwell in the wilderness and the other in the sea. In IV Ezra vi 49–52 and the Apocalypse of Baruch xxiv 4 the two beasts are said to have been created on the fifth day to be food for the righteous in the messianic age. The eschatological interpretation tends to confirm the mythological character of both beasts. The allusion in Enoch is particularly provocative. Enoch contains a number of other mythological allusions which preserve echoes of ancient pagan mythology. The juxtaposition of Behemoth and Leviathan in Job and in the post-biblical texts cited above suggests that Behemoth, like Leviathan in the Ugaritic texts, had a prototype in pre-Israelite mythology and that the monsters were connected in some ancient myth or played similar roles in different myths. Now, among the several monsters which the violent goddess 'Anat boasts of having conquered along with Leviathan there is mention of a bovine creature called *'gl il 'tk* which may be rendered conjecturally "the ferocious bullock of El" or "the monstrous, ferocious bullock" (the element *il* sometimes indicates the superlative; cf. D. Winton Thomas, VT 3 [1953], 209–24). Unfortunately, we learn nothing further about this particular beast in the Ugaritic texts so far recovered. However, the reference in Enoch to the effect that Behemoth is assigned to the wilderness recalls another Ugaritic myth. In the fragmentary text designated BH, El contrives a diabolical plot to undo his enemy, Baal. Laughing in his heart and chuckling in his liver, El sends out divine handmaids into the wilderness equipped with obstetrical paraphernalia and instructed there to give birth to creatures called "Eaters" (*aklm*) and "Devourers" (*'qqm*). The bovine nature of these monsters is explicit:

On them are horns like bulls	*bhm qrnm km trm*
And humps like buffalo,	*wgbtt km ibrm*
And on them the face of Baal.	*wbhm pn b'l*

As El had planned, Baal goes out into the wilderness and sees these beasts which arouse his instincts as a hunter. Somehow in the attempt to bag them, Baal himself is felled like a bull or a buffalo in a miry swamp and fever racks his body. With Baal thus incapacitated, drought and infertility ensue for a period of seven or eight years. We venture to suggest here, pending further study, that the monstrous bullock of the Ugaritic myths and Behemoth are both connected with the Sumero-Akkadian "bull of heaven" slain by Gilgamesh and Enkidu in the Gilgamesh Epic (ANET, pp. 83–85). While nothing is said in the Gilgamesh Epic of the Bull of Heaven having an anthropoid face (as in the Ugaritic characterization of the Eaters or Devourers cited above) still the frequent occurrence of bearded human-faced bulls in Mesopotamian glyptic art from Early Dynastic times on (cf., e.g., A. Moortgat, *Vorderasiatische Rollsiegel,* Pls. 23–26, and E. Porada and B. Buchanan, *Corpus of Ancient Near Eastern Seals,* 1948, I, Pls. IX–X [Nos. 53, 56, 57, 60] and XXII–XXVI), often in combat with a hero, suggest a connection of this figure with the Bull of Heaven in the Gilgamesh Epic and the bovine monsters with the face of Baal in the Ugaritic myth. Now, it is true that in the passage in Job there is no intimation of bovine character of Behemoth apart from the reference to its herbivorous nature in vs. 15c. It is also true, however, that the only real support for identification as the hippopotamus is contained in vss. 21–23. If vs. 23 were transposed to an appropriate position in the description of Leviathan, e.g., following xli 23, all suggestion of an aquatic or amphibious character for Behemoth would be removed. The reference to the lotus, the reeds, and the willows, vss. 21–22, could just as well characterize the haunt of a bovine creature. As a matter of fact, this is precisely the nature of the region around Lake Huleh which, according to the Ugaritic text cited in connection with xxxix 9a, teemed with buffalo. This was the marshy area where Baal was accustomed to hunt the great beasts with his bow. And it was in such a marshy area that Baal was felled by bovine monsters; cf. Ps lxviii 31 "the beasts of the reeds, the herd of buffalo" (*'abbîrîm,* the same word used in the Ugaritic myth [*ibrm*] to designate the creatures that felled Baal). Though the Ugaritic texts give no further indication that the locale of Baal's buffalo hunting and of his disastrous encounter with the specially created bovine monsters (in the Ugaritic texts all divine creation is depicted in terms of procreation; cf. EUT, pp. 49–54) are identical, still the marshy character of the place or places and the association with the known site (Samak=Semachonitis=Huleh) with buffalo makes the identification plausible.

15b. *as well as you.* Literally "with you." The clause "which I made" is not represented in LXX, but to omit it makes the phrase "with you" difficult to interpret. Ps lxxiii 22 presents a phraseological parallel which at first sight appears very striking: "*běhēmôṯ* I was with you." The context, however, gives no hint of a mythological allusion and it is likely that *bĕhĕmôṯ* means "cattle" as embodying stupidity; cf. xviii 3.

15c. The hippopotamus feeds both on river plants and on land, where it sometimes does extensive damage to crops. But the hippopotamus is not the only herbivorous animal. If Behemoth is a supernatural mythological creature, its herbivorous nature would suggest bovine characteristics.

16. The loins are the seat of strength, Nah ii 2, especially of the male as connected with virility and sexual power, but also of the female, Prov xxxi 17. To damage the loins is to weaken or render helpless; cf. Deut xxxiii 11; Ps lxix 24, as with Latin *delumbare*. Albertus Magnus, who regarded Behemoth as the natural animal representing sensuality and impurity, did not miss the suggestion of sexuality in this verse. "*Fortitudo eius in lumbis eius quantum ad masculum. In lumbis enim nervi sunt sensitivi, per quos semen a cerebro et a corpore descendens et tangens intima nervorum titillando libidinem concitat et vi delectationis sapientiae inclinat et subvertit.*" And 16b he applied to the female. "*Et virtus illius . . . in umbiculo ventris eius, quantum ad feminam. Matrix enim, cuius nervos tangit semen susceptum in coitu, conum habet ad umbiculum, et dum illi nervi tanguntur, femina intense delectatur . . .*" (quoted from Steinmann, pp. 334 f.). Thomas Aquinas understood Behemoth and Leviathan as the elephant and the whale, natural monsters in the literal sense but representing figuratively diabolical power. His comment on this verse as depicting the mating of the elephant is of more than Freudian interest. "*Describit autem coitum elephantis, primo quidem quantum ad principium libidinis, ex qua animalia commoventur ad coitum, cum dicit: fortitude ejus in lumbis ejus: nam ex lumbis sive ex renibus semen ad membra genitalia derivatur. Secundo describit figuram coitus: nam sicut Philosophus dicit in 5 Anim. cap. 2 'Patitur coitum femella elephantis et masculus ascendit' et hoc significat subdens: Et virtus illius in umbiculo ventris ejus, scilicet quia umbiculum magno virtus ne frangatur propter collusionem corporum tam magnorum. Animalia in quibus talis figura coitus non invenitur, dum coeunt, caudas inter tibias posteriores stringunt . . . Tertio describit organa coitu deserventia . . .*" (quoted from Steinmann, p. 339).

The term *šryr* here rendered "massive" may be the same as the *šrr* of Song of Songs vii 3 which is hardly the lady's navel. If the term is related to Ar. *sirr*, plural *asrār*, "secret(s)," *pudenda*, the term could apply to the privy parts of male or female.

17a. As applied to the tail of the hippopotamus, the hyperbole is extreme since the tail of this animal is absurdly small in proportion to its massive body. In the Gilgamesh Epic the Bull of Heaven brushed (?) Enkidu "with the thick of his tail" (ANET, p. 85, line 133). The term "tail" is inevitably suggestive of sexual sense in the light of similar euphemisms in several languages, e.g. German and Yiddish "Schwanz."

arches. The exact sense of the verb (*ḥpṣ*) is uncertain. It cannot have its usual sense of "delight, take pleasure, desire," etc. In Arabic *ḥpḍ* is used of bending wood. Since the animal's tail is likened to a cedar, this would seem an appropriate sense. The Arabic cognate of the Heb. *ḥpṣ* in the sense of "desire" means to "strive hard" for something. An erect tail is generally a sign of excitement and strength while a drooping tail indicates the opposite. Of course a rigid member could be bent up or down or sideways. The sexual connotations suggested by the wording of this verse have not been overlooked. Albertus Magnus remarks on the Vulg., *stringit caudam quasi cedrum, "Caudam vocat genitale membrum."*

17b. *thighs.* The cognate in Arabic has this meaning, but in the Targ. this word is used to translate "testicle(s)" (*'ĕseḵ*) in Lev xxi 20 and is retained, presumably in the same sense, in the present passage. Vulg. renders *nervi testiculorum eius perplexi sunt.* On this St. Thomas remarked, *"Haec autem ad diabolum litteraliter referri non possunt. . . ."*

18. *tubes . . . bars.* Cf. EUT, pp. 62, 79.

19a. Literally "He is the first of the ways of God." Peake and Szold supposed that the allusion is to the creation of cattle (*bĕhēmāh*) as first in order among the animals created on the fifth day, Gen i 23. Dahood's suggestion that "way" here means "power"—"He is the finest manifestation of God's Power" (TS 13 [1952], 593 f.; cf. I. B. Bauer, *Verbum Domini* 35 [1957], 222–27)—is attractive but not convincing. The same expression is used in Prov viii 22 of wisdom as the first of God's creative acts before the formation of the world. Taking the cue from this passage as well as from Enoch lx 7–9; Apocalypse of Baruch xxiv 4; and IV Ezra vi 49–52, the natural implication of the present line is that Behemoth was a special creation of God (El). This appears to be the strongest point in favor of the mythological interpretation.

19b. The text may be defective, but the above rendering is as literal as possible; cf. KJ, JPS, AT, and RSV. The clever emendation suggested by Giesebrecht and widely accepted (Dhorme, Moffatt, and CCD) alters every word of the line to produce "The one made taskmaster of his fellows" (CCD). This is scarcely more appropriate to the hippopotamus than the sense of the received text. The effort to explain the sword as the tusks of the hippopotamus, which he uses like a sickle to cut grass, strains the text as much as the imagination. The text as we have it suggests that the maker of Behemoth is also its slayer or conqueror. Rabbinic tradition elaborated this notion. In the messianic age, Behemoth and Leviathan are to furnish sport and food for the righteous. Pious Jews who shun pagan sports will be allowed to participate in the hunting of Leviathan and Behemoth (Midrash Rabba Lev xiii 3). When

Gabriel, according to one tradition, is unable to slay Leviathan, God will divide the monster with his sword. In another version, God will order Leviathan to battle with the "bull of the wilderness" and both will be slain (TB, Baba Bathra 75a; Pesiqta de Rab Kahana 188b).

20a. This line, taken with the following one, presents difficulties not always appreciated by interpreters. The usual expedient is to alter the word *bûl* (which occurs elsewhere only in Isa xliv 19 where it is used in connection with wood; cf. Akk. *bulû*) to *yĕḇûl*, "produce." Thus the sense would be "The produce of the mountains they bring him," or "Produce the mountains bring him"; cf. Ps lxxii 3 where the mountains are said to bring peace. A similar metaphor occurs in the Ugaritic myths, "The mountains will bring you much silver / The hills the choicest gold." What the mountains are to bring, or what product of the mountains is to be brought to Behemoth, is not clear. Presumably, if this emendation is correct, the allusion is to the herbage of the mountains delivered to the monster. This recalls the Midrashic interpretation of Ps l 10 which takes *bĕhēmôṯ* to refer to the primeval monster Behemoth (lying) upon a thousand hills (and feeding on them). Cf. IV Ezra vi 51, "And thou didst give Behemoth one of the parts which had been dried up on the third day to dwell in, where are a thousand hills" (cf. G. H. Box, *The Ezra-Apocalypse*, 1912, pp. 89 f.). A herbivorous monster would naturally (or supernaturally) require a prodigious amount of pasture and fodder. In the Ugaritic Text BH, it will be recalled, the bovine monsters are called "Eaters" and "Devourers." The Bull of Heaven in the Gilgamesh Epic apparently had a mammoth appetite and intake, for when Ishtar browbeat her father Anu into creating the monster Anu warned that there would be seven years of food shortage but Ishtar had already anticipated this and had stored seven years' grain and grass for man and beast (ANET, p. 85, lines 101–10).

Provocative as may be the line of interpretation suggested by the emendation of *bûl* to *yĕḇûl*, it is rendered dubious by the lack of congruity with the following parallel member of the bicolon, 20b. This latter colon is devoid of difficulty and clearly depicts a haunt where wild beasts sport, as Leviathan sported in the sea, Ps civ 26, and wisdom played before God, Prov viii 30. Now the term *bûl hārîm*, as Tur-Sinai noted, appears to be the equivalent of the common Akkadian term *bûl ṣêri*, "beast(s) of the steppe," which would make excellent synonymous parallelism with *ḥayyaṯ haśśāḏeh*, "the beast(s) of the field" in 20b. We cannot, however, go further with Tur-Sinai's interpretation of this verse which is highly fanciful. If we take our cue from 20b and interpret *bûl hārîm* as parallel and synonymous with *ḥayyaṯ haśśāḏeh*, it then becomes necessary to emend the verb of 20a to comport with the sporting (*śḥq*) in 20b. The only plausible emendation the present writer can suggest is to read *yišlāyû*, "they are at ease" (cf. xii 6), for MT *yiś'û-lô*, "they lift up/bring to him."

The various alterations of the text that have been made in the interest of the hippopotamus, such as changing "mountains" (*hārîm*) to "rivers" (*nĕhārîm*), do not merit serious consideration.

20b. There is no antecedent for the word "there," but it must refer to Behemoth's stamping grounds. The hippopotamus is usually dragged in with the explanation that its herbivorous nature makes it harmless to other creatures who blithely play about it. This would apply equally well to a bovine creature. LXX's reading *en tō tartarō*, "in Tartarus," for *šām*, "there," is of considerable interest in light of the use of *šām* with reference to the netherworld in i 21; cf. iii 17. The mythological associations of Behemoth are patent in the LXX's rendering of this verse, "And having gone to a steep mountain, he causes joy to the quadrupeds in Tartarus."

21a. *lotus*. Not the Egyptian lotus *Nymphae lotus*, which is a water lily, but the thorny shrub *Zizyphus lotus* (Heb. *ṣe'ĕlîm*, Ar. *ḍāl*) which flourishes in damp and hot areas from Syria to North Africa. This shrub is especially abundant around the Sea of Galilee.

21b. Cf. Ps lxviii 31; Isa xix 6.

22b. *wadi willows*. Cf. Lev xxiii 40; Isa xv 7, xliv 4; Ps cxxxvii 2. Identified as the *Populus Euphratica* which is common along the Jordan and all the streams and wadies of Palestine. The term "wadi" (*naḥal*), almost as strongly as Jordan in the succeeding verse, suggests a Syrian-Palestinian rather than Egyptian locale.

23b. This line is overlong. It may be reduced to size by dropping the verb *yibṭaḥ*, "he trusts," at the beginning of the line or the phrase "to his mouth" at the end of the line. As noted above, vs. 15a, this verse is the only basis for the assumption that Behemoth is aquatic or amphibious. Since the following line, 24a, is much too short, some critics, following Bickell and Wright, transfer "to his mouth," *'el-pîhû*, to 24a to fill out the line. This would effectively remove the image most critics see of the hippopotamus with nostrils just above the surface of the water. This recourse, however, does not solve the problem for the words "to his mouth" present still greater difficulty when transferred to the succeeding line. Critics who make the transfer have to emend or do violence to 24a in order to torture sense from it. The transfer of the phrase "to his mouth" is quite unnecessary. Dhorme (who accepts the hippopotamus) mentions the buffalo (Ar. *jāwāmiz*) to be seen on the banks of Lake Huleh with scarcely more than the muzzle protruding above the surface of the water. This would seem to eliminate the necessity of appealing to the hippopotamus here and elsewhere. With the rejection of the hippopotamus, the argument for emending Jordan to Nile (*yĕ'ōr*) collapses, as well as the necessity to explain that it does not really mean that stream specifically but is used merely as a type of any swift-moving stream. If the poet had in mind the marshy country in the vicinity of Lake Huleh (the canebrakes of Samak; *aḫ šmk* of Ugaritic; *yammā dĕsamĕḵā* of the Talmud; *limnē Semechonitis* of Josephus), then the Jordan may be taken literally. This is not to say that Behemoth is an ordinary buffalo wallowing in the swamps of the Upper Jordan. Even in depicting a mythological creature, the poet may and must use figures from the world familiar to him.

It is questionable whether *yardēn* here is to be taken as the name of the famous river; it may be a general term for a swift stream. Here and in Ps xlii 7 the definite article which is used in more than two hundred occurrences of *hay-yardēn*, "the Jordan," as the proper name is significantly absent. The Qumran Targum preserves a part of vs. 23, including the word *yrdn'* with postpositive determination:

] *yrdn' g'ph*
ytrḥṣ dy yqblnh

] the Jordan presses,
he trusts that he will receive it [ ].

S. Kaufman suggested that *g'ph* is a noun, the Western Aramaic (and Syriac) *gyp*, "shore," and rendered:

[Should] the Jordan [overflow] its bank,
he trusts. . . .

With the foregoing explanation, we may omit *yiḇṭaḥ* of 23b as it is frequently the case in Hebrew and Ugaritic poetry that a synonymous verb is omitted in the second element of a bicolon.

24a. As already noted, xl 23b, the first half of this verse is short and makes little sense. To augment the line both in length and in meaning, many critics prefix *mî hû*, "Who is he?", as omitted by haplography after the preceding *pîhû*, "his mouth." This is adopted as the best idea yet proposed. But what can be the meaning of "Who is he that can take him by/with his eyes?" It has been suggested (Ehrlich) that it is a matter of charming or fascinating the creature by staring at him. Often it is taken to mean "while he is looking." In keeping with the parallel line, some understand it to refer to capture by injuring the eyes or blinding the beast. Dhorme adopts an interesting interpretation, citing Herodotus (ii.70) who mentions a process of controlling a crocodile by plastering its eyes with clay. Kissane emends to *bim'ônô*, "in his lair."

A striking possible explanation of this puzzling line occurs to the writer belatedly as the result of experience and observation of game fishing. A large and powerful fish can be taken from the water and held with ease and safety by grasping it firmly by the eyes which produces complete paralysis. Leviathan, of course, is neither mere fish nor crocodile, but a supernatural marine monster which none but the bravest and mightiest god would dare grapple.

24b. *barbs.* The word (*môqěšîm*) is usually rendered "snare, trap." Since the verb "pierce" does not suit the action of a snare or trap, Ehrlich suggested emendation to *qimmôšîm,* "thorns." Dhorme regards it as intended irony that the description of the crocodile should begin with the trait with which that of the hippopotamus ends, the hippopotamus having nothing in common with those animals which one captures and holds by means of a cord passed through the nose. CCD omits the whole verse as out of place and a partial duplication of vss. 26 and 28. The verse is left where it is to show the awkward transition between the descriptions of the two beasts. The treatment of Behemoth is vestigial is compared to that of Leviathan and the two are joined in such a way as to create confusion. In IV Ezra vi 49 ff. there appears to be an attempt to undo the confusion of the passage here with the explanation that originally Behemoth and Leviathan were together in the water, but were separated because of overcrowding. "And you separated the one from the other, because the seventh part where the water was gathered together was not able to hold them (both). So you gave Behemoth one of the parts which had been dried up on the third day to dwell in, where there are a thousand hills."

The Qumran Targum, though well preserved at this point, is highly ambiguous.

bmṭl ʿynwhy yklnh
kbḥkh yzyb ʾph

The editors offer alternative interpretations of the first hemistich:

Le retiendra-t-on, *en couvrant ses yeux,* / *en enlevant ses yeux,*
(en le prenant) par ses paupières,
percera-t-on son nez, comme avec un hameçon?

The note explains that the form may be construed either as an infinitive of *ṭll,* "cover," or of *nṭl,* "lift, take," or that if *mṭl* is here a substantive (something which covers) one could perhaps think of the eyelids (paupières) of the animal. There is yet another possibility for *mṭl* which was overlooked by the editors and called to my attention by Mr. Bruce Zuckerman. The parallelism of *mṭl* and *ḥkh* (i.e. *ḥakkāh*), "hook," suggests that *mṭl* is also a substantive. The noun *měṭāl* is attested as some sort of weapon. In Targ. of I Sam xvii 6 it is used to render MT *kîdôn;* cf. xxxix 23a. The two lines of the verse thus present complete parallelism, spear with hook, eyes with nose, and the two verbs with meanings appropriate to the instruments in question. The translation of *ykln* as "Le retiendra-t-on?" appears to relate to the "hollow" root (*k*(*w*)*l*), "contain, restrain," which is inappropriate to *mṭl* as designating a weapon. Perhaps it is to be connected with the root *kly*, "come to an end," in the Pa'ēl or factitive stem meaning "destroy." The verb *yzyb* which corresponds to MT *ynqb*, "pierce," is problematic and the dictionaries provide no help; but it must have been intended in a sense roughly synonymous with *nqb*, "perforate." Connection with Heb. *z*(*w*)*b*, "flow," is ruled out on phonological grounds since the initial consonant was the interdental *d* which would be represented by *d*. Furthermore the sense "cause to flow" is not suitable to the context. The verb *zbb* in Arabic does not seem to offer any fitting sense, but the noun *zubb* is applied to the point of the beard and the penis. It is admittedly a dubious connection, but since the word must mean pierce, perforate, or the like, it may be legitimate to render it with an English term suggestive of double entendre:

With spear will you destroy his eyes,
With hook will you *prick* his nose?

If this seems too daring, one may simply assume that *yzyb* is a scribal error for *ynqb*.

xli 1 (xl 25H). *Leviathan*. As in iii 8, the allusion is to the marine monster called Lotan (*ltn*) in the Ugaritic myths. The ugaritic texts give no detailed description of Leviathan and it is difficult to tell because of the poetic parallelism whether the attributes mentioned apply to the same or different monsters. The relevant Ugaritic passages are given below in translation with minimum explanation of the context. In one of several communiqués between Baal and Mot (Death), the latter gives Baal the credit for having slain or conquered Lotan:

When you smote Lotan, the swift serpent,
Destroyed the serpent Twisty,
The Tyrant with seven heads . . .

In another instance, the goddess 'Anat claims to have dispatched this seven-headed dragon along with other assorted monsters. The goddess, Baal's ardent companion in love and war, is seized with apprehension of some threat to her consort and she says to Baal's messengers by the way of assurance of her loyalty and readiness to fight:

What foe has risen against Baal?
What enemy against the Cloud Rider?
Did I not smite El's darling Sea?
Did I not annihilate River the great god,
Did I not muzzle the Dragon? I muzzled him.

I smote the tortuous serpent,
The tyrant (?) with seven heads.
I smote El's darling——
Vanquished the monstrous, ferocious bullock,
Smote El's bitch Fire,
Annihilated El's daughter Flame ('nt III 34–43).

Although Lotan is not specifically mentioned in 'Anat's boasting, the repetition of identical terms in the two passages make it clear that the reference in part is to the same monster(s) which Mot acknowledged that Baal had slain. The apparent discrepancy here is very instructive. There were probably several versions of the major motifs of the myths and considerable freedom in their use. Since Baal and 'Anat are allies, it does not matter which one administered the *coup de grâce* to the enemy. Both the passages cited above contain words and phrases almost verbatim with Isa xxvii 1 which assigns to Yahweh the honor of slaying Leviathan in the *eschaton:*

> On that day Yahweh will punish with his great and strong sword Leviathan the fleeting serpent, Leviathan the tortuous serpent, and will slay the Dragon that is in the sea.

Ps lxxiv 12–14 mentions the heads of Leviathan without specifying the number:

O God, my king of old,
Doer of saving deeds in the earth,
You shattered Sea by your might,
Broke the heads of the Dragon on the water,
Crushed the heads of Leviathan,
Made him food for the wilderness folk.

The Dragon (Ugaritic *tnn,* Heb. *tannîm, tannîn,* and *tannînîm*) is mentioned also apart from Leviathan in Ezek xxix 3, xxxii 2 where it is applied metaphorically to Pharaoh. The sea serpent mentioned in Amos ix 3 may refer to the same mythical creature. The Ugaritic terms *bṯn/bšn* and the Heb. *nāḥāš* applied to Leviathan make the serpentine character of the monster a certainty. A Mesopotamian seal cylinder from Tell Asmar depicts a seven-headed dragon in the process of being subdued by two divine heroes. One attacks from the rear while the other battles the monster head on. Four of the dragon's heads are drooping, but the three upper ones are still erect with forked tongues protruding. The creature has six long tongues of flame rising along its back. The cylinder dates from the early Akkadian period, but certainly represents a prototype of the seven-headed serpentine monster Leviathan (cf. H. Frankfort, *Stratified Cylinder Seals from the Diyala Region,* Pl. 45, No.

478, and J. B. Pritchard, ANEP, 691). Equally interesting is a small shell plaque of unknown provenience (ANEP, 671) which depicts a god kneeling before a seven-headed fiery monster. The heads are serpentine and the body leonine with flames rising from the creature's back. The lowest head and neck appears to be drooping a bit, but the other six are still erect. There is something draped over the drooping neck, but it is difficult to tell just what it represents, perhaps a sword, a club, or a noose or muzzle. The only other mention of Leviathan in the OT is in Ps civ 26 which tells us nothing more than we already know, that Leviathan's playground is the sea. This is the passage in particular which suggests to some interpreters that Leviathan is the whale.

The supernatural character of Leviathan is abundantly clear from the data cited above. The Ugaritic myths, dating from the middle of the second millennium B.C., or earlier, show that the biblical allusions preserve bits and pieces of a complex and highly developed mythology. If the author of the present composition wished merely to exercise his poetic abilities on the subject of the power and ferocity of the crocodile, he surpassed his goal at the start with the use of the term Leviathan. The poem, it is true, does not mention multiple heads of the monster, but there are other features which indicate that Leviathan is more than an ordinary crocodile, whether of the Nile or the streams of Palestine The OT never mentions crocodiles, but they have been reported as seen or killed in the northern coastal streams Yarkon (Nahr ez-Zerqa) and Kishon. A town north of Caesarea was called Crocodilopolis (Strabo xvi.27) and a stream (the Yarkon?) Crocodilion (Pliny, *Nat. hist.* v.17). Cf. ICC, I, p. 359. The fact that many modern critics, in spite of the term Leviathan, understand the poem as the description of a crocodile indicates that there is some basis for this view. The mythological elements are ignored or passed over as hyperbole. The NOTES on the verses that follow will emphasize the mythological elements.

1–2 (xl 25–26H). Herodotus (ii.70) gives an account of the method the Egyptians claimed to have used to catch crocodiles. The hook was baited with a side of pork and a live pig beaten on the bank to attract the crocodile toward the bait. As soon as the beast was landed, its eyes were plastered with mud to make it easy to dispatch; cf. xl 24a.

1a (xl 25aH). *draw out.* The verb *timšōḵ,* "thou wilt draw out," is very similar to the Coptic word for crocodile, *temsaḥ,* which came into Arabic as *timsaḥ.* Delitzsch suggests that the poet makes a conscious play on the Egyptian word.

1b (xl 25bH). *tongue.* Herodotus (ii.68) expressed a popular belief that the crocodile has no tongue. The crocodile's tongue is attached immobile to the lower jaw. The emendation of *lĕšônô,* "his tongue," to *lĕ-šinnāw,* "to his teeth," adapted to the oral anatomy of the crocodile, presses a theory too far. This beast not only has a tongue, but is given to oratory; cf. vs. 27 and xli 4.

The Qumran Targum introduces the verse with the interrogative particle *h-:*

htgd tnyn bḥk'
'w bḥbl tḥrz lšnh

Can you drag Drake with hook,
Or with rope string his tongue?

The rendering of MT *lwytn,* "Leviathan," by *tannîn,* "Dragon," suggests that the Targumist regarded the terms as interchangeable. There is nothing to suggest that a mere crocodile was envisaged. MT *tašqîa',* "press down," is rendered by *tḥrz* (cognate with Ar. *ḫrz,* used of sewing with an awl) which is applied to the stringing of beads by boring a hole and squeezing the string through the hole. The same verb is used of the perforation of a thorn in the flesh, the sting of a wasp, and of poking one's neck through a window or door-hole. The passive participle *ḥărûzîm,* "pierced things," is applied to a necklace of beads in Song of Songs i 10.

2a (xl 26aH). *cord.* The primary meaning of this word (*'aḡmôn*) is "rush, reed," Isa ix 13, xix 15, lviii 5, and secondarily a cord of rushes or rush-fibers; cf. Gr. *schoinos.*

2b (xl 26bH). *hook.* Human as well as animal captives were held or led with hooks drawn through the nose, lips, or jaws; cf. II Kings xix 28; Isa xxxvii 29; Ezek xxix 4, xxxviii 4. Captives are thus depicted on Egyptian and Assyrian reliefs. The stela of Esarhaddon, e.g., depicts the great king holding the dwarfed kings Taharka (biblical Tirhakah) of Egypt and Ba'lu of Tyre by ropes attached to rings in their lips; cf. ANEP, 296, 447. In the Mesopotamian Creation Epic, when Ea liquidated or neutralized his foes, "He laid hold on Mummu, holding him by the nose-rope" (cf. ANET, p. 61, line 72). In the Ugaritic myth 'Anat claims to have "muzzled" the Dragon.

The Qumran Targum reads:

htšw' zmm b'ph
wbḥrtk tqwb lsth

Can you put a ring in his nose,
Or with your gimlet pierce his cheek?

The word *zmm* which renders MT *'aḡmôn* may be read as *zĕmām,* "muzzle," or *zĕmam,* "nose ring." The editors suggest that the noun *ḥrt* is to be related to the root **ḥrṯ* (Heb. *ḥrš*) "make incisions," "grave." It seems more likely that it is to be connected with Ar. *ḫrt,* "pierce, bore, perforate," *ḫurt,* "hole." The vocalization of the nominal form here used is uncertain, but its manifest meaning is clearly something like "awl," or "gimlet."

3 (xl 27H). We do not know of any episode in which Leviathan begs for mercy. However, in the Ugaritic myth which tells of Baal's defeat of the sea-god, the goddess Astarte does intervene on behalf of the fallen sea-god and rebukes Baal and shames him into making the Sea captive rather than completely annihilating him (cf. ANET, p. 131a).

The Qumran Targum reverses the order of the two hemistichs:

hymll 'mk bnyḥ
'w ymll 'mk bhtḥnnh lk

Will he speak to you with tenderness,
Or will he speak to you with supplication?

The addition of *lk*, "to you," at the end is redundant and may represent alternatives for expression of "to/with you."

4a (xl 28aH). *covenant.* The sort of covenant envisioned here is that of the vanquished with the victor, the vassal with the suzerain. Cf. G. E. Mendenhall, *Law and Covenant in Israel and in the Ancient Near East* (Biblical Colloquium, Pittsburgh, 1955).

4b (xl 28bH). *eternal slave.* Cf. Deut. xv 17; I Sam xxvii 12. The same expression is used in the Ugaritic texts; cf. ANET, pp. 138b, 145.

The Qumran Targum renders MT precisely:

hyqym qym 'mk
wtdbrnh l'bd 'lm

Will he swear allegiance to you,
Will you take him as eternal slave?

5 (xl 29H). Doves and sparrows are a favorite live plaything of children in the Near East.

D. W. Thomas (VT 4 [1964], 115–16) proposed on the basis of the parallelism to see in the word *lĕna'ărôṯeḵā*, "for your girls," a corruption of a word for "sparrow." By dropping the suffix and the feminine ending and changing the preposition *l* to *k* to agree with *kaṣṣippôr*, "like a bird," he arrived at the desiderated parallelism, "Canst thou play with him as with a bird (sparrow?), Or canst thou tie him with a string like a young sparrow (young sparrows)?" The Qumran Targum is preserved here and it confirms MT *na'ărôṯeḵā* in the sense of "your girls":

htḥ'k bh kṣ[pr']
[w]tqṭrnh bḥwṭ' lbntk

Will you play with it like a bird?
And tie it with a cord for your daughters?

The explanatory phrase *bḥwṭ'*, "with a cord," is an addition.

6a (xl 30aH). *mongers.* The unique form *ḥabbârîm* has the pattern of nouns denoting professions. While it may be related to the word *ḥăḇērîm,* "companions," it has here a technical sense. Tur-Sinai suggests that the term is to be related to *bêṯ ḥeḇer,* "granary, warehouse." As keepers of food warehouses, they would be something like wholesalers.

6b (xl 30bH). *hucksters.* Literally "Canaanites." The term originally designated the traders in the famous crimson cloth, whence the meaning "trade, merchant," as in Isa xxiii 8; Zech xiv 21; Prov xxxi 24; cf. W. F. Albright, "The Role of the Canaanites in the History of Civilization," BANE, pp. 328–62.

The Qumran Targum preserves a bit of the second half of this verse:

wyplgwn yth b'r[

And will they divide him in the l[and . . .]?

7 (xl 31H). *harpoons, spears.* Both these words (*śukkôṯ* and *ṣilṣal*) are unique. The former is usually related to *śikkîm,* "thorns," Num xxxiii 55 (cf. Ar. *šawkah,* "thorn," Akk. *šikkatu,* "point"). Thus the "thorns" are understood as darts, harpoons, or the like. The latter term is explained as related to the root meaning, "to vibrate" or "tingle" and the meaning "spear" is derived from the noise of the weapon as it vibrates in flight. Both these derivations seem dubious. Tur-Sinai has a novel interpretation. The *śukkôṯ* he takes to mean "cloves" and reading the preposition *bĕ* as part of the word *bĕṣilṣal* (which he takes as the Mishnaic *bĕṣalṣûl,* "shallot, dwarf-onion"), he serves up a gefilte fish:

Couldst thou stud his body with cloves,
with fish-onions his head?

40. YAHWEH'S SECOND DISCOURSE (*continued*) (xli 9–34)

XLI 9 "Lo, any hope is false; [xli 1]*
Were not the gods cast down at sight of him?
10 Is he not fierce when one rouses him? [2]
Who could stand before him?
11 Who could confront him unscathed, [3]
Under the whole heaven, who?
12 Did I not silence his boasting, [4]
By the powerful word Hayyin prepared?
13 Who can penetrate his outer garment, [5]
Pierce his double mail?
14 Who can open the doors of his face, [6]
Ringed round with fearsome fangs?
15 His back rows of shields, [7]
Closed with adamant seal;
16 Each sticks to the other, [8]
And no space intervenes;
17 Each welded to the other, [9]
They clasp inseparably.
18 His sneezes flash forth lightning, [10]
His eyes are like the glow of dawn.
19 From his mouth flames leap, [11]
Flames of fire escape.
20 From his nostrils issues smoke, [12]
Flame blown and blazing.
21 From his throat coals glow, [13]
Flame pours out his mouth.
22 In his neck dwells strength, [14]
Before him leaps violence.

* Verse numbers in Hebrew Bible.

23 The folds of his flesh are compact, [15]
Molded on him immovable.
24 His heart is hard as rock, [16]
Firm as a nether millstone.
25 At his terror the gods are affrighted; [17]
With consternation prostrate.
26 Who attacks, the sword avails not; [18]
Nor spear, dart, or javelin.
27 Iron he regards as straw, [19]
Bronze as rotten wood.
28 No arrow can put him to flight; [20]
Slingstones change to chaff on him.
29 Clubs he counts as splinters; [21]
Laughs at the javelin's whirr.
30 His undersides are sharp shards, [22]
A threshing sledge dragging the mire.
31 He seethes the deep like a caldron, [23]
Makes the sea like an ointment pan.
32 Behind him glistens a wake; [24]
One would think the deep hoary.
33 On earth is not his equal, [25]
One formed without fear.
34 He looks on all that is lofty, [26]
Monarch of all proud beings."

Notes

xli 9–11 (xli 1–3H). These lines are difficult and it is apparent that the text has suffered some sabotage intended to obscure gross pagan mythological allusions. For the difficulties and the numerous emendations proposed, cf. ICC, II, pp. 335 ff.

9a (1aH). *any hope.* Literally "his hope," i.e., the hope of any would-be assailant.

9b (1bH). The Masoretes have obscured the sense of the line by vocalizing the word *'ēl,* "God," or the proper name "El," as the preposition *'el,* "unto." Syr. and Symmachus read *'ēl* (*'ĕlaha* and *ho-theos*). Cheyne's emendation of *'el* to *'ēlîm* is very probable, as will appear presently. It does not matter greatly whether one reads *mar'āw,* "his appearance," or *môrā'ô,* "his dread" (i.e., the dread of him). The picture of God and/or the gods prostrated with fear recalls this motif which is elaborated repeatedly in the Mesopotamian Creation Epic. Of the monsters Tiamat created, it is said "he who beholds them shall perish abjectly." When Anu saw Tiamat and her cohorts, he could not face her and when he reported the situation to his father Anshar:

Speechless was Anshar as he stared at the ground,
Hair on edge, shaking his head at Ea.
All the Anunnaki gathered at that place;
Their lips closed tight, [they sat] in silence.
"No god" (thought they) "can go [to battle and],
Facing Tiamat, escape [with his life]." (ANET, p. 64, lines 86–91.)

The Ugaritic myth of Baal's conflict with the sea-god also presents a parallel to this motif. The sea-god sends his fierce messengers before the divine assembly with the demand that they surrender Baal whom they are harboring:

When the gods saw them,
Saw the messengers of Sea,
The emissaries of Chief River,
The gods lowered their heads
On top of their knees,
Even on their princely thrones.

(For discussion of the context of this episode and an interpretation, cf. EUT, pp. 27 f.) That the Masoretes would balk at vocalizing the text to preserve an allusion to a crude pagan myth is quite understandable. The consonantal text, however, is in good order and needs little alteration. We change only *'el* to *'ēlîm* and read the verb as plural. To leave the text unaltered would brand only El (God) as a coward, whereas all the gods (with the exception of the heroes Marduk in the Mesopotamian and Baal in the Ugaritic myth) were intimidated.

10a (2aH). Cf. iii 8.

10b (2bH). *him.* Reading with many manuscripts *lĕp̄ānāw* instead of *lĕp̄ānay,* "before me." Dahood, followed by Blommerde (who supplied the relevant bibliographical notes), construed the final *y* of *lĕp̄ānay* as the suffix of the third person.

11a (3aH). MT presents a lofty thought entirely out of keeping with the context. "Who ever came before me (with a gift) that I should repay?" The Apostle Paul quotes this version of the line in Rom xi 35. LXX, however, reflects a reading more in keeping with the context, *kai hypomenei=wayyišlām,* as in ix 4. Accordingly, we emend to *mî hû qiddĕmô wayyišlām.*

11b (3bH). MT again has an exalted expression of God's universal lordship. "Under all the heavens to me it (is)," i.e., belongs to me. For *lî* "to me," we read *mî*, "Who?"

Blommerde emended *hiqdîmanî* to *hiqdîmennî* and construed the final *y* as the third person suffix to produce the following sense:

> Whomsoever dares to approach him, I shall reward,
> What is under all the heavens shall be his.

12 (4H). This verse has remained very obscure. KJ's "I will not conceal his parts, nor his power, nor his comely proportion" is accepted in essence by most moderns. Moffatt's bold venture, "No hunter would survive to boast and brag of his exploits and his fine arms," is not hampered by rigid adherence to the text. JPS's "Would I keep silence concerning his boastings, / Or his proud talk, or his fair array of words?" is the most exact rendering of the text. The word *baddāyw* here does not mean "his parts, members," as in xviii 13, but "his boasting," as in xi 3; cf. Isa xvi 6, xliv 25 and lviii 13 (conjecturally); Jer xlviii 30, l 36. The use in Isa xliv 25 shows clearly the association of the word with heathen incantations. In the Ugaritic texts the root is used both as a verb and as a noun with the meaning "sing," "song." The real impediment to understanding of the text is the word *ḥyn* in the second line which is regularly explained as an anomalous form of the noun *ḥēn*, "grace, favor." The Masoretic vocalization of the word is passing strange. If the Masoretes had thought the word should be read *ḥēn*, why did they not so vocalize it? Tur-Sinai suggests that the word is to be related to the root *hyn*, as in Deut i 41, "You made bold to go up," and with Ar. *hayyin*, "light, lightheartedly contemptuous." Tur-Sinai, it seems, came close to the truth. I suggest that the troublesome word *ḥyn* represents an accidental corruption of a name or epithet of the god Koshar who is sometimes called *hyn* in the Ugaritic myths. The vocalization of this name is uncertain, but Ugaritic orthographic practice favors *hayyān* or *hayyīn*. Scribal confusion of *h* and *ḥ* is not surprising since the two letters are sometimes difficult to distinguish. This versatile deity Koshar serves in the Ugaritic texts as artisan, enchanter, and general factotum. It is he who supplied Baal with the wonder weapons by which the sea-god was laid low. The weapons, apparently some sort of missiles, were rendered effective by incantations pronounced by Koshar:

> Koshar fetched a "weapon"
> And proclaimed its name.
> "Thy name is Chaser.
> Chaser, chase Sea,
> Chase Sea from his throne,
> River from the seat of his dominion.

Bound from Baal's hand,
Like an eagle from his fingers.
Strike the shoulder of Prince Sea,
Between the hands of Chief River" (68:11–15).

This first weapon failed to shake the sea-god. But a second, dubbed "Driver," with a similar incantation, this time aimed at the head and between the eyes, struck home and toppled Prince Sea. Although Leviathan is not mentioned in the fragmentary Ugaritic myth which relates Baal's defeat of the sea-god, the connection of Leviathan with this episode is well established by the OT allusions as well as the Ugaritic texts. The use of incantations to ensure victory is an ancient and virtually universal practice. In the Mesopotamian Creation Epic, when Marduk set his face toward the raging Tiamat, "in his lips he held a spell." Tiamat, likewise, "recites a charm, keeps casting her spell." The passage cited by Tur-Sinai, Deut i 41, is provocative of speculation. The unique verb *hw/yn* is commonly interpreted as meaning "make light, think easy," etc., but this is a poor guess. The context suggests some sort of military preparation. Nothing is more necessary to such an undertaking than magical and religious rites to enhance the prospects of success. The use of the name of the master enchanter *hayyān* as the technical term for this activity suggests that the activity may have been resort to charms and incantations. This would explain why Yahweh was angered and refused to accompany his people to battle while they relied on spells associated with a pagan deity.

Dahood (*Psalms III*, second NOTE on Ps cvi 2) reads the negative particle *lô'* as the divine title *lē'*, "the Almighty," and translates the verse thus:

I the Almighty fashioned his limbs,
his powerful back and graceful build.

14 (6H). The crocodile's teeth are indeed fearsome. How much more so those of a supernatural monster like Leviathan! In the Mesopotamian Creation Epic, the formidable dentition of the monsters engendered by Tiamat is repeatedly mentioned.

15a (7aH). *His back.* Reading *gēwô* for MT *ga'ăwāh*, "pride."

15b (7bH). *adamant.* Following the interpretation of the LXX *hōsper smuritēs lithos.*

Dahood (*Biblica* 45 [1964], 399) took *ga'ăwāh* as "back" and found a synonymous parallel in MT *ṣar* which he read *ṣūr* and equated with Ugar. *ẓr* (*ẓu(h)r*), "back, top." Thus he arrived at the translation, "The back is a row of shields, the spine a closed seal." Despite the striking parallelism, it seems preferable to remain adamant with MT *ṣar.*

16b (8bH). *space.* Reading *rewaḥ* for MT *rûaḥ,* "wind, air." The Qumran Targum reads:

[ḥdh] lḥdh ydbqn
wrwḥ l[' t]n'wl bynhn

[Each] sticks to the other,
And air canno[t e]nter between them.

The interpretation of *rwḥ* accords with MT *rûaḥ,* "wind, air," as confirmed by the verb *'ll,* "enter," against the tentative conjecture that the word may have originally been intended to be read as *rewaḥ,* "space." The poet may well have been aware of the ambiguity. On other possible readings of *rwḥ* as *rewaḥ* rather than *rûaḥ,* cf. Dahood, *Psalms I,* third NOTE on Ps xviii 11, and *Psalms III,* fourth NOTE on Ps civ 3, and p. 305 (second NOTE on Ps cxl 11); cf. xv 30.

17 (9H). The Qumran Targum preserves this verse almost perfectly and renders it exactly, except for omission of translation of MT *yiṯlakkĕḏû,* "they grasp each other":

'nth lḥbrth ḥ'nn
wl' ytp[r]šn

Each grasps its companion,
And they cannot be separated.

The missing antecedent noun referring to the scales was feminine, as indicated by the feminine forms *'nth,* "a woman," and *ḥbrt,* "a (female) companion." The omission of one of the verbs in the second hemistich leaves the line too short. The verb *ḥ'nn* which serves to render MT *yĕḏubbāqû,* and perhaps also *yiṯlakkĕḏû,* is cognate with Ar. *ḥḍn,* "embrace." The nouns *ḥōṣen* and *ḥēṣen* occur in Isa xlix 22, Ps cxxix 7, in the sense of "bosom." In Neh v 13 *ḥōṣen* designates a part of one's apparel, a sash or girdle used for carrying money or other accessories, Akk. *ḫuṣannu;* cf. J. M. Myers, Ezra · Nehemiah, AB, vol. 14, first NOTE on Neh v 13, and CAD, VI, p. 259b, s.v. *ḫuṣannu.*

18a (10aH). *His sneezes.* Or perhaps "his nostrils," following Tur-Sinai. The onomatopoeia of the word (*'ăṭîšôṯāw*) is striking. These sneezes have provoked some learned comments on crocodilian allergy which appear to be based more on the supposed meaning of the text than on observation of the crocodile. The oft quoted passages cited by Bochart (*Hierozoicon* v.17) from Strabo (*hēliazontai kechēnotes,* xvii.39) and Aelian (*epi tēn ochthēn proelthōn kata tēs aktinos kechēnen, De nat. animal.* iii.11) do not refer to sneezing but to the crocodile's yawning or gaping in the sun. Only the presumption that the animal is a crocodile suggests that the poetic image is of the prismatic effect of sunlight on the spray from a crocodile's sneeze. Taking the monster as supernatural, the obvious reference is to the exhalation of flame in normal dragonesque fashion.

18b (10bH). Bochart cites Horapollon (*Hieroglyphica* i.65) to the effect that the Egyptians used the crocodile's eyes as the symbol of dawn because the crocodile swims with his whole body submerged except for the eyes which appear above the surface. The reddish eyes, or eyelids, of the crocodile are said to glow through the water. Again, rejecting the crocodile in favor of a dragon, we may interpret literally. Fire emanating from the eyes is not unbecoming a dragon. In the Ugaritic myth of the conflict between Baal and Prince Sea, the terrible messengers of the sea-god intimidate the entire divine assembly, except Baal, by their fiery appearance. Though the text is broken, the fire probably comes from their eyes. Ginsberg renders (ANET, p. 130):

> Fire, burning fire, doth flash;
> A whetted sword [are their e]yes.

Dahood (UHP, p. 41) suggested that a strong ellipse may be responsible for the refractory nature of the present verse which he rendered:

> His sneezings are as brilliant as the sun,
> And his eyes are as the twinklers of dawn.

According to Dahood, "The conjunction in the second half verse is also to be understood with *'ôr* in the first colon," i.e. the comparative particle *k*, "like, as," in *kĕ'ap̄'appê-šāḥar* is retroactive for *'ôr*, "light," taken to mean "sun."

The Qumran Targum is clear in the first half verse, but the end of the second is very uncertain:

> *'ṭyšth tdlq nwr'*
> *byn 'ynwhy kmmḥ p[r]'*

The editors translate:

> Son éternuement fait briller du feu
> entre ses yeux comme la verberation(?) de l'au[ro]re.

The end of the second line is highly problematic. Van der Ploeg proposed to see in *kmmḥ* the infinitive of an unknown verb *mḥḥ* which would be a secondary (iterative) form of *mḥ'*, in the sense "strike," hence the translation "comme la verberation(?)." The remaining letters *p[r]'* may represent *šprpr'*, "dawn," which in Oriental MSS of MT is written *špr pr'*. The Targ. of Isa lviii 8 translates MT *šaḥar* as *šprpr'*. (Jongeling questioned whether one must not read *kmmḥpr'*, "as (coming) from a cave," in which case the word would be attached to what follows.) The problems here are too complex to be treated in detail. One puzzling detail not discussed by the editors is the substitution of *byn 'ywnhy*, "between his eyes," for MT *'ênāyw*, "his eyes." The term "between the eyes" is not to be understood literally but is a poetic expression for head or forehead; it is now attested in Ugaritic (*Ugaritica* V, text 3, line 5) as a parallel to *riš*, "head," thus confirming the traditional understanding as to the proper placement of the phylacteries (Exod xiii 16; Deut vi 8, xi 18), not exactly between the eyes but well above on the forehead.

19–21 (11–13H). This is interpreted as hyperbolical description of the spray from the crocodile's breath as it breaks the surface of the water. But Peake comments, "The author may have embroidered his picture with reminiscences of stories of fire-breathing dragons"; cf. Rev ix 17.

19b (11bH) *Flames*. The word *kîḏôḏ* is hapax, but has a very plausible etymology as related to Ar. *k(w)d*, "emit fire." The nominal pattern, with repetition of the final consonant, is like that of *nîḥôaḥ*, "appeasement." Dahood (*Biblica* 46 [1965], 327) connected the word with Ugar. *kdd*, "child, son," *kîḏôḏê 'ēš*, "sons of fire," i.e. sparks, analogous to the *bĕnê rešep̄* of v 5. The sense remains unchanged: "From his mouth flames go forth, sparks (lit. 'sons of fire') escape." The Qumran Targum reads:

mn pmh lpydyn ypqwn
blšny 'šh yrṭwn

From his mouth flames come forth,
With tongues of fire they run.

The rendering of the troublesome *kydwdy 'š* with *blšny 'šh* complicates the textual problem.

20 (12H). Cf. II Sam xxii 9; Ps xviii 9 descriptive of Yahweh's theophany as a storm-god. Of the god Marduk it is said, "When he moved his lips, fire blazed forth" (ANET, p. 62, line 96). In the Ugaritic texts it is not stated that the dragon breathes fire, but among the monsters associated with the dragon that 'Anat slew are two females, one canine in form and the other unspecified, the one called Fire and the other Flame ('nt III 42–43); cf. NOTE on xli 1 (xl 25H).

20b (12bH). *Flame*. In previous editions of this work, the line was rendered "Like a pot seething over brushwood." It now seems better to take MT *kĕḏûḏ*, "like a pot," as *kîḏôḏ*, "flame," the singular of the word used above in 19b.

blazing. With Dhorme, reading *'ôḡēm* for MT *'aḡmôn*, "rushes"; cf. Akk. *agāmu*, "be angry," and Ar. *ajam*, "be burning hot." The Qumran Targum appears to support this revision in part:

mn nḥyrwh<y> ypq tnn
lkwš yqd wmgmr

From his nostrils issue smoke,
Flaming tow and live coals

The editors translated:

> De ses narines s'échappe de la fumée,
> comme de la paille brûlante et de l'encens brûlant.

The editors related the vocable *lkwš* to *kûš*, "rush, reed, cane" and construed the initial *l* as serving for the comparative particle. This interpretation was doubtless influenced by the MT *kdwd* and Targ. *hyk dwd'*, which took the initial consonant as the comparative particle, "like a pot." The word *lkwš*, however, is more likely to be connected with the post-biblical term *lek̲eš* which designates cedar fibers used for wicks and thus the Qumran Targum understood *kdwd* as a word for flame without the comparative particle. The editors interpreted the word *mgmr* as "burning incense," with reference to the Talmudic use of *magmār* to designate perfume produced by putting spices on live coals. It is not likely, however, that the monster's fiery breath was aromatic. The Arabic cognate *jamr* designates "live coals." The noun *g*[*m*]*ryn* is used in exactly this sense in the following verse of the Qumran Targum to render MT *gĕḥālîm*, "(live) coals."

> *npšh g*[*m*]*ryn tgs'*
> *wzyqyn ypqn mn pmh*

> His throat belches coals,
> Sparks issue from his mouth.

22a (14aH). Physical power resides in the neck, especially of large beasts; cf. NOTE on xv 26.

22b (14bH). *violence.* Following F. M. Cross, Jr. (VT 2 [1952], 163 f.) in emending MT *d'bh*, "languor," to *db'h* on the basis of the Ugaritic and the parallelism with *'ōz*, "strength." For the verb, LXX read *tārûṣ*, "she runs," instead of the unique *tād̲ûṣ* of MT. The verb *d*(*w*)*ṣ*, however, is attested in Syriac and Arabic in the appropriate sense of "move, leap."

The Qumran Targum reads:

> *bṣwrh ybyt tqph*
> *wqdmwhy trwṭ 'lymw*

> In his neck dwells his power,
> And before him runs vigor.

The reading *trwṭ* agrees with LXX, reflecting *trwṣ* instead of MT *tdwṣ*. The term *'lymw* which renders MT *d'bh* has connotations of sexual vigor characteristic of healthy youth, as seen in the Arabic cognate *ġalim*, "be overcome with sexual desire," and *gulâm*, *ġulâmat*, "boy," "girl," *ġulâmiyyat*, "prime of youth." (W. S. La Sor in a privately printed paper,

"Isaiah 7:14—'Young Woman' or 'Virgin'?" has made it abundantly clear that the term *'almāh* does not mean "virgin.")

23a (15aH). *folds.* Literally "falling parts," presumably the normally flabby and pendulous parts of the flesh and skin.

The Qumran Targum renders:

> *qply bšrh dbqyn*
> *nsyky[n 'lwhy] kprzl'*
>
> The folds of his flesh adhere,
> Cas[t on him] like iron.

24a (16aH). Cf. Ezek xi 19, xxxvi 26 on a stony heart as contrasted with a heart of flesh.

24b (16bH). The lower stationary millstone received the harder wear. The Qumran Targum preserves only vestiges of this verse, *wlb[h . . .] k'b[n . . .]*, "And [his] heart . . . like ston[e . . .]." The upper portable stone was handy for breaking an enemy's head, Judg ix 53; II Sam xi 21.

25a (17aH). *terror.* Cf. xiii 11a, xxxi 23b. The emendation to *miššĕṯô,* "at his hinder part" (Ehrlich), is groundless since the word *šēṯ,* "foundation," is applicable only to anthropoid posteriors.

gods. Aquila, Symmachus, Targ., and Syr. interpret the word as meaning "mighty ones." Vulg. has *angeli.* The emendation to *gallîm,* "waves," (Ehrlich, followed by Dhorme) is also misguided. The text is in good order and crystal clear. The cowering of the gods is a common mythological motif. In the account of the deluge in the Gilgamesh Epic, the gods were frightened and cowered like dogs against the wall of heaven (ANET, p. 94, lines 113 f.). In the Mesopotamian Creation Epic, the gods are given to violent display of emotions, fear, distress, anger, joy. The Ugaritic gods are also highly excitable. Mere anticipation of trouble is enough to throw the goddesses Asherah and 'Anat into a hysterical dither. The whole assembly of the gods, except the hero Baal, hide their faces on their knees from fear of Prince Sea's fierce emissaries. Even the doughty Baal is betimes seized with fear. It is not surprising that this raw bit from heathen myth should be found troublesome. This item is further proof of the mythological character of the monster who can throw the gods into panic.

25b (17bH). Both words of this line, *miššĕbārîm yitḥaṭṭĕ'û,* have continued to trouble. Rashi suggested the reading *mišbārîm,* "waves," and many moderns have followed a similar line and divided the word in two, *mišbĕrê yām,* "waves of the sea." Gunkel, in view of the Mesopotamian parallels, proposed the emendations *bišmê mārôm yiṯḥabbĕ'û,* "In the highest heaven they hide themselves." Similarly, Tur-Sinai read *môšaḇ rôm* for *miššĕbārîm* to produce the sense "they tried to placate him in their high seat." Actually there is no need to tamper with either word. The "breakings" do not refer to waves, but to the shattering effects of fear. The Vulgate was on the right track with the rendering *territi*. The term *šĕḇārîm* is either elliptical for *šeḇer moṯnayim*, "breaking of the loins," or else the word *motnayim* has been lost from the text through copyists' misunderstanding. The term *šiḇrôn moṯnayim* is actually attested in Ezek xxi 11 (6E); KJ with LXX and Vulg. renders the term literally and correctly, but other modern versions, including RSV, mistakenly change "loins" to "heart." The meaning of the expression is now clarified by the Ugaritic mythological texts which use the almost identical term to describe the sensations and manifestations of fear (ʿnt III 29–32):

When ʿAnat saw the gods	*hlm ʿnt tph ilm*
With her the feet trembled.	*bh pʿnm tṭṭ*
Behind the loins broke,	*bʿdn ksl tṯbr*
Above her face did sweat.	*ʿln pnh tdʿ*
The joints of her loins quivered,	*tġṣ pnt kslh*
Those of her back grew weak.	*anš dt ẓrh*

As for the verb *yiṯḥaṭṭĕʾû*, it is clear that the usual sense, "they purify themselves," is unsuitable, but there is no need to emend to *ḥbʾ*, "hide." Tur-Sinai's interpretation, "they tried to placate him," may have some support in the efforts to placate Tiamat in the Mesopotamian Creation Epic, but more acceptable sense is furnished by Ethiopic *ḥṭʾ* in the sense of "withdraw" and still better by Ar. *ḥṭʾ*, "cast down." The text thus makes excellent sense without the slightest emendation. S. R. Driver commented on Gunkel's brilliant emendation that it stands or falls with the mythological interpretation of Leviathan. Gunkel's insight has been confirmed by the appearances of Leviathan (*ltn*) in the Ugaritic myths, described in terms almost identical with those of Isa xxvii 1, but the emendation proves unnecessary.

26a (18aH). The emendation of *maśśîḡēhû*, "his attacker," to *taśśîḡēhû*, "it (the sword) attacks him" is quite unnecessary. The *casus pendens* construction is common.

avails not. Literally "does not stand."

28a (20aH). *arrow*. Literally "son of a bow."

31b (23bH). Naturally, the mention of an ointment pot or pan reminds the proponents of crocodilian exegesis of the scent glands in the animal's rear. But this has no relevance to the figure of boiling water or the seething mixture in an apothecary's pot as descriptive of the wake of the monster.

32b (24bH). *deep*. The use of *tĕhôm*, a designation of the primeval subterranean waters, to describe Leviathan's habitat may be regarded merely as a poetic figure. There is, however, nothing to suggest that the terms "sea" and "deep" refer to the Nile.

33 (25H). *earth.* Literally "dust." Sometimes a designation of the netherworld, cf. iv 19, vii 21, x 9, xiv 8, xvii 16, xix 25 (?), xx 11, xxxiv 15. Whether this is the case here is questionable.

Blommerde, following Dahood (*Biblica* 45 [1964], 410; UHP, p. 10) in the derivation of MT *ḥāṯ* from *ḫt'*, "shatter, crack," and reading *ḥăṭā'āṯ*, rendered:

> On earth is not his equal,
> made as he is without a flaw;
> every lofty being is afraid of him,
> the king of all proud creatures.

MT *yir'eh,* "he sees," Blommerde read *yārē'āh,* "it is afraid," and construed the following *hû'* as an independent pronoun in the accusative. The Qumran Targum preserves only the latter half of the second verse, and prefixes the conjunction *w* before the independent pronoun thus indicating that it goes with what follows and is to be construed as subject rather than object:

> *whw' mlk 'l kl rḥš*
> And he is king over every creeping thing.

The reading *rḥš* accords with Syr. and presumably reflects *šereṣ* instead of MT *šaḥaṣ*. This rendering was probably influenced by the notion that the creature in question is the crocodile. LXX read "And he is king of all those in the waters." The Ugaritic proof that Leviathan is a mythological monster (cf. iii 8, xl 25, xli 4) confirms MT *šḥṣ,* cognate with Ar. *šḫṣ,* "be high, lofty, sublime."

34b (26bH). *proud beings.* Literally "sons of pride"; cf. xxviii 8. This expression might seem to suggest that the creature in question is from the natural world, but in view of the many mythical features already noted this seems unlikely. The boastful Leviathan fits the specification of pride; cf. xli 4a.

41. JOB RECANTS; EPILOGUE
(xlii 1–17)

XLII 1 Then Job answered Yahweh:

2 "I know that you can do all things;
No purpose of yours can be thwarted.
[3 Who is this that obscures counsel without knowledge?]
I talked of things I did not know,
Wonders beyond my ken.
[4 Listen, and I will speak;
I will question you, and you tell me.]
5 I had heard of you by hearsay,
But now my own eye has seen you;
6 So I recant and repent
In dust and ashes."

7 After Yahweh had spoken these words to Job, Yahweh said to
Eliphaz the Temanite, "My anger burns against you and your
two friends; for you have not spoken truth of me, as did Job,
my servant. 8 So, now, take yourselves seven bullocks and seven
rams, and go to Job, my servant, and make a burnt offering for
yourselves, and Job, my servant, will pray for you, for I will accept him, so that I may not do anything rash to you; for you
have not told truth of me, as did Job, my servant. 9 So Eliphaz
the Temanite, Bildad the Shuhite, and Zophar the Naamathite
went and did as Yahweh commanded them. Yahweh accepted
Job 10 and restored Job's fortune when he prayed for his friends
and increased what he had twofold. 11 All his brothers and
sisters and former acquaintances called on him and had a meal
with him in his house; and they consoled and comforted him
for all the misfortune Yahweh had inflicted on him. Each one
gave him a qesita and a gold ring. 12 Then Yahweh blessed

Job's later life more than his earlier life; he now had fourteen thousand sheep, six thousand camels, a thousand yoke of oxen, and a thousand she-asses. 13 He had seven sons and three daughters. 14 He named the first daughter Yemimah (Dove); the second's name was Qeziah (Cinnamon); the third's name was Qeren-happuk (Horn of Kohl). 15 In all the land no women were to be found as beautiful as Job's daughters and their father gave them inheritance among their brothers. 16 After this Job lived a hundred and forty years and saw his sons and grandsons to four generations. 17 So Job died, old and satisfied with life.

NOTES

xlii 3a. This verse is almost identical with xxxviii 2 and is usually regarded as a misplaced variant. Driver, however, regarded it as an integral part of the text, supposing that Job here repeats the question previously put to him for the purpose of admitting the validity of the indictment. On the verb *'lm*, "be dark," cf. vi 16b.

4a. Cf. xxi 2, xxxiii 31.

4b. Identical with xxxviii 3b, except for the omission of the initial conjunction "and"; cf. xiii 22.

5a. *hearsay*. Literally "report of ear." The identical expression occurs in Ps xviii 45, but with different meaning; cf. xxviii 22.

5b. In what sense has Job "seen" God? Tur-Sinai's conjecture that an older version of the story related more of God's appearance seems rather unlikely. We must assume that Job is now convinced of what he had doubted, viz., God's providential care. He had hoped for the assurance that God was on his side and would vindicate him. This, he had insisted, xix 23–27, must come somehow—if not during his life, then later. Now that God has spoken directly to him, Job's demands have been met.

6. *recant*. It is usually explained that the object of the verb has been lost from the text. KJ and RSV follow LXX (*emauton*) and supply "myself." LXX actually gives a double translation of the verb but does not necessarily reflect any textual difference. Targ. adds an object, "my wealth." JPS supplies "my words." The latter is doubtless the correct interpretation. What Job now despises, refuses, rejects is his former attitude and utterances. The verb *m's* is not used of self-loathing. In ix 21 it is not himself, but his miserable condition that

Job finds distasteful. When the object of the verb is clear from the context, it does not need to be expressed; cf. vii 16. There is no reason to take the verb here in the sense of "melt, pine away," as in vii 5. Cf. L. J. Kuyper, VT 9 (1959), 91–94.

6b. Job is already sitting in ashes, ii 8. Cf. Isa lviii 5; Jer vi 26; Jon iii 6; Mic i 10.

The Qumran Targum preserves xlii 1–6 with some deviations from MT:

1 *'n' 'ywb w'mr qdm 'lh'*
Job answered and said before God
2 *yd't dy kl' tkwl lm'bd*
I know that you are able to do all
3 *wl' ytbṣr mnk tqp wḥkmh*
And power and wisdom are unlimited for you
xl 5 *ḥdh mllt wl' atyb*
I have spoken once and will not repeat
wtrtyn w'lyhn l' 'wsp
Even twice and to them I will not add
4 *šm' n' w'nh 'mll*
Listen, now, and I will speak
'š'lnk whtybny
I will question you and you answer me
5 *lmšm' 'dn šm'tk*
By hearsay I have heard of you
wk'n 'yny ḥztk
But now my eye has seen you
6 *'l kn 'tnsk w'tmh'*
Thus I am poured out and dissolved/smitten(?)
w'hw' l'pr wqṭm
And am become dust and ashes.

The editors note that the root *mh'* in *w'tmh'*—the *h* was inserted above the line between the *m* and '—is found here for the first time in Aramaic. It is, however, attested in post-biblical Hebrew in the Nip̄'al *nimhāh,* and the passive participle *māhûah,* "worn-out," and has an Arabic cognate *mahā,* "beat violently, be thin and watery." The latter sense "beat violently" may connect the root with *mḥ'* which is attested in all periods of Aramaic and has been shown by M. Held (JAOS 79 [1959], 171, n. 37) to be the exact correspondent of Akk. *maḫāṣu,* Ugar. *mḫṣ* and Heb. *māḥaṣ,* "strike down, slay." In Ezra vi 11 the form *yiṭmĕḥē'* is used of impalement. Whether in the sense of "be dissolved" as "be smitten," it is a strange interpretation of MT *wĕniḥamtî,* "and I repent." LXX rendered *kai etakēn,* "and I have melted," and like the Qumran Targum supplied a verb, *hēgēmai de emauton gēn kai spodon,* "and I esteem myself earth and ashes." Targ. added an unlikely twist, "and I am sorry for my children for they are dust and ashes."

7. Yahweh addresses Eliphaz, as the eldest of the friends; cf. xv 10. This verse presents difficulties. Some interpreters see it as an indication that the folk tale originally presented a pious and patient Job throughout, as in the Prologue, who continued to praise God and ignored his wife's advice to blaspheme and die. It has been suggested that the friends gave similar advice, which would explain the divine censure. How could the friends be condemned for such valiant defense of traditional dogma as they make in the Dialogue and how could Job be commended for his vehement attacks on their doctrine and the God they presumed to defend? How could God rebuke Job for speaking in ignorance and then commend him for having spoken the truth? Some interpreters attempt to explain this difficulty by taking the word in the Hebrew to mean "sincerity," but the word nowhere has this sense. The basic meaning is "correct." The almost identical expression occurs in I Sam xxiii 23 where RSV renders "sure information." Delitzsch notes that objective truth and subjective truthfulness are blended in the notion of what is "correct"; he suggests that the correct elements of Job's speeches were his denying that sin is always punished with affliction and his holding fast to his innocence despite his friends' attack. God approved this sort of truthfulness rather than the dissembling of the friends who could not admit Job's innocence without upsetting their neat system of doctrine. Job had indeed accused his miserable comforters of lying to defend and flatter God; and he suggested that an honest God would certainly reject and punish the pious sycophants, xiii 4, 7–11. If this verse refers to the arguments of the Dialogue, it is as magnificent a vindication as Job could have hoped for, proving that God values the integrity of the impatient protester and abhors pious hypocrites who would heap accusations on a tormented soul to uphold their theological position; cf. vi 14–30.

8. The friends are no longer present. Perhaps in the folk tale they had gone home after a time and left Job in his misery.

The sacrifice is rather large, indicating a grave concern; cf. Num xxiii 1, 4, 14, 29 f. For the schedule of expiatory sacrifices, cf. Lev iv. According to LXX and Syr., Job was to make the burnt offering for them, as he did for his sons, i 5.

accept. Literally "his face I will lift up"; cf. xiii 8. It would be in order for Job, as the offended party, to intercede, but cf. xxii 30 for Job's efficacy as mediator.

rash. Literally "folly," *nĕḇālāh.* Some critics find this word objectionable as applied to God's action since in common use it designates grave and wanton sin, almost always sexual offense; cf. Gen xxxiv 7;

Deut xxii 21; Josh vii 15; Judg xix 23, xx 6, 10; II Sam xiii 12; Jer xxix 23. It would be folly to emend this striking anthropopathism.

9. LXX has at the end of this verse a variation which may represent an original reading, "And he loosed the sin for them through Job."

10. *fortune.* Cf. Jer xxix 14, xxx 3; Ezek xvi 53, xxxix 25. This is the only occurrence of the idiom with the name of a person rather than a nation. The explanation offered by Ewald, that the word *šĕḇû/îṯ,* has nothing to do with captivity, but is cognate with the verb "return," *šûḇ,* is still the most satisfactory. Though the analysis of the idiom is uncertain, its meaning is clear; cf. R. Borger, ZAW 66 (1955), 315 f.

11. His prosperity again attracted his relatives and fair-weather friends; cf. xix 13.

qesita. An ancient unit of exchange of unknown nature and value, mentioned elsewhere only in transactions of the patriarchal age (Gen xxxiii 19; Josh xxiv 32). LXX renders *amnos,* "lamb," and *amnas,* "ewe" (cf. Lat. *pecunia,* from *pecus,* "cattle"), but perhaps corrupted from *mnā,* a mina; cf. the Arabic term *qisṭ.* It took a hundred qesitas to buy a sizable piece of real estate in the patriarchal age (Josh xxiv 32) so that one qesita from each visitor was more than a mere token gift.

ring. For the ears (Gen xxxv 4) or the nose (Gen xxiv 47; Isa iii 21).

The ending of the Qumran Targum differs considerably from MT and has closer affinities with LXX. The last column preserves seven lines which correspond roughly to vss. 9–11:

1 . . . .

2 *'lh' wšm' '[l]h' bqlh dy 'ywb wšbq*
. . . God. And God hearkened to the voice of Job and forgave

3 *lhwn ḥṭ'yhwn bdylh wtb 'lh' l'ywb brḥmyn*
them their sins on his account and God turned to Job with mercy

4 *wyhb lh ḥd tryn bkl dy hw' lh w'tyn lwt*
and he gave him double for all he had and they came to

5 *'ywb kl rḥmwhy wkl 'ḥwhy wkl yd'why w'klw*
Job all his friends and all his brothers and acquaintances and ate

6 *'mh lḥm bbyth wnḥmwhy 'l kl b'yšth dy*
with him food in his house and consoled him for all the misfortune which

7 *hyty 'lh' 'lwhy wyhbw lh gbr 'mrh ḥdh*
God had brought on him and each gave him a lamb

8 *wgbr qdš ḥd dy dhb*
and each a ring of gold

The last line corresponds to the ending of vs. 11 of MT and the scribe stopped at this point leaving half the space of the line and room for several more lines unused. Elsewhere in the document space is left only where there is a change in speakers, which is not the situation with xlii 11–12. It is thus possible, though not proven, as the editors cautiously note, that vs. 11 is the last of the Qumran Targum. In this case it presents the earliest of three stages of literary tradition of the ending of Job, MT being the second, and LXX, with its appendix translated from Syriac, the third.

13. The form of the numeral (*šiḇʻānāh*) is peculiar. Targ. construed it as a dual, thus doubling the number of sons without increasing the daughters. A surplus of girls ordinarily would be regarded as a calamity; cf. Ecclesiasticus xxvi 10–12, xlii 9–11. The pagan Arabs used to bury unwanted daughters at birth (cf. Sale, *The Koran*, pp. 199, 438). Job's daughters, well endowed with beauty and wealth, figure more prominently than the sons who are not even mentioned by name. Sarna (JBL 76 [1957], 18) suggests that the numeral *šiḇʻānāh* may be a genuine archaism related to the Ugaritic form *šbʻny*.

14. *Yemimah*. Cf. Ar. *yamāmah* for the Egyptian turtledove. LXX and Vulg. connect the name with *yôm*, "day." The dove was a symbol of feminine beauty:

My dove in the cleft of the rock,
In the cranny of the cliff,
Show me your form,
Let me hear your voice,
For your voice is sweet,
And your form fair (Song of Songs ii 14).

The dove's prodigious fertility and its conjugal devotion also made it an appropriate symbol of femininity. It also represented stupidity (Hos vii 11) and innocence (Matt x 16). It became a rabbinical symbol of Israel, as unjustly persecuted (Ps lxxiv 19; TB, Baba Qama 93a) and of the Holy Spirit (cf. Matt iii 16).

14. *Qeziah*. "Cassia," a variety of cinnamon used as perfume and along with myrrh and aloes as an ingredient of anointing oil, sacred and otherwise; cf. Exod xxx 24; Ezek xxvii 19; Ps xlv 9. (The identity of *qěṣîʻāh* and *qiddāh* [Exod xxx 24; Ezek xxvii 19] is certified by Targ. and Rashi.) In Prov vii 17, the adulteress says, "I have perfumed my bed with myrrh, aloes, and cinnamon (*qinněmôn*)." C. H. Gordon has related the name to a Ugaritic term for "bow," *qṣʻt*. "The shapeliness of a bow made it appropriate for a girl's name," (UT 19.2258). Dahood (UHP, p. 60) has taken *qṣʻt* to designate arrows rather than a bow, but

this is dubious; cf. Pope, JBL 85 (1966), 457. If *qṣʿt* means "arrow," it would not be particularly suitable for a girl's name. One may even harbor misgivings about "Bow" as a feminine name, despite the curvature.

Kohl. Powdered antimony was used as paint for the eyelashes, lids, and brows from very early times. This artifice heightened the already considerable seductive powers of the feminine eyes; cf. Jer iv 30; Ecclesiasticus xxvi 9. The use of such devices was not regarded favorably by the OT writers, because of its association with foreign and lewd women, II Kings ix 30; Ezek xxiii 40.

The names of Job's daughters represent natural feminine physical and spiritual charms enhanced by perfumer's and beautician's art. The naming of the daughters and the omission of the sons' names is reminiscent of Baal's children in the Ugaritic myths. The three daughters' names are several times mentioned as Dewy (*ṭly*), Earthy (*arṣy*), and Flashy (*pdry*), but the seven or eight boys (*ġlmm*) remain nameless. For interesting sociological parallels in the status of women between the patriarchal period of the OT and the world of Homer, cf. C. H. Gordon, "Homer and Bible," HUCA 26 (1955), 43–108.

The form *ymmt* occurs in Ugaritic as a variant of *ybmt,* in the goddess ʿAnat's epithet *ybmt limm* (*ymmt limm* in ʿnt III 9). In Hebrew *yĕḇēmāh* is the technical term for a brother's widow. The surviving brother (*yāḇām*) is obligated to take his dead brother's wife in levirate marriage and procreate (*yabbēm*) with her to ensure survival of the dead brother's name, Deut xxv 5, 7; cf. Matt xxii 24; Mark xii 19; Luke xx 28. ʿAnat's title *ybmt/ymmt limm* thus would mean something like Peoples' Procreatrix. Whether Job's Yemimah bears any relation to this epithet of the goddess is questionable.

15. *inheritance.* Normally daughters inherited only when there was no son, as in the case of Zelophehad who died leaving five daughters and no sons, Num xxvi 33, thus calling for special legislation, Num xxvii 1–8, xxxvi 1–12. Inheritance by the daughters when there are sons is thus remarkable and unique in the OT. This may be regarded as a token of the elevated status of women in the patriarchal society reflected by the Book of Job. For similar examples from the Homeric world, cf. Gordon, HUCA 26 (1955), 76–82.

16. LXX reads "And Job lived after the affliction 170 years" and then adds: "And in all he lived 240 (48) years." (Codex Vaticanus omits the extra eight.) Thus Job would have been 70 (or 78) at the time of his affliction, having come to the end of a grossly normal span of years (cf. Ps xc 10). MT's "140 years" then fits neatly into the scheme of double restitution of all Job's fortunes. Thus his added longevity was twice what he had before, or the equivalent of three lives. The LXX figure 170, and the resultant total of 240, may be

explained as confusion, conflation, or contamination of the implicit and expressed figures 70 and 140.

four generations. Joseph, who was credited with 110 years, saw only three generations of his descendants, Gen l 23. Presumably the four generations which Job saw did not include his first ill-fated progeny. To see one's grandchildren is the crowning joy of a full life; cf. Ps cxxviii 6; Prov xvii 6.

17. Cf. Gen xxv 8, xxxv 29; I Chron xxix 28. Delitzsch aptly notes that "The style of primeval history, which we here everywhere recognize, is retained to the last words." LXX adds: "It is written, however, that he will rise again with those whom the Lord raises up. This [man] is explained from the Syriac Book as living in the land of Ausis, on the borders of Edom and Arabia; formerly his name was Jobab. He took an Arabian wife and sired a son whose name was Ennon. But he himself was the son of his father Zare[th], one of the sons of Esau, and of his mother Bosorra, so that he was the fifth from Abraham. Now these were the kings that reigned in Edom, over which land he also ruled: first Balak, the son of Beor, and the name of his city was Dennaba; and after Balak, Jobab who is called Job; and after him, Asom, the governor from the country of Teman; and after him Adad, the son of Barad, who destroyed Midian in the plain of Moab, and the name of his city was Gethaim. And the friends who came to him were Eliphaz [a son of Sophan/r] of the sons of Esau, king of the Temanites; Bildad, son of Am(m)non [the son of Chobar], ruler of the Sauchaeans; Sophar, king of the Minaeans. [Teman, son of Eliphaz, ruler of Edom. This one is described in the Syriac Book as living in the land of Ausis, on the borders of the Euphrates; formerly his name was Jobab, but his father was Zareth from the rising of the sun.]" Obviously, these traditions are garbled and of dubious value. For a critical text and apparatus, cf. A. Rahlfs, *Septuaginta,* II, 1935, pp. 344 f.

INDEXES

INDEX OF AUTHORS

Abulfeda 3
Abulola 286
Aelian 340
Aeschylus LXX, LXXI
Albertus Magnus 323, 324
Albright, W. F. XXV, XXXIV, LXXXVIII, 4, 6, 23, 24, 47, 54, 66, 75, 168, 184, 199, 273, 302, 311, 334
Alt, A. LXXI
Anderson, B. W. XVI
Aquinas, Thomas 20, 323, 324
Arberry, A. J. 10
Aristotle 7
Arnold, W. R. LII
Augustine 21

Baker, J. LXXXVIII
Bar-Bahlul 46
Barclay, W. LXXXVI
Barton, G. A. XXVII, LXXXV, 141
Bauer, H. XXV
Bauer, I. B. 323
Baumgartner, W. 257
Beer, G. XLII, 32, 46, 297
Ben Sira, Jesus XL, 5
Ben Yehudah, Eliezer XLIX
Bertholet, A. LII
Beza, Theodore XXXI
Bickell, G. W. H. 297, 326
Billerbeck, P. 168
Blake, William 142
Blank, S. H. LXXVII
Blommerde, A. C. M. VII, 36, 37, 71, 72, 77, 79, 80, 81, 86, 92, 94, 102, 107, 108, 111, 115, 117, 123, 129, 130, 133, 152, 158, 159, 160, 167, 171, 173, 190, 193, 200, 209, 213, 219, 221, 238, 242, 248, 249, 256, 260, 268, 269, 275, 280, 283, 285, 287, 293, 294, 337, 338, 346
Bochart, S. 311, 320, 340
Bonnet, H. 214
Borger, R. 351
Bowen, R. L. 13
Box, G. H. 325
Boylan, P. 302
Bright, J. 47
Brockelmann, C. 248
Brooks, C. LXXXV
Browning, Robert 60
Brownlee, W. H. 144
Bruce, F. F. LXXXVI, LXXXVIII
Budde, K. 47
Buhl, F. 311
Burrows, M. XXIX, LXXX
Buttenwieser, M. LXXXV, 90, 183

Calderone, P. 107
Calvin, J. 21, 80
Cameron, G. 144
Caquot, A. LXXXVIII
Cassuto, U. 264
Chajes, H. P. 152
Cheyne, T. K. 47, 321, 336
Childs, B. S. 66
Chrysostom, John 21, 147
Clement of Alexandria XVI
Cohen, A. LXXXVII, 99
Cooke, G. A. 145, 220
Crook, M. B. LXXXV
Cross, F. M., Jr. XXXVII, XLV, 15, 44, 70, 251, 280, 343
Crum, W. E. 51
Cyril of Jerusalem XLII

Dahood, M. VI, VII, 35, 38, 43, 50, 61, 62, 66, 67, 71, 72, 75, 79, 81, 85, 86, 91, 92, 94, 99, 100, 101, 102, 106, 107, 115, 117, 118, 119, 123, 124, 126, 128, 129, 130, 131, 135, 136, 143, 146, 147, 151, 152, 153, 158, 159, 160, 166, 167, 168, 171, 172, 173, 177, 186, 191, 194, 199, 203, 209, 210, 214, 220, 222, 224, 229, 230, 232, 233, 243, 248,

250, 252, 257, 260, 264, 268, 272, 274, 275, 282, 284, 291, 292, 294, 297, 309, 310, 311, 312, 320, 324, 337, 339, 340, 341, 342, 346, 352
Davidson, A. B. LXXXV, 130
Daniélou, J. LXXXV
Delitzsch, F. LXXXV, 4, 38, 130, 260, 271, 276, 286, 287, 309, 331, 350, 354
Delougaz, P. 110
Dhorme, É. VI, XXV, LXXXV, 4, 16, 24, 30, 38, 51, 52, 65, 67, 134, 157, 159, 176, 177, 182, 183, 195, 205, 209, 210, 232, 243, 248, 250, 259, 261, 263, 264, 265, 271, 275, 276, 283, 294, 295, 301, 302, 308, 310, 314, 324, 326, 327, 328, 342, 344
Diodorus Siculus 200, 201, 310
Diringer, D. 143
Doughty, C. M. 12, 46
Driver, G. R. XLIII, LXXXVIII, 74, 108, 134, 143, 145, 153, 201, 265, 295, 296, 301
Driver, S. R. LXXXV, 144, 221, 286, 300, 345, 348
Duhm, B. LXXXV, 32, 91, 93, 134, 142, 178, 219, 273, 275, 297

Eerdmans, B. D. LXXXV
Ehrlich, A. B. 81, 152, 327, 344
Eissfeldt, O. XXVIII, XXX, 44, 110, 183, 302
Eitan, I. 107, 154, 172
Emerson, R. W. 190
Emmons, J. 235
Epiphanius XLII
Esh, S. 268
Etherius 4
Euripides LXX
Eusebius XXXIV, 23
Ewald, H. 52, 114, 351

Feinberg, C. L. LI
Finkelstein, J. J. 122
Fisher, L. R. 147
Fitzmyer, J. A. 66
Fohrer, G. LXXI, LXXXVI, 154
Foster, F. H. XLIX
Frankfort, H. LXXIV, 330
Frankfort, H. A. LXXIV
Freedman, D. N. LV, 15, 44, 70, 251
Freehof, S. B. LXXXVI
Fullerton, K. LXXI

Galling, K. 144
Gamaliel XLV, XLVI
Gard, D. H. XLIV
Gaster, T. H. 71, 280, 294
Gehman, H. S. XLIV
Gerber, I. J. LXXIII
Gerleman, G. 134
Gersonides 133, 143, 300
Gese, H. LXXXVI
Gesenius, W. 46, 76, 311
Giesebrecht, F. 324
Ginsberg, H. L. XXIII, XXVI, XXXI, XXXIII, XL, XLII, LXXXVIII, 47, 215, 243, 275, 280, 285, 291, 341
Ginzberg, L. 23
Glatzer, N. N. LXXXVI
Glueck, N. 200
Godbey, A. H. 308
Goethe LXXIX
Goetze, A. XXV, 235
Golénischeff, W. S. LI
Gordis, R. XXXVIII, XXXIX, LXXIX, LXXXIII, LXXXVI, LXXXVIII, 37, 91, 165, 168, 169
Gordon, C. H. 145, 161, 273, 291, 352, 353
Gordon, E. I. LVIII, LXXII
Graetz, H. 32, 200, 286
Gray, G. B. LII, 144
Gray, J. XXXIII
Greenfield, J. 61
Grelot, P. 151
Grene, D. 20, 32, 35, 56, 59, 60, 108
Gregory of Nazianzus XXXIV
Guillaume, A. XXXV, XXXVI, XLIX, LXXXVI, LXXXVIII, 12, 13, 33, 53, 71, 91, 94, 99, 106, 117, 160, 162, 167, 176, 190, 210, 219, 221, 251, 252, 259, 265, 271, 320
Gunkel, H. 30, 321, 344, 345
Gwyn Griffiths, J. 237

Harper, W. R. LII
Harris, Z. 169
Haussig, H. W. 295
Held, M. 52, 157, 349
Herder, J. G. XLVIII
Herdner, A. 235
Herz, N. 38, 212
Hillers, D. 75
Hitzig, F. 52, 301
Hoffmann, J. G. E. 297, 302
Hölscher, G. LXXXVI
Homer 30, 235, 281, 353

Honeyman, A. M. 261
Hontheim, J. 47, 297
Horapollon 341
Horst, F. LII, LXXXVI
Houbigant, C. F. 176
How, W. W. 10

Ibn Ezra XLIX, LI, 29, 73, 76, 90, 98, 100, 102, 111, 118, 129, 133, 137, 161, 168, 172, 178, 236, 238, 268, 272
Ibn Gabirol 125
Irwin, W. A. XXVII, LIII, LXX, LXXV

Jacob, B. 265
Jacobsen, T. LXXIV, 59
Jahnow, H. LIII
Jastrow, M. LXXXVI
Jaussen, J. A. 24, 302
Jepsen, A. LXXXVI
Jeshurun, G. 229
Jerome XLII, XLIII, XLVII, LXXVI, 22, 23, 201, 231
Jongeling, B. XIII, 341
Jonson, Ben 190
Josephus 3, 13
Joyce, James LXXIX
Jung, C. G. LXXXVI

Kaiser, O. 61
Kallen, H. M. XXXI, LXXXVI
Kapelrud, A. XXVI
Kaufman, S. VII, 160, 165, 181, 184, 193, 194, 210, 222, 327
Kaufmann, Y. XXIX, XXXVIII, LXXIX
Kazwini 309
King, A. R. LXXIII, LXXXVI
King, L. W. 285
Kinnier-Wilson, J. V. 21
Kissane, E. J. LXXXVI, 35, 36, 51, 54, 67, 263, 275, 327
Klostermann, 17
Klostermann, A. 152
Knight, H. LXXXVIII
Kohler, K. 46
Kraeling, E. G. LXXXVI
Kramer, S. N. XXVI, XXXIV, LVIII, LX, LXI, LXXIV, LXXVI, LXXXVI, LXXXVIII, 46, 59, 167, 251
Kuhl, K. XXX, LXXXV
Kuyper, L. J. LXXXVIII, 349

Lagarde, P. de 23
Lambert, W. G. XXXIII, XXXVII, LVI, LXI, LXII, LXIII, LXIV, LXXII, LXXVIII, 50, 65, 171
Larcher, C. P. LXXXVI, 143, 162, 176, 251
La Sor, W. S. 343
Lattimore, R. 20, 32, 35, 56, 59, 60, 108
Laufer, B. 309, 310
Lawrence, T. E. 237
Lee, Samuel 168
Le Hir, A. M. 252
Lewy, H. 281
Lewy, J. 281
Levy-Tokatly, Y. 290
Lindblom, C. J. LXX, LXXI
Lindhagen, C. 12, 59
Liverani, M. XXV
Löhr, M. LIII
Loretz, O. 122
Löw, Immanuel 220
Lowth, Robert LI, LII
Luckenbill, D. D. 4
Lucretius 60
Luther 144, 209
Luzatto, S. D. 10

MacKenzie, R. A. F. LXXXVIII
Maecklenburg, A. LII
Malraux, André 235
Marshall, St. J. 275
Martin, Annie 309, 310
May, H. G. LXX
Meek, T. J. 14
Meissner, B. 235
Mendelsohn, I. 233
Mendenhall, G. E. 333
Mercerus XVI
Merx, A. 20, 47
Michel, W. L. VII, 74, 135, 229
Migne, J. P. XXXI
Milik, J. T. 299
Milton XXXI, 82, 107, 164
Möller, H. LXXXVI
Moffatt, J. 90, 135, 222, 234, 242, 250, 274, 291, 300, 324, 338
Moortgat, A. 322
Molin, G. 312
Montgomery, J. A. 257
Moran, W. J. XLVIII, 136
Mowinckel, S. LII, 201, 202
Muilenburg, J. LII
Munn-Rankin, J. M. 99
Munster, Sebastian 300

Musil, A. 4, 7, 16
Myers, J. M. 340

Nachmanides 300
Nilsson, M. P. LXX
Nir, D. 290
Noth, M. XXIV, LXXXVI
Nougayrol, J. XXXIII, XXXIV
Nyberg, H. S. 275

O'Callaghan, R. T. 158
Oppenheim, A. L. 109, 110
Origen XLIII, XLIV, XLVII, 147
Orlinsky, H. XLIII, XLIV

Pargiter, E. LXIX
Parrot, A. 235
Paterson, J. LXXXVI
Peake, A. S. LXXXVI, 60, 263, 276, 298, 324, 342
Pedersen, J. LXXVII
Perles, F. 294
Pfeiffer, R. H. XXXI, XXXIV, XXXV, XLVIII, LXI, LXIII, LXIV, LXVII
Phillips, W. 13
Philo of Byblos 75
Picard, D. 11
Plato XXXI
Pliny 21, 23, 204, 214, 235, 287, 310, 331
Ploeg, J. P. M. van der XIII, XLV
Plutarch 282
Pope, M. H. LXXVII, LXXXVI, 36, 44, 151, 165, 176, 201, 215, 232, 281, 295, 353
Porada, E. 322
Preuss, J. 75
Pritchard, J. B. LXXXVII, 331
Pythagoras 183

Qimḥi, J. 133, 281
Quintens, W. 92

Rahlfs, A. 354
Raingeard, P. 282
Rashi (Rabbi Solomon Isaac) 20, 29, 46, 73, 90, 101, 102, 118, 123, 129, 130, 133, 134, 140, 143, 144, 158, 161, 172, 205, 209, 228, 231, 236, 238, 272, 344, 352
Reichert, V. E. LXXXVII
Reider, J. 314
Renan, Ernest XLVIII
Rinaldi, G. 190
Ringgren, H. LXXXVII
Robertson, E. 36
Robinson, H. W. LXXXVII
Robinson, T. H. LII, LXXXVII
Rosenthal, F. 310
Roth, W. M. W. 45
Rowley, H. H. XXVII, XXX, XXXI, LXXIII, LXXVI, LXXVIII, LXXXI, LXXXVII, LXXXVIII, 257
Rufinus XLII

Saadia XLVIII, 118, 175
Sale, G. 22, 352
Salles, G. 235
Sanders, J. A. LXXXVII, 269
Sanders, P. S. LXXXVII
Sarna, N. M. XXXIII, LXXXVIII, 62, 67, 130, 135, 136, 168, 169, 352
Savignac, J. de 24
Schaeffer, C. F. A XXIV
Schärf, R. R. LXXXVII
Scharbert, J. LXXIII, LXXXVII
Schechter, S. 60
Schloezer, A. L. XLVIII
Schultens, A. 20
Seneca 310
Sewall, R. B. LXXXVII
Shakespeare LXXIX, 237
Shapiro, D. S. LXXXVIII
Sievers, E. LII
Simeon-ben-Laqish XXX, 302
Skehan, P. W. LIII, LXXXVIII
Smith, J. M. P. 250
Smith, Morton XXXVIII
Sockman, R. W. LXXXVII
Soden, W. von 75
Säve-Söderburgh, T. 320
Sophocles LXX, 20, 32, 35, 55, 59, 60, 108
Speer, J. 147
Speiser, E. A. LXVII, LXIX, 23, 269, 273
Spiegel, S. XXIV, XXXIII
Stade, B. 31
Stamm, J. J. LXXIII, 144
Steinmann, J. LXXXVII, 323
Stevenson, W. B. LXXXVII
Stewart, J. LXXXVII
Stier, F. LXXXVII
Stockhammer, M. LXXXVIII
Strack, H. L. 168
Strabo 331, 340
Streck, M. 31
Sutcliffe, E. F. LXXXVII, 205, 269

Symmachus 209, 344
Szold, B. 143, 324

Tallqvist, K. 21
Taylor, W. S. LXXXVIII
Tebbe, W. LXXXIX
Tennyson 106, 125
Terence 35, 76
Terrien, S. LII, LIII, LXXV, LXXVI, LXXVII, LXXXVII
Theodore of Mopsuestia XXX, XLII
Theodoret of Cyrrhus XVI
Theodotion 209
Thomas, D. W. LXXXVI, 111, 247, 321, 333
Thompson, K. T. LXXXIX
Torczyner, H. LXXXVII; *see* Tur-Sinai
Toy, C. H. 321
Tromp, N. J. 146, 319
Tsevat, M. LXXXIII, LXXXIX, 250
Tur-Sinai, N. H. VI, XLIX, L, LXXXVII, 4, 10, 20, 51, 66, 67, 87, 97, 98, 99, 102, 109, 111, 118, 119, 135, 141, 143, 154, 157, 166, 168, 172, 177, 178, 183, 185, 186, 201, 234, 235, 236, 263, 270, 272, 273, 281, 291, 295, 302, 310, 314, 325, 334, 338, 339, 344, 345, 348

Van Beek, G. W. 13
Vaux, R. de 9, 59, 192, 233
Virgil 90, 114
Voltaire XLVIII

Weidner, E. 144
Weiser, A. LXXXVII
Wells, J. 10
Wetzstein, J. G. 107, 260, 309, 310
Wevers, J. W. XLIII
Williams, R. J. LXXIII, LXXXIX
Wilson, John A. LVI, LVII, LVIII
Woude, A. S. van der XIII, XLV–XLVI
Wright, G. E. LXXXVII
Wright, G. H. B. 274, 326

Xenophon 310

Yadin, Y. 312
Yeats, W. B. LXXIX
Yellin, D. 172
Young, G. D. LI

Ziegler, J. XLIII
Zuckerman, B. VII, 54, 135, 161, 181, 182, 276, 301, 328

INDEX OF SUBJECTS

Abba ben Kahana xxxii, 23
Abel lxxviii, 230
Abraham xxxii, lxxii, 11, 24, 125, 168, 228
Absalom 7, 209
Adam xxxii, 16, 22, 238
Adonis 237
Agag 300
Ahitophel 62
Akhenaton 72
Alalakh 6
'Aliy 148, 184, 207, 209, 274, 277
Alteration in person 260
Amalekites 7
Amarna Letters 5, 16, 219
Ammon 4
Ammonites xlviii, 7
Amnon 7
Amon-Re 298
Amorite 24
'Anah 24
'Anat xxv, xxxix, 15, 24, 33, 71, 74, 93, 137, 184, 229, 234, 306, 321, 329, 332, 345, 353
Angels 9, 116
Anshar 337
Anu 325, 337
Anunnaki 153, 337
Apil Adad 24
Apollo lxx, 42
Aqhat xxv, xxxix, 74, 167, 212, 236, 269, 306
Aqiba 59
Arabia 4, 13, 21, 24, 168
Arabia Deserta 13
Arabia Petraea 16
Arabic origin of the Book of Job xxxv, xlix, 117, 252
Arabs 7, 13
Aram 3, 4, 242
Aramaic xxxviii, xlv, xlvi, xlix, 251; *see also* Qumran Targum
Aramean 3, 7
Arcturus 70, 301
Arslan Tash Incantation 87, 285
Asherah 344
Ashtaroth 6
'Ashtart 61
Ashurnasirpal 14
Ashurbanipal 31
Astarte 333
Aton 72
Atonement, Day of 9
Aurora Borealis 287
Ausis 354
Awil-Nannar 235
Ayyab 6

Baal 33, 74, 184, 215, 221, 298
Babylonian Exile xxxv, xxxix
Babylonian Job xxiii, lxii
Babylonian Theodicy xxxvii, lxiv, lxvii
Baghdad Button (Jericho Rose) 21
Bahrein 4, 242
Balaam xxxii, 8, 30
Balak 354
Ba'lu of Tyre 332
Barachel 242
Barad 354
Bar Qappara xxxii
Bashan 6
Bear (constellation) 301
Behemoth xxii, xxix, lxxxi, 153, 320, 321, 322, 324, 325, 326, 327
Belt-wrestling 291
Bethenije 4
Bible de Jérusalem (abbr. BJ) 91, 143
Bit Yakin 14
Book of the Dead 227
Boötes 301
Bosorra 354
"Breaking of the loins" 345

Brotherhood of mankind 233
Buffalo 307
Bull of heaven 322, 323, 325
Bundle (of the living) 110
Buz 4, 242
Byblos 7

Caesarea 331
Cairo Genizah 5, 29
Caleb 12
Cancer 301
Canon XLII, 235
Carmel 108
Carneas 4
Cassia 352
Cassite period XXXIII, LXI
Chaldeans XXXII, XXXVI, 14, 55, 94
Chambers of the South 71
Channel (netherworld) 250
Chobar 354
Christ LXXV
Chronicles XLII
Chrysolite 204
Cock 302
Contest literature LXXII
Coptic XLIII, 51, 331
Coral 204
Cornelius Fido 310
Corona Borealis 301
Covenant 228
Cowering of the gods 333
Creation Epic 70, 141, 293, 332, 337, 339, 344, 345
Crocodile 320, 331, 340
Crocodilopolis 331
Cross LXXIV, LXXXII
Crystal 204
Cyprus 42, 125, 183, 200

Dahomey 110
Damascus 3
Damietta 202
Danel XXIV, XXV, XXXIII, 6, 11, 14, 165, 168, 212, 236, 306
Daniel, Book of XXXIII
Darius 10
David 9, 12, 110, 241, 292
Dawn 295
Death 111, 136, 192, 205, 251; *see also* Mot
Dedan 4, 12, 13, 24, 242
Deir Ayyub 4
Deluge 59
Demarous 264
Dennaba 4, 354
Denominative verbs from numerals 115
Dera' 4
Descent of Ishtar 296, 319
Deus ex machina XXXI
Deutero-Isaiah, *see* Second Isaiah
Deuteronomic Code 159
Devil 11
Devourers 293, 321, 325
Dhuneibeh 4
Dilmun 4, 46, 242
Dinah 23
Dishan 4
Divine assembly 251
Dog 219
Dolmens 183
Double-duty negative 119
Dove 352
Dragon 61, 329, 330, 331
Dreams 249
Dual, Canaanite 177, 238, 269
Duimes (Carthage) 145
Dusk 295

Ea 332
Eaters 293, 321, 325
Eclipse 29
Eden 201
Edom XLVIII, 3, 4, 23, 24, 200
Edomites XXXVI, XLVIII, 7
El XXIV, XXV, XXXIII, 15, 190, 203, 236, 282, 321, 324, 336
El-'Iṣ 4
El-'Ula 4, 13
Eldad 24
Eleazar, Rabbi XXXIV
Electra 60, 108
Elijah XXXVIII, LXXIX, 14
El-Kronos 282
Eloquent Peasant LVIII
'Elyon 147
Elysian Fields 252
Emendations of the Scribes 63, 242
Enclitic *-m* 38, 44, 62, 66, 85, 116, 119, 128, 151, 160, 166, 176, 212, 251, 281
Ein Gedi 306
Enki 59
Enkidu 322, 323
Ennon 354
Entemena 141
Enuma Elish 185
Ephraim 23

Ephron LXXII
Esagil LXIV
Esarhaddon 332
Esau XXX, XXXII, 4, 22, 354
Essenes 243
Eshmunazar 124, 183
Eskhuranib 200
Esther XLII
Etana 157
Ethiopia 13
Ethiopic XLVIII
Euphrates 7, 24
Execration Texts 6
Ezekiel XL, LXXVIII, 5, 11, 12
Ezion-geber 168, 200
Ezra XLII

Fables LXXII
Fatherhood of God 233
Fertility 152
Field-sprites 45
Filth 75
Fire-breathing dragons 342
Firstborn, crown prince 135
Flesh 236
Flood XXXVIII, 166, 175
Flute 224
Folly 16, 23, 228

Gabriel 23, 325
Gate (city) 42, 210
Gehenna 129
Gematria 46
Gentry 258
Gethaim 354
Gibeah 237
Gilgamesh XLI, 202, 237, 248, 322, 323, 325
Glass 204
Gold 204, 286
Gomorrah XXXVIII, LXXII, 237
Gonorrhea 236
Gravity 300
Greek Text XLIV
Greek tragedy LXX
Grief 15
Guardian angels 251
Gudea 67, 202
Gurpazaḫ 291

Ḫabur 24
Ḫadad 24, 185
Hades LXX, 16, 251
Hagiographa XLII
Halitosis 142
Hammurabi 165, 175, 179, 213, 235
Hand 85, 152
Hannah 22, 33
Hariscandra LXIX
Harp 224
Hattusilis 67
Hauran 3, 4, 260
Hawrōn 285
Heart 8
Hector 21
Heliopolis 214
Heracles 35, 55
Hermes 302
Herodotus 199, 214, 287
Hesperus 70, 292
Hexapla XLVII
Hijaz XXXVI
Hippopotamus 320, 322, 324, 326, 328
Hissing 195
Hodayot 151
Homosexuality 151, 236, 237, 269
Horus 237
Hosea XLIII, 55
Ḫubur 250
Ḫuleh 66, 307, 322, 327
Hyades 70, 301
Hyllus 35

Ibex 306
Ibis 302
Imprecatory Psalms 235
Inanna 319
India 168
Indian literature LXIX
Indra LXIX
Interpreter 251
Iron 201
Isaiah XLI, 12
Ishtar 67, 229, 237, 308, 325
Islam 167
Israel XXXV, XLII, 140

Jackal 224
Jacob 23
Jauf 4
Jebel el ʻAqra 183
Jebel el Naʻāmeh 24
Jehoshaphat 168
Jeremiah XLIV, LXXVIII, 4, 12, 27, 55, 115
Jericho Rose (Baghdad Button) 21
Jesus of Nazareth LXXVIII, 166

Jethro XXXII
Jewels 204
jinās 210
Job Stone 4
Jobab XXXII, 354
Job's daughters 352
Job's wife 21, 22
Johanan, Rabbi XXXIV
John the Baptist 136
Jonadab 93
Jonah XXXVIII
Jordan 327
Joseph 23, 354
Joshua XXXII
Joshua, Rabbi 190
Judah XXX

Karatepe 43
Keret XXV, XXXIII, 136, 165, 211, 212, 214, 234, 250, 270
Kerkuk 110
Kilamuwa 213
King's Ear 10
King's Eye 10
Kishon 331
Kiss 235
Knees 31
Kohl 353
Koran 22, 80, 281, 352
Koshar XXV, 30, 236, 338
Kronos 282

Labial change b/p 117, 203, 230
Lamech 44
Lamedh, of emphasis 136
Lament(ation) XLI, XLII, LXXI
Lebanons 53
Legitimation 31
Leo 301
Levi, Rabbi 302
Leviathan XXII, XXIX, LXXXI, 30, 55, 184, 201, 320, 321, 322, 323, 324, 325, 328, 329, 330, 339, 345
Lewdness 231
Lindwurm 202
Lotus 326
Lucifer 292

Makhir 22
Mami LXV, LXVI
Manasses 22
Marduk LXIII, LXIV, 70, 141, 171, 185, 202, 293, 337, 339, 342
Mari 6, 99
Marib 13
Markandeya Purana LXIX
Matteshub 291
Medad 24
Medain Saliḥ 4, 13
Mercury 30, 302
Meroë 13
Merodach-baladan 15
Mesha Stela XLVIII
Messiah LXXVI, 14
Methushelah 250
Metrics LI
Micaiah ben Imlah XXXVII, 9
Midian 24
Midianites 7
Mining 199, 200
Moab 4
Monotheism XXXVIII
Mons Casius 183
Mordecai 3
Moses XXXII, LXXII, 12, 47
Mot XXV, 75, 135, 136, 184, 192, 223, 251, 296, 329; *see also* Death
Moth 38
Mother Earth 16
Mount of Assembly 183
Mourning 15
Murashu 242
Mummu 332
Muslim 167
Muzzle 61

Na'amah 24
Naamathite 24
Nabatean(s) 23, 251
Nabonidus XXXVI, 14, 55, 71, 91, 94
Nabopolassar 14
Naboth LXXVIII
Nahor 3
Nahr ez-Zerqa 331
Narru LXVI
Nathan 3
Nawā 3
Nebuchadnezzar XXXVI, 11, 12
Nehardea 214
Nephilim 71
Nergal 42, 136
Netherworld 60, 75, 91, 111, 136, 182, 183, 250, 251, 296, 319, 346
New Year's Day 9
Niqmad XXV
Nile 202, 302, 331, 346
Nimrod 71
Nindar 67

Nineveh 247
Ningirsu 141
Nippur LVIII, 202
Noah XXIV, XXXIII, 6, 11, 168
Nomads 7
North Africa 199
North Syria 42
Nubia 13, 201, 204
Number idiom 44
Nuzi 109, 110, 291

Oath LXXVII, 153, 231, 238, 247
Ocean LXX
Olympus 183
Orphan 165
Ophir 168, 199
Orion 70, 301
Ostrich 224, 308, 310, 311

Palmyrene 251
Panamuwa 124
Parable 166
Paradise 46
Paraclete LXXVI
Patriarchal sagas XXXII, LXXI
Paul XLV, 37, 233, 337
Persia(n) XXXVI, 10, 11
Personal god LXXVI, 41, 146, 251
Pessimistic Dialogue LXVII–LXVIII
Peter 45
Philistia 4
Philistines 7, 200
Philo of Byblos 75, 302
Philoctetes 32, 59, 60
Phoenician XLVIII, 125, 169, 199
Phoenix 214
Physiologus 309
Pidray 299
Piel, privative 94
Pim 118
Piraeus 220
Pledge 128, 165
Pleiades 70, 300
Pluto 136
Poetry, biblical L ff.
Polonius 55
Potsherd 21
Prayer 252
Priam 21
Prince Sea 70, 71, 185, 341
Prometheus LXX, 115
Prosody L, LI
Prostitutes 269
Proverbs XLII, LI, LXXII
Providence 298
Psalms XXXVII, XLII, LI, LXXII, 100

Qarnayim 4
Qarnini 4
Qeren-happuk 348
Qeturah 24
Qeziah 348
Qinah LIII
Qoheleth XXXIX, LXXVIII
Qumran XL, XLV, 32, 143, 151, 192, 306
Qumran Targum VII, XLV, XLVI, XLVII, 151, 157, 160, 161, 165, 166, 167, 177, 181, 182, 191, 192, 193, 194, 196, 206, 210, 212, 219, 221, 222, 236, 242, 243, 248, 249, 250, 257, 258, 259, 260, 264, 269, 270, 272, 274, 276, 282, 283, 284, 291, 292, 293, 294, 295, 296, 297, 298, 299, 300, 301, 307, 311, 312, 313, 314, 318, 332, 333, 334, 339, 340, 342, 343, 344, 346, 349, 351
Qumran War Scroll 12

Rahab 60, 71
Rahmat 23
Ram 242
Ramses II 4
Ras Shamra, *see* Ugarit(ic)
Resheph 50
Retribution LXXXI, LXXXIII
Rosetta 202
Rubicon 15
Rubies 204
Ruth XLII, LXXI

Sabeans XXXII, 4, 13
Saints 251; *see also* Personal god
Salvation 222
Samak 66, 307, 322, 327
Samaria ostraca 209
Samaritans XVI
Samson 136, 231
Samuel 136
Sanchunjaton 302
Sarai's beauty 228
Sardinia 199
Sargon 13, 15
Sasi 5
Satan XVI, XXVIII, XXXVI, XXXVII, LXXIV, 9, 10, 11, 19, 20, 50, 73, 123, 231
Sauchaeans 354

Saul 9, 58
Sea(-god) 30, 61, 70, 71, 118, 333, 337, 338; *see also* Prince Sea
Seba 13
Second Isaiah XXXV, XXXVII, XXXIX, LXXIX, 32, 52, 91
Second Temple XXXIX
Secret service 10
Šelaḥ 250
Semachonitis 322
Semites XL, XLVIII
Sermon on the Mount 27
Serabit el Khadem 201, 202
Seth 237
Seven winds 281
Shaddai XXIV, XXVIII, XXXVIII, 43, 44, 147
Shaddayan 147
Shades 182
Shalmaneser 5, 308
Shamash LXVI
Sheba 4, 13, 24, 199
Sheikh Sa'ad 4
Sheikh Meskīn 3, 4
Shekinah 168
Sheol 108, 131
Shiva LXIX
Shuah 24
Shuhite 24
Siloam 250
Simeon-ben-Laqish XXX, 302
Sin (moon-god) 91
Sinai 200
Sinuhe 7
Sirocco 15, 285
Slavery 59, 233
Soapwort 75
Sodom XXXVIII, LXXII, 168, 237, 270
Sodomites 269
Solomon XXXIV, 4, 58, 168, 200
Song of Songs XLII
Sophar 354
South Arabia 13
Spain 199
Spitting 17, 129
Spittle 62
Spirit of God 242
Stones of fire 201
Storm 290
Styx 250
Suffering Servant XXX, XXXV, LXXIX, LXXXI, 12
Suicide LVI, LVII, 62
Suḫu 24
Sumerian XXXIV, XL, LI, LVIII, LX
Supererogation 168
Superlative 247, 321
Swaddling bands 293
Sword dance 158

t, infixed 252, 294
Taautos 302
Tablets, devotional 145
Ṭafīle 4
Taharka 332
Tannin 61
Targum 143, 167, 257, 258, 270, 299, 301, 307, 314, 328, 341, 342, 350
Tarshish 199
Tartessus 199
tauriyat 271
Tebūk 24
Tell Asmar 330
Tema XXXV, XLIX, 4, 13, 91, 94, 242
Teman 23, 354
Testament of Job 22, 231
Tetragrammaton XXXIX
Theodicy XV, LXII, LXVII, LXXIII, 50, 182
Theology, Near Eastern XXXVII
Theomachy 151, 181
Theophany XXII, XXVIII, 290
Thoth 302
Thunder 279
Tiamat 60, 70, 71, 141, 185, 293, 337, 339
Tiglathpileser 13, 307
Tigris 14
Tiḫut 302
Tirhakah 332
Titanomachy 151
Topaz 204
Trachis 35
Trachonitis 3
Transjordan 183
Trent, Council of XLIII
Tricola 79

u, indicative modal ending 108, 280
Ugarit(ic), mentioned throughout the book
Umpire 76
Unicorn 307
Uriah LXXVIII
Ursa Major 71
Uṣṣa 5

Uz 3, 4, 5
Uzziah 58

Vasishta LXIX
Venus 30, 237, 301
Vindicator 251
Virgin 228
Virgo 301

waw, apodoseos 80
waw, explicativum 242
waw, pleonastic 36
Wadi es-Saba 4
Watcher 11
Watusi 13
Widow 165
Wind storms 290
Wisdom XLI, LXXII, LXXVIII, 65, 66, 206, 242, 296, 325
Witness 251
Wrestling belts 291

y, third masculine suffix 73, 77, 80, 123, 125, 147, 159, 171, 173, 190, 256, 283, 294, 337, 338
Yahweh XVI, XXXVIII
Yamm XXV, 61, 70, 293; *see also* Sea(-god)
Yarkon 331
Yashar XXXII
Yaṣṣib 212, 271
Yaṭpan 74
Yemen 13
Yemimah 348

Zaphon 183, 275, 286
Zare(th) 354
Zekut Abot 168
Zelophehad 353
Zenjirli 43, 213
Zepho/i 24
Zerubbabel 12
Zeus LXX, 264
Zimran 264
Zimri 264
Zodiac 301
Zophar 24
Zulummar LXVI

INDEX OF WORDS

1. Akkadian

aban išāti 201
awat(u) 6
Ayabi-ilu 6
Ayabi-sharri 6
Ay(y)a-ḫammu/ḫalu 6
algamešu 204
Apil Adad 24
Aribi 13
ašlāku 75
Barik-ilu/i 242
Bil Adad 24
bûl ṣêri 325
bulû 325
Dadi-ilu 24
zaqāqu 200
ḫabḫu 221
ḫapāru 179
hurâṣu sagru 204
karpatu 159
karpu 159
ludlul bēl nēmeqi XXXIII, LXI, 171
manzaz pāni 171
manzaztu 281
maštāru 301
mušmîtûti 251
mušruššu 202
nazāzu 281
nasāsu 275
nâṣu 309
nêšu 202
samu 204
saparu 185
sagru 204
'mq 311
piāmu 118
šadū 44
ša-du-ya 147
šadû-ya-nu 147
šalḫu 250
šiliḫtu 250
šikkatu 334
šiṭir šamē 301
šiṭirtu šamāmi 301
šukênu 235
Šubši-mešrê Šakkan LXIII

2. Arabic

'ahrām 31
'aws 92
akala laḥmahu 236
'afiqa 94
'ufug 94
'br 145
'wb 5
'tm 145
balad 24
jabbār 71
jāwāmiz 326
jawzal 24
jibs 204
dāna 265
ḏāriyāt 281
ḏ(w)ḏ 281
ḏmr 264
hirām 31
wada' 251
waḍu'a 172
wallāhi 247
wḍ' 106, 199
ziqq 200
zrb 54
ḥabara 122
ḥawiyyat 295
ḥal(l)ūm 51
ḥarafa 190
ḥubbā 238
ḥmy 271
ḫrt 332
ḫb' 210
yamāmah 352
kayd 159
kalaḥa 46

mass 53
mazbalah 21
mṭṭ 75
saḥîfah 111
sirr 323
sufrat 144
'ās 193
'ubb 238
'zr 221
'ld 315
'nd 300
ġadda 81
ġalim 343
ġulâmat 343
ġly 223
fa 251
fa'ama 118
fâṣa 134
farḫ 221
fasīs 265
faššа 265
qiwām 167
qisṭ 351
raffa 184
rassaġa 271
šawkah 334
šḫr 311
šmr 249
tafala 17
tifl 17
timsaḥ 331

3. Aramaic
ḥdwt' 67
ḥdt' 67
ḥ'nn 340
ḥrt 332
ybl' 195
yḥl 260
yšr 306
mĕṭāl 328
mll' 210
mtyn 270
mṣbtn' 264
nĕpîlā' 71
'bq 251
piṯqā' 144
prsu' 264
ṣd' 257
qrm 300
šiḥnā' 222
šyt 299
trp 184

4. Hebrew
'ăḇaddôn 183
'abbîrîm 322
'āḏām 86, 115
'āḏām='āḏēm 238
'āḏām haq-qaḏmôn 115
'aḏām rāšā' 154
'ăḏāmāh 274
'ăḏônay XVI
'aḡmôn 332, 342
'aḥăra'y 146
aḥărôn 146
'Ayyāb 6
'aḵpā 101
'ammāh 101
'ămûnîm 94
'āpîq 94
'ărî 202
'aryeh 202
'ašpāh 312
'āšûr 166
'āwen 86
'ēḇeh 74
'ēḡel 299
'ēḏ 273, 275, 297
'eḥāḏ 173
'eḵep̄ 248
'ēl 43, 44, 191, 249, 336
'elep̄ 115
'elgāḇîš 204
'ĕlôah 43, 91
'ĕlôhîm 43
'ēmāh 101, 248
'ĕslāḡ 75
'Iyyôb 5, 6
'im 52
'imrô 154
'îš 91
'ôḇôṯ 66
'ôyēḇ 5
'ōkel 74
'omnām 257
'ōzen 243
'ôr 297
'ōreḵ yămîm 92
'ôš 92
'by 261
'wr 252
'yb 5
'kp 101
'ny 135
'rṣw 283
'sp 194
badd 135, 338

bāmāh 192
ba'aḏ 20
bāqār 12
bāśār 157
bĕhēmôṯ 320, 321
bĕḵōr māweṯ 135
bĕliyya'al 258
bĕlōṯ 108
bînāh 291
bḥr 172
bny 167
b'l 230
bry 283
brqt 201
ga'ăwāh 339
gab(b) 99
gāḇîš 204
gal 32
gĕḥālîm 343
gēw 220
gô'ēl 146
gōḇah 166
gōren 210
gôzāl 24
g'r 185
gr' 273
dereḵ 130, 186, 205, 272, 297
dîn 265, 271
d'w 243
hăḏōḵ 320
hawwôṯ 56
haskēn 167
heḇel 62
hwlyn 339
hwy 280
hll 182
hškm 8
htlym 128
wgy 140
wzn 243
zāhāḇ 204
za'ăqāṯî 124
zĕḵûḵîṯ 204
zĕmîrôṯ 263
zĕ'îr 268
zĕrô'a rāmāh 296
ziḵrôn 99
zimmāh 231
zmr 264
ḥabbârîm 334
ḥăzîz 205
ḥāḵām 93
ḥālîl 224
ḥallāmûṯ 51
ḥărāmôṯ 31
ḥārûl 220
ḥăsîdāh 308
ḥṭ' 346
ḥēḇel 306
ḥēḏer 281
ḥezyôn 250
ḥeleḏ 86
ḥēleq 129
ḥēn 338
ḥeseḏ 52
ḥēqer 258
ḥîḏāh 189
ḥîlāh 52
ḥôl 214
ḥōṣen 340
ḥōq 173, 205
ḥŏrāḇôṯ 31
ḥōšeḵ 117
ḥby 238
ḥbl 260
ḥbr 122
ḥbš 203
ḥwy 15
ḥzy 260
ḥṭ' 46, 345
ḥṭr 179
ḥlq 297
ḥlṣ 55
ḥlš 107
ḥnp 269
ḥps 324
ḥpš 203
ḥqq 143
ḥrp 209
ḥrs 55
ḥšb 55
ḥtt 183
ṭôḇāh 167
ṭôḵaḥaṯ 98
ṭ(w)ś 74
ṭḥn 231
ṭḥwt 302
yād='ād 238
yāh XVI, 111
yāhû XVI
yaḥṭōp̄ 71
yāqîṣû 108
yāqôṭ 66
yardēn 327
yĕhô XVI
yehô/yô-nāṯan XVI
yĕ'ōr 326
yēš dayyān 147

yĕšîšîm 92
yĕšû'āh 222
yeṯer 38
yirmĕyāh/yāhû XVI
yô XVI
yḥd 30
ykḥ 76
yṣ' 172
yṣwq 200
ysr 35
kabbîr 268
kāḇôḏ 17, 141
kad(d) 159
kālū-m 130
kāp̄ 101
kāpān 219
kāp̄îs 204
kattar 268
kelaḥ 46
kēn 76
kĕsîl 71
keṯem 204
kî 292
kîd 159
kîḏôḏ 342
kîḏôn 312, 328
kîḏór 117, 314
kîmāh 71
kinnôr 224
kip̄layim 84
kōaḥ 47, 72, 172, 219
kôs 159
klḥ 46, 219
kny 244
kr' 231
kry 55
ktr 268
l, emphatic 243
l, 'from' 268
l, intrusive 160
lammās 53
lē', l' 100, 107, 159, 193, 249, 268, 339
lēaḥ 47, 219
leḥem 51
lĕp̄ānîm 129
lip̄nê 33, 38
lô(') XLIV, 31, 42, 45, 77, 86, 173, 193, 249, 268, 339
lû' 31, 42, 76, 173, 243
lûaḥ 145
lqytn 332
lmw 166
ln 94
mă(h) 123, 228, 229
māweṯ 62
māḥaṣ 349
mallûaḥ 195, 220
manā/ôl 118
mās 53
ma'ăḏannôṯ 300
māqôm 124
marṣēp̄ 199
maśśā' 63
māšāl XXX, 129, 189
mĕzārîm 281
mēlîṣ 125
mĕlôšēn 72
mem, enclitic 72, 106, 129, 130, 134, 159, 160
mĕrērāh 124
mĕrîrî 29
mĕrōrîm 72
mĕrôrāh 124
mĕrôrôṯ 102
mĕšôp̄ēṭ 72
mibbĕlî-m šēm 38
miḏbār 176
minlām 118
mispar=missappēr 126
mispar 117
miṣwāh 172
miqneh 7
mirmāh 229
mišmār 61
mišṭār 301
miṯhallēḵ 11
môḵîaḥ 76
mōp̄eṯ 129
môreh 272
môṣā' 199
mûsār 269
m(w)ṭ 75
m'd 300
mr' 154
mrr 272
mṭ' 264
ne'ĕmānîm 94
nĕḇālāh 16, 23, 228
nĕ'îmîm 269
nep̄eš 62, 177, 222
nēṣaḥ 111
nešep̄ 30
nimraṣ 55
nôṣah 309
nôṣēr 193
nûḏ 24, 123
nhq 220

nhr 152
nzl 273
nḥr 311
nḥš 153
nḥt 250
nsk 293
nqm 146, 233
nts 221
saḏ 102
sāḡûr 204
sĕḡôr 204
sēp̄er 143
sĕp̄îaḥ 111
sîd 102
sôḏ 115
sikkāh 193
sld 52
spr 206
'ăḇērāh 231
'ăḇuddāh 7
'aḏ 14
'awlāh 56
'āṭîn 161
'ayir 86
'ayiš 71
'al 230
'al='ēl 285
'Aliy 148, 195, 207, 209, 275, 277
'almāh 37
'am 89, 258
'ammay-m 129
'ammîm 129
'ap̄ār 146
'ap̄'appayim 30
'ărāḇāh 307
'āš 38, 71, 106, 193
'ēl 80, 285, 287
'elem 37
'elyôn 160
'ênêḵā-m 134
'ēṣāh 291
'erkāh 203
'im 191, 230
'îr 11
'ōḏ 107
'ôzēr 221
'ôlām 99
'ōmeṣ 130
'ōp̄ereṯ 145
'ûgāḇ 224
'br 269
'd 107
'dn 300
'l 285, 287
'ly 148, 209, 223, 224
'lyw 275
'lyn 148
'lm 53, 166, 291, 348
'lṣ 308
'mm 90
'mq 311
'qb 380
'rbh 176
'rk 271
'rṣ 102
'zb 74, 79, 152, 309
p(a) 72, 124, 251
paḥad 310
paḵ 248
pānîm 129
paršēz 184
pĕnînîm 204
pere' 86, 176
pereṣ 124, 222
pîḏ 117
pîw 72
pîḵ 248
pîmāh 118
pirḥāḥ 221
piṭdāh 204
pd' 251
pyw 119
p'l/b'l 230
prḥ 221
ṣaddîq 168, 257
ṣalmāweṯ 124
ṣar 123, 339
ṣe'ĕlîm 326
ṣe'ĕṣā'îm 230
ṣippôr 24
ṣîṣ 106
ṣō'n 12
ṣôp̄ār 24
ṣûrî 123
ṣpy 117
qāḏîm 298
qeḏem 7, 172
qĕḏēšîm 269
qĕḏôšîm 41, 269
qesita 351
qešeṯ 153
qdm 31
qdr 53, 224
q(y)' 177
qn 234
qnṣ 133
qṣ't 352
qrṣ 248

rabbîm 35, 242
raḇ-kōaḥ 172
rāmîm 160
rā'ēḇ 135
ra'māh 311
rāqāḇ 106
rāšā' 176, 271
rĕḇîḇîm 274
rĕ'ēm 307
reḡeḇ 162
rewaḥ 339
reḥem 195
rĕnānîm 308
rĕp̄ā'îm 182
rĕšā'îm 295, 296
rîḇôṯ 98
rišp̄ê qešeṯ 42
rô'eh 166
rōṣ 124
rûaḥ 37, 62, 339
ruṭăp̄aš 252
rg' 185
rzm 116
rm 242
rmz/rzm 116
rṣw 283
rṣṣ 152
śāḏeh 44
śar'appîm 36
śāṭān 10
śĕ'ēṯ 98
śĕ'ippîm 36
śeḵwî 302
śîḥāh 114
śukkôṯ 334
śḥq 211
ś'rt 37
šadday 166, 191
šāw' 59, 119, 229
šaḥal 202
šaḥar 30, 295
šaḥaṯ 75, 251
šalgā' 75
šal'ănān 160
šām 16, 326
šĕḇā' 13
šeḇer motnayim 345
še-day 44
šēd 45
šĕḥāqîm 274
šĕḥîn 21
šeṭep̄ 298
šelaḥ 250, 269
šeleḡ 75
šemeṣ 186
šeqer 97
šēṯ 344
šikm 8
šip̄rāh 185
šô'āh 98, 221
šôḏ 45
šōham 204
šōḥad 232
šûṭ 10
šbb 294
šbm 61
šbr 294
šdd 44
šdyn 147
šwrtm 177
šḥw 16
šlm 295
š'r 210
špṭ 160
šrh 280
šryr 323
tāw 238
taḥaṯ 183, 259
tāp̄ēl 51
tĕ'ālāh 205, 298
tĕḇû'āh 232
têmān 71
tĕmîm dē'im 285
tĕmûnāh 37
tĕšû(')āh 223
tip̄lāh 17, 37, 51
tiqwāh 60, 66
tohŏlāh 37
tōhû 95
tōp̄eṯ 129
tô'ăpôt 168
tummātî 230
tûšiyyāh 43, 84, 223

5. Ugaritic
abn brq 201
aḫ 66
aḫr 27
ayab 6
ayaḫ 6
ayḫ 6
aklm 321
amt 101
arṣy 353
ibrm 322
il 321
iqnu 145

ur 252
ušn 92
bd 131, 313
bk 248
btlt 229
brlt 251
g 220
drkt 186
hyn 338
ḥl 214
ḫdw 30
ymmt 353
ẓr 339
ymmt 353
yr 206
kdd 342
krpn 159
ks 159
ktp 158
mḫṣ 349
ndd/ydd 281
nqmd XXV
'bṣ 151
'db 309
'Aliy 211
'm 191
'p'p(m) 30
'qqm 321
ġlm(m) 37, 353
ġlm 53, 166
pdry 353
pḫd 310
rb(b) 274
rimt 204
šb' 237
šskn 167
ṯir 237

INDEX OF BIBLICAL REFERENCES

Gen i 20 95
4 184
6 286, 296, 297
7 184
14 184
16 235
23 324
ii 6 273
7 37, 190, 242, 257
8 269
12 204, 269
21 135
iii 8 238
10 238
17–18 231
17–19 42
19 16, 37, 80, 259, 319
iv 7 98
10 124, 125, 230
12 231
24 45
v XXXII
vi 2 9
4 9, 71
vii 16 281
21 91
22 190
x 7 13
22 3, 242
23 3, 242
28 13
xi 1 94
xii 11 228
16 XXXII, 7
xiii 6 7
xiv 4–5 45
5 183
35 7
xv 14 27
20 183

(*Gen*)
xvi 12 86, 307
xvii 1 44
xviii 11
12 269, 300
21–33 168
22–23 11
22–32 LXXII
xix 237, 270
2 237
4 238
5 190
6–11 238
7 237
9 238
12 23
24 14
31 212
xx 3 249
xxi 12 37
xxii 9 100
13 XXXI
16–18 XXXI
20 242
21 3, 242
xxiii 3–16 LXXII
7 16
10 42
12 16
16 203
18 42
19 27
xxiv 15 14
16 176
35 7
47 351
xxv 2 24
3 13
7 XXXII
8 354
23 XLVIII

(*Gen xxv*)
26 27
31 194
33 194
xxvi 12 307
13 7
14 7
xxviii 20 209
xxix 1 7
18 59
31 31
xxx 22 31
30 12
43 12
xxxi 5 209
7 140
24 249
29 90
30 109
37 76
41 140
xxxii 5 XXXII
20 252
xxxiii 3 16
19 XXXII, 351
xxxiv 7 23, 350
27 212
xxxv 4 351
29 106, 353
xxxvi 11 23, 24
15 23, 24
28 4
33 XXXII
xxxvii 25 54
26 124
34 15
xxxviii 17–20 128
xxxix 6 73
xli 1 249
6 297
11 249
12 249
23 297
27 297
38 242
xlii 23 125
xliii 29 145
xliv 20 13
23 252
26 252
xlvii 28 106
xlix 6 30, 142
20 300
21 306

(*Gen xlix*)
24 190, 216, 294
l 10 25
23 31, 354

Exod iii 2 – iv 17 LXXII
iii 8 152
17 152
v 6 301
vi 3 44
6 146
ix 5 258
9 21
22–26 296
22–35 279
xi 5 231
xii 11 291
xiii 2 209
16 238, 342
18 209
22 290
xiv 3 93
31 12
xv 2 263
13 146
16 318
xvii 13 107
xviii 7 16
xix 16 279, 290
xx 3 12
17 231
21 29
xxi 2–11 233
10 273
xxii 2 179
9–10 227
14 58
21 165, 213
26 128, 165
31 219
xxiii 4–5 236
20 LXXVII
17 201, 204
xxix 10 201
xxx 24 352
xxxi 3 242
6 8
xxxii 11 87
18 107
32 109
xxxiii 22 101
xxxiv 7 159
22 8
xxxviii 8 286

(*Exod*)
xxxix 10 201, 204
13 203

Lev i 16 309, 310
iv 55, 350
xi 13 314
27 46
29 91
41 91
xiii 18 21
xv 2–15 236
xvii 5–7 46
xix 13 59
18 235
27–28 15
28 21, 234
xxi 5 21, 234
20 324
xxiii 36 8
40 326
xxv 5 299
25 146
39–55 233
48 146
xxvi LXXVII
16 230
19 303

Num v 20–22 227
23–24 102
vi 24 208
25 211
xi 1 14
16 301
xii 6 249
7 12
xiv 22 140
24 12
34 248
xv 22–29 55
39 230
xvi 15 175
22 92
35 14
xxii – xxiv 30
xxii 30 167
xxiii 189
1 XXXII, 8
4 350
7 190
14 XXXII, 8, 350
18 190

(*Num xxiii*)
22 168, 307, 308
29 XXXII, 8, 350
xxiv 189
3 190
8 168, 307, 308
10 194
15 190
17 272
20 190
21 190
23 190
xxvi 10 14
33 353
xxvii 1–8 353
16 92
18 242
xxix 35 8
36 8
xxxii 22 37
xxxiii 55 334
xxxiv 5 12
xxxvi 1–12 353

Deut i 22 282
15 301
41 338, 339
ii 6 55
10 183
11 183
20 183
21 183
30 70
iii 11 183
iv 19 235, 292
32 65
v 7 12
9 159
14 233
vi 8 238, 342
viii 5 250
9 200
ix 5 247
x 16 70
17 98, 258
18 270
xi 14 211
18 230, 238, 342
xii 15 306
xiii 1–5 250
7 19
18 230
xiv 1 15, 21
5 306

(*Deut xiv*)
12 314
26 51
xv 9 258
17 333
xvi 18 301
xvii 8 98
xviii 11 122
xix 6–12 146
14 175
16 146
xx 5 301
xxi 19–21 42
xxii 13–21 42
15 209
xxiii 17 269
xxiv 6–17 128
10–13 165
15 59
16 159
17 165
xxv 5 212, 353
7 353
9 129
xxvii 17 175
xxviii LXXVII
12 296
23 286, 303
27 21
29 44
30 231
32 90
35 21
37 189
49 74, 314
53 142
67 59
xxix 4 8
xxxi 17 101–2
xxxii 1 153
1–2 LI
2 LIII, 211, 274
4 65
10 95
11 214
13 209
15 118
22 232
23 50
24 29, 42, 91
30 70
33 152
35 161
39 44

(*Deut xxxii*)
41 153
42 14
xxxiii 9 73
11 323
17 307
24 209
25 153
29 70
xxxiv 5 12
6 162
7 47

Josh ii 18 60
21 60
vi 26 118
vii 6 15, 25
15 351
26 32
viii 29 32
ix 4 106
x 11 296
xi 5 24
xii 4 183
5 183
xiii 12 13, 183
xv 18 19
41 24
xxiii 10 70
xxiv 32 XXXII, 351

Judg v 15 134
vi 3 7
33 7
34 118, 213
vii 2 320
12 7
13 249
15 249
16 14
20 14
viii 10 7
19 142
ix 34 14
35 182
43–45 14
53 344
54 62
xii 3 99
xiv 4 248
8 120
18 12
xvi 21 231
xviii 25 32

(*Judg*)
xix 237
20 237
22 238, 258
22–26 238
23 237, 351
xx 6 351
10 351
40 99

Ruth i 12 44
17 231
20 190
iii 14 178
iv 1 209
1–11 42
4 250
4–6 146
15 7
19 242

I Sam i 1 3, 241
5 31
10 32
15 222
16 33
ii 5 7
8 43, 70, 269
16 194
iii 17 231
18 16
iv 2 271
12 25
19 306
vi 5 17
vii 10 279
ix 15 250
x 12 189
xi 2 228
11 14
xii 3 175
xiii 17 14
19–22 200
21 118
xiv 52 58
xv 32 300
xvi 7 80
21 9
xvii 6 328
7 200
10 279
16 247
43 219
xviii 4 15

(*I Sam*)
xix 5 99
xx 2 250
12 250
13 231
41 16
xxi 14 92
xxii 2 32
8 250
17 250
xxiii 23 350
xxiv 1 306
2 306
5 15
6 190
12 15, 261
14 189, 219
xxv 22 231
25 258
26 320
29 109, 110
33 320
xxvi 10 137
19 19
xxvii 12 333
xxviii 21 99
xxx 6 32
22 258
xxxi 4 62
12 210
13 25

II Sam i 11 15
16 115
23 74
iii 8 219
9 231
13 252
31 15
iv 2 212
v 3 228
24 37
vii 5 12
8 12, 32
22 205
27 250
ix 8 219
x 19 54
xi 21 344
25 14
xii 1 3
23 60, 111
xiii 3 93
7 7
8 7

(*II Sam xiii*)
12 351
19 25
20 7
31 15
32 13
xiv 5 176
11 146
14 154
24 252
28 7, 252
32 252
xv 4 212
xvi 9 219
10 71
13 25
xvii 8 32
11 319
23 62
xviii 14 250
17 33
21–33 74
22 99
29 209
xix 13 231
xx 1 123, 229
10 124
20 20
xxi 12 210
xxii 5 183, 251
8 184
9 342
29 29
34 306
35 153
xxiii 1 263
12 247
xxiv 1 XXXVII, 19
16 251

I Kings i 42 14
ii 8 55
19 16
iii 9 8
11 236
iv 23 306
30 XLVIII, 7
33 265
vi 20 203
vii 49 203
viii 31–32 227
ix 7 189
15–22 58

(*I Kings ix*)
19 58
26–28 168
x 2 199
11 168, 199
21 203
26 58
xi 3 7
24 212
xii 16 123, 229
xiv 11 219
24 269
xv 12 269
xvi 34 118
xviii 22 13
32 298
35 298
38 14
46 291
xix XXXVIII
12 37
18 235
xx 30 20
xxi 10 8, 258
13 8
19 219
23 219
xxii 9–23 XXXVII
10 42, 210
19 10, 251, 292
19–23 9
24 123
25 20
47 269
48 168

II Kings i 12 14, 153
ii 21 199
23 142
iii 19 45
25 45
iv 1 55
v 13 261
vi 30 124
31 231
vii 1 42
viii 13 219
20 92
ix 7 12
10 192
30 353
xi 4 228
xvii 13 12
14 70

(*II Kings xvii*)
16 292
23 12
xviii 20 92
26 XLVIII
28 XLVIII
xix 21 123
28 332
30 42
35 251
xxi 3 292
5 235
10 12
xxiii 5 235, 281, 301
7 269
11 235
36 242
xxiv 2 12
xxv 20 212

I Chron i 9 13
17 3
22 13
32 13, 24
36 23, 24
53 23
ii 9 242
25 242
27 242
xii 18 212
20 241
xx 4 183
xxi 1 XXXVII, 10
15 251
xxvi 7 241
xxvii 18 241
xxix 4 199
17 247
28 354

II Chron iv 20 204
22 204
vii 9 8
20 189
ix 20 204
xvi 10 102
xviii 9 210
31 19
xix 7 258
xxvi 11 58, 301
xxxii 6 209
18 XLVIII
30 199

Ezra iii 10–11 292
iv 21 92
v 3 92
vi 1 92
3 92
11 349
12 92
ix 3 15
5 15
11 12
13 92

Neh iii 15 250
v 3 128
5 90
13 340
vi 2 24
vii 3 184
viii 1 210
xiii 24 XLVIII

Esther ii 5 3
iv 1 15

Job i 1 – ii 8 XXXI
i 2 209
3 XXXII
4 209
5 XXXII, 22, 102, 350
6 19, 175, 247, 293
8 6, 36
9 111
10 20, 141
11 8
15 XXXII, 54
16 153
17 XXXII, XXXVI, 55
19 209
20 24, 25
21 32, 223, 326
22 37, 51, 178
ii 1 9, 175
3 6
5 8
7 142
8 142, 349
9 8, 190
9–10 XXXI
10 16
11 241
12 142
13 35
iii 3–10 LIII

(*Job iii*)
3–26 LXXI
4–6 82
5 117
7 120, 219
8 61, 70, 185, 200, 329, 337, 346
11 38, 51, 203
11–22 LXXVI
14 118
15 32
17 16, 106, 326
19 160
20 161, 252
23 141
24 38
26 106
iv 3 243
6 65, 235
7 161
8 257
8–11 LXXII
9 282
10 202, 213
12 186
12–15 250
12–16 62
17 70, 116, 182
18 14, 41, 116
19 33, 193, 346
21 46, 52, 59
v 1 251
1–7 LXXII
4 209, 234
5 230, 342
6 146
8 167
9 59, 71, 280
9–16 LXXI
10 205
11 269
12 52, 93, 114
14 95
17 LXXIX, 43, 250, 269
17–26 131, 167
22 211
23–26 65
26 219
vi 2 – vii 21 LXXI
vi 2 56, 230
3 60, 157
4 43, 124
5 220, 307

(*Job vi*)
6 92, 244
9 39
13 43
14–30 147, 350
16 291, 348
19 4, 13
22 XXXVI
24 260
25 247
26 157
27 129, 270
28 12
30 23
vii 105
1 81, 107, 108
4 30
5 51, 142, 224, 349
6 39, 52, 66
7 62, 73, 74
7–10 107
8 151
9 296
9–10 LXXVI, 81
10 151
11 79, 190
12 30, 109, 185, 203, 293
14 142, 250
16 73, 349
18–20 81
19 107, 109, 166
20 140, 165, 263, 276
21 248, 346
23 299
24 299
25 299
viii 2 50, 55, 65, 114, 190
3 43, 141, 257
4 102, 142, 209
5 36
8 116
9 106
11–19 LXXII
13 44, 153, 191
14 235
15 161
16 42, 136, 216
18 151
19 146
20–22 131
22 235

(*Job*)
ix 1–13 249
2 70, 85, 116, 182
4 287, 337
4–12 LXXI
5 LXXII
7 281
8–11 263
9 281, 300, 301
10 43, 258, 280
11–12 85
12 257, 272
13 30, 61, 181, 185, 203
14–17 171, 223
14–20 249
15–24 81
16 100
17 5, 223, 299
19 172
20 115, 285
20–24 287
21 79, 248, 348
22 256, 318
24 257
25 60
25 – x 22 LXXI
ix 26 195, 314
29 81
30 230
31 128, 165, 223, 250, 251
32 249, 258, 291
33 LX, LXXV, LXXVII, 42, 100, 125, 126, 146, 251
34 248
x 1 75, 190
2 260
3 109, 256
6 166
7 248
8 20
9 37, 319, 346
9–13 109
10 105
14 166
15 168
16–17 50
17 141
18–19 31
18–22 LXXVI
20 107
21 60, 91, 111, 126

(*Job x*)
21–22 296
22 91
xi 2 50, 90, 100, 114, 171
3 55, 313, 338
4–5 36
6 43, 223
7 287
7–9 263
7–10 90
7–11 LXXII
8 296
9 94
10 71
11 256
12 86, 90, 307
13–19 65, 131
15 168
17 131
18 44
xii – xiv 89
xii 2 95, 190, 258
2–3 56
2 – xiii 19 89
xii 3 97, 114, 115
5 235
6 XXXVI, 116, 326
6–10 298
7 265
9 XXXIX
10 LXXII
11 56, 256
11–12 LXXII
12 115, 242
13 92
13–25 LXXII, 249
15 205
16 43
17–21 258
17–25 XXXV
21 95
24 44
25 29
xiii 2 90, 114, 115
3 43, 171, 291
3–5 50
4 350
6 114, 120, 171
7 97, 131
7–11 129, 147, 350
7–12 116
8 44, 350
11 233, 344

(*Job xiii*)
15 XLIV, LXXV, LXXVII, 12, 260, 291
15–16 LXXVII
17 283
18 171, 247, 265, 271, 286
20 – xiv 22 89
xiii 21 248
22 291, 348
22–23 238
23 260, 291
23 – xiv 22 LXXI
xiii 24 141, 248, 259, 265
26 102, 115, 248
27 249
28 38
xiv 1–2 LXXII
2 106, 136
3 166
4 182
6 166
7 44, 136, 141
7–9 42
7–22 60, 81
8 146, 346
12 LXXVI, 147
13 258
14 58, 81
15 101
16 206, 229, 239, 258
21–22 159
xv 2 55, 190, 297
2–3 50
5 115
7 296
7–8 291
10 219, 242, 350
14 37, 106
14–16 182
15 41, 182, 210
15–16 37
16 256
17 100
17–35 LXXII
18 66
20–35 66
21 134
22 XLIX, 119, 153
22–24 161
23 117

(*Job xv*)
23–24 29
24 314
26 99, 124, 343
29 91
30 117, 136, 340
30–33 67
32 42, 66
34 14, 30, 161, 219
xvi 2 116, 162, 190
3 50, 65
4–6 157
6 – xvii 9 LXXI
xvi 6 228, 229
8 12, 129, 146
9–14 221, 223
12 62
12–14 50
13 50, 153
14 141
16 LIX, 30, 129, 142
17 248
19 LX, LXXV, LXXVII, 42, 146
19–21 LXXVI, 42 251
21 LX, LXXV, LXXVII, 42
22 LXXVI, 60, 272
xvii 1 LXXVI
4–5 147
5 52
6 189
8 120
9 33, 230
10 134
13–16 LXXVI
14 75, 161
16 346
xviii 2 86, 108, 109, 190
3 43, 108, 155, 250, 271, 323
3–5 50
4 75, 290
5–6 159
5–21 157
6 108, 113, 155
7 122
7–10 44
7–11 121, 135
7–12 110
8 141, 213, 291
8–11 165
10 44, 159

(*Job xviii*)
11 204, 286
13 43, 51, 111, 205, 224, 296, 338
13–16 217
14 134
14–15 161
15 XL, LXX, 12, 161, 250
15–16 LXXII
16 42, 216
16–19 67
17 243
18 155, 161, 216, 229, 235, 245
21 66, 161, 175, 217
22 250, 289, 296
22–23 209
23 226, 250
24 131, 217, 225, 229
26 109, 130, 217
27 217
28 38, 101
xix 1–2 LXVII
1–5 147
2 65, 101, 133, 126, 139
3 151
4 36, 164
5 50
6 151, 165, 248
6–12 221
7 44, 126, 131, 196, 223
7–9 42
7–20 LXXI
7–22 59, 79
8 117, 135, 287
8–10 33
9 213, 282
10 42, 136
11 248
12 124, 135, 212, 221
13 220, 351
14 57, 79
16 183, 201, 209, 225
18 219
19 220
20 142
21 52, 241

(*Job xix*)
21–22 145
22 52, 151, 236
23–24 238
23–27 348
25 LXIII, 125, 126, 146, 233, 346
25–27 LX, LXXVI, 251
xx 2 36
2–3 50
5 120
5–29 66
7 159
11 161, 346
14 124
17 209
18 308
19 75
22 159, 161
23 51
25 124, 161
26 14
26–28 159
28 161
29 66, 191, 229
xxi 2 348
5 318
6 XLII
7 46, 256, 268
9 283
10 172
11–12 158
12 224
13 60
14 166
15 166
16 166
17 134
18 194, 222
23–26 LXXVI
25 60, 190
31 12, 272
32 192
xxii 2 43, 233
2–4 263
3 43
6 175
6–9 190, 212
7–9 238
8 318
9 175
10 134

(*Job xxii*)
11 302
12 263
14 184
15 53, 256, 261
16 37
18 32, 159
20 14
22 172
24 203
27 252
27–30 LXXXII, 11
28 33
28–30 251
30 350
xxiii LXXI
2 LXIII
4 100, 238, 247, 265, 271, 286
5 249
6 72
7 LXXVII, 97
8–9 265, 287
9 259
10 LXXVII, 199, 248
11 230
13 71
xxiv 1 258, 265
2–17 263
3 270
4–5 298
5 307
6 271
7 234
8 252
9 270
12 263
13 259
13–17 30, 295
15 30, 231
17 133
18 74
18–20 191, 195
19–24 66
20 42
21 177
22–25 191, 195
23 258
25 73
xxv 2–6 LXXII
3 212
4 106, 116
4–6 37

(*Job xxv*)
5 116
6 116
xxvi 2–4 35, 190
3 43
5 296
5–14 LXXII, 182, 190
6 205, 232
7 286, 292
10 85
11 LXXII
12 30, 61, 71, 293
13 30
14 297
xxvii – xxviii XXXI
xxvii 1 189, 208
2 256
2–6 190
3 242
4 23, 299
4–6 230
5–6 248
5–14 190
6 19, 76
7 235
8 52, 120
10 43, 168
13 66, 154
17 230
18 38, 67
20 134, 159
21 223, 297
23 191, 195
xxviii 189, 199
3 85
8 202, 346
11 296
22 183, 296, 348
23 43
26 298
28 91
xxix LXXVII
xxix 1 – xxxi 37 LXXI
xxix 1 189
5 142
6 152
8 219
9 157, 235, 318
12 234
12–13 233
13 252
14 141, 239

(*Job xxix*)
15 35
18 XXXVI
19 67
xxx 211
1 XXXVI, 211
2 46
2–8 176, 298
3 XXXVI
3 30
4 195
8 38
10 129
12 141
13 50, 56
14 124
15 134
17 142
18 72
20 265
22 43, 244, 274
25 28
30 51, 142
31 224
xxxi 248
1 123
2 43
4 109, 258
5 256
11 37
12 183, 230
13–15 142
14 146
17 270
19 212
21 42, 270
23 98, 344
24 168
26 182, 286
26–28 XXXVI
31 143, 151, 157, 209, 236
35 290, 291
36 141, 300
xxxii 2 263
3 62
6 100
8 247, 282
9 35, 92
10 100, 243, 268, 285
14 100, 247, 276
17 100, 243

(*Job xxxii*)
18–20 35
21 98
xxxiii 4 190, 242
5 100, 286
6 37
7 101
9 256
10 102
11 102
12 318
14 259, 318
15 36
16–30 LXXIX, 270
18 250, 269, 296
19 44
22 75
23 125, 146
23–24 42, 125
28 75
30 252
31 257, 348
33 115, 257
xxxiv 2–4 263
3 91
5 190
7 116
9 43, 263
10–12 65
10–15 263
12 141
13 272, 296
15 319, 346
17 257
18–20 LXXII
19 98
20 89, 271
25 271
30 120
32 272
34–37 263
35 291
xxxv 2 62, 291
5 256
7 164
11 115, 135, 272
12 141
16 191, 260
xxxvi 2 100
3 243
3–4 243
4 243, 285
5 67
6 66, 190

(*Job xxxvi*)
7 43
9–12 LXXIX
10 250
11 LXVII, 60
13 66
15 250
16 19
17 165
18 19
22–23 318
23 257
26 258
27 43, 199, 297
27–33 205
28 86
29 285, 302
30 148, 184, 195
33 148, 184, 195, 302
xxxvii 2 186, 290, 302
2–5 318
3 205, 275, 298
4 302
5 179, 186
8 303
9 71, 296
10 XLV, 86, 268, 299
11 275, 318
15 275
16 243, 268
18 86, 247, 291
19 100
20 20
21 235
26 268
xxxviii – xli 265
xxxviii LXXI, 284
1 15, 318
2 53, 260, 346
2 – xxxix 30 318
xxxviii 3 101, 318, 348
4 70
6 70
6–7 184
7 9, 116
8–11 LXXII, 61
15 30
22 281
25 43, 205
26–27 205
27 220
31–32 71
32 71, 281

(*Job xxxviii*)
34 165
37 206
38 86, 162
39 250
39–41 LXXII
40 281
xxxix 318
5 93
7 211, 274
9 322
14 75
18 211
22 211
23 328
27 118, 276
27–30 74
xl 1 290
2 318
3 290
3–5 XXIX
4 157, 235
4–5 318
6 290
7 291
12 259
15 66, 133, 293
18 153
19 186, 297
20 16
23 66, 327
24 331
25 61, 71, 186
30 55
xli 1 30, 329, 342
3 205
4 30, 84, 313, 332, 346
12 30
17 98, 233
18 30
21 211
23 322
25 117, 146
26 201, 202
xlii 1 290
1–6 349
2–6 318
3 LXXX, 53, 166, 260, 291
4 101, 318
5 205, 318
6 XXIX
7–17 XXXI

(*Job xlii*)
8 XXXII, 8, 98, 251
10 XXXVI, 241
11 XXXII, XXXVI, XXXVII, XLV, XLVI, LXXXI, 24, 123
11–12 351
12 XXXII, 65
13 76
16 46, 106

Ps i LXXVII
1 130, 256
3 42, 102, 216
4 102, 151, 159, 194, 222
ii 5 143
7 173
iii 8 213
iv 4 8
6 60
7 211
vi 8 129
vii 6 146
8 272
9 275
13 50, 123
14 120
15 44
viii 62
3–4 182
5 75
8 321
ix 6 136
14 296
x 3 8
4 165, 166
8 178, 182
9 178
14 270
18 270
xi 2 38
4 31
7 252
xii 3–5 45
4 249
7 222
xiii 3–5 129
5 75
xiv 3 116
xvi 1 208
2 167
4 177

(*Ps xvi*)
5 159
6 294
11 158
xvii 3 172
5 172
12 36, 109
xviii 7 70
8 184
8–16 290
9 342
11 223, 340
12 275
13 279
16 275
19 270
28 90, 208
33 306
35 153
36 134
45 348
xix 302
2 292
3 100
3–5 28
7 224
9 282
13 55
xxi 6 318
xxii 2–19 LXXI
6 182
8 123
14 36, 123
16 146
18 206
19 55
21 36, 62, 307, 308
22–31 252
29 319
30 100
xxiii 260
1 LV
2 87
4 76, 124, 209
5 100
xxiv 2 292
4 230
6 252
xxv 4 158
7 102
12 212
14 115, 142
21 6
xxvi 4 53

(*Ps xxvi*)
9 194
10 232
xxvii 2 143
8 252
9 102
xxviii 26 298
xxix 280
1 9
2 129, 292
6 307, 308
xxx 252
8 102
10 146
xxxi 8 270
9 257
21 45
xxxii 6 298
9 81
xxxiii 3 252
7 303
11 291
13 166
15 260
19 135
xxxiv 13 60
17 136
xxxv 4 67
8 44, 98
10 234
14 224
26 67
xxxvi 9 208
10 252
11 175
xxxvii LXXVII, 151
2 106
6 172
7 211
9 73, 97
13 137
14 178
25 LXXVIII, 36
28 136
35 151
37 6
xxxviii XLI, LXXI, 250
2 50
3 50
7 224
12 141
15 171
18 135
19 129

(*Ps*)
xxxix 2 23, 61
13 111
xl 4 235
14 124
xli 11 129
xlii 4 33
5 79, 319, 222
7 183, 327
9 224
xliii 2 224
5 319
xliv 2 205
3 211, 320
24 259
25 102
xlv 4 291, 318
9 352
13 87
xlvi 3 128
7 209
xlviii 5 24
14 124
xlix LXXVII
5 189
7–9 252
10–13 235
11 260
14 136
16 131
18 119
l 3 290
10 124, 321, 325
20 142
21 271
li 7 106
8 302
9 248
17 67
lii 5 141, 230
8 42
liii 3 116
lv 2 53
15 142
23 151
lvi 9 167, 185
lvii 3 275
7 44, 213
lviii 235
1–5 157
2 94
3 284
4 50

(*Ps lviii*)
6 122
9 31
lix 18 264
lx 6 275–76
lxii 12 318
13 257
15 199
lxiv 7 50, 123
lxv 8 61
9 75, 199
14 172
lxvi 252
lxvii 3 130, 222
14 130
lxviii 3 222
5 270
6 213
8–9 290
14 290
23 61, 62, 219
31 322, 326
lxix 2–3 165
9 141
11 189
12 220
21 24
24 323
29 109, 110
33 167
lxxi 5 235
7 129
lxxii 3 325
5 108
7 108
10 13
12 212
15 13, 199
16 46
17 108
20 239
lxxiii LXXVII
3 157
6 172
7 118
11 165
19 134
20 151
22 133, 321, 322
25–26 LXXXIII, 100, 147
lxxiv 12–14 330
13–14 61
19 352

(*Ps*)
lxxv 3 70
4 124
5 124
7 107, 199, 268
9 159
lxxvi 4 42
lxxvii 3 171
15 318
17 61
17–18 279
lxxviii 2 189
7 235
19 142
26 71, 297, 313
37 230
39 60
48 42
49 251
64 192
lxxx 6 33
12 124, 161
lxxxi 4 184
16 209
lxxxii 1 9
5 29
lxxxiii 14 102
lxxxiv 3 109
4 221
lxxxvi 17 167
lxxxvii 4 71
lxxxviii LXXI, XLI, 102
3–7 183
9 141
10 182
11 183
11–12 60
13 296
14 259
15 102
17 50
19 141
lxxxix 7 9, 41, 115
10 181
10–11 61
11 71
12 292
13 318
17 124
24 124
28 135
30 108
37 108
40 124

(*Ps lxxxix*)
42 161
44 123
45 294
xc 39
2 115
3 80
6 106
10 353
9–10 66, 106
16 130
xci 4 101
6 29
11 208
11–13 251
13 202
xcii 10 124, 307, 308
12 42
12–14 214
xciii 3–4 61
5 92
xciv 19 37
xcv 4 168
8 70
xcvii 11 208
xcviii 1 318, 320
c 3 XLV
ci 2 130
5 72
cii XLI
3 65, 224
6 143
11 65
24 130, 271, 272
26 292
27 108
28 32, 272
ciii 4 146
5 214, 252
15 106
16 151
civ LXXII
1 318
3 340
5 70, 292
6 183
6–9 LXXII
11 43
18 306
21 LXXII, 265, 303
26 325. 331
27 LXXII
29 1 2, 257, 259
30 LXXII

(*Ps civ*)
32 LXXII
33 272
cv 4 252
cvi 2 339
cvii 93
4 93
7 93
14 93
16 93
18 296
27 95
29 37
33 199
33–36 93
34 307
40 93, 94
41 167
cix 235
42 44
6 10, 11
25 123
29 67
cx 3 252
cxi 10 206
cxii 4 208
9 124
cxiii 2 16
7 43, 269
cxvi 252
16 93
cxviii 14 263
22 292
cxix 7 247
11 172
30 212
37 130
57 297
69 97
70 118
83 297
97 114
99 114, 242
103 55
109 99
122 167
131 211
147 30
cxx 4 219
cxxi 3 75
7 208
cxxiii 2 141
cxxiv 5 183

(*Ps cxxiv*)
6–7 213
7 134
cxxvi 2 67
cxxvii 3 6
3–5 209
cxxviii 2 292
3–4 209
6 6, 353
cxxix 7 340
13 16
cxxxii 4 31
9 213
11 142
13 173
16 213
18 67, 213
cxxxv 7 281
cxxxvi 4 43
6 183, 291
cxxxvii 235
2 326
cxxxviii 4 130
cxxxix 1–6 172
3 167
5 76
7–10 172
8 183
9 30
11–12 258
13 16
13–16 80
15 16
23 37
cxl 6 134
cxli 3 61
cxliii 2 37, 106
2–3 292
cxliv 3 62
4 66, 106
6 50
13 12
cxlv 3 43
cxlvi 9 130
cxlvii 7 61
8 43
9 265, 303
cxlviii 2–3 292
6 205
7 61
cl 4 224

Prov i 2 203
7 205, 242

(*Prov i*)
20 312
27 221
ii 6 242
7 43
13 166
18 182
21 73
iii 7 6, 205
8 161
11–12 44
12 250
19 205, 292
20 274
21 43
25 98
33 65
iv 5 203
7 203
12 134
19 29
25 31
25–27 230
v 14 85
19 306
22 134
vi 1 128
4 31
6 265
7 301
16 45
17 116
21 238, 300
27–29 232
vii 4 131
6–27 231
9 30, 178
15 252, 319
17 352
18 308
20 184
23 124
viii 291
3 312
14 43
15–16 73
22 296, 324
25 115
27 166, 184
29 205
30 325
31 283
36 46
ix 10 203, 205

(*Prov ix*)
12 263
15 161
18 182
x – xvi LI
x – xvi LI
7 136
8 8
25 37, 194
30 73
31 242
xi 1 230
4 161
15 128
28 235
xii 3 42
4 106
12 42
21 36
xiii 9 134
xiv 4 308
16 6
30 42, 106
xv 11 183
19 33
33 242
xvi 6 6
15 211
16 203
26 101
32 116
xvii 3 199
4 243
5 233
6 353
18 128
28 98
xviii 1 43, 248
5 98
xix 2 46
6 87
18 44
21 291
28 258
xx 10 230
17 151
20 134
22 236
xxi 9 122
16 182
xxii 2 233, 234, 258
8 36
9 233
(*Prov xxii*)
26 128
29 9
xxiii 2 51
5 74, 98
10 146, 175
11 146
xxiv 12 257
17–18 236
20 134
31 220
34 11
xxv 20 252
21–22 236
24 122
28 116
xxvi 2 265
7 189
8 17
11 189, 219, 265
13 202
16 92
27 44
xxvii 3 50
20 183
21 199
xxviii 1 117
10 44
14 70
15 36
xxix 1 70
11 116
xxx 13 31, 116
14 274
15 45
17 314
18 45
18–19 314
24–31 265
29 45
10 204
xxxi 17 323
24 334
28 212

Eccles i 4 111
14 60
ii 14 166, 286
14–16 160
20 301
iii 11 53, 166
16 LXXVIII
19–30 160
20 111, 319

(*Eccles*)
v 5 236
14 16
vi 3 31
10 249
12 66, 106
vii 20 182
28 70
viii 4 71
13 66
14 LXXVIII
ix 5 111, 159
x 5 257
20 8, 257, 265
xi 2 45
5 80
9 252
xii 7 16, 257
18 123

Song of Songs i 10 332
12 15
ii 9 205
14 352
iv 9–12 237
16 71, 313
v 1 237
12 209
vi 9 212
10 224
vii 1 158
3 301, 323
viii 6 43, 111

Isa i 1 241
2 153
3 308
6 220
10 208
14 282
16 75
17 165, 240
18 75, 97
19–20 269
23 270
30 102
ii 4 76
iii 16 98
21 351
iv 3 109
v 2 45
5 124
6 298

(*Isa v*)
8 165
12 158
20 29, 131
24 42, 271
25 75
vi LXXII, 10
4 220
vii 3 298
11 85
14 37, 344
20 58
viii 14 134
16 111
ix 5 238
11 172
13 332
17 270
x 2 176, 270
18 276
26 73
xi 2 242
5 291
6–8 46
14 7
15 234
xii 2 263
xiii 6 44
10 70
12 199
13 70, 184
20 118
21 224
xiv 189
4 189, 190
9 182
11 161
12 107, 292
13 183
13–14 151
xv 2 273
7 326
xvi 2 214
6 338
14 59
xvii 2 87
12 258
14 134
xviii 1–2 74
5 120
xix 5 108
6 326
14 44, 95
15 332

(*Isa xix*)
16 234
17 291
18 XLVIII, 94
xx 3 12
xxi 13 13, 54
xxii 2 274
12 15
21 213
22 238
xxiii 8 334
xxiv 18 153
20 95
21 181
23 224
xxv 5 263
6 199
xxvi 7 33
14 182
20 108, 161
21 124
xxvii 1 61, 185, 186, 330, 345
8 297
xxviii 1 106
4 106
15 73
16 292
17 296
18 73
29 43
xxix 4 319
7 71
8 51, 151
15 165
22 109
xxx 8 145
20 272
26 44, 224
30 279, 296
31 220
xxxii 5 257
7 43
8 222
14 307
xxxiii 3 220
15 229
20 38
xxxiv 1 230
4 102, 108
5 181
7 307, 308
10 118

(*Isa xxxiv*)
11 292
13 224
xxxv 3 35
xxxvi 2 298
11 XLVIII
13 XLVIII
xxxvii 3 31
22 123
29 332
xxxviii 10 296
11 203
12 38, 39, 52
xl 2 58
6 106
7 36, 194, 282
10 318
12 205
13 272
20 106
22 166
23–24 258
24 38
25 52
25–26 116
26 181, 292
26–27 166
28 205
31 214, 252
xli 4 32
5 205
9 205
14 182
18 199
20 XXXIX, 91
27 74
29 60
xlii 3 152
5 230, 257
6 67
xliii 1 146
3 13
9 100
10 32
13 32
26 100
xliv 3 298
4 326
5 103, 244
6 146
16 313
19 325
24 146
24–28 93

(*Isa xliv*)
25 93, 338
27 93
xlv 4 244
8 274
9 80
14 13
15 259
17 13
23 173
xlvi 4 32
10 291
xlvii 2 231
14 220
xlviii 12 32
13 292
20 146
xlix 7 210
16 103
19 20
21 13, 30
22 340
l 6 129, 220
8 100
10 208
li 5 222, 318
6 108
8 38
9 61, 71, 181, 185
13 292
15 185, 210
16 292
17 159
18 67
19 24
23 140
lii 2 93
7 74
9 146
13 – liii 12 XXX, XXXV, LXXVI, 251
lii 15 44, 210, 235
liii 3 24
8 203
9 124, 192
10 46, 51
10–12 LXXXI
liv 1 176
5 102, 230
8 102
17 45
lv 10–11 173

(*Isa*)
lvi 10–11 219
lvii 4 123
10 301
13 62
15 140
17 102
20–21 117
24 102
lviii 4 194
5 332, 349
6–14 LXXVII
7 165, 233, 234
8 341
8–9 168, 252
9 101, 141
10 165
11 165, 199
12 32
13 338
14 168
lix 10 44
16 318, 320
17 213
lx 2 29
6 13
lxi 3 141, 264
4 32
lxii 1 172
lxiii 3 70
5 320
10 223
lxiv 5 102
lxv 20 46
22 230
lxvi 9 31
24 111

Jer i 1–10 LXXII
1 241
17 291
ii 24 307
25 301
iv 13 74
28 224
30 353
v 8 220
13 60
15 94
22 61, 205
28 118, 270
vi 4 59
11 142
16 166

(*Jer vi*)
20 13
26 349
vii 5–7 LXXVII
13 8
18 229
25 8
26 70
29 15
viii 2 192, 235
5 19
7 313
13 102
19 220
21 224
ix 17 31, 274
25 242
x 9 199
13 296
16 297
xi 7 8
19 47, 203
20 172
xii 1–2 157
13 231
14–17 LXXVII
16 167
xiii 16 17, 276
18 141
24 15
xiv 2 224
6 192
17 55
xv 2 192
3 219
5 24
10 55
12 153, 200
17 142
18 53
21 55
xvi 5 24
6 15, 21
xvii 1 145
5–8 LXXVII
6 307
7 235
8 216
9–10 20
xviii 5–12 80
12 301
16 24, 125
17 161

(*Jer xviii*)
18 45
21 192
xx 2 102
7 90
8 141
9 244
14–18 27
xxii 10 24, 192
19 192
xxiii 2–4 46
18 115, 142
22 115
24 258
28 250
xxiv 9 189
xxv 4 8, 12
9 12
15 159
19–20 4
23 4, 13, 242
xxvi 5 8, 12
14 351
19 8, 12
23 351
26 102
xxx 3 351
xxxi 8 213
17 14, 44
23 65
29 11, 159, 168
30 LXXVIII
35 185
39 292
xxxii 20 274
27 92
33 8
xxxiv 8–22 233
15–22 233
xxxv 14 8
15 8, 12
xli 5 15, 21
xliv 4 8, 12
16–19 229
xlvi 21 59
xlvii 5 15, 21, 311
xlviii 9 172
17 24
30 338
37 15, 21, 273
40 314
44 134
xlix 7 23
16 314

(*Jer xlix*)
17 194
22 314
28 7
32 242
35 216
l 27 137
34 146
36 338
li 5 37
19 300
26 292
64 239
lii 12 9

Lam i 5 140
7 294
12 140, 146, 161
20 224
ii 10 25
11 124, 224
13 85
14 51
15 123, 161, 194
19 222
iii 7 141
12 123
12–13 50
13 124
14 90, 220
15 72
26 211
29 44
30 123
45 75
58 146
iv 3 309
5 300
6 258
7 204
8 224
19 74
21 4
v 13 231
15 224
16 141

Ezek i 2 241
4 290
v 16 50
vii 18 15
19 161
viii 8 179
16 235

(*Ezek*)
ix 8 13
xi 19 344
xii 2 189
5 179
7 179
12 179
xiii 11 204
13 204, 296
xiv 12 168
14 XXIV, XXXIII, 6, 11, 168
20 XXIV, XXXIII, 6, 11, 168
xvi 26 236
39 141
40 85
53 351
xvii 2 189
3 309, 314
7 219, 309
xviii LXXVII, 11, 159, 168
2 189
12 165
xxi 11 345
29–30 137
xxii 7 270
20 145
xxiii 20 236
26 141
40 353
46 85
xxiv 3 189
8 124
xxv 3 313
4 7
10 7
13 23
xxvi 16 15
20 203
21 134
xxvii 12 199
16 204
19 352
22 13
30 25
36 134, 194
xxviii 2 151
13 201, 203, 204
14 201
17 151
19 134

(*Ezek*)
xxix 3 330
4 332
xxxi 4 298
6–10 151
7 151, 216
xxxii 2 330
18 296
xxxvi 26 344
xxxvii 6 300
8 300
11 44
xxxviii 13 13
4 332
9 221
22 204
xxxix 11 124
25 351
xl 3 – xliii 17 292
xlii 11 199
xliii 7 192
11 199
xlvii 12 102

Dan ii 249
14 92
24 212
34 258
41 264
iii 8 143, 236
10 92
12 92
14 257
29 92
iv 249
3 92
5 212
10 41
13 11
14 41
17 11
20 41
23 11
24 11
31 14
35 71, 272
v 12–13 242
21 307
27 230
30 271
vi 14 92
24 143, 236
27 92
vii 249

(*Dan vii*)
8 249
10 109, 251
20 249
viii 13 41
25 258
ix 6 12
10 12
26 298
xii 1 109

Hos i 5 216
ii 6 12, 141
20 46
iii 2 55
v 12 106
14 202
15 252
vi 1 44
3 211
4 8, 222
5 172
vii 11 8, 352
viii 6 294
7 36
9 176, 307
ix 1 32
16 42
x 4 231
7 195
8 231
13 36
xi 12 41
xii 1 41, 114
2 297
xiii 2 235
7 202
15 36, 297

Joel i 20 265, 321
ii 4 311
7 124
10 70, 184, 224
20 142
22 321
iii 8 13
16 70
17 116
iv 15 223

Amos i 3 153
3–13 44
12 23
ii 1–6 45

(*Amos ii*)
7 176
8 165
9 136
iii 3 24
6 52
7 12
iv 3 124
13 70
v 8 71
12 176
15 42
19 153
vi 5 158
13 4
vii 1–9 LXXII
viii 10 15, 29
1–3 LXXII
ix 2 108, 183
2–3 258
3 330
6 208

Obad i 9 23

Jon ii 183
3–6 165
iii 3 247
6 349
7 92

Mic i 3 70
8 224
10 349
ii 1 90
10 55
iii 1–3 43
4 141
6 224
v 1 123
4 45
5 45
vi 7 142, 152
9 43
15 230
vii 1 51
3 43
8 208
16 157, 235
17 91
18 19

Nah i 3 73, 290
8 298

(*Nah*)
ii 2 323
iii 3 153
7 24
15 14

Hab i 2 141
4 172
8 74, 314
13 20, 265
ii 6 189, 190
11 204, 230
17 321
iii 3 52
4 235
5 42
5–6 290
11 153
16 106

Zeph i 15 161
17 51
18 161
ii 1 109
15 194
iii 7 8
9 247
13 86

Hag ii 17 296
23 12

Zech i 6 12
16 292
ii 13 234
iii XXXVII, 10
iii – iv 10
iii 1 10, 11
1–2 9
2–6 238
3–5 76
8–9 238
iv 10
7 274, 292
10 10
vi 5 9
ix 1 274
9 85
14 290
16 276
x 1 206, 274
xi 12 203
xii 1 292
xiii 5 274